Computer Name

"COMP1

Hard Drive ☇ #18

NT 4.0

PC 1 # IP

10.1.23.200 = IP

Subnet Mask = 255.255.255.0

Domain name Server ⟶ DNS = 204.153.79.3

198.200.181.34

DMA = 5

Network Card = MADge Smart 16/4 A Ring Node

IRQ = 5

I/O = ~~A20~~ 0x0a20

Windows NT™ Server 4 Administrator's Guide

How to Order:

For information on quantity discounts contact the publisher: Prima Publishing, P.O. Box 1260BK, Rocklin, CA 95677-1260; (916) 632-4400. On your letterhead include information concerning the intended use of the books and the number of books you wish to purchase. For individual orders, turn to the back of this book for more information.

Windows NT™ Server 4 Administrator's Guide

Paul E. Robichaux

Bob Chronister

Jim Kanya

Sean Leinen

Ted Malone

Bo Williams

Prima Publishing

P

PRIMA is a registered trademark of Prima Publishing, a division of Prima Communications, Inc.

Prima Publishing® is a registered trademark of Prima Communications, Inc.
Prima Publishing. Rocklin, California 95677.

ISBN: 0-7615-0751-5

Library of Congress Catalog Card Number: 95-72642

Printed in the United States of America

97 98 99 BB 10 9 8 7 6 5 4 3 2

Publisher Don Roche, Jr.
Associate Publisher Ray Robinson
Acquisitions Manager Alan Harris
Managing Editor Tad Ringo
Product Marketing Specialist Julie Barton

Acquisitions Editor
Jenny Watson

Development Editor
Vangie Bazan

Project Editor
Robin Drake

Copy Editor
William L. Callahan

Technical Reviewer
Brady P. Merkel

Indexer
Sherry Massey

Cover Designer
Kari Keating

Dedication

Dedicated to Ann and Dave Robichaux, for their patient teaching of reading, writing, and the value of hard work.

—P.R.

Acknowledgments

Producing a book of this size and scope involves a large cast of characters. This book was actually written, edited, and produced by people in seven states! First and foremost, I'd like to acknowledge the work of the contributing authors: Bob Chronister, Jim Kanya, Sean Leinen, Ted Malone, and Bo Williams. Their work made this book what it is. Special thanks go to Jim Meadlock of Intergraph for contributing the foreword.

Books suffer or prosper as a result of their editors. I was fortunate to have a focused, professional team of editors: Vangie Bazan, Robin Drake, Brady Merkel, Jenny Watson, and Bill Callahan. All of them provided encouragement, advice, and an occasional attitude adjustment when needed.

My employers, Larry and Janie Layten of LJL Enterprises, were generous with their time, comments, and hardware throughout the writing and production process. Visit LJL's website at http://www.ljl.com for information on how you can secure your electronic mail against tampering and eavesdropping.

A large number of software vendors contributed material to the densely packed CD that accompanies this book. In particular, Stu Sjouwerman of Sunbelt generously gave us the full contents of Sunbelt's excellent Web site http://www.ntsoftdist.com, Eli Shapira was thoughtful enough to include a discount coupon for e.g. software's WebTrends package, and John Allen of Intergraph was instrumental in getting Intergraph's interoperability products onto the CD. My thanks to all the vendors who contributed material—vendors who provide evaluation or trial software make it easier for you to buy useful tools.

The Huntsville Coca-Cola Bottling Company deserves special mention for keeping local shelves stocked with plenty of Diet Coke, without which this book would never have seen print.

Last, but by no means least, my wife Arlene and son David were astonishingly patient and tolerant. My love and thanks go to them for helping, cleaning, cooking, babysitting, making backups, editing, and all the other myriad things they did to help me.

About the Authors

Paul E. Robichaux (paul@ljl.com) first started developing software on a TRS-80 Model I in 1978. By the time he finally wore out that machine, all the silver paint was worn off the keyboard. Since then, he has worked on projects as diverse as Ada compilers for the Navy, 3D network CAD programs, and cryptographic and security software, all on architectures ranging in size from 8-bit embedded microcontrollers to VAX clusters. His current job is keeping The Man out of your e-mail by writing cryptographic software for the MacOS and Win32 platforms.

Along the way, he has contributed to a number of books and magazines. His research interests include cryptographic protocols and systems, large-scale collaborative work environments, and Macintosh software development. His personal interests include reading cheap spy novels, high-performance aircraft, and enjoying time spent with his family.

Bob Chronister was born and raised in a small town in central Pennsylvania. His love/hate relationship with computers began with his first exposure to them in 1967, while working at Stanford University. After several sojourns into PDP11s, he has finally settled on Windows NT and seems to be spending more and more time with installing and maintaining systems. He has used and worked daily with Windows NT since the prerelease of Version 3.1. Bob writes Tricks & Traps for *Windows NT Magazine*. In addition, he runs three NT support forums on CompuServe and one on the *Windows NT Magazine* Web page (www.winntmag.com).

Since 1985, **Jim Kanya**, Jr. has been the Systems Manager for Cleaver Ketko, Gorlitz, Papa and Associates, Inc. (CKGP), a worldwide facility-planning, manufacturing engineering firm. His operating system experience includes VMS, CLIX, Aix, SunOS, DOS, Windows, Windows 95, and Windows NT. He has been heavily involved with many user groups, in particular the Intergraph Graphic Users Group (IGUG). He has held all offices in the Systems Operations SIG, conceptualized and managed the "IGUG Contributed Software Library CD-ROM" and is currently a member of the board of directors for the U.S. IGUG. In his not-so-spare time, Jim enjoys golf, music, woodworking, and reading.

Jim would like to thank his family—Sharon, Mary, Meghan, Alex, and Andrew—for their support during the writing of the book. Their support was a great help.

Sean F. Leinen is a senior systems specialist with the Systems and Network Services group of Intergraph Corporation. Sean is a Microsoft Certified Systems Engineer (MCSE) with product certification focus in the BackOffice family of products. He has sixteen years of experience in the computer industry. Having taken part in Intergraph's corporate move from UNIX to Windows NT, he is often sought by other corporations to help integrate Windows NT into their environments. He currently specializes in the specification, integration, and execution of Internet/intranet solutions for corporations.

Sean is an avid musician and is an active six-string electric bassist on the New York club scene. He uses his recreational time to play billiards and snooker, and enjoys using e-mail to intentionally evoke confused responses from acquisition editors.

Ted Malone has worked in the computer industry for more than 12 years, most of which has been devoted to the support of network operating systems. He holds the highest level of certification from both Microsoft (MCSE, MCT) and Novell (Master CNE, CNI), as well as certifications from 3COM. Ted's current position is as technical head of a computer consulting and training company in Scottsdale, Arizona.

Bo Williams was raised in Anniston, AL, and moved to the Huntsville area in 1986. A graduate of the University of Alabama in Huntsville in 1992 with a B.A. in Communication Arts, he has worked at Intergraph Corporation, where he writes user-level software documentation, since January, 1994. Bo is engaged to be married in May, 1997. In his spare time, he enjoys tropical fish, classic cars, and reading.

Contents at a Glance

Contents

Chapter 5   **Beyond the Installation**   **101**

Chapter 13   Safeguarding Your Data   331

Chapter 16 Managing Users and Groups in Domains 401

Chapter 27 Running Microsoft Internet Information Server 719

Appendix What's on the CD? 741

Foreword

Intergraph Corporation grew from a five-person consulting firm into the world's largest company dedicated to supplying interactive computer graphics systems, based on the strength and power of our software. Over the last four years, we made what analysts called a risky move by migrating our products, and the core of our workstation line, to Intel x86 machines running Windows NT. What led us to undertake this project?

In the early 1990s, the industry's direction started to shift. More and more customers were asking us how they could integrate their office productivity applications such as Microsoft Office with their CAD and graphics workflow. The Intel x86 platform was growing in capability and speed, but it lacked a suitable operating system—one with the power of UNIX.

When Microsoft announced that they were developing Windows NT, we realized that the combination of x86-based computers and Windows NT would provide us a way to build a "Technical Desktop"—a machine running Windows NT that could mix high-performance CAD and graphics tools with office productivity applications and off-the-shelf hardware. Windows NT provided a unique mix of features that our customers were demanding:

- *Ease of integration* with other operating systems, including the UNIX, NetWare, and Macintosh networks so prevalent in high-end CAD and publishing networks.
- *Scalability.* Windows NT transparently supports machines from single-processor 486-based desktop machines to four-processor Pentium Pro servers. Windows NT domains offer the same type of scalability for user and group account management across very large networks of 20,000 or more workstations.

- *Robustness:* Windows NT was designed to function well in large networks. It simultaneously allows multiple network protocols and cards to run on a single server, and it supports high-availability features such as hardware clustering and RAID.

- *Security.* All system operations can be logged and audited. The Windows NT File System (NTFS) supports a broad set of access controls, and Windows NT itself is certified C2-secure by the National Computer Security Center.

Other operating systems and hardware platforms have offered these attributes in various combinations, but Windows NT is the first to offer all four on a fast, widely available hardware platform—the Intel family. As a result of this combination, Windows NT is the perfect OS for demanding applications such as computer-aided design, digital video production, and large-scale database applications.

The future for Windows NT looks even brighter with the release of Version 4.0. Over the remainder of the 1990s, Microsoft will continue to migrate new features such as Internet integration into Windows NT's core; in conjunction with the still-rapid growth of graphics, network, and system hardware capabilities, Windows NT will increase its penetration into high-end networks in all sorts of applications.

Thanks to NT's features, our customers are successfully—and happily—using Windows NT for projects ranging from designing jewelry and goldwork for the Royal Family of the United Kingdom to designing submarines for the U.S. Navy to operating Enhanced 911 emergency dispatch services throughout the world. No matter your application, these same features can pay off for you.

Jim Meadlock

Intergraph

INTRODUCTION

Windows NT is becoming increasingly common on corporate desktops. Its stability, security, and scalability make it the right choice for many uses. This book will help you administer your Windows NT servers effectively and without wasted effort.

In short, this book was designed for one purpose: to provide solid technical information on administering networks of computers running Windows NT Server. From the ground up, our mission in writing this book has been to build a concise book containing useful information—without fluff, filler, or excess screenshots. You won't find discussions of things like the Calculator or WordPad applications here; you will find plain-spoken, down-to-earth information and a wealth of practical suggestions and tips.

Being concise doesn't mean that we left out important material, though. The book covers all aspects of Windows NT administration: setting up user accounts, groups, and domains; interoperating with NetWare, TCP/IP, and

Macintosh clients; planning effective backup and security policies, and running an Internet server with Microsoft's Internet Information Server software.

WHAT SHOULD YOU KNOW BEFORE READING THIS BOOK?

There are a few prerequisite skills you need to get the most from this book; however, even if you don't have all of them, you can still learn a great deal:

◆ You should already be comfortable with the Windows 3.x, Windows 95, or Windows NT 4.0 user interfaces, since we don't spend time discussing how to use them.

◆ You should be familiar with the basic hardware components of Intel-based computers.

◆ You should have experience using, if not administering, local area networks running the Windows Networking, NetWare, or TCP/IP protocols.

WHO SHOULD READ THIS BOOK?

One of the first steps in planning a book project is defining who makes up the book's audience. This book was no different. We identified three primary groups that compose our target audience:

◆ **Experienced system and network administrators.** A large number of companies and organizations have been happily using NetWare, UNIX, LAN Manager, OS/2, Banyan Vines, or Macintosh networking (among others) for a while. A growing number of these organizations are supplementing—or replacing—their existing networks with Windows NT servers. Readers who are already comfortable managing networks using these network operating systems (NOSes) will find frequent comparisons and contrasts between other NOSes and NT.

- **Experienced Windows NT Workstation users.** Although Windows NT Server has been relatively slow to penetrate the corporate marketplace, high-end desktop applications have been pushing Windows NT Workstation onto desktops at a quick clip. Software development, digital media editing, and computer-aided design applications such as Microsoft's Visual C++, Adobe's Photoshop, and Intergraph's Solid Edge have converted thousands of users to Windows NT. Windows NT Server is built on the same core as Windows NT Workstation, but the Server version adds a number of features that may be unfamiliar to Workstation users.

- **IS professionals and network planners.** This group will find that networks running Windows NT pose special challenges—and opportunities. Throughout the book, we've emphasized the role that Windows NT can play in enterprise networks, as well as pointing out tips and pitfalls for using Windows NT Server on smaller-scale projects. In addition, we've focused on providing information on performance measurement, tuning, and optimization to help you get the most out of your Windows NT network installation.

HOW TO USE THIS BOOK

The book is organized into eight parts, as detailed in the next section. Each part stands alone and includes a short introduction emphasizing the key topics it covers. Which approach you take to the book will depend on why you're using it:

- For comprehensive coverage, start with Chapter 1 and read straight through.

- For a quick exposure to the process of planning and installing Windows NT Servers on your network, read Chapters 3, 4, and 20.

- The most common system and network management tasks—managing printers, disks, and computers on your network—are covered in Chapters 6-11.

♦ If you already have another network operating system running and need to integrate Windows NT with it, see Chapters 21, 22, 23, and 24, all of which cover interoperating with other network operating systems.

♦ If you're adding Windows NT to your network so you can use it as an Internet server, read Chapter 12 (the security chapter), and then go on to Chapters 26 and 27.

♦ Domains are a key—but often misunderstood—feature of Windows NT Server. Use Chapters 14, 15, and 16 to help you plan, manage, and use domains effectively on your network.

♦ If you want to optimize your Windows NT Server installation, see the four chapters that make up Part VI: Watching and Tuning Performance.

WHAT'S IN THIS BOOK?

Besides the front matter (this introduction and Jim Meadlock's foreword) and a single appendix, the entire book is dedicated to the nuts and bolts of administering Windows NT servers. The book is broken into parts; each part focuses on a single topic you need to know to be an effective administrator. The following text details what each section covers.

Part I—Windows NT Server Fundamentals

Chapter 1 introduces Windows NT 4.0 by covering its historical development and feature set, including the features that differentiate it from Windows NT 3.51.

Chapter 2 explains the underlying architecture of Windows NT, including a discussion of the executive and kernel services that provide much of the system's flexibility and speed.

Part II—Installing Windows NT Server

Chapter 3 is devoted to the planning process you should follow before installing Windows NT on your network. It includes guidelines for choosing the right hardware for your needs.

Chapter 4 shows how to actually install Windows NT on RISC or Intel-based computers, as well as learning how to do specialty installs and how to troubleshoot failed installations.

Chapter 5 discusses what you'll see after a successful installation; it includes a brief tour of the Windows NT 4.0 user interface and a discussion of what files and services are installed and what they do.

Part III—Administering Windows NT Servers

The administration of Windows NT servers is the meat of Part III. **Chapter 6** gets you started by explaining how to create and manage user and group accounts with the User Manager for Domains. It also shows how to set up login scripts and user profiles for domain users.

Most networks have shared printers; **Chapter 7** teaches how to manage shared printers using Windows NT Server's security and sharing features.

Good mass-storage management is crucial to getting the best performance and reliability out of your servers. **Chapter 8** reviews mass-storage hardware and how you manage and control it in Windows NT.

A key difference between the Workstation and Server versions of Windows NT is the capability to remotely manage servers and workstations with the Server Manager. **Chapter 9** presents the Server Manager and teaches how to use it to control resource sharing, server connections, replication, and messaging.

Remote management is made more useful by the ability to install and use the Server Manager and other management tools on any Windows computer on your network; you can then manage your Windows NT servers from wherever is convenient. **Chapter 10** introduces the use of the remote management software, SNMP, and remote access tools like pcAnywhere and Remotely Possible.

The system registry is an often-misunderstood (and feared!) system component. **Chapter 11** explains what the Registry is, its purpose, and how you can use it safely.

Part IV—Protecting Your Network Environment

Networks often contain critical data, and you need to know how to protect it from loss or damage. **Chapter 12** exposes the fundamentals of Windows NT security policies and settings, and tells you what defaults are reasonable—and which ones are dangerous.

Even if your data is protected by security controls, you still need to protect it against accidental loss due to user error, hardware failure, or catastrophe. **Chapter 13** explains how to plan and execute backup and security plans that will safeguard your data even in the gravest extreme.

Part V—Managing Your Network with Domains

Domains are a concept unique to Windows NT, while workgroups have been around since LAN Manager 2.0. Learn the differences between them, and their relative strengths and weaknesses, in **Chapter 14**.

Once you've absorbed what a domain is and what it can do, **Chapter 15** will lead you through the process of planning, implementing, and running a domain model that makes sense for your network and organization.

Of course, domains are useless without users and groups to use them. **Chapter 16** expands on the concepts from Part III to teach you how to manage users and groups in a domain environment.

Part VI—Watching and Tuning Performance

Performance monitoring in many operating systems is an inexact science, but Windows NT provides excellent tools for tracking your servers' throughput. **Chapter 17** introduces the Event Viewer and Performance Monitor and tells you how to put them to work for you.

Chapter 18 expands coverage of the Performance Monitor by showing how to use it to monitor your network's health and performance; it also introduces the powerful Windows NT Network Monitor, formerly available only as part of Microsoft's Systems Management Server (SMS) product.

Measuring performance is good, but improving it is better still. **Chapter 19** provides you with the knowledge to do so—based on the measurements described in Chapters 17 and 18.

Finally, Part VI closes with **Chapter 20**'s detailed exposition of how to plan your network—including its remote access components—to handle the load you plan to impose on it.

Part VII—Integrating Windows NT with Your Network

Although DOS, Windows for Workgroups, and Windows 95 aren't meant to be network operating systems, many network clients run them. **Chapter 21** describes how to integrate them into your Windows NT network.

Because Novell's NetWare is still the most widely used network operating system in the world, Microsoft engineered Windows NT to work well with it. **Chapter 22** shows how to use the NetWare compatibility services to join your NetWare and Windows NT machines.

Many networks include Macintosh users. Windows NT can easily be configured to serve them as equals; **Chapter 23** shows how and points out some ways to smooth the cohabitation for both sides.

Two years ago, TCP/IP was a mystery to most networks; now, with the blossoming of the Internet, it's a key part of many networks. You learn how to make it work well with Windows NT **Chapter 24** shows.

Part VIII—Extending Your Network

Although Part VIII closes the book, it might be the most exciting part: It covers expanding your network to the world via the Internet and dial-up access. **Chapter 25** leads off this part by explaining how you can give dial-up networking access to clients using the Dial-Up Networking subsystem.

Chapter 26 expands your network's reach to include the global Internet; it shows how to research, choose, and configure an Internet connection that meets your needs.

Once you're connected, you'll probably want your system to serve as an Internet server—**Chapter 27** shows how to get the best use from Microsoft's Internet Information Server, included free with Windows NT Server 4.0.

WHAT'S ON THE CD?

Windows NT includes a wide spectrum of tools—but there are a large number of valuable third-party tools available. How can you find the right solutions? We've taken a step to make your job easier—the CD bound into the back of this book contains more than 30 NT-specific tools. Some are evaluation versions that expire after a set period; others are full retail versions that you can use without extra cost. Appendix A contains a complete list of the products; throughout the text, we've included cross-references to products on the CD. Here's a quick list of some of the included programs:

- ◆ *TCP/IP interoperability:* 30-day trial versions of Intergraph's eXalt X Window system server, DiskAccess NFS client, DiskShare NFS server, and Batch Services job scheduling tool

◆ *Remote access:* 30-day trial versions of Symantec's pcAnywhere/32 and Avalan's Remotely Possible/32 remote control software

◆ *Mass storage management:* A fully-functional version of Executive Software's Diskeeper Lite, plus a 30-day trial version of Quota Manager

◆ *Internet services:* A full 10-user version of software.com's Post.Office SMTP mail server, plus 30-day trial versions of e.g. software's WebTrends WWW log analyzer, the Pragma Systems Telnet server, and Process Software's Purveyor secure WWW server

◆ *Backup and security:* The fully-functional version of Symantec's Norton Antivirus for Windows NT, along with a trial version of the Kane Security Analyst and the Octopus fault-tolerance toolset

◆ *Server and network management:* Trial versions of Network Instruments' Observer network monitor, SomarSoft's DumpEvt event log analyzer, and the WhatsUp network watcher from Ipswitch

CONVENTIONS USED IN THIS BOOK

This book uses a number of typographical conventions to make it easier for the reader to understand how to use the commands, syntax, menus, and so on:

◆ Names of commands are presented in a special `computer typeface`— for example, the NT `CreateFile()` routine.

◆ Computer names (`semperfi`), directory paths (`\\butler\profiles\paulr\NTUser.man`), Internet addresses (`semperfi.ingr.com`), and TCP/IP addresses (`129.135.253.14`) also appear in this special typeface.

◆ Entries from the Registry, lines of command code typed at the prompt, etc. appear on a separate line for readability, and also use the computer typeface. Here's an example:

```
\HKEY_LOCAL_MACHINE\SYSTEM\CurrentControlSet\Control\Print
```

- ◆ Command syntax shows variables in `italic monospace`. Parentheses included in the monospace font are part of the command: `CreateFile()`.

- ◆ Terms being defined or emphasized appear in *italics* within regular text.

- ◆ Text that the reader is instructed to type appears in **`bold monospace`**. Unless otherwise instructed within the text, press the Enter key after completing the boldfaced entry.

- ◆ Menu commands and options are indicated with underlined hot keys and a vertical bar to divide menu levels: <u>O</u>ptions | <u>L</u>ow Speed Connection.

PART I

Windows NT Server Fundamentals

Chapter | 1

Introducing
Windows NT

In This Chapter:

* A Brief History of Windows NT
* Windows NT Features
* New Features in NT 4.0

Windows NT has become a very popular operating system (OS) in a relatively short period of time. Since its debut in 1993, it has gone from being dismissed as a resource-hogging OS that no one wanted to being the linchpin of Microsoft's enterprise strategy and the focal point for Microsoft's BackOffice suite of enterprise-level services.

This transformation is partly the result of Microsoft's willingness to keep developing and promoting NT despite its initially poor sales and partly the result of NT's continued technical growth. This growth has been matched by the expanding capabilities of PC hardware; a high-end system at NT's original ship date was a 486/66, but Pentium, Pentium Pro, and RISC systems now provide enough computational power and I/O capacity to make full use of NT's features.

This chapter describes what differentiates NT from other desktop and server operating systems:

* High performance, including support for native 32-bit applications, a faster file system, and full multitasking
* Support for large memory spaces, large disks, and multiple CPUs
* Security, auditing, and recovery features
* Ability to integrate with NetBEUI, Macintosh, TCP/IP, Novell NetWare, and LAN Manager networks

Before discussing these features, it's helpful to gain some historical perspective on how NT came to be designed the way it is.

> **NOTE:** Even though it's usually just referred to as Windows NT, WinNT, NT, or NTS, this book specifically covers Windows NT Server 4.0. Important differences between the Server and Workstation versions of NT are highlighted where necessary, but unless you see such a note, remember that we're only discussing NTS.

A Brief History of Windows NT

NT was designed to give Microsoft a vehicle for dominating both the desktop and server markets. In the mid-1980s, Microsoft and IBM reached an agreement to develop a successor to MS-DOS. This operating system was supposed to take full advantage of the Intel 80386 processor and its successors by running 32-bit applications, and the original agreement called for cooperative development of a robust, secure, high-performance OS that would finally provide a credible alternative to UNIX.

Unfortunately, the agreement fell victim to the intense rivalry between Microsoft and IBM. IBM continued work on what became OS/2 1.0, while Microsoft elected to start fresh, keeping only the Windows 3.x user interface. The "NT" designation came from Microsoft's vow to implement *new technology* as a base for its entry into the OS battle. This technology would make NT suitable for two primary environments: the high-performance desktop (for demanding applications like CAD and software development) and midrange servers.

To ensure that NT was suitable for both environments, Microsoft adopted a two-tier strategy. Windows NT Workstation (NTW) was the desktop operating system targeted at corporate users. NT Server (abbreviated NTS—it was originally called NT Advanced Server, or NTAS) included all the features of NTW, plus features designed to make it an ideal server operating system. Giving a cue to their intentions, Microsoft hired Dave Cutler to lead the NT development effort. Cutler was already known for his role as lead architect of another highly successful OS: Digital's VMS. While many IS managers and users (*especially* UNIX users) disdain VMS as clunky, verbose, and outmoded, it's a rock-solid, secure OS that handles millions of client/server transactions per day at sites all over the world. Microsoft wanted the same reputation for stability, performance, and protection that VMS has enjoyed for nearly 20 years.

The original Microsoft plan was to sell NTS as the scalable server OS for all layers of the enterprise, with NTW on power users' desks and Windows 3.1 or Windows for Workgroups everywhere else; NTS would replace Novell, Banyan, and UNIX servers while abetting Microsoft's efforts to put Windows 3.1 everywhere else.

1993: NT 3.1

In counterpoint to these lofty goals, NT got off to a relatively slow start. First, its original launch was delayed by more than a year as Microsoft missed its first two publicly announced ship dates. When Windows NT 3.1 was finally released in 1993, it opened to less-than-favorable reviews. NTW and NTS required many more system resources than Windows 3.1, and very few applications were available to capitalize on its new features. First-year sales were disappointing, and, compared to the strong sales of IBM's OS/2 2.x series, Windows NT appeared to be, if not an outright failure, at least a disappointment to Microsoft.

Despite this initially poor launch, Microsoft continued to back NT as its preferred vehicle for software development and application servers. One of Microsoft's strengths has always been incrementally improving software products. At the same time that Microsoft was working on addressing the weaknesses of NT 3.1, users and IS managers began looking forward to the day when NT's processor and memory requirements wouldn't be so onerous. The potential gains in performance, security, and administrative overhead that NT promised made it a very attractive platform—provided that suitable hardware was available.

1994: NT 3.5

Microsoft helped boost NT's acceptance by releasing Windows NT 3.5 in 1994. Version 3.5 was a much better performer than the original; at about the same time, the Intel Pentium processor family, with its ever-increasing clock speeds, began to make significant inroads into the desktop and server hardware markets. The Pentium finally provided an adequate amount of computing power for NT's demands. It also didn't hurt that Microsoft and its partners had been busy porting NT to a number of high-performance RISC architectures, including DEC's Alpha and the MIPS Rx000 series.

The first NT-enabled applications began to appear in 1994. Some were just Windows 3.1 applications that had been recompiled with 32-bit compilers (thus gaining significant performance under NT), but others, like Microsoft's Office and Visual C++, and Intergraph's MicroStation CAD package, took advantage of NT-only features like long file names, file system permissions, and the system registry. With applications available to help kindle user interest, sales of NT 3.5 continued to build steadily throughout 1994.

1995: NT 3.51

By early 1995, Microsoft had announced that one of the best ways to prepare applications to run under Windows 95 would be to ensure that they also ran under NT. Because NT was widely available to developers, many vendors took note and started making sure that their new releases would run well under NT and take advantage of its features where possible.

NTS began to make inroads into the server market in 1995 as well. Word began to spread that NTS was a good OS for serving data to Windows for Workgroups and Windows 3.1 clients. The release of NT 3.51 addressed some items on users' and vendors' wish lists—support for the PowerPC RISC CPU, improved support for PC Card drives and cards, and still more performance improvements. NT 3.51 also included the *Common Controls Library,* one of the key user interface components of Windows 95. Individual users and IS departments began to install NTS and NTW to see whether these operating systems would fit well into their enterprises, and to prepare for the coming of Windows 95.

1996: NT 4.0

Windows NT 4.0 is Microsoft's choice to be the primary desktop and OS in the enterprise, with Windows 95 relegated to laptop and home/small office uses and Windows 3.1 shoved off into the shadows. NT 4.0 keeps all the power, speed, security, and administration features of NT 3.51 and adds the user interface enhancements introduced in Windows 95. In addition, a number of architectural changes improve its usability and performance. Those changes are discussed in more detail in the later section "New Features in NT 4.0."

Windows NT Features

To evaluate NT's worth as an operating system, you must evaluate its features and how they apply to your users, network, and enterprise. What features make Windows NT a valuable OS? Let's examine some of NT's key selling points and see how they compare to other deployed operating systems.

32-Bit Architecture

MS-DOS was originally designed to take advantage of a particular processor: the 8-bit Intel 8086. As technology advanced, that 8086 begat the 16-bit 80286, which in turn grew into the 32-bit 80386, 80486, Pentium, and Pentium Pro. Processors grew more sophisticated, but for the most part, their operating systems didn't. NT was designed from the ground up to take full advantage of 32-bit microprocessors like the x86 family.

32-bit microprocessors like the Pentium and Pentium Pro are optimized for moving data around in 32-bit chunks. MS-DOS—and applications written for it—were limited by the 16-bit data size of the 80286. This limitation effectively throttled the CPU; even though 32-bit processors became very common in 1993 and 1994, the existing base of 16-bit applications kept Microsoft from converting its core Windows 3.x code.

Windows NT was designed from the start to be completely 32-bit. All the kernel and system code moves data in 32-bit blocks, and applications that are written to do the same can take advantage of the vastly increased performance that comes with moving twice as much data per instruction.

Of course, WinNT also supports most older 16-bit applications by running them in a *virtual DOS machine (VDM)*—in short, a DOS emulator. The VDM offers backward compatibility, but at a significant performance cost. In fact, running 16-bit code on the Pentium Pro is actually slower than running the same code on a Pentium; the Pro's internal CPU architecture slows down when forced to work with anything other than 32-bit data blocks.

Support for Large Memory and Storage Devices

Another lingering artifact of the MS-DOS/8086 connection was the 640KB restriction on memory size. XMS and EMS memory helped work around this limit, but users were still burdened with having to juggle drivers and software to stay within the 640KB boundary.

WinNT flattens the address space; instead of many 64KB segments—which programmers had to track like shepherds—the computer's RAM appears as one large, contiguous space. This use of *linear address space* means that programs can use memory without regard to what physical segment it's in, which greatly simplifies development. Users benefit because any piece of code can be loaded and run from any area of the address space—no more 640KB restrictions.

WinNT also includes seamless support for virtual memory, with a per-process address space limit of 4GB! Although this per-process allocation may seem ridiculously large, high-end machines that accept 256MB or more of RAM (like Intergraph's Intel-based ISMP servers and TDZ workstations) are becoming commonplace, and that means that memory-hungry applications will be with us for a while.

WinNT also supports very large storage devices—up to 4 terabytes (4,000 gigabytes) as a single device! Large disks can be combined to make one logical volume out of several individual disks. WinNT also supports *disk mirroring* and *striping*—two techniques for providing redundancy and faster data access that we'll examine in more detail later.

Multithreading, Multiprocessor, and Multi-Architecture Support

MS-DOS and Windows 3.x are tightly bound to each other and to a particular hardware architecture: the Intel x86 family. Since their appearance in the marketplace, operating system technology has evolved, but this tight binding made it very difficult to upgrade their fundamental architecture or to move them to other platforms. Microsoft included multiprocessor support, flexible multitasking, and support for different CPU types as critical parts of NT's design.

Multithreading allows programs to run as sets of *threads*; each thread is a single task within the program. For example, a server application can have one main thread that processes requests and spawns a new worker thread for each request it services. Breaking tasks down into threads enables NT to schedule the use of system resources more effectively; for server applications, it's much more efficient to use multiple threads within a single process than to adopt the UNIX model of creating a separate process for each request.

Multiprocessor support enables NT to run on computers with multiple CPUs. These multiprocessor machines were rare when NT 3.1 made its debut, but they are now common sights as manufacturers like Dell, Compaq, and Intergraph are shipping relatively inexpensive two-, four-, and six-processor servers and desktop machines. NT has the capability to distribute processes and threads to unused processors in a computer, and it automatically balances the CPU load to keep overall performance as high as possible. The thread scheduler automatically takes advantage of as many CPUs as are in the machine, with no extra work required of either the user or the application developer. Because Windows NT shares the system load across all available processors, it's sometimes called a *symmetric multiprocessing* (*SMP*) operating system; you'll often see SMP used to describe multiprocessor computers running Windows NT.

Multi-architecture support frees NT from dependence on Intel processors. Although the Intel processor family commands the lion's share of the desktop computer market, high-performance RISC workstations and servers still dominate some application areas, like digital video editing and CAD. NT was expressly designed to be portable to a wide range of existing (and future) CPU architectures; at present, NT is available for the MIPS Rx000 series, the Motorola/IBM/Apple PowerPC and the DEC Alpha CPU.

Security and Auditing

MS-DOS and Windows 3.x were originally designed to fit into the prevailing environment at the time—non-networked machines used by one user. In this environment, there's not much need for security features like those found in NetWare and UNIX. Because NT was intended to be used in a very different environment, it features more robust security.

NT's security features are based on the concept that every object in the system—a block of memory, a file, a user, or a network—can have access controls attached. These controls tell NT's security subsystem who may and who may not create, delete, modify, or access objects. These access controls are mandatory; that is, users can't bypass or ignore them.

The first and most obvious manifestation of NT's security subsystem is the login facility. Users have to log in to each individual workstation before they can do anything. Logins are verified against a distributed database of user account and privilege information. After a user is logged in, what that user can do is limited by access permissions on system objects.

The auditing subsystem can track successful and failed attempts to use objects in the system, or to set and change their permissions.

NOTE: The National Computer Security Center (NCSC) rates OS security according to a set of criteria called the Orange Book. WinNT earned a C2 rating (fairly high for an off-the-shelf, commercially-available OS) as a standalone workstation only. It doesn't meet the C2 criteria when NT's networking software is installed, whether or not it's active.

File System Support

The capabilities of an operating system's file storage system have a great influence over the overall security and performance of the OS. File and database servers are particularly sensitive to this influence, because their throughput depends heavily on the file system.

The MS-DOS file allocation table (FAT) file system was designed in an era of 180KB floppies and 5MB hard disks. Because of the 16-bit size limit (as well as other design compromises), FAT can be used only on volumes smaller than 2GB. The original FAT file system also lacks access controls, a way to set user permissions, and support for long file names. Windows NT partially addresses these difficulties; it allows the use of permissions on shared FAT volumes and (starting with Windows NT 3.51) it supports long file names on FAT partitions.

The NT file system (NTFS) remedies these deficiencies by providing a different architectural design for the file system. NTFS is designed to support volumes up to 4 terabytes without a performance penalty. It also includes support for long file names and volume names, and an extensive set of file permissions for local users and groups. NTFS also provides *journaling*; file system writes are logged. The Windows NT kernel automatically undoes write operations that failed partway through. Journaling increases the odds that the file system will stay in a usable state even after a crash or device failure.

NT was expressly intended to support different file systems via an installable file system interface that lets developers write high-level drivers to quickly integrate new types of file systems. In addition to NTFS and FAT file systems, NT can also serve volumes to Macintosh clients via the Services for Macintosh package; exported volumes appear to Mac clients just like native Mac volumes.

Connectivity Options

Windows has always supported Microsoft's own proprietary networking protocols: the *NetBEUI* interface for letting programs make network calls and the *Server Message Block* (*SMB*) protocol for communicating between clients and servers.

NT expands on that support by providing network software layers that provide AppleTalk, TCP/IP, and Novell NetWare support. These layers give NTS the capability to be a file and print server for Windows, LAN Manager, AppleTalk, OS/2, or Novell right out of the box. In addition, NTW clients can mount and use TCP/IP printers and NetWare volumes.

A number of third-party installable file systems let NT both serve and use *Network File System* (*NFS*) volumes. For example, Intergraph's DiskShare package lets you share volumes to NFS clients by sharing them from File Manager or Explorer, while their DiskAccess client allows you to browse NFS shares from the Network Neighborhood, Explorer, or anywhere you can browse Windows resources.

> **NOTE:** DiskAccess and DiskShare are both included on the accompanying CD.

These services in many cases can be gatewayed, so an NTS machine can offer a NetWare printer as a shared printer that any Windows networking client can see. The NTS NetWare compatibility layer takes care of translating NetBIOS requests from the print clients into NetWare packets for the print server. Figure 1-1 shows this gateway in operation. Requests from the Windows network clients on the left are translated into NetWare packets by the server. When NetWare packets come back in response, the server translates those as well. The Windows clients think they're communicating with Windows Networking servers, and the NTS machine handles all the protocol translation. NT also supports the Hewlett-Packard DLC protocol for communicating with shared printers that are on the network.

Windows NT was designed to allow these protocols to coexist on one computer, so a server running NTS could serve files to NetWare, Mac, and Windows clients. In addition, Windows NT can easily handle multiple network interface cards (NICs) in a single machine; you can bind protocols to specific adapters or run the same protocols on all adapters. When you install multiple NICs, Windows NT supports internetwork routing, so one NTS machine can route packets between multiple subnets—even if they're using different protocols.

Windows NT also includes support for connecting to remote networks via modem or ISDN. This support goes in both directions. Windows NT users can use the Dial-Up Networking (DUN) subsystem to reach corporate networks from home or at remote sites, while the Windows NT Server side allows an NTS machine to act as a dial-up server.

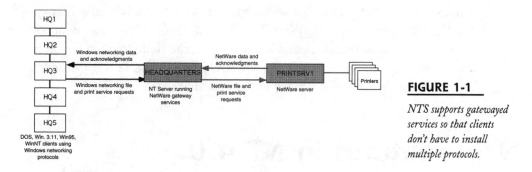

FIGURE 1-1

NTS supports gatewayed services so that clients don't have to install multiple protocols.

Focal Point for BackOffice

In 1995, Microsoft began to push its BackOffice concept: a unified family of server products—based on NTS—that could provide a wide array of services to the enterprise. Unsurprisingly, NTS has continued to be the focal point of this concept—although the individual server products can be used alone, they all require NTS. BackOffice comprises six products; each one provides a single class of service:

* NTS itself provides operating system, file, and print services.

* Internet Information Server (included with NTS 4.0) offers a mechanism for serving data to users on TCP/IP networks, including the worldwide Internet.

* SQL Server is a relational database engine intended to compete with offerings from Sybase, Oracle, and Informix.

* Exchange Server is the server end of Microsoft's Exchange messaging and groupware solution.

* SNA Server is a gateway product that allows Microsoft network clients to communicate with mainframes and minicomputers, using IBM's Systems Network Architecture (SNA) communications protocol.

* The newest piece of BackOffice is the System Management Server (SMS), an ambitious effort targeted at large networks. SMS is designed to provide centralized installation, auditing, and management of desktop software, as well as remote control of desktop hardware—giving network managers a single solution for managing machines on their networks.

Windows NT includes a number of features that were formerly reserved for UNIX or NetWare: integration with NetWare, TCP/IP, and AppleTalk networks; support for multiple users, file permissions, and logon security; the ability to run on multiprocessor computers; and support for large disks and RAM. Windows NT 4.0 also adds a number of key new features, as described in the following section.

New Features in NT 4.0

When the first rumors started to circulate about Cairo, the code name for the successor to NT 3.x, quite a bit of speculation was about what it would include. Magazine writers and online pundits started calling Cairo "NT 4.0," as it was to be a major upgrade to 3.x.

Since then, Cairo has moved from being a single release of software to a group of technologies that Microsoft will gradually introduce into future releases of NTW and NTS. The first group of Cairo technologies actually appeared in Win95; the revamped user interface (UI) and Plug and Play hardware support were originally slated for Cairo.

In the fall of 1995, Microsoft released a "preview" of NT 4.0 called the *Shell Update Release* (*SUR*). SUR basically added the Win95 user interface to NT, but it was released as unsupported software, and many applications didn't work with it. NT 4.0 includes a great deal more functionality than the SUR—some of which isn't immediately apparent. Unless otherwise noted, all the changes discussed in the following text are in both NTW and NTS.

NOTE: In October 1996, Microsoft announced that the followup to NT 4.0 would be released mid-to-late 1997. You should expect to see some Cairo features bundled into NT service packs. The first service pack (SP1) for Windows NT 4.0 was released in September 1996, and others will undoubtedly follow.

Windows 95 Interface

One change that's immediately obvious is NT 4.0's new look and feel. Microsoft has adapted the Windows 95 user interface look and feel NT 4.0 incorporates the Win95 shell components (the Start menu, Taskbar, desktop, and Explorer) as its own, including all the exported interfaces that other programs can use to extend the shell. The NT desktop also offers a revamped Task Manager and login manager.

NT 4.0 also includes the Win95 common controls and dialog boxes. The common controls were actually included in NT 3.51, but most NT applications weren't written to take advantage of them at the time. However, many Windows 95 applications can run on NT now that these controls are available. Finally, Version 4.0 of the Windows Help subsystem (which made its debut in Win95) has made the transition as well. Some of the user interface changes, like the right-click context menu, rely on extensions made to the Object Linking and Embedding subsystem.

Enhancements to Object Linking and Embedding (OLE)

For some time, Windows has supported the concept of embedding and linking data objects created by one application into another; this functionality, known as *Object Linking and Embedding (OLE)*, is the muscle behind the integration of Microsoft Office and a number of Office-compatible applications. OLE-capable applications can share data while preserving the appearance and native content of the shared data.

Network OLE extends the ability to link and share information across the network. Instead of requiring that the data objects be copied when their container is moved, Network OLE supports cross-network links. Microsoft stunned many observers by announcing that Network OLE—which most of the industry thought would be delayed at least until 1997—would be included in NT 4.0.

Network OLE allows OLE clients and servers to call OLE routines that are actually running on other machines on the network, instead of being limited to the same machine. For example, a large server running an OLE-capable CAD program could be an OLE server, serving CAD drawings to Microsoft Office users on network workstations. Users can share and modify data elements that reside permanently on the server. Network OLE transmits a representation of the data to the user's machine and allows the data to be edited remotely—transparently to the user! Network OLE isn't the only new networking and communications feature in Windows NT 4.0, though, as noted in the next section.

Networking and Communications

NT 4.0 includes some significant networking and communications capabilities that are new to the NT platform. The most promoted among these is Microsoft's *Internet Information Server* (*IIS*), a fast and well-featured server for Internet clients. Microsoft released it as freeware for NTS 3.51 in 1996, and it's included as part of NTS 4.0 as well.

NT 4.0 also includes full support for the *Telephony API* (*TAPI*). NT 3.51 supported a subset of TAPI, but full support means that NT 4.0 can run the Microsoft Exchange client and the new Dial-Up Networking subsystem—both of which are included. The *Messaging API* (*MAPI*) layer of NT 4.0 now supports the full set of extensions added for communicating with Microsoft Exchange servers.

In previous NT releases, you could map TCP/IP addresses to host names, using the Windows Internet Name Service (WINS), but if you wanted to use the Internet-standard Domain Name Service (DNS) protocol, you needed a third-party product. NT 4.0 includes a DNS service that integrates DNS with WINS to improve the mapping between computer names (`semperfi`), Internet addresses (`semperfi.ingr.com`), and TCP/IP addresses (`129.135.253.14`).

NT 4.0 also improves its integration with NetWare networks. NTW users can now run NetWare login scripts, and overall file and print communications with NetWare have been improved.

Architectural Changes and API Extensions

In addition to the changes discussed in the preceding sections—most of which are visible to users and administrators—there are some other, less visible changes at the system level in NT.

NT segregates processing into two areas. The kernel subsystem handles system processing; it's where the operating system itself runs, as well as its trusted processes. The *user* subsystem is where user programs and services run. In addition, there are other subsystems: the *Graphic Device Interface* (*GDI*) provides a way for applications to draw or print images and text, and the Win32 subsystem provides the actual interface between application-level code and the kernel.

The most talked-about change in NT 4.0 might be one that's invisible to users: the rearrangement of the user, kernel, and GDI subsystems. In NT 3.x, the entire Win32 subsystem ran as a separate process. This split caused some additional overhead, because calls to the GDI and user subsystems had to be routed through the kernel. But it also made NT very stable, because a crash in the Win32 subsystem wouldn't affect other applications.

For NT 4.0, adding the new shell and UI elements into the Win32 subsystem would have incurred an unacceptable performance decrease. To avoid slowing things down, Microsoft moved the NT 4.0 Win32 subsystem into the kernel's address space, as it is in Win95. See Figure 1-2 for a before-and-after comparison; the top half shows the design for older versions of Windows NT, while the bottom half shows the arrangement used in Windows NT 4.0. It remains to be seen whether this change will compromise NT's stability.

> For an exposition of the low-level details of Windows NT architecture, see Chapter 2, "Understanding Windows NT Architecture."

NT 4.0 includes a large number of new API routines. Some provide support for new shell features, like the ability to use the right mouse button to activate a *context menu* whose contents vary depending on what you click. Other API routines provide new services as part of the OS or incorporate support for features first introduced in Win95. Examples include partial support for Plug and Play, access to the groupware features of the Exchange server, and a consistent way for programmers to add new services to the context menu.

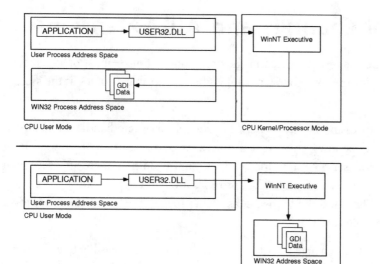

FIGURE 1-2

In NT 4.0, the Win32 subsystem moves from an independent process in user space into the system's kernel.

There are also some all-new APIs. The *Cryptography API* (*CryptoAPI* for short) provides a single unified interface for cryptographic system services. CryptoAPI makes it possible for application developers to include data security and authentication features in their application by using the system-provided security modules (or user-installed modules that follow the CryptoAPI specification.) By integrating cryptographic security at the OS level, Microsoft hopes to spur its use in application programs, thus providing greater overall security for Windows NT users and administrators.

The Win95 DirectX APIs, which provide direct access to graphics and sound hardware, are also included, although they aren't completely implemented. The Windows GDI subsystem is *device-independent*; any application can run on any device that supports the GDI, without knowing the particulars of that device. This portability imposes some performance overhead, and many vendors chose to implement drawing and sound routines using their own libraries—which were often incompatible with Win95 and Windows NT. DirectX was originally designed to give game and multimedia developers improved performance by letting them bypass much of the existing GDI API, but in a portable way that didn't require intimate knowledge of each type of display card. Other applications, like 3-D modelers and programs that manipulate sound, are starting to use DirectX calls as well.

Extended Hardware Support

Although most installations of NTW and NTS are on fairly ordinary Intel-based computers, several trends are moving new hardware capabilities into the NT world. The expanded availability (and reduced cost) of powerful RISC-based machines has made NT on RISC a much more common sight. RISC hardware and NT are natural partners, since NT requires a lot of system power to run effectively and well. When NT 3.1 first shipped, it supported only the x86 and MIPS processor families; in later releases, the Alpha and PowerPC processors were supported as well. As systems using these processors have become more common, application vendors have had an incentive to port their products from the Intel architecture.

NT 4.0 also improves on some other hardware features of 3.51. PC Cards are better supported. This support is important in light of the growing number of users running NT on laptop or portable computers, as well as the proliferation of desktop machines with integrated or external PC Card slots.

Another very useful feature is the capability to build hardware profiles. NT has always supported multiple-boot software configurations, but NT 4.0 adds support for multiple-boot hardware configurations. Each profile specifies which system services and drivers should be loaded, based on the hardware configuration. This capacity allows users whose machines can have different configurations—for example, notebook computers that can be docked to a desktop adapter—to switch between sets of drivers appropriate for each configuration.

A unique feature of NT is that, when run on RISC CPUs, it can emulate the Intel x86 instruction set. NT 3.x could only emulate a 286. NT 4.0 for RISC can now run enhanced-mode 386 applications.

Where to Go Next

This chapter provides an overview of NT's history and features, including three key features that make it a contender for use as an enterprise server OS:

* High performance and large capacity
* Support for enterprise-wide security and auditing

* Interoperability with Windows, Macintosh, TCP/IP, NetWare, and other common network protocols

The next chapter provides more details about NT's architecture and design, as well as how it supports enterprise-wide networking. There are some other chapters and resources which you may find useful at this point:

* Chapter 2, "Understanding Windows NT Architecture," discusses the details of NT's architectural underpinnings.

* Chapter 3, "Planning for Your NT Server Installation," addresses some points that you should consider before purchasing and installing your NT servers.

* Chapter 4, "Installing Windows NT Server," covers the process of installing NTS on Intel and RISC hardware, including upgrading from NT 3.51.

Chapter | 2

Understanding Windows NT Architecture

In This Chapter:

* The Windows NT System Architecture
* The Windows NT Networking Model
* The Windows NT Memory Model

Windows NT's architecture is fundamentally different from its 16-bit predecessors. These architectural changes give Windows NT its performance, stability, and security advantages, but the same changes have created some incompatibilities and quirks of which you should be aware.

Over the long term, Microsoft plans to unify all its operating systems by using a common 32-bit architecture. Unsurprisingly, this architecture very closely resembles that of Windows NT 4.0. This chapter examines this architecture, discussing the following topics:

* The fundamental parts of Windows NT's architecture: the kernel, hardware abstraction layer, and user-mode components
* The design of the network driver and service layers
* The Windows NT memory management system, including its virtual memory manager

The Windows NT System Architecture

Windows NT was designed to usurp UNIX's role in the OS marketplace. This role is really two distinct roles. On one hand, NT was intended to be a desktop OS for high-end users; on the other, it was designed to be a robust, fast, scalable server OS. To meet both of these objectives, NT was designed around a number of desirable characteristics (see Chapter 1, "Introducing Windows NT").

Windows NT is based on an *executive* that provides operating system services such as allocating memory, reading and writing disk files, and controlling access to objects in the system. The executive has several distinct parts, discussed later. First, it's important to understand the two different modes in which Windows NT can run code: *kernel mode* and *user mode*.

Kernel Mode Code

Most multiuser operating systems are based on the concept of a system *kernel*, a small piece of code that runs as a privileged program and answers requests for services. The kernel may use a special execution mode of the host CPU if it has one (like the PowerPC's supervisor mode); whether or not it does, it alone has direct access to system resources such as sectors on a hard disk. Processes that want to do I/O, allocate memory, and so on, do so by making requests to the kernel.

Windows NT provides similar functionality in its *Executive*. The Windows NT Executive provides system services to other subsystems and applications. The Executive runs in *kernel mode*. Code executed in kernel mode has full access to all objects and hardware in the system. This unrestricted access is necessary to implement capabilities like the security monitor and virtual memory manager. Not all the Windows NT system functions run in kernel mode; some are implemented in the protected subsystems, as discussed later in this chapter. The diagram in Figure 2-1 shows the Executive's major components and how they fit together.

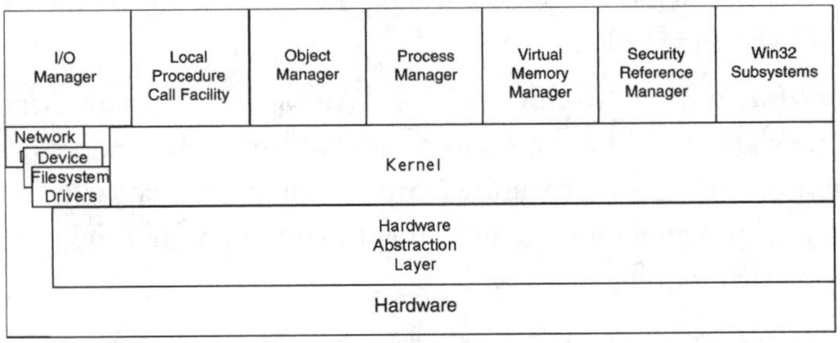

FIGURE 2-1

The Executive runs in kernel mode; its services allow subsystems to access system resources.

The Windows NT Executive

The Executive provides operating system services to subsystems and, through the various subsystems, to user applications. When a service request reaches a component of the Executive, NT runs the appropriate Executive manager in kernel mode. The manager fulfills the request (or returns a failure code if it can't perform the requested operation), and then the Executive leaves kernel mode and returns control to the caller.

The Executive is made up of nine components. Each provides a specific set of services to the NT subsystems (shown on the following page):

* The *Local Procedure Call (LPC) Manager* provides a mechanism that threads and processes can use to communicate with one another. Threads in one process can use LPC services to exchange data with threads in another process. LPCs are an optimized variation of the industry-standard Remote Procedure Call (RPC) mechanism, which NT also supports.

* The *Object Manager* creates, deletes, and tracks system objects. Each resource in the system (I/O ports, CPUs, disks, and so on) is represented by a unique object. The Object Manager is responsible for creating resource objects when a subsystem needs resource access and deleting objects when they're no longer in use. Access to objects is limited to authorized users.

* The *Process Manager* creates, deletes, schedules, starts, and stops processes and threads. In this role, it's responsible for implementing Windows NT's multithreading and multiprocessing capabilities. The Process Manager makes heavy use of the kernel's thread and task services.

* The *Security Reference Monitor* implements the lowest level of Windows NT security policies. It grants access tokens to processes and checks those tokens against the access control list for any Object Manager object that a user attempts to access. This access-based screening forms the foundation of the Windows NT security implementation.

* The *Virtual Memory Manager* provides the NT virtual memory subsystem. This manager allows processes to specify their working set size and to lock or unlock individual pages to maximize performance. It automatically provides a significant amount of optimization by constantly adjusting the working set of each running process.

The remaining four components—the I/O Manager, kernel, Hardware Abstraction Layer (HAL), and Win32 subsystems—are discussed separately.

I/O Manager

The *I/O Manager (IOM)* is designed to offer a standard method of accessing I/O devices, including floppy disk drives, hard disk drives, CD-ROMs, removable media drives, network interface cards, sound cards, and PC Card devices. The IOM depends on *device drivers*, which actually communicate with each other and with hardware devices. All the IOM does is accept I/O requests from subsystems and route them to the appropriate drivers for action. These drivers are portable, since they rely on the HAL for hardware access. In addition, every driver has a simple, fairly small set of commands that it must support.

Some devices, such as modems and printers, use single-layer drivers. The IOM sends a request to the driver, which sends it to the hardware device. File systems and disks use multi-layer drivers. When an application requests a block of data from disk, the request goes to the IOM, which sends it to the appropriate file system driver. That driver in turn translates the requests into a series of driver requests that it sends—via the IOM—to the driver for that disk family.

File systems are just another driver layer. Windows NT was specifically designed to make it easy to support new file systems by writing a driver for that file system type. By itself, NT supports the FAT, NTFS, and *CD File System* (*CDFS*) file systems. There are installable file system drivers for UNIX, NFS, and Macintosh volumes as well.

The IOM can dynamically load or unload drivers when requested. This makes it easy to enable or disable devices without having to reboot or shut down servers.

Kernel

The kernel provides a small set of services, called *primitives*, to other parts of the Executive. Primitives are the lowest level of operations available to Executive callers. Typical primitives do things like allocate a section of memory, allow multiple threads to synchronize their execution, and similar housekeeping tasks.

The kernel is the fundamental bedrock beneath Windows NT. It offers three critical services to other parts of the Executive:

* It schedules thread execution, controlling the execution order and priority for all active threads. It adjusts thread priorities dynamically both up and down, to balance the system's load as needed, and it automatically assigns threads to individual processors in multiprocessor machines.

* It catches interrupts and forwards them to the appropriate handlers. These handlers may be in the kernel (for things like I/O interrupts), a protected subsystem (for things like illegal memory accesses), or user programs (for things like floating-point overflow or underflow errors.)

*   It provides primitives for synchronizing operations on multiple processors, including semaphores, mutual-exclusion objects, and event objects. These primitives allow two or more threads to suspend themselves until some operation is complete.

The kernel is unique in another way—it can't be interrupted or preempted by other code. When the kernel is executing, it has complete usage of the CPU and doesn't share it; however, Windows NT spends very little time actually running any section code from the kernel, since the primitives are all small and fast.

Each of the Executive services makes calls to kernel primitives; however, the kernel primitives can call only other primitives and routines in the HAL—they can't call routines in other Executive services.

HAL

The *Hardware Abstraction Layer* (*HAL*) isolates all the hardware-specific code into a small, highly specialized bundle. The HAL provides functions for direct access to the machine's hardware subsystems; instead of making direct calls to move data between the CPU and external devices, the Executive and kernel call routines in the HAL. Because the subsystems call routines in the Executive to get hardware access, they are completely isolated from details of the hardware. In fact, Windows NT disallows direct hardware access for user-mode code (with the notable exception of the DirectX drawing and sound interfaces.)

Because the HAL is intimately tied to a particular hardware architecture, it has to be individually ported to each architecture that NT supports. There are at least three separate HALs for Intel x86-based systems alone—one for ordinary single-processor PCs, one for machines using the Corollary multiprocessor architecture, and one for machines using Intel's multiprocessor architecture—and that's not counting HALs for RISC CPUs! However, porting the kernel and the rest of the Executive goes faster, because their code doesn't have to be changed to accommodate the differences between the Intel x86 and, say, the PowerPC CPU.

Win32 Subsystem

In earlier versions of Windows NT, the Win32 subsystem was a protected subsystem like the OS/2, virtual DOS machine, and POSIX subsystems (described later). In order to implement the new shell and GUI functionality of NT 4.0, Microsoft wanted to reduce the amount of overhead caused by context switches between kernel-mode code and the Win32 subsystem. To accomplish this, the Win32 subsystem was moved into the kernel.

This move means that the Win32 subsystem has direct access to system services offered by Executive components. The original design protected other subsystems, and applications which used them, from badly-behaved code. The Win32 subsystem might crash, but that crash wouldn't affect the Executive or other subsystems. In Windows NT 4.0, code that causes the Win32 subsystem to crash can potentially disrupt the kernel and Executive, bringing down the entire machine. It remains to be seen whether this possibility really represents a net loss of stability, especially when balanced against the substantial performance improvement it offers.

The subsystem itself is made up of two components: the User subsystem (USER.EXE), which handles user interaction and processing of events generated by the user, and the Graphic Device Independent Drawing subsystem, usually abbreviated as GDI. GDI provides a way for programs to draw on printing devices, plotters, and displays of varying resolution and color capability without having to write special code for each device. User and GDI are used to build the entire Windows NT user interface.

User-Mode Code

By contrast with kernel mode, user-mode code has only limited access to system resources and services. The only way for a program running in user mode to receive a service like thread scheduling or memory allocation is to request it from the Executive.

System Services Layer

The *system services layer* (*SSL*) is the glue that binds together user-mode code and the Windows NT Executive. When an application or subsystem calls an NT routine, the call is translated into a message and passed into the SSL, which validates its parameters and either forwards it on to an Executive service or rejects it. This relationship is a client/ server system; the caller is the client, and the SSL is the server. When an application or subsystem makes an SSL request, the SSL can in turn make several requests to Executive services. For example, the NT CreateFile() routine causes the SSL to create a new file object through a call to the Object Manager. That object is then forwarded by the SSL to the I/O Manager to create a directory entry for the file.

The client/server nature of the SSL does add some overhead, which was the primary reason for moving the Win32 subsystem into the Executive proper. However, interposing the SSL between callers and the Executive allows the SSL to isolate the Executive from callers that require Executive services. The resulting stability and security benefits outweigh the performance decrease.

Protected Subsystems

Windows NT supports programs written using a number of programming interfaces. It can run 16-bit MS-DOS or Windows 3.x programs as well as 32-bit programs written for IBM's OS/2, the IEEE POSIX standard, and Win32. This flexibility is due to the NT *protected subsystems*, so named because they serve as a buffer between application programs and the SSL. Applications request services from the protected subsystems. If an OS/2 application crashes, it may affect the OS/2 subsystem, but it can't affect Win32, Win16, MS-DOS, or POSIX applications. In addition, individual processes that run in the same subsystem can't affect each other (except through the use of supported interprocess communication routines).

The SSL and Executive provide one set of behaviors for actions such as creating processes, allocating memory, opening files, and so on. The protected subsystems encapsulate these behaviors in code that emulates the behavior that the native applications expect. Figure 2-2 shows the relationship between applications, subsystems, and the Executive.

Each protected subsystem provides a set of interfaces that applications use, just like the native environment that the subsystem emulates. The subsystem's DLLs translate calls to native OS/2, POSIX, DOS, or Win16 routines into requests for Win32 or Executive services. The SSL services those requests as though they came from native Win32 applications.

The *Virtual DOS Machine* (*VDM*) and *Win16-on-Windows* (*WOW*) subsystems are worthy of special mention, because they're used most often. Each VDM provides a complete MS-DOS environment, including a command interpreter and 16-bit address space. Each MS-DOS program or shell actually gets a separate VDM. Because all VDMs share a single I/O and event queue, applications in separate VDMs can't multitask effectively.

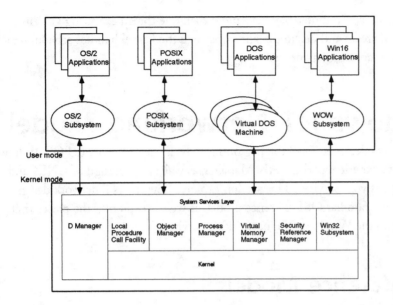

FIGURE 2-2

The protected subsystems provide different interfaces to the fundamental Executive services.

The WOW subsystem provides a Win16 environment for 16-bit Windows programs. WOW runs on top of a VDM, and it provides a way to execute several 16-bit Win3.x programs—each in its own thread—within a single Windows NT process. WOW also provides a facility for running each Win16 program in its own address space. This ensures increased stability for 16-bit applications, but imposes a small amount of overhead for each program. Running many such programs at once can cause all the programs to be unusably slow, because they all share a single VDM.

Applications

Applications aren't just programs like Imagineer or Microsoft Word. Windows NT services (managed via the Services Control Panel applet) and servers like the Microsoft Internet Information Server are applications as well. Native NT applications run in independent processes. These processes can communicate through the use of NT *interprocess communication* (*IPC*) system calls.

Each Windows NT application process has its own 4GB address space. Processes request services by calling Win32 system routines, which in turn make calls via the SSL to the Executive. Since the Win32 subsystem moved into the kernel's space, the additional overhead of calls to the NT 3.5 protected Win32 subsystem is gone. Because Windows NT is multithreaded, NT applications may have more than one thread executing at a time. Applications can create and delete threads as needed; the kernel handles scheduling all threads within an application's process.

The Windows NT Networking Model

Windows NT was designed from the beginning to be a network-oriented OS. It drew from Microsoft's experience with LAN Manager, as well as the design of UNIX and TCP/IP-based network services. This section explores how the NT network design corresponds to the familiar OSI reference model, as well as exploring the pieces that together make up the Windows NT networking services.

The OSI Reference Model

The *International Standards Organization (ISO)* defined the *Open Systems Interconnect (OSI) model* to provide an idealized reference model of how network communication takes place. Figure 2-3 shows the OSI reference stack. The dashed lines indicate protocols that can pass between equivalent layers. The only physical communication takes place via the actual physical network medium—the dark line at the bottom of the stack.

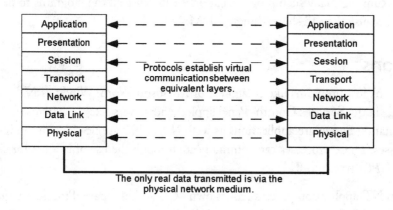

FIGURE 2-3

The OSI stack depicts an idealized network protocol stack.

Each OSI layer has a particular function and set of behaviors. Each layer provides services to the layers above it, and layers communicate directly only with the same layer on other machines. Here's a short synopsis of what each layer is responsible for doing:

* The *application layer* implements application-specific behavior, such as the FTP protocol or a Telnet session.

* The *presentation layer* controls formatting and data exchange behavior, such as byte-order conversions, data compression, and encryption. It's in charge of how the data is reformatted for presentation to the application layer.

* The *session layer* encapsulates network transmissions into "conversations" and controls synchronization and mode switching between the session's two endpoints.

* The *transport layer* provides reliable data delivery. It can also split data into packets and reassemble those packets on the receiving side.

* The *network layer* provides the services we think of as network services: routing, flow control, and so on.

* The *data link layer* controls transmission and retransmission of data. The data is formatted in accordance with the physical layer's requirements, and higher layers may reformat or modify it.

* The *physical layer* actually moves bits to and from some kind of network medium, whether it's a 10Base-T cable, a satellite link, or a modem connection.

Each OSI layer provides services that can be ordered and used to describe any arbitrary network implementation. Let's see how the Windows NT networking components fit into this model.

The Windows NT Networking Model

NT networking is built up of several layers, just like the OSI model. Each layer corresponds roughly to an OSI layer. This section examines them from lowest to highest to see how NT networking is layered.

NDIS Drivers

Microsoft's LAN Manager originally introduced what was at the time a revolutionary concept: the *network driver interface specification* (*NDIS*). Microsoft and Novell co-designed NDIS, which specifies how to write a single driver for a network card that will allow the card to support multiple protocols. This is critical for multi-protocol, environments, as without NDIS each network card would require independent—and perhaps incompatible—drivers for each supported transport. With NDIS, the NDIS-compatible driver provides a standard set of calls for managing the network card and its connection.

The NDIS driver must provide a way for the Windows NT I/O manager to request that network I/O is done. In addition, it must service the I/O interrupts generated when an I/O request starts or completes. NDIS drivers also manage physical layer issues such as media address assignments, and card-specific settings such as IRQ levels and the type of physical medium being plugged into the card. Thus the NDIS driver spans portions of the physical link and data link OSI layers.

Windows NT implements Version 3.0 of the NDIS standard, which is a full 32-bit redefinition of the original. NDIS 3.0 drivers are fully capable of running on multi-processor machines, and, when properly implemented by the card vendor, any or all of the NT transport protocols can use the NDIS driver to use the network card to move data.

Transport Protocols

The transport layer in the OSI model is equivalent to the Windows NT transport layer. Because the transport layer is responsible for moving data in usable chunks (as opposed to the lower layers, which move it in arbitrary chunks defined by the network medium), this layer is where the semantics of the network are defined.

Microsoft's networking protocols are built around the use of the NetBEUI transport, a proprietary Microsoft protocol dating back to MS-DOS 3.1. For greater functionality, Windows NT also supports the *NetBEUI-over-TCP/IP* (*NBT*) *transport*, which allows NetBEUI packets to be encapsulated and carried via TCP/IP's transport mechanism. NetBEUI can't be routed, but encapsulating it in TCP/IP overcomes this limitation by using TCP/IP's routing mechanisms. Furthermore, Windows NT provides direct TCP/IP transport as an option.

Additionally, NT can optionally support other transports, including Apple's AppleTalk, IBM's Digital Link Control (DLC), and Novell's IPX/SPX (provided by the Microsoft NWLink protocol stack). Although not all applications can use all transports, the transport mechanism is designed so that applications can use any transport with minimal extra effort. Furthermore, the transport layer used to move data is independent of the network medium and data link layer used to get it there.

File System Drivers

The Windows NT file system drivers operate at the OSI session layer. They provide a network interface to the NT file system (including the various types of file systems that NT supports.) As session layer components, they coordinate the movement of data between client and server, using Microsoft's *Server Message Block (SMB) protocol*, which was first introduced as part of MS-DOS 3.1 and is the standard Windows networking protocol. There are actually two separate file system driver components: the redirector and the server.

Redirector

The redirector reroutes file I/O requests to the network. It does so by using the NT I/O Manager's multiple layering support. An I/O request that should go over the network arrives at the I/O Manager and is automatically referred to the redirector, which starts the necessary I/O with the appropriate transport protocol and returns the results. The caller is unaware that this redirection has taken place.

Because the redirector actually implements a particular session-layer behavior, adding new redirectors to Windows NT allows it to support protocols other than SMB. Two notable redirectors that you'll see mentioned elsewhere in this book are the Novell NetWare redirector, which allows NTS machines to communicate with NetWare servers, and the Network File System (NFS) redirector, used to enable Windows NT to use files from NFS servers.

For example, when a user on a workstation named SEMPERFI tries to open a Word document stored elsewhere (let's call it \\HQMC\Manuals\FM1.doc), the IOM on SEMPERFI recognizes the requested item as a network item and calls on the redirector to service the I/O request. The redirector in turn assembles a network I/O request and sends it to the specified server with whatever protocol the redirector is currently using—in this case, HQMC. When the server returns data, the redirector passes it back to the IOM, which in turn gives it back to the original requestor.

Server

The server component is the redirector's partner. It receives, accepts, and handles requests that arrive at a server. These requests are generated by redirectors on client machines. It's the server's job to satisfy whatever I/O request the remote redirector is making. Just as with redirectors, Windows NT supports multiple servers, each implementing its own protocol. For example, a single NTS machine could run NWLink, AppleTalk, and NFS servers to serve the same files to each client type.

Drawing from the previous example, when SEMPERFI's redirector sends its request to HQMC, the server running on HQMC will generate a series of I/O requests to its own IOM. These requests get the data requested by the network I/O request and return it as a stream of network packets.

Application Programming Interfaces

The Windows NT application programming interfaces (APIs) provide services that allow applications to communicate between machines. These APIs correspond to the OSI model's application layer, and they're organized into services—for example, Windows NT provides named pipes as a service. Applications that use named pipes can open a pipe by specifying its name. The lower layers of the NT networking model, as described earlier in this chapter, handle formatting, transmitting, and guaranteeing delivery of the data. All the application has to do is read and write data from the pipe, and the rest is handled transparently.

In addition to named pipes, Windows NT supports TCP/IP sockets, mailslots (a VMS-style interprocess communications method), and network file I/O. Although file I/O may not seem to fit into this category, when an NT application opens a file that resides on a remote machine, the NT network subsystem handles all the details of moving data between the machines over the network. The application treats I/O to a network file identically with I/O to a locally stored file.

The combination of these services—NDIS drivers, transport protocols, file system drivers, and programming interfaces—provides the Windows NT implementation of the

OSI model. Each service provides some OSI functionality; when they're stacked together, they give you complete support for all seven OSI layers.

The Windows NT Memory Model

The Windows NT memory model is very different from the MS-DOS model with which most PC users are familiar. In the MS-DOS model, the address space available to programs is segmented into 64KB chunks. Moving data between chunks is difficult, and many programs and drivers depend on being loaded into the first 640KB of RAM to be usable. Fortunately, Windows NT has departed completely from the 64KB-segment model in favor of a less complex, more flexible scheme.

Windows NT doesn't segment the memory space like MS-DOS does. Instead, it offers each native NT process a 4-gigabyte address space. Of that 4GB space, 2GB is dedicated for system use, while the other 2GB is available to the application (in practice, all processes share the 2GB system area.) Applications can use this address space as a single linear range. For this reason, NT is often said to have a *linear memory model*.

The Windows NT Virtual Memory Manager

Because very few machines are likely to actually have 4GB of RAM, Windows NT implements *virtual memory*, a technique for mapping hard disk space into the address space of a process. The *virtual memory manager* (*VMM*), part of the Executive, handles all the address translation and mapping tasks required to make virtual memory work. Specifically, the VMM is responsible for the following tasks

* *Swapping* (moving unused data from physical RAM to disk and moving needed data from disk to RAM). Data is moved as 4KB *pages*, not individual bytes. The use of swapping allows processes to allocate and deallocate memory without regard to whether it's real RAM or virtual memory. Windows NT maintains one or more *paging files*, where it keeps the contents of virtual memory. These paging files are what NT uses to swap "to and from." You can have one paging file on every physical disk on your server, although placing paging files on slow disks slows the VMM's throughput. The VMM

stores and retrieves data in paging files transparently, and data stored there doesn't persist across reboots.

* Allowing processes to lock or unlock pages. Locking pages in RAM prevents them from being swapped, eliminating the swapping overhead. However, it also limits how much of a program can be in memory at once and how much RAM is available for other processes.

* Allowing processes to share memory by mapping the same virtual section into the address ranges of several processes. This *file mapping* allows applications to access data in files as though it were in memory; the VMM takes care of loading and unloading each page-size chunk of the file. Because I/O-to-RAM is much faster than disk I/O, mapping can significantly speed file operations. Furthermore, mapping is used to allow the Executive to load and execute executable code—the Executive maps the start of the file, and the VMM handles loading additional pages when needed.

* Efficiently deciding which pages can safely be swapped out and which ones should be retrieved, as well as adjusting the number of pages a particular process actually has in real RAM.

For more information on adjusting the VMM's settings, see "Tuning Virtual Memory" in Chapter 19, "Performance Tuning and Optimization."

Where to Go Next

This chapter provides you with an overview of Windows NT's architectural features—not all of which are directly visible to casual observers. It shows how NT divides processing between user-mode and kernel-mode code, what components make up the Windows NT Executive, and what the Executive does for its clients.

The next chapter moves on to considering factors that will influence how you deploy Windows NT in your network. Your understanding of the underlying NT design will help as you evaluate how much RAM, disk, and CPU power your servers need.

Here are some other resources that you may find useful at this point:

* Chapter 4, "Installing Windows NT Server," covers the process of installing NTS on Intel and RISC hardware, including upgrading from NT 3.51.

* Helen Custer's *Inside Windows NT* (Microsoft Press, 1993; ISBN 1-55615-481-X) is an exhaustive tour of the low-level features of Windows NT design and implementation. While it was written to cover NT 3.1 (and is consequently out-of-date), it offers a fascinating wealth of detail.

PART II

Installing Windows NT Server

Chapter | 3

Planning for Your NT
Server Installation

In This Chapter:

- ◆ The Importance of Planning
- ◆ Choosing the Right Hardware
- ◆ Choosing the Right Configuration
- ◆ Choosing the File System
- ◆ Defining the Server Role

Prior planning is critical for getting good value from your investment in Windows NT. Planning ahead maximizes your understanding of your requirements and minimizes the cost of meeting them. This chapter discusses the following planning topics:

- ◆ Why planning is the very first thing you should do
- ◆ How to choose appropriate hardware for your servers
- ◆ Some of the roles in which NTS servers can operate

Let's start by seeing why it's important to plan at all.

The Importance of Planning

Installing Windows NT in your network can be an expensive proposition: The software is expensive, it generally requires additional hardware, and it takes a significant amount of time. The best way to ensure a successful installation is to plan the installation thoroughly. In addition to reducing the initial adoption cost of hardware, software, and labor, proper planning will help you minimize two long-term costs: the labor cost of having people sitting idle or wasting time due to network or server failures and the lost opportunity cost you incur when you can't do business because your network isn't working. Even simple applications such as electronic mail can cost you thousands of dollars in lost time and productivity when they're not available. Of course, it would be silly to drive those costs to their absolute minimum while ratcheting up the total system cost for appropriate hardware, so it's important to strike a balance. Not every application on your network is truly critical, so you shouldn't equip every computer as though it were.

Equally importantly, prior planning can reduce the likelihood that you'll have to make costly changes later. For example, the idea of using one server as both a domain controller and a database server may sound appealing, until the database requirements grow to the point where the domain controller has to be moved elsewhere. The result: a costly and unnecessary move that could have been avoided by analysis of the cost (around $1,500 for an inexpensive P75 to act as a domain controller) versus the benefits (not having to spend several thousand dollars of people's time doing the actual move.)

The first step in your planning should be to understand clearly why you're installing Windows NT at all. A complete grasp of the motives behind the move will help you to figure out which costs and risks are safe and which are too expensive to bear. Common reasons for migrating to or adding seats of NTS include the following:

- Upgrading a network with Windows for Workgroups clients, but no (or few) centralized servers

- Replacing or supplementing NetWare or other network operating system servers

- Moving Windows for Workgroups (WfW) clients to either Windows NT Workstation or Windows 95 and simultaneously adding new, more powerful servers

- Implementing small-scale test beds of BackOffice services such as the Microsoft Exchange or SQL servers to test their usefulness before migrating the whole network

- Replacing existing database, file, and print servers with NTS

- Adding the capacity to quickly publish information on the Internet using Internet Information Server (IIS)

- Adding a distributed directory service that allows network-wide control of user logins on Win95, WfW, and NT

Some of these reasons involve whole-scale migration of an entire network, while others are smaller and less risky. If you have a clear idea of what objectives you hope to gain by including Windows NT on your network, you're ready to set milestones to measure how well you've succeeded.

In some industries, measuring success is easy. Race car drivers, Olympic athletes, and politicians get concrete and immediate feedback on their performance. In most computer-related fields, though, indications of success may be more elusive. If you start out knowing what you want to accomplish during your NTS installation, you'll be better prepared to know when you're done and how well you met your goals.

One way to start is by making a list of all the specific requirements that came out of your analysis in the preceding section. For example, if you're installing NTS to use NT domains for security and resource sharing on your network, your requirements might include "provide centralized control of user access rights" and "provide improved security for Accounting's data." Listing these specifics gives you a solid checklist. If you can check off all the items, your installation is a success. Following is a sample checklist. Where appropriate, it includes references to other chapters that can help you implement your plan:

- ◆ Do I have a clear estimate of the number of users who will use the new network? The number of computers? The number of physical locations to be linked?

- ◆ Have I identified the number of servers that will run Windows NT Server? What roles will each server play? Have I chosen appropriate hardware for each server?

- ◆ Is my network infrastructure appropriate for the network's purpose (Chapter 20)? Have I made provision for remote access (Chapter 25) and Internet access (Chapter 26), if desired?

- ◆ Can I subdivide the network into workgroups or domains (Chapter 14)? If the network requires domains, how will they be controlled, and will they need to share data or users (Chapter 15)?

- ◆ What access controls are appropriate for network data (Chapter 12)? Have I assigned appropriate user and group access permissions (Chapters 9 and 12)? Do I have adequate backup capacity and a plan to use it (Chapter 13)? What antivirus and physical security policies will I enforce?

- ◆ What client types will this network support, and how many? Do I have plans for integrating Windows NT with my existing NetWare, Macintosh, and TCP/IP clients (Chapters 21-24)?

Choosing the Right Hardware

The rate of change of PC hardware is probably faster than that in any other single industry (with the possible exception of software). Gordon Moore, co-founder of Intel, coined Moore's Law in the late '70s: "Computing power either doubles in speed or halves in price approximately every 18 months." Over the last two years or so, though, that 18-month period has become shorter—witness the price-to-performance ratios (at their respective introduction dates) of a 486/66 versus a 100 MHz Pentium!

Although hardware is changing very rapidly, you can still manage that change to your advantage by knowing what capabilities are important for your network servers. You're buying hardware to meet a need—service to your network. As long as the hardware continues to meet that need, it doesn't need to be replaced. Understanding the hardware and system attributes that differentiate servers means you can avoid unnecessary upgrades.

> **NOTE:** A brief digression, speaking of replacing hardware. Far too few companies realize the tangible and intangible benefits of donating amortized leftover hardware to local schools, churches, or charities. The donor gets a valuable tax break (as long as the equipment is depreciated) and the recipient gets badly-needed computer power. Thousands of homeless shelters, churches, and community organizations would be happy to have that old 286 that's gathering dust in the corner of your office.

What Makes a Good Server?

The answer to the question of what makes a good server depends heavily on individual situations. However, some starting points may help you refine your list of which attributes are most important to you:

- **System reliability.** No one likes unreliable hardware—especially not network managers. How badly would your network users be affected if any one of your servers had to be completely replaced due to failure? To what extent can you compensate for failed hardware by maintaining hot or cold spares? You should also consider the vendor's reputation and warranty policies. Some manufacturers include round-the-clock on-site service as part of their warranties; these can be very valuable in the event of a server failure.

- **Performance.** For the most part, network servers tend to be fairly high-performance machines. Most of their tasks are I/O- or network-bound, not CPU-bound, but database and WWW servers can burn a significant number of CPU cycles servicing requests. Think about the typical load a single user will put on your server: How many applications will that user be running? How many open files will she use at a time? Will she connect remotely? Then you can extrapolate that single-user load estimate to get an estimate of the total load on the server when it's full of users. The phone companies use statistical measurements to calculate exactly how many line pairs they need to reduce the number of dead calls (when a caller picks up the handset and gets no dial tone) below a desired threshold (say, 8 percent dead calls at peak usage). You can do much the same thing by analyzing what your users are using the server to do.

- ◆ **Expandability.** When loads on your servers start exceeding the performance criteria you've set, would you rather add another server, or expand your existing servers? Servers that are upgradeable to multiple processors, or that can be upgraded from a Pentium to a Pentium Pro, are well worth looking into. Make sure that your server has adequate RAM expansion potential, too, and don't forget to count slots to make sure that you can put in multiple network or remote-access cards if needed.

- ◆ **Architecture.** Don't forget that NTS runs on more than one type of CPU. DEC Alpha, and PowerPC-based servers can offer much better performance than Intel-based machines—often at a comparable cost (however, you should avoid MIPS-based servers, because vendors are no longer producing them for sale in the U.S.). If you're using NTS for an application server, you may be forced to stick with Intel because the applications you need to run haven't been ported; if not, however, you should consider the speed boost that a RISC server can provide.

Distinguishing Servers and Workstations

Until the early 1990s, PC network servers were most often just fast PCs with network adapter cards and lots of disk storage. Since 1994, however, most of the major PC manufacturers have introduced purpose-built servers. It's reasonable to wonder whether buying such a machine is worthwhile, especially when they can cost up to twice as much as a comparable desktop machine.

You may find that an ordinary PC will fit your needs; conversely, you may need a purpose-built server. Here are some common areas of difference between PCs and purpose-built servers that may make a difference in your application:

◆ **Expansion capability.** Servers typically have more expansion slots and drive bays than desktop machines, with the power supply and cooling capacity to match. For example, a server like Intergraph's InterServe MP-610 can be expanded from a "small" configuration (a single 150 MHz Pentium Pro, 64MB of RAM, 2GB SCSI disk, and a CD-ROM) to a "large one" (dual 150 MHz Pentium Pros, 1GB of RAM, 24GB of internal disk space, a CD-ROM, and a tape drive), all in the same physical cabinet—and that's without counting the 10 available PCI and EISA slots! By adding an external RAID array, you can increase the number of gigabytes available to many servers into the triple digits.

◆ **Architecture.** The server's architecture may be better suited to your needs than a desktop machine. For example, many servers support fast and wide SCSI-2, which is naturally faster at servicing file requests than an IDE or EIDE-based system. Servers that are designed to support multiple processors often include support for memory interleaving, error-correcting circuitry on the system's bus, and other exotic features that together increase system performance and reliability.

◆ **Availability and reliability features.** Server manufacturers have started taking cues from companies like Tandem and Stratus, the two biggest suppliers of fault-tolerant hardware. Stratus machines, which are often used in nuclear power plants, railroad switching centers, and other unforgiving applications, can sustain a failure of any system component—every piece of the system is dually redundant. They can call for help when the cabinet's opened, when the machine's temperature rises above a preset threshhold, or when a component is on the verge of failure. This kind of reliability once required expensive, purpose-built hardware, but it's now increasingly common to see servers with hot-swappable SCSI disks and other redundant components as well.

NOTE: The term *hot-swappable* refers to the ability to change out a single malfunctioning component without shutting down the computer. For example, most RAID cabinets support hot-swapping a failed disk; you can remove the bad drive and reinsert a new one without affecting other operations.

NTS servers can play a number of roles on the network, as indicated in the later section on network roles. Not every one of those roles necessarily requires a large, powerful server; for example, domain controllers, Domain Name Service (DNS) servers, and even Internet servers can easily be run on inexpensive workstations. Some servers may be critical to your business, while you may be able to do without the services offered by others.

To further clarify this distinction, consider this axiom: Any server whose loss would shut down your network (such as a centralized file server) is mission-critical; any server you could do without for a while (such as a backup domain controller) is not. With the cost of 75 MHz Pentium workstations dropping into the $1,400 range as of this writing, you should strongly consider desktop machines for your non-critical applications.

Of course, some servers have features that may make them compelling choices for your particular situation. For example, some manufacturers are now making servers that can mount in standard 19-inch equipment racks, and others offer built-in monitoring cards that can alert you via modem or pager when a component fails—a great help for environments where the server's locked in an equipment closet somewhere.

Choosing the Right Configuration

Even after you decide on a server that meets your reliability, performance, and availability needs, you still have to decide on an exact hardware configuration. Of course, the configuration you choose greatly influences the system's overall performance. This section discusses choices for each of the major server subsystems—including which subsystem types are unsuitable for production servers. Table 3-1 shows a brief summary of minimum and ideal configurations for several common server roles.

> **NOTE:** Many servers have network interfaces, disk controllers, and other peripheral interfaces integrated onto the motherboard. When done with careful attention to timing and bandwidth details (as in Intergraph's TDZ workstations), this integration can offer a nice performance bonus. The downside is that a failed component renders the whole machine inoperable; you can't just replace a PCI or EISA card and bring the machine back up.

Table 3-1   Recommended configurations for several types of servers.

Server Role	Minimum CPU	Minimum RAM	Ideal CPU	Ideal RAM	I/O Type
PDC (0 to 5,000 domain accounts)	486/66	32MB	Pentium/75	32MB	EIDE or SCSI
PDC (5,000 to 20,000 domain accounts)	Pentium/90	64MB	Pentium/133 or SMP	96MB	SCSI or SCSI-2
BDC	same as PDC	same as PDC	same as PDC	same as PDC	same as PDC
Internet server	486/66	32MB	Any Pentium or SMP	64MB	SCSI-2 or SCSI-3
Remote-access server	Pentium/75	32MB[1]	Pentium/90[2]	[1]	EIDE or SCSI
Database server	[3]	[3]	SMP	[3]	SCSI-2 or RAID
WINS, DHCP, or DNS server	486/66	32MB	486/66[4]	32MB	EIDE or SCSI

[1] 32MB is the absolute minimum; you should also allow 2MB for each connected user.

[2] For best RAS performance, use RAS coprocessor cards (as described in Chapter 25, "Providing Dial-Up Access") instead of an ultra-fast CPU.

[3] Consult your database vendor for recommendations; setups vary widely between vendors.

[4] These protocols are mostly bound by network bandwidth.

Processor and Cache

The CPU is usually the limiting factor for database servers, Internet servers, and application servers, because their tasks all depend on using the CPU to compute some results and return them to a client. Even though domain controllers, WINS and DNS servers, and other "supporting role" servers typically don't require as much CPU power, you should buy the fastest CPU *that makes sense for your application.* Remember that you can always upgrade individual components such as disks or video cards, or add more RAM, but your choice of CPU will be with you until you replace the machine.

The amount of on-chip primary cache your machines have will vary depending on their processor; any system you buy should have at least 256KB of secondary cache. A 512KB cache may improve performance for some computation-intensive tasks such as graphics rendering, but it may not be of tangible benefit for your file, print, or application server.

You should also consider buying multiprocessor or multiprocessor-upgradeable machines, as NTS and many NT applications can take advantage of multiple CPUs for better performance.

System Bus

The system bus provides the primary pathway for moving data between the CPU and peripheral devices such as video cards and disk controllers. Because of the central role it plays, the system bus design of your server has a large influence over the server's actual and potential performance. There are four primary bus types found in Intel-based servers:

- The *ISA* (*Industry Standard Architecture*) bus was designed for the original IBM PC/AT and its 80286 CPU. ISA buses are synchronized to an 8.33 MHz clock signal. Assuming zero wait states, it takes two bus clock cycles to move data. Because the ISA is a 16-bit-wide path, the maximum chunk transferred at any one time is two bytes. At best, the ISA bus is capable of only 4 million transfers per second. More importantly, the ISA bus has only 24 address lines to memory. This means that the maximum address range that ISA devices can directly access via *direct memory access* (*DMA*) is 2^{24}, or 16MB. Most servers use more than 16MB of RAM; bus-mastering cards expect to be able to take control of the bus for block transfers. ISA doesn't support either of these needs, so it would seem to be an outdated architecture with no role in server systems. Unfortunately, it's still common.

- The *Extended ISA* (*EISA*) bus improves on the ISA design (with which it's backwardly-compatible); EISA is a true 32-bit bus and can support DMA requests in up to 4GB of RAM. Unfortunately, it also uses the 8.33 MHz bus clock. At its best, it completes a data move in one bus cycle. Because its data path is 32 bits wide, 4 bytes can be moved at once. This translates to a maximum transfer rate of 33 MB/sec. EISA also adds some automatic configuration features to the ISA bus; these features were the precursor to the current Plug-and-Play hardware standard endorsed by Intel and Microsoft.

EISA is a major improvement over ISA, but is still significantly slower than the PCI bus; you should avoid buying servers or peripherals that require an EISA bus.

◆ The *Video Electronic Standards Association Local Bus* (*VESA-VL* or just *VL*) bus type was designed specifically for use with the Intel 80486 family. It has a maximum burst transfer rate of 133MB/sec and a sustained transfer rate of 66MB/sec. As its name implies, it was originally designed to provide a fast connection for video cards to use. It doesn't have the memory limitation of the ISA bus, and it's faster than the EISA bus. Unfortunately, the VL bus has very poor arbitration characteristics. A single device can "hog" the bus; typical VL devices often do just that. Because the VL design is intimately tied to the 386/486 bus architecture, it's not used much in dedicated server systems.

◆ The *Peripheral Component Interconnect* (*PCI*) bus was designed by Intel to support the Pentium and Pentium Pro CPUs with a fast, flexible bus; it has also been adapted by Apple, DEC, and a number of non-Intel manufacturers. PCI has several desirable characteristics for a high-performance bus. All transfers are burst transfers, and the length of the burst is negotiated on a device-by-device basis. The design of PCI devices isn't tied to the CPU type or clock rate. PCI devices are self-configuring; they automatically sense what devices are already present on the bus and choose settings that will avoid conflicts with those devices. Finally, PCI's maximum transfer rate is 132MB/sec on a 33 MHz bus and 528MB/sec on a 66 MHz bus.

Most new controllers and devices are based on the PCI bus. Its outstanding speed and ability to run on any PCI-compatible machine make PCI the bus of choice today for servers and desktop machines. FireWire and the Universal Serial Bus (USB) may supplant it in a few years; for the present, however, to maximize server performance you should choose a PCI bus system with PCI controllers.

CAUTION: If your server has to run special-purpose hardware that comes only in ISA or EISA versions (such as some data acquisition cards or WAN interfaces), make sure that your servers can accommodate those types of interface cards. Some PCI systems have EISA/ISA slots, and others don't.

Network Interface Controllers

Because servers serve data to clients over the network, the *network interface controller* (*NIC*) always plays an important part of a server's performance. The physical network infrastructure you already have in place will dictate what media type your NIC must support, but you still have some latitude in choosing the bus type, data width, and features for your NICs.

First, be sure to choose an adapter card that takes maximum advantage of your bus, no matter what physical medium you're using. If you're using EISA, put EISA NICs in them; likewise, use PCI adapters on PCI-bus machines. Just like system buses, NICs vary in how much data they can transfer at once. Modern PCI and EISA cards can move 32-bit-wide chunks of data to and from the system bus. Putting an 8-bit ISA adapter in a machine with a more capable bus will needlessly slow your network throughput.

Second, consider whether your network medium is likely to change. Although 10Base-T Ethernet is currently the dominant physical medium, inexpensive NICs that can switch between 10Base-T and 100Base-T are becoming common. Choosing cards of this type now can make your migration path to 100Base-T smoother in the future, by avoiding the need to buy new cards when you do migrate.

RAM

Microsoft claims that NTS will run in 16MB of RAM, and it will—but your disks will thrash mightily. 32MB is a more realistic minimum configuration. The server manufacturer specifies the speed and packaging type requirements for expansion memory; all you have to do is follow the requirements and select the appropriate quantity. The server's role will determine how much additional RAM you may need. Following are some guidelines for estimating your likely needs:

♦ For file servers, take the initial 32MB recommendation described earlier and add 1MB for each concurrent user you expect to have connected.

♦ For application or database servers, add however much RAM the application vendor recommends for acceptable performance.

◆ For *Remote Access Service* (*RAS*) servers, add 2MB for each user that can connect at any one time.

◆ For running any of the TCP/IP services, like the Domain Name Service, allow at least 4MB for each service you want to run.

Don't be surprised if your RAM requirements reach into the triple digits—but *do* make sure that your chosen server platform can accommodate RAM expansion above whatever amount you choose to install at first. You can approximate RAM requirements by using a formula recommended by Microsoft: 16 MB + (number of users × average number of open files per user × average size of data files) + (average number of applications run from the server × average size of applications run from the server.) This formula is imprecise, but it provides a good *minimum* value for use in your planning.

Device Controllers

As with network cards, mass storage controllers are available in several different varieties. The most common controller type is the *Integrated Drive Electronics* (*IDE*) interface and its variants, Rapid IDE and Extended IDE (EIDE). IDE-based drives and controllers are still in the majority and they tend to be less expensive than their SCSI counterparts. The chief disadvantages of the IDE interface are its relatively limited performance and expandability. Each individual IDE device must have its own onboard controller, and it can be difficult to get multiple devices to work together correctly.

The *Small Computer System Interface* (*SCSI*) and its variants (SCSI-2, Fast SCSI, Wide SCSI, and SCSI-3) are typically used in applications where performance and expandability are important. A 32-bit Wide/Fast SCSI implementation can offer up to 40MB/sec of bandwidth, which is adequate for almost all applications. Because each SCSI controller can drive up to seven devices (more with SCSI-3, or if the device supports SCSI sub-IDs), it's easy to configure large storage subsystems. Most RAID controllers on the market are SCSI-based, as are most high-capacity backup devices. Further, many non-storage peripherals (including scanners and printers) provide SCSI interfaces to take advantage of the capabilities of the bus.

Most purpose-built servers (and many workstations) include SCSI interfaces. SCSI should be the primary interface for your main servers. IDE or EIDE will work well for your second-line servers.

For more details on using and managing mass storage in your Windows NT servers, see Chapter 8, "Mass Storage Management."

Mass Storage Devices

The trend of disk-drive development greatly favors the consumer. Per-megabyte costs for 4GB disks now hover in the $0.17 range, and engineering improvements have steadily increased performance and storage capability without corresponding increases in cost.

The amount of storage you need will vary, depending on what your servers are going to do. A full NTS installation requires roughly 120MB, plus space for the system's paging file. You must also add space for storing user files, databases, or whatever else your server's going to serve; for file servers or large databases, it's not uncommon to see machines with 20+ gigabytes of active data in use.

The upper limit on how much storage you can put on your server is likely to be the number of drives your disk controller can handle. For example, a SCSI controller with six available addresses can easily handle up to 54GB of storage (six 9GB drives). Because a single server can use multiple disk controllers, the per-server limit is a function of how many slots the server has open and how big the disks are that are used on each controller.

Whenever possible, you should start relatively small. If you start a file server with, say, two 4GB drives, that leaves you free to buy larger-capacity, faster drives at some point in the future when you actually *need* more storage. Don't overbuy storage now, since it keeps getting faster and cheaper. Of course, for data-intensive servers, you'll have to buy adequate disk space *now* for your data, however large it may be. Second-line servers such as domain controllers can probably get by with the standard 850MB–1.2GB disks that most manufacturers provide as part of their standard configuration.

Modern hard disks are very reliable, but they have lots of moving parts, so they're still the one of the most failure-prone components in a server. You should consider keeping spare disks on hand for the inevitable failures. Critical servers should probably store data on RAID arrays (see Chapter 8 for full details on software and hardware RAID subsystems.) Make sure your backup system and policies can keep up with your storage, too; whatever backup subsystem you choose must be able to store as much data as your disks do, and you must be able to find files on the backups when you want to restore them.

Offline Storage

Depending on your application, you may need to archive large volumes of data and make it available on request at some time in the future. At the very least, you'll need offline storage to back up your servers' data and configuration files.

Offline storage devices cover a huge range of performance, capacity, and cost, from the humble 1.4MB floppy at the low end to *Digital Linear Tape* (*DLT*) drives that can back up 30–40GB at up to 80MB/sec. Mid-range offline storage includes cartridge drives, optical drives (which come in a wide range of capacities, from 128MB up to 4.6GB), and a variety of tape formats, including 4mm and 8mm tapes and 3M's increasingly popular Travan cartridge tape format. As with most other technologies, offline storage mechanisms keep getting faster, less expensive, and more reliable as time passes.

There are four interrelated factors that you can use to judge the merits of offline storage technologies for your network. These factors are often shown visually in a diagram like the one in Figure 3-1 (although longevity isn't included, because it varies by media type).

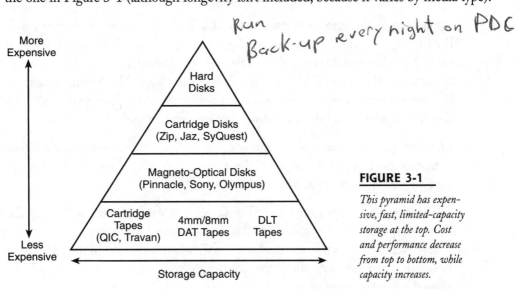

[handwritten annotation: Run Back-up every night on PDC]

FIGURE 3-1

This pyramid has expensive, fast, limited-capacity storage at the top. Cost and performance decrease from top to bottom, while capacity increases.

Which weight you give these factors depends on your network needs. Let's see what they are and what they mean:

+ *Cost per megabyte* is a measure of how much money it costs to store a megabyte of data. This measure doesn't reflect the fixed cost of the drive—

just the media needed. It's related to capacity, because the amount of data a piece of media can hold often determines its cost.

♦ *Longevity* measures how long your data will be readable. This factor is tricky; most of the storage systems now on the market are so new that no one knows whether their media will be usable in 20 years.

♦ *Read/write performance* measures how fast the device can back up or restore data. This performance is often inversely proportional to media capacity, as some media may require sequential access.

♦ *Capacity* designates how much data a piece of media can hold; a single back-up device may be able to use different-capacity media. Capacity and cost are linked. In general, as the capacity of a media type increases, its cost per megabyte decreases.

In general, cost and capacity are inversely related to performance. For example, a 4mm DAT tape costs about $11 and can hold up to 4GB of data, compared to $700 or so for a 4GB hard disk, but the disk is at least two orders of magnitude faster than the tape.

Depending on the amount of data you need to back up, a simple tape drive may suffice. For backing up individual servers, putting a tape drive on each server can be a viable alternative to a central backup device. Backup speeds are maximized by putting the back-up device on the same SCSI bus as the device being backed up; unsurprisingly, doing backups across the network from a disk on one server to a tape drive on another is much slower than backing up the same disk to a tape drive on the same machine.

Large optical drives, such as the Pinnacle 4.6GB line, are becoming a good alternative to tape in the under-5GB size range, because opticals offer a good compromise between media cost, longevity, speed, and size.

For large data stores, you need an offline device that will allow you to back up the entire store with minimal intervention—backups that require human attention often don't get done. Several manufacturers make "jukeboxes" (which work like music jukeboxes) or autoloaders that can (with the proper backup software) automatically load a new tape when the previous one is full.

Most high-capacity offline storage devices have SCSI interfaces; SCSI offers better throughput than parallel-port or IDE-based devices, and for backing up a large server you'll need the speed.

Choosing the File System

As discussed in Chapter 1, "Introducing Windows NT," one of NT's features is support for several types of file systems. As shipped, NTS supports two file system types: the MS-DOS file allocation table (FAT) file system and the NT File System (NTFS.) Each of these file systems has particular strengths and weaknesses; knowing what they are will help you choose the proper one for your servers.

FAT

The FAT file system was originally designed for use with the first versions of MS-DOS. The operating system tracks which files are using which sectors on a disk by keeping score in an allocation table, hence FAT's name. Despite its age, FAT is still the default file system used with NT, and the only file system supported by Win95 and MS-DOS. In addition, NetWare still uses FAT as its primary file system.

Pros: FAT is portable, as Win95, MS-DOS, Win3.11, NetWare, Linux, Macintosh, and OS/2 clients can all mount, read, and write FAT volumes. This portability makes it a good medium for exchange. The NT implementation of FAT supports long file names.

Cons: FAT is much slower than NTFS, and it can't support partitions larger than 2GB. FAT doesn't provide local security like NT's access controls and file permissions do. (You can still apply share permissions to shares on FAT volumes, however.)

NTFS   NT allow Security on NTFS/FAT Doesn't

NTFS was designed from the start to be a fast file system for use in a fast OS; in addition to its speed advantage over FAT, it provides robust security and data redundancy features. However, NTFS file systems are hard to use with most other client types, and there's no way to set up a machine with multiple operating systems unless the boot partition is FAT.

Pros: NTFS provides file system journaling for data recovery, along with long file names, file permissions, and superior speed. NTFS volumes can be up to 4 terabytes in size, and they can be exported to appear as Macintosh volumes.

Cons: Setting up multiple-boot machines requires a FAT boot partition. OS/2, NetWare, and Win3.x clients can't directly use NTFS partitions.

> **TIP:** There's a free third-party redirector, NTFSDOS, which allows DOS and Win3.1 users to use network-mounted NTFS file systems. When installed, NTFSDOS makes files on NTFS partitions available, but users can't use long file names or rely on NT access permissions.

Defining the Server Role

NTS machines can function in a number of roles. File and print services are standard parts of NTS; however, there are a number of other uses for NTS servers besides just serving files and printers. Let's examine some of the roles your servers can play on your network.

Primary Domain Controller

The *primary domain controller* (*PDC*) serves as the central source of user account information within a domain. There can only be one PDC per domain, and the PDC must be running NT Server. When you install Windows NT Server, the setup program lets you choose whether you want the computer to act as a PDC, a backup domain controller, or an ordinary server.

All domain login requests are validated against the PDC's account database; the PDC can also serve user login scripts or profiles to other machines in the domain. Centralizing this data on one machine allows all domain computers to have access to it. This setup lets users log into a consistent desktop environment from any computer in the domain, although the PDC plays no role in validating logins to local accounts on individual workstations.

The PDC can be a dedicated server, or it can share a machine with other services. Because its service is a key part of domain management, many networks prefer to dedicate a machine to be the PDC.

Backup Domain Controller

When a domain's PDC fails or needs to be taken off-line, users won't be able to log in or access shares that depend on domain security. In recognition of this possibility, NTS allows other NTS servers within a domain to act as *backup domain controllers* (*BDCs*). Each BDC in a domain gets periodic updates from the PDC, so that all BDCs have an up-to-date copy of the domain security database. When the PDC fails, domain computers will automatically send authentication requests to a BDC; you can also manually promote a BDC to make it the domain's PDC at any time.

Because the BDC has minimal duties unless and until the PDC fails, most BDCs are run on servers that already have another primary role.

For more information on planning, using, and managing domains, see Chapters 14, 15, and 16.

Application Server = Member Server

Many NTS installations use NTS as a platform for providing application services to end users. These services include messaging and electronic mail, Internet and intranet services, and database management services, as well as software that end users use to conduct the organization's business. Some server roles, such as the PDC, are required for the network to function at all; application servers are usually the servers that run the business operations. Examples include accounting software, customer and sales tracking databases, and engineering analysis tools.

Because end users depend on application servers to get their jobs done, these servers are usually dedicated to their tasks. It's common—and a good idea, if your budget permits—to keep enough spares to be able to replace at least one failed application server; these spare parts should be in addition to any spares that you stockpile for replacing other servers.

Service Server   Does bulk of work

The last category of server roles is a catchall; it includes system and network services that provide useful services to network clients. For example, the Windows Internet Name

Service (WINS) server, which maps NetBIOS computer names to TCP/IP addresses, can run on any NTS machine. Other examples include the TCP/IP protocol's Domain Name Service (DNS) and *Dynamic Host Configuration Protocol* (*DHCP*) services, and the *Microsoft License Services* server that tracks software licensing throughout all domains of an enterprise.

These services provide extra functionality to network clients; by contrast with application servers and domain controllers, users can still do productive work when these services aren't available. Many NTS sites put all the service functions on a single machine. Such a concentration keeps the services from degrading performance on more critical machines, but renders them vulnerable to a single-machine failure.

Where to Go Next

This chapter introduced you to the planning process necessary before moving your network to Windows NT. By planning ahead, you can avoid unnecessary expenses, outages, and inconvenience. Once you have a complete plan to guide your migration, you can proceed with confidence in the knowledge that you are acting with forethought. In the next chapter, we discuss how to install Windows NT on Intel and RISC hardware—including how to upgrade servers running Windows NT 3.51. Following are some other chapters that you may find helpful before proceeding:

♦ Chapters 12 and 13 can guide you in designing an effective, easily-administered set of security plans to guard your network and its data.

♦ Chapter 20, "Estimating and Planning Networks," covers processes you can use to decide how much network capacity you need.

Chapter | 4

Installing
Windows NT Server

In This Chapter:

- ◆ A Brief Introduction
- ◆ Installing a New System
- ◆ The Upgrade Process (RISC or Intel)
- ◆ Network Installation
- ◆ What If Problems Arise?

How do I...

One of the most frequent problems with Windows NT is simply the installation of the operating system itself. Many older computers have chipsets that are incompatible with installing or running Windows NT. This chapter examines the issues involved in dealing with the installation process.

Windows NT 4.0 can be installed in several ways. The first is simply a local installation that can be new or an upgrade. All aspects of the installation are available locally. The second is more complicated and involves gaining access to files over the network. As in the first case, this can also be an upgrade or a new installation. For large installation bases, 4.0 offers much improvement in unattended installations and setups that will install NT for a user. Let's begin by examining the various steps of an installation.

A Brief Introduction

In many respects, this should be the shortest chapter in this book. Much has been done by Microsoft to ensure an easy and straightforward installation. In spite of this effort, the installation process isn't always straightforward. Before getting into the nuts and bolts of the install procedure, we need to examine some of the changes that have occurred in the continuing evolution of Window NT.

New Features in Version 4.0 That Affect Installation

The changes in 4.0 are substantial. Many of the changes influence the installation process:

- As Figure 4-1 indicates, even the initial screen is different.

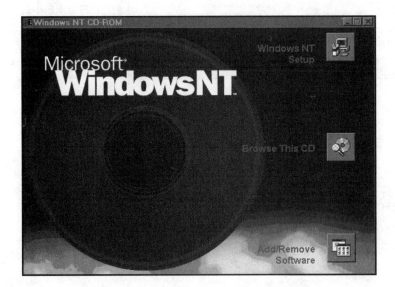

FIGURE 4-1.

The new install screen in NT Server 4.0.

The installation CD is an auto-run CD which you can boot for the installation procedure (if the motherboard BIOS allows booting from CD-ROM). In the past, running an installation from a CD was exclusively a RISC option.

- Wizards have been added to make the use of the server more friendly. Figure 4-2 shows an example of the administrative wizards.

  These wizards provide very fast and automated access to standard server-based administrative chores such as adding users and changing security.

- Some device drivers are no longer supported directly by Microsoft; these drivers are now in the driver library. Figure 4-3 shows various types of files present in the driver library. For storage devices, these files must be prepared before an install is done. We'll describe the process for creating an installation disk for legacy drivers.

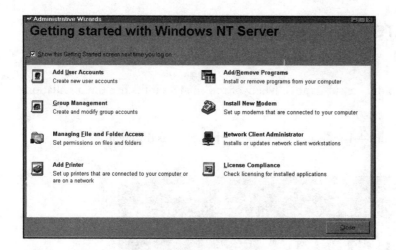

FIGURE 4-2.

Administrative wizards add a new ease of use to those not familiar with Windows NT.

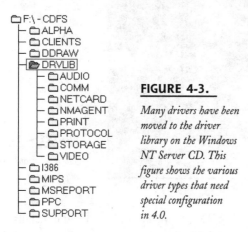

FIGURE 4-3.

Many drivers have been moved to the driver library on the Windows NT Server CD. This figure shows the various driver types that need special configuration in 4.0.

◆ The driver that controls all IDE components is ATAPI.sys. Atdisk is no longer used. If you upgrade from Version 3.51, you'll receive a message that Atdisk loaded improperly; you'll have to disable it in the Windows NT Control Panel.

◆ Hardware profiles have been added, enabling you to set specific profiles for booting into NT and actually somewhat changing the installation procedure. For example, if you use a notebook as a special server to carry from site to site, you can boot into NT in various ways, depending on the hardware differences needed. You'll get a prompt to press the space bar to choose the proper profile when you boot the system. Although seemingly trivial, the hardware profiles make it very easy to maintain different boot sequences on the server.

- You can now log onto an NT domain by enabling the Logon Via Dial Up Networking option in the Logon dialog box. This would enable a server to log onto a remote domain via Dial-Up-Networking.

- Although not visible in NT, the User and Graphic heaps have been moved to the kernel. This move eliminates one layer of client/server complexity and (for example) makes the ensuing video faster. Unfortunately, this change also means that drivers need to be reconfigured and recompiled. In other words, many drivers from Version 3.51 won't work in Version 4.0. (Interestingly, some 3.51 SCSI drivers will work in 4.0, but printer and video drivers won't.)

- NT 4.0 no longer natively supports HPFS. If you are using this file format, you must convert it to NTFS.

Specific differences between the installation of Version 4.0 and previous versions include the following:

- Greater use of installation wizards makes most of the installation painless.

- If the installation fails in the GUI portion, a reboot restarts the setup.

- You no longer specify printers on setup. All printers are set up once Windows NT has been installed and is running properly.

There are far more changes in 4.0 than those just listed. The ones listed are significant to the installation process. Two additional points must be emphasized:

- NT 4.0 won't install on older 386 machines. The minimum machine for NT is now a 486. In addition, you need a minimum of 12MB of RAM on an Intel machine and 16MB on a RISC machine.

- NT 4.0 will not install from 5$\frac{1}{4}$-inch floppies, and can't be installed totally from floppies. For a succssful installation, you need access to a local or network CD-ROM.

> **TIP:** For servers, it seems reasonable to use SCSI components wherever possible. It is possible, however, to add an EIDE CD-ROM for the installation of files and applications onto a server. You can install an inexpensive EIDE CD-ROM (for example, an Atapi 1.2-compliant CD-ROM onto the primary IDE channel as a master device). The NT 4.0 install process will see the drive and load the necessary driver. The cost of a quad-speed CD-ROM is under $80.00.

Know that ✓

What Is the Install Process?

The installation (or just *install*) process is divided into various steps or procedures. First of all is the *text (or DOS) phase*, which copies files and establishes a boot-up facility either on floppy disks or the hard drive. The second phase (the so-called *GUI phase*) actually loads drivers and runs in the true *Windows NT phase*. The following steps explain the basic installation procedure:

1. The initial part of the text mode involves booting into the installation process. There are several ways to accomplish this. The most obvious is booting from the install floppies. Likewise you can access the installation CD from the DOS prompt and start the installation by running winnt (or winnt /b, which copies the boot files to a hard drive rather than floppy drives) from the I386 directory. If you're upgrading the installation from Windows NT 3.51, you can run winnt32 in the same manner. Likewise, you can run winnt or winnt32 with /u to perform an install in unattended mode. Common switches used for the winnt and winnt32 commands are summarized in the following table.

Switch	Description *Barebones set. Command is Win NT*
/s:*sourcepath*	Specifies the location of the Windows NT files.
/i:*inf_file*	Specifies the filename (no path) of the setup information file. The default is DOSNET.INF.
/t:*drive_letter*	Forces Setup to place temporary files on the designated drive.
/x	Prevents Setup from creating Setup boot floppies. Use this option when you already have Setup boot floppies.
/b	Places the Setup boot files on the system's hard drive rather than on floppy disks.
/ox	Specifies that Setup create boot floppies for CD-ROM installation.
/u	Upgrades your previous version of Windows NT (settings stay the same) in unattended mode.
/u:*script*	Similar to /u, but provides a script file for user settings rather than using the settings from the previous installation.
/r:*directory*	Installs an additional directory within the directory tree where the Windows NT files are installed. Use additional /r switches to install additional directories.
/e:*command*	Instructs Setup to execute a specific *command* after installation is complete.

On RISC-based machines, the install process is somewhat different. For example, NT is installed onto Alpha-based machines by running applications directly from the CD (and you don't use switches such as /b). These differences will be detailed in the appropriate sections.

The setup will run automatically and will boot onto the install CD if the system BIOS supports this feature. If an install CD isn't found (unless you're running the winnt or winnt32 methods from an install directory), the install will abort after Disk 3.

2. When given the choice between Default and Custom, choose the Custom Install method. This option enables you to see and select the applications that are being installed.

3. Verify the system components that the detection procedure summarizes for you. If the list is incorrect, restart Setup. When the system displays the message Setup is inspecting your computer's hardware configuration, press F6. This action should allow you to bypass autodetection of the hardware; you can then indicate the components that are present. (At this point, you can also install legacy SCSI drivers, etc.)

4. You will be asked to choose file formats. Many people suggest that you have a small FAT partition as drive C: so that you can do file maintenance via DOS. However, installing a FAT partition is a violation of C2 security (if that's important to you). Use NTFS wherever possible, especially with modern large drives (greater than a gigabyte).

5. If the drive hasn't been formatted, you will be given the opportunity to partition and format the drive. Even if you ask for NTFS, the initial format is FAT and then it's subsequently converted to NTFS on the next reboot.

6. Select the directory to which NT will be installed. Using the default name (winnt) is a good idea (you can change the drive).

7. Enter your name and your company name.

8. Enter the Administrator password. *This is very important.* Choose a password that's at least seven characters long and has a nonsense symbol in it.

9. Supply a unique name for the computer—that is, a name that doesn't exist elsewhere in the network or domain.

10. When the network portion of the install continues, you are given the following choices:

    ◆ Do not connect the computer to the network at this time

    ◆ This computer will participate on a network via (default):

        ◆ Wired directly to a network via ISDN or a standard network cable

        ◆ Remote access via a standard modem

    This is a marked change from previous setups and reflects the new wizard incorporation. Unless you have prior knowledge of a problem with a network interface card (NIC), there should be no problem joining a network. On the other hand, there are cases where NT is installed and crashes only when the network driver is initialized. A server needs an NIC. If there are suspected problems, install the Msloopback adapter; after NT is running, install the NIC. If you know that the NIC is okay, continue with the installation process.

11. Now we come to our first serious choice. What NIC is on the server? By the way, a server by definition must have a network card or other means of providing for "serving." For some NICs, autodetection can return a null set. If the setup crashes as a result of autodetection, detect the NIC manually.

> **NOTE:** Some NICs that traditionally use jumpers for IRQ and I/O status now use software configuration. A common NIC in this category is the NE 2000 clone, as well as the one from Microdyne. You *must* configure the card via the DOS utility before installing NT, or the default IRQ and I/O might be totally incorrect. If you choose IRQ 5 and I/O of 300, NT will apply it, but will not be able to verify it. Make sure that you know all the IRQs and settings that you intend to use, and make sure that they are correct. If using any ISA IRQ on a PCI system, make certain that you have told the BIOS to reserve that IRQ for ISA.

12. Choose the networking protocol. The install defaults to IPX/SPX and NetBEUI. The former is needed if you are using interconnectivity to a Novell network. The latter works well in a Microsoft environment. My choice, however, is TCP/IP, because it's the fastest growing of the protocols. If you do choose a TCP/IP protocol, you are asked if you have Dynamic Host Configuration Protocol (DHCP) to install or connect to. This of course is dictated by the network environment into which the machine is being installed.

For more information on configuring TCP/IP and DHCP, see Chapter 24, "Interoperating with TCP/IP Clients."

TIP: If you need to route a protocol, note that NetBEUI isn't routable but both TCP/IP and IPX/SPX are.

13. The server installation defaults to installing as a Primary Domain Controller (PDC). You can set up the installation as a Backup Domain Controller (BDC), but this option presupposes the existing presence of PDC on the network. Finally, you can install as a standalone server.

    This isn't a trivial choice; it requires planning. A server can't be promoted to a PDC—instead, a new installation is needed.

14. When asked to determine the time zone you're in, set the system information accordingly.

15. The final issue of note is establishing the video configuration. This is easier in Version 4.0 than in previous versions. You simply select the resolution you want. You will be asked to reboot. After rebooting, you can change the resolution on-the-fly, but changing to a larger font, etc., requires a reboot.

Choosing a File System Type

The *FAT* (*file allocation table*) format was originated for the 8088 (IBM XT) system. It obviously is well-supported, and has many support applications. The table is composed of links to the data blocks that describe a file. In addition to the FAT, a duplicate FAT assists in fault-tolerance. Because FAT is 16-bit, there are serious problems with large drive sizes. As the size of drive increases, so does the cluster size. With drives larger than 520MB, cluster sizes jump to 16KB, 32KB, or even 64KB. This would mean that a file with size 1 would occupy up to 64KB on the hard drive. Furthermore, only a few attributes are maintained, and this eliminates the use of security in FAT.

NTFS was designed from the ground up as a superior file system. Unlike FAT, NTFS maintains both a *master file table* (*MFT*) and a mirror of that table. In addition, a file log is maintained to allow file recovery. Most importantly, all information about the files is maintained in the MFT. Accordingly, the information necessary to locate a file is maintained only in the MFT. NTFS also maintains extensive attributes for files; thus, group and individual security can be maintained in the MFT. Finally, cluster size is no problem in NTFS. In all circumstances, I recommend using NTFS, if the partition involved is greater than 500 megabtyes and is only used by NT.

Unlike previous versions of NT, NTFS can be formatted with larger cluster sizes to avoid excessive fragmentation. The following box shows a capture of the new capabilities of the FORMAT command in NT (including floppy drive support).

```
FORMAT drive: [/FS:file-system] [/V:label] [/Q] [/A:size] [/C]
FORMAT drive: [/V:label] [/Q] [/F:size]
FORMAT drive: [/V:label] [/Q] [/T:tracks /N:sectors]
FORMAT drive: [/V:label] [/Q] [/1] [/4]
FORMAT drive: [/Q] [/1] [/4] [/8]
 /FS:file-system Specifies the type of the file system (FAT or NTFS).
 /V:label Specifies the volume label.
 /Q Performs a quick format.
 /C Files created on the new volume will be compressed by default.
 /A:size Overrides the default allocation unit size. Default settings
         are strongly recommended for general use.
 NTFS supports 512, 1024, 2048, 4096, 8192, 16K, 32K, 64K.
 FAT supports 8192, 16K, 32K, 64K, 128K, 256K.
 NTFS compression is not supported for allocation unit sizes above 4096.
 /F:size Specifies the size of the floppy disk to format
         (160, 180, 320, 360, 720, 1.2, 1.44, 2.88, or 20.8).
 /T:tracks Specifies the number of tracks per disk side.
 /N:sectors Specifies the number of sectors per track.
 /1 Formats a single side of a floppy disk.
 /4 Formats a 5.25-inch 360K floppy disk in a high-density drive.
 /8 Formats eight sectors per track.
```

Notice the changes in cluster sizes for NTFS. In Version 3.51, the maximum cluster size was 4096. For users that deal with large file sizes (such as video files), the small clusters could produce fragmentation. The larger cluster size more effectively handles large file sizes.

> **CAUTION:** It's generally stated that NTFS works by putting files in a space that is as large as the file. This isn't the case. NT actually sticks the file in the next available space (leaving a gap), regardless of size. Examination of fragmentation indicates that performance degradation starts being noticeable at 30 percent of drive capacity.

Installing a New System

When you consider the purchase of a new system, you need to be aware that not all systems support installing or running Windows NT. In fact, installing onto a new computer requires you to purchase hardware that has been tested by Microsoft to work with Windows NT 4.0. The information that's essential here is on the hardware compatibility list, which can be found at the Microsoft Web site (www.microsoft.com).

The Hardware Compatibility List (HCL)

Microsoft publishes a Hardware Compatibility List (HCL) that details devices that have been tested under NT Version 4.0. Read this list carefully before purchasing a system or building your own clone. The HCL is significant in that Microsoft gives official support to the devices on the list. While appearing somewhat constraining, the HCL is an excellent jumping-off place.

If you purchase a clone from a vendor, make sure that it will run NT. In fact, if the vendor won't pre-install NT on it, think twice about buying the system. Without a doubt, Windows NT is the best stress test of hardware I have ever seen. NT virtualizes hardware and requires drivers to be exact. Many system crashes have occurred due to nonstandard devices. In fact, it can be argued that any server in a critical environment should be a leading brand, such as Hewlett-Packard, Compaq, or Digital Equipment (to name a few). When you use proprietary hardware, specialized drivers or fixes are needed from the manufacturer. Make certain that these drivers are in fact available in a timely fashion.

New Installation on Intel

The installation of NT 4.0 onto a new system is very straightforward. In fact, the procedure is easier than upgrading a previous install. Simply use hardware that has the proper drivers and is currently supported. Given the recent decline in memory and CPU prices, I recommend using, as a minimum, a Pentium 100 with 32MB of RAM. Use standard NICs and video cards. Unless special requirements dictate, don't worry about getting the latest and greatest video cards.

> **NOTE:** The basic rules of Windows NT apply here. Be certain that you know what you are installing as—Server, Primary Domain Controller (PDC), or Backup Domain Controller (BDC). You can elevate a BDC to a PDC, but you can't elevate a server without a new installation.

These are the steps in the installation process:

1. Gather the basic installation data:
   - Motherboard type and BIOS date
   - CPU type and number, including stepping number (usually on the bottom of the CPU)
   - Major SCSI controller cards, with firmware versions and date
   - Network cards, including IRQ, memory address, and I/O (if ISA)
   - Make note of any special exclusion of IRQs, etc. in BIOS

2. Insert the CD and the first setup floppy and begin the installation procedure. You'll be prompted for disks 2 and 3. As you make various choices, be certain to record the most significant selections. Be certain to place the information in a protected place because of the potential security risk with the Administrator password. Of special note:
   - Record all drives, partition sizes, and file system types.
   - Record Administrator password.

CAUTION: Be *certain* that all hardware configurations match the list you have prepared.

As stated earlier, the installation proceeds in two basic phases: the hardware detection phase/file copying (text or DOS phase), and configuration (NT or GUI phase). After the first phase, the system will reboot. This reboot is the first place that a failure typically occurs. In general, the installation shouldn't present any problems, assuming that you have entered all the proper information. The various system messages and their meanings are summarized in a later section, after we deal with upgrade installations.

TIP: Using legacy drivers? To create a floppy disk for installing a legacy driver from the driver library, format a floppy and label it `Drivers disk`. Copy the files from the appropriate directory onto the floppy. For example, if you're installing on an Alpha, be sure to copy files from the Alpha directory on the CD. Boot into Setup; as soon as you see the message `Setup is inspecting your computer's hardware configuration`, press F6 and manually add the driver.

New Installation on RISC

The essential difference in installing on RISC (we'll use an Alpha as an example) is the initial part of the installation. The drive has to be prepared for the install. You do the following:

1. Turn on the system and allow the ARCS BIOS to load.
2. Insert the Windows NT CD in the CD-ROM
3. From the Boot Options menu, choose Enter Setup and press Enter.
4. Using the Setup menu, choose Run a Program and press Enter.
5. Type `cd:\alpha\arcinst.exe` and press Enter.
6. Choose Configure Partitions and press Enter.
7. Finally, choose Create Partition and press Enter.

8. If more than one drive is present, you're asked to choose the drive. Drives are defined by their SCSI IDs.

9. You'll be asked for a partition size. Most people suggest using a 5MB partition, but I suggest using slightly larger ones (10MB).

10. The partition is formatted, and you're asked to press a key to continue. When asked whether this is a system partition, type **Y** and press Enter. You are now ready to install Windows NT.

11. Press Esc to return to the Setup menu. Choose Run a Program again, type `cd:\alpha\setupldr`, and press Enter. From this point, the installation is nearly identical to that on Intel machines.

In general, the installation procedure just described is the same for all RISC machines. In certain cases, specific machines may require additional steps for the installation procedure.

If the machine doesn't have the proper drivers on the CD, the manufacturer may be able to provide the proper files. If Setup can't determine the type of computer you have, you'll be presented with several options. Select Other and press Enter. Put the manufacturer's disk into the floppy drive and press Enter. Be certain that the choice you make matches the hardware and version of NT. This will copy the essential HAL (hardware abstraction layer) onto the system. Follow the remaining directions (and be certain to read the manufacturer's instructions).

> **NOTE:** When installing, make sure that the firmware version of the system is correct for NT Server 4.0. For a Digital system, check the release notes on their World Wide Web site at `http:/www.windownt.digital.com`. The latest drivers and firmware revisions are also there.

> **TIP:** The system partition is formatted as FAT so that it can be read by the system. In such a situiation, there's no security on the system partition. You can use Disk Administrator to protect or secure the system partition.

The Upgrade Process (RISC or Intel)

For most servers, hopefully, the upgrade process will be from NT to NT. Technically, you can't upgrade another OS to NT *en toto*, but you can make systems coexist.

You can easily upgrade NT 3.51 servers to 4.0. If the 3.51 system has gone through numerous service packs and customization of the Registry, an upgrade may in fact fail or be subject to corruption. In general, it's easier by far to do a new installation than attempt an upgrade. The upgrade process is the same as the new installation. You can run the boot floppies or use the winnt or winnt32 command.

> **TIP:** It's always easier to install from a local hard drive than from a CD-ROM or over the network. You can copy the appropriate folder off the CD (for example, I386) to your local hard drive, and then install from there with the winnt32 application. This will require an additional 100MB of space (actually, 90MB for the Intel files).

You can upgrade both NT 3.51 Workstation and 3.51 Server to 4.0 Server. You can't upgrade a 3.51 Workstation or Server to a PDC or BDC. On the other hand, a 3.51 PDC or BDC can be upgraded to a 4.0 PDC or BDC.

> **TIP:** To be sure that all is okay when upgrading, make a second installation of Windows NT on a different drive and prepare a boot floppy. If the upgrade fails, you can boot to the second NT installation and do a tape restore. It's always best to install NT onto a drive different from the one(s) with the applications and data drives.

> **TIP:** When you have successive failures loading Windows NT, the signatures on the drive can get really corrupted. If SCSI, I routinely do a low-level FORMAT and then a new FDISK and FORMAT. Many times, the failed installation works fine after that.

Upgrading from Windows NT 3.51

It's easy to upgrade 3.51 to 4.0. The following should be done before the upgrade:

1. If the system is on a UPS, remove the software before upgrading.

2. If there are any TSR-like files present (for example, a backup agent), disable them before upgrading.

3. If you're using any remote boot software, remove it before upgrading.

4. Remove any network-controlling applications such as pcAnywhere 32 or Remotely Possible32.

5. Make a fresh backup of the 3.51 installation before proceeding.

6. Copy the I386 directory (or whichever directory is appropriate for your machine) from the CD to a local drive and run winnt32 /b (diskless and thus faster) from that directory.

   If you don't have sufficient room on the hard drive (remember that you need to copy the installation files, about 55MB for the Intel platform, and then install them to a temp directory for the upgrade), run the Setup disks. I suggest a minimum of 160MB free space for the total upgrade (170MB for RISC).

7. The rest of the installation is easy. Simply follow the instructions that are presented to you.

> **NOTE:** Server requires a minimum of 148MB free for INTEL and 158MB for RISC machines. Always err on the high side.

Upgrading from Windows 95

Windows 95 can't be upgraded to Windows NT. You can install NT into a different directory, but most applications will have to be reinstalled into NT. Run the Setup disks as discussed previously, and install Windows NT into a directory separate from Windows 95. Applications can't be migrated from Windows 95. Microsoft suggests *not* installing Windows 95 and Windows NT on the same server. In fact, this is excellent advice.

Upgrading from Windows for Workgroups/Windows 3.1x

In this case, copy the I386 directory onto the local hard drive. Exit to DOS and then choose the Install Server option. The installation will suggest that you install into the windows directory. This will then allow you to migrate your applications to NT. The installation will proceed as a new installation, with the exception of migrating applications.

When you boot into NT as a non-administrator, you're asked if you want to migrate win.ini and control.ini settings as well as groups. This works very well—however, it's not a good idea. Windows 3.1x systems start getting all kinds of weird settings in the ini files. A more appropriate migration is to copy the appropriate sections of the Windows win.ini into the NT win.ini. You can then copy the DLLs from Windows into the winnt\system directory (don't overwrite any files) and also all necessary ini files. You can then create a new folder and copy icons to this new folder (see the next chapter for details). This sounds like a laborious task—and it is. The alternative is to reinstall the applications.

Network Installation

The entire issue of a network installation is simply gaining access to a shared CD-ROM or an installation directory. The first and most obvious method is simply upgrading a system that's already on the network. Gain access to the necessary folder or CD, go to the appropriate folder, and run either winnt or winnt32 with or without the switches described earlier. You can also copy the appropriate folder (I386, for example) to your local hard drive, and perform the installation as described earlier. This type of installation will work on Windows for Workgroups/Windows 3.1x, Windows NT 3.51, or Windows 95 (but see the earlier caution about this).

CAUTION: All of these network installations require valid licenses for the installations.

A more extreme case occurs when you install Windows NT 4.0 onto a system and you don't have an existing installation or network connection. The easiest way to accomplish this type of installation is to install from a DOS boot floppy—strange as it might seem. The DOS boot floppy happens to have all the necessary files to make the network connection and access the NT 4.0 install files.

Make a DOS boot floppy by booting to a DOS machine and running the SYS command. This copies the necessary boot files to the floppy. On a 4.0 server, choose Start | Programs | Administrator Tools | Network Client Administrator. Choose the option to make an installation disk. Follow the instructions (have the System Administrator tell you what the specifics are for your network) and fill in the necessary information about NICs, protocols, and installation shares. (Make sure that you have proper security privilege for the necessary installation shares.) Edit the necessary files to be sure that all parameters are correct. Finally, edit all files to be sure that all information is correct.

Chapter 21, "Working with Windows and DOS Clients," reviews the process of creating an installation disk for an over-the-network install.

After editing the autoexec.bat file on the floppy, the file should look as follows:

```
path=a:\net
a:\net\net start
net use z: \\BOBSPLACE\CD-ROM
z:\I386\winnt /b
```

This file will invoke the necessary network boot files and log onto the server BOBSPLACE and its share called CD-ROM. The system will then run the winnt /b file from the I386 directory.

The setup.ini file has the necessary information for the boot. This is the text of the file:

```
[network]
filesharing=no
printsharing=no
autologon=yes
computername=BOB
lanroot=A:\NET
username=BobC
workgroup=Bobsplace
```

```
reconnect=no
directhost=no
dospophotkey=N
lmlogon=0
logondomain=Bobsplace
preferredredir=full
autostart=full
maxconnections=8

[network drivers]
netcard=elnk16.dos
transport=ndishlp.sys,*netbeui
devdir=A:\NET
LoadRMDrivers=yes
[Password Lists]
```

With this scenario and one of the NICs detailed above, you can boot onto the network with Netbeui, TCP/IP or IPX/SPC and gain access to the network 4.0 server CD and begin an over-the-network installation.

Unattended Installation

One of the options in using winnt or winnt32 is the use of the /u switch (unattended). Normally the syntax would be winnt32 /b /u:Unattend.txt where Unattend.txt is the answer file. On the server CD, there is in fact an example of the unattend.txt file. In the following example, access has been obtained via a DOS boot to a client distribution share mapped to drive Z:

```
z:\I386\winnt /u:unattend.txt
```

where the unattend.txt file reads as follows:

> **NOTE:** The unattend file is copied into the I386 directory where it replaces the example provided. This change allows a custom unattended installation to occur.

```
[Unattended]
OemPreinstall = no
Method = "express"
ConfirmHardware = no
NtUpgrade = no
Win31Upgrade = no
TargetPath = "*" ;indicates a default directory WINNT
OverwriteOemFilesOnUpgrade = no
;The above dictates the installation of a new installation. The
;assumption here is that there is a single drive and the
;installation is to the C:\WINNT directory. Notice that all
;the normal feedback is negated.


[GuiUnattended]
!SetupApplications = "no" ;no applications are being setup
!DetachedProgram = ""
!Arguments = ""
!AdvServerType = "SERVERNT" ; being installed as a server
!TimeZone = "(GMT-06:00) Central Time (US & Canada)"
!SetupNetwork = "yes"


[LicenseFilePrintData]
!AutoMode = "PerSeat"


[UserData]
!FullName = "Bob Chronister"
!OrgName = "Chronister Consultants"
!ComputerName = "BOB15"
!ProductId = "xxxxxxxxxxxxxxx"


[DomainData]
!AutoDomain = "BOBSPLACE" ;can also be JoinDomain
; JoinDomain = BOBSPLACE


[TransportData]
```

```
!InstallNWLink = "0" ;do not install IPX/SPX
!InstallNetBEUI = "1" ;Install Netbeui
!InstallTCPIP = "0" ;do not install TCP/IP
;or simply InstallProtocols = NetBeui


[NetworkAdapterData]
!AutoNetOption = "ELNK3ISA509"
;3COM509 ISA NIC used here.

[AdapterParameters]
!AutoNetInterfaceType = "1"
Transceiver = "0"
!AutoNetBusNumber = "0"
IoBaseAddress = "768"
InterruptNumber = "10"

[Display]
ConfigureAtLogon = 0
BitsPerPel = 16
XResolution = 640
YResolution = 480
VRefresh = 70
AutoConfirm = 1
;obviously this is being installed as standard
;VGA. This is an excellent installation choice.

;The assumption also was that the hard drive in question was
;either an EIDE drive or a drive listed in the SCSI section of
;the TXTSETUP.SIF file.
```

The easiest place to see the utility of the unattend.txt file is in automatic upgrades. If the installation line Ntupgrade = yes is found in the [Unattended] section, all settings will remain the same and the server will be upgraded to 4.0. All selections after Ntupgrade = yes will simply be ignored.

Installation via SMS

Many large networks running Windows NT and related desktops also have the Microsoft System Management Server installed. This application uses SQL to store information about all the computers, software and hardware, that it can detect. With this intact and a key server available for central distribution (site for the shared files), you can easily send out upgrades (force them, actually).

Using SMS, you can create a job—in this case, upgrade 3.51 servers to 4.0 servers—that pushes installations over the network. In other words, the installation is done automatically to SMS clients. SMS also can perform queries across the network and thus find all the machines that have the appropriate hardware and software for the upgrades.

The basic concept in SMS is to create a package containing file information and then create a job to handle the distribution. For present purposes, the use of SMS to install Windows NT Workstation Version 4.0 would require several tasks. (Please note the proper chapters in the Microsoft SMS manual; of importance are Chapters 7, 10, and 11, dealing with queries, packages, and jobs.)

Once you perform a query that will tell you which systems are the ones you want to upgrade, you're ready to continue. In this case, make a query to detect the specifics of the systems that you want to upgrade to NT Server 4.0. You then create the appropriate *PDF* files (package definition files). These files form the basis of the installation.

The first task is to determine which machines will be upgraded to Server 4.0. Assuming that you have all the necessary inventories on hand, you know which machines you want to upgrade or install Windows NT Workstation 4.0 on. If you don't have such a list available, you need to sort the machines or run specific queries to determine the machines that will be upgraded. Define these systems as a Machine Group for use in the distribution phase.

The second task is to prepare a PDF to handle the updates. In many respects, a PDF is the same as an answer script for an unattended installation. Although no specific NT 4.0 scripts are available as yet, SMS 1.2 has several scripts for NT 3.51. The following is a modified PDF file that will install NT Server 4.0:

```
[PDF]
Version=1.0
```

```
[Automated NT (x86) Setup]
CommandLine=ntencap /NTs winnt32.exe /U:ntupgrd.400
CommandName=Automated Upgrade of (x86) NT Client
UserInputRequired=FALSE
SynchronousSystemExitRequired=TRUE
SupportedPlatforms=Windows NT 3.51 (x86)


[Manual NT (x86) Setup]
CommandLine=ntencap /NTs winnt32.exe /B /S:.
CommandName=Manual Upgrade of (x86) NT Client
UserInputRequired=TRUE
SynchronousSystemExitRequired=TRUE
SupportedPlatforms=Windows NT 3.51 (x86)


[Automated NT (Alpha) Setup]
CommandLine=ntencapa /NTs winnt32.exe /U:ntupgrd.400
CommandName=Automated Upgrade of (Alpha) NT Client
UserInputRequired=FALSE
SynchronousSystemExitRequired=TRUE
SupportedPlatforms=Windows NT 3.51 (Alpha)


[Manual NT (Alpha) Setup]
CommandLine=ntencapa /NTs winnt32.exe
CommandName=Manual Upgrade of (Alpha) NT Client
UserInputRequired=TRUE
SynchronousSystemExitRequired=TRUE
SupportedPlatforms=Windows NT 3.1 (Alpha)


[Automated NT (MIPS) Setup]
CommandLine=ntencapm /NTs winnt32.exe /U:ntupgrd.400
CommandName=Automated Upgrade of (MIPS) NT Client
UserInputRequired=FALSE
SynchronousSystemExitRequired=TRUE
SupportedPlatforms=Windows NT 3.51 (MIPS)
```

```
[Manual NT (MIPS) Setup]
CommandLine=ntencapm /NTs winnt32.exe
CommandName=Manual Upgrade of (MIPS) NT Client
UserInputRequired=TRUE
SynchronousSystemExitRequired=TRUE
SupportedPlatforms=Windows NT 3.51 (MIPS)


[Automated Win Setup]
CommandLine=w16ntupg winnt.exe /U:unattend.400 /W /S:.
CommandName=Automated Setup of Win16 Client
UserInputRequired=FALSE
SynchronousSystemExitRequired=TRUE
SupportedPlatforms=Windows 3.1


[Manual Win Setup]
CommandLine=w16ntupg winnt.exe /B /W /S:.
CommandName=Manual Setup of Win16 Client
UserInputRequired=TRUE
SynchronousSystemExitRequired=TRUE
SupportedPlatforms=Windows 3.1


[Automated DOS Setup]
CommandLine=dosntupg.exe winnt.exe /U:unattend.351 /S:.
CommandName=Automated Setup of DOS Client
UserInputRequired=FALSE
SynchronousSystemExitRequired=TRUE
SupportedPlatforms=MS-DOS 5.0, MS-DOS 6.0, MS-DOS 6.2, MS-DOS 6.21, MS-DOS 6.22


[Manual DOS Setup]
CommandLine=dosntupg.exe winnt.exe /B /S:.
CommandName=Manual Setup of DOS Client
UserInputRequired=TRUE
SynchronousSystemExitRequired=TRUE
```

```
SupportedPlatforms=MS-DOS 5.0, MS-DOS 6.0, MS-DOS 6.2, MS-DOS 6.21, MS-DOS 6.22


[Package Definition]
Product=Windows NT Server
Version=4.00
Comment=Microsoft Windows NT Server 4.00
SetupVariations=Automated NT (x86), Manual NT (x86), Automated NT (Alpha),
➡Manual NT (Alpha), Automated NT (MIPS), Manual NT (MIPS), Automated Win,
➡Manual Win, Automated DOS, Manual DOS
```

You then create a package to install the software. From the Package window in SMS, choose File | New and import the appropriate PDF described above (*server**folder**filename*). When the package is imported, the Package Properties dialog box returns. Choose Windows NT Server. Just as in the unattended installation, you need access to a distribution share that you enter in the source directory. Be certain to make this an automatic setup. Choose OK and the package is ready to be run. In this example, we'll only deal with an upgrade. Notice that in the automated scripts for installing Server in the PDF file above, there are references to the file ntupgrd.400. An example of ntupgrd.400 follows:

```
; This script file is an example script for facilitating
;upgrading NT. If the TCP/IP protocol stack is present on the
;machine being upgraded then the UpgradeEnableDhcp paramater must
;be correctly specified in order to fully automate the upgrade.
[Unattended]
;Method = custom ¦ express
Method = express

;ConfirmHardware = yes ¦ no
ConfirmHardware = no

;NtUpgrade = manual ¦ yes ¦ no ¦ single
NtUpgrade = yes

;TargetPath = manual ¦ * ¦ <path>
```

```
TargetPath = *


[GuiUnattended]
; Specifies if TCP/IP protocol is to use Dynamic host configuration pro
;!UpgradeEnableDhcp = YES ¦ NO
!UpgradeEnableDhcp = YES


;!DetachedProgram = ""


;!Arguments = ""


!ProductId = "*** *******"
```

In this particular example, any NT Server (MIPS, Alpha or Intel) will be automatically upgraded to NT Server 4.0. In reality, making the Ntupgrade=yes should produce an automatic upgrade with settings intact.

To create the job, open the Jobs window and choose File | New. For the present example, define a comment similar to this: Push upgrade of all NT workstations in the * machine group where * is the name defined earlier. Make certain that all necessary files including scripts are copied to a network share on which SMS Service Account has proper access.

Choose Run Command on Workstation. Click the Details command and choose the proper package in the Package window. In the machine group you have defined, enter the name of the specific machine group you have defined. In the send phase, you can choose to place the files directly on the target, and go through a server to which the systems to be upgraded have access. Assuming that you have chosen to copy all files to the targets, you then issue the command you choose in the Run window, in this case automated setup of NT client. Schedule the job; if necessary, make it mandatory. All should be automatic from now on.

The next time the user of a target machine logs on, the scheduled job appears. When the job is completed on the client, the upgrade will be finished. This type of over-the-network upgrade is called a *push* upgrade because the job is pushed onto the client rather than being initiated by the client.

What If Problems Arise?

As with all types of computer issues, it becomes important to distinguish between hardware and software failures. With Windows NT, this isn't always possible. Several fundamental procedures can be followed, however. The following example shows how to use the procedures.

An upgrade of a 3.51 server to 4.0 failed consistently near the end of the process. In all cases the BSOD (Blue Screen of Death) referenced a SCSI driver but the crash always occurred when the system logged onto the network.

Hardware:

- ◆ Mylex PCI/EISA motherboard with 32MB RAM and a Pentium 66
- ◆ Mylex EISA DAC960 Raid controller with three hard drives and 4MB of RAM cache, running RAID 0
- ◆ ATI mach64 video controller
- ◆ NCR (now Symbios) 825 SCSI controller with a single hard drive
- ◆ Cogent eMaster PCI NIC

The problem:
During the upgrade, all appeared to go well. The system was part of a domain. After the upgrade, an attempt was made to reboot, 4.0 appeared on the screen, and then the infamous blue screen of death (BSOD) with all problems pointing to the DAC960 driver. Since this was an important server on the network, the installation needed to be recovered quickly.

The solution:
Assuming that the problem was related to connecting onto the domain, the machine was booted locally. In fact, there was no problem doing so. The Cogent card was removed and a 3COM 3C590 fast Etherlink card substituted. The machine was rebooted and an attempt was made to join the domain. Another BSOD followed immediately. Still no functional server. The July DAC960 driver from Mylex was copied to the \system32\driver directory, after renaming the 4.0 driver. The system was rebooted into the network and all was fine.

In all cases, you can adopt a strategy to examine installation problems. This strategy is very simple and involves common-sense steps. Never try to solve problems in a complex manner. Always search for the best common solution to the problem. Specially, try the following:

Technique 1: Examine the issue and determine the most likely cause. If a system won't boot onto a domain, don't assume that it won't boot locally.

Technique 2: If you have a complex system, simplify it. Remove any unnecessary cards such as sound cards, etc.

Technique 3: If you're using a high-end specialized video card, remove it and use a common card.

Technique 4: If you're using a SCSI bus master, make certain that the drivers will recognize that card.

Sometimes, no matter what you try, the system will crash in the kernel mode. These crashes are serious enough that the exception handlers can't maintain system integrity. In such cases, NT stops and the infamous BSOD appears. These screens are actually diagnostic and you can use them to help troubleshoot the problems.

Common Crashes

STOP 0x0000000A IRQL_NOT_LESS_OR_EQUAL. A pointer in a driver or process incorrectly pointed to a memory address that it had no permission to use. This problem can be caused by both hardware and software, but typically it's driver-related.

STOP 0x000000 KMODE_EXCEPTION_NOT_HANDLED. As the name states, a trap occurred in the kernel and the system crashed. When I have seen these crashes occur, it was always a non-revved driver for a SCSI controller. Be certain to get all proper drivers and hardware.

STOP 0x0000007F. This usually indicates that a hardware fault has occurred. Look at memory, disable all internal and external cache, remove cards, and finally try a new motherboard (preferably a different one).

INACCESSIBLE HARD DRIVE. If SCSI, make certain that all cables and terminators are correct. If the drive is a 7200 RPM drive, it may overheat. Make sure that adequate ventilation and cooling are available. Check the boot sector for viruses (I've seen it before). If the drive is a large EIDE, make certain that LBA is enabled and the drive set to proper master/slave configuration. If LBA isn't enabled, you need to set it and redo FDISK and FORMAT.

Where to Go Next

This chapter dealt with many of the installation issues of Windows NT Server 4.0. Hopefully, sufficient detail was given to allow an easy new installation or upgrade. Common problems and solutions were provided where available.

Here are some other resources that you may find helpful at this point:

♦ Chapter 5, "Beyond the Installation," explains many of the features of 4.0 that can be changed to fit your specific needs.

♦ Chapter 6, "Managing User and Group Accounts," explains how to manage access to the server—especially if the server is a domain Controller.

♦ Chapter 9, "Managing NT Servers," explains how to manage the server effectively.

♦ There are a few Web sites that deal with installation issues and solutions. One particularly useful location is the *Windows NT Magazine* site at www.winntmag.com.

♦ Always read the documentation that comes with Windows NT. Some people complain that the material isn't thorough, which is true, but you can find many useful tips and information.

Chapter | 5

Beyond the Installation

In This Chapter:

- Installed Components
- Understanding the Boot Process (Intel)
- Understanding the Boot Process (RISC)
- A Quick Review of the Default Services

How do I...

After Windows NT 4.0 has been installed, many of us have the daunting task of understanding what we're staring at—even worse, trying to customize what we see. For many network administrators, simply seeing My Computer and Network Neighborhood on the desktop is unacceptable. All these interface issues can easily be civilized.

Installed Components

The most dramatic change in Windows NT 4.0 is obviously the interface. Much has been written about its superiority over the Version 3.51 interface. In fact, however, parts of the interface are useful and parts may not be as functional as those in 3.51. Fortunately, both Program Manager and File Manager are still available in NT 4.0. Before continuing with an explanation of how to change the interface, it's important to discuss the changes that have occurred that provide the new interface.

By the way, the Winlogon setting in the Registry has the value of explorer.exe, which is what makes the interface look like Windows 95. You can restore the familiar Program Manager interface (although this isn't supported by Microsoft) by making a small change in the Registry. The appropriate Registry entry is as follows:

```
HKEY_LOCAL_MACHINE
  \Software
    \Microsoft
      \WindowsNT
        \CurrentVersion
          \Winlogon
            \shell
```

Change the word shell to progman.exe to use the old interface.

The Windows NT Interface

One very good aspect of the new interface is that it's very easy to customize. This includes customizing the Taskbar as well as most of the other aspects of the screen. The default interface has a simple appearance, with certain applications on the left side of the screen and the Windows Taskbar at the bottom of the screen, shown clearly in Figure 5-1.

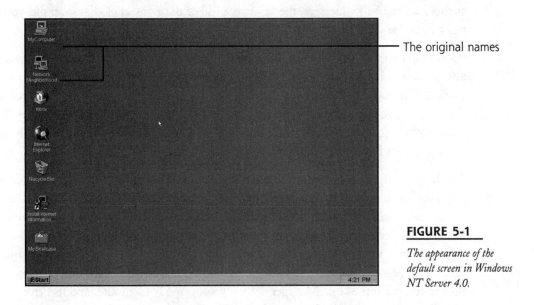

The original names

FIGURE 5-1

The appearance of the default screen in Windows NT Server 4.0.

As a matter of convenience, it seems appropriate to change the name from My Computer to the machine name. To accomplish this, simply right-click the My Computer icon and you easily can rename to the machine name (see Figure 5-2).

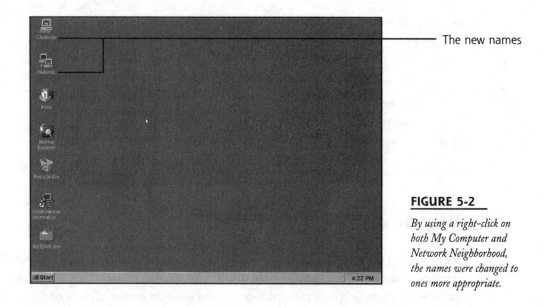

The new names

FIGURE 5-2

By using a right-click on both My Computer and Network Neighborhood, the names were changed to ones more appropriate.

The important feature used to make these changes is the right-click. Throughout the customization of the interface, the key is the use of the right-click. For example, you can right-click the window background and change the video properties.

As an important adjunct to customizing the names of programs on the desktop, you can also place new programs and shortcuts on the desktop. Shortcuts are references to a program, and have various properties that can be viewed by right-clicking the shortcut icon. For example, you can place a shortcut to Microsoft Word on the desktop; double-clicking the shortcut takes you directly to the specified program. Figure 5-3 shows a highly customized server interface with many server applications.

The key to adding applications to the desktop is the right mouse button and Windows Explorer. You can open Explorer and drag executable files to the desktop, which is an easy way to customize the appearance of the desktop. There's a better approach than using Explorer, however. My Computer (hopefully, you've renamed it) allows you to explore one drive at a time, while still allowing you to copy applications from your hard drives to the desktop. When you use Explorer, you cache many icons; consequently, Explorer is very slow in comparison to File Manager. When you open My Computer and its drive C: icon, the icon caching is very limited and the process is faster (and thus easier to use).

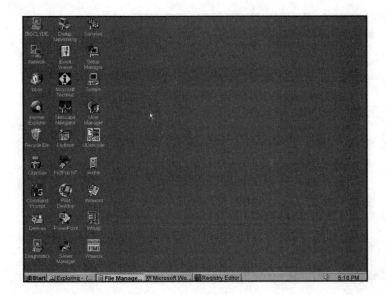

FIGURE 5-3

The desktop of a highly customized Windows NT 4.0 server. This desktop has many server applications very handy and ready to use.

Figure 5-4 shows the default appearance of a directory. The files in the directory are shown with only file name and icon, rather than the details about the files that you're used to from File Manager. This problem is easily overcome. Click the next-to-last button on the window's toolbar. Now all the files are displayed with their normal extensions (assuming that you have selected the proper options (choose View | Options | Show All Files and clear the Hide Files of these types check box). This more typical appearance is shown in Figure 5-5.

Using either Explorer or My Computer, you can drag a file and place it on the desktop. Such an approach may seem tedious, but it's not. When you copy the executable file, you're actually copying a shortcut to that file. This method has advantages because you can apply switches to shortcuts very easily. For example, you can create a shortcut called winnt32 /b, which includes the /b switch. This can't be set as a run option.

One final point about the use of My Computer. If you right-click a file, you can obtain a menu of options concerning a file. As Figure 5-6 shows, this is an impressive amount of options that you can use to perform various operations on the file.

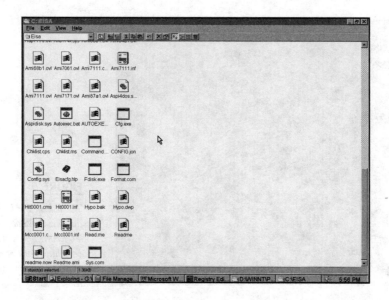

FIGURE 5-4

The icon appearance of a folder on drive C:.

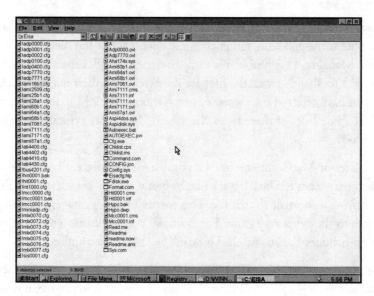

FIGURE 5-5

The same folder, shown in list mode. If you checked Show Extensions in the Options dialog box, you now see a list of all files.

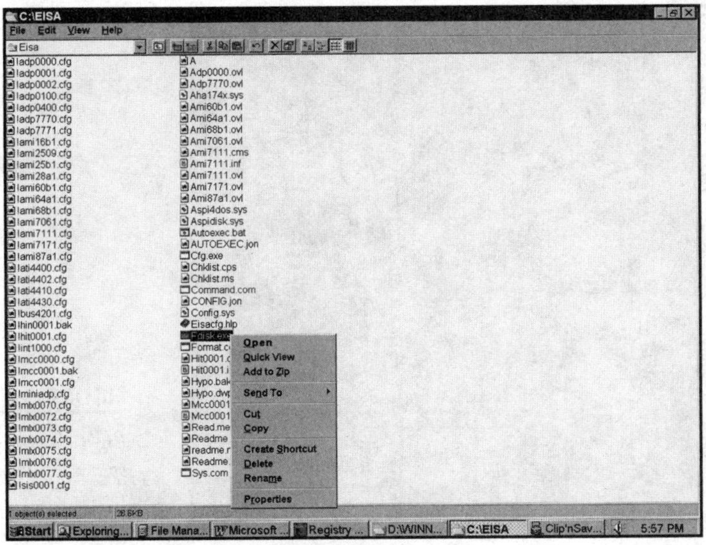

FIGURE 5-6

Right-clicking reveals a lot of information about that file. You can also create a shortcut to that file and drag it to the desktop.

TIP: Once you have the desktop configured as you want, you can copy it to the Taskbar or the Start menu. Open the My Computer window. Choose View Toolbar. On the toolbar, click open the drop-down list and select Desktop (it's at the top of the list) to change the My Computer window to a Desktop window, displaying your shortcut icons. This desktop can then be "dragged" to either the Taskbar or the Start menu. This makes it easy to use any of your shortcuts when you have other applications open and obscuring the view of the desktop.

If you accidentally delete a icon or rename something on the desktop incorrectly, you can right-click the desktop and undo these changes, as shown in Figure 5-7.

You can also right-click a file and get all the salient information on the file by clicking Quick View. The resulting data can help you appreciably in understanding the specifics of any program on the desktop. For example, looking via quick view at an executable file can show you header information, import tables, date stamps, and many other file sttributes that can be valuable if problems arise.

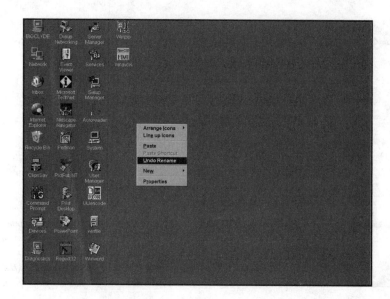

FIGURE 5-7

Right-click the desktop to open a pop-up menu. In this case, Undo Rename is highlighted.

Customizing the Start Menu

The Start menu supplies nearly everything you will ever need to run Windows NT 4.0. When you click Start, you get an application list and a program/setting list. Separating them is a horizontal line in the pop-up box, as shown in Figure 5-8.

The Help program on the bottom half of the Start menu provides the basic help issues for all of Windows NT. It's very handy indeed. The adjacent Find program finds computers, files, or folders. Settings gives you access to the Control Panel, printers, and the configuration of the Taskbar (see the next section for details on the Taskbar). The document list shows the last 15 files that you worked on. Clicking one of the files opens that file. In short, the crucial files for setting up and running Windows NT 4.0 are on the bottom half of the menu by default.

Clicking the Programs item on the Start menu reveals all the programs that you have installed on your computer and on your account. If you have installed onto an NT network, you will have both a network and a local account. In such a case, the personal programs of the two accounts probably will differ.One such list of programs is shown in Figure 5-9.

You can easily add programs and shortcuts to the Start menu. Open Explorer and find the application that you want to add. Copy the program icon (or a shortcut) to the Start menu by dragging the file and dropping it on the Start button. This application will be above the horizontal line on the Start menu.

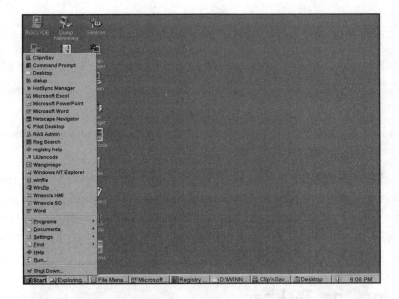

FIGURE 5-8

The Start menu showing applications above the line and programs/settings below the line.

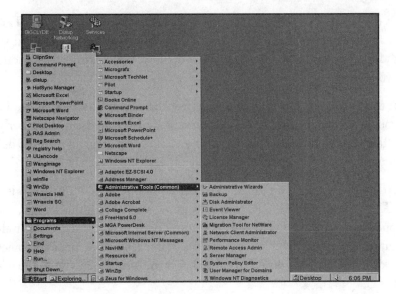

FIGURE 5-9

Clicking the Programs item shows you the programs installed on your computer and allows easy access.

If you right-click the Start button, you can open all applications. This fact implies that you can open your personal applications and not common ones. When you choose Open All Users, you open the common applications. In both cases, you can drag and drop applications on the Start button.

> **TIP:** Drag and drop shortcuts rather than the executable files to the desktop. If you accidentally drag the icon representing an application to the trash can, you'll delete the application. This isn't the case with a shortcut. In addition, a shortcut can have switches, an application can't.

It's prudent to keep the number of applications on the Start button to a reasonable number. Too many simply clutter up the interface.

Finally, if you click Start | Settings, you can open the Taskbar settings. The Start menu is part of the Taskbar. In the window that opens after you choose this option, you'll see the Start menu listed; you can add, remove, or set the advanced properties of the applications listed on the Start menu. These capabilities enable you to control the applications on the Start menu quite easily.

Customizing the Taskbar

The Taskbar is the last part of the interface that we'll discuss here. Basically, the Taskbar enables you to access any open application. Recall that you can also drag the desktop to the Taskbar and, assuming that you don't close the desktop, the desktop will stay on the Taskbar after you reboot.

You can resize the Taskbar by moving the mouse over the edge of the Taskbar. Resizing is important if you have enough applications open that you can't read them all properly. You can also move the Taskbar to other positions on the desktop by dragging, but the default (bottom) position is probably the most logical place.

By default, the Taskbar is always on top of the other items on the desktop, which is very inconvenient. The easiest way to use Taskbar is to auto-hide it. With this feature, you can work on an application with the full screen. When you need to access the Taskbar and the Start menu, simply press Ctrl+Esc. To close the Start menu, click any unoccupied part of the Taskbar. You can also display the Taskbar by moving the mouse to the edge of the screen.

Moving the mouse over an application button on the Taskbar displays information on the specifics of the application. For example, if you have Word for Windows open with a document on-screen, moving the mouse pointer over the button for Word on the Taskbar displays a ToolTip with the name of the file being edited.

The final important aspect of the Taskbar is the right-click feature, with which you can tile, cascade, and minimize windows. If you right-click the Taskbar and choose Properties, you end up at Taskbar Properties—the same place you would go by choosing Start | Settings | Taskbar. More importantly, by right-clicking and choosing Task Manager, you open a very powerful window with which you can control processes and applications (very similar to the version that shipped with the 3.51 Resource Kit). Figure 5-10 shows the Task Manager. The Task Manager windows shows a list of the applications or processes currently running. The End Task button gives you control over the current application.

FIGURE 5-10

Right-clicking the Taskbar and then choosing Task Manager shows a much enhanced Task Manager in comparison to that in Version 3.51.

By clicking the Performance tab in the Task Manager, you can display a miniature version of some of the critical aspects of Performance Monitor (see Figure 5-11). The basic aspects of the system memory and CPU utilization are shown in some detail. This feature can help you keep track of many of the performance issues of your system.

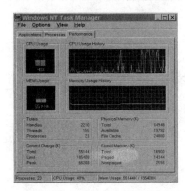

FIGURE 5-11

System performance information displayed on the Performance tab in the Task Manager window.

TIP: If the utilization percentage is consistently above 80 percent, you may need to consider upgrading to a faster CPU. (See Chapter 17,"Monitoring System Performance," for more detail.)

Choosing a File System

With the release of Version 4.0, certain aspects parts of the file structure in Windows NT changed. No longer is HPFS (High Performance File System) officially supported in NT. If you have a system using HPFS and you upgrade to NT 4.0, you need to change the format prior to upgrading (you can only convert FAT to NTFS in 4.0). This fact obviously means that you need to do a backup of all files on the partition and then reformat it.

Several file structure strategies are possible:

♦ The simplest method is to keep all file structures the same. You simply choose either FAT or NTFS. Both have clear advantages and disadvantages (for details, see Chapter 12, "Windows NT Security Fundamentals").

♦ The second choice is to have a small FAT partition with the rest NTFS. This is a good option, but having a FAT partition violates a major aspect of C2 security. This may or may not be important to you.

♦ Some users keep equal volumes of FAT and NTFS. The choice of using FAT or NTFS is one of user or network preference.

The following list shows the main advantages and disadvantages of FAT and NTFS systems:

FAT Advantages

♦ Allows nearly all operating systems to access the partitions.

♦ The most universal file format; widely accepted.

FAT Disadvantages

♦ No security attributes to protect files.

♦ No automatic disk-restoration feature.

♦ Poor cluster size management.

NTFS Advantages

 ♦ Supports file-based security.

 ♦ Logs activities to restore disks in case of problems (automatic disk restoration).

 ♦ Supports extended attributes.

 ♦ Excellent cluster size management.

NTFS: Disadvantages

 ♦ Recognized fully only by Windows NT (other OS support is read-only).

 ♦ You can't boot DOS from the hard drive.

TIP: After Windows NT 4.0 is installed, you can add support for HPFS for editing the Registry. (This may or may not be a good idea because it's clearly not supported by Microsoft.) Before editing the Registry, of course, make certain that you have an up-to-date emergency repair disk (ERD). Run `Rdisk /s` to make a current ERD.

The following steps show the Registry editing that has to be done for this to work:

1. Copy the NT 3.51 `pinball.sys` to `%SYSTEMROOT%\System32\drivers`.

2. Start the Registry Editor and open the following key:

    `HKEY_LOCAL_MACHINE\SYSTEM\CurrentControlSet\Services`

3. Add the key `Pinball`.

4. Highlight the `Pinball` key and add the following values (case-sensitive):

    ```
    ErrorControl: REG_DWORD: 0x1
    Group: REG_SZ: Boot file system
    Start: REG_DWORD: 0x1
    Type: REG_DWORD: 0x2
    ```

5. When this is complete, reboot the machine. **Note:** This change is not supported by Microsoft in any way (you will not be able to obtain technical support from Microsoft if problems arise)!!

Initial Folders (Directories/Subdirectories)

Windows NT installs with various *primary* and *secondary folders* (directories and subdirectories). The default installation directory is WINNT. Regardless of the drive on which you install, for a new installation it's a good idea to accept the default WINNT directory choice. The other major folder created at installation is the Program folder, where most applications will be installed. This folder replaces the win32apps folder that many of us still have around from our Version 3.5 days.

The bulk of the folders that are installed are secondary folders within WINNT. The most significant of these folders are profile, system and system32.

The profile folder contains individual user account information. Under each user, including default, are other folders. NT defaults to these folders when an application saves or opens an file. For example, Word for Windows 95 saves by default to the logged on user's personal directory (user\personal). Although a logical choice, this default makes it difficult for multiple users on a computer to share the same documents.

The system folder typically contains the DLLs for 16-bit applications. The folder consequently is usually very small.

The system32 folder, on the other hand, is the heart and soul of Windows NT. Here the fonts (typefaces), the 32-bit DLLs, and all system configuration files are stored. The most important secondary folders are the drivers and the configuration folders. Little here has changed from Version 3.51.

System Partition Files

For the proper startup of Windows NT 4.0, certain specific files and drivers must load and function properly. The following sections describe these files, which generate the NT system on boot.

NTLDR

After Windows NT has been installed on the system, NTLDR is loaded from the boot sector of the hard drive. All operating systems on the drive are loaded by NTLDR; that is, NTLDR allows DOS or Windows NT to load. If NT is chosen, NTLDR actually does much of the loading of Windows NT components.

OSLOADER

The OSLOADER file is the RISC counterpart of NTLDR. As discussed in the later section "Understanding the Boot Process (RISC)," the functional boot of a RISC machine is far easier than that on the Intel platform.

boot.ini

boot.ini is the system file used to create the choice screen that is seen early in the boot process. A typical boot.ini file looks like the following, which allows the choice of booting to Windows NT server or DOS:

```
[boot loader]
timeout=5
default=multi(0)disk(0)rdisk(0)partition(2)\WINNT
[operating systems]
multi(0)disk(0)rdisk(0)partition(2)\WINNT="Windows NT Server
➥Version 4.00"
multi(0)disk(0)rdisk(0)partition(2)\WINNT="Windows NT Server
➥Version 4.00 [VGA mode]" /basevideo /sos
C:\="MS-DOS"
```

To translate these lines, you need to understand *ARC* (*Advanced RISC Computing*) terminology (see the later section "Building a Boot Disk"). The syntax of boot.ini is actually a derivation of the RISC boot process or ARC terminology. The basic ARC syntax is as follows:

```
controller(w)disk(x)rdisk(y)partition(z)\path
```

To make matters very simple, the controller name is either SCSI (very infrequently used, and mostly seen with multiple controllers) or multi, which indicates machines that find drives via BIOS, and is the typical term used even with SCSI controllers.

disk(x) is used only with SCSI terminology and indicates the ID of the appropriate drive. For example, if you boot from the first drive on the bus, disk would be (0); from the second drive, disk would be (1).

rdisk(y) is used with multi terminology. It refers to the ordinal number of the drive on the adapter. If you boot from the second drive, rdisk(y) would be rdisk(1).

partition(z) refers to the partition containing the active Windows NT folder. The numbers start with 1. For example, in the boot.ini discussed earlier, both the 3.51 and the 4.0 folders are on drive E: or the third partition of the first drive.

> **NOTE:** When multi is used, the drive is loaded via INT 13 (BIOS disk interface). Due to current limitations with FAT, this limits a boot drive to 2 gigabytes in size.

NTDETECT.COM

The file NTDETECT.COM is an exclusive Intel-based program. It examines the hardware and generates a list; this list is then incorporated into NTLDR. Subsequently, the list forms the hardware aspect of the Registry. This is the key hardware detection file in the boot process.

BOOTSECT.DOS

If you dual-boot DOS or one of its variants, BOOTSECT.DOS is used to boot into the older operating system. In general, this is the boot sector that existed before Windows NT was installed.

NTBOOTDD.SYS

If you use SCSI terminology in boot.ini, you need to copy the boot SCSI driver to the root drive and rename it NTBOOTDD.SYS. This file enables devices to be attached to the boot controller. It's seldom used anymore because of the limited use of the SCSI terminology in boot.ini. The primary use of SCSI is on boot disks (see the later discussion of boot floppies for details).

Understanding the Boot Process (Intel)

The Windows NT boot process has several parts. First, platform-specific components (Intel; Alpha, MIPS, PowerPC) are loaded. Following this specific component loading, common NT components (the ones that are the same in all platforms) are loaded. This process is complex and involves many modules. Throughout the entire process, improper hardware or drivers can cause a fatal kernel error or Blue Screen of Death (BSOD).

Phases of the Boot Process

When you turn the system on, the system runs its POST (Power ON Self Test). This is typically called the pre-boot phase. The system must then assemble a specific set of variables that enable NT to load. This phase is typically called the *boot phase*. As the boot phase progresses, NTOSKRNL.exe is loaded, which begins the kernel phase. This kernel phase has four subphases; all concludes with a successful logon. The following sections describe each of the phases in detail.

Order of File Loading

When a computer boots, it goes through a set of phases. The first noticeable phase is the *POST (Power-On-Self-Test)*. During this phase, hardware is listed and placed in the CMOS tables. After this occurs, the hard drive is scanned for the Master Boot Record (MBR) and the necessary programs are run. NTLDR is initialized and reads boot.ini. This is the start of the *boot sequence*.

NTLDR first loads the flat memory model currently limited to 4 gigabyte of memory (Windows NT is 32-bit, so the amount of memory that can be addressed is 2^{32}).

NTLDR then loads the file system drivers so that the hard drive can be read. These drivers are for FAT and NTFS by default.

NTLDR then reads boot.ini and gives the user the boot screen to choose an operating mode. Normally this is Windows NT (perhaps several versions) and DOS (if you dual-boot). If you choose DOS, NTLDR simply passes control to BOOTSECT.DOS. If you choose NT, however, NTLDR loads the next module, NTDETECT.COM, which scans all the associated hardware and passes the information to the System hive in the Registry.

NTLDR then loads NTOSKRNL.exe and the *kernel phase* of boot begins. During this time, four distinct events occur (this total phase is called the *NT boot phase*):

+ The *kernel load phase* begins with the kernel (NTOSKRNL.exe) being loaded and is followed by the loading of the *Hardware Abstraction Layer* (HAL.dll). The System hive generated by NTDETECT.COM is then loaded and the appropriate drivers loaded into memory. (You notice this phase as the dots progress across the top of the screen).

♦ In the *kernel initialization phase*, all the drivers loaded into memory are initialized. The System hive is examined once more, and all necessary drivers loaded. Obviously, these drivers are considered high-level drivers (for example, a specific SCSI driver)and not kernel-mode drivers (for example, ntfs.sys). The CurrentControlSet aspect of the Registry is saved and a clone set generated. At this time, all hardware is configured in the Registry.

♦ In the *services load phase*, the session manager (SMSS.EXE) is started, and the sequence of events dictated in the bootexecute key in the Registry is executed. Typically this includes an autochk.exe application, but it could also be a conversion of FAT to NTFS if that mode was selected. Next, the page file is set by the session manager (the pagefile is generated each time NT boots). The CurrentControlSet is written to the Registry. This phase concludes with the loading of the Win32 subsystem—the fourth phase.

♦ The *Win32 subsystem* starts with the Winlogon process (WINLOGON.EXE). Importantly, local security authority is started, and the familiar Ctrl+Alt+Del screen is displayed. When a user logs on successfully, the clone set becomes the Last Known Good set. (For details on the Last Known Good, see Chapter 11 "Working with the Windows NT System Registry."

Understanding the Boot Process (RISC)

The RISC boot process differs from that of the Intel platform. First of all, the boot device is written to non-volatile RAM, which the resident firmware reads during the pre-boot stage of initialization. The firmware then searches the first sector of the boot drive to determine whether the drive is bootable. A query is then made of the file structure to ensure that it's supported. After this, OSLOADER.EXE is loaded, and the hardware collected at POST is passed to it. Obviously, NTDETECT.COM isn't needed on a RISC machine because much is done in firmware. When all these steps are accomplished, NTOSKRNL.exe is loaded; the remaining boot processes are nearly identical.

Troubleshooting the Boot Process

Typically problems concerned with the inability to access a drive are due to issues with hardware or corrupted Master Boot Records (MBR). Many times the errors are due to viruses in the boot sector (`inaccessible hard drive` error) or corrupted individual files. In the latter case, check the hardware including cables and drives.

Here are the most common issues (in boot order):

◆ If `NTLDR` is missing; you get this message:

```
BOOT: Couldn't find NTLDR
Please insert another disk.
```

◆ If `NTDETECT.COM` is missing, the following message appears on the boot loader screen:

```
NTDETECT V1.0 Checking hardware ...........
NTDETECT V1.0 Checking hardware ...........
```

◆ If `NTOSKRNL.exe` is corrupted or missing, the following message appears immediately after the Last Known Good option appears:

```
Windows NT could not start because the following file is missing or corrupt
\winnt\system32\ntoskrnl.exe
Please reinstall a copy of the file
```

◆ If `bootsect.dos` is missing or corrupt, the following message is displayed after the Last Known Good screen:

```
I/O error accessing boot sector file
multi(0)disk(0)rdisk(0)partition(1):\bootsect.dos
```

In all these cases, you can use the repair facility in Setup to examine and fix the boot sector drives. Although you don't need a repair disk to fix an NT installation, it's far easier if you have a new ERD. If you have an NT boot disk, you can boot into NT.

The system responds differently if there are problems with `boot.ini`:

◆ If the file is missing, `NTLDR` immediately tries to boot NT. If NT is in the default `\winnt` folder, the boot will probably work. If another directory is used, the following message shows up immediately following the Last Known Good screen:

```
Windows NT could not start because the following file was missing or corrupt:
\winnt\system32\ntoskrnl.exe
Please reinstall a copy of the above file.
```

♦ If `boot.ini` contains an improper path, the following message appears:

```
OS Loader V4.0
Windows NT could not start because of a computer disk hardware configuration
➥problem. Could not read from the selected boot disk. Check boot path and disk
➥hardware.
Please check the Windows NT documentation about hardware disk configuration and
➥your hardware reference manuals for additional information.
```

In these cases, you need to edit `boot.ini`. Remove its hidden and system attributes and change the improper syntax. If you can't access `boot.ini`, you need to install a new version of NT (to a different directory) and thus gain access to an NTFS partition containing `boot.ini`. You still need to manually edit the file.

Building a Boot Disk

If you use mirroring for boot drives, it's always a good idea to create a floppy boot drive. In general, it's important to have a boot disk to recover from a physical disk failure. For example, if you boot Windows NT on `drive 2` and `drive 1` fails, a boot disk will allow you to boot to `drive 2` from the floppy drive. It's very easy to make a boot floppy for both Intel and RISC computers.

Format a floppy in Windows NT. For Intel-based machines, copy `NTLDR`, `boot.ini`, `NTDE-TECT.COM`, and, if appropriate, the boot SCSI driver (copied and renamed `NTBOOTDD.SYS`). For RISC-based machines, copy `OSLOADER.EXE` and `HAL.dll` to the floppy disk. In both cases, the floppy disk must be formatted in Windows NT.

> **NOTE:** Prior to copying the files, remove all system/hidden/read attributes. After copying, restore the attributes for both the source and copied files.

The primary use of a boot floppy is to bypass a corrupted boot sector. Only the files copied to the floppy will be loaded from the boot floppy. All other files are found on the hard drive and must be intact. If any such files are likewise corrupted, the boot floppy won't work.

As an example, let's examine a boot floppy that has been created to repair a damaged primary drive of a mirrored set. Assume that we'll use this floppy to access the secondary or shadow drive. For simplicity's sake, we'll do this in SCSI terminology. boot.ini will read as follows:

```
[Boot loader]
timeout = 30 ; this is the default timeout in seconds
default = scsi(0)disk(0)rdisk(0)partition (1)\winnt="primary drive"
[operating systems]
scsi(0)disk(0)rdisk(0)partition (1)\winnt="primary drive"
scsi(1)disk(0)rdisk(0)partition (1)\winnt="shadow drive"
```

In this scenario, the primary drive is on the first SCSI controller (0) and the shadow drive is on the second controller (1). In both cases, the SCSI ID is 0. In both cases, NTBOOTDD.sys is also needed on the boot floppy. Booting to the first OS boots to the primary drive; booting to the second OS boots to the duplexed drive. Using such a boot, you can load NT from either the primary or duplexed drive, independently of the status of the other hard drive. Simply choose the first (primary) or second (secondary or mirrored) drive.

A Quick Review of the Default Services

We have so far ignored the critical services that are loaded during installation. During Windows NT setup, a default set of services is installed. Some of these services are critical to the functions built into Windows NT. A brief description of the major services will help you understand these basic aspects of Windows NT functionality.

The Browser Service

The *browser service* is far less critical in Version 4.0 than it was in Version 3.51. (Much of the browser function can be accomplished by Explorer.) The browser service basically maintains a list of network resources that can be passed on to an application. This list of resources includes computers, printers, and similar sharable devices.

On any network, there's always a system that contains the master resource list. This system is called the *master browser*. Every time a potential master browser comes online, an election is held to determine which system will be master browser. If a master isn't found, a new one is established. During this election, the resource list is passed to all eligible systems. (For more details on the master browser and elections, see Chapter 14, "Workgroups, Domains, and Browsing Explained.")

The Workstation Service

The *workstation service* on a Windows NT system allows that system to access network resources. This service is the redirector service, and basically allows one computer to gain access to another computer. The workstation service runs in privileged mode and can call other services directly.

The Server Service

The *server service* allows the creation of shared network resources. This service also has privileged access to other services. Unlike the workstation service, the server service doesn't connect to other computers. This service basically uses other services to gain access to the data in files and then passes the data to a requesting client.

The Alerter Service

When a problem occurs with a resource, the *alerter service* simply notifies selected computers and users of these administrative alerts. Typical messages cover loss of power and the use of a UPS, or problems in accessing a drive because it has crashed, is no longer available, or has gone offline.

The Messenger Service

As the name implies, the *messenger service* is used to send and receive messages sent by administrators or the alerter service. In order to send and receive messages, this service has to be running.

All these services are essential for the proper functioning of Windows NT. Without them, the network won't function properly. Messages won't be delivered and NT simply won't function in any meaningful way. Without proper files being loaded, NT won't boot; without proper services loaded, it won't work.

Where to Go Next

This chapter describes the new Windows NT 4.0 interface and how to customize it. The basics of boot process are presented, as well as basic troubleshooting. In addition, the text discusses the essential services that are loaded automatically. As you can imagine, additional information is widely available. Following are several key sources:

- ◆ Obviously, the Microsoft Web site has much up-to-date literature and plenty of fixes for Windows NT. The site is www.microsoft.com, and includes hot fixes and service packs.

- ◆ Although Microsoft has officially left CompuServe, the WINNT forum on CompuServe still has a lot of very useful information and discussion.

- ◆ The www.wintmag.com site is dedicated exclusively to Windows NT. There are troubleshooting and product sections on the site.

- ◆ The Windows NT Resource Kit from Microsoft contains many utilities and information not found in the standard documentation. Beginning with NT 4.0, the kit includes separate Server and Workstation versions.

PART III

Administering
Windows NT Servers

Chapter | 6

Managing User
and Group Accounts

In This Chapter:

- Understanding Users and Groups
- Managing Users and Groups
- Setting Account Policies
- Controls for Individual Accounts
- Controls for Entire Domains

How do I...

Windows NT is the first Windows operating system to offer any sort of usable multiuser access control, security, or logon functionality. As with UNIX and NetWare, Windows NT workstations require that users log on. Administrators can assign users to individual groups that, in combination with user policy settings, determine where users can go on the network and what they can see and do while there.

This chapter explores:

- The fundamental principles behind the Windows NT user and group accounts
- What built-in accounts and groups exist, and what powers they have
- How to manage user and group accounts on single machines and single domains
- How to manage user policies and profiles to control user access and environment settings across your network

You use the User Manager for Domains application to create, remove, and manage user and group accounts; throughout this chapter, we describe how to use User Manager for Domains to manage your own set of users and groups.

Understanding Users and Groups

The Windows NT account-management features depend on two separate classes of accounts. *User accounts* link a set of identifying attributes with a set of permissions for resource access. The central attribute of a user account isn't its name, but its NT *security identifier* (*SID*); other identifying attributes include the list of groups to which an account belongs, and a human-readable account name. User accounts can provide access to resources on a single machine or spread across many domains in a large enterprise network. Windows NT, Windows 95, and LAN Manager clients can use Windows NT user accounts to give and restrict access to shared resources and workstations; in addition, the Windows NT–NetWare compatibility services detailed in Chapter 22, "Interoperating with Novell NetWare," enable you to use Windows NT accounts with NetWare services.

Group accounts are the second class of account that Windows NT supports. You can aggregate users into groups, which consolidate users into units where all members have the same permissions and rights. By using groups, you can control permissions so that they're consistently applied to all members of the group. This centralization greatly simplifies managing related sets of users—for example, all the users in your accounting department need permission to print to the department's printer, but not necessarily to other printers across the hall.

Both user and group accounts operate in *domains*. A domain is merely a collection of machines that share a common security database; this sharing allows one user account to access resources throughout the entire domain. Throughout the rest of this chapter, we mention how user accounts can interact with domains. Using, planning, and managing domains are covered in Chapters 14, 15, and 16; you may find those chapters helpful as you proceed.

Rights and Permissions

Throughout this chapter, I'll talk about rights and permissions. A *right* grants the user power to do certain things on the entire system; rights apply to all instances of whatever objects the right can affect. For example, an account that has the Debug Programs right can use this right on any program running on the server. By contrast, a *permission* allows the user to do certain things to a specific object. Because Windows NT creates system objects for files, network devices, hardware devices, and accounts (among other things), permissions can be applied to individual instances of many system components. For example, the owner of a shared directory such as f:\source\daily\headers can assign Read permission to one group and Full Control permission to another. These permissions extend only to that object—not to other directories at the same level or on other disks.

Understanding User Accounts

Windows NT user accounts map an *entity* (whether it's a person, or a piece of software that needs access privileges) to a set of *attributes*. The most important attribute is the *security identifier* (*SID*). All the permissions and attributes attached to the account are carried via the SID, much like a UNIX user id (uid). Unlike uids, however, SIDs can't be reused. When you create a new account, a new SID is assigned; if you later delete that account and create another one with the same name, the two accounts will have different SIDs, and any resources with permissions for the old account will need to be reset to allow access to the new SID.

The most basic set of attributes for an account are the ones that identify the user to the system and to other users: the account user name, password, full name, and description. There are also a set of *attribute flags* that control whether the account is usable, when (or if) it expires, and whether the user can or must change the account password.

In addition to these attributes are several groups of characteristics that you can use to allow or deny certain behaviors:

- ◆ *Logon restriction attributes* let you restrict what hours of the day an account can log on, as well as from which machines it can log on.

- ◆ *Group membership attributes* specify to which groups an account belongs; this in turn determines what extra permissions accounts have, and how— or whether—accounts from one domain can use resources in another.

- ◆ *Profile and policy attributes* control what environment settings an account has, as well as which settings it can change. Each account can have its own account profile script that executes at logon; in addition, each account, group, and machine can have policy settings that override the default. Editing account policies is covered in detail later in this chapter.

Global User Accounts

Global user accounts are ordinary domain accounts. New accounts default to being global. Each user's account will ordinarily be a global account in that user's home domain. Global accounts can be used to access shared resources or log on interactively to machines in the domain, and they can be put into local or global groups and shared between domains. (For more details on using and managing global accounts in groups and across domains, see Chapter 16, "Managing Users and Groups in Domains.")

Local User Accounts

Local user accounts are intended to allow users from other domains to access resources within your domain. Users in other domains can connect to shares in your domain by using the local account's name and password, without there being a trust relationship between those domains and your own. Local accounts can't be used to log on interactively—only to access resources. You can't add local user accounts to local or global groups in the domain, so they can't be exported to other domains. (For more details on using local accounts in domains, see Chapter 16.)

Understanding Group Accounts

Windows NT groups provide a way to group users with similar rights and/or permissions. By assigning the desired rights and permissions to a group, you avoid having to manage permissions on every individual user account; instead, you control access privileges by adding and removing user accounts in the groups on your system. For example, you can control who can administer a computer by changing the membership of the computer's built-in Administrators group.

Local Groups

Local groups under NTS confer permissions and rights to all machines in a domain. Local groups often contain user accounts from the local workstation or server; these accounts have access only to the local machine and its resources.

However, local groups can also be maintained at the domain level, in which case they're local to the entire domain. Any member of the group can use resources available to that local group on any computer in the domain.

In their domain role, local groups can include user accounts or global groups from any trusted domains. One simple way to grant access to groups of users from a trusted domain is to put those groups into a local group in your domain. Local groups can't contain other local groups, and they can only be used within the domain of the server they're created on. Local groups can grant permission to use shared resources, and they can also be granted group rights, like the power to create new accounts in a domain.

Global Groups

In addition to local groups, NTS also offers *global groups*. Global groups can contain users from the domain in which the global group exists.Global groups provide a simple way for you to collect users with similar access requirements; for example, you can put all the engineers into a global group and then grant that group access to your CAD servers and plotters. As Chapter 16 explains, other domains can use your domain's global groups to allow sharing data between domains.

Global groups can't contain local or global groups, and they can't be used to confer rights, only permissions. These restrictions mean that when you allow users from a global group in another domain to use resources in your domain, the other domain's administrator can't grant rights to her users. This prevents unauthorized changes to your network by keeping other domain administrators from granting rights to themselves or their users that you don't want them to have.

Built-In User Accounts

Windows NT automatically creates two user accounts, Administrator and Guest, during installation. however, the built-in accounts are created automatically and can't be removed or renamed.

Administrator

The *Administrator account* is the most powerful account on an NTS machine. The Administrator has complete access to devices and files, and can take ownership of resources even when they belong to other users. Unlike the UNIX superuser account, the Administrator must first take ownership of objects or files before changing their security settings. The Security Reference Manager creates corresponding entries in the security accounting log, indicating what has taken place.

The Administrator account also has the power to grant and deny any set of rights to any user or group account. Furthermore, this account can't be locked out or denied logon access, and its password has the "never expires" flag set. If you forget the account password, and don't have another account in the Administrators group, the only way to regain administrative access to the server is to reinstall NTS.

> **CAUTION:** Because the Administrator account is all-powerful, it is *critical* that you set a good password for the account. Don't use an empty password, system, administrator, or any other easily guessed word or phrase. As you'll see later, most system management can be done by users who are members of the various Operator groups, so you should limit the number of people who have use of the Administrator account. You can also rename the Administrator account to prevent attacks based on the account name from succeeding.

Guest *this on test*   *Guest account is disable by default*

By contrast with the Administrator account, the Guest account has very limited abilities. For starters, NTS disables it at install time (although it's normally enabled on NTW machines), and you must manually enable it to permit guest access to your servers—if in fact you want to allow it at all. While you can rename it and change its rights and permissions, you can't delete the Guest account. Guest is only in the Domain Guests group (on machines that participate in a domain); by default, the Guest account's password can't be changed and won't expire unless you change these settings.

> **CAUTION:** The Guest account allows untrusted users entry to your system. You should turn it off. If you're running the Internet Information Server or another service that normally allows anonymous access to your server, make sure that you use the accounts recommended for the service instead of Guest.

Built-In Groups

Windows NT includes 11 distinct groups as part of its standard installation on machines in a domain; NT machines that are being used in workgroups don't have some of these groups. These groups can be categorized according to use: Some are for system management, while others are for controlling user access. First let's review the system management groups.

Administrators

The *Administrators* group contains users who have full control over the server's hardware, software, accounts, and groups. Administrators are the only users who can add, remove, or change the rights assigned to local and global groups. In addition, they can create and edit domain user and group accounts. Administrators members can manipulate user files, but they're still restricted to the NTFS permissions set by the files' owners. However, administrators can bypass NTFS permissions altogether by taking ownership of the files, thus giving them full access—but this leaves a security audit trail in the system's auditing log.

This group is local, so when you add members to it you're allowing them only to administer the machine that owns the group. This is a useful way to give users control over their desktop machines without granting them too much power A similar group spans the entire domain; we'll cover it next.

Domain Admins

The *Domain Admins* group is automatically added to the local Administrators group on every NTS and NTW machine in a domain. By adding your domain administrator's accounts to the Domain Admins group, they gain administrator rights on all NTS and NTW machines in the domain. If you want to limit an account to managing a single machine, put the account directly in that machine's Administrators group; if you want the account to manage all machines in the domain, put it in Domain Admins instead.

The Operator Groups

Because many system management functions require specific rights that fall short of the Administrator's broad range of powers, NTS includes four Operator groups that offer

Know This

subsets of Administrator rights. You can better secure your servers by putting users with management responsibilities into specific Operator groups instead of just putting them all into the Domain Admins or Administrators groups:

♦ The *Account Operators* group grants the right to create and modify local groups, global groups, and user accounts. However, members of Account Operators can't modify membership of the other Operators groups or the Administrators and Domain Admins groups, and they can't alter user accounts of members of any of those groups.

Basically, Account Operators can create new accounts for domain users and change their passwords and privileges, but they can't add or remove rights for groups, and they can't tamper with any of the *real* administrator's accounts to get better access rights. The Account Operators group is a local group.

♦ *Backup Operators* have the access needed to do backups of the machines in a domain; they can shut down and restart servers and workstations in a domain, and they can back up and restore machines without requiring read access to files and partitions on the server. The Backup Operators group is a local group.

♦ *Print Operators* can control the use of printers within your domain by sharing, unsharing, and modifying printer queues and entries. The Print Operators group is a local group, but you may need to add its members to a separate global group if you want to put printers on other workstations in your domain.

♦ *Server Operators* have adequate rights to manage server hardware—they can start and stop services, make backups, run the Disk Administrator, and shut down and restart the server when necessary. This group is a local group.

♦ The *Replicator* local group contains accounts that have access to the Directory Replicator service. If you're using Directory Replicator, put the system account you're using for replication into this group on each exporter or importer. (For complete details on using the Directory Replicator service, see the section "Controlling Directory Replication" in Chapter 9, "Managing NT Servers.")

Know This

The User Groups

NTS also includes four groups dedicated solely to grouping and granting permissions to user accounts. These groups allow you to quickly grant consistent permissions and rights to a set of users just by adding them to the appropriate group:

♦ *Guests* is a group for guest accounts. Because this group is a local group, it normally contains only the Domain Guests global group. Most Windows NT installations don't make any significant use of the guest account; one exception might be when you want to give users of a trusted domain very limited access to resources in another domain.

♦ The *Domain Guests* global group contains those accounts that you want to have guest access within your domain. Normally it only contains the Guest account (which is disabled by default on NTS machines). Unless you want to enable guest access, you can leave this group as is and not add any other accounts.

♦ The *Domain Users* global group contains users from your domain. While not every user in your domain must be in this group, users who aren't in the group won't have access to other domain computers or computers in trusting domains. By default, all accounts are automatically added to this group when they're created.

♦ The *Users* local group holds users who have user access to an individual machine. Members of the Users groups can log onto, shut down, and lock workstations, and they can create and modify new local groups on workstations as well. However, they don't have privileges to access servers.

♦ By default, each machine in a domain has the Domain Users group in its Users group, so that any domain user can log onto any machine. You can also add individual accounts to this group when you want users to be tied to a single machine.

♦ Finally, the *Everyone* group is worthy of a mention. It's not really a group—you can't add or remove its members, and it doesn't appear as a group in dialog boxes for setting access controls or permissions. However, it serves as a placeholder that represents *all* users in a domain. When you give access to a resource to Everyone, that is literally what you're doing: granting identical access to every user in the domain. Older versions of Windows NT gave "Full Control" access to Everyone by default. This permissive setting allowed all users to see and modify files in a share. Fortunately, NTS 4.0 no longer does so, thus removing a potential security nightmare.

> **NOTE:** The Power Users group is specific to NTW and doesn't exist under NTS. Power Users' rights are a mix of the Operator groups with a few Administrator privileges thrown in, but NTS segregates these permissions to make secure administration easier.

Special Groups

A number of other built-in groups may be of use or interest to administrators. Their membership is dynamic; as users connect and disconnect on the system, the contents of each group changes. These groups are created as part of the NTS installation, and you can't rename or remove them. You can use them when you assign share permissions. These are the groups:

♦ The *Interactive* group contains all users who are interactively using an object from the console. Ordinarily, there will be one account in this group at any time—the logged-on console user. The group will be empty when no one is logged onto the console.

♦ The *Network* group contains all users who are using an object (such as a file or printer) over the network. This group can contain zero or more accounts, depending on how many users are accessing the object.

♦ The *System* group doesn't contain any user accounts. Instead, it allows the operating system to control access to its own resources by restricting that access to members of the System group.

Managing Users and Groups

In NTS, you manage user accounts with the User Manager for Domains, which allows you to create, edit, remove, and manipulate user and group accounts on your Windows NT network. The differences between the vanilla User Manager (installed on NTW machines) and User Manager for Domains (installed as part of NTS) are small; in brief, User Manager for Domains adds domain capacity to the base User Manager application so that you can do the following:

- ◆ Browse, create, edit, and remove user accounts in any domain where you have administrative rights, not just on the local machine
- ◆ Browse, create, edit, and remove group accounts for both local and global groups
- ◆ Create local and global groups and grant or deny them various rights
- ◆ View and set domain trust relationships for domains you can administer

The coverage in this chapter focuses on the user and group functions of User Manager for Domains; controlling domain trust relationships is covered in Chapter 15, "Planning and Using Domains and Workgroups."

Using User Manager for Domains

The main User Manager for Domains window is shown in Figure 6-1. The top pane of the window shows all the users accounts on the local machine and the domain, while the bottom pane shows all the local and domain groups. You can control the sort order used to display user accounts in the top pane with the View menu's Sort by Full Name and Sort by Username commands.

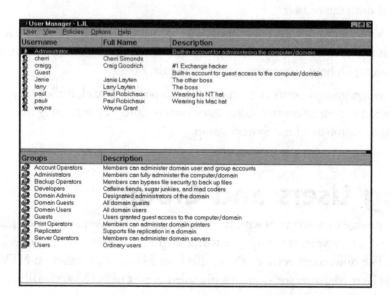

FIGURE 6-1

The User Manager for Domains main window lists users in the top pane of the window and local and global groups in the

You can browse other domains on your network with the User | Select Domain command; when you select a domain, the program displays the groups and users in that domain, although you can't modify them unless you have administrative rights in that domain.

Because NTS supports a centralized user account database on the domain controller, multiple users can edit user and group accounts at once. The User Manager for Domains will periodically update the display to reflect changes made by other network users; you can manually update it at any time with the View | Refresh command.

Sometimes you may need to administer your user or group accounts across a low-speed connection. You can tell User Manager for Domains not to update your display by selecting the Options | Low Speed Connection command; when you do, the user and groups panes will display a message telling you that updates have been suspended. You can still select users and commands from the User menu, but the normal summary panes won't reflect your changes. As soon as you disable Options | Low Speed Connection, the display will resume its periodic updates.

There are two other useful commands in the Options menu: Confirmation, which toggles whether User Manager for Domains will ask you to confirm actions such as deleting users, and Save Settings on Exit, which tells User Manager for Domains to save your option and window settings when you exit the program.

Adding Accounts

You add new user accounts by completing the New User dialog box (see Figure 6-2), which appears when you use the User | New User command. At minimum, you must specify a user name. Although all the other fields are optional, it's a very good idea to set an initial password for the account. You should also fill out the Full Name and Description fields; this makes it easier to identify accounts in the system's network browsers, as well as in the User Manager for Domains itself.

When you create an account, you must also set its password policy. Three of the four check boxes below the user information section control password selection and expiration:

- ♦ When the User Must Change Password At Next Logon checkbox is checked, the user will be forced to specify a new password when she next logs in. This option ensures that users won't leave their accounts with the default password, which is often an easy-to-guess word or phrase.

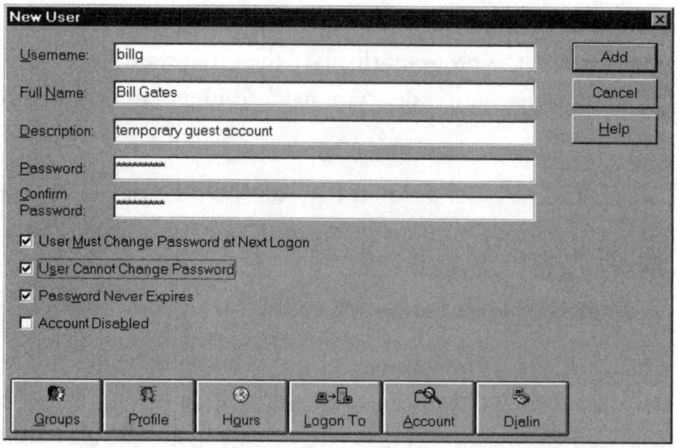

FIGURE 6-2

In the New User dialog box, you assign permissions and user identification to a new account.

♦ Conversely, the User Cannot Change Password check box prevents the user from changing the account password. Because regular password changes are an important part of security maintenance, you should use this box sparingly. Some services (such as the Print Services for Macintosh service discussed in Chapter 23, "Interoperating with Macintosh clients") must run in their own user account; these dedicated accounts should have the "cannot change" option turned on to prevent accidental or malicious password changes from denying access to the service. The "must change" and "cannot change" options are mutually exclusive.

♦ The Password Never Expires check box overrides the Windows NT password aging mechanism so that the minimum and maximum password ages you set in the Account Policy dialog box don't apply. Use this option for system accounts, for services like the Directory Replicator and the Macintosh file and print service tools, but make sure that ordinary user accounts have expiring passwords to prevent an old password from being used to launch a security exploit.

♦ The fourth checkbox, Account Disabled, renders the account unusable without deleting it; when disabled, accounts can't log on or be used to authorize access to resources. Because deleting an account is irreversible, you should use this option instead of deleting accounts unless you're certain that you won't need to restore permissions set using the original account.

The buttons at the bottom of the dialog box represent categories of permissions and rights for the new account; you can use them to configure the account the way you want before adding it to the account database. For a detailed description of how to set these properties, see the following sections, each of which covers a group of properties.

Once you've established account settings the way you want them, click Add to actually add the account to the user database. If you have more accounts to add, you can do so—just click Add after each one.

Disabling Accounts

It's often necessary to remove an account's ability to access resources on your network. In some network operating systems, you can just delete the account and reinstate it later if it's needed. Because Windows NT accounts each contain a unique security ID, this strategy won't work. If you have a user account named FRANK and you delete that account, any resources that had granted access to that account will remove that access—but if you later want to reactivate the account, you'll need to reassign permissions to every resource for which the account previously had access.

The preferred solution is to disable the account. Disabled accounts can't log on interactively or over the network, so they can't be used to gain access to shares or computers. However, when disabled, an account keeps its SID, so you can easily re-enable it later without needing to reset permissions. You can disable an account simply by selecting the Account Disabled check box in the User Properties dialog box (refer to Figure 6-2). After the account is disabled, you can re-enable the account at any time by deselecting the Account Disabled option.

Deleting Accounts

Even though you can disable accounts, there may be cases where you want to delete an account and remove its access controls. To delete user accounts, select the accounts you want to remove and use the User | Delete command on the User Manager menu. User Manager will warn you that, once you delete an account, even creating a new account with the same name won't restore access to objects that have granted permission to the account you're deleting—even though the names are the same, the old and new accounts will have different SIDs. Once you confirm that you understand, you may (if Options |

Confirmation is on) be asked to confirm the deletion; once you confirm it, the account will be deleted *permanently*.

Setting User Account Properties

Once you create an account, you can change its properties at any time by using the User Properties dialog box, which appears when you select a user account and use the User | Properties command. This dialog box is nearly identical in appearance to the New User dialog box (refer to Figure 6-2); the primary difference is that the User Properties dialog box won't allow you to edit the user name. Instead, you can rename an account with the User | Rename command.

To modify an account's password, full name, or description, use the corresponding fields of the dialog box. The other account property settings are available via the six buttons at the bottom of the dialog box. The Groups button displays a dialog box with which you control which groups the account is in; the Profile, Hours, Logon To, Account, and Dialin buttons are described in separate sections later in this chapter.

Creating and Deleting Groups

Groups in the current domain are shown in the bottom pane of the User Manager for Domains window; you can switch to another domain with the User | Select Domain command. The basic process for creating local and global groups is similar, but there are a few significant differences, because the type of entities that can be in each group type are different.

The User | New Global Group command brings up the New Global Group dialog box, as shown in Figure 6-3. Enter the group's name and a short description in the provided fields. The group name can be up to 20 characters long, and it can't be the same as any user or group name in the domain *or* on the local machine. Once you create a group, you can't change the name, so plan ahead. Next, use the Add and Remove buttons to set the group's membership by moving account users between the Members and Not Members lists. Note that you can add only user accounts, not groups, to the global group.

Creating a new local group is quite similar; in this case, you use the User | New Local Group command, which brings up the New Local Group dialog box shown in Figure 6-4. You name the group and give it a description the same way as you do for global groups. You use the Add and Remove buttons to change the group's members in much the same way, except that the Add button brings up a separate dialog box. The Show Full Names button looks up the full name of each user and group in the Member field and display the full name instead of just the domain and account name. When you use the Add button, you get the standard Add Users and Groups dialog box, which you can use to add any users *or groups* already defined within the domain. Local groups can contain both users and global groups.

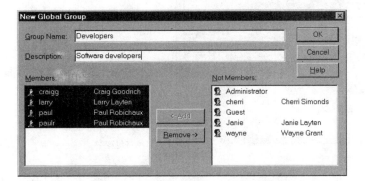

FIGURE 6-3

Create new groups with the Add Global Group dialog box by specifying which users should be added.

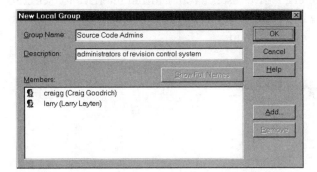

FIGURE 6-4

Use the New Local Group dialog box to create new local groups.

Controlling Group Membership and Properties

User Manager enables you to set properties for local and global groups on your domain and servers. The most important of these properties is membership; you control which accounts are in each local or global group on your network. You can put accounts into a group when you create it as previously described, or you can modify the groups' properties at any time. To change a group's properties, select it and use the User | Properties command.

Local and global groups each have their own properties. The Local Group Properties dialog box is shown in Figure 6-5. In this dialog box, you can edit the group's description and membership. The <u>A</u>dd button summons the standard Windows NT Add Users and Groups dialog box (shown in Figure 6-6), and the <u>R</u>emove button lets you remove accounts currently in the group.

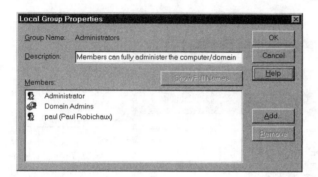

FIGURE 6-5

The Local Group Properties dialog box lets you control who is in the group.

The Add Users and Groups dialog box is like the standard Open, Save, and Print dialog boxes that Windows NT offers; it gives users a standardized interface for selecting users and groups. The dialog box is used in User Manager for Domains to select members when creating a new local or global group.

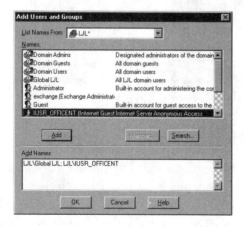

FIGURE 6-6

The Add Users and Groups dialog box lets you control which users and/or groups make up the new group.

The List Names From list lets you select the domain or workgroup whose members you want to view. The user and group names are listed in the Names pane; each entry has an icon to indicate whether it's a user account, a local group, or a global group. You can see the members of a group by selecting the group and clicking the Members button; you can also search the current domain for an account with the Search button.

There are two ways to add accounts to the Add Names field: Select one or more names and use the Add button, or type the names into the Add Names field. In either case, when you click OK the accounts you've selected will be added to the access control list for whatever operation you were performing.

By contrast to the Local Group Properties dialog box, the Global Group Properties dialog box shown in Figure 6-7 allows you to add only users who already have domain accounts. Move users between the Members and Not Members fields to establish who is in the group and who isn't.

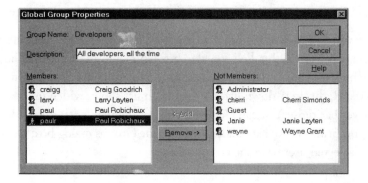

FIGURE 6-7

The Global Group Properties dialog box lets you add and remove existing domain accounts for a global group.

Setting User and Group Account Rights

Rights enable you to give users and groups persistent permissions that apply to all objects on a system, not just to individual files, shares, printers, and so on. You control which users have which rights in two ways:

◆ When you assign users to groups, they gain all the rights given to that group, so you can control account rights by setting the group's rights.

◆ You can also directly grant or deny specific rights directly to user accounts.

Each local and global group in the system can have a set of rights associated with it. For example, the Account Operators group has a certain set of default rights. If you want a user account to have those same rights, you can add the account to the group and avoid making any changes to the user account's rights. This strategy keeps you from letting users have rights they no longer need; all you have to do to remove special rights on an account is remove it from the group that has those rights. Although there are a few exceptions (noted later), for the most part you can assign rights to groups as you please; you can then move users into groups that grant them the rights they need.

The alternative approach is to grant rights directly to users. This approach offers very fine-grained control, because you can give users exactly the rights you want them to have. There are significant disadvantages to this method, though. The first is that you must assign rights to every user you want to have those rights. Although this process may not be bad for small workgroups, it gets vastly more difficult as your user base gets larger. Another problem is that you must be proactive about taking away rights from accounts that no longer need them. Because the rights are attached directly to the account, there's no way to automatically deny a previously granted right on several accounts at once.

Whichever strategy you choose will require that you use the Policies | User Rights command and the associated User Rights Policy dialog box (shown in Figure 6-8). The dialog box shows you in which domain you're granting rights; when you choose the right you're interested in with the Right drop-down list, the Grant To list shows which users and groups currently have that right. You can change the list of grantees with the Add and Remove buttons. Add brings up the standard Add User or Groups dialog box; Remove quietly removes the selected user or group from the list.

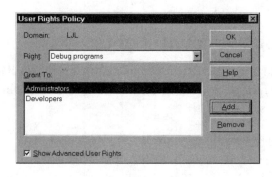

FIGURE 6-8

Use the User Rights Policy dialog box to grant or deny rights for users or groups.

NTS offers no fewer than 27 separate rights that groups and users can have. The rights are divided into two groups: *standard rights*, which always appear in the User Rights Policy dialog box, and *advanced rights*, whose display is controlled by the Show Advanced User Rights check box in the User Rights Policy dialog box. The standard rights are just that; they control common actions that several groups or users may need to perform on a particular machine. By comparison, the advanced user rights are quite a bit more esoteric; most of them are available only to Administrators. Some rights are normally not assigned to any group, but they're listed because the executive uses them internally.

CAUTION: There is rarely any reason to change any of the advanced rights settings. You may cause significant security vulnerabilities by altering them.

Local Profiles are home

Managing User Profiles and Environments

user.
g

Profiles are collections of settings that apply to user accounts. For example, a user's profile tells the system which items are in the program groups of the Start menu, which icons are shown on the desktop, which Windows Messaging profile to use, and so on. These settings are stored in the system Registry, and each user has at least one profile of her own—for users with no profile, the system copies the default profile to make a user-specific profile. *Customize Desktop*

Profiles are a foreign concept to many Windows and DOS users, who are accustomed to having a machine dedicated to each user. In that kind of environment, there's no reason to use profiles, because each user can customize her machine the way she wants. Readers who have experience using UNIX or NetWare, on the other hand, will appreciate why profiles are useful, even on PCs—profiles let you divorce the user's environment from the individual machine and make it into a floating environment that the user can use, no matter what machine she logs into.

In addition to creating profiles that make the user's desktop environment available on multiple machines, Windows NT enables you to assign *mandatory* user profiles to some or all users. These profiles, along with the other policy settings that you control with the System Policy Editor (see the later section on System Policy Editor), provide a valuable source of control over user environments. A user who has a mandatory profile assigned to her is forced by the system to use the settings in that profile.

In addition to profiles, the user's environment setting may specify a *home directory*—a central storage space for the user's files and data. Each user may have an individual home directory, or several users can share a single directory.

You manage user profile and environment settings with the User Environment Profile dialog box (see Figure 6-9). To open this dialog box, use the Profile button in the User Properties dialog box.

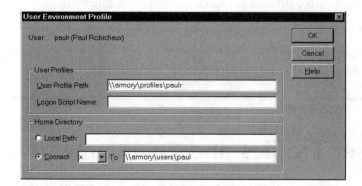

FIGURE 6-9

Set the user's default directory, logon script, and environment with the User Environment Profile dialog box.

The most common use of profiles and home directories is to put all the user profiles and data files onto centralized servers. When you set each account's profile path and home directory to point to these servers, users gain consistent environments and access to their files, no matter which workstation they physically log onto. You gain the ability to quickly back up all users' data and to minimize the number of different places you must go to make environment changes when they're needed.

> **NOTE:** Of course, if you centralize profiles and file storage, you must be very careful to ensure adequate redundancy and backup for the servers to avoid knocking all your users offline in the event of a server failure.

Using User Profiles

User profiles in Windows NT include all the user's settings: screen color schemes, persistent connections for shared disks and printers, and so on. In Windows NT 4, these profiles can be stored on a central server so that users keep their familiar desktop appearance and work environment no matter where they log on. When the user makes changes, those changes are saved to the central server so they're available next time the user logs in. Profiles that follow users around like this are called *roaming profiles*. There's also a twist: You can make roaming profiles *mandatory*, so that users can change them but can't save the changes when they log off.

To store roaming profiles on a central server, you have to create a share on the server and grant Full Control for Everyone permission on the share (since roaming users need to be able to update their profiles over the network.) Once you've done so, you should specify the path to that directory, plus the user's profile file name, in the U̲ser Profile Path field. Normally, this path should be a UNC path; for example, if `\\butler\profiles` is the directory where profiles are stored, `\\butler\profiles\paulr` would be the profile path for a user named `paulr`. The profile itself must be stored as a file named `NTUser.dat` for a roaming profile or `NTUser.man` for a mandatory profile. The full profile for user `paulr` would thus be `\\butler\profiles\paulr\NTUser.man`.

> **TIP:** To make a user's profile mandatory, just rename it to `NTUser.man`; most often you'll copy a standard canned profile into each user's directory, and then rename it.

> **NOTE:** Windows NT 3.51 stores profiles in a single file, and Windows NT 4.0 stores them in a directory. If you want users on your network to keep their profiles when logging into 3.51 and 4.0 machines, specify a *profile file* (that is, a file whose name ends with `.man` or `.dat`.) If you're supporting profiles only for Windows NT 4.0 users, specify the profile directory without a filename or extension.

When the user logs in, Windows NT fetches the user's profile from the specified server and compares it to the local copy of that user's profile, if one exists. Local profiles might exist if the user is on a portable that's not always connected to the network, or if that user has customized his environment while disconnected from the network. If the profiles are different, the Windows NT logon process presents the user with a dialog box listing the available profiles; the user gets to choose which one to use. When the user logs out, changes made to roaming profiles are stored on the central server; changes made to mandatory profiles are ignored.

Using Logon Scripts

In addition to profiles, you can have your accounts run an executable logon script each time they log on. This script can be a batch file or executable, and it can do things like map drives or run programs to prepare the operating environment. A user's profile establishes his or her desktop appearance and settings immediately; it's the first thing that takes place during a logon. After the profile is loaded, the logon script executes. Logon scripts can do literally anything that an executable program can do (subject, of course, to NT security restrictions).

For a programmer, a logon script might synchronize the local machine's source code files with a central server. For an accounts payable clerk, it might display a summary of the previous 10 transactions posted. Users can create their own logon scripts, but it's much more common for network administrators to create these scripts. You can create simple scripts using a text editor and the NT batch language; you can also write executables using whatever programming tools you prefer.

To set a logon script for a user account, type its name in the Logon Script Name field in the User Environment Profile dialog box. The Windows NT logon service combines the name you type and the logon script path to find the script; the logon script name you supply can include subdirectory names, too. The default logon script path is %SYSTEM-ROOT%\SYSTEM32\REPL\IMPORT\SCRIPTS, but you can change it by using the Logon Script Path field in the Directory Replicator properties dialog box, as detailed in the section "Controlling Directory Replication" in Chapter 9.

> **TIP:** The NTS 4.0 NetWare Migration Tool can convert NetWare 3.x and 4.x logon scripts for use on Windows NT servers; see Chapter 22 for more details.

For logon scripts to be most useful, they must be available to all computers the user can log onto. The Directory Replicator service (covered in more detail in Chapter 9) provides this service as a built-in option. Normally, you'll put all the logon scripts for a domain's users on either the primary or backup domain controller. The server where you put the scripts will export them to other computers in the domain. When you specify a path in the Logon Script Path field of the Directory Replicator dialog box, the Windows NT logon manager will use that path, plus the script name for that user account, to find the script.

Here's what you need to do to replicate logon scripts effectively:

1. Put your domain users' scripts on a single NTS machine. You'll get the best performance if you put them on the primary domain controller, but you can use the backup domain controller or any server in the domain. We'll call this machine the *script server*.

2. Configure the script server as a replication exporter. Export the directory where you placed the scripts to all machines in any domain where your users can log on. Determining which machines to export to can be tricky; you may want to start with the default of exporting to all machines in the same domain.

3. Make each Windows NT server or workstation in the domain import the script server's export directory. Note that NTW machines must import scripts to this default directory:

   ```
   %SYSTEMROOT%\REPL\IMPORTS\SCRIPT
   ```

   NTS machines can use another directory, but it's best to keep the default so that you don't have to reset the <u>L</u>ogon Script Path in Server Manager for each machine in the domain.

Setting User Home Directories

It's often useful to centralize users' directories on file servers instead of leaving them scattered around on individual machines. Instead of requiring that you use a logon script to connect network shares to a particular drive letter, Windows NT gives you the ability to set the default user directory as part of the environment profile. The Home Directory section of the User Environment Profile dialog box lets you specify how to handle default directories.

> **NOTE:** If you have a NetWare gateway product installed, there may be additional options in the Home Directory section—see Chapter 22 for complete details.

If you select the Local <u>P</u>ath option, you have to supply a local directory with the name you specify on each machine. This local path must exist on *every* machine when the user logs in. For example, if a user's local path is set to d:\users\paul, Windows NT expects to see that directory, already existing, every time that user logs into any domain computer.

A better alternative is to use the <u>C</u>onnect option, to specify that you want the user's home directory to be connected to a predefined drive letter. For example, you can have all users' home directories mapped from the server to drive Z: by specifying **Z** as the drive to connect to and giving the UNC path to the user directory.

> **TIP:** One neat feature is that User Manager for Domains will expand %USERNAME% to the user's actual name if you use it in this dialog box. This is very useful when setting home directories for multiple users at one time. You can select a group of users, bring up the User Environment Profile dialog box, and specify a path like \\accounting\users\%USERNAME% rather than entering the user name separately for each account.

Setting Account Policies

You can apply a number of policy settings to individual user accounts or to all accounts in a domain; these policies control what users may and may not do with their accounts. Some policies apply to the account itself; others restrict what users using the accounts may do.

There are three primary types of policies. In general, there's not much overlap between the classes:

◆ *Individual account policies* apply to individual accounts and cover such things as restricting when users can log on.

◆ Policies that apply to all accounts in a domain, such as how long a password is valid before it must be changed, are called *account policies*.

◆ *System policies* apply to selected users, groups, or machines in a domain. Examples of system policies include whether users can change desktop settings, whether computers will allow remote registry updates, and what audit policies are in effect in a particular domain. You control system policies with the System Policy Editor, which is covered in Chapter 16.

Controls for Individual Accounts

You can apply three sets of restrictions to individual accounts: logon time restrictions, logon workstation restrictions, and remote access restrictions. Each class of restrictions imposes limits on what a user account can do, as described in the following sections. These settings apply only to the accounts on which you put them; if you want to apply them to a group of users, you can do so with the System Policy Editor (described shortly).

Logon Time Restrictions

It's often useful to restrict the hours during which a user account can log on. For example, some sites reserve time each week during non-business hours to allow for backups, server maintenance, or hardware upgrades, and it's best to prevent logons during those time periods. You can control what times users can log on *to the server* with the Logon Hours dialog box, which appears when you click the Hours button of the User Properties dialog box (see Figure 6-10).

You can select individual hours or blocks of time on the same day by clicking and dragging; if you click on the name of a day, all hours in that day will be selected, and if you click in an hour slot, that hour will be selected throughout the week. Finally, you can click the blank bar above Sunday to select all hours of the week. Once you've selected the hours for which you want to control access, click the Allow or Disallow buttons to permit or deny logons during that time.

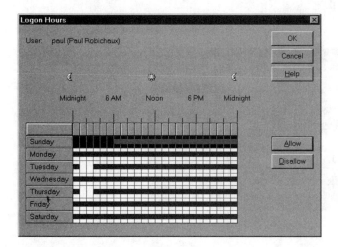

FIGURE 6-10

Use the Logon Hours dialog box to set the hours when an account may and may not log on.

> **TIP:** What happens to users who are still logged in when the clock hits the start of a disallowed period? You have two choices: You can either force them to log off immediately or allow them to stay logged on. These settings are controlled by the Account Policy dialog box, as described in the later section "Controls for Entire Domains."

Logon Workstation Restrictions

Under ordinary circumstances, any global account in a domain can log onto any computer in that domain. There are two ways to restrict where users can log on. The first is to create only local accounts on individual computers that users need to access. If you have a small number of users that you want to restrict, or a small number of machines that you want to be restricted, this solution may work. The more general solution, which takes advantage of Windows NT domain features, is to set specific restrictions on accounts with the User Manager for Domains.

You control which machines user accounts can access with the Logon Workstations dialog box, shown in Figure 6-11. This dialog is activated by the Logon To button in the User Properties dialog box. When the User May Log On To All Workstations button is selected, as it is by default, the account is usable from any domain computer. When the User May Log On To These Workstations button is selected, you can enter up to eight workstations from which the user account can be used. Logon requests on workstations that aren't listed will fail.

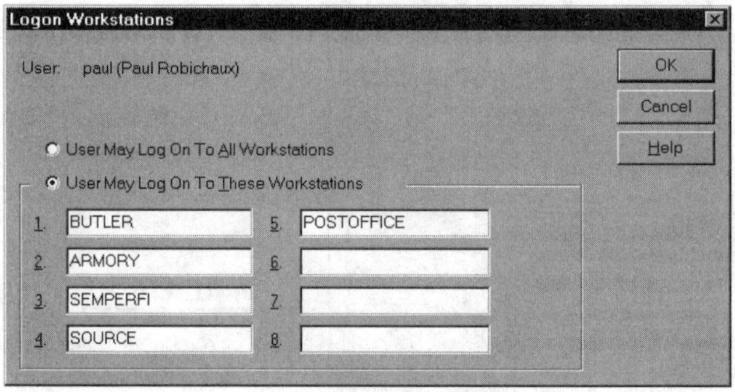

FIGURE 6-11

You can restrict which machines users can use to log on to their domain accounts with the Logon Workstations dialog box.

NOTE: If your NTS machine is running the NetWare compatibility package, you'll see additional options in the Logon Workstations dialog box. These options allow you to apply the same logon restrictions to NetWare workstations as you can to Windows networking clients. These options aren't shown here, but they're documented in the User Manager online help and in Chapter 22.

Remote Access Restrictions

Many sites now choose to allow remote users to gain network access via the Windows NT Dial-Up Networking feature. However, you may want to deny remote access to certain accounts, or to require a security callback to prevent unauthorized use. You can set these restrictions in two places: via the Dial-Up Networking service's Remote Access Admin application or the User Manager for Domains.

NOTE: For complete coverage of using Remote Access Admin to set permissions for dial-in access, see Chapter 25, "Providing Dial-Up Access."

The Dialin Information dialog box is shown in Figure 6-12; you access the dialog box by clicking the Dialin button in the User Properties dialog box. When the Grant Dialin Permission to User check box is not selected, the user can't log on over a dial-up connection; when the option is checked, the user will have dial-up access.

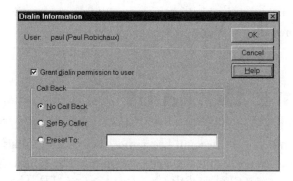

FIGURE 6-12

The Dialin Information dialog box gives you control over user access to dial-up networking.

The Call Back section of the dialog box lets you require that incoming calls from this account set up a callback connection, where the Dial-Up Networking server will hang up on the user after logon and call back at the number specified. The default setting is No Call Back. If you use Set By Caller, the user has to tell the dial-up server what number to use for the callback; if you use Preset To, the server will always call the user back at the preset number.

> **CAUTION:** Microsoft warns that using Preset To will prevent users with multilink capability from establishing connections using more than one phone line or ISDN channel at a time. Furthermore, using Set By Caller removes most of the security benefit of using callbacks; its use is recommended only if you need it for some reason, such as to reduce telecommunications charges for long-distance users.

Setting an Account's Expiration Date

It's often useful to set a predetermined expiration date on an account that you know will be needed only for a certain period. For example, accounts for temporary employees and interns shouldn't remain available after the user has moved on. You can set the expiration date to any arbitrary date with the Account Expires section of the Account Information dialog box. To see this dialog box, use the Account button in the User Properties dialog box. Ordinarily, accounts never expire; if you choose the End Of radio button and enter a date, the account will be disabled at the end of that day (actually, a few seconds before midnight).

After an account has expired, it becomes disabled just as it would if you manually disabled it as described in the preceding section.

Controls for Entire Domains

Microsoft calls controls that apply to accounts—instead of users—*account policies*. They don't restrict what rights or permissions the account has; rather, they control things such as how old the account's password can be before a change is required. The Policies | Account command displays the Account Policy dialog box (see Figure 6-13). The settings you choose in this dialog box apply to *all* accounts in the domain, but you must manually set account policies for each domain you want to control. When you change these poli-cies, they apply at the next opportunity for each account; for example, if you change the minimum password length to 8, users with 7-character passwords won't be affected until they next change their passwords.

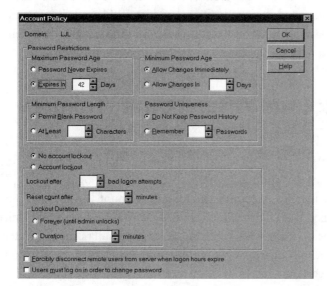

FIGURE 6-13

The Account Policy dialog box lets you set password and lockout behavior for accounts in the domain.

The settings in this dialog box give you a great deal of flexibility for setting account security policies to best meet your needs while maintaining good security. Although the dialog box is intimidating at first sight, the options are grouped logically, as described in the following sections.

Password Restrictions

The settings in the Password Restrictions section of the Account Policy dialog box govern what sort of restrictions Windows NT enforces on user passwords:

♦ The Maximum and Minimum Password Age sections control how old a password can get before Windows NT forces a change, as well as how long the password must be in effect before it can be changed. The default (rather permissive) settings are to expire passwords in 42 days, and to allow changes at any time.

- ◆ The Minimum Password Length options let you impose a lower limit on password length. Good security practice suggests at least an eight-character minimum length and an expiration period of 30 days or less.

- ◆ The Password Uniqueness options let you tell the Windows NT logon sub-system to keep a record of what passwords users have chosen in the past, so that it can reject recycled passwords. Password history files can keep users from using two passwords, say ch3vy and f0rd, and just changing between them at each password expiration, so you should turn on this option.

Locking Out Accounts After Logon Failures

You can control the lockout policy that applies to accounts with an excessive number of logon failures. A logon fails when the password specified for the username is incorrect; each time the wrong password is specified for an account during a logon attempt, NTS tracks it as a failed logon. The No Account Lockout and Account Lockout radio buttons in the Account Policy dialog box control whether this feature is enabled at all. Unless you change it, NTS doesn't lock out accounts when logon attempts fail (although it does log all failed logon attempts in the Security section of the system's Event Log.) If you want to freeze accounts after a certain number of failed attempts, make sure that the Account Lockout option is selected, and then put the number you want into the Lockout After ... Bad Logon Attempts field.

You can also require a "cooling-off" period with the Reset Count After ... Minutes field; this option lets you specify, for example, that attempts that occur more than five minutes apart don't count together toward the number of failures allowed before a lockout.

The Lockout Duration section of the dialog box lets you specify whether locked-out accounts stay disabled until manually enabled, or until a certain amount of time has passed.

Miscellaneous Settings

Remember the earlier discussion about setting logon times? In the Account Policy dialog box, the option called Forcibly Disconnect Remote Users from Server When Logon Hours Expire lets you tell NTS whether it should kick off users who are already logged in when the clock hits their no-logon time, or whether they should be allowed to stay connected.

The option called Users Must Log On in Order to Change Password, when set, forces a user to complete a successful logon before he can change his password. If the password expires, the user won't be able to log on to change it—that means that an administrator or Account Operator has to change the password. Deselecting this option lets a user log on even when his password has expired, so that he can change the password.

Where to Go Next

This chapter explored how Windows NT distinguishes between different classes of user and group accounts, how to control account behavior by setting user account and group properties, and how to restrict access by setting the appropriate properties.

The next chapter details how to share printers on a network, including how to control access to those printers based on user and group permissions. Later chapters explain how to build an effective set of domains and an access policy that secures your data.

Here are some other resources that you may find useful at this point:

- For coverage of controlling how users get access to shared resources, see Chapter 9, "Managing NT Servers." Printer access control is covered in Chapter 7, "Printer Management."

- Chapter 16, "Managing Users and Groups in Domains," discusses several strategies for organizing your users into groups in one or more domains.

- Chapter 12, "Windows NT Security Fundamentals," explains how to set up workable but safe permissions to allow access to authorized users, while protecting your network and data from unauthorized use.

Chapter | 7

Printer Management

In This Chapter:

- Windows NT Server 4.0 Printing
- Understanding the Printing Process
- Printer Types
- Connecting to Printers
- General and Device Settings
- Configuring Printers
- Printer Security
- Special Printing Considerations
- Troubleshooting the Printing Process

How do I...

Windows NT Server 4.0 (NTS) brings all the printing pluses to the table that were found in previous versions of NT. It's easily configurable, which enables you to customize NTS 4.0 to suit a particular network configuration. It's versatile, providing built-in network interface support. Also, a favorite NT 3.51 printing feature is alive and well in NTS 4.0—one server with many installed printer drivers can be used by many workstations with no installed printer drivers.

This chapter discusses the following topics:

- Printer hardware and network interfaces
- Creating, connecting to, and sharing printers
- Printer configuration, management, and security
- Printer troubleshooting

> **NOTE:** Throughout this chapter, the term *printer* frequently refers both to the physical output device and to the logical printer used by the Windows NT Server 4.0 printing management tools. Where it isn't readily apparent from context which meaning is being used, *printer name* refers to a logical printer, and *physical printer* refers to a physical output device.

Windows NT Server 4.0 Printing

The most striking difference between the Windows NT Server 4.0 printing system and earlier versions of NT is the new interface in NTS 4.0. It's easier than ever to manage printing resources. Everything you need is at your disposal in one place—the Printers window, accessed either through the Control Panel or the My Computer window.

There's also one important behind-the-scenes change. Like many other Windows NT components, the NTS 4.0 printing system has undergone a complete re-architecture from earlier versions of NT. The NTS 4.0 printing system runs in operating system kernel space, rather than user space. Consequently, the printing system runs a little faster.

Understanding the Printing Process

When you print a job, the job flows from the client to the server to the printer. Unless a malfunction occurs somewhere along the way, this process appears quite simple, and for many users, it is. Frequently, users aren't interested in *how* their documents print—they simply want them to print. However, much happens behind the scenes that can interest a Windows NTS 4.0 administrator.

Print Flow

When a job is printed, it isn't sent directly from the submitting machine to the printer. Rather, it's stored in the spooler on the print server. Think of the spooler as a waiting room for print jobs. Jobs wait in the spooler until a printer becomes available.

Windows NT Server 4.0 print jobs are often (inaccurately) said to wait in a *queue*. This term is a bit misleading. A queue implies linearity; jobs wait in single file, and are processed in the order in which the server received them. But an NTS 4.0 print server can spool and release many print jobs simultaneously. Moreover, it can manage jobs intelligently, considering security, efficiency, and so on.

Figure 7-1 shows the events that occur when you submit a print job to a printer name.

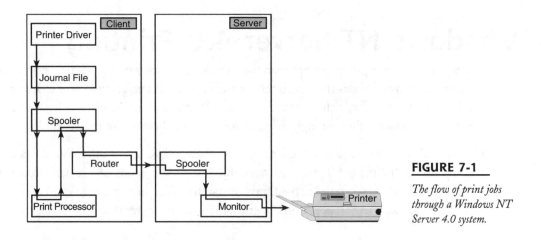

FIGURE 7-1

The flow of print jobs through a Windows NT Server 4.0 system.

First the client machine loads the appropriate printer driver. Then the *Device Driver Interface* (*DDI*) generates a journal file. This journal file contains hooks to the just-loaded printer driver. Next, the spooler (WINSPOOL.DRV) moves the journal file to the print processor (WINPRINT.DLL). The processor generates raw data consistent with the selected physical printer, completes the rendering begun by the spooler, and returns the data to the spooler. The spooler moves the data to the router, and the data leaves the client machine.

When the data arrives at the server machine, it enters the server's spooler. The server's spooler sends the data to the monitor (HPMON.DLL or LOCALMON.DLL). The monitor directs the data to a port, and a spool file is written. The directory in which the spool file is written is determined by the DefaultSpoolDirectory Registry key value, which is located in the following key:

HKEY_LOCAL_MACHINE\SYSTEM\CurrentControlSet\Control\Print\Printers

When the data leaves the monitor, it goes to the printer, and the job prints.

In most cases, it's not necessary to change the spool directory. Generally, you should change it only if you have an administrative reason to do so (if you want to use another hard drive as a dedicated print spooler drive, for example).

Printing and the Registry

Because you can do so much with the Printers window, it's generally not necessary to use the Registry to manage Windows NTS 4.0 printing. However, some characteristics, such as the spool file directory mentioned above, are controlled only from the Registry.

All Registry entries relevant to printing are located in the following key:

```
HKEY_LOCAL_MACHINE\SYSTEM\CurrentControlSet\Control\Print\Printers
```

Here are some settings that you may want to examine:

♦ BeepEnabled. The BeepEnabled setting can be set to 0 (off, the default setting) or 1 (on). When a remote job encounters an error on a print server and BeepEnabled is on, a beep occurs each time the job is retried (every 10 seconds).

♦ DisableServerThread. The DisableServerThread setting can be set to either 0 (false, the default setting) or 1 (true). When set to 1, the browse thread on the current machine is disabled. The thread is used to notify other print servers that the printer exists.

♦ FastPrintSlowDownThreshold and FastPrintThrottleTimeout. The default setting for FastPrintThrottleTimeout is 2,000 milliseconds (two seconds). When the JobPrintsWhilstSpooling setting is enabled, some printers pause if they don't receive data for a timeout period. To counteract this problem, the spooler throttles back data sent to the printer when FastPrintSlowDownThreshold is reached. Then FastPrintThrottleTimeout causes 1 byte per defined period to go to the printer until FastPrintSlowDownThreshold is exceeded.

♦ FastPrintWaitTimeout. The default setting for FastPrintWaitTimeout is 24,000 milliseconds (24 seconds). When JobsPrintsWhilstSpooling is enabled, the port thread synchronizes with the spooling application. The FastPrintWaitTimeout setting determines how long the port thread waits before it aborts the current job and moves to the next print job.

◆ NetPopup. The default setting for NetPopup is 1 (enabled). When set to 1, a pop-up message appears on the server for remote print jobs. To disable the pop-up message, set NetPopup to 0.

◆ NetPrinterDecayPeriod. The default for the NetPrinterDecayPeriod setting is 3,600,000 milliseconds (one hour). This setting specifies how long to cache a network printer. The cache presents the list of printers when the browse dialog box is used.

◆ PortThreadPriority. The default setting for PortThreadPriority is THREAD_PRIORITY_NORMAL. This setting enables you to set port thread priority. Port threads are the threads that output to printers.

◆ PriorityClass. The default setting for PriorityClass is 0. This setting determines the spooler priority class. If this value is empty or left at 0, the default is enabled (9 for servers, 7 for workstations). If a new value is set, it becomes the server priority class.

◆ SchedulerThreadPriority. The default setting for SchedulerThreadPriority is THREAD_PRIORITY_NORMAL. This setting enables you to set the priority of the scheduler thread, which assigns jobs to ports. It can be set to THREAD_PRIORITY_NORMAL, THREAD_PRIORITY_BELOW_NORMAL, or THREAD_PRIORITY_ABOVE_NORMAL.

For more detailed information on putting the Registry to work for you, including adding Registry keys, editing Registry keys, and Registry editing cautions, see Chapter 11, "Working with the Windows NT System Registry."

Printer Types

A printer can either be physically attached to a print server or connected directly to the network, just as a workstation might be. This section presents information on ports and network interfaces.

Printer Interfaces

Printers are physically attached to print servers through parallel ports or serial ports. When data transmission is parallel, characters are sent simultaneously along separate data lines. With serial transmission, data is sent bit by bit.

This section gives a brief overview of parallel ports and serial ports, and covers information you need to use ports effectively with NT Server 4.0. For a more detailed description of parallel ports and serial ports, refer to your dedicated hardware documentation.

Parallel Ports

The parallel port was originally designed as an easy way to add a printer to a system. Over the years, hardware and software developers have generally agreed that this is a pretty nifty thing to do with the parallel port, as printers and parallel ports still work well together today with minimal fuss.

Your PC is probably equipped to support one parallel port—called *LPT1* (the *LPT* designation comes from a shortening of *Line PrinTer*). If you need more, adapters are generally available that will add LPT2 and LPT3. If you decide to do this, make sure that you can set the additional parallel ports to interrupts that aren't used by the server.

The cable that connects a printer to a parallel port should be as short as possible. To ensure reliable operation, the cable should be no longer than 25 feet. In some circumstances, you may find it possible to print with a cable longer than 25 feet, but to do so will almost certainly slow things down considerably. Worse, data integrity can't be guaranteed with an overly long cable, due to retransmission problems. If data takes too long to reach the printer, the server may decide that the printer is not responding. Unpredictable behavior on the server, at the printer, or both is usually the result.

When you configure a parallel port, either during or after printer installation, you can specify the Transmission Retry setting in the Configure LPT Port dialog box, as shown in Figure 7-2. To access the Configure LPT Port dialog box, click Configure Port on the Ports tab. The *transmission retry* is the time, in seconds, that the server waits for printer communication before deciding that the printer isn't responding. The default is 90 seconds.

FIGURE 7-2

Parallel port settings.

Serial Ports

Serial ports can be as difficult to install and configure as parallel ports are simple. As mentioned earlier, a big advantage of parallel ports is that they're dedicated printer connections. However, because serial ports were never designed as dedicated printer connections, different printers often use the serial port differently, so finding the right cable can be a challenge. Furthermore, many mice and other peripherals use a serial port, so hardware competition can quickly become fierce.

Your PC probably has two serial ports—COM1 and COM2 (the *COM* designation is a shortening of *com*munications). If you need additional serial ports, adapters are generally available to raise the number of serial ports to 8, 16, or even higher. However, because many serial card manufacturers don't yet support Windows NT, it's a good idea to check for Windows NT support before you buy. The Windows NT Hardware Compatibility List (HCL), a list of hardware that Microsoft has thoroughly tested and found to be compatible with Windows NT, is a good resource with which to start. You can find it at Microsoft's Web site (http://www.microsoft.com).

Serial communications take place bit by bit. To ensure reliable operation, the cable between a serial port and a printer should be no longer than 75 feet.

When you configure a serial port, either during or after printer installation, you can set baud rate, data bits, parity, stop bits, flow control, and some advanced settings (see Figure 7-3). To access the Settings for the COM1: dialog box, click the port on the Ports tab and click Settings.

FIGURE 7-3

Serial port settings.

The following list describes these settings.

♦ *Baud rate* is the measure of the rate, in bits per second, at which the serial port operates. 9600 is a standard setting for most printers. Check your printer documentation to see how high you can set this value. The higher this setting, the faster the print time.

♦ *Data bits* control the number of bits of data per transmitted character. You'll almost always set this to 8, as a setting of 8 enables support for most character sets and graphics.

♦ *Parity* is a simple error-detection method that rarely comes into play with printers. Generally, you can set this at None with no consequences.

♦ *Stop bits* flag the end of a serial character. It's usually most efficient to set this at 1, as this setting uses the least amount of the total capacity of the serial cable.

♦ *Flow control* determines the mechanism by which the server and the printer tell each other when data is ready to be transmitted or received. Generally, this mechanism is through dedicated wires in the serial port hardware itself. If this is the case, choose Hardware. Other options include XON/XOFF, in which software signals are used; and None, in which no flow control at all is used.

Click the <u>A</u>dvanced button in the Settings dialog box to configure parameters for additional serial ports, including interrupt numbers and port addresses.

Network-Attached Printers

Connecting printers directly to the network has its advantages. For the most part, server hardware capacity issues are eliminated. You don't need to worry about locating a printer a certain distance from its server or running out of physical ports. Also, when you connect a printer directly to the network, the need for dedicated cables and connectors is reduced, as a printer connects just like a workstation or server does. Moreover, largely because of the elimination of extra hardware, in most cases a network-attached printer performs faster than one attached to a parallel or serial port. Data can enter and leave the printer more quickly because it uses only high-efficiency network cabling for transmission.

Network-attached printers must use protocols supported by NTS 4.0. Two NTS 4.0-supported protocols in widespread use are DLC and TCP/IP, as described in the following sections.

DLC

Data Link Control (*DLC*) is an IBM-developed protocol adopted by Hewlett-Packard and other companies for printer communications. It's a transport protocol, which means that if an error occurs during transmission, it will detect the error and retransmit. Originally, it was used almost exclusively to communicate with Hewlett-Packard printers attached directly to a network via a JetDirect card. However, most manufacturers now equip their printers to emulate Hewlett-Packard hardware. If you take advantage of this emulation, you can use DLC to control those printers as well. Install DLC from the Networks utility in Control Panel.

When you install a DLC printer, that printer's server is the only machine on the network that needs to have the DLC protocol installed. Other machines on the network can connect to and use the printer without having the protocol installed locally.

DLC printers have network-unique card numbers. Generally, you must know a DLC printer's card number to establish a connection to it. Refer to the online documentation delivered with the DLC protocol for more information.

TCP/IP

Transmission Control Protocol/Internet Protocol (*TCP/IP*) began at the Department of Defense in the 1970s. Thanks to its open design and the explosive growth of the Internet, it's now everywhere. For more information on TCP/IP interoperability, see Chapter 24, "Interoperating with TCP/IP Clients."

In the printing realm, you can use TCP/IP to print to UNIX print queues, as well as TCP/IP printers on the network. NTS 4.0 can manage a TCP/IP printer only on the print server, with workstations connecting to a TCP/IP printer using the same protocol they use to connect to the server, as shown in Figure 7-4.

When the TCP/IP print services are installed, you create a TCP/IP printer by printing to the LPR (line printer remote) port. Make sure that you can ping a printer with its name before you define the printer. To ping the printer by name, you must register the address properly in DNS.

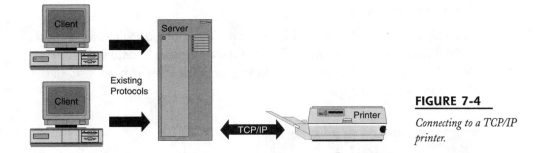

FIGURE 7-4

Connecting to a TCP/IP printer.

Mismatched IP addresses can be a problem with TCP/IP printing, just as they can be with other applications of TCP/IP. When you define the printer destination, make sure that you uniquely link the destination printer and the server name. Consult the TCP/IP printing online documentation for more information.

Network Ports

When you install or configure a network printer, you can use one of the following ports:

- ◆ **AppleTalk Printing Devices.** This port is available when the AppleTalk protocol is installed.
- ◆ **Digital Network Port.** This port is available when the TCP/IP or DECnet protocols are installed.
- ◆ **Hewlett-Packard Network Port.** This port is available when DLC is installed.
- ◆ **LPR Port.** This port is available when the Microsoft TCP/IP Printing service is installed.

Working with Local Printers

A *local printer* is a printer that's controlled by your machine. Local printers can include

- ◆ A printer physically connected to a port on your machine
- ◆ A printer connected directly to the network, but controlled from your machine
- ◆ A printer that outputs directly to a file
- ◆ An association of multiple printer names with different properties that each output to the same physical printer

Creating Local Printers

In earlier versions of Windows NT, to set up a local printer, you created a printer in Print Manager. In Windows NTS 4.0, the Add Printer Wizard walks you through this process. Double-click Add Printer in the Printers window to start the wizard (shown in Figure 7-5).

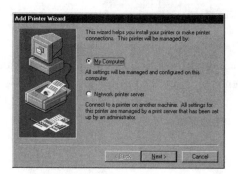

FIGURE 7-5

The Add Printer Wizard.

When the Add Printer Wizard starts, choose My Computer and click Next. The wizard asks which port you want to use for the new printer. If you want to use a port that isn't listed, click Add Port for additional options. When you're done, click Next. The Add Printer Wizard asks for the manufacturer and model of the printer you are installing, as shown in Figure 7-6.

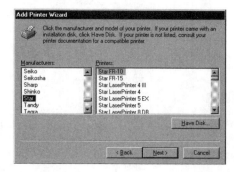

FIGURE 7-6

Selecting the printer manufacturer and model.

After you have selected your printer, if you want to use the driver built intoNTS 4.0, click Next. If you want to install a driver from manufacturer-supplied floppy disks, click Have Disk and follow the prompts. After the driver is installed, the wizard asks you to name the printer (see Figure 7-7).

FIGURE 7-7

Naming the printer.

Give the printer a name of no more than 32 characters—including spaces—and indicate whether you want this printer to be your default printer. Then click Next. The wizard asks you whether this printer is to be shared on the network, as shown in Figure 7-8. If you plan to share it, give it a share name of no more than 12 characters, including spaces.

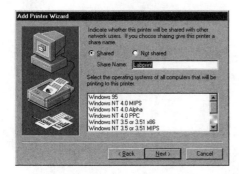

FIGURE 7-8

Sharing the printer.

An enhancement new to Windows NT Server 4.0 is the selection of printer drivers for other operating systems. You can use the list to tell the wizard which operating systems will print from this printer. The wizard will intelligently ask for driver files for each operating system you choose, so be sure to have them handy. You'll probably have these files either on your original operating system delivery media or on media delivered with your printer. If you didn't get the operating system from media in your possession (for example, if you downloaded it from a vendor's FTP site), you may be able to retrieve printer drivers in the same way that you installed the operating system. If not, contact the operating system vendor and/or printer vendor for assistance.

> **NOTE:** If you have MS-DOS clients on your network and you intend for them to be able to use this printer, give it a share name that conforms to the 8.3 MS-DOS file-naming convention.

When you're finished, click Next. The printer is installed.

Sharing Local Printers

One of the options you have when you install a printer with the Add Printer Wizard is whether to share the printer on the network. Frequently, shared printers are initially installed as shared printers. However, if you choose not to share a printer during installation, you can share the printer after it's installed with the Sharing tab in the Properties dialog box for the printer, as shown in Figure 7-9.

FIGURE 7-9

The sharing options.

On the Sharing tab, click Shared and give the shared printer a share name. The share name doesn't have to be the same as the printer name, but you may find it helpful if they are the same. Remember that a share name must be 12 characters or less, including spaces, while a printer name must be 32 characters or less, including spaces.

If Windows systems other than PC Windows NT 4.0 systems will use the shared printer, you should also indicate on the Sharing tab which other kinds of systems will use it. Make your selections from the list at the bottom of the dialog box, and click OK. You'll be prompted for system files for these other operating systems, so be sure to have them ready. Once this process is complete, these PC non-Windows NT 4.0 systems will load necessary server files to their system printing directories automatically when they connect to the print server that controls the shared printer.

Connecting to Printers

You can use a printer controlled by another machine by connecting to the printer. This section describes connecting to a Windows NTS 4.0 printer from a Windows NT system. It also describes connecting to a printer when either the client or the server is a non-Windows NT system.

Connecting from a Windows NT System to a Windows NTS 4.0 Printer

Connecting from a Windows NT workstation to a Windows NTS 4.0 printer shows Windows NTS 4.0 at its finest. With Windows NTS 4.0, its not necessary to load printer drivers individually onto every Windows NT workstation on the network. Rather, the NT workstations use the drivers on the server. Furthermore, if you want to update a particular printer driver, you update it only on the server. All the NT workstations on the network begin using the new driver automatically. Quite handy—that roar you hear out there is the sound of several administrators with hundreds of Windows NT seats cheering in agreement!

To connect to a shared printer, double-click Add Printer in the Printers window. The Add Printer Wizard appears (see Figure 7-10). Select the Network Printer Server option, and click Next. The Connect to Printer dialog box appears (see Figure 7-11).

FIGURE 7-10

The Add Printer Wizard for adding a network printer.

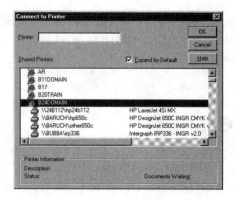

FIGURE 7-11

The Connect to Printer dialog box.

The Connect to Printer dialog box shows the shared printers available on the network. To connect to one, double-click its name or highlight it and click OK. That's all there is to it—you're connected!

Too easy? Must be a "gotcha" somewhere? There is, but it's not a big one. With a driver stored at one central location, each workstation must access it every time a workstation prints. This normally isn't a problem, but if more than a few workstations grab the driver simultaneously, network performance can suffer slightly. However, this phenomenon must be particularly acute to measurably impact the network for any length of time. In nearly all cases, the housekeeping benefit of having one driver to maintain and update outweighs this slight problem.

You can also print from a Windows NT 4.0 workstation to a Windows NT 3.51 server. To do this, log on to the NT 4.0 workstation, using an account with administrative privileges on the Windows NT 3.51 server. Open the Printers folder, and connect to the Windows NT 3.51 server. Select the printer for which you want to add a Windows NT 4.0 driver, and install the driver normally. Select the alternate drivers you want to install, click OK, and you're done.

Connecting from a Non-Windows NT System to a Windows NTS 4.0 Printer

Connecting from a non-NT system to an NTS 4.0 printer isn't quite as easy as NT to NT, but it's usually not very painful.

Windows 3.1/Windows for Workgroups

With a Windows 3.1/Windows for Workgroups client, you can connect to a Windows NTS 4.0 printer the same way you would connect to a Windows for Workgroups server printer. The necessary printer driver must be installed on the Windows 3.1/Windows for Workgroups client.

MS-DOS and OS/2

With an MS-DOS or OS/2 client, you can connect to an NTS 4.0 printer from the command line. Type the following command:

```
net use port \\server\sharename
```

where *port* is the name of the port you want to use, *server* is the server controlling the printer you want to use, and *sharename* is the name of the shared printer. For example, you might type this:

```
net use lpt1: \\ntprsrv\hplaser
```

where lpt1 is the port, ntprsrv is the server, and hplaser is the printer you want to use. The necessary printer driver must be installed on each MS-DOS or OS/2 client.

Macintosh

If Services for Macintosh is installed on the server, Macintosh users on the network can use Windows NTS 4.0 printers. Services for Macintosh includes a PostScript-compatible printing component. With this component, a Macintosh user can use the Chooser to talk to any Windows NTS 4.0 printer on the network—as if the printer were an Apple LaserWriter.

Connecting Windows NT Server 4.0 to a Non-Windows NT Printer

If you want to use Windows NTS 4.0 to connect to a printer that isn't controlled by Windows NT, you must install a driver for the printer locally on the NT system. Use the Add Printer Wizard to connect to the printer. The printer name you create simply feeds into the queue of the printer on the non-Windows NT system, using the locally-installed NT driver.

General and Device Settings

This section describes the General and Device Settings tabs of the Properties dialog box for the selected printer. These tabs contain controls for basic printer settings.

General Settings

The General tab of the Printer Properties dialog box contains several controls for configuring general information (see Figure 7-12).

FIGURE 7-12

The general settings.

You can put whatever you feel will best help you as an administrator in the Comment and Location fields. The Driver controls enable you to select a different driver for the printer.

The Separator Page button lets you create a *separator page*—a page that prints at the start of every job on the printer. See the later section "Separator Pages" for more details.

The Print Processor button allows you to specify the print processor datatype. Generally, you see only WINPRINT in this list. If another installed software package needs a different datatype, that software package will add it to the list as an option. See the documentation for that package for more details.

The Print Test Page button is handy for printing a test page after you change a printer's configuration.

Device Settings

When you look at the Device Settings tab of the Properties dialog box, you see a list of the printer's hardware characteristics, as shown in Figure 7-13.

FIGURE 7-13

Device settings.

The contents of this list vary, depending on the printer. You can use your printer documentation as well as your own knowledge about your network to ensure that all of these settings are as you'd like them.

Configuring Printers

The following sections describe some tools and techniques you can use to help you manage your Windows NTS 4.0 printing resources effectively, including scheduling, spooling, and security.

Printer Scheduling

The Scheduling tab of the Properties dialog box enables you to control when a printer is available on the network (see Figure 7-14). You can control a printer's priority in relation to other printers on the network, as well as its spooler behavior.

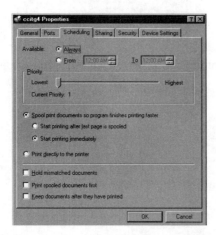

FIGURE 7-14

Scheduling options.

NOTE: Keep in mind that, in some ways, the functions of the Scheduling tab can be used as security measures. They're described separately from security functions here because they have purposes other than security, and because they have their own tab in the Properties dialog box.

Setting Printer Hours

With the controls at the top of the Scheduling tab, you can control the hours during which a printer is available. There are advantages in making a printer available only during certain hours. For example, if you have two printer names assigned to the same physical printer, you can make one of the printer names a low-priority printer, and make it available only late at night for long jobs, such as inventory reports. When a job is submitted to the low-priority printer name outside its available hours, the job waits in the spooler until the printer is available. This is an excellent technique for ensuring that the printer is used effectively during the course of a day.

If you want the printer to be available all the time, click Al_ways.

Setting Priorities

The _Priority slider control adds another level of scheduling. If you have two printer names assigned to the same physical printer, and the available hours of the two printer names overlap, you can independently set the priority for each printer name. If a job is submitted to each of a physical printer's printer names simultaneously, the job submitted to the printer name with the highest priority prints first. Also, remember that you can give a physical printer as many printer names as you like. You can set the priority differently for each of these printer names. Priorities are numbered 1 through 99, with 99 being the highest. A job with a priority of 99 will print before a job with a priority of 71, for example. The default value is 1.

Setting Spooling

The spooling controls in the bottom half of the Scheduling tab enable you to control how the spooler operates. The advantage of spooling is that it enables you to return to your application more quickly. When spooling is enabled, an application doesn't feed a print job directly to the printer, one piece at a time. Rather, it sends the entire job to the spooler. The spooler then feeds the job to the printer a piece at a time. In most cases, this means that your application will relinquish control of the job more quickly, and thus return you to your work more quickly.

With the appropriate controls, you can choose whether the spooler begins printing immediately (after the first page is spooled), or whether it waits for the entire job to enter the spooler.

The options at the bottom of the Scheduling tab are available only when spooling is enabled:

- If Hold Mismatched Documents is checked, any documents entering the spooler that don't match the currently loaded form are held until you can make a change.

- If Print Spooled Documents is checked, jobs that have finished spooling print before jobs that are still spooling, even if the still-spooling jobs have higher priorities.

- If Keep Documents After They Have Printed is checked, jobs stay in the spooler even after they're printed. This may be a good idea if you have reason to believe that a job might cause a problem on the printer, because you can reprint it directly from the spooler rather than fussing with the application again. However, this is generally best left unchecked to conserve spooler resources.

To disable the spooler, select Print Directly to the Printer.

Printer Security

With the Security tab in the Properties dialog box, you can control permissions, auditing, and ownership for the printer (see Figure 7-15). You can use permissions, auditing, and ownership in conjunction with scheduling functions to present printer resource to the network that behave exactly as you want. This section describes the options.

FIGURE 7-15

Security options.

Setting Printer Permissions

Printer permissions enable you to control who uses which printers on the network, as well as what they can do with that equipment. There are four different levels of access a person or group can have:

◆ **No Access.** Members can't do anything with the printer.

◆ **Print.** Members can print documents with the printer.

◆ **Manage Documents.** Members can print documents with the printer, as well as pause, resume, restart, and delete documents.

◆ **Full Control.** Members can do anything with the printer, including print, control document settings, manage documents, and change printer permissions and properties.

To configure permissions for a printer, click the Security tab of the Properties dialog box for that printer, and then choose Permissions. The Printer Permissions dialog box appears, as shown in Figure 7-16.

FIGURE 7-16

The Printer Permissions dialog box.

All the groups or users that have any permissions for the printer are visible in the Name list. To change permissions, highlight a user or group and use the Type of Access drop-down list to choose the new access type.

> **NOTE:** Be sure to leave at least one group with Full Control access. If you don't, you won't be able to change permissions in the future.

To add a user or group to the permissions list, click Add. The Add Users and Groups dialog box appears, as shown in Figure 7-17.

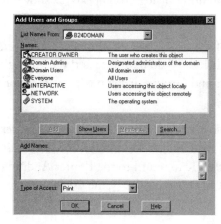

FIGURE 7-17

Adding groups.

To add a group to the permissions list, select the permission that you want to give the group. Then click the group, click Add, and click OK. If you want to add a person to the permissions list, click the Show Users button. A list of all user groups on the system appears. Scroll through the Names list until you find the user you want, and double-click it.

To remove a user or group from the permissions list, highlight the user or group in the Names list and click Remove.

Auditing

To keep up with what different groups or users are doing with network printers, you can audit printer events. Logs of printer events are recorded in the Event Viewer (it's in the Administrative Tools group window).

Audit information can help you in a number of ways. For example, it can help you make decisions about printer configuration. If an office bay contains six printers, you could discover through auditing that two of these printers receive most of the bay's print jobs. You may find this undesirable—especially if all six printers are intended for the bay's use. Because your audit information has painted an accurate picture for you of what happens in the bay, you might choose to move the four seldom-used printers to another location where the need for them is greater. Or you can reconfigure permissions and/or printing hours to "nudge" the bay into using all six printers.

To set up auditing for a printer, open the Security tab in the Properties dialog box for the printer, and choose Auditing. The Printer Auditing dialog box appears, as shown in Figure 7-18.

If the options in the Events to Audit area of the dialog box are dimmed, you haven't yet selected the groups and/or users to audit. Click the Add button to add the groups or users that you want to audit. The Add Users and Groups dialog box appears (see Figure 7-19).

In the Names list, either click a user or group and click Add, or double-click a user or group. The users or groups are added to the Add Names list. Do this for all the users or groups that you want to audit, and then click OK to return to the Printer Auditing dialog box, where the name(s) you have added will be shown in the Name list (see Figure 7-20).

FIGURE 7-18

The Printer Auditing dialog box.

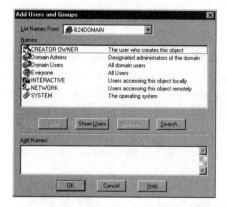

FIGURE 7-19

Adding users and groups.

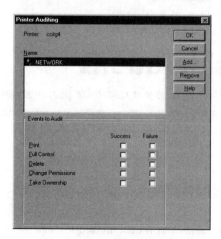

FIGURE 7-20

Enabling the auditing options.

Notice that the options in the Events to Audit area of the dialog box are now available. To audit different events, depending on the group or user, simply click the group or user for which you want to change auditing options. Then use the check boxes to set the options. Do this for each group or user and then click OK. Auditing is now enabled. If you want to audit all users, select Everyone.

To stop auditing a user or group, click the user or group in the <u>N</u>ame list and click Re<u>m</u>ove.

Taking Ownership

By default, the person who initially creates a printer is its owner. However, if you have Full Control, you can take ownership of a printer. Click Ownership to display the Owner dialog box, as shown in Figure 7-21. Click <u>T</u>ake Ownership, and it's yours. You can now control the printer as if you had originally created it. Click <u>C</u>lose to exit the Owner dialog box without taking ownership of the printer.

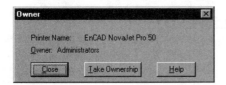

FIGURE 7-21

The Owner dialog box.

Special Printing Considerations

Windows NTS 4.0 includes several capabilities to help you maximize printing productivity. This section describes multiple printer names, printer pools, status messages, and separator pages.

Giving a Printer Multiple Names

You may find it advantageous to give a physical printer on the network more than one printer name. This plan enables you to set up different options for each of the printers, such as printing hours and access, depending on how you configure each name. This feature is also useful if you'd like to set up one printer name for network use and another printer name for local use.

To give a physical printer another name, simply use the Add Printer Wizard. As you use the wizard, select the same port and driver that the other printer name uses, and ensure that the settings are as you'd like them to be for the new printer name. When you finish, the physical printer is available under the new name.

Even though they are associated with the same physical printer, the two printer names are independently configurable. For instance, you can configure the second printer name to use a different paper tray. Or you can configure the second printer name to be available only at night. To network users, there are two printers out there—each with its own distinct behavior.

If you need many different configurations for the same physical printer, you can give one physical printer as many different printer names as you like. To do this, repeat the same steps with the Add Printer Wizard.

Pooling Printers

Pooling identical printers on the network can save time. When you have several identical printers on your network, you can pool them together under the same printer name. This way, if you send a job to that printer name, the first available printer in the pool will print it. You set up this feature with the Ports tab in the Properties dialog box for each printer.

> **NOTE:** A printer pool can be a valuable tool, but it's more efficient in some circumstances than in others. For example, firing off seven very long documents to a pool of three printers won't win you any friends in the office, as all three printers will start jobs and be tied up for an extended period of time. Such an activity is also quite memory-intensive, and may compromise network performance at all locations. On the other hand, this same three-printer pool could be helpful if several people need to print several short documents each throughout the course of a day. Generally, it's in these and similar situations that pools can be helpful.

Plan pools with care. A pool can be more of a liability than an asset if the printers in it are scattered throughout a 20-story office building, for example. Also remember that a job submitted to a pool will be printed by the first available printer in the pool. It's impossible to predict which physical printer in a pool will print a job. Use your judgment and knowledge about your situation to determine how printer pools can best help you.

Status Messages

Status messages appear on users' workstations as pop-up dialog boxes. They inform users of printer events, such as job completion or an offline printer.

To enable status messages on Windows NT, simply start the messenger service. (It's on by default.) On Windows 95, run WINPOPUP.EXE. This program is in the Windows directory.

It's unlikely that the appearance of a status message would interfere with program execution on a user's workstation, as it's only a dialog box that requires a click for dismissal. However, if you have concerns, you can disable the messages. To disable the messages, disable the messenger service on the workstation.

Separator Pages

Separator pages are extra pages that print before each print job. If a printer receives a lot of jobs, separator pages can help users keep their jobs separated with minimal confusion. A separator page can contain just about anything—the job number, the user's name, the date, or a message to the printer's users. A separator page file must be located on the machine that controls the printer for which you're specifying a separator page.

Three separator page files are delivered with Windows NTS 4.0. You can use one of those, edit one and save it as a new file, or create your own.

A separator page file is a text file that uses variables to determine output. It includes an escape character—a character that denotes a function rather than text to be printed in the separator page file. The escape character (a pound sign, for example) should be all by itself on the first line of the separator page file. The remaining lines should be the variables, with parameters when applicable. The variables are as follows:

#B#S	Prints text in single-width block characters.
#D	Prints the date on which the job was printed.
#E	Ejects an extra page from the printer.

#F*path*	Prints the contents of the file in the *path*.
#H*ss*	Initiates a printer-controlled sequence where *ss* is a hexadecimal code sent directly to the printer. For more information, consult your printer documentation.
#I	Prints the number of the job.
#L*mmm*	Prints the specified message (*mmm*).
#N	Prints the name of the person who submitted the job.
#*x*	Skips *x* number of lines. *x* must be between 0 and 9, inclusive. When you put in 0 for *x*, printing is moved to the next line.
#T	Prints the time at which the job was printed.
#U	Turns off block printing (enabled by #B#S).
#W*ww*	Sets the character width (*ww*) of the page. The default value is 80; the maximum value is 256.

To use a separator page, open the General tab of the Properties dialog box for the printer and click Separator Page. The Separator Page dialog box appears, as shown in Figure 7-22.

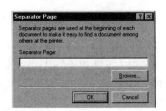

FIGURE 7-22

The Separator Page dialog box.

Click Browse and use the Browse dialog box to select a separator page file. (Look in the SYSTEM32 directory for the three separator page files delivered with Windows NTS 4.0— PCL.SEP, PSCRIPT.SEP, and SYSPRINT.SEP.) After you make your selection, click OK. The separator page file is enabled for the printer.

To create your own separator page file, use a text editor such as Notepad to open a new file. Establish an escape character—the character that tells NTS 4.0 that the next character is an instruction—and put it all by itself on the first line of the file. Be sure to choose a character that you won't need for anything else in the file (don't use a variable, for example). Use your chosen escape character and the variables described earlier in this section to create a custom separator page file. Save it and select it in the same way that you would select a separator page file delivered with Windows NTS 4.0 (as described in the preceding paragraph).

To stop using a separator page file for a printer, open the Separator Page dialog box and delete the entry in the Separator Page field.

Troubleshooting the Printing Process

Windows NTS 4.0 is a robust and reliable printing platform. However, from time to time things won't go quite the way you want. This section explores a few common pitfalls and what you can do to recover from them.

Failing to Communicate

When a communication problem occurs between a printer and a server, the printer and the server can't "see" each other.

Can't Create the Printer

When you simply can't create a printer (dialog box controls for doing so are dimmed), it's a problem with privileges. Remember, you must be an Administrator or a Power User to create a printer. Log out and then log back on with the correct privileges, and you'll be able to create the printer.

Can't Connect to the Printer

Once in a while, you may try to connect to a printer and get a message that says `Could not connect to the printer: The remote procedure call failed`. It's a rare occurrence, it's not your fault, and it almost always follows a period of intense printer configuration activity—especially adding and removing printers. A "failed remote procedure call" just means that you've baffled the Registry. Close the error message box, log off, and log back on again, and the connection should work perfectly.

Other Problems

What if the server and the printer can see each other, but nothing's happening or the output is erratic? It must be either the software or the hardware. Some trial-and-error is involved but, with a little creative sleuthing, you can often find the problem.

Software problems can be related to the printing software (driver, port specifications, and the like) or the application software. If you can print from other applications, suspect the application software. If printing works erratically or with unexpected results, you may have a printer driver installation problem. Try deleting and reinstalling both the driver and the printer.

Hardware problems are frequently easier to diagnose because hardware problems are more often "all-or-nothing" problems. When you can't print from any application, using any driver, and have tried again after a reboot, suspect either network or printer hardware. The printer's inner workings could be jammed, or a cable could be bad. Check to see whether the printer works in another port. If so, that's strong evidence for a bad port on the server.

Where to Go Next

This chapter explored the Windows NT Server 4.0 printing resources and how you can effectively manage them as an administrator on a network.

The next chapter examines the ins and outs of mass storage devices on NTS, including device types and disk management.

Here are some other resources that you may find useful at this point:

- ◆ For a detailed treatment of how you can make the Registry work for you, go to Chapter 11.
- ◆ Chapter 12 presents in-depth coverage of Windows NTS 4.0 security policies and configuration.
- ◆ For more on incorporating non-Windows NT 4.0 clients into your network, see Chapter 21.

Chapter | 8

Mass Storage
Management

In This Chapter:

- An Introduction to Drives and Terminology
- Mass Storage Interfaces
- Configuring Device Controllers and Devices
- Optimizing Disk Performance

How do I...

An Introduction to Drives and Terminology

As Windows NT has emerged from its original obscurity, more and more users are confused by its supposedly large hardware requirements, including system RAM and hard drive space. By the same token, the cost of these components has decreased. So what do you buy? What constitutes excellent (or even decent) drive choices for Windows NT? All these excellent questions are subject to significant hype and opinion. Windows NT uses memory and drives like any other operating system (OS). In certain cases, the drives that you purchase may have special OS-specific firmware, but this is seldom a problem on a PC. What does help in choosing hardware is an understanding of how the hardware—specifically, in this case, the storage media—works.

Over the past several years, a great revolution has happened to storage devices. Drives have gotten smaller in size, faster in transfer rate, and bigger in capacity. Within a few months, 23 gigabyte drives will be available; with a Fiber Channel Interface, these drives will have data transfer rates approximating 50-70 megabytes per second. For those of us that started with 40MB MFM hard drives, such a size and performance are unimaginable.

Storage devices are somewhat misunderstood. They include—but are not limited to—hard drives, magneto-optical (MO) drives, tape drives, CD-ROMs, and drives that use jukebox libraries. These latter are usually MO drives or tape libraries. Recently, RAID (Redundant Array of Independent Disks or sometimes Redundant Array of Inexpensive Disks) has become very popular, as has clustering (in clustering, redundancy is carried to the extreme; for example, two computers can share the same hard drives). We'll deal with each of these topics prior to considering configuration issues.

A hard drive can be considered a permanent repository for data. *Permanent* simply means that when the computer is turned off, the files are still present for later retrieval. The basic mechanism by which a drive works is actually very simple. A drive consists of a platter (or multiple platters) that spin. A read/write head travels across distinct concentric circles that travel from the center to the periphery of the platter (which is rigid and accounts for the name *hard drive*). Information is conveyed by an electrical current sent to the read/write head, and this current magnetizes particles on the platter tracks. During a read phase, the head passes over the magnetic fields, resulting in inductive currents in the head coils. Such currents are the actual binary stored bits of data. All these read/writes occur in a sealed environment that is dust-free. When the computer is turned off, the magnetic changes to the drive are maintained. Although this is a simplistic view of hard drive mechanics, it shows that a hard drive is dependent upon several basic components:

- ◆ The rotation speed dictates the read/write speed of the device.
- ◆ The electrical components dictate the type of drive.
- ◆ The number of platters dictate the size of the drive.

All these elements are related to developments in many fields. To give you a comparison of some devices: A standard floppy drive rotates at 360 RPM; fast SCSI drives rotate at 7200 RPM and will probably soon get faster. We're all aware of the speed of transfer of a floppy drive. The 7200 RPM hard drives, simply based upon rotation speed, are 20 times faster than a floppy drive (7200/360=20).

Although the hard drive was first developed in 1973 by IBM (the so-called *Winchester drives* with two 30MB disks, reminding folks of the Winchester 30/30 rifle—hence the name), it was not until the development of the XT in 1983 that hard drives started becoming popular. In the 13 years since then, development has really skyrocketed.

Mass Storage Interfaces

For all practical purposes, there are only two drive types that should be considered today. These are *IDE/EIDE* (*Intelligent Drive Electronics* or *Enhanced IDE*) and *SCSI* (*Small Computer System Interface*). There is no purpose gained at all by discussing the older MFM/RLL/ESDI drives.

IDE and EIDE

IDE started as part of the *CAM* (*Common Access Method*) specification in the mid-80s and was submitted for formal approval to ANSI in 1990. The CAM standard was adopted in 1994 as the X3.221-1994 specification. The IDE drive requires a very inexpensive controller and is sent from the factory with specific settings that don't need to be changed. The price war started by IDE has seriously eroded the use of other platforms.

As implemented originally, the IDE drive was controlled by a *PIO* (*programmed I/O*) *card*. In this design, all data transfers are handled by the CPU. There's no handshaking at all in such transfers, and the transfers aren't synchronized. Data is transferred in 512-byte sectors, and nothing can use the CPU until the transfer is complete. There are serious limitations to this design.

Everyone adopted the original WD1003 controller, which was controlled by the INT13 BIOS call. This turns out to be a limitation of 1024 cylinders, 16 heads (although supposedly 255, the task file registers are limited to 16), and 63 sectors. This turns out be a 528MB limit on drive size. (The size of a drive is actually limited by DOS. DOS 4 supported 128MB hard drives. DOS 5 and higher allowed the use of a larger cluster size, 8192 bytes, which raised the 128MB limit to 536MB, or 528 real size.) There were only primary/secondary configurations and the ability to add many components simply wasn't present. All drive activity was CPU-dependent, thus not allowing much multitasking.

The Enhanced IDE specification was introduced by Western Digital in 1994. EIDE circumvents many of the problems in IDE. First and foremost, EIDE uses *LBA* (*Logical Block Address*) to translate the cylinder, head, and sector information into a 28-bit block, much as is done in SCSI translation schemes. This LBA is used by BIOS to set up an enhanced drive parameter table that's read by the system. The actual formula used for the translation is as follows:

```
LBA=[(cylinder × max. head number × selected head) × sectors/track + (sector-1)]
```

When this formula is used, the number of cylinders is lowered and the number of heads is increased. In this way, the size of the drive is translated to the system. For example, instead of a 1.2MB drive having 2450 cylinders and 16 heads, it now has 610 cylinders and 64 heads.

The other major changes included faster transfer rates via mode changes (simple increases in internal specifications) in PIO, and even faster ones yet using the Mode 4 PIO or Mode 2 DMA transfers. To be practical, EIDE drives need to be connected to a fast bus. Intel realized this and started supplying on-board PCI chipsets that contained EIDE control in 1994. All in all, the EIDE standard has done much to increase performance with a minimum increase in cost.

The EIDE standard also incorporates support for four devices. The primary channel is designated for hard drives and the secondary for slower devices such as CD-ROMs and tape devices. In each situation, a device is either *slave* or *master*. The primary channel uses IRQ14 and the secondary uses IRQ15. With this expansion and the use of the back-wardly-compatible 40-pin ribbon connectors, the speed of the transfer limits length of the cable to 18 inches.

As far as Windows NT is concerned, the most dramatic change in EIDE support is the incorporation of the *ATAPI (Advanced Technology Attachment Packet Interface)* standard. In Windows NT 4.0, all EIDE devices are incorporated into the ATAPI driver, whereas prior versions used ATAPI for CD-ROMs but ATDISK for EIDE hard drives. Currently, built-in support is limited to hard drives and CD-ROMs, with tape-device support being driver- or vendor-specific. From a technical perspective, the major change seen in ATAPI is the incorporation of packet-based transport rather than computer architecture that was seen in IDE. In other words, ATAPI runs SCSI-II commands over an IDE interface (there is no support for command queuing, multiple *LUN*s (*logical units*), or disconnect features found in SCSI-II). The advantage of this SCSI-on-IDE model is that future standardized drivers will address ATAPI as well as SCSI. EIDE devices are basically using an abbreviated version of the SCSI-II command sets. In fact, soon such companies as Adaptec will be supporting ATAPI devices. Currently such drivers and applications are in development.

Starting in 1995, a new specification is being developed. This is the *ATA-3 (Advanced Technology Attachment)* improvement to the EIDE effort. Improvements will include the handing of large drive sizes (137 gigabytes, to be exact), fast transfer rates via mode 4 or more likely DMA 2, and the inclusion of tape and CD recorders. As this technology matures, it will be interesting to see the outcome. Such concepts as terminators to reduce noise and echo are being considered (showing the SCSI heritage). More importantly, the specification allows multitasking to occur.

It seems apparent that IDE has in fact come a long way. There's no doubt that it will suffice for small servers, limited to small file servers that get few simultaneous queries. However, because it currently lacks multitasking and simultaneous I/Os, EIDE simply doesn't meet the requirements of a high-end server, such as a SQL server or other server that has many simultaneous queries. Be prepared, however, for an onslaught of cheaper devices for use on servers.

SCSI

SCSI began in 1980 as the *Shugart Associates System Interface* or *SASI*. The entire concept was based on an inexpensive interface to handle drives. In 1982, the ANSI committee started working on the first SCSI specifications. The adoption of the SCSI hard drive by Apple started the SCSI acceptance. Today we are looking at SCSI-I, SCSI-II and SCSI-III specifications. In reality, only SCSI-II and SCSI-III are of any interest to us.

The reason SCSI is of importance in the server area is the fact that it's device-independent. The computer to which the device is attached doesn't need to know anything about the device. (This independence is very important, and provides much of the basis for RAID systems, discussed shortly.) The SCSI specification provides a specified language to communicate across the bus, and all devices are treated as logical units. Each device can have eight logical unit numbers (LUNs). For example, a CD-ROM jukebox could have an ID of 4 and have eight platters in it.

SCSI is a peer-to-peer implementation, allowing devices to communicate with all other devices. Unfortunately, many special devices need drivers to fully utilize device functions. These drivers, termed *device drivers*, are essential in Windows NT. For example, only recently have drivers become available to write to CD-recorders in NT.

How does SCSI work? SCSI uses a defined set of signals over a defined set of lines. In the standard SCSI-II bus, there are nine control lines and nine data lines, with the rest of the lines (except number 25) forming ground lines. In such a configuration, you can see that all signals are in fact 8-bit. With the advent of wide SCSI, the number of data lines went from eight to 16. There is even some discussion of moving to double-wide or 32-bit

SCSI. This is unlikely to occur until the bus and cable types are agreed upon. We'll discuss the future of SCSI shortly.

> **TIP:** The decision of whether to buy wide or narrow SCSI can be reduced to simple bandwidth issues. A controller doesn't have sufficient bandwidth to run several fast SCSI-II drives efficiently. One drive always waits for the other. This isn't the case with wide SCSI. Transfer rates are another example where wide SCSI shows an advantage. SCSI-II drives seldom exceed 5–6 meg/sec transfer rates, while wide drives can approach 10–11 meg/sec. For sheer performance, buy wide SCSI—even better, the new Ultra Wide SCSI, which has even more bandwidth than wide SCSI.

The entire SCSI system is based on a controller that uses an onboard processor. Most of these processors are RISC-based and they assist in the transfer of information from devices to the parent system. (Remember, devices on a SCSI bus are system-independent. They aren't reported to the system BIOS and indeed are controlled by the SCSI card.) If a file is needed, the system (the *initiator*) informs the controller, and a request is sent over the bus to the appropriate *responder*. This device acknowledges the request and fills it. During this process, the device can go offline to find the file, and then inform the controller that the file is found. This ability to go offline is called *disconnection*. During the time of disconnection, a different request can go over the control lines. Thus, the basic nature of SCSI is a multiprocessing one, so it stands to reason that servers in general have all been SCSI-based.

> **TIP:** When information is being sent to memory, the SCSI busmasters use *Direct Memory Access* (*DMA*) to transmit information into main memory. In the initial design of the ISA bus, there are only 24 data lines. DMA is then limited to 2^{24} megabytes of access (16MB). All memory above 16MB must be buffered below 16. Although Windows NT does a decent job of the buffering, there's no reason to use an ISA controller on a server. Use PCI or EISA and avoid the memory limitations of the ISA bus.

SCSI Terminology

Certain terms in SCSI systems need elaboration:

- **Single-ended SCSI.** In single-ended SCSI (by far the most popular), the signals are determined by voltage relative to a common ground. This signal can be 5 volts but typically is considered present if it exceeds 2.5 volts relative to a ground of 0. A signal is considered negative if the voltage on the bus falls below 0.4-0.5 volts. As is easily seen, the crucial step in setting up a SCSI bus is the control of proper voltages on the bus. Since the bus is voltage-related, all cables must meet the SCSI specifications and length limits. The specification states 19 feet as the limit, but in reality fast SCSI and fast wide SCSI should be limited to about 10 feet.

- **Differential SCSI.** The major difference between differential and single-ended SCSI is the manner in which signals are determined. Instead of a comparison to ground, all voltage is read by contrasting the voltage between two lines. This provides better control of the signal; as a consequence, cables can be longer (up to 80 feet or so). This version of SCSI isn't very popular and devices are hard to find. Unfortunately, you can't mix differential and single-ended devices.

- **Termination.** Termination simply refers to stopping the signal at that point and also providing a good ratio between low and high signals. Having proper termination on the bus is mandatory. Some users refer to this issue as *SCSI voodoo*. In reality, termination is straightforward. Always use active terminators, since they're specified in SCSI-II and they provide the control of bus voltage. Most devices have onboard terminators and you can disable/enable them via jumpers or removing the resistor packs (basically inline resistors). You can also have the bus or the device provide the power to the terminator. Wherever possible, have the bus provide termination power. A properly terminated bus has a termination at each end. If you use both internal and external devices, the last physical device (both internal and external) needs to be terminated, and termination removed from the controller card. With most modern controllers, this is all set in firmware. For example, the Adaptec controllers are all configured by using Ctrl+A as the card POSTs or by setting an EISA configuration utility. (When the card "POSTs," it communicates with all the devices and sends this information to the system BIOS. It's analogous to a system being turned on and doing its POST.) Newer cards actually provide automatic determination of termination.

> **TIP:** It's actually easier to terminate the cable than a device. External terminators are very popular and easy to find. Some vendors are now shipping internal cables that are also terminated. These cables and terminators allow easy maintenance of SCSI buses.

◆ *SCSI ID.* Each SCSI device needs a unique identifier (*ID*). The higher the ID, the greater the priority given to the device. For this reason, most SCSI cards have an ID of 7. Drives are given the lowest priority in part because they're faster than other components on the bus. The boot drive is 0 and the next drive is usually 1. Tape drives are in between, typically 3 or 4, and CD-ROMs are given the highest priorities. All these IDs are set with jumpers. The first block (0) is 1, the second is 2, and the third is 4. Combinations are easily determined.

The bus works very simply. Commands are started by the initiator. Devices go offline (if they allow it) and do their jobs. If contention occurs, the device with the highest number gains priority. All this is handled through arbitration. The basic states of the bus are as follows:

◆ *Bus free.* Nothing is on the bus. This is the state that happens when all commands are finished.

◆ *Arbitration.* The situation in which multiple requests are being handled and the system must decide who has priority. This is determined by the ID. After arbitration, the system enters the select or re-selection phase.

◆ *Selection.* The system selects the appropriate device and then chooses what information, when it will be sent, and where it's going. In all cases, the initiator and the target communicate based on ID. When all is selected, the target asserts a Busy signal on the bus and then occupies the bus until the task is finished.

◆ *Re-selection.* After a target goes offline, it's re-placed on the line by this process.

♦ *Command phase.* The target requests a command from the initiator. The command byte is sent, and the device can go offline to complete the task. The target interprets the command and finds the data block. This is then followed by the data-in phase.

♦ *Data in/Data Out.* For data in, the target asks for data to be transferred to the initiator. In data out, the target receives information from the initiator.

♦ *Status phase.* A complex phase in which the status of the ongoing task is described. This is usually success or failure but also includes busy, command completed, and others.

♦ *Message in/message out.* In this optional phase, messages are sent between the initiator and the target. In all cases, the command `complete` is sent at the end of a job.

SCSI functions very well. The internal SCSI language is well described and covers the basic mechanisms of device operation. On the other hand, it should be apparent that a lot of communication is necessary for the bus to function properly. This language is referred to as *SCSI overhead* and it is essential for multiprocessing. On a single task, EIDE is faster. The last topics that will be considered are the SCSI specifications and where SCSI seems headed in the near future.

SCSI Specifications

SCSI-II is really built on the SCSI-I specification. SCSI-II actually evolved from the *Common Command Set* standard that defined much of the functions for hard drives. This was seen as an opportunity to add other command sets. Specifically, command sets were set for CD-ROMS, jukebox arms (media changers), scanners, and communications. In addition, the command sets were expanded. Several very important features were added:

♦ Terminator resistance was reduced from 132 ohms to 100 ohms. This was done because most cables didn't match the 132 ohm resistance. Unfortunately, manufacturers of cables continue to make cables that aren't to SCSI-II specification, and some adapters (for example, early 1542Cs from Adaptec) had serious problems with the inexpensive cables.

♦ Bus arbitration is no longer optional—in fact, is mandatory.

♦ Parity checking is mandatory.

♦ Optional features added include command queuing, which allows up to 256 commands to be placed in a queue so that the device can complete many requests without asking the initiator. The ability to tag the commands allows priorities to be assigned to commands. All of this was designed to enhance SCSI I/O.

♦ Fast SCSI was added, allowing the standard 50-pin connector to handle up to 10MB in synchronous mode.

♦ Wide SCSI was added; this kept the command set as 8-bit, but the data path was opened to 16-bit. A 68-pin connector was added to support wide SCSI.

SCSI-III was started before SCSI-II was finished. The basic reason: improve functionality and transfer rates. This set of specifications are very exciting and will offer great functionality and speed to servers. Some important additions include:

♦ Support for Fast 20 devices (UltraSCSI) that allows 20 meg/sec transfers over 8-pin devices and 40 meg/sec over wide SCSI.

♦ Support for SCSI commands over Fiber Channel. This addition adds transfer rates up to 100 meg/sec over nearly 100 feet of cable.

Support was added for FireWire or the 1394 bus. Among other additions, FireWire adds the ability of data and commands to coexist on the bus at the same time.

All of these additions will be upon us very soon; here we'll discuss the new specifications in more detail.

NOTE: SCSI-III also adds specifications for tapes and printers, jukeboxes, multi-media, RAID, and graphics (scanners in particular). It is a very thorough specification.

FCAL, USB, and FireWire

It is well known that the current bus design has very serious speed limitations. Unless some drastic change is made in fundamental design, only very serious RAID configurations will be able to supply needed I/O to such new systems as Pentium Pro 200s or Alpha 500s. Fortunately, such design is in the works.

Fiber Channel-Arbitrated Loop (FC-AL)

The Fiber Channel Arbitrated Loop (FC-AL) is a recent addition that stems from the Fiber Channel Specification Initiative started in 1993. Unlike the standard SCSI, the FC-AL is actually a loop connected to the backplane in two separate places. This allows rapid transfer of data from device to device. In a single-channel design, FC-AL can send information at 100 meg/sec; in dual channel, 200 meg/sec. Such bandwidth eliminates most of the complaints dealing with SCSI overhead. In addition, FC-AL supports up to 126 devices. Expect early implementations of FC-AL to be UltraSCSI drives, etc., maintained on the FC-AL architecture. This should prove to be very efficient and fast (and available toward the end of 1996). With the soon-appearing 23 gigabyte Elite drives from Seagate, a loop comprising 63 drives (on a single loop) would result in 1449 gigabytes of storage. This should satisfy most user demands.

Universal Serial Bus (USB)

Although not in competition with FC-AL, the Universal Serial Bus has received a lot of attention lately. USB devices attach to the USB via a port on hubs. When a device is detected, the hub indicates the addition or removal of a USB device in its port status. Hosts periodically query the hub to determine the cause of the status message. When the hub receives the query string, it tells the host which port. The host then issues a control pipe command and addresses the device using the USB default address.

The host identifies the device attached to the port and notifies the software of the arrival or removal of the device (or function). In the 1.0 specification, the devices stipulated are slow devices rather than fast ones. The advantage of the USB specification is in the elimination of port setups and IRQ-I/O contention.

FireWire (or the 1394 Initiative)

FireWire is proposed as a low-cost serial bus. It was developed originally by Texas Instruments and Apple, and was approved as an IEEE standard at the end of 1995. FireWire can handle SCSI protocols and has several interesting features:

- ◆ It's Plug and Play compliant (perhaps one reason Microsoft supports it so fully).
- ◆ It allows hot plugging of devices.
- ◆ The implementation is *isochronous*, meaning that slices of bandwidth can be assigned to each device.

Unlike other protocols we're discussing, FireWire uses a memory model of interaction. SCSI, as you recall, supports channels. In FireWire, all devices are viewed as memory-type transactions and are accessed directly by the CPU.

Other Options

In addition to the standards just mentioned, others are emerging. Paramount among these is the *Serial Storage Architecture* (*SSA*) designed by IBM. SSA has an excellent design, but it's currently unclear how broadly its support will be implemented.

Fast devices will emerge soon as UltraSCSI or fiberoptic. The first use of these drives in new technology will be SCSI over fiberoptic cable. In this case, FireWire isn't currently a contender, as it doesn't support fiberoptic currently. In the near future, we'll see new generations of motherboards and components, probably developed as FC-AL (or related). Such devices will be fast, and will in fact redefine server abilities.

Each of the discussed designs has advantages. FireWire is by far the cheapest. FC-AL has the fastest physical layer, but is the most expensive. In addition, FC-AL supports the longest cable length. Finally, Fiber Channel affords the greatest flexibility in mapping protocols to a common physical layer.

The next year will prove to be very interesting. The SCSI protocols will be run over fiber optic cables, and serial rather than parallel SCSI will be released.

Configuring Device Controllers and Devices

It is very important to configure optimally drives and controllers so that Windows NT will run properly. Many users complain of CD-ROM recognition issues with EIDE. SCSI devices also need proper configuration and termination. Windows NT virtualizes hardware and all must be to specification.

EIDE

The safest way to set up EIDE drives is to put the drives on the primary channel. While this restricts the system to two hard drives, 4 gigabyte drives have just been introduced and LBA enables their use in NT. I don't recommend using EIDE on a server, but clearly it can be done. Save the secondary channel for CD-ROMs, being certain to obtain drives that are ATAPI 1.2-compliant.

Mixed Buses

Many users like booting off a small EIDE drive onto NT installed to a SCSI hard drive. While this does work, mixing buses can cause serious bus contention. Unless there are extremely compelling reasons, don't mix EIDE and SCSI hard drives.

SCSI

New controllers and devices are very easy to set up. (Avoid legacy controllers.) EISA is okay, but all the better controllers are PCI. Obtain a controller with onboard BIOS control. For example, the Adaptec 2940 and 3940 controllers can be configured by onboard SCSI utilities that can be found by simply pressing Ctrl+A at post (boot) time. The new "U" series will even allow the setting of multiple boards with a single Ctrl+A. Invest in quality controllers.

By convention, SCSI IDs need to follow specific standards (we'll exclude Microchannel in this discussion because it's no longer supported). The controller needs the highest priority and is assigned an ID of 7. The boot drive is assigned the lowest priority (ID0) and subsequent drives start at 1. DAT drives are usually given intermediate IDs, with 3 or 4 being the most common. CD-ROMs typically receive IDs of 5 or 6. Whatever you decide to set up, be consistent across servers.

Serious attention must be given to cables and termination. The best currently are from Granite, but they're expensive. On the other hand, cheaper cables that don't work are actually *more* expensive. Keep cable length to a minimum. When in doubt, use the diagnostic cables from Granite. You need to minimize noise and echo on the bus or data corruption will be insured.

Whenever possible, terminate the bus and not the device. For example, on an external chain, put a terminator on the second SCSI connector and not on the device. Once more, buy a good active terminator. There are internal cables that are also terminated, although these are relatively difficult to find. Newer SCSI controllers actually automatically determine the best termination for the bus. If you use a combined wide/narrow controller, only use two of the ports at one time.

Troubleshooting Examples

I recently added a hard drive externally and can't access it. It simply doesn't show up anywhere.

The termination is still most probably enabled on the controller; you need to remove the termination either via software or removal of the terminator packs.

I added a second drive, and now the system hangs at boot time.

Make certain that there are no duplicate SCSI IDs on the bus.

I added a wide hard drive to my external chain and placed it last on the chain. The performance is less by far than I expected.

You probably have narrow devices before the wide device. This essentially makes the wide device narrow as well. Place the wide drive first on the chain.

I just added a SCSI chain to my system and now I see four instances of one drive. What's the problem?

Check to see whether the cables and termination were the culprit. Simplify the bus and make certain that all configurations are proper.

I just added an old slow CD-ROM to my SCSI bus. The system now hangs during initialization.

The CD-ROM probably doesn't support synchronous data transfers or parity. Disable them for the ID in question.

Disk Administrator: Partitioning and Formatting

Disk Administrator (*DA*) is the major feature in Windows NT that allows the manipulation of partitions, formatting, drive and CD-ROM labels, volumes, and stripe sets. Understanding what it can and can't do is key to the use of hard drives in Windows NT 4.0.

Partitioning drives is very easy in Windows NT. All the work is done either at the command line (for special cluster sizes) or Disk Administrator . Little has actually changed since Version 3.51, but DA does have a new interface and customization characteristics.

Figure 8-1 shows a system with three new unpartitioned hard drives added to an Alpha server. Drive 3 is highlighted; and under the partition menu on the toolbar, an extended partition has been chosen for the drive.

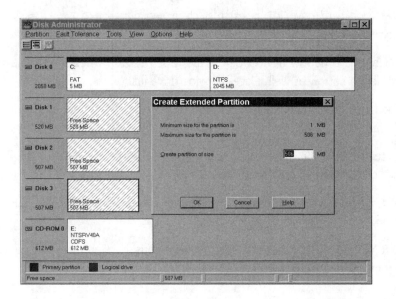

FIGURE 8-1

Using Disk Administrator to assign an extended partition to a "raw" drive. The figure shows Disk 3 selected and the size returned as a minimum-maximum. The whole drive was selected in this example.

Once the partition has been created, if it's a primary partition, it's automatically assigned a drive letter. If it's an extended partition, you'll need to create logical drives as shown in Figure 8-2.

TIP: As a general rule, set up only one primary partition on a computer. If you add more drives, it's easier to maintain standard drive lettering without mixing drives and partitions in a confusing manner. In all cases, a letter is assigned to a primary partition before an extended partition. In such a situation, drive C could be the primary partition on drive 0 and drive D could be the primary partition on drive 3. Keeping drives and partitions as simple as possible is a good idea.

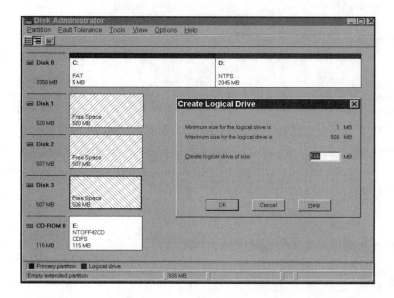

FIGURE 8-2

Creating a logical drive with Disk Administrator. In this case, the whole drive was selected.

After changing the partition information, you need to save the configuration. There are two ways to accomplish this. You can choose Partition | Commit Changes Now, or you can simply exit DA. Figure 8-3 shows the result of using the Commit Changes method.

TIP: When using a Syquest SCSI drive, don't try to commit the changes with the Partition menu. It won't work, because the drive is removable. Exit DA and you will be given the option of saving changes. Enter Yes and you can now format the drive.

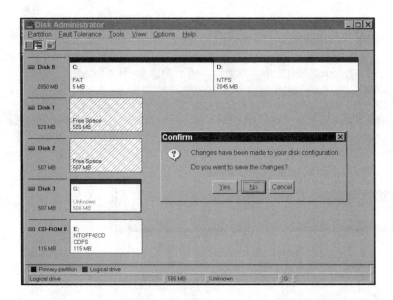

After the information has been updated, a dialog box suggests updating the Registry with `Rdisk.exe` in the `system32` folder (see Figure 8-4). In fact, this is a mandatory procedure if you want to save the current configuration information.

FIGURE 8-4

After changing drive information, this dialog box suggests updating the Registry information with `Rdisk.exe`.

The final step in adding a new drive is to format the drive. After the partition has been made and saved, you can choose Tools | Format. Upon doing so and answering Yes to the standard format warning, you'll see a progress dialog box (see Figure 8-5).

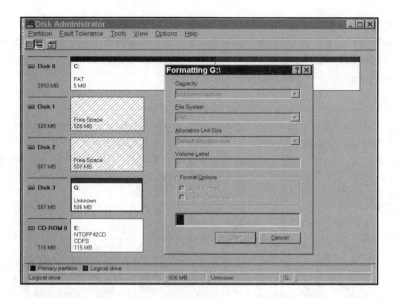

FIGURE 8-5

The progress window showing the formatting of drive G.

TIP: If you are using large files and you want to optimize cluster size, set the partition and then format at the command line. The syntax is as follows:

```
FORMAT drive: [/FS:file-system] [/A:size]
 /FS:file-system — Specifies the type of the file system
➡(FAT or NTFS).
 /A:size Overrides the default allocation unit size.
➡Default settings are used by DA and should not be changed
➡for normal use (you cannot compress a drive formatted over
➡4096).
 NTFS supports 512, 1024, 2048, 4096, 8192, 16K, 32K, 64K.
 FAT supports 8192, 16K, 32K, 64K, 128K, 256K.
```

For example, if you are storing large video files, small clusters will increase the amount of fragmentation on the drive. Increase the cluster size accordingly. If the files are large TIF or CAD files, use the largest allocation unit. In general, however, it's best to stay with the 4096 default size.

Deleting partitions is the exact opposite of what has been discussed so far in this section. In DA, you highlight the partition and choose Partition | Delete. You'll be informed that the drive and all its files will be deleted. If you choose Yes, the partition is removed, but the removal isn't permanent until you save the changes.

> **TIP:** When you attempt to delete a partition, you're informed that the partition can't be removed because it can't be locked for exclusive usage. If you have any pointer in the system that's related to the drive in question, this indeed can be a troublesome problem. Make sure that no obvious pointer is directed to the drive. Obvious ones include those in Explorer or File Manager.
>
> If you find that it's still impossible to delete the partition, no matter what you do, there are several options available. Sometimes the `Fdisk` program that ships with DOS 6.22 or higher will work. You can also use the `delpart.exe` file that was released by Microsoft and works similarly to `fdisk`; it allows you to delete an NTFS partition. If the drive is a SCSI drive, you can do a low-level format on it. You can find `delpart.exe` on CompuServe in the `WINNT` forum.

Fault Tolerance

Fault tolerance is a very complex issue. It involves configuring hard drives, configuring hardware in general, and planning for disaster recovery and prevention. This section examines the issue of hard drive redundancies and their value in Windows NT 4.0.

It has been estimated by several independent sources that the amount of data storage is increasing 50 to 100 percent per year. These estimates are alarming. Not that many years ago everyone was using a 40MB hard drive and it seemed massive. Today we're worrying about gigabyte data files. With this explosion in storage size, disk arrays have become more and more prominent. Quite simply, a *disk array* is a logical grouping of drives that is designed to be faster, be fault tolerant, or both. The most common of disk arrays is *RAID* (*Redundant Array of Independent Disks*). In reality, the concept of RAID is too narrow, and we'll really discuss fault-tolerant storage in a broader sense.

Fault tolerance, as the name might suggest, is the capability of a system to handle disasters in such a way that continuous operation is maintained. Needless to say, considerable effort is required to provide such capability. In fact, there are several approaches to accomplishing this tedious chore. The first one we'll consider is hard drive management or RAID.

RAID

RAID can be discussed in several manners. One is the classic, almost 10-year-old configuration of hard drives only; the other consists of drives and accessories such as power supplies. The latter method truly starts providing fault tolerance, but no single entity provides complete crash resistance.

Almost every book that discusses RAID assumes that all you need to know are the levels of RAID—and the discussion nearly always stops there. The major concern should be not what RAID *is* but how you *use* it. For completeness, however, we do need to define various terms, including RAID levels.

The following list describes the levels of RAID:

♦ Just a bunch of drives—This is nothing more than placing drives together for convenience. There is no implied fault tolerance in this level. In Windows NT, this is termed a *volume*.

♦ Level 0—Believe it or not, RAID 0 is closer to "Just a bunch of drives" than to the other RAID levels. No consideration is given to fault tolerance, and the sole purpose of this array is a speed increase. The increase in speed has serious shortcomings (discussed shortly). In RAID 0, the data are striped across drives, allowing for simultaneous I/Os to all the drives. As the number of drives increases, so does the speed of the array and the risk of data loss. Use RAID 0 only when performance and not data integrity is the compelling reason.

♦ Level 1—RAID 1 is perhaps the best of all levels. All writes of data occur onto at least two drives. In other words, Drive A is duplicated onto Drive B. When both drives are on the same controller, this process is termed *mirroring*. When the drives are on separate controllers, the process is called *duplexing*.

There are several important considerations about RAID 1. It's generally an option in operating systems; in fact, you can accomplish both mirroring and duplexing in Windows NT 4.0. Undeniably, RAID 1 provides the greatest redundancy in RAID. Unfortunately, RAID 1 is also the most expensive of standard RAID levels. In today's business world, a simple RAID 1 solution may be cost-prohibitive.

NOTE: An additional level of RAID is sometimes discussed: RAID 0 + 1 (sometimes called RAID 10). In this configuration, you first establish RAID 0 arrays and then mirror them. Doing this allows redundancy and speed but the cost increases dramatically.

- RAID 2—RAID 2 is very seldom used. Striping is accomplished at the bit level, bringing about serious overhead and expensive.

- RAID 3—Like RAID 2, RAID 3 is seldom used. All correction data are maintained on a single drive, and information is striped across the remaining drives a byte at a time. For this level to function properly and at optimal speed, drive spindles need to be synchronized. There's no need to consider Level 3.

- RAID 4—This level is similar to RAID 3, with the exception of data being striped at the block level. Like RAID 3, there's no compelling reason to use it.

- RAID 5—RAID 5 is actually a compromise level. Striping is at the block level, and error correction is distributed across all drives. This level uses the simultaneous writes seen in levels 0 and 1, but parity data are distributed across all drives, resulting in increased overhead. As we'll see shortly, RAID 5, implemented properly, is an ideal start at maintaining some level of fault tolerance.

Creating Software RAID Arrays (Sets) in Windows NT

Windows NT server allows you to enable pre-RAID (volume set), RAID 0 (striping), RAID 1 (mirroring) and RAID 5 (striping with parity)—all via the operating system. RAID 0 and 1 are acceptable, but using RAID 5 at the OS level is foolish and asking for serious disaster-recovery issues. If any file or process is locked onto the drive, you can repair it. Windows NT won't let you replace the drive. This is never the case with hardware-based RAID.

Volume sets are termed "just-a-bunch-of-drives" by many RAID vendors. To create a volume set, you simply highlight unpartitioned drives and create a volume set from the Partition menu. Unlike the other arrays, a volume set can be expanded at any time by adding an unpartitioned drive to the set. A volume is really nothing more than a design of convenience. It offers no fault tolerant advantage at all.

To use software RAID 0 in Windows NT software, select unpartitioned drives by clicking one, holding down the Ctrl key, and clicking the rest. After selecting the drives, choose Partition | Create Stripe Set. Figure 8-6 shows three drives selected and the Create Stripe Set dialog box. Note that you can create drives using as much of the total size as you want.

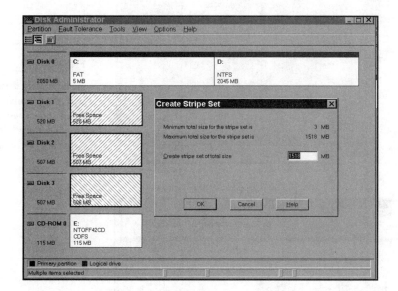

FIGURE 8-6

Using DA to create a stripe set or RAID 0.

After creating the stripe set, you have to commit the changes. Doing so requires a reboot, and then you can format the set. You can use Tools | Format as in conventional formatting, or use the command prompt methods discussed earlier. This formatting is shown in Figure 8-7.

Figure 8-8 shows the final formatted stripe set. (Notice the skip between the CD-ROM with drive E: and the set with drive G:—a network drive was mapped to F:.) Simply disconnect the mapped drive and reassign a new drive letter with the tools in DA.

Once a RAID set has been set up, you can save the array information to a floppy drive. This is a mandatory procedure in case you ever lose any information about the set and need to re-create it (see Figure 8-9).

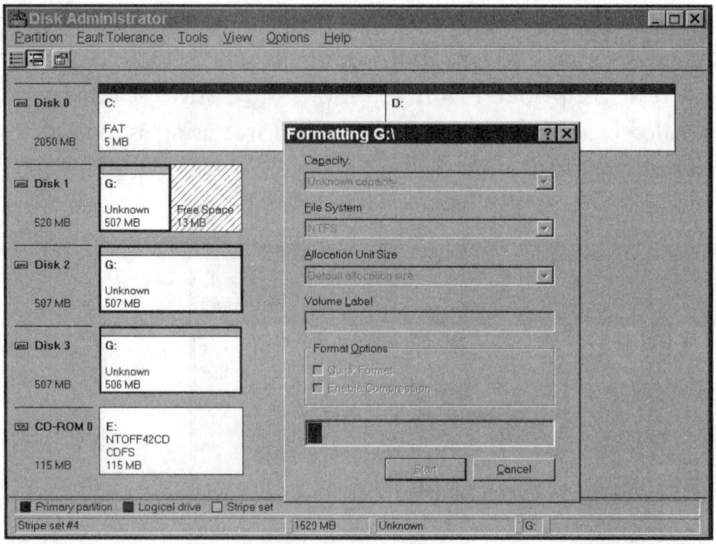

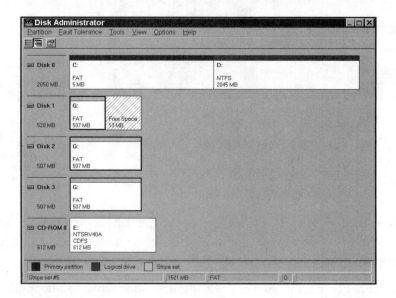

FIGURE 8-7

Formatting the stripe set with Disk Administrator. Notice that all partitions are of equal size. The largest drive has 13MB free space.

FIGURE 8-8

The finalized and formatted stripe set on the Alpha server.

To create a RAID 1 or RAID 5 set, use the procedure just described. After selecting the drives, choose Fault Tolerance | Mirror or Fault Tolerance | Create Stripe Set with Parity. Figure 8-10 shows the creation of a stripe set with parity (RAID 5).

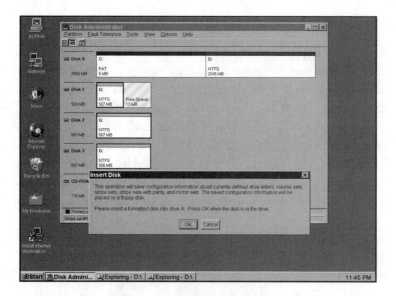

FIGURE 8-9

This figure displays the save feature available for arrays. If you choose to use any stripe set based on the built-in tools in NT, this step is mandatory.

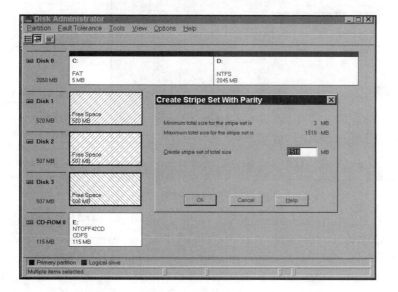

FIGURE 8-10

Creating a RAID 5 array in Disk Administrator. Note the same ability to alter the size of the set as seen in RAID 0.

TIP: When you use three drives to set up a RAID 5 array, the actual space available for data is only two of the drives. In all parity drive sets, one drive can be considered the parity drive.

Setting Up RAID in Hardware

For all practical purposes, RAID is strictly a SCSI implementation. This of course brings us back to system independence. If you create a hardware device that in turn creates and controls a disk array independent of NT, then Windows NT should accept the configuration communicated to the system by the controller. Figure 8-11 shows a view of Disk Administrator running on an NT server. Notice that drive C: is listed as a 1530MB hard drive. This drive was created on a Mylex DAC960 and is a RAID 0 drive composed of three drives. All control of I/Os and overhead is maintained by cache on the controller. Furthermore, the controller has a RISC processor. It should be obvious that recovery from disaster in RAID 5 is far easier to regenerate than in software-based RAID.

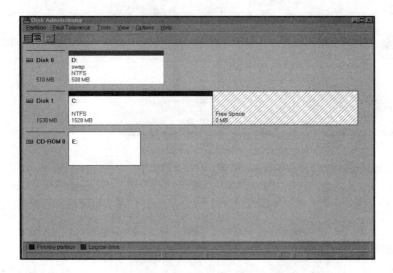

FIGURE 8-11

A hardware-maintained RAID 0 array is seen here in Disk Administrator. Note the absence of a stripe set appearance.

Hardware RAID exists in several configurations. You can obtain a RAID controller from Mylex, DPT, AMI, and a few other vendors. These allow you to attach drives and build your own RAID enclosure. You can also purchase preconfigured RAID enclosures. These also come in different configurations. Of interest here is the emergence of Auto-RAID, which asks you several questions and offers the best RAID configuration for your situation. In the next year or so, these Plug and Play-like RAID setups will become more common.

Entry-Level RAID Enclosure

These configurations consist of an external enclosure with a power supply, drives, and SCSI controller. Many of these enclosures are quite adequate for small LANs, but they don't offer much fault tolerance to an enclosure crash. The second level is a redundant level. There are two power supplies and the system is designed to handle an enclosure disaster. The upper-level RAID arrays offer internal power supplies to the bus, allowing data to be written to the drives. In reality, what becomes the major issue is how much you're willing to spend to provide system integrity. The top tier of hardware support is found in the clustering now provided by Digital Equipment. This clustering consists of RAID enclosures with dual controllers that can be attached to two separate computers. Failure of one brings about an automatic switch to the other.

Some RAID Facts

Table 8-1 shows a comparison of the performance of RAID levels based on the use of four gigabyte Barracuda drives from Seagate. All calculations are based on standard formulas.

Table 8-1   Summary of performance with wide SCSI hard drives.

Factor	RAID 1	RAID 5
Capacity for use	16GB	16GB
Number of drives	8	5
Overhead	50%	20%
Concurrent reads	8	5
Concurrent writes	4	2.5
Maximum random reads	575	360
Maximum random writes	285	135

Most discussions of RAID use mean time values to discuss fault tolerance. The common mean time values used to discuss RAID functionality are as follows:

- ◆ MTBF—Mean time before failure (before any component in the system fails). In general, this value predicts the frequency of repair of a system or system component.

- MTRF—Mean time to reduced function. This reflects a loss of a component that causes a reduced functionality in the array. Data can still be accessed but at noticeably inferior levels of performance.

- MTDA—Mean time of data availability. This is the mean time to failure of non-redundant components, causing the data to simply become unavailable.

- MTBDL—Mean time between data loss. The average time before components fail, resulting in loss of both data and error correction.

- MTBFR—Mean time between failure and recovery. Obviously, this is the true test of fault tolerance, and is usually ignored in the planning of RAID systems. In reality, this factor is perhaps the most salient of them all.

Although these five values seem somewhat obscure, they are the true predictors of fault tolerant storage methods. As one might predict, using the operating system to provide RAID levels results in very low mean time values and repair values.

There are a few numbers that you should know. MTBF (Mean Time Between Failures) values for common system components (all numbers are based on standard industry figures):

Hard drive	300,000-500,000 hours
Adapter	200,000-300,000 hours
Array controller	300,000-1,000,000 hours
Power supply	50,000-300,000 hours

As you can see from this list, parts that you don't expect to fail (for example, the power supply) are perhaps the first to fail. As you might expect, as the number of components increases, there's a corresponding decrease in the MTBF. As a conservative estimate, four hard drives in an independent array might have 100,000 operation hours of actual use. Five drives configured as RAID 5 (same storage space as the four independent drives) might have 75,000, and eight drives configured as RAID 1 would have only 50,000 operation hours. Conversely, the time to data loss would be the exact opposite. The independent drives would get 100,000 hours of use. In a RAID 5 array, two drives would have to be lost at the same time; in RAID 1, four drives would have to be lost. These redundancies provide great data protection, but need more repairs. These factors weigh very heavily in determining your plan for fault tolerance.

The performance issues that count now are the MTDA and the MTBFR. If you lose a power supply (high risk), you'll lose access to the data until the power is restored. Clearly, redundant power supplies are a good start at eliminating a common failure problem. The optimal design would be dual power supplies with full power redundancy.

True fault tolerance is dictated by the MTBFR. In the ideal situation, this number would be zero. Component failure would never be seen, because the redundancy would provide seamless switchover. Unfortunately, many high-end hardware solutions are so dramatic in their ability to repair that Administrators aren't aware of the problem until a second component fails. For this reason, it's essential to have a decent messaging system to alert the user of failures.

The use of software RAID increases dramatically the time between failure and repair. In some cases, the repair simply can't be made. In such cases, a new installation of the OS must be done and the data contained on the RAID drives restored from tape. In such cases, there is always a gap between the backup and the restore; hence, data is never up-to-date. In hardware configurations, the RAID can actually fix itself if there are spare drives present. The parity information is used to fix the missing drive; at this time, there's a system slowdown.

The latest high-end RAID configurations actually allow real-time configuration and repair. Drives can be added and RAID levels switched totally independently of the operating system. One such example of this type of enclosure is the SuperFlex 3000/DRG system from Storage Dimensions. Obviously, you pay a premium for such a system. On the other hand, being able to dynamically expand and configure might be very important to a business that can't afford downtime.

One word of caution should be given to the use of cached controllers. Typically NT doesn't get along with RAM on controllers. In this case, however, the RAM is being used to handle the RAID overhead. The latest array controllers like the Mylex DAC960PD use 15 nsec SRAM (Static RAM). Generally speaking, 16MB RAM on the controller should be adequate.

Practical Solutions

Assuming that money is limited, some measures can be taken to keep the MTBFR to a minimum. First of all, obtain a dual-channel SCSI controller and mirror the boot drive. Prepare a boot floppy that will allow you to boot to either the primary or the secondary drive. This will provide a means of booting into a viable copy of NT and then accessing an external RAID array. The overhead is present but is acceptable.

If you don't want to use mirroring, there are other alternatives. First of all, you'll still maintain your data on a RAID 5 enclosure. You can protect the data by using an online data replicator such as Octopus. The top of the line Octopus product supports automatic switchover. If system 1 fails, system 2 simply takes its place.

Ideally, you would design the server in such a manner that the operating system was on a hardware mirror and the database on a separate RAID 5 enclosure. This design would maximize redundancy safety. It's possible with some devices to do a three-way mirror.

If money is no object, the dual controller configurations allow system 1 and system 2 to share the same hard drives. Using clustering, you are protected locally—combined with Octopus, you can actually replicate the system to a distant cluster.

Optimizing Disk Performance

In any system, there's always a balance between cost/performance and risk. If speed is your main concern, RAID 0 becomes an option, but the data on the RAID will be in serious jeopardy of loss. The best overall strategy to optimize performance is to separate drives and devices, based on speed and function.

Disk and Controller Strategies

Windows NT functions to a large extent via thread and thread handling. Each thread is assigned a priority; a thread with a higher priority can interrupt a thread with a lower priority. In fact, a client thread that spawns a server thread is preempted by the server thread. (This is why video and printer drivers have been moved to ring 0, to avoid unnecessary thread disruption.) Ideally, you optimize NT by providing separate paths for disruptive threads.

First of all, place the operating system and its page file on a controller or channel by itself. You can also place utilities and related applications on this drive, but use only applications that aren't speed-sensitive.

Secondly, place all data and applications on a separate drive on a different controller or channel. For example, a convenient entry-level server would have a 2GB boot drive on channel A of an Adaptec 3940uw and all applications on a larger drive (for example,

4GB) on channel B. Because this card allows multiplexing, both channels can be active at nearly the same time. In this manner, activation of the page file on channel A won't be very preemptive (destructive) to tasks on B.

> **TIP:** A page file is supposed to be equal to the amount of RAM on your system plus 12MB, necessary for NT to run. Therefore, if you have 64MB RAM, your page file should be 76MB. In reality, having twice the memory seems to be a better choice. If you have 128MB RAM on a dual Pentium Pro 200, you need 256MB of page file.

Finally, place all slow devices on a separate controller. For this configuration, you can use a 3940u and put DAT drives and CD-ROMs on one channel, and devices such as a CD-R on the other channel. Setting up systems with hardware as described here can dramatically improve computer performance.

Where to Go Next

This chapter deals with the intricacies of drives and other storage devices in Windows NT. The differences between SCSI and EIDE are discussed in detail. Understanding the components and what they can do enables you to set up systems with decent performance. No longer will you suffer serious disk trashing and system slow downs.

For more useful information on drives and bus configuration, consult the following sources:

- ◆ The Intel Web site at www.intel.com has excellent information on processors and bus configurations. Be prepared to search diligently because documents can be well hidden.

- ◆ The Web site at www.cem.ch/HIS/fcs/storage.htm has excellent information about FC-AL drives and companies.

- ◆ The Adaptec Web site (www.adaptec.com) presents some excellent information on FireWire, as well as other SCSI-related data.

Chapter | 9

Managing NT Servers

In This Chapter:

- Using the Server Manager
- Controlling Resource Sharing
- Controlling Notification and Messaging
- Controlling NT Services
- Controlling Directory Replication

How do I...

Windows NT servers can do a lot: share files and printers, offer logon and security services, give network users access to a range of data. As a direct result of this flexibility, there's a lot to learn about administering and managing computers running NTS.

This chapter starts by introducing you to the NT Server Manager application, the central point for administering your servers, and covers the following topics:

- The Server Manager and its capabilities
- How to share file system resources from the NT desktop, the Explorer, and the Server Manager
- How to regulate resource usage by setting permissions and monitoring users
- How to control directory replication and other system services on servers in your domain

Let's begin by examining what the Server Manager application can do to help ease your administrative workload.

Using the Server Manager

You can think of the Server Manager as a central control console that can configure any NT workstation or server in your domain. Server Manager provides you with a single interface that enables you to monitor and control the operation of computers in your domain. All of its capabilities duplicate what you can do with individual tools, but Server Manager offers it wrapped up in a single package.

For any server or workstation in your domain, you can use the Server Manager to do all of the following:

 ◆ See what shared resources the computer is offering, and which users and computers are connected to them

 ◆ Create new shares, change permissions on existing shares, or stop sharing

 ◆ Start, stop, or configure NT services running on workstation or server

 ◆ Use directory replication to synchronize data between machines automatically

 ◆ Send messages to users on the workstation or server

 ◆ Control which events cause administrative alerts to be broadcast or logged

> **NOTE:** Server Manager also allows you to promote or demote domain controllers and add or remove domain accounts for computers. These features are discussed in Chapter 15, "Planning and Using Domains and Workgroups."

Server Manager Basics

Microsoft adopted a standard look and feel for all the NTS Manager utilities, so the Server Manager looks very much like the User Manager for Domains and the other Manager applications. The main window for the Server Manager is shown in Figure 9-1. The window's title bar indicates the domain you're looking at; if you restrict display to workstations or servers only, the title bar indicates that fact as well. The Computer column lists the NetBIOS name of each machine displayed, the Type column tells you its type (PDC, BDC, server, and so on), and the Description column displays whatever description the computer owner has specified (if any).

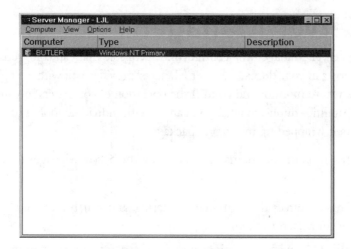

FIGURE 9-1

The Server Manager provides a simple way to watch and control servers and workstations within your domain.

The Computer menu's commands operate on the selected machine; they're discussed in the following sections.

You can control which types of machines appear in the list by using the View menu. Choose View | Servers to display only NTS servers, View | Workstations to display only workstations, or View | All to show all machines in the domain (even Windows 95 and Windows for Workgroups machines). You can also restrict the display to machines that are actually members of the domain you're interested in with the View | Show Domain Members Only command. Finally, as with all the other Manager utilities, you can refresh the list at any time with the View | Refresh command.

The Options menu—another fixture of NT's Manager utilities—enables you to tell the Manager when you're using a slow connection, whether you want the settings from this session to be saved for the next one, and what display font you prefer. The Options | Low Speed Connection option is very useful over slow links, because it tells the Manager not to refresh as often. Each refresh generates a wave of network traffic, as the Server Manager has to send out a query to see who's on the network.

> **TIP:** The Low Speed Connection option is useful even when you're not using a low-speed network, because it reduces overall network traffic. If your computers aren't constantly going up and down, you may not need continuous updates and can save the bandwidth.

Administering Remote Computers

Server Manager is particularly valuable because it allows you to administer machines remotely in your domain. Any of its commands can be used on a remote machine by first selecting the machine you want to administer in the Server Manager main window. You can control machines in other domains where you have administrative rights, also, by choosing the domain of interest with the Computer | Select Domain command, and then selecting the appropriate computer.

Controlling Resource Sharing

Windows networking clients can individually control which of their file and print resources they share, but Server Manager also provides the domain administrator a way to control sharing of resources on machines within the domain. Equally importantly, you can monitor which users are using which shared resources.

Your primary vehicle for controlling sharing in Server Manager is the Properties dialog box (see Figure 9-2), which appears when you choose Computer | Properties or select Properties from the pop-up menu that appears when you right-click a computer in the Server Manager main window.

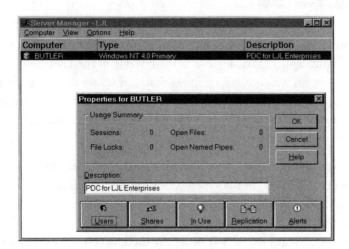

FIGURE 9-2

The Properties dialog box summarizes resource usage on the selected computer and gives you a row of command buttons to use for calling up more details.

The five buttons at the bottom of the dialog each display a dialog box with more information on the selected item, as well as buttons to control that item's status. The Users, Shares, and In Use buttons are discussed in the following sections; the Replication and Alerts buttons are covered later in the chapter.

Monitoring Connected Users

Using the Users button in the Properties dialog box displays the User Sessions dialog box (see Figure 9-3), which shows which users on which computers are connected to shares on the target machine. It also shows a summary of all the resources on the target machine, so that you can see at a glance which shares are getting the most (and least) use.

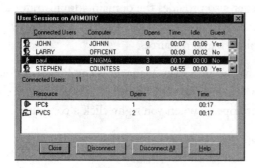

FIGURE 9-3

The User Sessions dialog box shows you which users are using which shared resources; it also gives you a way to quickly disconnect any user of a share.

Clicking the Shares button in the Properties dialog box displays the Shared Resources dialog box, shown in Figure 9-4. This dialog box is the obverse of the User Sessions dialog box; instead of focusing on which users are using shares, it shows the shares first, and then who is using them. Each share is listed with its name, the number of current connections, and the path to the file or device being shared. The middle of the dialog box lists individual users who are using the selected share.

Choosing the In Use button in the Properties dialog box shows you only the shares that are currently in use by domain users (in the Open Resources dialog box, shown in Figure 9-5). This feature boils down the content of the Shared Resources and User Sessions dialog boxes into the really important stuff—who's doing what with which shares. This data gives you insight into which shares are heavily or lightly used, which in turn can tell you when it's time to move resources to another, less-heavily-loaded server. It also enables you to find out which users are actually using resources as opposed to just staying connected to them—valuable knowledge indeed, because Windows NT may be licensed per user in your installation!

The Open Resources dialog box lists each open resource, along with who opened it, what permissions are active (read, delete, execute, and so on), the number of locks on the resource, and the path to the directory, file, or device that's actually in use.

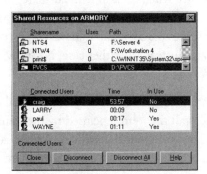

FIGURE 9-4

The Shared Resources dialog box summarizes all the resources being made available by a particular machine.

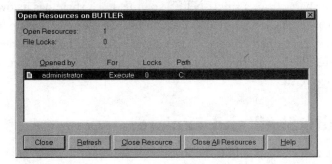

FIGURE 9-5

The Open Resources dialog box shows which users are doing what.

The Close Resource and Close All Resources buttons in the Open Resources dialog box forcibly close connections to the selected resource without affecting other connections.

CAUTION: These buttons are dangerous because forcing a close may interrupt a data transfer in progress or cause a client or server to fail. Use them sparingly.

Creating New Shares

One of the key features of NT's networking is the ability of individual users to share or stop sharing resources at any time. Users have full control over what data they offer to others, because they can share (or not) any item on the computer. In addition, they also have a fair degree of control over the security of their shares. Because peer sharing is decentralized, though, it's hard to track resource usage or maintain good security; in addition, it can be difficult to realize good performance when each individual shared machine, and its network connection, are also being used for everyday work tasks. To solve these problems, many organizations centralize their shares onto a small number of powerful servers and let users access files from these shares instead. In either case, NT provides a consistent user interface for creating new shares.

Shares can contain a single directory or the entire contents of a *volume* (a physical or logical disk). When a share is created, it includes all the items enclosed by the item being shared. There's no way to exclude contained items from being shared. You can create new shares for individual items contained within another shared item and give the new shares different permissions.

Figure 9-6 shows a set of shares from a single NTFS volume. Each share has its own permissions; for example, SourceCode is accessible to users in the Development group but no one else. Notice that the share named Pending doesn't allow access to the directories that contain it. Of equal interest is the fact that the BugDatabase share allows users to use the Defects share, but not vice versa.

Sharing from the Shell and Explorer

The fastest way to create a new share is find the folder or volume you want to share and right-click its icon. Choose Sharing from the pop-up menu, and the object's Properties dialog box will appear, set to the Sharing tab. An example Properties dialog box is shown in Figure 9-7. To start sharing the object, deselect the Shared As radio button. If you choose to share, you can specify a share name and comment in the appropriate fields; this information will be displayed to network browsers. The default share name is the same as the folder or volume name (although you'll get a warning if the name is longer than eight characters).

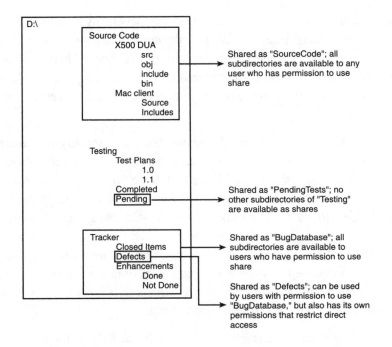

Shared as "SourceCode"; all subdirectories are available to any user who has permission to use share

Shared as "PendingTests"; no other subdirectories of "Testing" are available as shares

Shared as "BugDatabase"; all subdirectories are available to users who have permission to use share

Shared as "Defects"; can be used by users with permission to use "BugDatabase," but also has its own permissions that restrict direct access

FIGURE 9-6

Each shared directory has its own set of permissions.

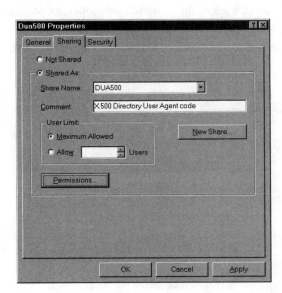

FIGURE 9-7

The Sharing tab is where you set sharing options for a new or existing share.

The User Limit section of the Sharing tab lets you specify how many concurrent users can use the share. If you select Maximum Allowed, the number of connections allowed will depend on the number of available client access licenses (although shares offered by NTW machines are limited to 10 concurrent users.) You can also specify an absolute number of connections, but if it's larger than the number of licenses the license limit will apply instead.

Choosing the New Share button pops up a dialog box that allows you to create another share for the same resource. You can specify a different name, comment, connection limit, and permissions. At first glance, this seems like an odd capability—the new share is just another reference to the original object being shared. However, you can use multiple shares of the same object to grant different permissions to different groups of users, or to restrict the number of users in a particular group who can use the share. For example, you might grant unrestricted access to your Developers group for a share containing source code, but allow read-only access to a maximum of five users from the TechWriters group. This approach means that you can avoid lumping together all the groups that need access into one new group. Instead, create a share for each group.

Once you create multiple shares for a resource, the Share Name field on the Sharing tab becomes a drop-down list, so you can select the share whose properties you want to change. The Remove Share button also appears; it will remove the share entry for the currently selected share. Figure 9-8 shows the sharing options for a directory with more than one share.

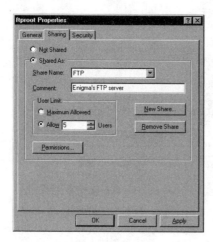

FIGURE 9-8

Adding multiple shares to a single resource enables additional sharing controls.

Sharing from the Server Manager

You can also manage shares offered by a domain computer by selecting it in Server Manager's main window and using the Computer | Shared Directories command. The Shared Directories dialog box (pictured in Figure 9-9) lists all currently shared directories for the selected machine, including the special administrative shares like IPC$ and C$. This dialog box allows you to change the properties and permissions of shares, create new shares, or stop sharing a resource at any time.

The administrative shares enable you, as administrator, to connect to computers and administer them, even if nothing is shared. By default, Windows NT creates a named share for each drive letter; the name is the drive letter plus a dollar sign. Thus, a machine with drives C:, D:, E:, and F: will have administrative shares named C$, D$, E$, and F$. Administrative shares don't appear when you browse a computer; you must explicitly name the share you want when connecting. In addition to the shares for disks, Windows NT creates shares for remote administration (the IPC$ and RPC$ shares) and printer management.

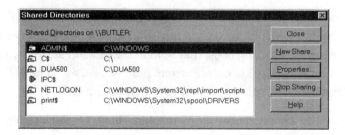

FIGURE 9-9

The Shared Directories dialog box shows you a complete list of all the shared resources on the server you're viewing.

To create a new share, click the New Share button and specify the share name, the path to the shared resource on disk, and the number of users you want to be able to connect simultaneously. You can also specify an optional comment that users browsing the network will see in their browse list next to the share name. Once you've established your share settings, you can use the Permissions button in the New Share dialog box to set the share's permissions, or you can click OK to create the share immediately.

Setting Share Permissions

You can't change permissions of administrative shares. However, you can use the System Policy Editor to keep the system from creating some administrative shares. Full details on using the System Policy Editor are provided in the section titled "Setting Domain-Wide User Policies " in Chapter 16, "Managing Users and Groups in Domains." To turn off administrative shares, perform the following steps:

1. Start the System Policy Editor and open the policy for the computer (workstation or server) that you want to modify. You can open the Default Computer policy to set policy for all machines in the domain.

2. In the Properties dialog box, select the Windows NT Network item, and select its Sharing subitem. You'll see two settings: Create Hidden Drive Shares (Workstation) and Create Hidden Drive Shares (Server).

3. Turn the options on or off as appropriate; when they're off, Windows NT won't create administrative shares for disks. When you're finished, click OK. The policy update will be sent to all domain computers at the next update.

NT allows you to assign permissions to shared resources in a number of ways. But all the methods share a common dialog box for actually setting the permissions. Don't confuse share permissions with file system permissions; they're independent and are set by two different methods. (For more information on file system permissions, see "The NT Security Model" in Chapter 12, "Windows NT Security Fundamentals.")

No matter which method you use to actually set permissions, there are some things you should remember when doing so:

♦ The default setting of Everyone having Full Control access is probably too permissive for most uses. Unfortunately, there's no way to keep it from being the default. Be sure to set appropriate permissions when you first create a new share; allowing the Users and Domain Users groups to have Read permission is probably a reasonable start for most data.

♦ Because permissions for shares within a domain depend on domain security, users on computers that aren't part of the domain (such as Macintosh, Net-Ware, or LAN Manager users) will need access to a domain account so that they can supply a valid user name and password to reach the share.

♦ Accounts that don't have the "Access this computer from network" right for the machine holding the share won't be able to use it.

> **NOTE:** For information on what permissions are available, and some reasonable defaults for your shares, see the section in Chapter 12 called "Permissions Versus Rights."

Using the Access Through Share Permissions Dialog Box

The Access Through Share Permissions dialog box is shown in Figure 9-10. The Access Through Share field shows the share name you used when you created the share, and the Owner field shows the account name of the owner (if an account has taken ownership of the directory being shared). The Name list shows all users or groups with access to the share, along with what permissions they've been granted.

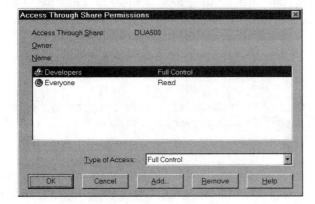

FIGURE 9-10

The Access Through Share Permissions dialog box is used everywhere you can set permissions on shares.

> **NOTE:** For details on using the Add Users and Groups dialog box, see the section "Controlling Group Membership and Properties" in Chapter 6, "Managing User and Group Accounts."

You can change permissions for an existing entry in the Name list by using the Type of Access drop-down list. You remove user permissions with the Remove button. To add entries to the list, use the Add button, which brings up the standard Add Users and Groups dialog box, with one addition—the dialog box features a drop-down list at the bottom that allows you to select what access you want the newly added users or groups to have.

Setting Permissions from the Shell and Explorer

NT 4.0's user interface is much more consistent than its predecessors, so the method you use to get to the Permissions dialog box is the same whether you apply it in the shell or from within the Explorer. Right-click the folder you want to share, and then click Sharing. The Properties dialog box for the share you selected will open to the Sharing tab; click the Permissions button to display the Access Through Share Permissions dialog box, and then set permissions as described in the preceding section.

Setting Permissions from the Server Manager

You can edit the properties of any listed share by selecting it in the Shared Directories dialog box (refer to Figure 9-9) and clicking the Properties button. The Share Properties dialog box (whose contents are identical to the Sharing tab of the Properties dialog box for a directory) enables you to change the path, comment, user connection limit, or permissions of the share.

> **NOTE:** You can't change the share name reported to other computers without removing the share and recreating it with a new name.

When you set permissions on a share through the Share Properties dialog box, you'll see the standard Access Through Share Permissions dialog box (refer to Figure 9-10). By default, new shares allow Everyone (one of NT's built-in groups) to have full access to your files. You can add and remove permissions for individual accounts, domain accounts, and domain groups, using the Add and Remove buttons.

Disconnecting Users From Shares

Under some circumstances, you might need to force users to disconnect from shares they're using. For example, you might be shutting down a machine to replace a failed or failing component, or you might have to restore data from tape while users are connected to the share where that data resides. There are a number of ways to forcibly disconnect users from the shares they're using:

- The Disconnect and Disconnect All buttons in the User Sessions dialog box (refer to Figure 9-3) allow you to summarily kick off one or all users of a selected resource. Just select the connected user or resource, and use the appropriate button.

- The Shared Resources dialog box (refer to Figure 9-4) also includes Disconnect and Disconnect All buttons, which work like the ones in the User Sessions dialog box.

CAUTION: Never disconnect users without warning them with the messaging facilities discussed in this section. Abrupt disconnection can cause data loss for the client *and* the server, because data requests may not be completed before the connection is lost.

Controlling Notification and Messaging

NT provides two services for sending and receiving alerts: *Alerter* and *Messenger*. The Alerter sends alert messages to other machines on the network the sending of these alerts can be triggered by security events, user session problems, printer problems, or power failures (when a UPS is connected). In addition, you can send messages using the Server Manager or the Server Control Panel. The Messenger service receives messages sent from other machines running the Alerter service. Normally, both of these services are always running on NTS and NTW machines.

TIP: You can send messages to Macintoshes in your domain, too, but you must do so from the MacFile control panel. See Chapter 23, "Interoperating with Macintosh Clients," for more details.

Controlling Outgoing Alerts

The Alerts button in the Properties dialog box (refer to Figure 9-2) provides a way for you to specify where administrative alerts are sent. Choosing the Alerts button opens the Alerts dialog box, as depicted in Figure 9-11. The Send Administrative Alerts To list shows which machines and users will get alert messages; you can add or remove items from this list using the New Computer or Username field and the Add and Remove buttons.

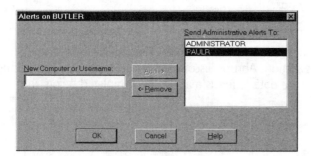

FIGURE 9-11

Specify who gets notification of administrative alerts with the Alerts dialog box.

TIP: Every situation that can trigger an administrative alert also makes a record in the Event Log. You can safely turn off administrative alerts for most occurrences because the Event Log is keeping them for later review.

Sending Messages to Domain Users

You can also send messages to users connected to any machine in the domain. The message will be caught and displayed by a service on the client. This feature is very useful in conjunction with the Disconnect buttons in the Shared Resources and User Sessions dialog boxes, since you should always notify remote users before disconnecting them. (See the earlier section "Controlling Resource Sharing" for more details on forcibly disconnecting share users.)

To send a message, use the Computer | Send Message command. When the Send Message dialog box shown in Figure 9-12 appears, type your message into the Message field, and click OK to send it.

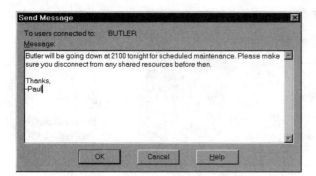

FIGURE 9-12

The Send Message dialog box lets you send a message to all users connected to a domain computer.

> **CAUTION:** Users who aren't connected to a computer when you send a message won't get the message. Send Message is best used for short-notice alerts announcing reboots,or notifying users that a WAN link has failed.

Controlling NT Services

Each NT workstation or server in your domain will be running a number of NT services, such as the Browser, Workstation, and Alerter services. Many third-party software components, like the popular EMWAC World-Wide Web server, are delivered as services as well. Services run all the time, whether or not a user is logged into the console. Users can log on across the network and interactively without affecting the services' behavior, although a logged-in user can control services if she has adequate permissions. When services are run using the built-in System account, they can be run securely without a user logged in at the console by running under the System account. Services can be administered by users logged into the console of the machine that's running them (via the Control Panel's Services applet) or through the Server Manager.

The user interface for the two components is identical. This section covers the Services dialog box from Server Manager, but all the instructions also apply to the Services Control Panel applet. The Server Manager's Computer | Services command displays the Services dialog box, which looks exactly like the Services applet. This dialog box allows you to start, stop, and configure services on a particular machine (see Figure 9-13).

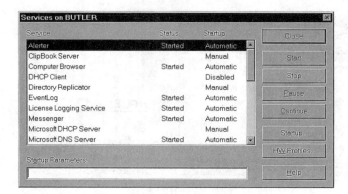

FIGURE 9-13

The Services dialog box shows you what services are running on the target and lets you start, stop, or configure any of them.

The Services dialog box contains a list of all the installed services on a machine. Each entry tells you the vendor's service name (which usually bears no resemblance to the cryptic 8.3 name of the service executable), whether it's running or not, and under what conditions it will be started. The buttons on the right-hand side of the window allow you to control individual services. Here's what they do:

- The Start and Stop buttons start and stop the selected service. NTS requires you to stop its system services (including but not limited to DNS, DHCP, and WINS) before restoring their data files from a backup. You must stop services before you remove or overwrite their executable files; this means that you must be careful to stop a service before you upgrade, remove, or replace it.

- The Pause and Continue buttons suspend and resume execution of a service. While a service is paused, it can't answer any requests and consumes no CPU time, but it's not stopped—just sleeping. (NTS actually pauses the service by blocking all of its threads.)

- The Startup button and the Startup Parameters box give you a way to control when the service starts up and what arguments are passed to it when it does. Whatever parameters you put in the Startup Parameters box are passed to the service on its command line when it starts. Figure 9-14 shows the Service dialog box.

FIGURE 9-14

*Use the Service dialog box
to specify when a service
runs and what account it
runs under; in this example,
the Directory Replicator
service is being set up to
run automatically.*

The options in the Startup Type section of the dialog box control when the
service is started, and the Log On As options control what user account the
service runs as. Services normally run under the standard system account;
when they do, you can choose whether to allow them to interact with the
desktop by posting messages, presenting dialog boxes, and so on. Other
services, though, such as the replicator and many WWW server services,
expect to run as a particular account. You can allow them to do so by selecting
the This Account radio button and choosing an account from the provided
list. You'll also have to supply the password for the account to be used.

CAUTION: Remember that a service running under an account has the same
security privileges as that account! Be careful about running services in anything
other than the standard system account.

◆ The H<u>W</u> Profiles button in the Services dialog box enables you to use the
resulting Service dialog box shown in Figure 9-15 to specify whether the
selected service should be enabled or disabled for a particular hardware
profile. For example, you might want to disable the DHCP client service
when you're running your notebook in its away-from-the-desk
configuration. For each hardware profile you've registered, you can enable
or disable the selected service with the <u>E</u>nable and <u>D</u>isable buttons.

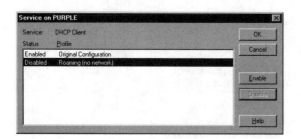

FIGURE 9-15

You can specify that services be enabled or disabled, depending on your hardware configuration.

One final note: Changes that you make in Server Manager's Services dialog box are immediate. The target machine will receive and execute the instructions immediately, so be careful about what you're doing. For example, if you stop a service on another machine, that service will stop without any chance for you to confirm your command; if you mistakenly stop a service or disconnect a share, you'll need to use Server Manager to redo whatever you mistakenly did.

Controlling Directory Replication

It's often desirable to synchronize data between servers. For example, logon scripts, user profiles, and Web pages are most useful when they can be accessed transparently from any of a number of servers on a network. NT offers an automatic synchronization service that works between directories on different machines. This service, called the *Directory Replicator* (or just the *replicator*), copies changed files from an *export server* to an *import server*. You can think of the exporter as the source and the importer as the target, if you like. Any NT machine can be an importer, but only NTS machines can export data; because this is a server function, you use the Server Manager to control it.NTS machines can actually be both importers and exporters. A single NTS machine can re-export the same data it imports, or it can export a completely different set of data.

Figure 9-16 shows export and import relationships between four computers in a domain. By default, the export server on ARMORY exports all subdirectories of the base path to all importers in the domain. FORTRESS exports a different base path to one machine only; that machine, ENIGMA, is running Windows NT Workstation, so it can import but not export data.

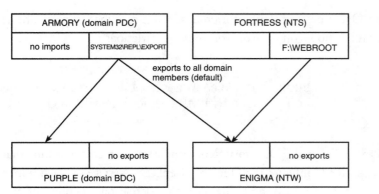

FIGURE 9-16

Domain computers can export and import data in a variety of ways.

The replicator copies only files that have changed since the last replication, and it won't copy files that are open. It can back up only ordinary files and directories, not special files like the NT Registry or a SQL Server database. Because of these limitations, it's not suitable for use as a general-purpose backup tool; however, replication is perfect for mirroring the contents of a Web server, FTP site, or other service. It's also by far the best way to replicate logon scripts throughout a domain, so that all users can use their individual logon scripts on any workstation.

Understanding the Directory Replicator Service

The Directory Replicator service is a single NT service that runs on both exporters and importers. The same NTS machine can be both an importer and an exporter. On exporters, the service periodically checks the export folder (the default folder is %SYSTEM-ROOT%\SYSTEM32\REPL\EXPORT) and sends a broadcast notification when its contents change. Each exporter can make available for export only a single folder and its enclosed items.

When running as an importer, the service listens for change notification messages. When it receives one, it initiates copying of the changed files over the network, after waiting a random length of time. Because all importers choose random wait periods, the exporter doesn't get overloaded immediately on broadcasting a change notification.

To use the replicator, you must enable the replication service by using the Services dialog box described earlier. Before you do so, there are two things you must do. The first step is to set up an account for the service to use. The replicator account must be a domain account (so that all machines in the domain can use it), and it must be a member of the domain's Backup Operators and Replicator groups. Make sure that its password never expires, and that it has no logon time or workstation restrictions.

> **NOTE:** For complete instructions on adding user accounts with the User Manager for Domains, see the section called "Using User Manager for Domains" in Chapter 6.

Next, you need to configure the Directory Replicator service on each machine that will be an importer or exporter. Configure the Directory Replicator service on each importer or exporter to start up automatically and to log on as the user account you just created. You can use the instructions in the earlier section "Controlling NT Services" to do this from a single Server Manager session on one of your machines. The Server Manager will automatically start the Directory Replicator service if it's not already running on a machine you've set up as an importer or exporter, but you must still set it to use the proper account and to start automatically after a reboot.

Once you've created an account and enabled the service, you're ready to configure your importers and exporters.

Setting Up Export Computers

Exporters provide data that's copied to importers. Only NTS machines can be exporters. Each exporter can export only a single directory, called the *base directory*, and its subdirectories; by default, the base directory is as follows:

%SYSTEMROOT%\SYSTEM32\REPL\EXPORT

Because you can export only directories that are children of the base path, you may want to use a different directory as the base path. You can also configure your applications to store the data you want replicated in subdirectories of the base path.

> **NOTE:** Remember that every file in the directory tree rooted at the base path will be copied to the importers whenever the file changes. This process can quickly overwhelm your network, so be careful about what files and directories you put in the base path.

> **TIP:** The Directory Replicator is smart enough to copy new files that are added to the base path, so you don't have to have any files there when you configure your exporters.

Configuring an export server requires three simple steps, in addition to the two steps listed above:

1. In Server Manager, use the Computer | Properties command to open the Properties dialog box (refer to Figure 9-2), and then click the Replication button to display the Directory Replicator dialog box.

2. Select the Export Directories radio button. In the From Path box, enter the base path you want to use. Remember that you can export only a single directory tree on each NTS server. See Figure 9-17 for an example of how this dialog box looks.

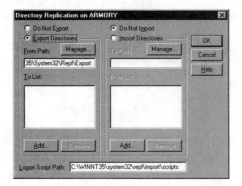

FIGURE 9-17

The Directory Replicator dialog box gives you control over the import and export behavior of any domain computer.

> **NOTE:** The Directory Replicator service doesn't have to have read permission to the files it's replicating, because its account is in the Backup Operators group.

3. Tell the Directory Replicator which machines you want to export to by adding them to the list in the To List box. The default is to export to whatever domain the exporter itself is in; if that's all you want to do, don't change the entries in the To List box.

If you click the Add button, you'll see the standard domain selection dialog box, from which you can select the domain or machine to which you want to export. If you add one or more explicit export targets, you'll turn off the default of exporting to the local domain.

You can take finer control over how exports are performed by using the Manage button to trigger the Manage Exported Directories dialog box (see Figure 9-18). Each exported subdirectory under the base path is listed in the dialog box, along with the subdirectory's name, how many file locks are currently active, how the Stabilize and Subtree settings are set, and how long the directory has been locked (the Directory Replicator service won't replicate locked files).

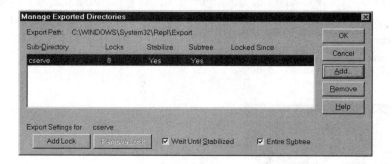

FIGURE 9-18

You can view and set exported directory behavior with the Manage Exported Directories dialog box.

Here's what you can do with the Manage Exported Directories dialog box:

- You can lock or unlock individual subdirectories. If the number of locks on a directory is greater than zero, nothing will be exported from that directory or its subdirectories until the lock count returns to zero. Select the directory you want to lock or unlock, and then use the Add Lock or Remove Lock button to change the lock count for the selected directory. You might lock a subdirectory if you know that its contents will be changing, or if you want to prevent the data it contains from being duplicated elsewhere on the network.

- The default export behavior is to export a file as soon as it is unlocked and has changed since the last export. You can force the Directory Replicator to wait until at least two minutes have passed without changes before exporting anything in a subdirectory. This waiting period reduces network overhead by grouping updates together once the directory's contents have settled. To force this waiting period, select the Wait Until Stabilized check box, or deselect it to allow immediate export of changes.

♦ By default, any subdirectories of the base export path will automatically be exported as well. If you want to limit export to the base directory and the files it contains, deselect the Entire Subtree check box.

Setting Up Import Computers

Importers pull data from the corresponding exporters and give it a safe, redundant home. The copied data goes into a base directory just as with the exporter. The default import base directory is as follows:

`%SYSTEMROOT%\SYSTEM32\REPL\IMPORT`

A single importer can import from one or many exporters; each imported directory is stored as a subdirectory of the base path.

> **CAUTION:** Make sure that the device that holds the importer's base directory has enough space to accept all the files from its exporters. If the Directory Replicator doesn't have enough space, it won't copy the changed files (though it will log an error message in the Event Log).

Configuring an importer is very similar to configuring an exporter. In total, there are three steps to complete to get started (not counting the step of configuring the Directory Replicator service itself):

1. In Server Manager, use the Computer | Properties command to open the Properties dialog box (refer to Figure 9-2), and then click the Replication button to display the Directory Replicator dialog box (refer to Figure 9-17).

2. Select the Import Directories radio button. In the To Path box, enter the base path you want to use. All directories that you import will end up as subdirectories of this base

3. If you want to import directories from machines in a different domain, or only from specific machines, use the Add button under the From List box. As with

exporting, by default NT will allow imports from any machine in the same domain. If you change the contents of the From List box, however, you have to explicitly add the machine's domain back to the list, or the importer won't import from machines in that domain.

> **CAUTION:** The import directories' contents are overwritten every time a replication occurs. Any changes you make to data in the import directories will be lost.

You can also control some per-directory settings for importers. The Manage Imported Directories dialog box, shown in Figure 9-19, is quite similar to its exporter counterpart described earlier.

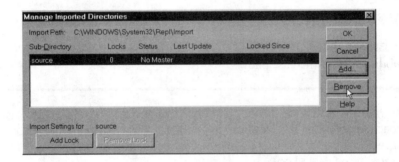

FIGURE 9-19

Like its counterpart for exporters, you can use the Manage Imported Directories dialog box to view and set imported directory behavior.

The per-directory status in the Manage Imported Directories dialog box shows the directory name, lock count, and lock start times just as for exports, but there are two additional items: a status column and a column showing the time of the last update:

- The Status indicator shows the import status for that directory:
    - A blank status indicates that the directory has never been replicated; this is usually due to a misconfiguration of either the exporter or importer.
    - A status of OK means that the importer is getting normal replication updates from its exporter, and that the replicated data matches the original data.

◆ The No master status means that no exporter is exporting to this import directory; this is often the result of someone turning off replication on the export server.

◆ The most serious status is No sync. This code means that files have been replicated, but the data on the exporter and importer don't match. This can happen due to network or server failures, but the most common culprit is an open file on either the importer *or* the exporter. Remember, the Directory Replicator can't replicate open files—when the lock count in the lock column is greater than zero, the directory can't be copied.

◆ The Last Update column shows the time and date of the last successful replication to the directory. If the export server is stabilized, this will indicate only the last update time; if the exporter isn't stabilized, this time will match the time of an individual file in the target base path.

◆ You can add or remove import locks with the Add Lock and Remove Lock buttons (they work like the options in the Manage Exported Directories dialog box). Like export locks, when the lock count on an import directory is greater than zero, nothing will be imported to the directory. Other than that, this dialog box is primarily for viewing—not changing—the import settings.

Additional Registry-Only Replication Settings

Some of the settings that control Directory Replicator behavior exist only in the Registry. While most sites won't need to change these settings, some may. All these keys are in the following location:

HKEY_LOCAL_MACHINE\SYSTEM\CurrentControlSet\Services\Replicator\Parameters

NOTE: For more information on editing data in the Registry, see Chapter 11, "Working with the Windows NT System Registry."

The Interval parameter specifies how often an exporter should check the export directory for changes. The default is 5 minutes, but the value may range from 1 to 60 minutes. If files in your export directory change at predictable intervals (for example, when hourly reports are generated), you can increase this interval to reduce unnecessary checks.

The GuardTime parameter tells the replicator how long to wait since the last file change before sending a change notice. This parameter is used only when the Wait Until Stabilized option is selected in the Manage Exported Directories dialog box. Its value can range from 0 (send changes immediately) to half of the Interval value.

Pulse controls when the exporter will resend change notices. The change notices are sent even when no changes occur, so that importers know whether they missed any updates due to network outages. The value can range from 1 to 10 and is used as a multiplier of Interval. For example, a Pulse value of 3 (the default) combined with an interval of 30 minutes means that redundant change notices will be sent every 90 minutes.

Where to Go Next

This chapter explains how to manage Windows NT servers using the Server Manager tool. In particular, it shows how to create and set permissions on shares, how to control system services, and how to replicate data between servers using the Directory Replicator service. These tasks are often necessary in networks of Windows NT servers.

The next chapter describes how to use Windows NT's management tools such as the Server Manager and User Manager for Domains to manage computers over the network or remotely. It also shows how to use Microsoft's WWW-based management tools.

Here are some other resources that you may find useful at this point:

♦ Chapter 12 explains the fundamentals of Windows NT security, including recommendations for file system permission settings.

♦ Chapters 14 and 15 explain how to plan, configure, and use domains and workgroups to organize servers and computers on your network.

Chapter | 10

NT Server
Management Tools

In This Chapter:

◆ Using the Server Administration Tools

◆ Managing with Simple Network Management Protocol (SNMP)

◆ Managing Remote Sites

How do I...

Though it's true that Windows NT Server can be used as both a file server and as a platform from which to manage the network, most network administrators don't run NT Server as their desktop operating system. Most administrators use Windows NT Workstation or Windows 95 as their desktop operating system. For this reason, Microsoft has provided a method of managing NT from the desktop when that desktop is either Windows 95 or Windows NT Workstation.

Included with Windows NT Server are client-based administration tools that the administrator can install on her workstation and use to manage the NT Server as if she were physically sitting at the console. These tools include the User Manager for Domains, Server Manager, Event Viewer, DHCP Manager, and WINS Manager. These tools should be sufficient to perform most administrative tasks without physically sitting at the server.

> **NOTE:** Previous versions of NT Server included tools that could be used to manage NT from Windows 3.1 and Windows for Workgroups. These tools aren't included with NT 4.0 but can still be used if you can locate them (they're on the NT Server 3.51 CD-ROM).

This chapter covers the following topics:

♦ Installing and using tools from Windows NT 4.0 Workstation and Windows 95

♦ Installing and configuring the SNMP agent in Windows NT Server

♦ Managing remote servers with the server tools

♦ Using the new Web Administration Tool, which enables you to use a standard Web browser to manage most of the server properties

Using the Server Administration Tools

Microsoft provides server management tools for both Windows NT Workstation and Windows 95 on the NT 4.0 Server CD-ROM. These tools include the most-commonly-used administration tools and are installed via the Network Client Administrator tool, located in the Administrative Tools group on the Start menu.

Using Network Client Administrator

The Network Client Administrator is a utility that enables you to copy the server administration tools to a shared directory on your server so that they can be installed from the client. This tool is also used to create client installation disks. (See Chapter 21, "Working with DOS and Windows Clients," for more information on this topic.)

Start the Network Client Administrator by choosing Start | Programs | Administrative Tools to display the opening screen, as shown in Figure 10-1.

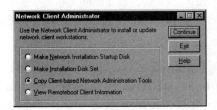

FIGURE 10-1

The Network Client Administrator enables you to copy the server administration tools to an installation directory that can be accessed by the client.

The option called Copy Client-Based Network Administration Tools starts the process of configuring the shared directory on your server. Figure 10-2 shows the next screen in the process.

FIGURE 10-2

Configuring the installation point for the Network Client Administrator utilities.

You have the following options:

♦ Path—The path to the source files for the client administration tools. Point to either the NT Server CD-ROM or a previous installation of server tools.

♦ Share Files—Use this option if you haven't previously shared the files for server tools. This option shares the specified path.

♦ Copy Files to a New Directory, and then Share—This option copies the files from the specified path to the directory you indicate in the Destination Path text box, and then shares that directory with the name you indicate in the Share Name text box.

♦ Use Existing Shared Directory—Select this option when you have previously copied the files to a server and you want to specify that server as the installation point for the administration tools.

After you have selected the appropriate directory, click OK and then Continue. The system will copy the files, configure the directory, and report back when the process is completed (see Figure 10-3).

Click OK to close the dialog box and choose Exit to close Network Client Administrator. The client administration tools have been copied from the CD to the specified directory and are shared with the specified name. You're now ready to install the tools on to the client.

FIGURE 10-3

Once the directory has been configured, the system tells you it's ready to proceed.

Installing the Client Administration Tools

Once the server is configured to share the directory for the client administration tools, you're ready to install them on the client. Windows NT 4.0 ships with client administration tools for both Windows 95 and Windows NT Workstation clients.

The following list describes the tools included for Windows NT Workstation:

DHCP Administrator	Manages DHCP servers within the domain. Its file name is DHCPADMN.EXE.
RAS Administrator	Manages the Remote Access Service (RAS) and RAS users within the domain. Its file name is RASADMIN.EXE.
RPL Manager	Manages the Remote Boot Service on servers within the domain. Its file name is RPLMGR.EXE.
Server Manager	Manages server properties within the domain. Its file name is SRVMGR.EXE.
User Profile Editor	Manages User Profile properties. Its file name is UPEDIT.EXE.
User Manager	Manages user properties within the domain. Its file name is USRMGR.EXE.
WINS Administrator	Manages WINS servers within the domain. Its file name is WINSADMN.EXE.

NOTE: Because Event Viewer is part of NT Workstation, it doesn't need a special version copied for server administration.

These are the tools included for Windows 95:

Event Viewer	Enables you to read the event log on servers within the domain.
Server Manager	Manages server properties within the domain.
User Manager	Manages user properties within the domain.

Regardless of the platform on which you install the tools, you have an extensive help library that covers just about any management topic that you need.

Installing Administrative Tools on Windows NT Workstation

To install the Administrative tools on Windows NT Workstation, make sure that you are logged into the machine as a user with administrative rights. Connect to the shared directory on the server where you installed the client tools, change to the WINNT directory, and run SETUP.EXE. This action launches the client administration tools installation utility, which is simply a DOS batch file (see Figure 10-4). Once the program runs, it tells you to create shortcuts from the desktop for the programs that you want to place on the desktop, such as User Manager for Domains or Server Manager.

FIGURE 10-4

The Client Administration tools for Windows NT Workstation are installed via a DOS command file.

After installing the tools, you need to create shortcuts to the tools so that you can find them more easily when needed. The simplest method is to use Explorer to create a new program group and add that group to the Start menu. For example, to install User

Manager For Domains into a new program group called NT Server Administration, follow these steps:

1. Right-click an empty area of the Windows Taskbar and choose Properties from the pop-up menu.

2. In the Taskbar Properties dialog box, click the Start Menu Programs tab and select the Advanced button to open an Explorer window showing the Start Menu folder.

3. Navigate to the Programs group and double-click to open it.

4. Choose File | New | Folder to create a new folder in the Start Menu\Programs group. Name this folder NT Server Administration.

5. Double-click the new folder to open it; then choose File | New | Shortcut to open the Create Shortcut Wizard.

6. Choose Browse and navigate to the folder \WINNT\SYSTEM32.

7. Double-click USRMGR, click Next, give the shortcut the name User Manager, and click Finish. This process will create a new shortcut in the NT Server Administration folder that points to User Manager for Domains.

8. Repeat this process for each of the following tools that you want to use: DHCPADMN.EXE, RASADMIN.EXE, RPLMGR.EXE, SRVMGR.EXE, UPEDIT.EXE, WINSADMN.EXE. Choose OK to dismiss the Taskbar Properties dialog box when you're finished.

The NT Workstation versions of the Server Administration Tools are now installed and ready to use.

Installing Administrative Tools on Windows 95

To install the tools on Windows 95, you must first connect a network drive to the shared directory on the server. Next, open Control Panel and double-click the Add/Remove Programs icon. Click the Windows Setup tab and then select Have Disk. Type the path to the Windows 95 directory on the client installation share you created earlier. Choose OK to install the Windows 95 Server Administration Tools. Windows 95 will automatically modify the Registry and create a program group on the Start menu for the server administration tools.

The Windows 95 versions of the Server Administration Tools are now installed and ready to use (see Figure 10-5).

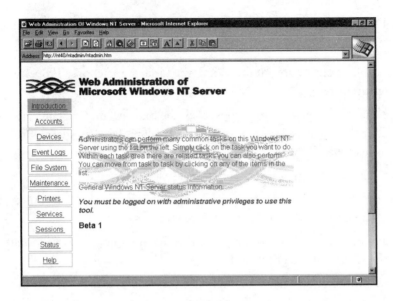

FIGURE 10-5

The server tools are now available on the Programs menu.

Using the Client-Based Server Administration Tools

Regardless of the client platform on which the tools are installed, using them is basically the same as if you were using them on a server. Here are some guidelines that you may want to take into consideration:

♦ Remote Access—If you're going to use the tools on a workstation that's using RAS to connect to the network, make sure that you select the option for low speed connection, so that the system doesn't try to build a browse list for everything that you select. This will help speed the response time of the tools across a slow modem connection. The downside is that you'll have to type the name of any object that you want to manage.

♦ Domain Membership—If you are using a workstation that isn't a member of the domain (for example, a workstation connected via RAS), make sure that you're logged into your workstation with the same user name and password as your domain account, to ensure that you have the appropriate access to the object you want to manage.

♦ Security—If you're using the tools on Windows 95, enable user profiles, so that the tools are available on the workstation when you log on. You may also want to set a system policy that requires the user to enter a valid user ID and password to run Windows.

Managing with Simple Network Management Protocol (SNMP)

To this point in this chapter, we've been concentrating on managing server properties from a client workstation. This type of management allows you to perform basic administration tasks and perform changes as situations demand. Another type of management that you may need to perform is to collect performance data on a particular workstation, or to verify that a particular device is functioning correctly. These types of tasks are best performed with a Simple Network Management Protocol management station.

The *Simple Network Management Protocol* (*SNMP*) is part of the TCP/IP protocol suite, and was designed primarily to manage bridges and routers. SNMP has grown tremendously during the last several years and has been expanded to manage just about any device on the network, including Windows NT-based computers. The devices that can be managed and what you can do to them vary, depending on the management software you choose. Microsoft's management agent enables you to query basic items, such as CPU utilization and contact information, the location of the system, and who to call for questions.

SNMP consists of two main components: a *management agent*, which is a piece of software that runs on a device to be managed, and a *management console*, which is the software that controls the devices being managed. Microsoft doesn't provide the management console software, so you'll need a third-party solution such as (on the high end) IBM's Netview or Hewlett Packard's Openview, or (on the lower end) Intel's LANDesk manager or Castlerock's SNMPC.

Microsoft provides the management agent software, which is included with both NT Workstation and NT Server. Installation of the agent is covered later in this chapter.

SNMP Operational Overview

SNMP management consoles communicate with SNMP agents by requesting information via a GET or GET-NEXT command, or by setting certain parameters via a PUT command. Optionally, the management console can be configured to send a community name with each command. This community name acts as a password, in that only agents configured with the same community as the manager will respond to commands from the management console.

SNMP management agents are configured to report on various parameters as defined by the *Management Information Base* (*MIB*) that has been installed on that client. The MIB also defines which parameters the management console is allowed to change. The only communication that the agent will initiate with the management console is in the form of a TRAP message. A TRAP is generated when a specific parameter has exceeded a specific threshold (such as CPU utilization exceeding 80 percent).

Depending on the management software that you decide to install, the options with which your management console can interact can range from simple to very complex. Microsoft's SNMP agent uses a standard MIB called *MIB II* and includes support for some Microsoft-specific DHCP and WINS information. Most management software comes with its own agent software that you install on each client, but Microsoft's agent is fine for basic management, such as reporting CPU utilization, or finding out who the "contact" is for a particular machine.

Installing the SNMP Agent

To install the Microsoft SNMP agent software, open the Network Properties dialog box by right-clicking the Network Neighborhood icon and selecting Properties. Then click the Services tab, choose Add, and select the SNMP Service (see Figure 10-6).

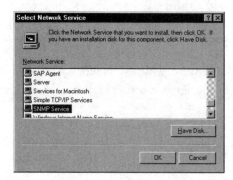

FIGURE 10-6

Select the SNMP Service from the list of available servers to install SNMP.

Choose OK and specify the path to the Windows NT source files. After the system finishes copying the files, it posts the SNMP Properties dialog box shown in Figure 10-7.

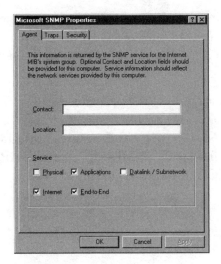

FIGURE 10-7

The SNMP Properties dialog box allows you to configure each SNMP parameter.

Configuring the SNMP Agent Software

Type the name of the system contact in the Contact text box. This name will be sent to SNMP management consoles that request the system contact information. (It's a good idea to include the telephone number on this line as well.) Fill in the system location in the Location box. These parameters are optional, but are especially valuable when the SNMP management console is located at a remote site. You should also indicate the types of services provided by the computer on which you're installing the SNMP service:

- Physical—Select this option if the computer provides the physical connection to the network. (Usually selected when the computer is a RAS server.)

- Applications—Select this check box if the computer is an application server. (Generally used with SQL Server or Exchange Server.)

- Datalink/Subnetwork—This option specifies that the computer provides the logical connection to the network. This box is checked by default.(This option is used when the computer is not a RAS server, but provides a network service such as file or printer access.)

♦ Internet—Use this option if the computer provides routing services. (Generally used when the computer is configured as a router with RIP enabled.)

♦ End to End—This selection indicates that the computer is capable of using connection-oriented services to the network such as named pipe communications. (Generally used on domain controllers to facilitate tracking of logon requests.)

Once you have selected the appropriate options, select the Traps tab. (See Figure 10-8.) Here you define the destination addresses for the management console or consoles in the Trap Destinations box. In the Community Name box, specify the community name to send along with the trap messages. Microsoft supports SNMP over either TCP/IP or NWLINK, so the address can be either a TCP/IP address or an IPX address.

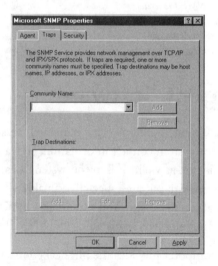

FIGURE 10-8

The Traps options enable you to specify the destination of any trap messages sent from your workstation and to specify the community name used when sending a trap.

Once you have specified the destination addresses and community names to be used when sending a trap message, select the Security tab as shown in Figure 10-9. Here you have the option of specifying an *authentication trap*, which means that the computer will send a trap to its configured managers if an SNMP manager configured with the wrong community name attempts to communicate with the agent. Use the other options shown here to configure the list of accepted community names and managers. You're required to specify a community name to include with any trap message send. A common community name that can be used is public, although you're free to use any word that you want.

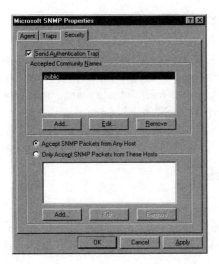

FIGURE 10-9

Configuring the security options available to SNMP agents.

Once these options are configured appropriately, click OK and then Close. Choose Yes to restart your computer. The SNMP agent software will be installed and ready for any SNMP management console to start managing it.

Managing Remote Sites

SNMP is very good for providing a mechanism for the NT Administrator to keep track of the workstations and networking devices on her network. However, SNMP isn't very adept at performing basic administration tasks, such as adding a new user or changing a user's rights. When administering remote systems, you have to use the tools provided by Microsoft.

Networks are getting larger and staffs that manage them are getting smaller. Because of this trend, you need a method for managing sites that are in phyically separate locations—from a single, centralized location (such as a corporate headquarters). Windows NT was designed with this goal in mind, and, with the exception of hardware-specific tasks, there are very few tasks that you can't accomplish remotely with the provided management tools, either server- or client-based.

Managing Remote Servers

Using Server Manager on a remote server is almost as easy as using it on a local server. The main difference is that you'll most likely want to bypass any network browsing by selecting Low Speed Connection from the Options menu of any management tool you're using, unless your remote sites are connected via high-speed connections.

Managing Remote Shares

You can use either the Windows NT Explorer or Server Manager to manage remote shared directories. You'll most likely find Server Manager to be easier, as it doesn't require reading directories. The downside here is that you have to know the path of the directory that you want to share.

Managing with Non-Microsoft Client Platforms

To manage a Windows NT server, you may assume that you either must be sitting at that server's console or running a Microsoft Windows desktop operating system with the appropriate server tools installed. Because these methods require a relatively high-bandwidth connection to manage the server effectively, sometimes the management process is difficult.

Microsoft has taken this problem into consideration and developed a new tool for managing NT Servers. The *Web Administration Tool* was designed to work with any "standard" HTML browser. The tool can be found on Microsoft's Web site at
`http://www.microsoft.com/ntserver/webadmin.htm`.

Several third-party tools are also available to perform "remote control" management of an NT server from any client capable of running the program. Examples include Symantec's PC-Anywhere32 and other programs that support Windows NT for remote control. Be sure to select a remote control package that will operate with both your server and your client environment.

Using the Microsoft Web Administration Tool

The Web Administration Tool uses the Microsoft Internet Information Server (IIS) and an ISAPI DLL to allow limited access to the server's management utilities from any HTML browser that supports client authentication. The beauty of this tool is that it will allow you to perform most management tasks from any client platform that can support a Web browser—for example, a Macintosh. The following lists describe the tasks you can perform with the Web Administration Tool.

Account Management tasks:

♦ Create and delete user accounts, including those with access to the File and Print Service for NetWare(FPNW) service.

♦ View and change user properties.

♦ Change user passwords.

♦ Disable (and enable) user accounts.

♦ Create and remove groups, as well as manage group properties (including adding and removing users).

♦ Add and remove workstations in the domain.

Share Management tasks:

♦ View shares for all installed file services, including FPNW and Macintosh-compatible volumes.

♦ Change permissions on shares.

♦ Create new shares for all installed file services.

Session Management tasks:

♦ View current user sessions.

♦ Delete user sessions.

♦ Send messages to connected users.

Server Management tasks:

♦ Shut down and reboot the server.

♦ Change services and driver configuration properties.

- ◆ View all event logs.
- ◆ Save server configuration to a data file (dump configuration).
- ◆ Take a snapshot of server activity.
- ◆ Take a snapshot of any Performance Monitor counter.

Printer Management tasks:

- ◆ List and manage print queues.
- ◆ Pause or flush a specific print queue.

The Web Administration Tool requires that IIS be installed on each server that you want to manage via HTML.

Because the Web isn't traditionally a secure environment, the Web Administration Tool supports not only the use of Windows NT challenge/response (CHAP) authentication, but also the use of the *Secure Sockets Layer (SSL)* to ensure that the management is indeed secure. SSL can be used only when you have generated a site certificate for your server, but does provide the most secure environment for management.

Installing the Web Administration Tool

To install the Web Administration Tool, you first have to install IIS. After IIS is installed, you must configure it to support either basic or NT challenge/response password authentication. To configure IIS for password authentication, start the IIS Management Tool (Internet Service Manager) and double-click the WWW service for the server on which you want to install the Web Administration Tool. This action opens the Properties dialog box for the WWW service, as shown in Figure 10-10. Select the authentication type you want to use and click OK. Currently, only Microsoft's Internet Explorer supports NT CHAP authentication. If you want to use a browser other than Internet Explorer, select basic authentication.

After IIS is installed and configured, use a Web browser to connect to Microsoft's Web site and select the platform for which you want to install the Web Administration Tool. The file for Intel platforms is called Webadmin.exe and is available at http://www.microsoft.com/ntserver/webadmin.htm. (This is a self-extracting installation program.) After you download the program to a temporary location on your hard disk, double-click the program to run it and display the license agreement. If you agree with the license, choose Yes to continue the installation. After the files have been extracted to a temporary directory, Setup starts (see Figure 10-11). The installation program copies the appropriate forms into the IIS directories, modifies the system Registry with the appropriate values, and prompts you to exit to Windows when it's done.

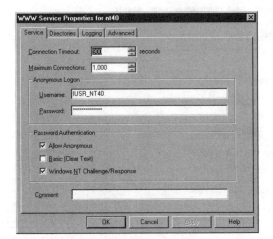

FIGURE 10-10

Use the Internet Service Manager to configure the client authentication type to either basic or NT challenge/response for the Web Administration Tool to work properly.

FIGURE 10-11

The installation process for the Web Administration Tool consists of this dialog box.

After the Web Administration Tool is installed, you're ready to manage your server from any Web browser that will support user authentication.

Using an HTML Browser to Manage the Server

To use the Web Administration Tool, start your Web browser and point it to the following path on your server:

```
http://server_name/ntadmin/ntadmin.htm
```

Be sure to enter a user name and password with administrator privileges when prompted. This will bring up the main screen of the Web Administration Tool, as shown in Figure 10-12.

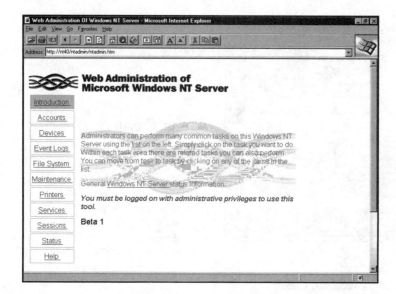

FIGURE 10-12

The Web Administration Tool as viewed from Internet Explorer 2.0.

Using the tools contained within the Web Administration Tool is much the same as using the "normal" tools for Windows NT Server. Each server that you want to manage via the Web Administration Tool must have both IIS and the Web Administration Tool installed on it.

This tool's best use is probably by administrators who are forced to manage servers that exist across slow links. Because the Web Administration Tool makes use of the ISAPI interface, it's a bit slower to perform the same tasks as the "normal" tools, but the speed is more than made up by the fact that you can now manage servers across slow links and have the management programs run remotely.

Another very good advantage to the use of this tool is that it can manage the server from any workstation that has access to a Web browser. This gives the administrator the flexibility to solve problems quickly that would otherwise have to wait until he could get to a workstation that had the administration tools installed.

Where to Go Next

This chapter explains how to install the management tools on a client workstation and how to install and configure the SNMP service, concluding with a discussion of the new Web Administration Tool from Microsoft. For related information, consider the following sources:

◆ For more information regarding the use of the server tools, see Chapter 9, "Managing NT Servers."

◆ For more information regarding the use of SNMP to monitor the system, see Chapter 18, "Monitoring Network Performance."

Chapter | 11

Working with the Windows NT System Registry

In This Chapter:

- ◆ Understanding the Registry
- ◆ Editing the Registry
- ◆ Other Registry Utilities

How do I...

Stated most simply, the Windows NT Registry is a database of settings that control the operation of the Windows NT operating system and applications that reside on the computer. In a perfect world, administrators would never have to edit the Registry to modify or even add entries; Windows NT does a great job of ensuring that the Registry is in tip-top shape!

As an administrator, however, you realize that today's computing environment is far from perfect and sometimes you have to change system settings. For example, you may have these types of situations:

- ◆ A user accidentally changes colors on her desktop so that everything is black.

- ◆ You want to change the default condition of many settings such as the Shutdown option not appearing on the default logon window for servers.

- ◆ You need to modify the security of Registry keys for Windows 95 applications (the Windows 95 Registry doesn't have security for keys in its Registry—this has been a problem for users attempting to run Windows 95 applications under Windows NT).

These types of situations require you to edit the Registry.

If you are an administrator new to Windows NT, you probably won't edit the Registry very often. With additional experience, however, most administrators like to tweak their systems. This means making changes to the Registry. In either case, it's very helpful for administrators to understand the basics as well as the more advanced concepts of the Registry.

This chapter takes you on a trip through the Registry and the utilities that help you manage it. The chapter covers the following topics:

- The structure of the Registry
- How to find values and edit data
- Security in the Registry
- Registry utilities that aren't delivered with Windows NT

Understanding the Registry

The Registry has been around since the beginning of Windows NT development. If you were a Windows 3.1 user or administrator, you probably remember the chaos that occurred with INI files. These files were text files that held initialization information for Windows 3.1 and Windows applications. Unfortunately, the files were easy to modify, they were easily corrupted, and all Windows applications created their own INI files, filling the Windows directories with those files.

The Registry was the NT developer's answer to these and other problems. The information that was previously found in the INI files is now found in the Registry. In fact, it worked so well that the Windows 95 product group copied many of the concepts of the NT Registry.

> **NOTE:** Although many of the concepts, hives, keys, and even values of the Windows NT Registry have similarities within the Windows 95 Registry, they aren't binary compatible. (You can't copy the Windows NT Registry to a Windows 95 machine and expect it to work.) In addition, although a Windows NT key may look similar to a Windows 95 key, Microsoft didn't attempt to ensure that values are the same. Before you make a change to a value, be sure to look at the documentation.

Registry Basics

The Registry is a binary database of the settings that Windows NT and its applications need to start and operate. Because the Registry is a binary file, the only way to edit it is with the Registry Editor provided by Microsoft or with programming tools. As an administrator, you should focus on using the Registry Editor.

> **CAUTION:** Because the Registry holds all your configuration information, it's crucial that you don't delete any entries or enter information for any of the values without proper knowledge. A corrupted Registry could force you to reinstall Windows NT Server, thus losing previous settings for NT or applications that reside on this machine.

The Registry Editor isn't found on any of the default menus. You must run the program to begin using the editor. In Windows 4.0, Microsoft released two versions of the Registry Editor. One version has the same functionality as the Windows 95 Registry Editor; the other has the same functionality as the Windows NT 3.51 Registry Editor. We'll expand on this topic later, but because of the limitations of the Windows 95 Registry Editor in a Windows NT environment, we'll focus on the Windows NT Registry Editor.

Using the Registry Editor (REGEDT32.EXE)

Remember that the Registry Editor isn't found on any of the default menus in Windows NT. You must run a special program to begin using the Registry Editor. Here's the command name:

```
%SystemRoot%\system32\REGEDT32.EXE
```

You can add it to the Start menu for easy access.

Because changing Registry entries can cause damage to your system, however, we recommend that you review the Registry in Read Only mode until you're familiar with its workings. To open in Read Only mode, choose Options | Read Only Mode and make sure that a check mark is next to this option (see Figure 11-1). Using this feature can prevent accidents while allowing you to become familiar with the Registry.

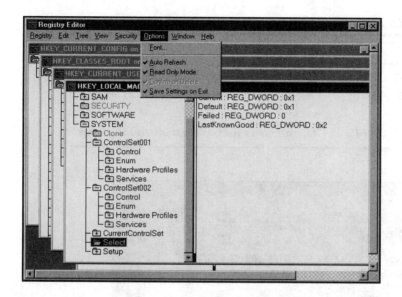

FIGURE 11-1

The Registry Editor allows users to view the Registry in Read Only Mode.

TIP: A very good way to prevent unauthorized users from modifying the Registry is to change the protections on the Registry Editor. Assuming that you're using NTFS, this strategy is very effective—and easy. Change the Registry Editor so that domain and local administrators are the only groups with access to the Editor.

The Registry Editor uses an Explorer-like interface to display five cascaded windows (see Figure 11-2). Each of these windows depict one of the predefined Registry subtrees for Windows NT. Think of these subtrees as the root directories of the five areas of the Registry. The following sections describe the keys.

Table 11.1 shows the five predefined subtrees with a brief description of each.

Table 11.1 Predefined subtrees in Windows NT 4.0.

Subtree	Contents
HKEY_LOCAL_MACHINE	Information about the local computer.
HKEY_USERS	User profiles from users who have logged on to the local system.

continues

Table 11.1 Continued

Subtree	Contents
HKEY_CURRENT_USER	The user profile from the user currently logged on.
HKEY_CLASSES_ROOT	Object Linking and Embedding (OLE) information for the local machine.
HKEY_CURRENT_CONFIG	Information for the configuration used at startup.

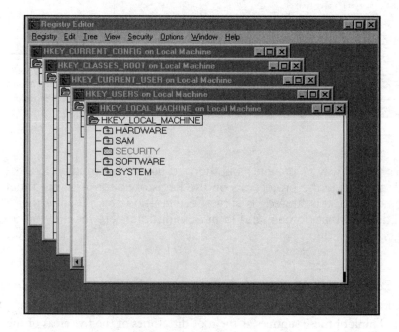

FIGURE 11-2

The Registry Editor provides a standard interface for viewing and modifying the Registry.

HKEY_LOCAL_MACHINE

The HKEY_LOCAL_MACHINE window shown in Figure 11-3 holds configuration information about the local computer. This information includes hardware configuration, security data, and details about the software loaded on the machine. The information in the hardware subkey is created dynamically each time the system is started. The program

NTDETECT.COM detects the hardware and places the hardware information in the Registry. Because it's re-created at startup, this information isn't saved in the Registry. This also means that any changes to these keys won't be saved.

The Security Account Manager (SAM) holds security information for the local machine. If the machine is a domain controller, SAM holds all the security information for the entire domain. As of Version 4.0, the operating system, by default, will no longer allow you to view or modify the security information. As an administrator, you can change security values to view this information, but it is in a binary format.

The software subkey contains information about the software loaded on the local machine. This information is usually machine-dependent and doesn't conflict with information in the HKEY_USERS. If there's a conflict with HKEY_USERS, the information in HKEY_USERS will be used.

The system subtree holds information used to start the system. This topic is discussed shortly.

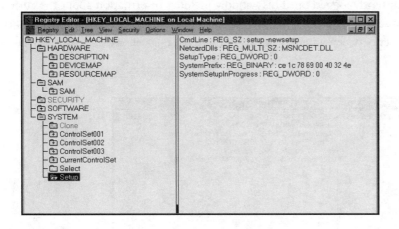

FIGURE 11-3

The
HKEY_LOCAL_MACHINE
subtree.

HKEY_USERS

The HKEY_USERS window contains user profiles from users who have logged onto that machine locally (see Figure 11-4).

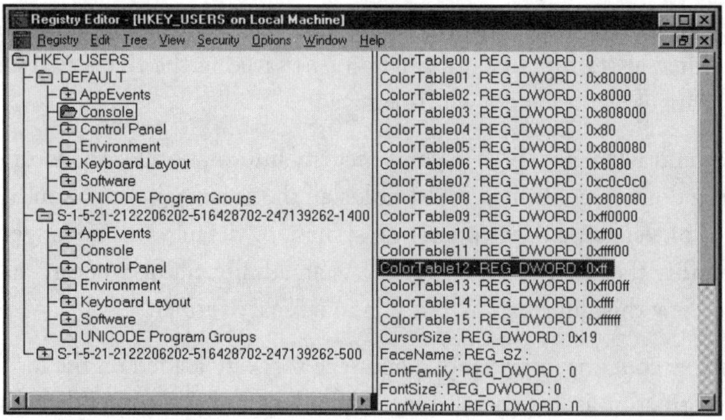

FIGURE 11-4

The HKEY_USERS *subtree.*

HKEY_CURRENT_USER

HKEY_CURRENT_USER (shown in Figure 11-5) is a mirror of HKEY_USERS key. When a change is made to one, the change is made to the other. This key holds the user profile of the user who is currently logged on. This window includes information about the current user's desktop settings, printers, network connections, and software configuration. If there's a conflict between an entry in this key and HKEY_LOCAL_MACHINE, this key takes precedence.

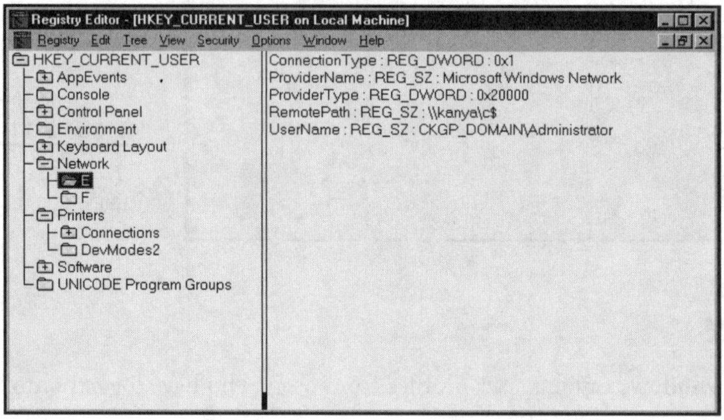

FIGURE 11-5

The HKEY_CURRENT_USER *subtree.*

HKEY_CLASSES_ROOT

Figure 11-6 shows the HKEY_CLASSES_ROOT key, which holds information on object linking and embedding (OLE). This key mirrors the HKEY_LOCAL_MACHINE\Software\Classes sub-key. The duplication of information in the Registry is another method that Microsoft used to ensure fault tolerance in Windows NT.

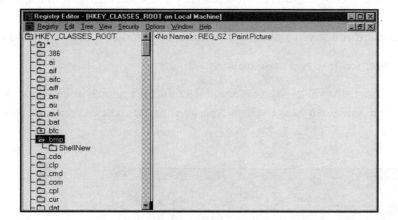

FIGURE 11-6

The HKEY_CLASSES_ROOT *subtree.*

HKEY_CURRENT_CONFIG

To display information about the current hardware configuration at startup, open HKEY_CURRENT_CONFIG (see Figure 11-7). This key was added in Windows NT 4.0 along with the availability of hardware profiles.

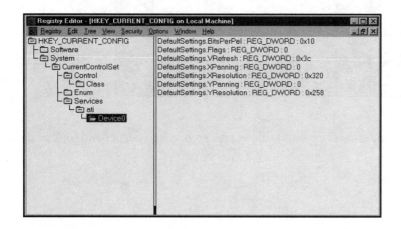

FIGURE 11-7

The HKEY_CURRENT_ CONFIG *subtree.*

Parts of the Registry Editor Screen

An understanding of the subtrees is basic to working with the Registry. As you work with the Registry more, you'll understand the subtrees better. Next, we need to go deeper into the subtree window and define each part of the entry.

Figure 11-8 shows the elements of the Registry. The left pane of the window holds the keys. If you look at the highlighted example, the key in the left pane is simply called `WindowMetrics`. This key holds information about the border width of windows. If you were to document this key, you would say that it can be found under the following listing:

`HKEY_USERS\.DEFAULT\Control Panel\Desktop\WindowMetrics`

The right pane holds the values, data type, and data. In the example in Figure 11-8, `BorderWidth` is the value, `REG_SZ` is the data type, and `1` is the data. Keys can have many values.

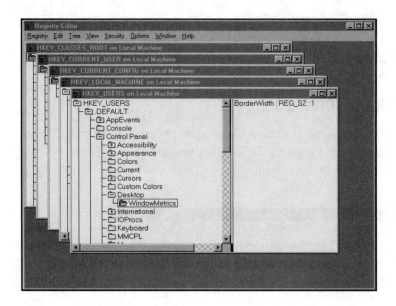

FIGURE 11-8

An example value and its three fields.

Now that you understand keys and values, let's go one step deeper and look at the data types.

Understanding Data Types

There are five different data types for the Windows NT Registry. Each data type uses a different format. The following list describes the data types for Registry entries:

♦ REG_BINARY—Raw binary data, this is usually hardware component information or security information. If you see Registry data in this data type, avoid editing the data. Binary data isn't easy to modify, and the developers of Windows NT put some data in this format so that users couldn't change it. The following example holds information about the subkey's component:

```
ComponentInformation : REG_BINARY : 00 00 00 00...
```

♦ REG_DWORD—A number that's four bytes in length, usually seen as parameters for device drivers and services. The following example is the interrupt for SCSI port 0:

```
Interrupt : REG_DWORD : 0xe
```

♦ REG_EXPAND_SZ—An expandable data string—text containing a variable to be replaced when called by an application. For example, if a key depended on the file program.exe in the user's home directory, the value would be %HOMEPATH%\program.exe.

This allows Windows NT and its applications to use the variable instead of hard-coding a username. The value in the following example shows where Windows NT will look for media clips:

```
MediaPathUnexpanded : REG_EXPAND_SZ : %SystemRoot%\Media
```

♦ REG_MULTI_SZ—Multiple-string values containing lists or multiple values in a readable format. This example holds information about the system BIOS version:

```
SystemBiosVersion : REG_MULTI_SZ : BIOS Version 1.00.09 AX1T
```

♦ REG_SZ—A simple character string. This is the type of data you will edit the majority of the time. The following example holds the directory path for *SystemRoot*:

```
SystemRoot : REG_SZ : C:\WINNT40
```

Understanding Hives

Thus far, this section has looked at subtrees, keys, values, and data types. Let's go back to the big picture and examine the hives.

The majority of the Registry is stored on the local hard drive in six files, as shown in Table 11.2. These files are called *hives*. Hives enable administrators to back up files (more on this later) and load parts of the Registry from remote machines. The hives are found in the %*SystemRoot*%\system32\config folder.

Table 11.2 lists the hive files and their corresponding Registry keys.

Table 11.2. Hive files.

Key	File Name
HKEY_LOCAL_MACHINE\SAM	SAM and SAM.LOG
HKEY_LOCAL_MACHINE\SECURITY	SECURITY and SECURITY.LOG
HKEY_LOCAL_MACHINE\SOFTWARE	SOFTWARE and SOFTWARE.LOG
HKEY_LOCAL_MACHINE\SYSTEM	SYSTEM and SYSTEM.ALT
HKEY_USERS\DEFAULT	DEFAULT and DEFAULT.LOG
HKEY_CURRENT_USER	USERDIFF and USERDIFF.LOG

You may notice that some of these files have no extensions; others have extensions of LOG or ALT. The next section provides details on both types of files.

Fault Tolerance in the Registry

One of the first design goals of Windows NT was to make the operating system able to survive power outages and system crashes. Because the Registry is such an integral part of Windows NT, fault-tolerance is also found in the Registry.

Figure 11-9 shows a file without an extension and a file with a LOG extension. Windows NT first writes the change to the LOG file. The LOG file is used with the file that has no extension to provide fault tolerance. Let's look at a change to the SOFTWARE hive. When a user or an application requests a change to the HKEY_LOCAL_MACHINE\SOFTWARE subtree of the Registry, Windows NT first writes the change to the SOFTWARE.LOG file. Once that change is complete, the hive file is marked as being "in transition." The hive file named SOFTWARE is then modified and the SOFTWARE hive file is marked as complete. If the system crashes while the SOFTWARE hive file is in transition, Windows NT uses the SOFTWARE.LOG file to complete the changes.

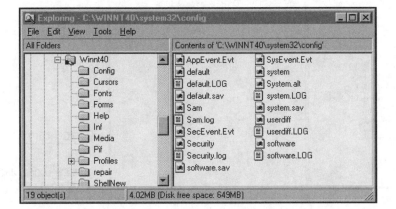

FIGURE 11-9

The Registry is stored in hive files.

The exception to this process is the System hive, because the System hive is more critical to the startup process. The System hive has an ALT file instead of the LOG file. The ALT is a copy of the System hive. Changes are written to the System hive first, and then to the ALT file. In the event of a system crash during a change to the System hive, Windows NT uses the ALT file as the System hive. The difference between this method and the LOG method is that the changes don't have to be made again.

Using the "Last Known Good" Configuration

Another example of fault tolerance in the Registry can be found in the concept of the Last Known Good configuration.

The HKEY_LOCAL_MACHINE\System subkey holds any information required to start the system (that isn't dynamically created). Figure 11-10 shows that under the System key are subkeys called ControlSet### and a CurrentControlSet. Each of the ControlSet### keys holds information used to start Windows NT on a previous occasion. Windows NT saves between two and four control sets. To find out which ControlSet### your system considers Current, Default, Failed, or LastKnownGood, look under the Select key. This Key has those values and a number in the data field. The number refers to the ControlSet number that corresponds to the value.

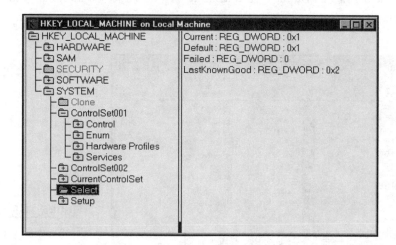

FIGURE 11-10

The HKEY_LOCAL_MACHINE \System *subkey.*

The CurrentControlSet is a link to one of the ControlSet### keys. Normally, after a user logs on to a Windows NT system, the data in the ..\Select\Current value is moved to ..\Select\LastKnownGood and the new ControlSet number is placed in ..\Select\Current.

If changes are made to the system and the system won't restart correctly, you open the Hardware Profile/Configuration Recovery menu. To access this menu, press the spacebar during startup just after you see the message OS Loader V4.00 on the top of the screen. You'll be given a list of configurations (you know them as ControlSets) and asked to choose one. After you choose a configuration, the data in the ..\Select\Current value is moved to ..\Select\Failed and the data in ..\Select\Current is changed to the selected ControlSet number.

In Figure 11-10, the Select key holds the values for the current configuration, default, failed, and "Last Known Good" configurations. Notice that the data is simply a number. Each value is a pointer to a control set.

Windows NT considers a logon to the local machine as a "good" configuration. Once the logon is successful, Windows NT abandons the previous Last Known Good configuration and makes the current configuration the Last Known Good configuration.

TIP: An administrator can determine what Windows NT uses for the "good" configuration criteria. To modify this, the administrator must have a program that checks something and reports back a value. For instance, let's say that the Windows NT server is a Web server. A program could be written to ensure that the Web software and Internet link are working on the server. This way, if a Registry entry change stops the Web software or the Internet link, you can roll back to the Last Known Good configuration. Once the program is complete, add this key:

```
HKEY_LOCAL_MACHINE\SYSTEM\CurrentControlSet\Control\
BootVerificationProgram
```

Place the path and name of the program in the value of this key. You then need to modify the following key:

```
HKEY_LOCAL_MACHINE\SOFTWARE\Microsoft\WindowsNT\CurrentVersion
    \WinLogon\ReportBootOK
```

Change the value to 0 to disable the automatic verification program.

Editing the Registry

Now that you understand the basics and internals of the Registry, let's go to the Registry Editor and make a change.

Earlier sections of this chapter discussed the Windows NT Registry Editor, REGEDT32.EXE. This is the Registry editor that you'll use most often in Windows NT. Another Registry Editor ships with Windows NT 4.0; however, it is named %SystemRoot$/REGEDIT.EXE. This is a look alike to the Windows 95 Registry Editor, but REGEDIT.EXE is a different executable than the Windows 95 version.

As mentioned earlier, REGEDT32.EXE is the preferred Registry Editor for Windows NT. There are a couple of good reasons to use REGEDIT (the Win95 look alike editor) rather than REGEDT32 (the NT editor):

◆ REGEDIT's Find function works much better than the Find function in REGEDT32. REGEDT32 only lets you search for keys, but REGEDIT allows you to find keys, values, data, or any combination that you need (see Figure 11-11)! This is a very powerful tool that would have been a great addition to REGEDT32.

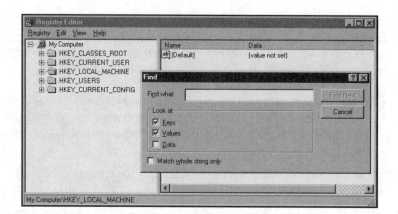

FIGURE 11-11

*The Windows 95 Registry
Editor (*REGEDIT.EXE*).*

♦ The other reason to use REGEDIT is that it has the Explorer interface "look
and feel." All the root keys are open in a single window, as opposed to
REGEDT32, which opens one window for each of the five root keys. REGEDIT
also allows you to right-click the key, data type, or data for a quick menu.

On the other hand, REGEDT32 gives you more power when working with the
Windows NT Registry. REGEDT32 includes the ability to look at and
modify the security of each key (more on this later), open hives, open the
Registry as read-only, and auto-refresh the screen. You should use the
REGEDT32 Editor as your primary Registry Editor.

CAUTION: Remember that if you put invalid data in the Registry, you run the risk of
corrupting your system. While you are learning the Registry, open the Registry in
Read Only mode, as described earlier in this chapter. When you're sure you're ready
to modify a value, simply open the Options menu and deselect the Read Only
option.

Whenever you modify the Registry, be sure to double-check your change before
choosing OK. As a carpenter might say, "Measure twice; cut once." If you apply this
standard to editing the Registry, you'll look twice at everything you want to modify
before you commit the change. You can't undo changes; any changes that you commit are written directly to the Registry. If you make a mistake, you must retype the
data to correct the mistake.

The Registry is a tool that Microsoft thought only experienced users would use—you
must be responsible with it.

Why would you ever want to edit the Registry? In many cases, editing the Registry is the *only* way to correct a problem.

Editing a Value

Let's try to apply what we know about the Registry and modify a value. Suppose that you have a print server in a locked room. Under normal circumstances, no one logs into the server locally; it just sits there and spools print jobs. Occasionally the machine's spooler might stop, however, requiring shut down and restart. Instead of logging on simply to restart the system, it would more convenient to restart from the logon screen.

One of the differences between Windows NT Workstation and Windows NT Server is that the logon process in Workstation allows users to reboot without logging on, while the Server's logon dialog box doesn't allow a shutdown until someone logs onto the system. This setup is simple to change, if you know where it is. This value is found under the following key:

```
HKEY_LOCAL_MACHINE\SOFTWARE\Microsoft\WindowsNT\CurrentVersion
➥\Winlogon\ShutdownWithoutLogon
```

If you set the data to 1 the menu option will appear; set the data to 0 to disallow the option.

Finding the Key

For example purposes, let's assume that you don't know where in the Registry this setting is located, but heard about it from a friend. Your friend remembered only that the key had Winlogon in it somewhere and that Shutdown was part of the value. The first task is to guess which key to search. Ask yourself, "Where *should* this value be?" Because it has to do with the machine and isn't a user setting, you should probably start your search in the HKEY_LOCAL_MACHINE key.

To use the Find feature to locate the key you need, choose View | Find Key to open the Find dialog box. For this example, you would type **winlogon** in the Find What field and deselect the Match Whole Word Only check box, as shown in Figure 11-12.

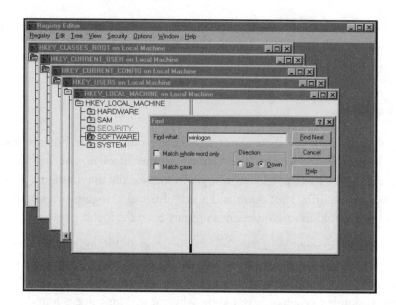

FIGURE 11-12

The Find dialog box.

NOTE: If you guessed incorrectly, just search another root key. You haven't changed any settings, so no harm was done by searching. You may even find other useful keys for future projects.

The Find function should locate the Winlogon key on its first attempt. The left side of the screen shows the keys and the right side of the screen displays the value and data. Looking at this screen (shown in Figure 11-13), you can see that the only value that begins with Shutdown is ShutdownWithoutLogon. This value certainly sounds like what you want!

Remember that the Find function in REGEDIT is much more powerful than that in REGEDT32. If you knew only that the value had shutdown in it somewhere, REGEDT32 couldn't locate the value for you; it only searches keys. REGEDIT would let you find information in the key, value, data, or any combination of the three.

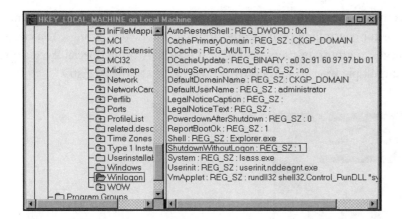

FIGURE 11-13

The Registry Editor has located the key containing Winlogon.

Changing the Value

Now to modify this value. The easiest way to edit the string is to double-click the value, which opens a dialog box where you can edit the string. Change the 0 to 1 and exit the dialog box. The next time you attempt to logon, you'll see the shutdown option!

As you can see from the previous example, editing the Registry is easy—maybe *too* easy. To prevent users from changing keys in the Registry, you can use the Registry's built-in security, as described in the next section.

Maintaining Security Within the Registry

Because the Windows NT architects wanted a high level of security, they built security features directly into the Registry. This plan enables administrators to use the security within the Registry regardless of whether they're using a high-security file system like NTFS or a low-security (some people say "nonexistent security") file system like FAT. The Registry's security model uses the privileges and groups assigned in User Manager.

NOTE: REGEDIT doesn't allow you to view or modify security in the Registry. You must use REGEDT32 to work with the Registry's security features.

To view or modify security settings, open the Security menu. Notice that the menu includes options for controlling permissions, auditing, and owner settings. You can grant separate privileges to groups or users. As Figure 11-14 shows, the Special Access option even gives you multiple ways to split up what users can do to the Registry.

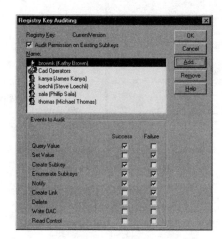

FIGURE 11-14

Auditing options within the Registry.

The Special Access values are described in Table 11-3.

Table 11-3. Special Access values.

Option	Enables a User or Group to...
Query Value	Read a value from a Registry key.
Set Value	Set a value in a Registry key.
Create Subkey	Create subkeys below the current key.
Enumerate Subkeys	Identify subkeys.
Notify	Audit events from a key.
Create Link	Create a symbolic link to another key.
Delete	Delete a key.
Write DAC	Write a Discretionary Access Control list (DAC).
Write Owner	Take ownership of a key.
Read Control	Access the security information for a key.

With this degree of access control in the Registry, you can give users access to almost anything (or prevent access). Be very careful when making changes, though. You may stop a user from accessing something she needs to use on the Windows NT machine.

The default security established within the Registry during the initial load of Windows NT is usually appropriate. The most common reason to change the security settings is to open up protections on a subtree to allow a Windows 95 application to write to a protected area of the Registry.

Because the Windows 95 Registry doesn't have internal security, the developers of Window 95 applications tend to ignore security within the Registry. Of course, this fact hurts Window NT users. If something works for the user who loaded the application, but other users can't access the function, it's usually Registry security that makes the difference.

We recommend that you contact the software developer to find out which key(s) require security changes. Once you have this information, highlight the key and choose Security | Permissions to open the Registry Key Permissions dialog box, as shown in Figure 11-15. This dialog box displays the current users, groups, and their permissions. This dialog box looks and functions just like the Security dialog box in Explorer, except for the extra Special Access values.

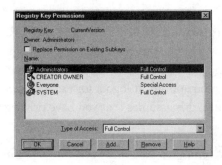

FIGURE 11-15

Setting Registry key permissions.

The Registry also enables Administrators to audit Registry events. Administrators can audit any key or subkey for any user or group attempting to make a change to the Registry. These events are defined by the list of Special Access values just described. Audited events appear in the security log of the Event Viewer on the local machine. Be careful, though; the more items you decide to audit, the more work you create for the operating system. You can slow a machine down tremendously by auditing everything in the Registry.

By Auditing events in the Registry, you can view what users are attempting to change, or use the auditing information to track which keys an application changes when it loads or is in use.

The final option is to change the owner of a key (see Figure 11-16). As in Explorer, you can take ownership of a key or subkey. In the previous example regarding the Window 95 applications, a quick fix is to have the user having problems with the application take ownership of the key. This usually fixes the problem, but any other user attempting to use the application will have the same problem.

FIGURE 11-16

Changing the key owner.

Security is available only on a key or subkey level. Permissions, auditing, and ownership aren't available on a value or data level.

Remote Registry Editing

One of the most powerful features in the Registry Editor is the ability to edit a Registry hive of another computer over a network. Any change you can make to your Registry locally, you can make over the network to another computer. If you want to change all the servers on your network so the shutdown option appears at logon, for example, you can do it from the comfort of your desk. Of course, this assumes that you have privileges to access the other computer and its Registry.

When you open the Registry on the remote computer, you only open two predefined keys: HKEY_USERS and HKEY_LOCAL_MACHINE. You can only look at or change keys to which you have access. Administrators can access and change any key.

You'll appreciate this feature most when a user changes his settings and introduces some kind of problem at the same time. For instance, if a user changes his desktop color scheme so that he can no longer see anything on-screen, an administrator can edit the Registry over the network and fix the problem. If you don't have the ability to modify the Registry over the network, this kind of change requires logging into the machine under a different username and changing the data.

Another instance in which this capability would come in handy is if you wanted to change the location of some standard drives. Suppose that the corporate data server is named SERVER1 and you need to move the data to SERVER2. As an administrator, you have to coordinate changing the share name from SERVER1 to SERVER2 for each user. This can be accomplished easily over the network by editing the network connections in HKEY_USERS. The other way to do this is to walk to each machine and log the user off the machine, log on with an administrator account, make the change, log off, and have the user log back on.

You can also use this feature as a diagnostic tool. Many times, a user will have a problem that you can begin to look at through the Registry. This allows you to work from your desk, with your reference material in front of you, while the user can continue to work on something else.

As you can see, although this is a short section in the book, the concept of remote Registry editing is powerful! Keep this ability in the back of your mind while you administer your machines. You'll find many uses for it in the future.

Other Registry Utilities

CAUTION: This section discusses utilities that are available in the Windows NT Version 3.51 Resource Kit. At press time, we were unable to get any information about a Version 4.0 Resource Kit, although Microsoft mentions it on their Web site. Although we expect that this Resource Kit will eventually become generally available, there is no guarantee that the utilities in the Resource Kit will work like those in the earlier versions.

To give you some utilities with which to work while the Resource Kit is unavailable, however, this section documents applicable utilities from the Version 3.51 Resource Kit.

Although the tools delivered with Windows NT are good for normal administration of the Registry, other tools are available for Windows NT Registry administration. These tools can be found in the Windows NT Resource Kit. The Resource Kit is usually a great purchase for anyone administering Windows NT machines. The Resource Kit provides additional documentation for Windows NT and a CD-ROM full of utilities that don't ship with the operating system.

REGENTRY.HLP

The most useful utility is the file REGENTRY.HLP. This help file holds all the documented Registry keys and values. The help file explains where the key or value can be found, describes the valid data for each key and value, and lists the range and default values for the data. Many users ask how to learn more about the key and values in the Registry—Figure 11-17 shows why this is the place!

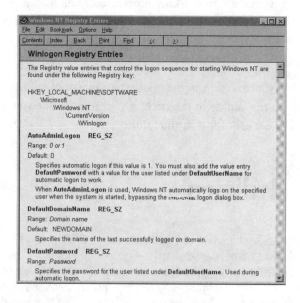

FIGURE 11-17

The Registry Entries help file in the Windows NT Resource Kit is the best place to learn about different Registry keys and entries.

REGBACK and REGREST

REGBACK.EXE and REGREST.EXE are tandem utilities from the Resource Kit. The two utilities enable users to back up and restore Registry files to floppy or hard disks. Microsoft recommends that users back up the Registry files to tape with the standard Windows NT Backup utility. In fact, it's a good idea to include in your backup scheme the directory where the Registry files reside. Many administrators forget about backing up these files because they're in a special location. If you don't have a tape drive, you should use these utilities.

Both of these utilities are console applications; this means that you have to use a console (or DOS) window to run the program. REGBACK creates a full backup of any or all active subkeys of the Registry while the system is running. By default, REGBACK backs up all the active hives from the %SYSTEMROOT%\SYSTEM32\CONFIG directory. Any hives that aren't active can be copied with the copy commands in Windows NT. The syntax of the command line to backup the files is as follows:

REGBACK *pathname*

where *pathname* is the drive and path where you want the backup files to reside.

REGREST restores Registry files that were created with REGBACK. REGREST reloads the entire hive; you have to reboot before you see the changes. The program renames instead of copying, so the files must be on the same volume for the rename to work. Here's the syntax for the command:

REGREST *Newfilename Savefilename Hivetype Hivename*

Newfilename is the filename for the backup source. REGREST will use this file to replace the old hive file. *Savefilename* is the location and filename where the current Registry hive will be saved. *Hivetype* is either machine or users, depending on which hive you're trying to restore. Here's an example:

REGREST c:\backup\user c:\backup\olduser.sav user user

REGINI

REGINI is the final utility we'll talk about in this chapter. Think of REGINI as a script language for the Registry. REGINI enables you to type the key, value, and data once and then repeat the changes again and again. You can copy this script file around the network and make changes to the Registry of different machines.

> **CAUTION:** This chapter has repeatedly mentioned how dangerous modifying the Registry can be. Before you use the REGINI file you create, *be sure* that it's correct. Using this type of script file can make changes much faster then you can clean up the mess afterward!

Let's say that management has decided that security must be increased. As part of this process, they note that the username of the last user to logon successfully shouldn't be displayed when a user attempts a logon.

To fix this problem, you would start by creating an INI file. We'll call the example file SECURE.INI. Open your favorite editor and place the following two lines in the file:

```
\Registry\machine\software\microsoft\windows nt\currentversion\winlogon\
➥dontdisplaylastusername = REG_SZ 1
```

As this example shows, REGINI isn't case-sensitive. Once you have typed the text, save the file as SECURE.INI. To make the change, start the console window and type the following commmand:

```
REGINI SECURE.INI
```

The output of the command should look something like this:

```
00 0000 KeyName: \Registry\machine\software\microsoft\windows nt
➥\currentversion\winlogonUpdated value for Key:
➥\Registry\machine\software\microsoft\windows nt
➥\currentversion\winlogon\dontdisplaylastusername = 'REG_SZ 1'
```

Although this output looks cryptic, it tells you that the command was successful. Any other message is a potential problem.

Sometimes using REGINI isn't the best option. If you want to change anything in the HKEY_CURRENT_USER key, for example, you would have to access it through HKEY_USER when using REGINI. To change a key as the current user of my workstation, I would have to type the following entry:

```
\Registry\user\s-1-5-21-2122206202-51648702-247139262-1001\É
```

The portion starting with s-1-5 is how I'm known to the Windows NT Registry. This may not be a problem to type once, but if you wanted to make batch changes to all users on the network, you would have to go to the Registry to find this entry for each Windows NT user.

As you can see, REGINI is a great tool to change entries in a consistent manner.

Where to Go Next

The chapter explained the basics of the Windows NT Registry, how to find and data, the security within the Registry, and utilities that aren't delivered with Windows NT.

For more information, try the following sources:

◆ Microsoft has introduced a new tool with Windows NT Server 4.0 to modify Registry settings for a domain full of computers—it's called System Policy Editor. See Chapter 16, "Managing Users and Groups in Domains," for more information.

◆ The Windows NT Resource Kit is filled with 150+ pages of documentation on the Registry. You also receive the software on the CD-ROM that accompanies the Resource Kit documentation set. This is definitely a must-buy if you are interested in the Registry.

◆ The Microsoft Knowledge Base (`http://www.microsoft.com/kb`) is a good place to find answers to problems; these answers will most likely send you to the Registry.

◆ Online newsgroups and other electronic forums also provide good information about keys and values. Because Microsoft has discontinued support on CompuServe, the place to be is `msnews.microsoft.com`.

PART IV

Protecting Your
Network Environment

Chapter | 12

Windows NT Security
Fundamentals

In This Chapter:

◆ The NT Security Model
◆ Permissions versus Rights
◆ Auditing Events in Windows NT

How do I...

Security is often a misunderstood concept. Many people seem to feel that security is simply protecting files from unwanted users. Security is much more than that. In simple terms, security is the ability to protect a computer and all its resources. In other words, if you don't place the computer in a secure physical environment, you have immediately violated a basic tenet of security. Windows NT doesn't have a thing to do with this very basic level of security, but it certainly represents an important aspect of basic security. As far as Windows NT is concerned, security means protection of all files, objects, and resources.

Windows NT 4.0 (along with its previous versions) is designed to work with C2 security (designed by the Department of Defense in 1985). Basically, C2 security for NT is concerned with four basic features:

◆ Secure logon that's difficult to circumvent
◆ The ability of the owner of a resource to dictate who can gain access to the resource, and what they can do to it
◆ The ability to allow auditing of security-related events and to choose the events to be audited
◆ The ability to prevent access to memory after files have been written to a hard drive

The NT Security Model

It's Monday morning and you turn on your workstation. You're faced with a screen asking for your password. You enter the password and suddenly you're on an NT domain. You can search your e-mail, access data and work files, and even use several printers. Interestingly, none of the files or printers are physically connected to your system. How does all this come about? What has transpired that allows you access to files and printers? What occurs during the logon process?

First and foremost, Windows NT uses a mandatory logon, which means that each user must supply a unique name and password to log onto the computer. In this case, unique means that there are no duplicates of the name and password in the domain. This logon is actually the start of a very important series of events on the domain. First of all, during this process, all user-mode programs are suspended. This means that no one can create an application that can copy credentials as you logon. Likewise, a user can have more than one name and password. This allows multiple profiles and desktops to be used on the computer and the domain.

The logon screen is the first evidence of security in Windows NT. You may find it interesting that Microsoft uses the Ctrl+Alt+Delete sequence for the logon. This was chosen, obviously, for its unique ability to also boot systems. When you successfully log onto Windows NT, the security subsystem creates an *access token* for you. This token is composed of the username, group membership, and related information. When the token is granted, you can access the system. To be specific, the logon involves the following processes:

1. The dialog box is posted.
2. The Security Accounts Manager (SAM) queries the security database to determine the validity of the user and the password.
3. If the account is active and the information is correct, the security subsystem creates the access token and passes it back to the `Winlogon` process.
4. The `Winlogon` process calls the `win32` subsystem and a new process is presented to the user—the Explorer-based process.

The logon process is summarized in Figure 12-1.

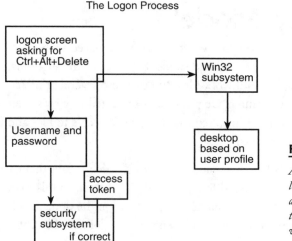

The Logon Process

FIGURE 12-1

A model showing the logon process succeeding and an access token passed to the win32 *subsystem, with the desktop being generated.*

Obviously, the generation of the access token has a great deal of importance to this entire process. The access token contains the security ID of the logged-on user, the group IDs of the user, and user privileges. If you can use printers that are remote to your system, permission was granted to you because your access token matched the printer's *Access Control List* (*ACL*). This is the next important aspect of domain access and permission.

The ACL is a list of access entries that describe an object. Objects include folders, links, printers, processes, network shares, devices—even threads. For you to print a file remotely, the network administrator had to give you permission to use that printer and file. This information is carried as an access entry in the ACL. If the access token agrees with the entries in the ACL, you can print the file. If the access token doesn't agree with the ACL, you are denied access to the printer. Figure 12-2 shows a diagram of how the ACL works.

The NT security model is based for the most part on attributes of NTFS (discussed shortly). Chapter 4, "Installing Windows NT Server," notes that NTFS has the capability to maintain many different attributes in its file structure. In fact, NTFS security can be both local as well as shared These attributes control the security on the file/directory/sub-directory objects. One immediate feature of NT security is thus the ability to control its granularity; that is, permission can be assigned to group or to a user. Group permission is less granular than is user permission. Throughout the assignment of security, an administrator has control of security granularity.

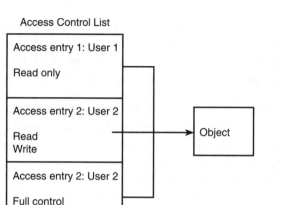

FIGURE 12-2

This model of an ACL has multiple entries about an object.

NOTE: Before dealing with the basics of the NT security model, I should point out that you can maintain a degree of security on FAT systems though network user shares. Obviously, this isn't a very sophisticated security setup, and not granular at all, but it *is* present.

As implied in the preceding statements, the NT security system is simply the central managing of objects by means of a *gatekeeper*. Paramount to the security is the Security Descriptor (SD) of an object. The SD contains the owner information, the discretionary ACL and the system or auditing ACL. Thus, the gatekeeper must know the user (hence, logon dictates who is on the system), and must match the security descriptors on objects (files, threads, printers etc.) with the user. At all times, a "deny" descriptor takes precedence over an access descriptor. For example, if Paul is a member of two groups, one that has access to files in a directory and one that doesn't, Paul can't access the directory.

Let's examine the workings of the gatekeeper model.

NTFS functions to maintain permissions by using combinations of individual permissions:

- ◆ Read (R)
- ◆ Write (W)
- ◆ Change Permissions (P)
- ◆ Delete (D)
- ◆ Execute (X)
- ◆ Take Ownership (O)

For the most part, the standard attributes you see on directories and files are combinations of this list. These are combined first for the directory and second for the file. An example would be Read (RX). In this case, (RX) means that a user can read contents of files in the directory and can execute applications in the directory.

To work with NTFS security, a user must have been given access to files and directories; if not, he or she can't access and use the files. When files are created in a directory, the security of the directory is passed on to the file. This scheme can create confusion. If you place security on the file and then secure the directory, the original security is intact. In other words, the file security overrides the directory security.

In addition to the User information, there's an additional aspect of the default security in Windows NT. An administrator can take ownership of any object. Indeed, administrators have default access to the root administrative share (for example, C$). These shares are visible only to administrators. As such, an administrator can take ownership of any file on the system. This ability is very important on an NT network and gives complete potential control of everything to an administrator.

NT security affects the entire operating system and comprises many components. Initially, we'll discuss the following:

- The logon process
- The Local Security Authority (LSA)
- The Security Account Manager (SAM)
- The Security Reference Monitor (SRM)
- Discretionary Access Controls

The Logon Process

The logon process sets the stage for all subsequent security. When a user logs onto a domain controller (or Windows NT in general, but we're discussing servers and domains here), the user enters a name and then a password. This information is passed via the security subsystem to the SAM, where the information entered is compared to a central database. If a match occurs, the logon is authenticated and all other aspects of the logon are completed. These aspects include the assignment of a user directory and the execution of any logon scripts.

NOTE: The logon name is not case-sensitive. *Bob* is the same as *bOb* or *bob* or *BOB*. The password, however, is case-sensitive. If the password is *smith*, entering *Smith* will result in denial of access.

TIP: Passwords are easy to make, easy to crack, and easy to forget. Many of the cracking schemes simply pass all the words in a dictionary to the logon process. You can make a reasonably secure password by combining words with a nonsense character. If I log on as Bob Smith and use *Bob Smith* as my password, it's easy to figure out. But if I use *Bob&Smith* as my password, it gets harder. *Bob&Smith^* is even harder. Design a password that's easy to remember but has nonsense characters in it.

Once the logon has been authenticated and finished, the user is then assigned an *access token*. This token contains all the essential user information, *Security Descriptor* (*SID*), groups, and the user name. The access tokens form the basis for much of NT security.

From this point on, the access token is associated with everything a user does. For example, if the user attempts to open a file or use a printer (remember, both are treated as objects), the access token (plus process used) is checked against the *access control list* (*ACL*) for that object. If validation occurs, the process is allowed to continue and the file is edited, for example. If the validation doesn't occur, the process is denied, and the user is informed that she doesn't have the proper authority to conduct the process.

The Local Security Authority (LSA)

The *Local Security Authority* (*LSA*) is the basis of security in NT, and is commonly called the *security subsystem*. We don't need to spend much time with this topic, but understanding what it does is at the very center of understanding security. This subsystem generates tokens, allows users to use the system, and, most importantly, provides interactive users' services. The final thing that it controls (and that we'll discuss in detail shortly) is the audit process. If someone ever asks you what process controls security, it's the LSA. In the earlier example, the security subsystem was described in conjunction with an access token.

The Security Account Manager (SAM)

In simplest terms, SAM maintains the security account database. This database has all the user and group information. SAM handles two very important tasks: It does the comparison of the logon user and password with the database, and it provides the SID (security identifier) for the logged-on user.

> **NOTE:** When an account is deleted, the SID is retired. If you subsequently use that account name again, the original privileges are lost. All SIDs are unique.

As you might expect, there are two basic types of SAMs: those that are used locally and those that are used on a network. The central SAM is maintained on the Primary Domain Controller (with replication to the Backup Domain Controller if present) and the local is maintained on the local system.

> **TIP:** Never assume that your domain logon name and password will work if you boot locally. Always be certain to add the user or group in both databases.

> **NOTE:** The logon process can be more complex than just described. In a set of domain trusts, a logon can be accomplished by a trusted server. For example, if you attempt to log onto a server that is a trusting server to another domain, and the trusting SAM can't validate you, you are then passed to the trusted domain server for validation. This is called *pass-through validation*.

The Security Reference Monitor (SRM)

The SRM is the enforcer of the access validation code. It protects resources or objects from unauthorized access or modification. This security component enforces all access validation and audit policy in the LSA. In fact, the SRM is the sole source of validation policy on the system; that is, it implements the security and is the security enforcer. Every object in NT has an access control list (ACL). The ACL consists of ACEs (Access Control Entries) that have a SID (individual or group) and a list of actions allowed to that object. Every time a user attempts to access an object, the SRM checks to see whether the user SID matches an ACE list. If so, the task continues because there was a security match. In short, the Security Reference Monitor (SRM) is the Windows NT Server component responsible for enforcing the access validation and audit generation policy held by the Local Security Authority subsystem. The Security Reference Monitor contains the only copy of the access validation code in the system. This setup ensures that object protection is provided uniformly throughout Windows NT, regardless of the type of object accessed.

Discretionary Access Controls

This is really the last topic we need to consider to get an understanding of how the security in NT works. The discretionary access controls do as their name implies; they allow the owner of an object to set specific security descriptors for an object. For example, if you create a file called outline.doc, you're the owner of that file. If you use the Windows NT Explorer, you can right-click the File and choose Properties. A dialog box opens as shown in Figure 12-3. Click Permissions, and you can add specific permissions to that file, including special access that can allow Bob to edit the file but not Paul. (As you recall, the security in Windows NT is granular from file to subdirectory to directory to drive.)

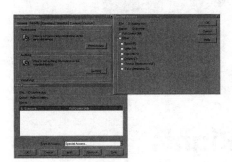

FIGURE 12-3

The security dialog boxes for the file outline.doc.

It seems apparent that the security in NT is very flexible and powerful. It's also easy to get confused by its implementation. A careful implementation of security is essential for proper network functioning.

Brief Summary

Although daunting to the user, the security in NTFS and NT is reasonably straightforward. Think of objects that have user-assigned attributes and an enforcer that checks these attributes against a user's security identifier.

All is made even easier from an administrator's point of view, because a wizard for file and directory (folder) management is present in the administrator tools (see Figure 12-4).

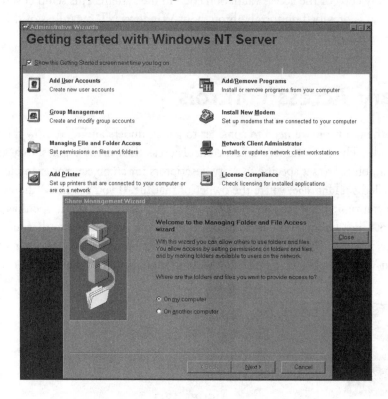

FIGURE 12-4

This wizard allows rapid and easy access to file/folder security.

Permissions versus Rights

The User Rights policy manages the rights granted to groups and user accounts.

Rights allow users who are logged onto an NT system the ability to perform certain tasks. Rights apply to the system as a whole. *Permissions* are different from rights and apply to specific objects. You can have the right to log on but not permission to use a file or printer.

Windows NT comes with user groups that have built-in rights. It's always best to assign a user to a group rather than have totally granular security by dealing with individual user accounts.

NTS offers 27 separate rights that groups and users can have. The rights are divided into two groups: *standard rights*, which always appear in the User Rights Policy dialog box, and *advanced rights*, whose display is controlled by the Show Advanced User Rights check box in the User Rights Policy dialog box.

The standard rights are just that; they control common actions that several groups or users may need to perform on a particular machine. Table 12-1 lists the standard rights—what name User Manager gives the right, what the right allows users to do, and which groups have the right by default.

Table 12-1. The standard user rights can be granted to any user or group.

Name	Given to which groups?	When granted, allows you to...
Access this computer from network	Administrators Everyone	Log on and access shared resources over the network.[1]
Add workstation to domain	Administrators Account Operators	Add workstation accounts to the domain's security database so the workstation can use domain accounts and groups.[2]
Back up files and directories	Administrators Backup Operators Server Operators	Back up files and directories without respecting file permissions.[3]
Change the system time	Administrators Server Operators	Reset the system's hardware clock.[3]
Force shutdown from a remote system	Administrators Server Operators	Not implemented in NTW or NTS 4.0.

continues

Table 12-1. Continued.

Name	Given to which groups?	When granted, allows you to...
Load and unload device drivers	Administrators	Load or unload device drivers without restarting the machine.[3]
Log on locally	Account Operators Administrators Backup Operators Print Operators Server Operators	Log on at the system console.[3]
Manage auditing and security log	Administrators	Control which security operations leave an audit trail entry.[3]
Restore files and directories	Administrators Backup Operators Server Operators	Reload backed-up files and directories without respecting file permissions.[3]
Shut down the system	Account Operators Administrators Backup Operators Print Operators Server Operators	Force shutdown of system processes and cleanly shut the machine down.[3]
Take ownership of files or other objects	Administrators	Reassign the ownership setting of a file from its current setting to indicate that you own the objects.[3]

[1] *When granted for servers in a domain, this right applies to all domain controllers; when granted on an individual workstation, it applies only to that workstation.*

[2] *This right can't be taken away from its default groups, so they're not listed as available in the User Rights Policy dialog box. Those groups can grant this right to other users.*

[3] *When granted in a domain, this right applies to the domain's PDC and BDC; when granted on individual workstations or servers, it applies only to that machine.*

By comparison, the advanced user rights are quite a bit more esoteric, but essential for applications that need to act as a service (for example, Network Backup Applications); most of them are available only to Administrators. The advanced rights are listed in Table 12-2. Some rights normally aren't assigned to any group, but they're listed because the Executive uses them internally. For example, most backup programs give a backup user the right to log on as a service.

CAUTION: There's rarely any reason to change any of the advanced rights settings unless specific applications call for changes. You may cause significant security vulnerabilities by altering these rights.

Table 12-2. The advanced user rights can be granted to any user or group.

Name	Given to which groups?	When granted, allows you to...
Act as part of the operating system	None	Gain access to system services by direct access to functions in the Executive.
Bypass traverse checking	Everyone	See the directory and file structure of a share, even if you don't have read permission.[1]
Create a pagefile	Administrators	Create a new virtual memory paging file on a system disk.
Create a token object	None	Create a new access token for a system object; every object has a token that controls who can use it.
Debug programs	Administrators	Access debugging information about NT or current processes.

continues

Table 12-2. Continued.

Name	Given to which groups?	When granted, allows you to...
Generate security audits	None	Necessary to generate a security audit log.
Increase quotas	Administrators	Necessary to increase object quotas.
Increase scheduling priorities	Administrators	Increase the priority of a process, thread, or process group.
Lock pages in memory	None	Force NTS to keep some virtual memory pages in physical memory to avoid swapping.
Log on as a batch job	None	Allows a user to log on using a batch queue application.
Log on as a service	None; usually assigned to individual accounts	Run background service processes as though they were logged in.
Modify firmware environment values	Administrators	Modify settings in the computer's CMOS area or in configuration EPROMS of interface cards; needed to run programs like an EISA-bus configuration tool.
Profile single process	Administrators	Gather performance data on an individual process.
Profile system performance	Administrators	Run Performance Monitor and gather system-wide performance information.

Name	Given to which groups?	When granted, allows you to...
Replace a process-level token	None; used by POSIX subsystem	Replace the system access token on a process object with another; effectively allows a process to change ownership.

[1] *When granted in a domain, this right applies to the domain's PDC and BDC; when granted on individual workstations or servers, it applies only to that machine.*

Default Permissions and Rights

Windows NT has built-in user rights. Some can be configured; some can't. Table 12-3 shows the configurable rights and group assignment for a server functioning as a domain controller. (Note that the Replicator group isn't included because there are no default members of this group.)

Table 12-3. Standard user rights assigned for specific groups; can be changed on domain controllers.

Rights	Administrators	Server Operators	Account Operators	Print Operators	Backup Operators	Everyone
Log on locally	X	X	X	X	X	
Log on over network	X					X
Take ownership of files	X					
Manage security and audit logs	X					
Manage the system clock	X	X				
Shut down the system	X	X	X	X	X	

continues

Rights	Administrators	Server Operators	Account Operators	Print Operators	Backup Operators	Everyone
Shut down remotely	X	X				
Perform backups	X	X			X	
Perform restores	X	X			X	
Add device drivers	X					
Add workstations to a domain	X					

In contrast to this list, Table 12-4 shows the standard user rights that can't be changed on domain controllers. Note that this list doesn't apply to the groups Users and Guests. (The Replicator group isn't included because there are no default members of the group.)

Table 12-4. Standard user rights assigned for specific groups; can't be changed on domain controllers.

Non-changeable Rights	Administrators	Server Operators	Account Operators	Print Operators	Backup Operators	Everyone
Assign user rights	X					
Manage auditing	X					
Create and manage global groups	X		X			
Create and manage local groups	X		X			
Create and manage user accounts	X		X			
Lock the server	X	X				X
Override lock	X	X				
Format a server hard drive	X	X				
Create common folders	X	X				
Share and unshare folders	X	X				

Non-changeable Rights	Administrators	Server Operators	Account Operators	Print Operators	Backup Operators	Everyone
Share and unshare printers	X	X		X		
Create and manage local groups	X		X			

These tables can be expanded to include workstations and servers that aren't part of a domain. There is little difference with the exception of the Power User Group. A power user can do all that a user can do, but also can control his or her user accounts and share directories and printers.

Access Control Lists

The access control list, as stated earlier, is a list of users and groups with their permissions. Each user or group consists of a discrete entry in the ACL termed the Access Control Element. The basic elements comprising the ACEs are *access allowed*, *access denied* and *system audit*. The degree of granularity is determined by the specifics of the permissions allotted. For example, you can authorize access at the root directory or folder (as in the case of the Administrator), at the folder/subfolder level, at the file level, and, in the case of printers or ports, at the object level.

It's important to realize that the ACL is accessed only when a object is opened or used. For example, if an administrator changes the permission to a file from Full Control to Read Only, any user who has the file open at the time of the change will have full control until he or she closes the file and then reopens it.

User, Group, and Object Permissions

Remember that all operating system resources are considered objects. These objects can be created, protected or monitored. All is under the control of the object manager, which deals with folder (directory) objects, file objects, thread objects, object objects (printers, for example), port objects, and so on. In all cases, permissions to gain or restrict access to an object can be granted by the owner or administrator. In addition, each object can be monitored as to use and resource. Given this incredible flexibility, how can permission be assigned to protect the system and its resources but also be easy to maintain? You simply deal with groups and the built-in rights discussed earlier.

It's common to place users in more than one group. In doing so, try not to use conflicting security. For example, if a user is a member of two groups and one group has access to a file but the other group is denied access to a file, the denial will be the one used. Likewise, if Group 1 has Read Only rights to a file but Group 2 has Full Access, Full Access is given to a user who shared by both groups.

User/Group Privileges

With the User Manager for Domains, you can easily assign a user to a pre-defined group. The important groups include the following list for a standalone server:

♦ **Administrators.** These accounts can manage all local groups, assign user rights, take ownership of any local file or resource, and basically control all aspects of the system.

♦ **Backup Operators.** A backup operator can perform a backup and restore in the absence of read/write permissions on files.

♦ **Power Users.** Users who can share directories and printers on the machine.

For domains, the list increases with several very powerful groups. These groups generally have control throughout the entire domain.

♦ **Domain Admins.** This group is a global group but also is a member of each local group on any Windows NT servers or workstations on the domain. This group has blanket administrative power throughout the network.

♦ **Account Operator.** This group is composed of users who can manage domain user and group accounts. This group is very limited in functionality.

♦ **Server Operators.** This group has much the same functionality as an Administrator, but they can't control security, nor can they start and stop services. This group is primarily designed to keep servers running. They can't create or manage users.

♦ **Print Operators.** This is a confusing group because a Print Operator can do more than simply control printers. This group can log onto and shut down servers.

Setting Up User Accounts

Much has been written about setting up user accounts on networks. With NT, this is actually very easy. The primary tool for this process is the User Manager for Domains. The only thing necessary in filling this out is the adoption of a uniform scheme of assigning users. In small LANs, you can use abbreviations or first names; in larger ones, adopt some variation of the last name as a starting point. Remember, all users must have unique names and passwords.

> **TIP:** By far the easiest way to manage users is assigning them to groups rather than treating them as individual users. If the security of the user has to be altered in any way, it doesn't affect the security of the group.

> **CAUTION:** No one can read passwords; they're encrypted with a one-way scheme. If a user loses a password, no one can tell him what the password is. Of course, an administrator can create a new password.

You can create a new group very easily and then highlight it and assign the rights that you want. For example, Figure 12-5 shows a group called workers being assigned specific user rights. With careful planning, you can form a group that's more specific to your needs than any of the built-in groups.

When you add a user to the server or domain, you simply highlight the group for which you want to make the user a member, and click Add. The Group Memberships dialog box is shown in Figure 12-6. In all cases, you can select a primary group if more than one group is chosen.

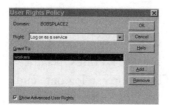

FIGURE 12-5

The assignment of user rights to the newly created user group called workers.

FIGURE 12-6

The standard Group Memberships dialog box.

One change in NT Version 4.0 is the ability to set dial-in security for a user. This allows the user to dial into the network with the dial-up networking program (see Figure 12-7). To do this, you simply select the option called Grant Dialin Permission to User.

FIGURE 12-7

The Dialin Information dialog box for a user assignment in User Manager for Domains.

Understanding Local Security Issues

Before discussing the minimum security setup, we need to consider one additional aspect. Many times it's essential to protect the resources of the domain. In this case, you are worried about resource deletion or alteration or the system corrupted by a user. A new tool has shown up in NT Version 4.0. This powerful tool is the *System Policy Editor*. With this tool, you can easily lock displays, desktop, and so on. This editor can make it easy for you to form mandatory profiles so that all desktops on the network look the same and only administrators can change desktop resources.

Understanding Profiles

We've already discussed the difference between local and domain logons. As might be expected, logging onto a domain results in profiles that are specific to the domain controller. Logging on locally uses local profiles. By the same token, changes to the local profile are only stored locally. Logging onto the domain will not show the changes made locally.

There are two basic types of server-based profiles: *personal profiles* and *mandatory profiles*. Unlike previous versions of Windows NT, this version stores profiles in the form Ntuser.DAT and not .usr files. Personal files allow you to store desktop information on the domain controller and therefore centrally. (When stored on the PDC, the profile files are called *roaming profiles* and they can follow you to any workstation.) Mandatory files are stored in the form Ntuser.man. This file is read-only. When a user logs on to a domain and has a mandatory profile, he or she can change the profile, but no changes are ever permanent. This makes it convenient to set restrictions on the mandatory file and use it for several users. These restrictions can be set for global usage.

You can change the type of profile from local to roaming by use of the User Profile tab in the System applet in Control Panel. This also allows you to copy profiles, delete profiles, or change from local to roaming. This tab is shown in Figure 12-8.

FIGURE 12-8

The User Profile tab in the System applet in Control Panel.

Suggested Permissions and Security Steps

When you setup security in NT, certain fundamental issues and policies need to be addressed. Some of the options are obvious, others aren't. The following list represents the major items to consider:

♦ All NT systems and domains have Administrators. This is a known user and it can't be deleted. You can rename Administrator, however. If you do so, hackers can't access the Administrator or Administrative shares.

♦ In the User Manager for Domains, use the Account Policy Editor and set the Lock Out option to a reasonable number, such as 5. This of course means that after five failed attempts to enter a password, the system is locked up and only the administrator can unlock it. This often-overlooked setting enables you to minimize risk caused by hackers on a LAN or WAN.

♦ The domain administrator must access the roles played by everyone on the network. If a new user needs to have administrator privilege, simply add the user to the Domain Admin group. Likewise, every user you create on a domain becomes a member of the Domain User group. Beyond this, the only other domain group is the Domain Guest group, which has no members by default. It's not a good idea to enable the Domain Guest account. The account can be used to hack into your network.

♦ Global groups can be used to allow users to gain access to local workstations. Simply place the user in a global group and then place the global group into the local group of appropriate computers. This plan allows many users access to several local machines. When used with a roaming mandatory profile, everything will look the same, regardless of the computer used.

♦ If you need to assign permissions on Windows NT workstations, create a global group and assign that group permission to access a workstation or group of workstations. Alternatively, place the global group in the necessary local groups.

♦ Global groups can be placed in local groups. Local groups can't join other groups. Although seemingly trivial, this setup can be used to gain easy domain-wide access.

♦ If you place all users into groups, you can then further restrict privileges of a user and not influence other members of that group. See Chapter 16, "Managing Users and Groups in Domains," for details on the issues of users and groups.

Once all groups have been determined and all users placed in groups, all you need to worry about is the assignment of privileges by file owners and administrators. In all cases, not assigning permission to an object is the same as denying access to that object. This enables you to deny access through simple neglect. In other words, plan to worry about user and group access to objects. From this point on, permissions become straightforward.

> **NOTE:** Not assigning permission may sound the same as denying access to an object. From an administrative perspective, of course, an explicit deny (No Access) isn't the same as not assigning permissions to an object. But the user can't tell the difference.

Remember, denial always wins out. If a user is a member of a group that has full read/write privilege over a file, but the user is denied access to the file, the denial prevents the user from accessing the file despite the group privilege. This strategy enables you to use levels of security granularity to control group/user access to objects.

The easiest strategy then uses explicit access to objects to control all access. (This of course presupposes that you have minimized the number of administrators on the network, because an administrator can gain access to a file and even become owner of the file.) Try to set up the network in such a manner that most files/folders are simply not shared and root directories never are shared. Make specific directories/folders that are to be shared and assign group access to them. For example, if you use an accounting application that stores data centrally, you can create an Accounting group and give that group access to the data. Other groups won't be able to access it. Such context and security will do much to minimize risk to your data when using NTFS as the file structure.

> **TIP:** Try to not mix shades of security to users. For example, if a user has read-only access to a file but a group of which the user is a member has full access to the file, so does that user. Use group access and privilege only.

Suppose that you have a drive with several folders. Folder 1 is called accounting and folder 2 is called sales. How can you assign security to the drive? What strategy should you take?

First of all, assume that the drive is NTFS. (The security on FAT is problematic at best.) It seems obvious that there are two groups of users that will access the drive: salespeople and accountants. If the folders will be accessed exclusively by either salespeople or accountants, assigning security is straightforward. Simply create groups called `sales` and `accounting` and place all users in the appropriate groups. The easiest way to create security in this system is to create two shares. You grant access to the `sales` share to the `sales` group but deny access to the `sales` share to the `accounting` group. Do the same in reverse with the `accounting` share.

But what if some salespeople need access to specific accounting subdirectories or folders? It's important that all files are organized logically in the folder. You can exclude users from some files or subdirectories but give them access to others. If the files are organized in logical directories, this added complexity is no problem.

Now what would happen if you had a user that always tried to change everything? You can simply deny access to that user for any specific file or folder. In this way, you give explicit rights to that user to access certain files but deny the user access to others. This can be done on a file-by-file basis. As is evident, the degree of access is determined by creating making shares with specific degrees of access. Much of this strategy simply reflects the organization of the domain administrator.

Auditing Events in Windows NT

By default, auditing is disabled in Windows NT. This should never be the case. Auditing should be enabled but with some degree of restraint. In User Manager for Domains, choose Policies | Audit; Figure 12-9 shows the basic audit policies that should be routinely assigned. Under normal circumstances, don't enable Process Tracking because this will fill the Event Log very rapidly and also provide unnecessary overhead to the Windows NT network.

Several of these choices need explanation:

◆ File and Object Access—You need to enable this option to use auditing of files and objects such as printers. It's more important to see failures than successes.

◆ Use of User Rights—This option monitors the use of special privileges and, in this case, their failures. It also monitors failed attempts to use rights not assigned to users.

◆ Security Policy Changes—This option enables you to keep track of all changes that have occurred to the security subsystem. Here you need to keep track of failures as well as successes.

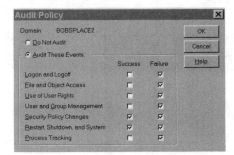

FIGURE 12-9

The suggested auditing events that are enabled in User Manager for Domains.

Throughout this process, bear in mind that you can audit both directories and files. These audits can be set up in the My Computer window or in Explorer. In both cases, right-click, choose Properties, choose the Security tab, and then click the Auditing button. This is also related to the built-in granularity of the security in Windows NT. Figures 12-10 and 12-11 show auditing options for both directories and files. To view the results of the auditing (see Figure 12-12), you use Event Viewer's Security menu.

FIGURE 12-10

The audit screen for directories.

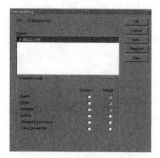

FIGURE 12-11

The audit screen for files.

Date	Time	Source	Category	Event	User	Computer
5/30/96	11:26:29 AM	Security	Object Access	562	SYSTEM	BIGCLYDE
5/30/96	11:26:29 AM	Security	Object Access	560	BIGCLYDE	BIGCLYDE
5/30/96	11:26:29 AM	Security	Object Access	562	SYSTEM	BIGCLYDE
5/30/96	11:26:29 AM	Security	Object Access	560	BIGCLYDE	BIGCLYDE
5/30/96	11:26:29 AM	Security	Object Access	562	SYSTEM	BIGCLYDE
5/30/96	11:26:29 AM	Security	Object Access	560	BIGCLYDE	BIGCLYDE
5/30/96	11:26:29 AM	Security	Object Access	560	BIGCLYDE	BIGCLYDE
5/30/96	8:42:21 AM	Security	Object Access	562	SYSTEM	BIGCLYDE
5/30/96	8:42:21 AM	Security	Object Access	560	BIGCLYDE	BIGCLYDE
5/30/96	8:42:21 AM	Security	Object Access	562	SYSTEM	BIGCLYDE
5/30/96	8:42:21 AM	Security	Object Access	560	BIGCLYDE	BIGCLYDE
5/30/96	8:42:21 AM	Security	Object Access	562	SYSTEM	BIGCLYDE
5/30/96	8:42:21 AM	Security	Object Access	560	BIGCLYDE	BIGCLYDE
5/30/96	8:42:21 AM	Security	Object Access	562	SYSTEM	BIGCLYDE
5/30/96	8:42:20 AM	Security	Object Access	560	BIGCLYDE	BIGCLYDE
5/30/96	8:42:20 AM	Security	Object Access	562	SYSTEM	BIGCLYDE
5/30/96	8:42:20 AM	Security	Object Access	560	BIGCLYDE	BIGCLYDE
5/30/96	8:42:20 AM	Security	Object Access	562	SYSTEM	BIGCLYDE
5/30/96	8:42:20 AM	Security	Object Access	560	BIGCLYDE	BIGCLYDE
5/30/96	8:42:20 AM	Security	Object Access	562	SYSTEM	BIGCLYDE
5/30/96	8:42:20 AM	Security	Object Access	560	BIGCLYDE	BIGCLYDE
5/30/96	8:40:23 AM	Security	Object Access	562	SYSTEM	BIGCLYDE
5/30/96	8:40:01 AM	Security	Object Access	562	SYSTEM	BIGCLYDE
5/30/96	8:40:01 AM	Security	Object Access	560	BIGCLYDE	BIGCLYDE
5/30/96	8:40:01 AM	Security	Object Access	562	SYSTEM	BIGCLYDE
5/30/96	8:40:01 AM	Security	Object Access	560	BIGCLYDE	BIGCLYDE
5/30/96	8:39:35 AM	Security	Object Access	562	SYSTEM	BIGCLYDE
5/30/96	8:39:35 AM	Security	Object Access	560	BIGCLYDE	BIGCLYDE
5/30/96	8:39:35 AM	Security	Object Access	562	SYSTEM	BIGCLYDE
5/30/96	8:39:35 AM	Security	Object Access	560	BIGCLYDE	BIGCLYDE
5/30/96	8:39:32 AM	Security	Object Access	562	SYSTEM	BIGCLYDE
5/30/96	8:39:32 AM	Security	Object Access	560	BIGCLYDE	BIGCLYDE
5/30/96	8:39:32 AM	Security	Object Access	562	SYSTEM	BIGCLYDE

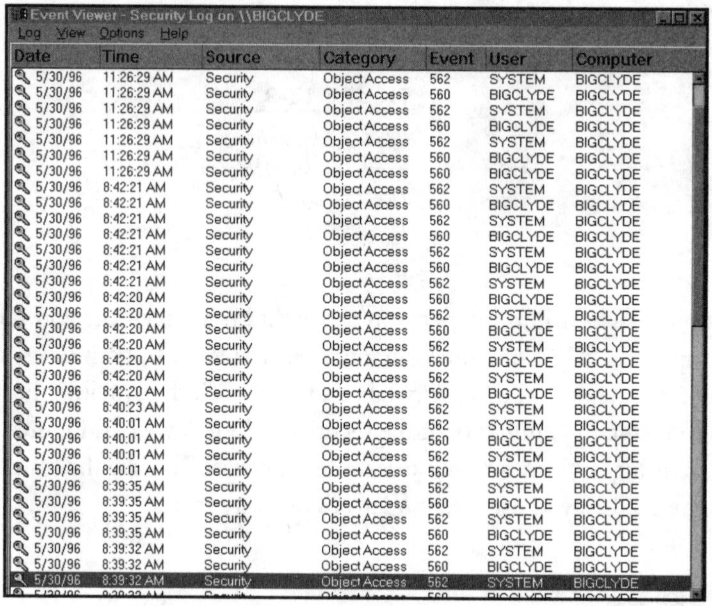

FIGURE 12-12

The security log as seen in Event Viewer. Notice that both system and user events are recorded.

TIP: Many networks are set up so that a domain controller also functions as an application server. This is far from optimal. If you analyze the consequences of auditing, you can see that overhead is added to the controller operation. In many cases, the auditing is essential and should remain in use. Therefore, it seems logical not to use a PDC (or BDC, for that matter) as an application or file/print server. This is especially true on larger networks.

In addition to auditing files, you can audit printers and network shares. All of these are done through My Computer, by right-clicking the resource in question. Choose Sharing and then Security; if local, go directly to Security. With these basic procedures, it's very easy to set up the exact auditing that's deemed appropriate for your system.

> **TIP:** Don't try to enable file security on a drive that has the swap file on it. In all cases, you won't gain access to that file and will have to abort the security.

Where to Go Next

This chapter presented many of the internal aspects of security in Windows NT. In fact, much of this basic material is also fundamental in assigning access to printers, files, and folders. As such, security is a recurring theme in NT.

Other chapters expand on the issues raised here:

♦ For coverage of controlling how users get access to shared resources, see Chapter 9, "Managing NT Servers." Printer access control is covered in Chapter 7, "Printer Management."

♦ Chapter 16, "Managing Users and Groups in Domains," discusses several strategies for organizing your users into groups in one or more domains.

♦ Chapter 6, "Managing User and Group Accounts," goes into detail in maintaining and setting user and group accounts, which then become an important part of the ACL used to control all access.

Chapter | 13

Safeguarding
Your Data

In This Chapter:

- ◆ Planning for Security and Redundancy
- ◆ Backing Up and Restoring Data
- ◆ Protecting Against Viruses
- ◆ Maintaining High Availability
- ◆ Recovering from Emergencies

How do I...

As information systems have become more important to the daily business operations of companies, the importance of network security risk has increased dramatically. A complete treatment of every aspect of network security planning would require a book at least as thick as this one, and there are several good ones on the market (see the section "Where to Go Next" at the end of the chapter for more details.) However, you can—and *should*—do some fairly straightforward planning now to get you started toward building a safe, secure network.

> **TIP:** When the subject is security, it's easy to go overboard and try to get perfect security—at a high cost. You should only be as paranoid as it's cost-effective to be. Weigh the cost of security measures against the cost of damage, corruption, or loss of the data you're securing.

This chapter will help you safeguard data on your network by doing the following:

♦ Introducing you to the fundamentals of security and redundancy planning

♦ Explaining hardware and software options for small- and large-scale network backup

♦ Teaching you how to diagnose and repair crashed servers using the Emergency Repair Disk and the Windows NT diagnostic tools

Planning for Security and Redundancy

Security and redundancy protect your network against intrusion and irreparable data loss. Good planning maximizes the potential that you'll be able to prevent a loss (where that loss is preventable—it won't help with earthquakes, fires, and the like). It also improves the likelihood that you'll be able to recover from any unpreventable loss.

The most common cause of data loss is the failure of a mass storage device. Modern hard disks are very reliable, but since they're based on rapidly rotating assemblies which rely on very fine tolerances, they are more prone to failure than solid-state devices like CPUs or RAM. Accordingly, let's start by discussing how you can protect your data by devising a workable backup plan.

Planning an Effective Backup Strategy

Accidents happen: Components fail, and users will occasionally overwrite or delete things they wanted to keep. The best insurance against these inevitable but unpleasant occasions is a good backup-and-recovery plan.

Much of what you do for your plan depends on your backup application and hardware configuration. Doing incremental backups over a fast backbone results in a far different strategy than simple pull backups over a standard 10BaseT passive hub. How you decide to implement backups will dictate disaster recovery, general restoration of files, and storage of media. The following guidelines provide some general insight to developing a sensible strategy.

To start, map out what data you keep on which servers. Some servers (for example, a print server or a machine dedicated to sharing a scanner) may not need any backup because they don't have any important data. On the other hand, file and database servers are sure to have things you want to keep. Once you know what data is where—and how much space it takes—you can decide on the best way to replicate it for archival and retrieval. Once you've done that, here are some other things you need to do as well:

♦ In addition to backing up the data, you must also *regularly* make sure that you can restore data from your backup media. Silent backup failures are the second biggest cause of irreparable data loss, second only to failure to make backups in the first place.

♦ Make sure that your backup plan includes training multiple people on how to restore archived data. What if a server fails while you're on vacation in Hawaii? In that case, you'll be glad that someone other than you knows how to reload the database from a backup, so you can enjoy an uninterrupted vacation.

♦ Don't forget the physical security component of your backup-and-recovery plan. Keep at least one set of backup media offsite so that you're protected against fire, theft, alien invasion, or unexpected damage.

Security Policies

You can use a number of security policies and procedures to enhance the overall security of your network. This section provides some detailed ideas on the kind of policies you need to consider:

♦ Physical security
♦ Network security and access controls
♦ Recovery planning

NOTE: In addition to plans and good intentions, security requires that you enforce the policies you create. Keep enforcement concerns in mind as you review the following sections.

Physical Security

Most IS managers have a good understanding of physical security requirements. After all, companies have been running their mainframes in climate-controlled, limited-access rooms for more than 30 years, so most of the problems and concerns are pretty well understood. However, you may be tempted to brush off physical security concerns because they don't seem to apply to your network.

Don't. Fire, flood, theft, or vandalism can disable your servers just as easily as a virus, a hacker, or a bad system component. The odds are excellent that your organization already has a physical security policy; whether they do or not, your planning should at least include the following tactics:

- Ensuring that servers are located in a physically secure area, away from unwanted visitors

- Providing adequate fire protection (preferably by some means other than water sprinklers)

- Guaranteeing a reliable backup supply of power—this may be a UPS, or your building may offer a standby power system to cover you during outages

If at all possible, consider placing your NTS servers with any other "big iron" you may have nearby; mainframe rooms are usually designed with these concerns and more in mind. The new seal of approval for the National Computer Security Association (NCSA) for rating WWW servers security includes criteria for whether and how the server is physically secured.

Network Security and Access Controls

One of the chief selling points of Windows NT Server is its strong built-in security support. Notice that I said security *support*—the security features won't help if you don't use them. Here are some suggested starting points:

- Use NTFS file systems whenever possible to get the benefit of their access controls and auditing features. See Chapter 12, "Windows NT Security Fundamentals," for full details on NTFS access controls.

- Structure your domain trust relationships and user access permissions so that everything is denied except what you have specifically permitted. The alternative—permitting everything except what is specifically denied—

is poor security practice, but it's also the NT default in most cases. (See Chapters 15 and 16 for suggestions on how and when to use domain trust relationships.)

◆ Be careful to restrict remote access users to only those permissions that they actually need. This strategy minimizes the risk that a successful break-in will compromise something important.

Recovery Planning

Most people prefer not to think about awful disasters in their workplace. If your network is critical to your company's survival, however, consider this: What would happen if your building burned to the ground tonight? What about if a tornado hit it? Maybe your office is in an earthquake-prone area?

Recovery planning can help insulate you from potential loss. Residents of Miami (Hurricane Andrew) and parts of California (the Northridge and Loma Prieta earthquakes) can testify to the concrete effects of what these unforeseen events can do to business networks. Prior planning can't stop the whirlwind or make the ground stop shaking, but it can greatly ease the process of returning your business operations to normal.

Your recovery plan should be just that—a step-by-step, detailed map of how you would reconstitute and recover your network capabilities in the event of a catastrophe. Your plan should incorporate a full inventory of the physical hardware you have (Hint: How would you prove to your insurance company what you'd lost?), as well as the data stored on it. Be sure to keep backup copies of important paper documents such as invoices and network maps. The plan might include provisions for setting up operations at an alternate site, if necessary.

Finally (and this is the part most people *really* don't like to think about), your recovery plan *absolutely must* allow for the possibility that you might not be available to help put the pieces back together. For example, does anyone other than you know the administrator's password for your servers? What about the configuration passwords for your routers? Failure to keep a record of the password puts your network at immense risk, because there's no way to recover the domain database or NTFS-protected files if you can't log onto the machine as an administrator.

The goal for your recovery planning is this: to capture whatever would help your company start over if your *entire network* was totally destroyed overnight. Any information, hardware, software, or knowledge that you'd need should be covered in your plan. A final note: Write down your plans and make sure that copies are kept in a safe place.

Making Your Network Fault-Tolerant

Fault tolerance is a very complex issue that, in part, is dictated by network demands. If a particular network is used as part of a large retail business, downtime can be very expensive or even prohibitive. In such a case, money spent to prevent downtime is a smart investment. On the other side of the continuum, the so-called SOHO (small office/home office) scenario may not be so critical, and only marginal investments required. In either situation, several factors stand out:

♦ All systems need some type of redundancy. Every experienced consultant or integrator has been asked to restore data to a system that ostensibly was "unimportant" but after the crash was deemed crucial.

♦ All systems can fail. There's no such thing as an absolutely protected network. Redundancy is expensive. The degree of redundancy that you choose must balance cost and degree of risk that you're willing to assume.

♦ Backups don't insure fault tolerance. In fact, backups are a very small part of the overall equation.

♦ In today's complex networking that involves LAN, MAN, GAN (local area networks, metropolitan area networks, global area networks) and Internet connections, fault tolerance is composed of many individual facets, including intrusion-prevention by packet filtering/firewalls, virus detection and elimination, crash prevention, file retrieval, and planning.

Fault tolerance is as the name implies; the ability to continue functioning if a fault or error occurs. Remember, the time between the fault and the recovery dictates the level of fault tolerance. So how can you plan ahead?

♦ Prevent unwanted physical access. No system is secure that can be accessed directly.

♦ Use redundancy throughout the network. If you use a PDC, have at least several BCDs if the network is large. The same holds true for DHCP. If your network uses a large database, have the database mirrored so that access is always insured. If the network is always being accessed remotely, use both the Internet and direct dial-up access (RAS server).

♦ Plan physical as well as software redundancy—of the simplest yet most practical nature. For example, placing each drive in a RAID enclosure on a separate power supply is foolish. Having redundant automatic fall-over power supplies (when one fails, the other takes over automatically) for the entire enclosure is an excellent idea.

♦ Operating systems can be rebuilt; databases can't. Invest your resources judiciously.

♦ Hardware redundancy is mandatory, but it must be monitored actively. Having part of a system go offline is okay, but having several parts go offline can lead to true disaster. Any hardware redundancy should be capable of remote administration and monitoring.

♦ File backup and retrieval is perhaps the most-described and -discussed aspect of fault tolerance, and probably the part that's most poorly enabled on a network. Always be certain to set up a regimented and thorough backup strategy.

Backing Up and Restoring Data

Although acceptable for local backups, NTBackup is not acceptable for network-based backups. There's no provision for remote backup of the Registry or active files. Granted, the application is getting better with each release of NT, but using it to ensure network integrity is foolish.

Choosing a Backup Method and Strategy

Much of your strategy and implementation is dictated by the software chosen. For example, if you use more than one backup device at a time, you want an application that allows concurrent use of these backup devices (Cheyenne's ArcServer, Seagate's Storage Exec and Legato's Networker). If you want to back up large amounts of data that are always changing, but you have a very small window of time to back up the data, you need an application that keeps track of files and performs incremental backups. Such an application would be able to restore any file without you having to hunt for that file. All such applications are available for Windows NT.

The most important thing to consider is the strategy used for the backup. Leaving a single tape in any backup device and overwriting each night is ludicrous. The easiest rotation scheme is the grandfather/father/son method. In this scheme, you rotate tapes in a very controlled manner. Typically there are 19 tapes used. On each day you use the same tapes, but the monthly tape is retired. The following table shows this scheme.

	Monday	Tuesday	Wednesday	Thursday	Friday
Week 1	Tape 1	Tape 2	Tape 3	Tape 4	Tape 5
Week 2	Tape 1	Tape 2	Tape 3	Tape 4	Tape 6
Week 3	Tape 1	Tape 2	Tape 3	Tape 4	Tape 7
Week 4	Tape 1	Tape 2	Tape 3	Tape 4	retired

As another option, you can purchase an application that will use a database and a tape library to maintain a large set of files and maintain tapes for you. This alternative is very enticing but also very expensive (in the neighborhood of $10,000–$30,000, depending on the type of system).

Regardless of the scheme adopted, be serious about it. Failure to have backups always results in catastrophes at the worst possible time. Saving a few dollars now can cost thousands later.

Another sought-after but seldom used alternative to backup is the use of Hierarchical Storage Management (HSM). HSM is a simple concept that allows you to migrate files, based on usage. Files that are actively used remain with the fastest components and drives. Files that are inactive for a defined amount of time are migrated to successively less available media. For example, files can be migrated to optical disk after three months and then to tape after an additional three months. While commonly practiced on mainframes, HSM is new to the PC world and not much used even though an excellent idea. Products with current HSM support are ArcServer and Storage Exec (formerly Storage Manager).

Choosing Backup Hardware

Many types of hardware are available for backup. These devices can be grouped into three basic categories:

◆ Devices for standalone systems

◆ Devices for moderate networks

◆ Devices for enterprise networks

Devices for Standalone Systems

This group is represented by QIC drives and low-end SCSI drives. QIC standards are for quarter-inch tapes and represent an inexpensive drive design. Most of these drives don't support file compression and aren't suitable for serious backups of networks. Likewise, the inexpensive SCSI drives are more for workstations than networks. These devices are in the $200–$500 dollar range and give you 10–15 meg/min backup rates.

Devices for Moderate Networks

This group consists of the DAT drives and the 8mm drives. DAT refers to the basic tape design. These tapes actually adhere to *Digital Data Storage* (*DDS*) standards; they're not "digital audio tapes" even though they are termed *DAT drives*. There are currently DDS-1 and DDS-2 specifications (DDS-3 is under development). The primary difference between them is capacity: 90-meter maximum for DDS-1 and 120-meter maximum for DDS-2. DDS-2 supports better compression schemes than DDS-1 and can store more data. Try to obtain decent DDS-2 drives such as the HP C1533a. This DAT drive costs under $1,000 dollars and should consistently give you 40 megabyte/minute locally and 20+ across a 10BaseT network.

> **TIP:** When you go shopping for drives, don't believe the rates and capacities cited. The numbers typically are for marketing purposes and deal with backups of idealized data, not real data. Low-end drives typically achieve 10–20 meg/min locally. The DDS-2 drives such as the C-1533a will back up at about 40 meg/min locally. The DLT devices for the enterprise will average near 100 meg/min for local backups.

Devices for Enterprise Networks

This group of drives consists of 8mm, DLT drives with and without tape libraries, and DAT drives with tape libraries. *Digital Linear Tape* (*DLT*) represents a major advance in tape construction and longevity. These tapes can withstand 500,000 passes through a tape drive and have a shelf life of 10 years, which far exceeds 4mm designs. Many 4mm tapes need to be retired after 50–100 uses. The 8mm tapes are better, with the new Mammoth systems from Exabyte nearly matching the performance of DLT tapes.

In addition, these drives offer large amounts of storage (10GB to 40GB). These features allow excellent data streaming (where data-in speed matches drive speed, so fewer stop/start interrupts occur to the drive). No matter what DLT brand you purchase, Quantum makes all DLT engines.

The 8mm devices typically have been seen as viable only on high-end LANs. This situation is changing rapidly. The advantage of 8mm drives is capacity: With reasonable compression, a single tape should hold about 10GB of data. The newly released mammoth drives from Exabyte represent a significant advance in speed and storage for 8mm drives.

The tape libraries available from such vendors as Exabyte and Qualstar offer much in convenience. The Qualstar devices are very sophisticated and allow the use of standard tape drives with enhanced access and control. For convenience and sheer enterprise capabilities, tape libraries are mandatory.

Tape systems are now showing up based on RAID sets. The purpose of these systems is to increase capacity and speed. Using such devices, tremendous backup and restore rates can be achieved. These types of devices, whether DAT, 8mm, or DLT, are very expensive but well worth the cost if time is at a premium.

Magneto-Optical Drives and Writable CD

If you want to use an intermediate storage system as suggested in HSM, nothing is more appropriate than the new magneto-optical (MO) solutions and CD-Rs. MO drives have become more respectable in the past year, with speeds approaching that of standard hard drives. The older SCSI-I MO devices were very slow. In addition, software such as Disk Extender from Optical Technology Group allows the management of large MO jukeboxes with ease and speed. Likewise, files that are routinely used as templates but don't change themselves can be burned onto CDs and used in CD jukeboxes, which Disk

Extender also manages very well. In short, central management of data resources can be very efficient and fast if designed properly. These devices are technically not backup devices, but certainly can be used as part of intermediate storage.

Protecting Against Viruses

Little thought is given by most administrators to virus protection in Windows NT. It has been assumed for a long time that NTFS was virus-resistant. In truth, it is, but other factors come into play. If a server is booted from a DOS floppy that has a boot sector virus on it, the boot sector of the hard drive can become infected, at which point NT will no longer boot. In addition, if the primary partition is FAT, viruses can multiply extensively (not true in NTFS). Finally, viruses are now showing up in document files and not simply executables. Accordingly, it's appropriate to consider steps that ensure the safety of any server—and, in fact, of any system on the network.

The best way to deal with the problem of viruses is prevention—with a combination of virus scanner and control of physical access.

The primary virus threat these days seems clearly to be Internet-related. The best approach to preventing virus infestation is to implement the following strategies:

- No user can install software without explicit permission.
- All files going to and from the Internet are scanned for virus signatures (this will slow down access, but the safety of the network must prevail).
- All systems that are backed up fall under a routine virus scanning.
- Virus signature lists are updated frequently.

Establishing a Virus-Protection Plan

The first aspect of virus security is preventing physical access to all essential servers and systems. It seems reasonable to go so far as to disable booting from floppy devices. Unfortunately, this strategy isn't enough. You can purchase virus protection applications from many vendors. One of the most established is Innoculan from Cheyenne Software. This application is installed as a service and can be used to screen systems on the network.

For Windows 95 machines as well as DOS and Windows/WfW that are attached to NT servers, it's imperative that some type of virus protection be implemented. To do this, establish network rules that have to be followed. For example, disable floppy drive support or make it impossible to boot from a floppy drive. Use mandatory profiles and let the users know that all changes to their systems must be done centrally rather than at their machine. In any event, make certain that users understand the consequences of using floppies contaminated with some type of virus.

Many antivirus applications are available for Windows NT, including offerings from Cheyenne, Symantec, and others. Of particular need are those applications that can be included in firewalls and proxy servers.

Dealing with Existing Viruses

What do you do when afflicted with a virus? First you have to understand what signifies a probable virus infection. One is fatal error code 0x4,0,0,0. Any time you suddenly receive a message about an inaccessible drive, you should think about a possible virus infection. The treatment is to scan all potentially infected hard drives with a good virus scanner; many such programs are available (Norton AntiVirus, MacAffee, FProt, etc.).

If a virus is found, get rid of it. If this doesn't work, boot to a clean (non-virus-infected) DOS boot floppy that also has FDISK.EXE and run FDISK /MBR. This should repair the boot sector. After this, you probably will have to run the install disks and repair the boot sector. (Boot to the install disk but choose Repair rather than Install. When given the option, choose Repair Boot Sector.)If all else fails, reformat the drive, reinstall NT, and do a tape restore.

Maintaining High Availability

High availability is simply the use of redundancy to minimize downtime. In fact, no magic elixir exists that provides availability. Yet you can plan ahead and achieve reasonable availability with minimal resources. The easiest way to look at these issues is to define various levels of availability based on downtime:

   ◆ **Downtime isn't critical.** For this situation, availability can be restored by having suitable tape backups and necessary hardware components. Simply turn off the system, replace the hardware, do a new installation, add the appropriate tape driver, and restore to the old directory, making certain that all necessary boot applications (NTLDR, NTDetect.COM, BOOT.INI, and BOOTSEC.DOS, if appropriate) are also restored.

♦ **Downtime isn't critical but needs to be as small a window as possible.** When you install NT Server, also install a bare minimum workstation to a separate hard drive. You want the workstation for sheer boot speed and maximum performance. If the system goes down, fix the hardware or handle other issues as appropriate, boot to the workstation, and do a restore of the server applications and operating system.

♦ **Minimal downtime is essential.** The easiest solution for this setup is to have serious redundancy built into the network with suitable backup servers and automatic switch-over applications such as Octopus. If a critical server goes down, the backup will immediately take over.

♦ **Downtime is unacceptable.** The present solution to this arrangement is hardware-sharing as is done with Digital's Clustering. In this scenario, drives are shared by more than one computer; if a system goes down, immediate local backup is available. To protect the system completely, all critical servers need to be replicated offsite. Octopus works with Clustering to produce this effect. Obviously, this configuration is very expensive.

Mass Storage Redundancy

Within the near future, nearly every server will have some form of redundancy for data protection. The best and most simple implementation of this protection is to mirror the operating system and stripe the data files with parity. All this redundancy needs to be accomplished in hardware and drives available on the unit so that rebuilds can be done from within Windows NT. As long as the systems remain running, data should always be accessible.

Uninterruptible and Backup Power Supplies

The most common causes of system failure are related to power supplies or power failures. For true redundancy, you need power supplies that automatically switch over. If one goes out, the other immediately takes over. This is commonly overlooked on systems, but the power supply is the most likely part of a computer system to fail.

For average networks, an intermediate solution is to use an *uninterruptible power supply* (*UPS*) or uninterruptible backup unit. These are made by APC, Triplite, and several other manufacturers. You need one large enough to give you about 30–45 minutes of use. Smaller ones simply shut down the system in 5–10 minutes. The APC units and their Powerchutes work fine in Windows NT 4.0. These units are far superior to the standard UPS applet that ships with 4.0.

Recovering from Emergencies

Many of us have experienced the infamous Blue Screen of Death (BSOD)—some of us often enough to think blue is not a nice color. In reality, the BSOD can be used to determine the cause of the crash. Whenever a system running Windows NT has a hardware problem, inconsistency, bad drivers, and so on, the system displays a message about the problem. Such a screen is typically called a *trap screen* or *kernel crash*. In essence, the integrity of the NT kernel has been compromised and the system needs to be rebooted.

With the Control Panel's System applet, you can dictate within the startup/shutdown settings how the system behaves when a crash occurs. Several factors dictate the outcome:

- ◆ You need to have the system reboot and write the memory dump to `%systemroot%\memory.dmp`. Because this is a dump of all the memory, you need to have virtual memory (`pagefile.sys`) equal to the amount of memory in the system plus the amount of memory necessary to run NT—as a general rule, the amount of memory plus 12MB.

- ◆ Systems set up to debug crashes use special checked files that can determine the cause of the crash. These files are large and slow and don't appear in most versions of Windows NT. The necessary files do exist, however: they are the `symbol` files on the CD in the `support\debug` folders. Copy the appropriate `symbol` folder to the `%systemroot%` directory.

- ◆ Either set up a remote debugger or use the `dumpexam` utility to determine the cause of the crash. In general, a system debugger is the best approach, but isn't always possible.

Interpreting Crash Dump Messages

Debugging simply means determining what pointer in a stack references an invalid memory address (that is, points to non-paged rather than paged memory). The first several lines of the crash typically tell you the cause of the problem. You can use the code that is returned and search the message base that can be obtained via TechNet or some similar tool.

The stop message may be somewhat daunting to an end user, but experienced technicians can use the information to help determine the cause of a crash. This message has several components based on the message ID, which in turn dictates the cause of the crash. For example, a crash identified as 0x0000000A is a memory crash that has four strings with it: a memory address, an IRQL address, a "for" string, and a "from" string. You need to relate the messages to the exact driver that is the cause.

You can also set up the dumpexam utility (on the CD in support\debug\platform). If you copy the symbol files and have a memory dump, you can use the dumpexam utility to change the file into a memory.txt file that you can read.

There are several common stop messages. Unfortunately, there is no single problem that might cause the stop, but several alternatives can be used to address the crash. The following list of messages includes possible causes and solutions.

◆ 0x0000000A (IRQL_NOT_LESS_EQUAL). This stop message is often thought to be IRQ-related. In fact, it means that a pointer to a *process internal request level* (*IRQL*) is generally pointing to a region of memory that is too high. This is a kernel mode trap, and can be caused by many things. The most common causes are bad drivers, mismatched SIMMs, or bad memory or cache. Occasionally DMA conflicts can cause the crash.

   Solution: Remove all unnecessary cards, particularly network cards. Make certain that all SIMMs are matched. When in doubt, do a crash dump analysis.

◆ 0x0000007B (Inaccessible_Boot_Device). This message is catastrophic. In order of occurrence, this is caused by incorrect setup parameters of an EIDE drive causing INT13 calls to fail, boot sector viruses, repeated failed installations, or installation on an unsupported SCSI controller with an improper driver.

Solution: Make sure that LBA is enabled with large EIDE drives. This is a very common problem on older IDE systems. Run antivirus applications that check the boot sector. On some FAT-based drives, you can run FDISK with the /MBR switch to restore the boot record. If you've tried several installations and the problems seem progressively worse, finally culminating in an inaccessible_boot_drive message, the problem is very similar to having a virus in that the boot record or allocation tables have become corrupted. In these cases, the best solution is a FORMAT and reinstall. If you're using a new SCSI controller but haven't prepared the drive for that controller, you can get a failure to boot message. Be certain that all SCSI cards and drives are properly configured.

◆ 0x0000001E (Kmode_Exception_Not_Handled). The most common cause of this kernel trap is a hardware or driver crash, typically related to a SCSI card or driver. In rare occasions, this can be caused by legacy NICs and drivers.

Solution: During installation of Windows NT Server 4.0, the installation will warn you about legacy NICs. Take these warnings seriously. If this stop message occurs, change to a newer NIC. If you're using SCSI cards that aren't approved by Microsoft, make certain that all drivers are current with NT.

◆ 0x0000007F (Unexpected_Kernel_Mode_Trap). This message typically occurs with a severe hardware problem. It can be caused by bad SIMMs, bad controllers, or even a bad motherboard.

Solution: This is a trial-and-error issue. Remove all unnecessary boards and see whether the problem goes away. If not, reduce the memory to the least amount possible to determine whether the SIMMs are the problem. Replace the SIMMs, if possible. As a final resort, try a new motherboard.

◆ There's no consistent pattern to the stop messages; they occur after you've added more SIMMs.

Solution: You probably have added marginal SIMMs to your system. Move the new bank of SIMMs to bank 0. In most cases, the new memory will crash outright. You need new memory.

Using the Emergency Repair Disk

During the installation of Windows NT Server 4.0, you were offered the option of preparing an Emergency Repair Diskette or Disk (ERD). This step should be mandatory. You can repair a crashed NT installation without an ERD, but the ERD is far more bulletproof.

Boot into the install process. Instead of installing, choose Repair an Existing Installation. As the repair process unfolds, you are asked if you have an ERD. Insert the disk; then you can repair system files, the Registry, and the boot sector. In general, you only repair system files and the boot sector. Repairing the Registry reverts the system to the last time the ERD was totally updated.

You can update the repair information with the Rdisk.exe command, which should be placed via Explorer into the Administrator folder. Rdisk doesn't update the ERD completely, but if you use the /s switch the system updates everything in the same manner as the original installation. Simply place a disk in the floppy drive and run Rdisk /s.

What the ERD Restores

The ERD contains the following files:

- ◆ autoexec.nt helps initialize DOS applications in NT.
- ◆ config.nt helps initialize DOS applications in NT.
- ◆ ntuser.da_ is a specific user profile.
- ◆ sam._ holds the Security Account Manager.
- ◆ security._ is the security database.
- ◆ setup.log is setup information.
- ◆ software._ contains software-configurable settings.
- ◆ system._ contains system-specific settings.

You can use the ERD to fix computer- and user-specific settings. In doing so, you lose all custom settings and new hardware/software configurations; that is, everything that has been changed since the ERD was last updated. To run the ERD, run the installation procedure (see Chapter 4, "Installing Windows NT Server"). When offered the choice, choose Repair. You will be asked for an ERD. When running this program, be certain to use only the necessary portions of the repair procedure. In general, fixing the boot sector or system files will suffice, but security can likewise be repaired.

What the ERD Doesn't Restore

The ERD won't repair many third-party applications. It's very important, in the case of a repair, to have a backup present for restoring. In other words, a repair won't restore the whole Registry. A common repair process would be as follows:

1. Run the Windows NT 4.0 installation and choose Repair.
2. Repair the necessary files.
3. Boot into NT and restore the Registry.
4. Reboot NT.

This method has saved the lives and reputations of many NT service personnel.

Using the "Last Known Good" Boot Setting

The Last Known Good entry is maintained in the Registry as a REG_DWORD value. This value is in HKEY_LOCAL_MACHINE \SYSTEM\Select; it specifies a particular control set that is known to have been booted successfully. If you install an application or driver that causes NT to crash on booting, you can press the space bar when instructed and choose the Last Known Good boot to go to a previous configuration of NT that booted successfully. (For details on using the Last Known Good, see Chapter 11, "Working with the Windows NT System Registry.")

As in many cases, use this ability very carefully. You might lose far more than you anticipate. For example, you'll lose any application or customization that you have just added. This is one reason to always have a recent backup.

Using Microsoft's Diagnostic Software

Windows NT ships with several applications that can make diagnosis of problems easier. The most common is the Diagnostic applet included in the Administrator folder. This application is very similar in content to the Microsoft Diagnostics (MSD) executable that ships with DOS. In extent, however, this application is far superior to MSD. If you consistently have crashes that make no sense, check to see whether you have overlapping I/O addresses or IRQs. For example, it's not uncommon to have a PS2 mouse pointer disappear on a Pentium SMP computer. Typically this happens during periods of heavy processor activity when you suddenly move the mouse. The mouse has lost its IRQ. Checking the IRQ assignments might show you that IRQ 12 is assigned to the mouse and also to the APIC logic of the SMP configuration. In this case, there's little that you can do (and the problem is less frequent in Version 4.0), but at least you can get a decent idea as to the cause. The Diagnostic application is important enough that it should be placed on the desktop.

WinMSD tells you nearly everything about the system you're using. You can determine DMA, IRQs, and I/Os (see Figure 13-1). There's also information about the video card and the CPU. The status of services is displayed—whether running or not. In short, WinMSD is a superb diasgnostic tool.

FIGURE 13-1

WinMSD can show details about IRQs and their properties installed on a system.

In conjunction with the Diagnostic application, use the Event Viewer. Specific types of errors may be shown in the Event Viewer. These errors can help you in system diagnosis. For example, the Event Viewer may tell you that a Digiboard card failed to initiate because of an overlap with a video card. You can look in the Diagnostic application and find the possible overlap with the video card, and perhaps find an appropriate I/O address.

Likewise, you can use the Devices and Services Control Panel applets to help you diagnose a problem. If a mouse fails to function, you can look in the Devices Control Panel applet to see what mouse drivers are installed on the machine. Then you can try a different mouse driver.

Two more diagnostic tests are included on the Version 4.0 CD in the Support folder: Hqtool and SCSItool. Both of these files need to be made into floppy disks on your system with a makedisk.bat file. You boot to these floppy disks; diagnostics then are run on your system that indicate potential installation problems. Interestingly, these are DOS boot floppies that you can use (making a licensed copy of DOS unnecessary).

> **NOTE:** Several aspects of these utilities may report information incorrectly. For example, if you have 128MBof RAM on the system, the applet will most likely tell you that you have 64MB. This is actually a DOS limitation.

Making an NT Boot Disk

Although seldom used, a boot disk is a very valuable floppy disk to possess. Furthermore, it's very easy to make:

1. Format a floppy disk.
2. Copy the files NTLDR, boot.ini, and NTDetect.COM to the boot floppy. (These files are probably hidden system files; you'll need to remove the attributes before copying the files, and then reset the attributes after the copy process is finished.) In some cases, it's more efficient to use the SCSI rather than multi terminology for boot.ini. In that case, you need to copy the SCSI boot driver to the boot floppy as NTBootDD.sys. (See Chapter 8, "Mass Storage Management," for details on these system files.)

You can use this boot floppy to bypass sick but present boot drives, to go to mirrored drives rather than primary ones, and to bypass corrupt master boot records. The boot floppy is like the ERD in that it should be mandatory with all NTFS systems.

Where to Go Next

As you can see, the time needed to plan for data safety and recovery may never pay off—but, like insurance, the investment is well worth the potential safety benefits if you ever need it. This chapter introduced you to some fundamental concepts in data safety, including some basic aspects of security and redundancy planning, a discussion of choosing a backup system and strategy, and coverage of repairing damaged or crashed machines. While you may never have to use these skills and plans, it's far better to have them and not need them than to need them and not have them.

There are some other resources which you may find helpful at this point:

♦ Chapter 12, "Windows NT Security Fundamentals," explains access controls and user permissions so that you can properly apply them to network resources.

♦ The National Computer Security Association (NCSA) offers a wide range of security publications and services to members and non-members alike. Check out their Web page at http://www.ncsa.com/.

♦ The *Disaster Recovery Yellow Pages* (Stephen Lewis; The Systems Audit Group, Inc., 1996) is a fascinating if somewhat unsettling guide to services such as emergency computer rental, document dehumidification, trauma counseling, and other disaster-related resources.

PART V

Learn this

Chapter

Managing Your Network with Domains

Chapter | 14

Understanding Workgroups, Domains, and Browsing

In This Chapter:

- ◆ Workgroups
- ◆ Domains
- ◆ Browsing Services

One of the key features that differentiates NT from other Windows operating systems is its support for managing collections of users and computers, not just individuals and standalone machines. Workgroups provide a simple, painless way to share resources on a small scale. For bigger networks, you can use NT domains to set up a network of servers and clients with centralized account management and control of users' access rights. You can also control the privileges given to users from a particular domain who want to access resources owned by another domain. This chapter provides the following coverage:

- ◆ An introduction to workgroups and domains, beginning with an overview of their respective features and uses
- ◆ A glimpse of NT's network browsing services

The details of how you use workgroups and domains, plus how you can tune browsing behavior to minimize network traffic, are covered in Chapter 15, "Planning and Using Domains and Workgroups."

Workgroups

Workgroups form the backbone of Microsoft's Windows networking services. The original LAN Manager for DOS introduced the concept of a loose association of computers that could share information without a centralized server. This type of service is often called *peer-to-peer networking*, because computers in a workgroup are all equally able to share and use resources. Windows for Workgroups, Windows 95, and Windows NT all improved on the original concept by better integrating access to shared resources into the shell, File Manager, and Explorer.

Workgroups Explained

Workgroups provide a convenient way to group computers that need to be able to share resources. To join a workgroup, all an individual computer has to do is claim to be part of the workgroup—there's no administrative control. Users are free to access shared resources without any centralized servers, and there's no central store of privilege or accounting data.

Although the name "Windows for Workgroups" suggests that Windows NT is not for workgroups, NT supports workgroups quite well; NT, Windows 3.1, and Windows 95 machines can be freely intermixed in a single workgroup. Furthermore, computers that don't directly support NT domains, such as Windows for Workgroups, the Macintosh, and OS/2, can use the domain just like a workgroup; instead of using the domain's access control resources, though, the domain controller imitates a workgroup's master browser.

Because workgroups don't have a centralized controller, trying to find the server or shared resource you want is easy—as long as there aren't many choices available! Even a medium-size LAN with 50 machines can make it difficult to find a share unless you already know its full name. To solve this problem, all the Windows variants provide a way for users to see a list of available servers and the resources they're offering to share. Depending on the Windows variant you're running, the list may appear in the Connect Network Drive dialog box of the File Manager, the Network Neighborhood, and the Explorer. Shared printers and devices also appear in applications that can display them.

Although there's no explicit central server, workgroup machines register their available resources by broadcasting announcements to the *master browser* of the workgroup. The master browser listens for these announcements and keeps a list of workgroup members and their available shares. When a client needs to display a list of workgroup computers (as in the File Manager or Explorer), it sends a request to a special network address registered by the master browser. In return, it gets a list of the available servers. This process is called *browsing*, and it's explained in more detail in the later section " Browsing Services."

Where To Use Workgroups

Workgroups are very easy to use; all you have to do is tell each computer you want to be in the workgroup to claim membership in it (using the Change button on the Identification tab of Windows NT's Network Control Panel applet), and the workgroup will spring into existence with no further action on your part. Because they're easy to set up and manage, they are useful for environments where many machines come and go—as in a pool of laptops or machines that move around frequently. Workgroups are further useful in small islands of isolated machines or in organizations where users can administer their own machines and the centralized control of a domain isn't needed or welcome.

However, using workgroups involves some compromises. When you use workgroups to group NT machines, you give up the centralized user account database that gives NTS much of its power. Workgroups can't share user accounts between machines, and there's no equivalent to the grouping and inter-domain access controls that domains offer.

A typical use for a workgroup is maintaining a set of machines that are used to demonstrate products at trade shows. Because machines are constantly being sent out and brought back, the membership of the workgroup varies, depending on which machines are currently away at shows. The need to segregate demo machines from the corporate network—to avoid introducing viruses to the network and accidentally leaking private data onto a demo machine—argues against letting these machines take part in a standard domain. Instead, they can be networked together in a workgroup as shown in Figure 14-1. In this example, a single Windows NT Workstation machine serves as a file server that all clients can use.

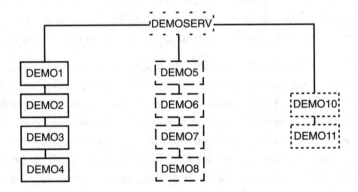

Windows NT Workstation

LAN Manager 2.x

Windows for Workgroups 3.1x

Windows 95

FIGURE 14-1

A workgroup can contain NTW, LAN Manager, OS/2, WfW, and Win95 computers.

Domains

If a workgroup is like a loosely knit group of acquaintances, a domain is more like a Marine Corps battalion: Not just anyone can join, and resources within the group are centrally managed and administered. Domains are managed by domain controllers, and each computer or account within the domain has specific resource access privileges assigned by the owner of the resource. NTS servers within a domain share logon, privilege, and account data so that all the servers in a domain share a common set of knowledge about what users can do. Individual machines within the domain can still maintain their own local accounts and permissions, in addition to the domain-wide database.

Domains aren't limited to Windows NT computers; OS/2, WfW, and LAN Manager 2.x clients can join domains, using the domain's ability to impersonate a workgroup. Computers running Windows 95, Windows NT Workstation, and Windows NT Server can act as full participants in the domain—meaning that, unlike the WfW and LAN Manager clients, they can use the domain's security database for user authentication and access control.

Domains Explained

The Windows NT Directory Services (NTDS) subsystem provides distributed, replicated access to user profiles and access rights. This means that users can log onto an entire network or domain with one user name; any network share can validate that user's access rights from the directory, so users have transparent access to resources from a single network-wide logon.

NT domains provide a key part of the NTDS subsystem. You can think of a domain as a workgroup with a replicated user database and security features—domains represent a convenient way to group users and resources for controlling access in a consistent manner. The domain administrator has total control over what privileges domain users have on the machines in their domain, as well as controlling what access rights users from other domains have.

Each NT domain has a *primary domain controller* (*PDC*). The PDC can be any machine running NTS; it maintains the master copy of the domain's security account manager (SAM) database, which contains user and permission data. Every other NTS machine within the domain keeps a copy of the SAM database as well, but the PDC's copy is the only one that can be changed. Changes ripple out from the PDC to other servers.

> **TIP:** You may have thought that only BDCs kept a copy of the SAM database. All servers do—but their copies are read-only. If your BDC fails, another NTS box can still authenticate logons, but you can't make any changes to the SAM database.

The first NTS machine you install on your network will become the PDC; you must specify during installation that it should be a domain controller. Once you've done so, other NTS machines will automatically contact that PDC for copies of the SAM database. In addition, the PDC will automatically synchronize itself with the *backup domain controller (BDC)* for the domain, if there is one, as well as with PDCs and BDCs in other domains.

> **NOTE:** Logon information is replicated to all NTS servers in a domain, so that even if the PDC and any number of BDCs are simultaneously unreachable, users can still log on, as long as at least one server remains up. When this happens, users will see a warning message, indicating that the primary domain controller couldn't be contacted, and an entry will be made in the Event Log.

Trust relationships between domains are just what the name implies: a database of rules that specifies what permissions a given domain is willing to give to users from other domains. There are four models for handling trust relationships between domains; we'll see them in more detail in the next chapter.

The PDC maintains all the user account data for users in the domain. Because user accounts are maintained at the domain level instead of the individual machine level, users can log onto their "home" domain from any workstation on the network (unless, of course, you've restricted user accounts so they must log on—or can't log on—from particular machines).

The BDCs get database updates from the PDC to keep their data synchronized with the PDC. When a PDC fails, you can easily promote a BDC to PDC so that you can continue to update your security database; when the original PDC is back up, you can demote the ex-BDC back to its backup role.

When to Use Domains

Domains are the preferred network grouping for many applications. Because they provide a shared database of user, security, and audit data, you don't have to manually manage accounts on individual machines. You also can set up domains so that users can access resources outside their home domain through a trust relationship.

Domains may not be the best choice for small networks, which can often function well as workgroups. If you don't need the benefits of the replicated SAM database, workgroups have less overhead, because they don't require domain controllers.

Browsing Services

Domains, workgroups, and individual machines form a hierarchy. Domains contain other domains, workgroups, and individual machines; workgroups contain individual machines, and the individual machines share their local resources. Any of these machines may have file systems, printers, or other things to share. To avoid confusion, we'll call machines with resources to share *sharers* instead of servers. Each sharer sends out network broadcasts announcing its computer name and what it has available to share. Figure 14-2 shows a sample network segment composed of a domain named WEATHER that in turn contains two workgroups, FORECAST and SATELLITE. Each machine in the figure can share any of its local resources.

> **NOTE:** NT domains appear as ordinary workgroups to Windows 95 and Windows for Workgroups machines, because those operating systems don't have any knowledge of domains. Resource browsing works just like it does on true NTS domains, but NTS can't validate permissions like it does for members of an NT domain.

Each workgroup or domain designates one computer as a *browse master*. In keeping with the decentralized nature of workgroups, workgroup computers elect the browse master for their workgroup. Within a domain, the domain PDC is always the domain browse master. If the workgroup is contained within a domain, the PDC will also act as the workgroup's browse master.

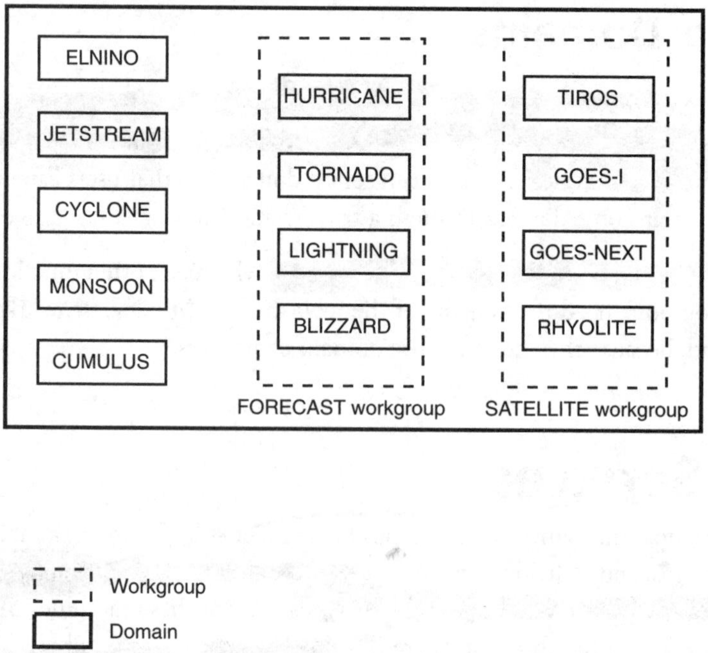

ELNINO		
JETSTREAM	HURRICANE	TIROS
CYCLONE	TORNADO	GOES-I
MONSOON	LIGHTNING	GOES-NEXT
CUMULUS	BLIZZARD	RHYOLITE
	FORECAST workgroup	SATELLITE workgroup

- - - - Workgroup

———— Domain

FIGURE 14-2

A domain can contain servers, computers, and workgroups; in turn, the workgroups are made up of computers.

The browse master listens to broadcasts from sharers and keeps an up-to-date list of advertised resources that workgroup and domain members can access. Individual clients query the browse master to get the current browse list; in fact, this is how the Network Neighborhood and File Manager's Connect To Network Drive get their information. The browse master listens for requests on a special network address reserved by Microsoft for browse master use; this is why browsing continues to work even when a new browse master is elected. For more details on how browser election works, see the later section "Master Browser Elections."

The browse master's list contains every machine that the browse master sees on the network. This is where the workgroup concept comes in: By default, clients start by viewing the resources offered by sharers in their own workgroup or domain. Resources from sharers in other workgroups appear beneath additional levels in a tree control, so that users can quickly select the workgroup in which they're interested.

In a further layering, NT domains also have a *domain master browser* (*DMB*) that collects information from the browse masters of each workgroup within the domain. Each master browser sends out announcement requests. When the domain master browser gets such a request, it asks the master browser for a list of the resources available in its workgroup.

Figure 14-3 shows the collection process; in the figure, CYCLONE collects browse data from the FORECAST and SATELLITE workgroups, and then makes it available to all computers in the domain, including workgroup members. If a FORECAST user wants to see what's in the SATELLITE workgroup, her Workstation service can get the list for SATELLITE from the domain master browser.

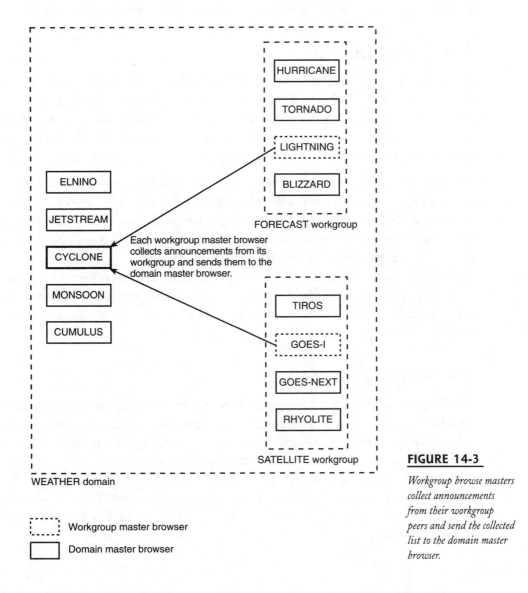

FIGURE 14-3

Workgroup browse masters collect announcements from their workgroup peers and send the collected list to the domain master browser.

How Browsing Works

The NT Browser, Server, and Workstation services implement the browsing and sharing behavior discussed in the preceding section. There are similar components for Windows for Workgroups, Windows 95, and LAN Manager network computers. Each component provides a portion of the NT peer networking services; let's examine what they do.

The Server Service

The Server service plays several roles in NT's networking subsystem. It answers requests from network clients, including requests to create files, read or write data in a file, or get directory or volume data. Server is responsible for periodically broadcasting packets that announce the availability of shared resources. These broadcast packets identify the computer name, share name, and UNC path of the resource being offered.

The server service is actually implemented as a Windows NT file system driver. As described in Chapter 2, "Understanding Windows NT Architecture," file system drivers in Windows NT can be layered, and the server service is actually layered atop the ordinary disk drivers. When a network request arrives, the server service turns it into a stream of disk I/O requests. Although the server service could have been implemented as a stand-alone process, making it a file system driver allows it to run as part of the kernel-mode executive code. Therefore, the server service has direct access to the file system and network caches, and can often serve data without calling the Win32 subsystem at all, resulting in better performance.

The Workstation Service

The Workstation service is also called the *redirector*, because its function is to redirect local I/O requests to a server somewhere on the network. The redirector does so transparently to the caller; applications aren't usually aware that their data is being furnished by a redirector-server connection instead of a standard file system driver. Like the Server service, the redirector is implemented as a file system driver. In fact, the redirector implements a network-based file system. I/O requests go over the network instead of to a local disk, but the semantics and behavior of the redirector's service are identical to those of a physical file system.

The Browser Service

The redirector and Server services provide the core capability of routing file I/O requests over the network. However, this capability needs a user interface as well; without one, users would be hard-pressed to identify the network resources they wanted to use. The Browser service is responsible for handling all aspects of browsing, including triggering or voting in elections for browse masters (described shortly), and querying the appropriate browse master to get a list of browseable resources when the user requests it.

Understanding Browsing

Browsing is an important service, because it enables users to find the resources they want to use. As you've seen, browsing requires a substantial infrastructure to work properly; let's examine some parts of that infrastructure in more detail.

Browse Masters

The *browse master* (or *master browser*, the terms are interchangeable) is the central repository for browse information. Each computer with resources to offer sends a broadcast packet over its network connection. The master browser listens for these packets and uses them to build a complete list of available resources within the workgroup or domain.

There are actually two kinds of master browser: the *domain master browser* (*DMB*) serves as the master browser for an entire domain. By default, the domain master browser is always the domain's PDC. BDCs or ordinary servers in a domain can act as master browsers, as can machines in workgroups. In domains, the master browsers synchronize their browse lists with the domain master browser. There's only a single master browserper workgroup, however.

Workgroups and domains can also have two other types of browsers: *potential browsers* and *backup browsers*. Potential browsers are computers that could be directed to become backup or master browsers if no other machine could be elected. Backup browsers help reduce the browsing load by handling queries within a workgroup. In workgroups, there's one master browser, plus one additional backup browser for each additional 32 machines.

In domains, each master browser connects to its domain master browser at regular intervals (every 12 minutes, by default) to synchronize browse lists. The master browser sends its accumulated browse list to the domain master browser and receives the domain-wide browse list in return. This ongoing synchronization ensures that all domain or workgroup computers have access to an up-to-date browse list. However, it can also generate unwanted network traffic when the domain includes machines connected by WAN or dial-up links.

> **NOTE:** You may wonder whether memory takes a hit with all of this exchanging of info. Not really; each browser caches the browse list in RAM, but it's fairly small. Network bandwidth can be wasted, though.

Browsers

Each domain computer can display the contents of the browse list to its users through a number of methods, including the Network Neighborhood, the Explorer, and the File Manager. When you open one of these components, the software calls a NetBIOS routine that asks the master browser to enumerate a list of available servers. The master browser complies by passing back the contents of the browse list for the selected workgroup or domain, as well as a list of other available workgroups or domains. The client then uses this information to display a list of shares, computers, domains, and workgroups for you to browse through.

Master Browser Elections

Because the workgroup concept itself is democratic, it's no surprise that members of a workgroup can "elect" a machine to be the workgroup's master browser. From time to time, you may see Event Log messages saying that an election was forced. Don't worry; these elections are normal and can be triggered in a number of ways:

◆ When the current master browser is shut down normally, it forces an election so that another browser will take over.

◆ When any machine in the workgroup can't locate a browse master, it starts an election.

◆ When any potential master browser starts up, it starts an election to see whether it should become a master.

In each case, the actual election is started by one machine sending out an *election packet*, which contains several fields that identify the machine by name, specify what its role is (domain controller, potential master browser, etc.), and what operating system it's running. All other master browsers and potential master browsers receive this packet and compare its data to their own. The process is very much like a poker game: If any recipient has a "better" set of data than the machine that sent the election packet, it sends out its own election packet and the election restarts. In general, more powerful roles win the election. An NT PDC will always win an election in its domain; BDCs beat out Windows 95 or Windows for Workgroups machines. In the case of a tie, the participants use the amount of time since their last reboot as a tiebreaker. If those times are identical, as a last resort the dispute is resolved by comparing their computer names. Lowest alphabetical name wins.

If the original sender doesn't get a response to its election packet, it's most likely because no other machine can beat it. The sender will try up to three more times (for a total of four election broadcasts) before declaring itself the winner and becoming the master browser. Whichever machine assumes the master browser role immediately starts listening to the special NetBIOS address reserved for master browsers.

Browser Contention

Windows for Workgroups, Windows 95, and Windows NT machines can all interoperate in domains and workgroups, but there are some occasional rough spots. One such problem is *browser contention*—two or more machines simultaneously try to act as master browsers, or a browser somehow can't interoperate with others on the network. The most common symptom of browser contention is an empty list of available resources.

One common cause of contention is the case where a Windows for Workgroups machine is taking part in an NT domain as a backup browser. If the WfW user isn't logged into the domain, that machine may not be registered as part of the domain. If the domain master browser goes down, it will promote the WfW machine, but if that machine isn't logged into the domain at the time, it won't be able to build the browse list. The fix for this situation is to make sure that the WfW user has logged into the domain with a valid domain account, or enable the Guest account in the domain so the WfW machine can use it instead.

Another cause of contention, Windows 95-specific, stems from Win95's interface for setting workgroup and domain membership. Win95 can simultaneously be in an NT domain and a WfW/Win95 workgroup, and it's possible to set a different name for each in the Network control panel. When the names are different, Win95 may not properly log on to the domain, so browsing will either show no resources or resources in the workgroup. The cure is to explicitly force Win95 to log onto a domain by using the Log On to a Windows NT Domain check box in the Configuration tab of the Client for Microsoft Networks Properties dialog box.

Where to Go Next

This chapter describes the features and roles of domains and workgroups. Because browsing is a subtle and often misunderstood topic, this chapter presents detailed material explaining how it works. In the next chapter, you encounter the fundamental domain models and learn how to apply them to structure your network by using domains. The chapter also describes how to control browsing to best suit your network environment. Later on, you see how to divide users into groups within and between domains, as well as how to tune your network for best performance.

Here are some other resources to consider:

♦ At this point, you may find the discussion of Windows for Workgroups and Windows 95 clients in Chapter 21, "Interoperating with Windows and DOS Clients," to be useful, as that chapter covers the specifics of having WfW and Win95 machines as workgroup and domain participants.

♦ Chapter 15, "Planning and Using Domains and Workgroups," covers the details of how you can plan, set up, and use domains and workgroups to organize your network.

Chapter | 15

Planning and Using Domains and Workgroups

In This Chapter:

- ◆ Domain Trust Relationships
- ◆ Domain Models
- ◆ Using Domain Controllers
- ◆ Managing Domains
- ◆ Controlling Network Browsing

How do I...

One of the key features that differentiates NTS from NTW is its support for managing collections of users and computers, not just individuals and stand-alone machines. By using NT domains, you can set up a network of servers and clients with centralized account management and control of users' access rights. You can also control the privileges given to users from a domain who want to access resources owned by another domain. This chapter covers the following topics:

- ◆ Understanding the five basic domain models and choosing the proper ones for your network
- ◆ Managing and administering domains using the User Manager for Domains application
- ◆ Creating and operating primary and backup domain controllers

- Understanding and using domain trust relationships
- Controlling the behavior of the browser service and its related components.

CAUTION: It's worth mentioning a few noteworthy limitations at the beginning of the chapter, because they can cause problems:

- The first NTS machine you put on your network must be a domain controller.

- Once you install NTS, you can't change a domain controller into a non-controller or vice versa without reinstalling NTS.

- Once you put a domain controller in a domain, you can't move it to another domain name without reinstalling NTS.

Domain Trust Relationships

NT provides trust relationships to allow administrators greater flexibility in specifying which users can use resources. Without trust relationships, each domain would need its own list of trusted users and groups; to add a user to multiple domains, someone would have to add that account to a group on each domain.

Instead of this labor-intensive process, a trust relationship can be established between any two domains so that users who are trusted in one domain can gain access to resources in the other *without logging onto that domain*. One logon—on the user's home domain—can permit the user access to all domains that trust her home domain. Figure 15-1 shows an example logon. For clarity, throughout this section we'll use a small example network with two domains: ENGINEERING and MARKETING.

Because of the way trust relationships work, it's useful to distinguish the *truster* from the *trustee*. Let's call the domain that's being trusted the *trusted domain*, and the domain that's being told that it can trust the trusted domain the *trusting domain*.

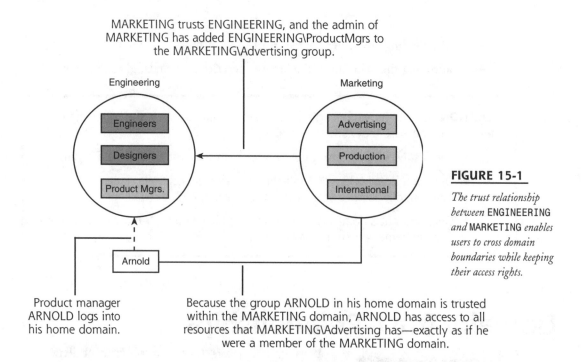

MARKETING trusts ENGINEERING, and the admin of MARKETING has added ENGINEERING\ProductMgrs to the MARKETING\Advertising group.

FIGURE 15-1

The trust relationship between ENGINEERING *and* MARKETING *enables users to cross domain boundaries while keeping their access rights.*

Product manager ARNOLD logs into his home domain.

Because the group ARNOLD in his home domain is trusted within the MARKETING domain, ARNOLD has access to all resources that MARKETING\Advertising has—exactly as if he were a member of the MARKETING domain.

Understanding Trust Relationships

When you trust another domain, that literally means that you are personally trusting the administrators of that domain. Your domain will honor logon and access authentications for users and global groups from that domain. If they're careless with their access policies, you may end up with unwanted users accessing resources in your domain. While you may not have much choice, be aware that creating a trust relationship between your domain and another creates a trust relationship between you and the other domain's administrator, too.

To establish trust relationships, you need the cooperation of the other domain's administrator. You can specify your MARKETING domain to trust ENGINEERING, but the ENGINEERING administrator must also allow your domain to trust his. This is true even if the trust relationship is one-way.

NT's trust relationships are one-way. If domain SALES trusts domain MARKETING, that doesn't mean that MARKETING trusts SALES—you may trust your sister to come over and feed your cat while you're out of town, but she may not trust you to feed her prize piranha when *she's* out of town. There's an additional wrinkle not found in human trust models: A domain must have permission to trust another domain before it *can* trust that domain. The domain administrator can give or revoke such permission at any time, but without it one domain can't be made to trust another.

Real-life trusts aren't *transitive*. If Alice trusts her coworker Bob, and Bob trusts his friend Cheryl, that doesn't mean that Alice trusts Cheryl. Likewise, NT trusts aren't transitive. Each trust relationship is a one-way link between one pair of entities, and no more. If you want two domains to trust each other, that requires two separate one-way trust relationships. This property is quite useful in situations where you want one domain to access resources in another without reciprocation; for example, the internal audit division might have access to the ACCOUNTING, FINANCE, and LEGAL domains, but not vice versa.

When to Use Trust Relationships

Trust relationships enable you to grant access quickly to groups of users maintained in other domains. The extent to which you use trust relationships depends on the environment in which your domains exist. By their nature, trust relationships force you to cede some control over your own domain; when you trust another domain, you're allowing that domain's administrator to designate which users in his domain have access to your resources. In addition, if your network uses the multiple-master or complete trust models, maintaining trust relationships can take a substantial amount of time (depending, of course, on the number of trust relationships you choose to use).

Trust relationships offer two important benefits:

- They decentralize access controls by moving them to the levels where they can be managed most effectively. If your network includes several physical sites, each with its own domain, allowing users from the NEWYORK domain to access resources in the HONGKONG domain is simple and can be directly accomplished by the domain administrators.

- The properties of trust relationships make it easy to replicate real-world access controls, like the fact that an auditing group may have access to many departments' shares, but not the other way around.

Using Trust Relationships

Trust relationships are managed with the User Manager for Domains (first presented in Chapter 6, "Managing User and Group Accounts"). The process of managing trust relationships is fairly simple; the more difficult part is deciding which domains your domain should trust and be trusted by. After you arrive at that decision, handling relationships falls into two categories: making new trusts and breaking old ones, as described in the following sections.

Making Relationships

Two steps are required to create new trust relationships. First, the trusted domain must permit another domain to trust it. For example, to establish trust from MARKETING to ENGINEERING, you start by telling ENGINEERING to allow MARKETING to trust it, and then you tell MARKETING to establish trust in ENGINEERING. You accomplish this with the following procedure:

1. In the domain that will *be trusted* (ENGINEERING in our example), use the Policies | Trust Relationships command in the User Manager for Domains. The Trust Relationships dialog box opens. Click the Add button next to the Trusting Domains field. The Add Trusting Domain dialog box appears, as shown in Figure 15-2.

FIGURE 15-2

Use the Add Trusting Domain dialog box to tell your domain that it has permission to trust another domain.

2. Specify which domain you want to allow to trust you by typing its name in the Trusting Domain field. Type a password into the appropriate fields (remember that the passwords must match). Click OK.

Now that you've set up the first half of the relationship, you need to give the password to the other domain's administrator, because she needs it to establish the trust.

> **CAUTION:** Don't make the trust password the same as your administrator password, because you have to give the trust password to other administrators.

Now that you've told ENGINEERING to allow MARKETING to trust it, you (or the other domain's administrator) still must tell MARKETING to do the trusting:

1. In User Manager for Domains, select the domain that's *granting trust*, and then choose Policies | Trust Relationships to display the Trust Relationships dialog box. This time, click the Add button to the right of the Trusted Domains list.

2. The Add Trusted Domain dialog box appears, as shown in Figure 15-3. Enter the name of the domain you want to trust, enter the trust password, and choose OK.

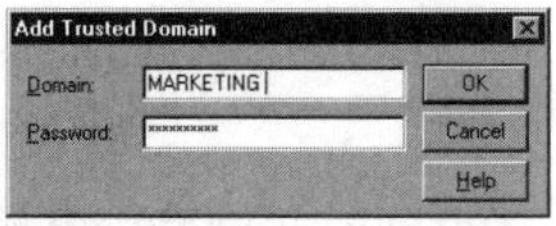

FIGURE 15-3

Use the Add Trusting Domain dialog box to tell the other domain that it should trust yours.

After you close the Add Trusted Domain dialog box, the new domain appears in the list of trusted domains. The User Manager for Domains records the trust relationship in the domain SAM database, and the trusting domain accepts the trusted domain for authentications. A dialog box will open to tell you that the trust relationship has been successfully established. If it doesn't appear, the trust relationship failed. Check the Event Log for errors, and then try to reestablish the trust.

Breaking Relationships

There are two steps to removing a trust relationship, just as when establishing a new trust relationship. To completely break a trust relationship and keep it from recurring, you must tell *both* the trusted and trusting domains to end their relationship.

In both cases, you break the relationship by using the Trust Relationships dialog box. Instead of using the Add button, though, you must select the domain for which you're removing the trust relationship, and use the appropriate Remove button. The trusting domain must stop trusting the domain that it trusts, and the trusted domain must stop allowing the trusting domain to trust it.

Domain Models

An impossibly large number of ways exists to organize your network into domains, but Microsoft claims that the possible groupings all fall into one of four basic categories. (There's actually a fifth configuration, as indicated in the following discussion.) Which arrangement is best for you depends on several factors that we'll explore in the following sections, along with the good and bad points of each. Remember that these are just categories; you'll probably choose a variation on one of these models. Let's start by examining each of the five models, and then look at some factors that you should consider when deciding which model is best for you.

The No-Domain Model

Without at least one NTS machine serving as a PDC, you can't use domain security features. If you don't have any NTS machines on your network, this is the trust model you're using. If you do have NTS machines, unless at least one is a domain controller, each server is an island unto itself. Without domains, there's no way to concentrate user or group information on a server somewhere; instead, you must configure each individual workstation's user accounts and access settings individually. For users to log onto any machine on the network, each machine must have identical user information—which must be manually maintained. Figure 15-4 shows what a no-domain setup looks like.

FIGURE 15-4

If you have no NTS domains, each workstation or server is an independent entity.

Accounting   Marketing   Engineering

The no-domain model is appealingly simple. Like each of the other models, however, it has its pros and cons:

- *Pros:* With no domains, you don't need domain controllers. This approach makes sense if you have many more clients that can't use domains than you have NT machines. For example, in a network of mostly NetWare machines with a few computers running NTW and NTS, it makes sense to forgo the overhead of domain controllers in favor of a workgroup.

    This approach may also be suitable for NTW-only networks if the NTW machines don't need to share user accounts.

- *Cons:* The lack of a central home for user and logon information makes more work for you. Because security and logon information isn't shared, it must be kept on each workstation. The amount of overhead required makes this alternative fairly rare.

- *Recommendation:* The security and administrative benefits you gain from using domains make them worthwhile unless you have a very small number of workstations that you don't mind configuring individually, or you really don't need centralized control over logon policies and access rights. Think very carefully about adopting this strategy.

The Single-Domain Model

In a single-domain environment, there's only one primary domain controller, which is shared by all machines in the domain—no matter how many machines that is. (There should also be a backup controller, but it doesn't count because it just mirrors the primary controller.) This lone controller keeps all user account and access information for all machines within the domain. Figure 15-5 shows an example of a single-domain configuration.

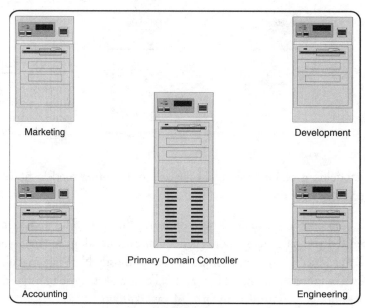

Marketing

Development

Primary Domain Controller

Accounting

Engineering

Main Domain

FIGURE 15-5

With one PDC, all the domain's logon requests are funneled to a central controller.

The single-domain model is the simplest domain-based model. It requires the least over-head of any of the domain models, but it's best suited for specific circumstances. Here's an overview of its good and bad points:

♦ *Pros:* Single-domain setups are good for smaller networks, because they're easy to administer. You can administer any server in the domain from any machine in the domain, and there aren't any trust relationships to create or maintain. You gain the benefits of having all your security and user account data in one central location. You can easily split a single domain into multi-ple domains as your network grows by moving computers (but not domain controllers) from the single domain into other domains with new PDCs.

♦ *Cons:* Unfortunately, with a single domain you lose the ability to group ser-vices or machines together; Engineering, Accounting, Finance, and Sales are all lumped together in one big überdomain. This loss of granularity in turn causes a loss of network performance due to increased browsing. Every browse query must go to the PDC for resolution, because it's also acting as the browse master, so the PDC can be bogged down. Users see long lists when they browse the domain. In addition, if your domain stretches across WAN links, the added browsing and broadcast traffic over the WAN will make performance suffer further.

♦ *Recommendation:* Use single-domain configurations only when you have a small number of machines that don't need to be grouped at any lower level. Single-domain groups are also appropriate for "islands" of machines, as in a test lab or other environment where machines are connected together but not to your organization's LAN. The browsing overhead caused by having a single PDC makes this model inappropriate for sites with machines connected by WAN links; instead, consider setting up a single domain at each site and establishing trust relationships between them in a multiple-master configuration.

The Master Domain Model

In the master domain model, the network has a separate "master" domain (hence the name) that contains all user, group, and security data. The "slave" domains, which can be organized however you'd like, refer all logon requests to the master domain's controller. Of course, these subdomains can contain sharers and workstations, but all security and accounting functions are kept within the master domain.

In this model, user accounts are defined as global accounts by the master domain; the master domain administrator can group accounts in global groups as needed. In turn, each of the subdomains can choose to which user accounts and global groups to grant access. An example master domain network is shown in Figure 15-6.

♦ *Pros:* This approach maps well to the common situation of having a central MIS or IS group that "owns" network access. The IS group can create and manage network-wide user accounts, and individual departments can still control which of those accounts can use their resources. As an added bonus, the subdomains can still create local accounts that allow intra-domain access to their data. Human resources and engineering groups, to name two, are often *very* reluctant to grant other people control over their servers, so don't underestimate the power of this advantage.

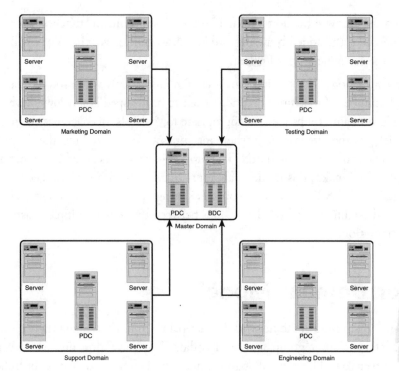

FIGURE 15-6

The master domain keeps security information; the subdomains trust the master domain but not each other.

♦ *Cons:* The downside to having a single domain that controls logon and group data is the establishment of that domain as a choke point. Because all logon requests have to go to the master domain, network traffic between segments increases. For this reason, the master domain model isn't well suited to use over WAN links or networks where there's a slow connection between the subnets containing the master and slave domains. Worse still, if anything happens to the PDC of the master domain, no one will be able to log on unless there's an available BDC—which may or may not be the case, depending on why the PDC has gone down.

♦ *Recommendation:* If you need the administrative benefits of a single domain while still allowing individual departments control over their machines, consider the master domain as a possible solution. Be sure to provide adequate redundancy in case your master PDC or BDC fails, and be aware of the added potential for network congestion over WAN links.

The Multiple Master Domains Model

Multiple master domains solve the choke point problem that plagues the master-domain model by having more than one master domain. All the master domains trust one another, and each subdomain trusts all the master domains. You can think of this model as having two groups of domains: a group of masters and a group of subdomains. Figure 15-7 shows a representative multiple master domain configuration.

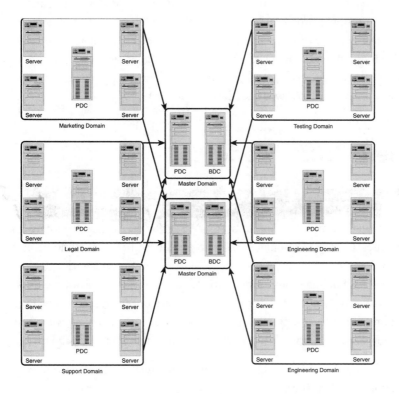

FIGURE 15-7

In the multiple master domain model, there are several master domains; each slave domain trusts all the masters, and the masters may have trust interrelationships as well.

◆ *Pros:* Using multiple masters relieves you of the single-master choke point, so redundancy and performance are both better than the single-master model. Individual subdomains can still keep control over their own resources, and you can still create trust relationships between subdomains where needed. This model works well for geographically distributed networks, because each physical location can have its own master; all the local subdomains can use it without putting traffic onto the WAN.

♦ *Cons:* Because all the masters must trust each other and the subdomains must trust all masters, this solution can require a fairly large number of trust relationships. Organizing users into groups can pose problems, too. Each subdomain must have a local group that containsthe global groups from the master domain that you want to have subdomain access. Finally, multiple master domains can be expensive if your PDCs and BDCs don't act in any roles other than domain controller.

♦ *Recommendation:* If your network covers a number of physical sites, and if the user-grouping problem doesn't cause you trouble, this model's a good alternative because of its increased redundancy and performance. You can establish one master domain per site or large organizational unit (say, a division of your company), and then install subdomains for smaller units (departments, teams, or whatever is appropriate.)

The Complete Trust Model

The complete trust model is simple to explain, but can be difficult to administer. Each domain has individual trust relationships with every other domain it wants to trust. The number of trust relationships required to do this can grow very quickly—a network with 4 domains requires 12 trust relationships to enable full trust between all domains, but a network with 5 domains needs 20, a 6-domain network requires 30, and a 10-domain network requires 90! The maximum number of relations for a set of N domains is expressed by calculating n $(n-1)$. Trust relationships are one-way, so this maximum reflects full bidirectional trust between all domains—which not every network needs. Figure 15-8 shows a small network where the domains are linked by complete trust.

♦ *Pros:* This model allows exact control over trust relationships, even in very large domains. If you often grant one-way trust between domains and you don't need or want to have most domains trust each other, this model may suit your needs. For example, it's easy to set up a system where the Engineering domain can have read-only access to the Manufacturing domain and full access to the Marketing domain, but not vice versa. This model also does away with centralized control, because each domain can decide which other domains to trust.

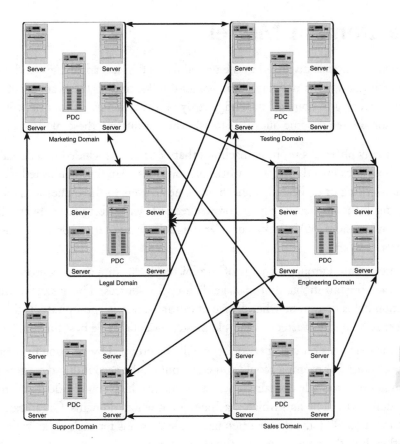

FIGURE 15-8

The complete trust model allows maximum control over trust relationships, but requires a larger number of relationships than the other models.

- *Cons:* As the number of domains grows, so does the number of relationships needed for full trust. Because these relationships have to be added and maintained manually, this option can cause a lot of additional work for each domain's administrators. Operationally, the lack of centralization may cause problems if each group is responsible for maintaining its own relationships, because relations often need to be two-way. Politically, this model may cause problems because it's decentralized, and there's no role for MIS to play in managing the domains.

- *Recommendation:* For many uses, this option requires too much manual administration to be useful. However, it provides the most control over trust-granting between domains, and is well suited to networks where multiple sites are connected by an internetwork.

Choosing a Domain Model

Each of the domain models discussed in the preceding section has advantages and disadvantages. As with many other network administration tasks, finding the best way of dividing your network into domains depends largely on the structure of your network and your organization. Here are some questions to ask when evaluating these models:

1. How many physical sites have machines that need to be included in a domain? Are these sites linked by fast networks or slow ones? Are they connected via dial-up networking or dedicated connections? The answers to these questions tell you how much the impact of network browse requests will affect your network. If you have one or more WAN links, consider the multiple master or complete trust models.

2. Is there a central group in charge of administering all computer resources, or does each organizational unit manage their own resources? The answer to this question helps determine what degree of centralization is appropriate. If the answer is "yes," the master or multiple master model may be best for you.

3. Can the machines on your network generally be grouped by function or organizational unit? For example, could you easily put all the accounting department's machines into a single domain? These answers may help you decide how large your domains will be and which machines go in which domains. Organizations with many small domains can often use single domains for each organization, and then link them with trust relationships as needed.

4. How is information shared between departments? Are there clearly defined needs, or ad hoc requirements that change often? These answers tell you how much maintenance of trust relationships your network will require, as well as guide you in building global and local groups. If the requirements change often, the complete trust model gives you the most flexibility, at the cost of additional administrative overhead.

Using Domain Controllers

After you've determined how many domains you need and what domain model is best for you, you're still left with the task of managing the domain, its controllers, and its member computers. You do this with the Server Manager, first introduced in Chapter 9,

"Managing NT Servers." Server Manager contains a number of features expressly for managing domains, but some tasks require other tools. Let's look first at how you install, configure, and use domain controllers.

Domain controllers are easy to use once you get them installed. As long as they're working—which is most of the time—they are pretty much invisible and go unnoticed by most users. Even when a domain controller fails, the replication of logon data and the availability of backup servers means that you may not suffer any downtime as a result. However, to be prepared, you need to know how to manage the controllers in your domains.

> **CAUTION:** You must choose whether each NTS machine in your network is to be a domain controller *before you install NTS*. If you install NTS and specify that the server is a domain controller, you can't "un-controllerize" it without doing a complete reinstallation of NTS. Likewise, you can't turn an ordinary server into a domain controller without reinstalling.

What Domain Controllers Do

All computers running Windows NT store user account information, including passwords and access privileges, in the *security account manager* (*SAM*) *database.* The SAM is a protected subsystem that handles authenticating requests for access to all objects in the system. In concert with the security reference monitor, the SAM is responsible for checking logon requests for both interactive and network logons.

Each NT machine has its own private SAM database that stores account information for accounts local to that machine. When a user logs on, the NT logon subsystem compares the logon request against the data stored in the SAM. If the user has authorization to log on, the request succeeds. Domain computers can also access a *domain SAM*, which is stored on the domain's primary domain controller and made available to all domain members. When a user logs onto the domain to which the machine belongs, an authentication request is sent to the domain controller, which checks the request against the domain SAM. If the request succeeds, the domain controller tells the logon workstation to accept the logon.

For this scheme to work, the domain SAM must be centralized so that there's only one version of the account data. In NT domains, all changes to the SAM database go through the User Manager for Domains, which is smart enough to send its changes directly to the domain controller no matter where it's run. Because keeping the domain SAM on a single machine would cause all logon requests to fail if that machine became unavailable, NT automatically replicates the domain SAM to one or more backup domain controllers. If the primary controller fails, authentication requests from domain computers are automatically routed to an available backup.

Primary and Backup Controllers

The *primary domain controller* (*PDC*) is the master repository of security information. As mentioned, it holds the domain SAM and uses it to authenticate access requests for interactive and network logons. The PDC for a domain can answer logon requests for computers in the domain or computers in trusting domains; the request routing is automatic in all cases.

To maintain redundancy and allow logons to continue when the PDC is down, one or more NTS machines on the network can serve as a *backup domain controller* (*BDC*). Each BDC keeps a replicated copy of the domain SAM database. The PDC periodically synchronizes its database with its BDCs. In normal operation, logon requests are serviced by the PDC or any available BDC; however, if the PDC fails, you can promote a BDC server to the PDC role.

When you promote a BDC server, it becomes the PDC, and the old PDC (if it's still on the network) will automatically be demoted to a BDC. If the outgoing PDC is off the network, you may have to manually demote it when it comes back online.

Synchronizing Controllers

Unlike some other NTS system services, the domain controller's software is supposed to broadcast changes in the domain SAM database to the BDCs right after they happen. This approach ensures that all BDCs have correct information in their local caches; as you add and remove users in a domain, the changes get propagated so that new users can log on and deleted users can't. This automatic synchronization normally works well.

But just because the PDC is *sending* these updates, that doesn't mean that all servers in the domain have *received* them. If your domain spans a WAN, or if one or more BDCs are offline when a change is made on the PDC, the PDC database and the servers' copies can become disjointed. You'll notice this if you get complaints from new users that they can't log on, or if you make group changes that don't show up on particular servers.

To force a BDC to resynchronize with its domain controller, select the server in Server Manager and choose Computer | Synchronize with Domain Controller. The selected BDC will request an up-to-date copy of the domain SAM database from the PDC. This process affects only the selected server, but you can also synchronize all servers in a domain by selecting the PDC for the domain. The menu command changes to Synchronize Entire Domain; choosing this option it forces the PDC to update all BDCs and PDCs of trusting domains with an up-to-date database.

Controlling Domain Controller Replication

Distribution of the domain SAM database is controlled by the Netlogon service. Under ordinary circumstances, Netlogon uses a 128KB buffer for copying the database, and replicates the database whenever it changes. If your PDC and BDC are connected by a slow network link, these settings can consume a large portion of your available network bandwidth.

The ReplicationGovernor parameter controls this behavior *on the BDC*; the PDC just copies data according to the BDC's request, so the change has to be made on each BDC where you want the change to apply. There are two keys to which this value can be added: one for standard NetBEUI networking, and a second one that's used when you choose to use the NetBEUI-over-TCP/IP transport, NBT. These keys are located in the following places, respectively:

```
HKEY_LOCAL_MACHINE\SYSTEM\CurrentControlSet\Services\Netlogon\Parameters
```

```
HKEY_LOCAL_MACHINE\SYSTEM\CurrentControlSet\Services\Tcpip\Parameters
```

In either case, you can add the ReplicationGovernor parameter, which is a REG_DWORD value ranging from 0 to 100. Its value represents a percentage; the percentage applies both to the 128KB buffer size and to the frequency at which update requests may be broadcast by the BDC. For example, a value of 25 specifies that a BDC should use a 32KB buffer (25 percent of 128KB) and that a replication request can be on the network no more than 25 percent of the time.

> **CAUTION:** Don't set this value to 0! If you do, the PDC will never synchronize with the affected BDC.

Promoting and Demoting Controllers

In ordinary circumstances, the PDC and BDCs for a domain will quietly process logon requests without calling attention to their presence. However, when the PDC fails, you lose the ability to make changes to the domain security database—so you can't add, remove, or change user accounts. Although the BDCs can answer logon and authentication requests, a BDC can't act as a PDC unless it's promoted.

To promote a BDC to be the primary domain controller, select it from the list in the Server Manager window, and then choose the Computer | Promote to Primary Domain Controller command. If the original PDC is online, Server Manager demotes it to backup status and passes domain controller authority to the BDC you selected. In addition, the incoming PDC will synchronize its database with the outgoing PDC before the demotion occurs, to maintain consistency. That computer's domain database becomes the master copy. When you promote a BDC because the PDC has failed, the synchronization step won't occur.

Because the existing PDC is demoted automatically when you promote a server, there's normally no specific way to demote a PDC except by promoting another server. While this setup may seem odd, it's actually a useful feature, because it prevents you from demoting the PDC and leaving your domain with no controller. Because demotion happens automatically, going back to the original PDC after temporarily promoting another server is simple—just promote the old PDC and it automatically resumes its former role.

Recovering from a Controller Failure

Sometimes, no matter how hard you try to prevent it, your primary domain controller will fail. When it does, it presents a special problem. The domain SAM database sometimes can't be restored from a backup, even if the backup software correctly backed it up—and some don't!

The simplest way to recover a crashed PDC requires some foresight—you must have an available BDC. Remove the crashed machine from the network, and then promote a BDC to PDC. This process ensures a smooth transition without loss of logon or security services. Once you've got the crashed machine off the network, restore from a backup or by reinstalling NTS. If you reinstall, remember that using the same machine name still generates a different security ID, and be sure to specify that the machine will be a BDC. (For more details on potential problems that can occur when you assign a new security ID to an existing machine, see "The Security Account Manager" in Chapter 12, "Windows NT Security Fundamentals.")

If you restore the crashed machine by reinstalling NTS, you can promote it to PDC; the Server Manager automatically demotes the existing BDC. If you restore from a backup, however, or if the failure didn't damage the disk, when you reconnect the machine it still will think it's the PDC. This situation will cause domain logon requests to fail until you get back to having only one PDC for the domain. To fix this problem, select the original PDC in the Server Manager and choose Computer | Demote to Backup Domain Controller. The selected machine is forcibly demoted, and your network logons will begin working again. It's a good idea to resynchronize the domain after taking this action, because it ensures that the recovered server will have an up-to-date copy of the domain SAM database.

Managing Domains

The earlier section "Using Domain Controllers" discussed how to use the Server Manager to promote and demote domain controllers. However, there are other domain management tasks that you need to perform, including creating domains, adding and removing domain computers, and managing trust relationships. Let's examine how you do each of these.

Creating New Domains

Creating a new domain is fairly straightforward, if somewhat limiting. NTS won't let you create new domains on-the-fly. Instead, you can create a new domain only by installing (or reinstalling) NTS on a machine, and specifying that you want to make the machine a primary domain controller by clicking the Controller in New Domain radio button in the Domain Settings dialog box.

Later in the installation process, you'll be prompted for the domain name to be created. You must specify a new, unique domain name. The NTS installation process creates the domain SAM database and configures the server as a PDC—including having the new PDC broadcast its status to other servers added to the domain later. You'll also be prompted to specify a password for the domain's Administrator account. Don't confuse this account with the Administrator account for the server you're setting up; the domain administrator account enables you to administer the domain controller from other machines in the domain, but the server's administrator account enables you to control only the behavior of that individual server.

> **CAUTION:** NTS and good planning each impose limits on domain names. NTS requires that domain names be unique on your network (no computer, workgroup, or domain can have the same name as your new domain.) Because you can't move domain controllers between domains without reinstalling NTS, make sure that you have chosen a meaningful domain name so that you don't have to change it later. Changing the domain name for the server is the same to NTS as physically moving the computer to another domain.

For the first NTS machine you put in a domain, you *must* make it a PDC so that the new domain will have a PDC before any other machines attempt to join the domain. This rule is especially important if you'll be installing other NTS machines, because the NTS setup program expects to see a domain controller on your network unless the machine you're installing is to be a PDC.

Adding a BDC to an Existing Domain

The best way to minimize the impact of a PDC failure is to have at least one BDC ready to take over if the PDC fails. Even if your domain is small, it's worth considering the advantages of having a BDC available in case the worst happens to your PDC. However, you need to decide which machines will be BDCs before you start installing software, because you can't turn an ordinary server into a domain controller without reinstalling NTS.

When you install NTS, you can choose whether you want your server to be a PDC, a BDC, or a plain NTS server. As noted earlier, the Controller in New Domain button in the Domain Settings dialog box is used when creating new domains; use the Backup Domain Controller button instead if you want to make the new server into a BDC for the domain. Be prepared to provide the domain administrator's password during the installation process, because the installation will ask you for it in order to add the BDC to the domain.

Managing Domain Membership

Each computer in a domain must have its own account in the domain SAM, so you can't just arbitrarily add machines into a domain. Instead, you must create accounts for them before they can join and gain access to the domain SAM database. Likewise, you must update the domain SAM database when a computer leaves the domain permanently. You also have to update the old and new domains when you move computers between domains. All of these cases are covered in the following sections.

Adding Computers to a Domain

There are actually two ways to get the accounts in a domain created: the first is to create the account at the time you tell the client to join the domain, and the second involves using the Server Manager to add the account manually.

In either case, you add the client workstation to a domain by using the Identification Changes dialog box shown in Figure 15-9. You access this dialog box by opening the Network Control Panel applet, clicking the Identification tab, and clicking the Change button.

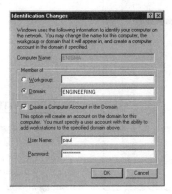

FIGURE 15-9

The Identification Changes dialog box is where you specify to which domain or workgroup a particular machine belongs.

Instead of selecting the Workgroup radio button, select the Domain radio button and enter the name of the domain this computer is joining. If there's already a domain account for the computer in the domain it'sjoining, just click OK and the computer will join the domain. If not, there are two ways that you can create the computer account. You'll have to do one or the other before the new machine will be able to join:

♦ The first method—and easier of the two methods to do on the client—is to use the options in the bottom half of the Identification Changes dialog box to create the new computer account. If you have administrative rights in the domain, select the option called Create Computer Account in Domain; then enter the user name and password for an account that has Account Operator or Administrator rights in the domain. When you click OK, the PDC adds a new account for the new domain member and then logs the computer into the domain. If you don't have administrative rights to the domain you want to join, you'll have to contact someone who does, and have him or her add a domain account for you.

♦ The second way to get the account in place is to add the computer account directly in the Server Manager by using the command Computer | Add to Domain. This command opens the dialog box shown in Figure 15-10.

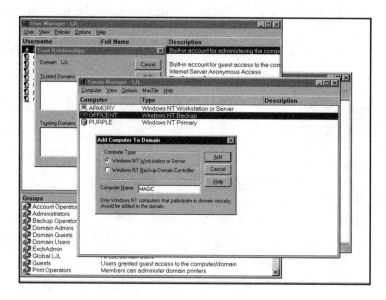

FIGURE 15-10

Use the Add Computer To Domain dialog box to tell the PDC for which machine you want to create an account.

Use the Computer Type radio buttons to specify which type of machine you're adding, type the machine's name in the provided field, and click OK. If the name is unique, NTS creates the computer account on the PDC. You still have to go through the steps at the beginning of this section to tell the client which domain to join.

Moving Computers Between Domains

To move a client (whether it's running Windows NT Workstation, NTS, Windows 95, Windows for Workgroups, or even the Mac OS) from one domain to another, follow these steps:

1. Deactivate the computer's account in its current domain. (See the next section to learn how to do this.) Once you do this, you lose any access controls and group memberships tied to that computer's domain account, so be sure it's what you really want to do.

2. Use the Server Manager to create a new account for the computer in its new domain. This step is optional; if you skip it, though, you have to add the account as part of the next step.

3. Tell the computer to join its new domain as outlined in the earlier section "Adding Computers to a Domain." If you're prompted to reboot, do so, and then log onto the new domain.

Unfortunately, there's no way to move NT domain *controllers* between domains. Because SIDs are unique, the PDC has a unique SID for the domain itself. When you move a PDC or BDC, there's no way to change the SID of the domain it "belongs to" in the domain SAM database without re-creating it from scratch. The only way Microsoft provides to do that is to reinstall NTS on the machine being moved. Make sure that the machine is on the right subnet *before* doing the install, so that Setup can find the correct PDC to get the domain installation data. Then specify which domain to join in the Network applet when NT Setup displays it.

Removing a Computer from a Domain

There may come a time when you need to remove a workstation from a domain. Perhaps the machine has failed and won't be replaced, or it's been stolen. Whatever the case, you can easily remove domain computers by using the Server Manager. To remove an unwanted machine, select the target computer; then use the command Computer | Remove from Domain to remove it.

> **CAUTION:** Once you delete a computer from a domain, that SID is gone forever. If you install a machine with the same name as the deleted machine, it will get a new SID at installation time, so don't count on keeping the same permission data for a domain computer after you delete it.

Using Non-NT Machines in a Domain

If you have only Windows NT machines on your network, all your clients can be in domains and everything works just as Microsoft intended. In reality, though, even diehard NT shops like Intergraph still have some number of Windows 95, Windows for Workgroups, or even LAN Manager 2.x machines. Wouldn't it be nice to let these machines participate in NTS domains?

Windows for Workgroups machines can only *partially* participate in domains. WfW can browse resources in NT domains, but it can't take advantage of NT's security features. You tell a Windows for Workgroups machine to use a domain by specifying the domain name instead of a workgroup name in the Network applet in Control Panel. For WfW machines to browse a domain, though, there must be at least one WfW machine in the domain already because the client WfW browsers require a WfW domain member to act as a master browser.

To enable your WfW clients to access domain resources, open the Network applet and click the Startup button. When the Startup Settings dialog appears, select the check box called Log On to Windows NT or LAN Manager Domain, and then enter the name and password for the domain you want to access.

Windows 95 machines can participate in NT domains almost as well as NT machines, provided that you have created a domain account for each computer. The procedure for creating domain accounts for Win95 machines is identical to that outlined in the earlier section "Adding Computers to a Domain." Once you have created an appropriate account, tell Win95 to log onto the domain using the account. Open the Microsoft Client for Windows Networks in the Network applet, turn on the Domain check box, and enter the name of your NT domain.

> **TIP:** Even "foreign" clients—in this case, IBM LAN Server and NetWare—can use domain resources. Although neither LAN Server nor NetWare can directly interact with NT domains, you can allow them access to a domain by creating local users within the domain. Each LAN Server or NetWare user should have a corresponding local user account on the NT domain; you should group these users together to allow maximum control over permissions and access rights.

Controlling Network Browsing

As described in Chapter 14, "Understanding Workgroups, Domains, and Browsing," network browsing is an important service. Without it, users would be required to manually find resources they wanted to use. In the extreme, users would even have to manually update lists of resources made available by network computers.

The network browsing components in NT are complicated, and a number of subtle issues can make managing browsing behavior fairly troublesome. This section points out the most common browsing pitfalls and tells you how to correct them.

Controlling Browse Master Updates

Browse masters can generate lots of network traffic. Each *master browser* (*MB*) has to update its *domain master browser* (*DMB*) periodically; likewise, the DMB must transmit its collected list of resources back to the MBs. This traffic can clog ISDN or Frame Relay links; worse, it can cause your WAN to reopen dial-up connections needlessly. By default, this synchronization happens every 12 minutes, but you can control the frequency with two Registry entries in this Registry hive:

`HKEY_LOCAL_MACHINE\SYSTEM\CurrentControlSet\Services\Browser\Parameters`

The first value, `MasterPeriodicity`, controls how often each master browser contacts its DMB. The value is expressed in seconds, so the 12-minute default provides the standard value of 720. You can set this value as low as 5 minutes (300 seconds) or as high as 49 days and 17 hours (millions of seconds), but a value of 20–45 minutes would be more realistic. For best effect, you must change this value on every NTS machine in your domain, because any machine could be elected as the browse master at any time. Changes to this value take effect immediately.

The other value, BackupPeriodicity, controls how often backup browsers contact their master browser. The value range is the same as MasterPeriodicity. Unlike its counterpart, though, BackupPeriodicity doesn't affect WAN traffic, because backup browsers are always on the same subnet as the master browser they're backing up. Also unlike MasterPeriodicity, changes to this value don't take effect until your next reboot.

Controlling Browsing Announcements

Machines with available resources to share announce their availability just like browsers do; in fact, these server announcements are what the browsers listen for, collate, and rebroadcast. These announcements can cause unwanted network traffic, but you can control the frequency at which servers announce what resources they're making available via two Registry parameters that you can add in the following hive:

HKEY_LOCAL_MACHINE\SYSTEM\CurrentControlSet\Services\LanmanServer\Parameters

The Announce parameter indicates the frequency, in seconds (from 1–65535 seconds—up to 18 hours, 12 minutes, 15 seconds) at which a server should broadcast an announcement. The default value of 4 minutes is reasonable for most networks, but if your network's shares and servers change less often, increasing this time reduces the amount of bandwidth consumed by these announcement packets.

To avoid network collisions and reduce overhead, the Server service adds a random variation to the Announce time. The amount of variation permitted is controlled by the AnnDelta parameter, which can range from 0 (meaning that the value of Announce is used exactly) to 65535 milliseconds (meaning that the interval specified by Announce can vary by approximately 65 seconds either way.)

Disabling the Printer Browse Thread

When you create a new printer share in NT, the print spooler spawns a broadcasting thread that repeatedly announces the share's presence. All print servers on the network can receive this message and use it to add the new printer to their printer list without any human intervention.

To make sure that print servers have consistent resource lists, each print server also broadcasts its list of known printers so that other servers can ensure that their lists are complete. The combination of these two broadcasts can cause unneeded broadcast traffic; once a printer is established and the servers have all "seen" it, there's no need to keep retransmitting the data.

You can disable the printer browse thread on each machine that has a printer to share. You may also want to disable it on each centralized print server. If you do, be aware that when you add new printers they won't show up in browse lists until you re-enable the browse thread.

Disabling the thread requires adding a new value to the Registry. Here's what to do:

1. Open the Registry Editor and navigate to the following location:

    `\HKEY_LOCAL_MACHINE\SYSTEM\CurrentControlSet\Control\Print`

2. Choose Edit | Add Value and add a new REG_DWORD value named `DisableServerThread`.

3. Give `DisableServerThread` the value 1 to disable the server thread or 0 to allow the spooler to restart it. Changes you make won't take effect until you next restart the affected machine; even after that, it may take as long as 60 minutes for all print servers to resynchronize themselves.

Hiding Servers from Network Computers

At times, you may want to keep human browsers from seeing a particular server on your network. If you want to hide a machine from view, you can do so by adding a Registry key. Although this change keeps the server from appearing in the browsing user interface, users who know the UNC path to the server's resources can still access it. To hide an individual server, you have to add a new value to its Registry. Follow this procedure:

1. Open the Registry Editor and navigate to this location:

    `\HKEY_LOCAL_MACHINE\SYSTEM\CurrentControlSet\Services\LanmanServer\Parameters`

2. Choose Edit | Add Value and add a new REG_DWORD value named HIDDEN.

3. Give HIDDEN the value 1 to hide this machine or 0 to make it visible again. Changes you make won't take effect until you next restart the affected machine.

Browsing on Subnets and WAN Links

Each subnet of a large network has its own master browser. This approach ensures that clients on the same subnet can see resources for that workgroup, but it introduces difficulties for users who want to browse resources on other subnets. Because the PDC is also the domain master browser, it's responsible for solving this problem by collecting announcements from each subnet's local browse master and making the collection available to clients on any subnet.

Figure 15-11 shows a small network with two domains, HEADQUARTERS and ENGINEERING. HEADQUARTERS contains two subnets: one for the accounting department and one for the marketing department. Each subnet has its own master browser, determined by elections (as described in Chapter 14). In this example, ACCT5 and MKT1 are the subnet master browsers. The domain PDCs act as the domain master browsers. Every machine is a potential browser, and HQ3 and MKT4 have been elected as backup browsers.

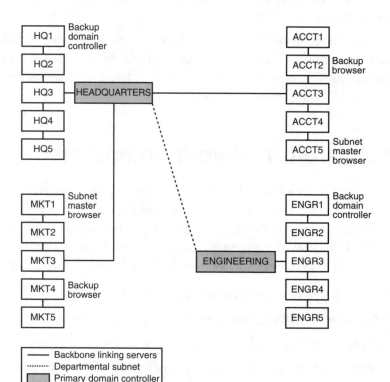

FIGURE 15-11

Networks with multiple domains and subnets have several types of master browsers.

Subnets

If the PDC and some of its domain clients are on different subnets, the clients won't be able to browse the PDC unless you add an entry for the PDC to the clients' LMHOSTS file. There's another subtle trick, too. As in Figure 15-11, suppose that your network has two domains, HEADQUARTERS and, on different subnets. Members of HEADQUARTERS won't be able to browse computers in ENGINEERING unless the domain master browser (usually the PDC) of HEADQUARTERS has an LMHOSTS entry for ENGINEERING's PDC. Workgroups aren't subject to this problem because they can't span subnets.

> **NOTE:** For more details on how subnets work, see "Subnetting Your Network" in Chapter 19, "Performance Tuning and Optimization."

Wide Area Networks (WANs)

WAN browsing is limited to Windows 95 and NT machines if the WAN spans more than one subnet (as it almost always will). The requirement for LMHOSTS entries is true for WAN browsing as well. In addition, WAN links are particularly sensitive to network traffic caused by browsing. You can alleviate much of this traffic by tuning the Registry parameters listed in the preceding sections; in addition, directory replication and replication of the WINS and SAM databases can cause significant traffic. If you're using a WAN link, make sure that you've set the replication times to reasonable values, based on the frequency of changes to the contents of your databases. Chapter 19 has complete details on configuring WINS and SAM replication timing and frequency.

Where to Go Next

This chapter explores the fundamental domain models and how to evaluate them in light of your network's needs. In addition, it describes how to create and administer domains, domain controllers, and trust relationships. This knowledge should enable you to design and execute an effective domain strategy for your network.

The next chapter extends your domain knowledge by using local and global groups to manage users within and between domains. Following are other resources and chapters that you may find useful:

- The basic concepts of domains, workgroups, and browsing are covered in Chapter 14.
- Chapter 16 is all about the proper use of local and global groups and user accounts in both single- and multi-domain networks.
- Chapter 6 provides more details on using the User Manager for Domains for common administrative tasks.

Chapter | 16

Managing Users and Groups in Domains

In This Chapter:

- Groups and Domains
- Users and Domains
- Setting Domain-Wide User Policies

How do I...

Windows NT provides facilities for grouping user accounts so that all users in a group have consistent permissions and rights. Groups can be local to a single computer or they can apply across an entire domain—or even between trusted domains. Properly establishing domain groups is a key part of using Windows NT on your network.

Chapter 6 shows how to set up and manage user and group accounts, and Chapters 14 and 15 describe how to set up and manage domains. This chapter explains how to combine these activities to manage user and group accounts effectively across and between domains. It covers the following topics:

- The differences in scope between local and global accounts and local and global groups
- How to use groups within a single domain or across multiple domains
- How to manage user rights and permissions by using local and global groups
- How to use the System Policy Editor to control what settings domain users can change on their workstations

Groups and Domains

Windows NT groups and domains work well together. Without groups, the only way to control user permissions, rights, and access to domain resources is to do so for each individual account. For domains with more than a handful of users, this quickly becomes prohibitive. Without domains, groups would have to be manually created on each machine in a group to ensure consistent access, and there would be no easy way to coordinate access between subnetworks.

Local Versus Global Groups

Windows NT's groups come in two kinds: *local* and *global*. They differ in two key ways: their scope and their permissible contents. Local groups can be used in an entire domain (their home domain), but are not visible to other domains. Local groups can contain both users from their home domain and global groups from any domain. Global groups are visible to all domains on a network, but they can contain only users from the domain that created the global group. Let's explore the group scopes and uses in more detail to illustrate exactly how they differ.

Local Groups

Local groups can contain domain user accounts; they can also contain global groups and user accounts from any trusted domain. All computers in the domain can use that domain's local groups for controlling resource access. They are local to the domain in that they aren't visible outside their home domain, and unlike global groups, they can't be used to grant permissions in trusting domains.

Including a global group (from a trusted domain) in a local group (of a trusting domain) enables user accounts in the global group access to resources in the trusting domain. This intermixing gives the trusted-domain administrator control over what user accounts are in the global group and the trusting-domain administrator control over what access the group members have.

Global Groups

All computers in a domain can use that domain's global groups for controlling access to resources. Global groups can only contain user accounts from within the domain that defines the global group; you can't add users from other domains, nor can you add local groups.

As with local groups, all computers in a domain can use that domain's global groups for controlling access to resources, but global groups can also cross domains. Any domain which trusts your domain can include your global groups in its local groups. This ability gives you an easy way to aggregate users who need access to resources in another domain: put them in a global group in your domain, then let the other domain's administrator grant appropriate access to that global group.

Groups and Domains: An Example

Figure 16-1 shows our sample domains from Chapter 15, ENGINEERING and MARKETING, plus two new domains: HEADQUARTERS and ACCOUNTING. The arrows indicate trust relationships (for example, the arrows going from the domains to HEADQUARTERS indicate that all domains trust HEADQUARTERS.) The dark blocks indicate global groups, while the light blocks indicate local groups.

Let's see what conclusions we can draw, based on the knowledge about local and global groups you gained above:

- ◆ Each domain has at least one local group. These local groups contain domain users from the local group's home domain and global groups from trusted domains (including the home domain.) Users in the local groups can access resources only within the domain. For example, the Accountants group can use resources in ACCOUNTING, but not in ENGINEERING, even though ENGINEERING trusts ACCOUNTING because the Accountants group is a local group.

- ◆ Some domains have global groups, which can be granted access to resources in other domains. The Engineers and Designers groups are allowed to use printers in ACCOUNTING and MARKETING, just by the ACCOUNTING Domain Administrator adding access to printers for ENGINEERING\Engineers and ENGINEERING\Designers.

- ◆ Domain trusts override group memberships; you can only put global groups

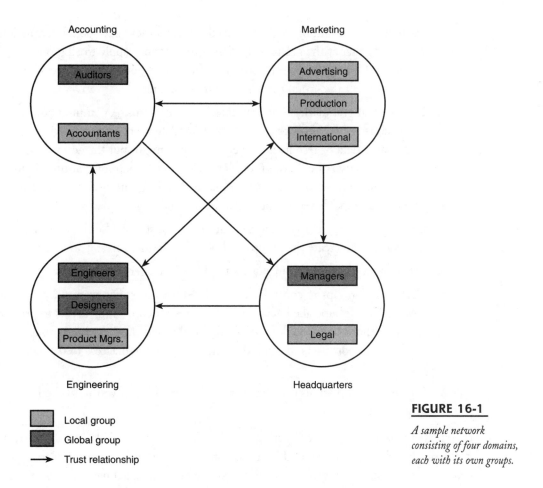

FIGURE 16-1

A sample network consisting of four domains, each with its own groups.

from domains you trust into your domain's local groups. All domains trust HEADQUARTERS, but HEADQUARTERS doesn't trust any other domain— so ENGINEERING\ProductManagers can't access resources in HEADQUARTERS after all.

Managing Groups in a Single Domain

Managing groups in a single domain is a simple 4-step process. With careful planning, the groups you create now can be used in the future, even if you add more domains to your network. Let's examine the steps in detail:

1. Create user accounts for all the users you want to have access to domain

resources. You might or might not need to assign them any special permissions; you can do that at the group level if the same settings apply to all group members. *Do* assign account restrictions (for logon hours, dial-in access, and so on), because the group can't impose those settings.

2. Decide what granularity is appropriate for your groups. A common (and useful) approach is to build groups so they accommodate users who all need access to the same data or resources. For example, you might put the accounting department's users into two groups: an Accounting group for granting them access to accounting data and a 3rdFloor group for granting them access to printers and tape drives on their floor of the building.

3. Create global groups according to your plan from step 2. Use the User Manager for Domains to create the groups and put users in them to suit your requirements.

4. Set rights for the new groups using the User Manager for Domains.

5. Create local groups to control access to local resources. For example, you could create a local group called AccountingPrinters for controlling access to printers served in the ACCOUNTING domain. Add global groups to these local groups where needed to import users in other domains and give them access to the local resources.

6. Finally, set permissions on whatever local shared objects you want the local groups to be able to use.

If you later expand your network with additional domains, the global groups you created in the original domain can be used in those domains. If instead of creating global groups you had created only local groups within the single domain, you'll have to regroup users in global groups to grant cross-domain access.

Managing Groups Between Domains

Managing groups in a multi-domain environment is more complicated than in a single domain, but much of the additional complexity comes from having more users spread across more domains— the basic administrative principles are the same. The best strategy is to group users first in global groups as described above. Once you have built global groups within each domain, you can build local groups within each domain, using that domain's user accounts plus any appropriate global groups from other domains.

> **NOTE:** Before you can use global groups or users between domains, you have to create the inter-domain trust relationships you want to apply on your network. See "Using Trust Relationships" in Chapter 15 for more details.

First, start by creating user accounts (if you haven't already), then dividing them into groups based on their access needs. While doing so, you may find that a diagram like Figure 16-1 helps you visualize which groups and resources already exist in each domain. Because the purpose of putting users in a global group is to allow that group access to other domains' resources, your diagram should include printers and file servers in all domains so you can see what resources users might need to reach.

Next, create the global groups in each domain. You can think of these groups as ambassadors: they travel from their home domain to another domain to use resources there, but the group's membership and access rights are controlled by the home domain. Don't forget to create global groups for the home domain, too.

Once you've created global groups defining which users in a domain need to reach other domains, you can do one of two things with them. The easiest route would seem to be to add those global groups to the Domain Users group of any domain you want them to access. By doing so, you grant the global group members the same access granted to home domain accounts. However, this can impose some security risks; you may not want all members of ENGINEERING rooting around in ACCOUNTING's file servers. The alternative—and preferred—solution is to create local groups in each domain, then put global groups in them to restrict access. For example, creating a local ACCOUNTING\PrinterUsers group, then putting ENGINEERING\Developers in it, could allow developers to use Accounting's printers without giving them unwanted access to other resources.

If you do choose to create new local groups for users, you can add global groups or individual user accounts from other domains to the local groups. As explained in the section on Local User Accounts, you can even allow access to users from untrusted domains.

Users and Domains

If you use groups and domains together, you might not need to do direct management of user accounts at all (except for occasionally creating or deactivating accounts.) However, there are some circumstances where managing user accounts directly is desirable or even necessary. Before we start in on them, let's begin with the different scopes user accounts can have.

Global versus Local User Accounts

Like groups, user accounts have two distinct flavors: *local* and *global*. Local accounts are limited to use within their home domain and have relatively limited abilities. Global accounts, the standard account type, can be used throughout the domain and are restricted only by the rights and permissions you apply to them. There are other, more subtle differences that are discussed in the remainder of this section.

Global User Accounts

Global user accounts are standard domain accounts. A global user account is an account in the user's home domain and provides access to all resources in the domain. By default, new accounts are global accounts when they are created; they remain that way unless changed. Global accounts can be used to access shared resources or log on interactively to machines in the domain. They can be put into local or global groups and shared between domains.

Local User Accounts

In contrast with global accounts, which can be used across and between domains, local accounts are more restricted. They're designed to be used so that individual users in untrusted domains can use resources in your domain. For example, the administrator of ENGINEERING could create a local account for the technical writer working on the top-secret Project X; the local account would let the tech writer reach needed resources without requiring ENGINEERING to trust the newly added DOCUMENTATION domain.

Local user accounts don't appear in the Add Users and Groups dialog box, so they can't be added to local or global groups in the domain. They can be used to access resources, but can't be used to log on interactively. The combination of these limitations means that local accounts can't be re-exported to other domains or used to interactively log onto or access your domain's machines. Despite these restrictions, though, they offer a useful way to grant limited access to users in untrusted domains.

Managing Users with Global Groups

Global groups provide the most portable way to group users, because any domain can grant access to global groups from all domains it trusts. Creating global groups is easy, because the only users you need (or can) add are those already in your domain, and you don't have to do anything special to allow other domains' administrators to use them. Use global groups when you want to accomplish the following tasks:

♦ Lump users with similar access requirements together so that you can assign permissions to them consistently

♦ Create sets of users who need access to resources in other domains

Managing Users with Local Groups

By contrast with global groups, local groups are limited to use within a single domain. Despite this lack of portability, though, local groups provide a means to give other domains' user accounts access to your resources. You can put individual user accounts or global groups from a trusted domain into your domain's local groups. Once you do, your domain treats those user accounts as though they're part of your domain. Use local groups when you have these objectives in mind:

♦ Assemble sets of user accounts for resource control without making them available to domains which trust your domain

♦ Allow user accounts in domains you trust to use resources within your domain

♦ Assign permissions and rights to multiple user accounts at once and with consistency, even when some of those user accounts are in other domains

Once you kow how and when to put users into local and global groups, you can also set policies for what those accounts and groups can do. These policies can apply to individual machines or across an entire domain. The next section shows how to devise and apply these policies.

Setting Domain-Wide User Policies

One advantage of NT's domain system is that it allows you to set up user policies that are available on all computers in a domain. These policies allow you to specify settings and restrictions for the shell and other system components. For example, you can set the policy for a group of users prohibiting them from shutting down any machine or running any application not on a list of approved tools.

The System Policy Editor is the tool for managing these policies, whether they apply to a single machine or an entire domain. Many of the configurable settings in the System Policy Editor were settable through the NT Registry in earlier releases of Windows NT, but you had to know they were there to use them. Setting a consistent policy on multiple machines through the NT Registry required a System Administor to spend more time in the Registry editor than normal humans should have to tolerate.

System Policy Editor stores each policy as an independent file which you can copy and apply as needed. You can even attach policy templates, which contain groups of related policy settings, to your System Policy Editor application. This mechanism allows developers of Windows NT applications to provide a group of policy settings that you can use to control use of their applications.

You can think of System Policy Editor as a trimmed-down Registry editor, because using it to edit policies on remote systems is similar in concept to editing a remote machine's Registry. Once you create a policy, you can apply it remotely to one or several machines, or you can apply it locally on each machine you want to update. Computer policies end up in the HKEY_LOCAL_MACHINE Registry subtree of each machine, while user and group policies are stored in the HKEY_CURRENT_USER and HKEY_LOCAL_USER subtrees.

System Policy Editor includes one very useful improvement over the regular Registry editor: It caches changes and doesn't apply them until you tell it to. You can always back out of an ill-advised change by closing your policy file without saving it.

Policies are usually stored in the Netlogon share of the PDC for a domain and replicated to the BDCs. The System Policy Editor works in concert with the Registry to push policy updates out to all machines where they're applicable. You can store policies on any NTS machine, though you'll still need to replicate the policy directory to the PDC if you want updates to be automatic.

The actual mechanics of setting policies are fairly simple; they can be condensed into four steps:

1. Define your policies and their application. At a minimum, you should review the list of policy settings in System Policy Editor and decide which settings apply to all machines or accounts. You can decide on policies down to the individual account level if you wish.

2. Create a new policy and the user, group, and computer entities that the policy will restrict.

3. Tell each domain computer to enable remote policy updates.

4. Use System Policy Editor to set the policy controls you desire for each user, group, and domain computer.

Let's start by examining how the System Policy Editor itself works, and how you can use it to create a new policy and the objects where the policy applies.

System Policy Editor Basics

System Policy Editor is a little different from the other Windows NT service and system managers. Instead of giving you a tree view of the servers you're managing, à la the DHCP or WINS Managers, you get a Macintosh-like icon view of the items in the policy you're managing. The main screen of System Policy Editor, showing a new, untitled policy, is shown in Figure 16-2. Each icon represents policy settings for a user, group, or computer.

There are a few basic operations you'll need to know before we start setting policies. You can display the properties of any of the items in the window by double-clicking it, or by selecting an item and choosing the Edit | Properties command. You can use the commands in the View menu to toggle the way items are displayed between using large icons (the default), small icons, a standard Win95-style list view, or a multicolumn detailed view.

When you first launch System Policy Editor, you'll see a blank window. You have to open an existing policy (using the File | Open Policy command), create a new policy with the File | New Policy command, or open the local Registry (the end repository of policy settings on each machine) with File | Open Registry before you'll see a display like that in Figure 16-2.

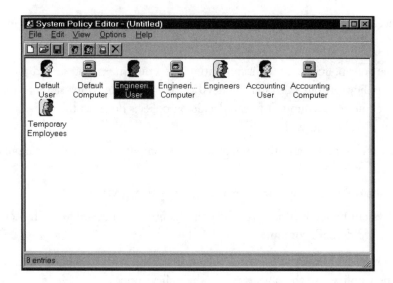

FIGURE 16-2

The System Policy Editor main window shows you icons representing user and computer policies.

Creating New Policies

The first step in creating a new set of policies is normally to create a new policy with File | New Policy. When you do, you'll see a window that's blank save for two items: Default User and Default Computer. These defaults have special meaning; whatever changes you make to Default User percolate out to the HKEY_CURRENT_USER Registry subtree of all users on all computers in the domain. Likewise, whatever you set in Default Computer is used as the default for HKEY_LOCAL_MACHINE on all domain computers. If your policies apply equally to all machines and users, you can set the Default items' properties and leave it at that. In most cases, however, you'll want to apply different policies to different machines, users, or groups. Before you can change the properties for these items, though, you must tell System Policy Editor about them.

Adding and Removing Users, Groups, and Computers

Once you've created a new policy, the next step in setting up policies for your domain is to define the entities you want the policies to affect. The Edit menu offers three commands for this: Add User, Add Computer, and Add Group. Each command brings up a simple dialog box; Figure 16-3 shows the Add Group dialog box as an example. You can type the name into the name field, or use the Browse button to display the standard Windows NT user, group, or computer browser dialog boxes and make a selection from the browser list.

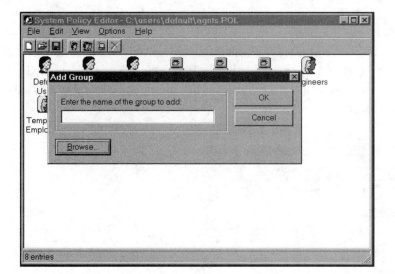

FIGURE 16-3

The Add Group, Add User, and Add Computer dialog boxes are all simple and similar. The Browse button brings up the standard system browser for selecting a name.

Each user, group, or computer you add appears in the Policy window, either as a text entry (in Details or List view) or as an icon. Users, groups, and computers have distinctive icons, and the icon title reflects the user, group, or computer name that you've assigned. This name must match the entity that the policy will restrict; for example, if you have a domain group named SALES, the corresponding group item in System Policy Editor must have the same name if you want the policy settings to apply to that group.

You can also remove items from the policy scope by choosing the item or items you want removed and using the Edit | Remove command. You're asked to confirm the removal before it actually occurs. Don't worry, though; removing items from a policy in System Policy Editor doesn't remove them from the user, group, or domain databases, just the policy itself. It also doesn't change whatever values are currently set in the Registry of each target machine.

Setting Policies

You can see, and change, the policy settings for an item by selecting the item and using the <u>E</u>dit | <u>P</u>roperties command to open the Properties dialog box for that item. Each Properties dialog box shows a tree control with the properties broken down by component; for example, the Temporay Employees Properties dialog box shown in Figure 16-4 shows two subcategories of settings for the Windows NT Shell item, Custom folders and Restrictions. In addition to the tree list, there is a settings pane at the bottom of each dialog box. When you select a tree item that has multiple policy controls associated with it, you'll be able to set those individual controls in the bottom pane. You may also see explanatory text, depending on the option.

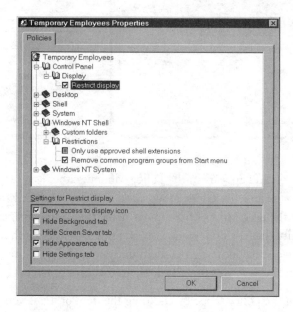

FIGURE 16-4

The Temporary Employees Properties dialog box is an example of how the Properties dialog boxes group related items in a tree structure.

The complete list of policy settings is likely to change with every release of NTS, and there are too many settings to cover in detail here. Each category of items has its own group of settings. For example, computers have groups for NT network, system, printers, and remote access policy controls, among others, while users have policy controls which govern their access to the NT shell and desktop. However, all the settings have a consistent interface.

Modifing Policies On Individual Computers

You can use the System Policy Editor to change policy settings on an individual computer running Windows NT (either Workstation or Server.) To do so, you must have administrative privileges on that machine. Here's how to do it:

1. In System Policy Editor, use the File | Connect command to open the remote computer's Registry. The Users on Remote Computer dialog box will appear.

2. Select the user for whom you want to set policy. (Only users who are currently logged in will appear in the dialog box.) Click OK.

3. The System Policy Editor will create a new policy window with Local Computer and Local User icons. These represent policy settings that will apply *only to the machine you're connected to.*

4. Make changes to the policies as needed. When you're done, use the File | Save command to make the changes permanent.

5. Close the connection to the remote computer with the File | Disconnect command.

Distributing Policies to Domain Computers

Once you've enabled each machine in your domain, you still have to get the policies onto the individual machines. The easiest way to do this is to store the completed policies on the PDC and let Windows NT do the work for you. To make this approach work, you must save the policy in a specific location and give it a specific name. When you save the policy, put it in the Netlogon share of your PDC and name it NTconfig.pol. When this file changes, NT will push the changes out to target machines with no action on your part.

You can also store policy files on any other server in your domain. However, you must be sure to tell Windows NT where to get the policy update file. To do this, you'll have to set the correct update mode and path on each individual machine in the domain as described in step 3 of the section above.

Here's how to set up each computer for allowing remote updates:

1. On the target machine, run the System Policy Editor and use the File | Open | Registry command. You'll see a window with icons titled Local User and Local Computer; there may be others, depending on whether you've already set some local policies with the Registry editor.

2. Open the Local Computer icon, then expand the Network and System policies update icons. The Remote Update box must be checked before the computer will accept remote policy updates. Check it.

3. If you want the Registry editor to receive error messages from the remote machine, check Display Error Messages. If you plan on storing policy files on the PDC's `Netlogon` share, leave Update mode set to Automatic; if instead you want to load policies from a machine other than the domain PDC, set Update mode to Manual and fill in the full path to the location of the policy files (you should use a UNC path to avoid requiring a hard-mapped drive letter.)

Once you've done steps 1-3, the Local Computer Policy dialog box looks like Figure 16-5.

FIGURE 16-5

Before you can set policies on a remote machine, you must tell that machine to accept remote updates.

NOTE: In either case, you should use the Directory Replicator service to replicate the directory where you're keeping the policy files to the PDC and all BDCs in your domain. For complete instructions on how to set up replication importers and exporters, see the section titled "Controlling Directory Replication" in Chapter 9, "Managing NT Servers."

Setting Group Policies

When you create a group in System Policy Editor, the policy settings you create will apply automatically to all members of that group. If you have users who are members of multiple groups, though, you may run into a conflict between policies for different groups.

System Policy Editor allows you to set group priorities; the highest-priority group's policy settings take precedence over others for users who belong to more than one group. The Options | Group Priority command displays the Group Priority dialog box, shown in Figure 16-6. Each group in your policy will appear in the Group Order list; you can reorder groups with the Move Up and Move Down buttons.

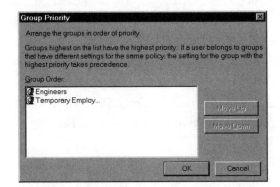

FIGURE 16-6

The Group Priority dialog box allows you to control which group's policies should take precedence.

Using Policy Templates

You can attach new policy templates to your System Policy Editor. These templates contain groups of related settings. Microsoft provides two templates with NTS 4.0, and application vendors have the tools needed to create their own custom templates so you can set policies for their applications. For example, if you install a new accounting package, the vendor may choose to include a policy template that you can use from System Policy Editor to control user actions in the accounting software.

You manage templates with the Options | Policy Templates command. Although the command is always active, you can only attach or remove templates when no policy documents are open. The Policy Template Options dialog box lists all the currently attached templates and gives you Add and Remove buttons for attaching and detaching templates. Once you attach a new template, its settings will be visible in all policy documents.

Where to Go Next

This chapter describes what differentiates local and global groups and local and global user accounts. It also shows how to use the appropriate account and group types to manage users and groups in both single and multiple domains within a network. The chapter closes by explaining how to use the System Policy Editor to apply consistent policies to computers, groups, and users within a domain.

A number of other chapters are relevant to this material:

 ◆ Chapter 6, "Managing User and Group Accounts," covers the nuts and bolts of using User Manager for Domains to create and control user and group accounts for single or multiple domains.

 ◆ Chapter 9, "Managing NT Servers," discusses the process of creating and managing group accounts using the User Manager for Domains.

 ◆ Chapter 11, "Working with the Windows NT System Registry," covers how you can edit policy settings on individual machines using the Registry Editor instead of System Policy Editor.

 ◆ Chapter 12, "Windows NT Security Fundamentals," covers the Windows NT permissions and rights that group accounts can confer on their users. You may be surprised at what defaults the system applies to new accounts.

 ◆ Chapter 14, "Workgroups, Domains, and Browsing Explained," and Chapter 15, "Planning and Using Domains and Workgroups," reveal how domains work and how you can set up a multidomain network effectively.

PART VI

Watching and Tuning Performance

Chapter | 17

Monitoring System Performance

In This Chapter:

- ◆ Using the Performance Monitor
- ◆ Monitoring Unusual Events
- ◆ Using the Task Manager

How do I...

For most networks, there will come a time when things just don't run fast enough. This unhappy milestone can arrive due to a number of factors: Too many users, underpowered servers, or insufficient network bandwidth are frequent culprits. Although this saturation point may be inevitable, there's no reason it should surprise you when it arrives. Careful and regular use of Windows NT's performance monitoring tools can warn you of potential bottlenecks before they impact your users and networks.

This chapter shows how to use the Windows NT Performance Monitor to gather and display performance statistics for your computers. It also explains how to keep tabs on warnings, error messages, and informational notices that software components can add to the event log. It closes with a brief overview of the Windows NT 4.0 Task Manager, which is a substantial rework of its predecessors from Windows NT 3.51 and earlier.

Using the Performance Monitor

Part of keeping track of your servers' health is being able to monitor their performance on an ongoing basis. This monitoring can help you predict when you will need more network bandwidth or computational power, and it can give you early warning of performance bottlenecks. Windows NT Server (NTS) includes a versatile performance monitor with which you can see instantaneous charts of any number of system parameters. If you prefer, you can choose to get periodic reports, logs, or alerts when parameters exceed values you define.

Objects, Instances, and Counters

The Performance Monitor is based on three concepts: objects, instances, and counters. Performance Monitor monitors *objects* in the system. Each object represents some physical or virtual item in the system. Objects include physical devices such as printers, executable code such as system services or the Exchange server, or system resources like RAM or network bandwidth. Each type of object may have one or more *instances* of the object; for example, if you have four CPUs in your server, you'll have four instances of the Processor object. You can monitor each instance of an object independently of its brethren, and you can watch any combination of objects and instances at once.

Counters are specific parameters you can monitor for an object and its instances. Each counter represents some measure associated with an object or instance. For example, the Physical Disk object (which has one instance for every hard disk on your machine) has counters for, among others, both the average and instantaneous bytes per minute written and read to the disk. Some counters, like the TCP and ICMP counters, are installed when you install the SNMP service. Some system objects don't have counters at all; objects that don't have counters can't be monitored with Performance Monitor.

Like most of the other NTS administrative tools, Performance Monitor can monitor counters on other computers in the domain. In the Add dialog box that you use to add counters, you can type a computer name into the Computer field, or use the browse button to surf your network to find the computer you want.

> **TIP:** To keep users on other machines from viewing Performance Monitor counters on your servers, use the Registry Editor to open the following key:
>
> HKEY_LOCAL_MACHINE\SOFTWARE\Microsoft\Windows NT\CurrentVersion\Perflib
>
> Select the Perflib key, then use the Registry Editor's Security | Permissions command to remove the permissions entry for Everyone. After you restart NT, users on other machines won't be able to view the server's Performance Monitor counters unless they're in the Administrators or System groups.

Performance Monitor Basics

The Performance Monitor's main window is shown in Figure 17-1. This figure shows a chart of the paging file usage, number of virtual-memory page faults per second, and processor utilization for a lightly loaded NT server. The toolbar at the top of the window provides buttons for choosing between the four data types that Performance Monitor can display: charts, alerts, reports, and logs. There are also toolbar buttons for adding and removing counters to the displayed data and setting display options. The rest of the window's contents vary depending on the data type you've chosen.

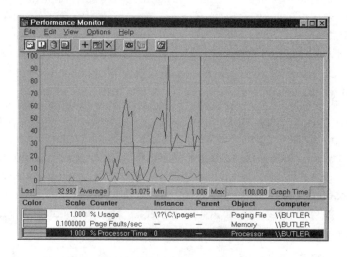

FIGURE 17-1

The Performance Monitor displays the performance data you specify in a single window; you can display charts, reports, logs, or alerts.

Performance Monitor *charts* are line graphs that depict the selected counter values graphically. Each line on the chart has its own color and scale; all chart lines are plotted on a 0-100 scale, so a counter with a scale of 1.0 represents data from 0-100, while a counter with a scale of 2.0 would represent the range between 0 and 200. In Chart mode, there's a legend at the bottom of the window that identifies the color for each displayed counter and the instance, object, and computer that the counter represents.

Alerts are alarms that you can set to trigger when a counter value exceeds or falls below your threshold. You can specify a program to be run when the alert triggers. Performance Monitor displays alerts as an Event Viewer-like list, with the date, time, object, instance, and alert condition displayed for each entry. There's also a legend at the bottom to indicate which alerts in the list are which.

Logs are files of data containing counter values. Performance Monitor will log data at an interval you specify, or only when you explicitly request it. Log files are primarily useful for saving data for later viewing, although there are also third-party tools like SomarSoft's DumpEvt for analyzing the logs or converting them into a format suitable for use in a database.

Finally, you can view data as *reports*, which are text-only summaries of the counters you select. Each parameter's value is shown as its true value, without scaling. By default, Performance Monitor updates reports every 5 seconds, but you can change this interval or use manual updates.

Performance Monitor supports using all four data views at once. You can switch between them with the commands in the View menu or the first group of four buttons on the toolbar. Each view can have different counters in it; for example, you might simultaneously set alerts on your TCP object's Connections Reset and Connection Failures counters, then use a chart to view the Connections Active and Segments/Second counters. Because each data view is independent of the others, you can set display options for each view and load and save the view's counter settings at any time. Performance Monitor also provides a way to save all the active views into a single *workspace* that you can reload later. Let's examine each of the Performance Monitor data types in more detail.

Charts

Charts show you the value of a set of counters over time, and they're the clearest way to visualize trends in the counter values. Refer to Figure 17-1 for a sample chart with three counters. You can display as many counters as you like. When you first start Performance Monitor, the chart view will be active by default, but you can switch to it with the View | Chart command or by clicking the Chart toolbar button.

You can add parameters to the chart with the Edit | Add to Chart command, or by using the Add toolbar button. When you do, you'll see the Add to Chart dialog box, pictured in Figure 17-2.

You can choose the computer whose data you want to monitor by typing a computer name into the Computer field, or using the browse button to select a machine from the network. The Object drop down list lists all the objects that can be monitored on the selected computer. Once you select an object, the contents of the Counter and Instance fields will change to show which counters are available and what instances (for objects that have instances) you can monitor. You can use the Explain button to display a short summary of what the counter measures.

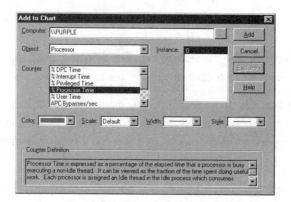

FIGURE 17-2

The Add to Chart dialog box lets you select an object, instance, and counter for monitoring, as well as the color, scale, and style used to display its data.

The Color, Scale, Width, and Style drop down lists control the appearance of the selected counter on the graph. Style and width settings are mutually exclusive; each instance that you add to the chart can have its own color, style, and scale.

> **TIP:** You can change the display style and color for any counter by double-clicking its entry in the chart's legend, or by selecting it in the legend and using the Edit | Edit Chart Line command or the Modify toolbar icon.

Once you've added counters to the chart, you may want to change the chart's update frequency or appearance. The Options | Chart command displays the Chart Options dialog box, shown in Figure 17-3. The Legend, Value Bar, Horizontal Grid, Vertical Grid, and Vertical Labels checkboxes control whether those elements are displayed on the graph; the Vertical Maximum field lets you set the upper limit of the graph, which Performance Monitor uses in conjunction with the scale for each counter. The option buttons in the Gallery group allow you to choose between a line graph and a histogram. Finally, the Update Time group gives you a way to control how often the graph's updated. Specify the interval for updates in the Interval field, or select the Manual Update button to turn off automatic updating.

Logs

Logs are permanent records of the performance statistics you choose to store. You can reload log files and use them in Performance Monitor just like real-time data, or you can dissect the logged data with an analysis tool for further scrutiny. The Log view, which you

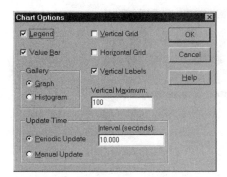

FIGURE 17-3

The Chart Options dialog box gives you control over the chart's update rate and appearance.

can display with the View | Log command or the corresponding toolbar button, isn't much to look at—just a plain list of the object and computer being logged. The Log view does include the log file name, the update frequency of the logged data, and the log's size and status.

Unlike the Alert and Chart views, there's no way to select counters or instances for logged data. When you select an object, all counters are logged for all instances; this makes it possible for you to come back later and review any parameter of the selected object. Because of this difference, the Add to Log dialog box (which you access via the by-now-familiar Edit | Add to Log command) is very simple. It only allows you to choose an object; there are no other settings.

Once you've added the desired objects to your log, though, you need to specify the logging options you want with the Options | Log command. The Log Options dialog box looks very similar to the standard Save File dialog box; the biggest difference is the addition of the Update Time group and the Start Log button. Use the upper portion of the dialog box to pick a log file. You can create a new file at any time. If you select an existing file the new data will be appended to the file's contents. As with alerts and charts, use the Update Time group to tell Performance Monitor how often to capture logged data. Performance Monitor won't actually log anything until you click the Start Log button. Once you do, Performance Monitor will collect an initial set of data, then keep collecting data at the interval you specified. To stop logging, you must reopen the Log Options dialog box and click the Stop Log button. Figure 17-4 shows a log in progress.

While the log is open, there's an additional command unique to Log view. The Bookmark toolbar button (which looks like an open book) allows you to add a comment to the log at its current point. You'll be able to see the comment when you reload the log file.

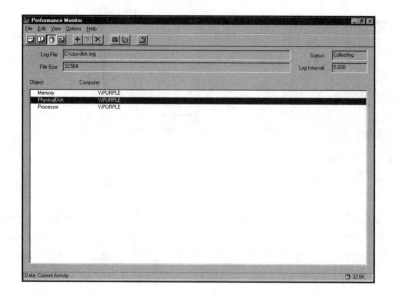

Reports

Reports are a useful tool for summarizing the current state of several parameters. Unlike charts or alerts, reports just show the counter values without any interpretation or scaling. Reports group the displayed values first by computer, then by object. If you select multiple instances of an object, each instance gets its own column.

> **NOTE:** Performance Monitor doesn't provide any scrolling features, so if you monitor more than a few instances of a counter, some data will be invisible. The workaround? Don't monitor more instances than you can see displayed on your monitor.

You add counters to your report with the Edit | Add to Report command, or the toolbar button. The Add to Report dialog box only allows you to choose a computer, object, instance, and counter to display (although it does have the Explain button you saw above.) The Report view doesn't give you any way to change the formatting or style of the displayed report. Figure 17-5 shows a sample report view.

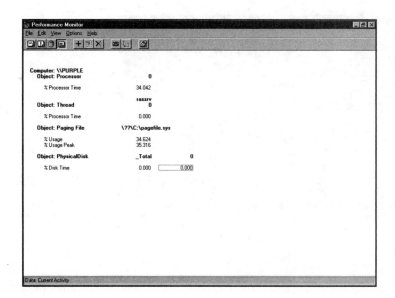

FIGURE 17-5

The Report view shows a tabular summary of your selected counters.

Alerts

Alerts are most often used to signal a network manager when some condition goes out of preset limits. For example, a sudden drop in the number of TCP/IP segments sent or received might signal a network outage. The Performance Monitor alert facility allows you to set thresholds for counters and log exceptions when the counter falls above or below the threshold. You activate the Alert view with the View | Alerts command, or with the Alert toolbar button. When the Alert view is active, you'll see a summary of alerts, with each entry listing the alert's date and time, the value that triggered the alert, the threshold value for that alert counter, and the object, instance, counter, and computer that the value measures.

You add counters to the Alert view with the same commands as for a chart, but the Add to Alert dialog box (shown in Figure 17-6) is slightly different. The process of choosing a computer, object, instance, and counter is identical, but there are some additional settings that are specific to alerts. The Alert If group controls the alert trigger; you can choose to trigger alerts when the counter value exceeds or falls below your threshold. The Run Program on Alert group gives you a way to start an external application (say, a tool that will page you or send you e-mail) when the alert is triggered.

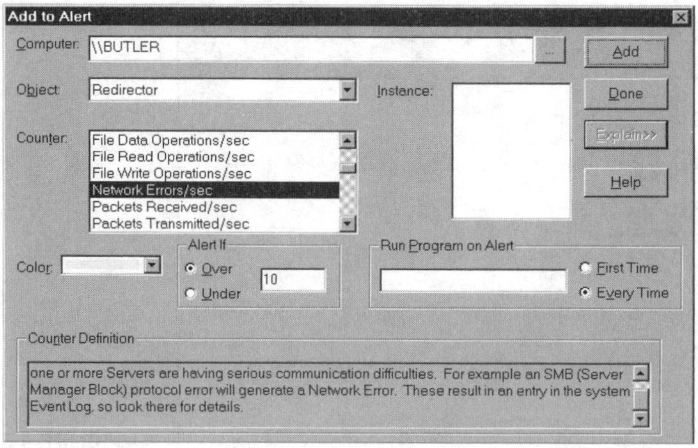

Add to Alert

Computer: \\BUTLER   ...   Add

Object: Redirector   Instance: Done

Counter:
File Data Operations/sec
File Read Operations/sec
File Write Operations/sec
Network Errors/sec
Packets Received/sec
Packets Transmitted/sec

Explain>>

Help

Alert If   Run Program on Alert

Color: ⊙ Over [10]   ○ First Time
           ○ Under   ⊙ Every Time

Counter Definition
one or more Servers are having serious communication difficulties. For example an SMB (Server Manager Block) protocol error will generate a Network Error. These result in an entry in the system Event Log, so look there for details.

FIGURE 17-6

Set alert triggers for counters with the Add to Alert dialog box.

TIP: You can change the threshold, display color, and external program settings for any alert counter by double-clicking its entry in the Alert view's legend, or by selecting it in the legend and using the Edit | Edit Alert Entry command or the Modify toolbar icon.

Like charts, the Alert view has some options you can set to control how alerts are displayed and handled by Performance Monitor. The Options | Alert command displays the Alert Options dialog box, shown in Figure 17-7. The Switch to Alert View checkbox tells Performance Monitor to change the active view to Alert whenever an alert occurs. The Log Event to Application Log checkbox will force Performance Monitor to add an entry to the Application section of the system's event log (this is in addition to any logging done by the software which controls the counter). You can specify that alert messages should be sent to a particular Windows machine on the network by using the Network Alert group. As with Chart view, you can set the update frequency for the alert list.

ON THE

CD

NOTE: An evaluation version of Ipswitch Software's WhatsUp is included on the CD. WhatsUp monitors system parameters you select and can notify you via e-mail or pager when a parameter goes out of range.

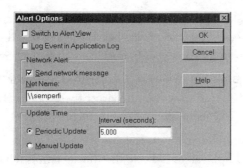

FIGURE 17-7

The Alert Options dialog box lets you control what happens when an alert occurs.

Gathering a Performance Baseline

To make informed decisions about your computers' performance, you need to compare the current performance data against a standard set of data. The process of building a set of data for comparisons is called *baselining*; when you establish a baseline for your servers' performance, you are really establishing a set of measurements indicating how your machines were running at a fixed time.

The biggest advantage of a good baseline is that it's repeatable. Once you choose a set of meaningful parameters, you can monitor them over time and compare the effects of changes in your network. At any time, you can go back to your baseline measurements and trace exactly when your network load rose above a certain percentage, or when your disk controller became the bottleneck on your main file server.

Choosing What to Monitor

Because Performance Monitor can monitor so many different objects and counters, choosing the right set can be difficult. However, some counters provide data that's more immediately useful than others. The counters listed below represent a good starting point for building a baseline.

◆ The Browser object's Announcements Total/Sec counter: This counter totals the number of server and domain announcements per second. High values may indicate that your network's carrying unnecessary browsing announcements; you can reduce the volume by following the steps described in Chapter 15, "Planning and Using Domains and Workgroups."

- The Logical Disk objects' `% Disk Time` counter, which records the percentage of time the disk is in use. Values above 50-60% indicate heavy usage of that disk; you might see performance gains from adding additional disks or controllers.

- The Logical Disk objects' `Avg Disk sec/Transfer` counter, which measures the average elapsed time of a disk read or write. The larger these values, the longer it's taking to satisfy disk I/O requests.

- The Memory object's `Pages/sec` counter counts the average number of system page faults per second. High values indicate that the system is relying heavily on virtual memory; adding more RAM will boost performance.

- The Memory object's `% Committed Bytes In Use` counter reflects what percentage of available virtual memory space is actually in use. High values indicate that the system is using more of its allocated page file space; when this value hits 75%, you should increase the page file size. Note that this value is an instantaneous measure, not an average.

- The Network Segment object's `% Network Utilization` counter shows what percentage of the network bandwidth is being used. High values tell you that it may be time to split your segment into subnets.

- The Paging File object's `% Usage Peak` shows the high-water mark for use of the system's page file. You should monitor the `Total` instance for this counter. When it reaches or exceeds 75%, you should consider increasing the pagefile size.

* The Processor object's `% Processor Time` counter reflects how much time your CPUs are spending doing something besides running the Idle thread. The higher this number, the busier your CPU. When it gets above 70%, you should consider adding additional processors or reducing the load on the machine by moving some services to other computers.

- The Redirector object's `Current Commands` counter indicates how many file service requests are waiting for the redirector. If this number consistently exceeds the number of network interface cards in your server, that means your server is acting as a bottleneck because it can't service requests fast enough.

- The Server Work Queue object's `Queue Length` counter indicates how many server requests have been queued for later handling. This count is a snapshot, not an average, but a sustained value greater than 4 indicates that the system processor can't keep up with the pace of arriving requests.

◆ The System object's `% Total Processor Time` counter totals the percentage of time that processors in the system are busy running user or system threads. This counter directly reflects the CPU load on your servers; when it reaches 50%, you should begin considering adding additional processors or servers.

There are a large number of other counters which may be appropriate for your particular network. The best way to find the right set of baseline parameters is to use your knowledge of your network, applications, and users to pinpoint which objects and counters represent scarce resources. For example, if your network has to support intra-office video conferencing, the Network Segment's `% Multicast Frames` and `% Broadcast Frames` counters can tell you what fraction of your network bandwidth is being used to carry that traffic. Likewise, if you have other special situations—file servers with large image or CAD files, heavily populated database servers, and the like—there's bound to be a counter in Performance Monitor that will give you useful data.

Setting Up Baselining

Once you've decided on a set of counters to monitor, you can use the Performance Monitor commands to create charts, alerts, reports, and logs that capture the data you want. You might want to save these views as workspaces so that you can keep a collection of views available as a group; you can also save independent views to enable mixing and matching different groups of counters quickly.

Once you've collected an initial baseline of data, make sure you save it somewhere for future reference. If you create a log file with Performance Monitor, you can back it up once it's created and then restore it when you want to compare your original system load with the current load. The frequency with which you want to compare the baseline data with new data will determine how long an interval you need to log and how long you need to keep the logged data.

Gathering Performance Snapshots

Although building a performance baseline is important, it's also time-consuming. Sometimes you may need to see how much network bandwidth is being used by your new Web server, or how much idle time is available on a particular system's processor.

These instantaneous measures are often called *snapshots*. Like their namesake, snapshots reflect system performance at a moment in time, as opposed to representing performance in a historical context like a baseline.

Setting up snapshots is straightforward: choose the objects, instances, and counters you want to monitor, then create Performance Monitor views which display them. You can save these views so that you can repeat the snapshot measurements at a future time, or you can keep them up only long enough to see the values that interest you.

Note that many counters are *instantaneous*; that is, they display a specific value from a specific point in time, not a running total or average like other counters. Performance Monitor identifies which counters are instantaneous in the Counter Definition field of the Add dialog box (refer to Figure 17-2).

Exporting and Analyzing Data

Whether you gather data as part of a long-term baselining effort or in a series of quick snapshots, it is often useful to analyze the data you gathered using tools other than Performance Monitor. Databases and spreadsheets, for instance, offer analytical tools that make it possible for you to examine your data in a wide variety of forms not supported by Performance Monitor.

Exporting Data

When you have an active view (that is, one which is monitoring at least one counter) in Performance Monitor, the File | Export command becomes active (although its name will change to reflect the type of view you're using.) With this command, you can export the data generated the current view's contents. When you choose the command, you'll see the standard Save File dialog box. The Save as type drop down list allows you to select whether you want the data saved with ASCII tab characters or ASCII commas as field delimiters. Which option you select depends on what program you're using to read the exported data; in either case, the exported file will include a header listing the date, time, interval, counter, instance, and computer name for the exported data. The format of the export file's contents will vary; for charts, it's a simple table, but alerts include a line for each time the alert triggered. Once you've exported the data, you can import it into a spreadsheet, graphics package, or database and manipulate it according to your needs.

Printing Charts

Oddly, Performance Monitor doesn't directly support printing charts, alerts, or reports. If you want hardcopy of these views, you'll have to generate it yourself by taking a screen shot of the window and printing it. You can do this with the standard Windows Alt+PrtSc key combination, which copies the active window image to the clipboard for use in Paintbrush or another image editing program. You can also use a screen capture utility to grab the image and save it to a file or send it straight to a printer.

ON THE

CD

> **NOTE:** An evaluation version of TechSmith's SnagIt/32 screen capture tool is included on the CD. SnagIt allows you to grab a single window or the full screen and save it to a file, print it, or copy it to the Clipboard.

Monitoring Unusual Events

Many other server operating systems, notably various flavors of Unix, include a system log that applications and system components can use to log informational messages, warnings, and failure notifications. Windows NT includes the Event Logger service, which allows any application, driver, service, or other executable code to put messages into the central log.

In Windows NT, events are grouped into *event classes*. These classes group messages by severity, so that informational messages and security warnings can be tracked individually. NT supports 5 different event classes:

- ◆ *Informational* messages are just that—they tell you what the application or system component thinks you should be told. These messages are purely advisory and don't usually require any action from you. A typical message might indicate that the event logging service has successfully started up or that a master browser election was forced due to a PDC startup.

- ◆ *Warning* messages warn you that an out-of-limit condition was detected in some component. Warnings may indicate that you need to reconfigure or fix something; they can provide early alerts of problems like misconfiguration of a network service. For example, the SNMP service will log a warning if it detects that you're trying to send traps to a nonexistent machine, and the system keeps track of disk space and logs warnings when space on a physical disk runs low.

- *Error* messages report actual execution errors in a system component. These messages almost always require you to fix something. Drivers which can't find the devices they drive often report errors, and other system components can log errors to notify you of problems more serious than those logged as warnings. For example, when a network card's driver can't be loaded, the NT I/O subsystem will log an error message to warn you.

- *Success audit* messages indicate that an operation, like logging in or accessing a share, was successful. Success audit messages are informational, but they aren't useful to many administrators. By default, Event Viewer masks these events, so you have to explicitly enable them to see them in the list.

- *Failure audit* messages are the opposite of success audit messages; they indicate that some operation failed. You'll see these when user logons fail, when users can't authenticate themselves to use shared resources, and in other similar cases. Like errors, these messages may require some action on your part. Most often, these errors occur because a user tried to do something for which she didn't have adequate authorization rights.

NOTE: You can only see success and failure audit messages when you're viewing the log of a machine on which you have administrative privileges.

In addition to the five event classes, the Windows NT event logger facility offers three log sections: System for system components like device drivers and network services; Security for security-related messages; and Application for messages generated by individual applications like IIS or SQL Server.

You view the output from the Event Logger service with the Event Viewer application. Event Viewer allows you to sift through logged events on local or remote machines, filter out the ones you don't want to see, and sort them according to your interests.

ON THE

CD

NOTE: An evaluation version of Somar Software's DumpEvt is included on the CD. DumpEvt allows you to dump some or all system events (depending on your selection criteria) from the Event Log into a text- or comma-delimited file suitable for analysis in a spreadsheet or database.

Using the Event Viewer

As its name implies, Event Viewer is designed to let you view; so, most of its functionality focuses on customizing what you see to your tastes. The main window of Event Viewer is shown in Figure 17-8. By default, Event Viewer opens with all event classes in the System log listed, with the newest events at the top of the list.

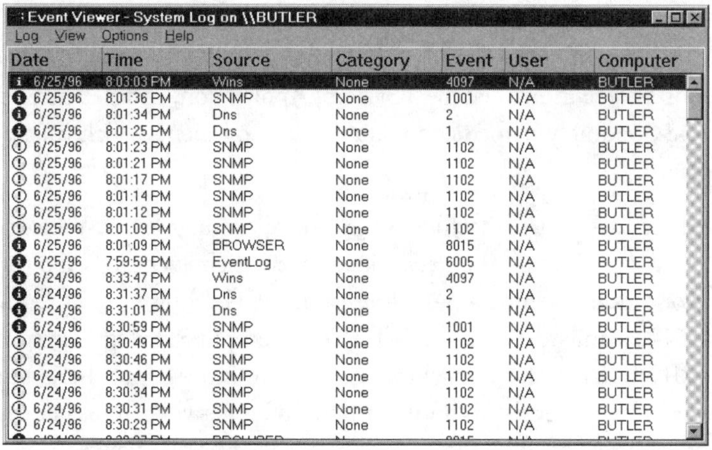

FIGURE 17-8

The Event Viewer is your window into the system's event log.

For each event, Event Viewer displays eight columns of information as follows:

- Event Class
- Date of the Event
- Time of the event
- Source of the Message
- Event Category
- Event ID
- User
- Computer

The first column displays a small icon indicating the event class. It is followed by the date and time when the event occurred. The Source column shows the name of the component that generated the message; this name isn't always the same as the executable file, especially for Windows NT services. The Category column allows applications to group related events by assigning them the same category; for example, a web server could group all access control errors into an "Access" category so they'd be displayed together. Most System and Security events will have "None" in this column. The Event column shows the numeric event ID assigned by the developer to that event. Finally, the User and Computer columns show the user account and computer which owned the process which generated the error.

Choosing Which Log to View

Event Viewer supports three individual logs: System, Application, and Security. Each of these logs has a correspondingly named command in the Log menu which causes only that log to be displayed.

In addition to the three logs on the machine where you're running Event Viewer, you can also connect to remote machines on the network and view their event logs too (provided you're logged into your local machine as an administrator.) The Log | Select Computer command brings up the standard Windows NT Select Computer dialog box; you can either type the NetBIOS name of the machine you want to browse into the Computer field, or use the Select Computer list to browse through the network. In either case, you can check the Low Speed Connection box to tell Event Viewer that you're using a slow link and that it should slow down its update frequency. Once you've established a link to a remote machine, its log will be displayed exactly as it would if you were running Event Viewer on its console.

Viewing Event Details

The Event Viewer main window presents a summary of each event, but the Event Logger service stores some additional data that you can view. Double-clicking an event in the Event Viewer main window, or selecting an event and using the View | Detail command, brings up the Event Detail dialog box as shown in Figure 17-9.

This dialog box contains the same information as the single-line summary, but it includes any data logged by the component itself. This additional data is often useful for isolating the exact cause of an error or failure. The Next and Previous buttons at the bottom of the dialog box let you cycle through the events before and after the currently displayed one.

FIGURE 17-9

The Event Detail dialog box shows complete details of the selected event, including any data logged by the logging service.

Filtering Unwanted Events

Because there are so many components in NTS, and because administrators have little control over what gets logged, the logs can contain much more data than you really want to see at a given time. Event Viewer includes a filtering facility that lets you focus only on the events of interest to you.

The first level of filtering is provided by the separation of events into three logs, as discussed above. The second level comes into play when you use the All Events and Filter Events commands in the View menu. The default is for Event Viewer to show all events in the log, and that's what View | All Events does. For those times when you want to be more selective, the View | Filter Events command will display the Filter dialog box shown in Figure 17-10.

> **TIP:** When filtering is on, Event Viewer will tell you by adding "(Filtered)" to the window's title. Filters stay in effect until you turn them off, so if your log suddenly looks bare, check for unwanted filtering.

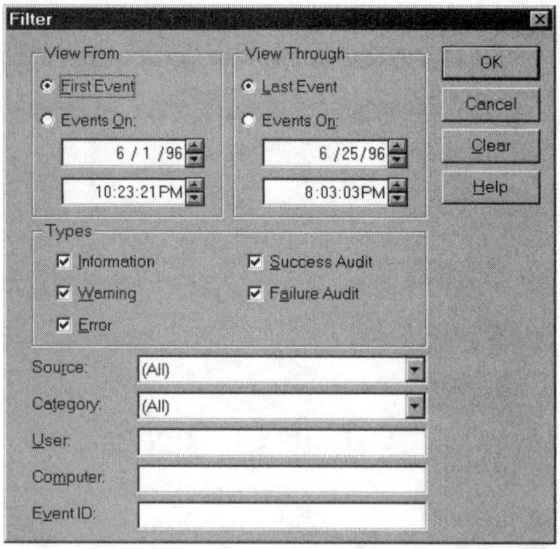

FIGURE 17-10

The Filter dialog box lets you screen out uninteresting or unwanted events from your Event Viewer display.

You can filter events by date, event class, source, category, user, computer, or event ID. These filters are additive, so you can filter by any combination of these criteria. You make your wishes known to Event Viewer via the groups in the Filter dialog box; here's what they do:

◆ The View From and View Through groups let you specify a range of time for event selection. By default, the First Event and Last Event buttons are selected, so you get all events in the log. You can go from the log's start to a specified time by using First Event and specifying a time in the View Through group; by contrast, you can start at a specified time in View From and continue to the end of the log with Last Event.

◆ The Types group lets you restrict the displayed events to the classes you select. By default, all five classes are selected.

◆ The Source and Category fields let you filter events based on the component which reported them and the category reported by the component. These fields are combo boxes so that you can quickly choose from the legitimate component and category names without fear of mistyping.

◆ You can see only those events generated by a particular user or computer by specifying the targets in the User and Computer fields. When these fields are blank, Event Viewer won't include them as filtering criteria. Unless you're connected to a remote computer's event log, you should leave the Computer field empty.

♦ The Event ID field lets you weed out all events that don't match the unique event ID of the event you're interested in. This ID is reported by the component and is unique to that particular event.

Sorting and Searching the Event Log

In addition to filtering events so you see only the ones that interest you, Event Viewer lets you change the sorting order and search for interesting events. The sorting order is controlled by the View menu's Newest First and Oldest First commands; each of these will resort the display according to your choice.

> **TIP:** When you choose the Options | Save Settings On Exit command, Event Viewer will save your filtering and sort settings and use them the next time you launch Event Viewer.

The View | Find command displays the dialog box shown in Figure 17-11; it is similar to the Filter dialog box, except that it doesn't allow you to search for events based on the time they occurred. Enter your search criteria in the dialog box and choose Find Next to find the next occurrence. You can toggle the search direction with the Direction group's Up and Down buttons, too.

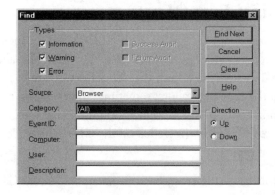

FIGURE 17-11

The Find dialog box lets you search for the next event which matches your specification.

Controlling Log File Disk Usage

Event Viewer allows you to control how much disk space the event log uses, as well as what to do when the allotted space fills up. There are a large number of components that log events, and a busy network or server can quickly accumulate more events than you can view (or make sense of), even with filtering.

You control how events are kept in the log with the Log | Log Settings command. For each of the three logs (Application, System, and Security), you can set a maximum log size (in 64Kb increments). The default size of 512Kb is adequate for most uses.

You can also specify what the event logger should do when the log is full:

♦ Overwrite old events, starting with the oldest one still in the log

♦ Overwrite events older than the specified number of days

♦ Never overwrite logs; this option requires that you manually clear the log when it fills, or no new events will be captured

Because these settings apply individually to each of the three logs, you can customize the log's disk usage to your needs. I recommend setting the "do not overwrite" option for the security log so that you can review it periodically as suggested elsewhere, but the default of overwriting the oldest event first is fine for the other two logs.

The Log | Clear All Events command gives you an easy way to flush the entire log. Event Viewer will ask you if you want to save the event log to an archive file before the actual clearing occurs; if you say yes, then you'll have a file you can reload at a later time for further review or analysis.

Dumping and Reloading Event Logs

You may find it useful to save your event logs for further analysis. For example, most systems in security-minded environments (the U.S. government, banks, stock firms, and so on) dump their logs periodically and archive them for a year. This allows them to review the system's behavior leading up to the time of a failure; sometimes the event log can provide valuable clues. Another common application for event log dumps is the use of a third-party tool like Somar Software's DumpEvt (included on the CD), which allows more detailed filtering and sorting of events.

You can save the current set of events using the Log | Save As command. In the Save As dialog box, you can use the Save as type drop down list to save the file as a native Event Viewer file (with an extension of `.evt`) or as plain or comma-delimited text (with an extension of `.txt`).

If you save the file in text form, the event data will be included, but the binary event data that appears in the Event Detail dialog box won't be. If you have any filters active, they won't be applied—what you see in the Event Viewer window is what will be written to disk. You can also save the logs when you use the Log | Clear All Events command.

Of course, saving the logs wouldn't be of much use without a way to reload them at some time in the future. That's what Log | Open is for. When you open a saved log file, Event Viewer will ask you to choose between displaying the System, Application, and Security logs. It's a good idea to use a naming convention when saving the files so that you'll know which event log you're loading; one good way to do so is to name the files SYS, APP, or SEC, plus the date when they were generated, as in SYS961002.EVT.

Although Event Viewer allows you to open any type of file, if you try to open a non-.evt file it will fail and report that the event log file is corrupt.

Using the Task Manager

In earlier versions of Windows NT, the Task Manager was a simple modal window listing running tasks and providing you a way to switch to or end any task. Although more flexible tools were available to developers, there wasn't a good way to manage process priorities or even to get a quick glimpse of system performance without learning to use the Performance Monitor.

This situation has changed in Windows NT 4.0, which includes a new Task Manager application that gives you more control over machine processes. Unlike Server Manager and Performance Monitor, Task Manager is limited to controlling processes on the local machine. However, it's still a useful tool for watching and affecting the state of applications and processes on your computers.

Task Manager Basics

To invoke the Task Manager, right-click the Taskbar and choose the Task Manager command. The Windows NT Task Manager's main window is shown in Figure 17-12. The Applications, Processes, and Performance tabs each have a view associated with them; the figure shows the Applications view, which is the closest equivalent to the old-style Task Manager interface.

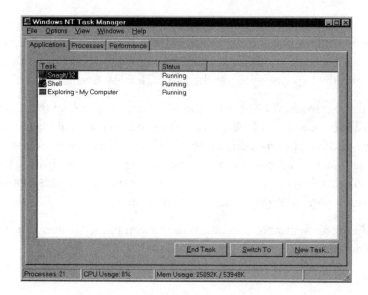

FIGURE 17-12

The Task Manager's three tabs let you view applications, individual processes, or performance data.

Each active application is shown, along with a status that indicates whether the application is still running. You can use the End Task, Switch To, and New Task buttons to start, stop, or swap tasks just as with the original Task Manager interface. You can also click the right mouse button on an application to display a context menu which allows you to maximize, minimize, switch to, or kill the application.

One nice touch to this incarnation of Task Manager is the window status bar at the bottom of the window; it summarizes the current process, CPU, and memory load. You can also control whether the Task Manager stays atop all other applications and what it does when you minimize it with the Options menu's commands. Task Manager also adds a small green bar graph to the tray on the right end of the Taskbar; this graph shows the CPU load, and clicking it will maximize the Task Manager application when it is hidden.

Monitoring Processes

The Processes tab, whose associated view is shown in Figure 17-13, lists individual processes in the system. Some of these processes belong to Windows NT, while others are user applications or services. Each process is listed by name, along with whatever other parameters you've chosen to monitor. You can change the columns displayed with the View | Select Columns command (see Figure 17-14).

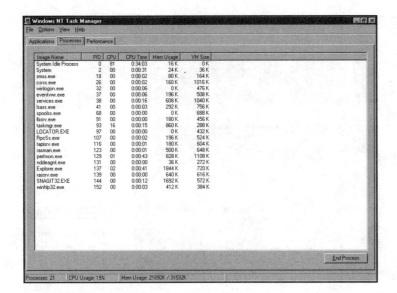

FIGURE 17-13

The Processes tab in Task Manager lets you view resource usage of individual processes.

FIGURE 17-14

Selecting columns.

Clicking on the column headers sorts the list by the value of that column. You can use the End Process button to terminate the selected process; you can also right-click any process in the list and kill it, debug it (if you have a debugger installed), or change its system priority.

Monitoring CPU and RAM Usage

Perhaps the most welcome feature of the new Task Manager is its Performance tab, featuring a graphic display of memory and CPU usage as shown in Figure 17-15. The CPU and memory usage graphs work like charts in Performance Monitor; they chart the utilization values at intervals you specify with the View | Update Speed and View | Refresh Now commands. The data area at the bottom of the window summarizes memory and resource usage.

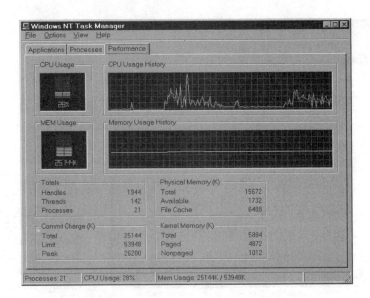

FIGURE 17-15

The Performance tab in Task Manager offers a dynamic view of memory and CPU usage.

The CPU and MEM Usage graphs show instantaneous usage, while the History charts show usage over time. You can expand either set of graphs by double-clicking them; the data area will disappear and the selected graph's scale will increase to fill the window. Double-click the graph again to return to the normal display.

Where to Go Next

This chapter describes how to use the Performance Monitor, Task Manager, and Event Viewer to track of your systems' performance and resource usage. These tools can provide insight into what's happening with your computers. This insight can be invaluable when you're searching for the cause of a performance problem or trying to plan upgrades.

At this point, you may find some of these chapters and resources useful:

♦ Chapter 18, "Monitoring Network Performance," is devoted to using Performance Monitor and other tools to monitor network-specific performance items.

♦ Chapter 19, "Performance Tuning and Optimization," provides details on adjustments to improve your system's performance.

♦ Chapter 3, "Planning for Your NT Server Installation," covers planning steps you should take to ensure that you are buying adequate hardware to avoid bottlenecks altogether.

Chapter | 18

Monitoring Network Performance

In This Chapter:

- ◆ Using the Performance Monitor
- ◆ Using the Network Monitor

How do I...

Most Windows NT Server machines are used as network servers and, in that application, their performance is tightly coupled with the performance of the networks they use. Network performance influences the server's performance, and the server's use of the network impacts other network clients.

Chapter 17, "Monitoring System Performance," discusses some of Windows NT's performance measurement tools. This chapter shows how to use the Performance Monitor to gather and display statistics that reflect your network's performance and loading. You'll also learn how to use the Network Monitor application to monitor, filter, and analyze traffic on your network.

Using the Performance Monitor

Chapter 17 shows how to use the Performance Monitor application and suggested counters to use in forming a good starting baseline for long-term performance measurement. In this section, we'll discuss the other objects, instances, and counters which you can use to watch your network's performance, including an explanation of what they measure.

Useful Built-In Objects, Instances, and Counters

Performance Monitor includes counters for a wide range of objects and their instances. Several of these counter sets report on network-related performance; each one is listed below, along with what instances, if any, it supports and a list of its most important counters.

The Browser Object

Instances: The Browser object has no instances, since there's only one browser per Windows NT server or workstation.

> **NOTE:** Instances are used to distinguish between different objects of the same type. Because there will never be more than one brower per Windows NT server or NT workstation, it isn't necessary to identify *which* browser. For the browser (or any system-unique object), the instances identifier doesn't add any information—once you know that the object is THE Browser, you already know it is browser #1. Consequently, we say that the Browser object has no instances, even though logically we might say it has one.

What it does: It measures the number of announcement, response, and election packets sent, received, and missed by the Browser service on the selected machine.

Key counters:

- ◆ Announcements Total/Sec indicates the total number of announcements sent and received per second.

- ◆ Enumerations Total/Sec counts the number of server, domain, and other enumeration requests per second. Each enumeration request requires the recipient to send back a list of all of the requested items (servers, master browsers, or backup browsers) it knows about. High values indicate a large amount of network browsing traffic on this subnet.

The Redirector Object

Instances: Like the Browser object, the Redirector object has no instances.

What it does: The Redirector object monitors performance of the network redirector, which redirects I/O requests for data served by network servers to the appropriate server.

Key counters:

- ◆ CurrentCommands indicates the number of requests waiting for service; when this value is greater than the number of network adapters in your system, it means that either the server is too slow to keep up with the request rate or that the redirector is too busy for the current network adapter.

- ◆ Network Errors/Sec indicates the arrival rate of network errors; if this counter is above zero, look in the Event Log for the error message.

The Server Object

Instances: None.

What it does: The Server object measures statistics for the server service, which answers network I/O requests from redirectors on other machines.

Key counters:

- ◆ Bytes Total/sec indicates the total number of bytes sent by a server; if you sum this value for all your servers, you can measure what fraction of your network bandwidth is in use. When the threshold reaches 50% of your available bandwidth, it's time to start considering ways to conserve or increase that bandwidth.

- ◆ Sessions Errored Out indicates how many sessions failed due to network errors.

- ◆ Work Item Shortages: Each request from a client is represented by a *work item*. The server process maintains a pool of work items for servicing requests; each incoming request uses a work item until the request is finished. The Work Item Shortages counter indicates when the server has more requests to process than it has available work items.

The Server Work Queues Object

Instances: One instance per installed CPU, plus one instance for blocked work requests.

What it does: The Server Work Queues object measures statistics for work requests sent by network redirectors to the Server service on this server and breaks down Server object counters to individual thread instances.

Key counters:

◆ `Bytes Total/sec` indicates the total number of bytes sent by a server.

◆ `Sessions Errored Out` indicates how many sessions failed due to network errors.

◆ The `Work Item Shortages` counter indicates when the server has more requests to process than it has available work items. This counter will always have a zero value for the blocked work request queue, since by definition these requests aren't using any work items.

The Network Segment Object

Instances: One or more per installed network adapter.

What it does: The Network Segment object measures throughput, error rate, and other metrics for installed network adapter cards.

Key counters:

◆ Total `bytes received/ sec` indicates the total amount of data received by an individual adapter. This value will vary depending on the load on your server.

◆ `% Network utilization` sums the amount of available bandwidth used on this network segment. Values about 50% indicate that you need to consider subnetting or traffic reduction to improve bandwidth availability.

The TCP, UDP, ICMP, and IP Objects

Instances: None.

What they do: Count throughput, error and rejection rates, and other parameters for Windows NT's TCP/IP implementation.

Key counters: Each individual object includes counters for total throughput and the number of errors which occurred during sending or receiving data.

The NBT Connection Object

Instances: One—the Total instance.

What it does: Measures throughput in the NetBEUI over TCP/IP (NBT) transport protocol, often used in mixed Windows & TCP/IP networks.

Key counters: Bytes Total/sec counts the total amount of traffic generated by NBT requests and responses.

Additional Counters

When you install additional network protocols on your NTS machines, you may also gain access to Performance Monitor counters specific to the new protocols. For example, when you install the Services for Macintosh package (as described in Chapter 23, "Interoperating with Macintosh Clients"), part of the installation is an AppleTalk object; this object has an instance for every network card to which AppleTalk is bound. In turn, each instance has a set of counters for the AppleTalk network protocol.

These protocol-specific counters usually include a common set of measures indicating how much virtual and physical memory is being used by the protocol drivers, as well as measures unique to that protocol. For example, the AppleTalk counter set includes counters for the number of Zone Information Protocol (ZIP) and Datagram Delivery Protocol (DDP) packets received per second.

Ongoing monitoring of these counters will tell you if and when any of these values pass out of limits. When they do, that indicates a problem. Sometimes these problems can be resolved by adding faster hardware; in other cases, though, you need more detailed data—perhaps data specific to a single network protocol. The Network Monitor is like a zoom lens: it can focus in on individual bytes on the network, or zoom out to give you protocol-by-protocol summaries. Let's see how it works.

Using the Network Monitor

NTS 4.0 includes a powerful network monitoring software package. This package, descended from Network General's Sniffer line of network monitors, lets you capture, trace, and analyze network traffic on your Ethernet, Token Ring, or FDDI network.

Some features in the NTS Network Monitor are disabled, but the version included with Microsoft's Systems Management Server (SMS) is full-featured.

NOTE: An evaluation version of Network Instruments' Observer is included on the CD. Observer is a full-featured, easy-to-use network monitor with a number of graphing and capture features missing from Microsoft's offering.

Introducing Network Monitor

The main purpose of Network Monitor is to allow you to see what traffic is passing on your network at the protocol and packet levels. As such, it's not a tool for the casual user, and we'll only cover the rudiments of using it here—using a network sniffer well is somewhat of an art form.

The main Network Monitor window is shown in Figure 18-1. There are a large number of widgets, buttons, graphs, and panes, displaying a smorgasbord of data. Each Network Monitor capture window (so called because you use it to capture frames of network traffic) represents a single network interface card (NIC); if you have more than one NIC, you'll have more than one capture window within the Network Monitor window. Each capture window is titled with the adapter's device name (for example, \Ethernet\Net1) and contains four panes. In the upper-left corner is the Graph pane, which displays bar graphs of usage and timing parameters. Immediately below it is the Session Stats pane, which displays statistics for the currently active network session. The Total Stats pane takes up the right-hand side next to the Graph and Session Stats panes; it displays a summary of network and capture statistics. The bottom of the window is ordinarily taken up by the Station Stats pane, which shows overall statistics for the computer being monitored.

Any of the panes can be shown or hidden. All four panes are shown in the default configuration, but you can hide or show any of the panes with the Window menu or the second group of buttons on the toolbar. Table 18-1 shows the toolbar buttons; they're not exactly self-evident.

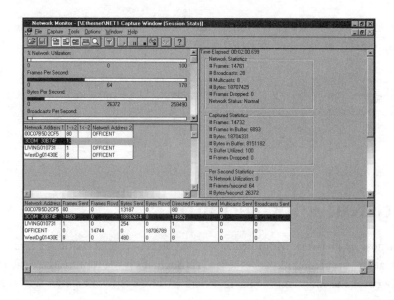

FIGURE 18-1

The Network Monitor main window consists of four panes which display different sets of network data.

Table 18-1   Toolbar buttons in the Network Monitor window.

Button	Name
	Open
	Save
	Toggle Graph Pane
	Toggle Total Stats Pane
	Toggle Session Stats Pane
	Toggle Station Stats Pane
	Zoom Pane

Button	Name
	Edit Capture Filter
	Start Capture
	Pause/Continue Capture
	Stop Capture
	Stop & View Capture
	Display Captured Data
	Help

You can customize the panes' display to suit you; each of the columns in the Session Stats and Station Stats panes can be resized, and you can reorder the columns by dragging them with the left mouse button into the order you want. You can also customize how Network Monitor displays captured data; see the later section "Viewing and Analyzing Captured Data" for more details. One final note: in either the capture window or the summary window, you can save the current view settings, fonts, colors, column widths, and so on with the Capture or Display menu's Save Configuration command.

Installing Network Monitor and the Network Monitor Agent

The NTS installation doesn't default to installing the Network Monitor or Network Monitor Agent, nor does it provide you a way to ask for it during the install. If you want to monitor network traffic on your server, or if you want any of your NTW or NTS machines to be monitored by an SMS server running the SMS Network Monitor, you need to install the Network Monitor package on the machines to be monitored.

There are actually two components you can install: the Network Monitor Agent component, which has only the Network Monitor agent software, or the Network Monitor Tools and Agent component, which includes the Network Monitor application with the Network Monitor agent software. If you want to monitor an NTS or NTW machine, install the Network Monitor Agent software. If you want to run the Network Monitor itself, install the Network Monitor Tools and Agent component instead.

In either case, the steps needed to add network monitoring capability are similar to those required for installing SNMP:

1. Open the Network Control Panel applet and choose the Services tab.

2. If the menu shows "Network Monitor Agent" or "Network Monitor Tools and Agent", the Network Monitor Agent has already been installed, so skip on to step 4.

3. Click the Add button; when the Select Network Service dialog box appears, select which package you want to install on this machine, then click OK. NT Setup will prompt you for the path to the installation media, then it will copy the files you've selected. After the installation is finished, you will be reminded to restart before the new components become active.

4. To start the Network Monitor Agent service, open the Services Control Panel applet and look for the "Network Monitor Agent" entry. If you just installed Network Monitor, the service will be listed as a manual startup service. Click the Startup button, then set the Startup Type to Automatic and click OK. Finally, click the Start button to start the Network Monitor Agent.

Capturing Network Data

Before you can analyze traffic, you must capture it. Network Monitor's Capture menu furnishes commands for configuring how capturing works, from how much data can be captured to what data is filtered during the actual capture. Once captured, data can be written to disk and filtered or analyzed later.

Network Monitor copies data from the network card's onboard buffer to its own RAM buffer. The size of this buffer and the speed of your computer determine how much data you *can* capture and how much of the data from the wire you *actually* capture. The Capture | Buffer Settings command brings up the Capture Buffer Settings dialog box, with which you can specify how much RAM will used for the capture buffer as well as how much of each incoming frame to capture. Use the Buffer Size field to allocate a chunk of RAM for the network copy buffer.

> **TIP:** You should specify a buffer no larger than the amount of free RAM you have when running Network Monitor; if your buffer is too big, Windows NT will use its virtual memory subsystem, and the resultant swapping will cause a large number of dropped frames.

You can increase the effectiveness of your buffer by telling Network Monitor to capture only the part of the network frames that interest you. By default, Network Monitor captures the entire frame, but you can use the Frame Size field to capture only the first N bytes of the frame, skipping over the application-specific contents if you don't need them.

Since network data can arrive at speeds up to 100Mbps, your computer may fail to capture some packets if it can't keep up. Network Monitor offers two ways to capture data; *normal* mode keeps the statistics panes in the window up to date as data arrives, and *dedicated* mode freezes the statistics panes and minimizes the Network Monitor application to maximize your capture rate. To toggle between the two options, use the Capture | Dedicated Capture Mode command.

Setting Capture Triggers

Network Monitor allows you to set triggers that will automatically take some action when the condition you set becomes true. For example, you can set a trigger to stop capturing data when a particular pattern occurs. You might do this to get details on an FTP session that keeps failing to certain hosts; seting a capture trigger that stops the capture when the session completes.s you to capture only the protocol data of interest.

You set capture triggers with the Capture Triggers dialog box (see Figure 18-2), which appears when you choose the Capture | Trigger command.

The Trigger On group offers you five choices for when the trigger should occur:

◆ The default is Nothing, which means nothing will happen. (The other choices are more interesting.)

◆ Pattern Match causes a trigger event when the pattern you specify in the Pattern group occurs in a frame.

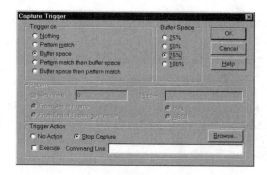

FIGURE 18-2

The Capture Trigger dialog box is where you link network events to actions you want taken.

♦ Buffer Space causes a trigger event when the percentage of the buffer in use hits the value you specify. You're limited to choosing space in 25% increments.

♦ Pattern Match Then Buffer Space links a pattern with a buffer space limit. Network Monitor will first watch for the specified pattern; when it occurs, it will fire a trigger when the buffer utilization reaches the value you set.

♦ Buffer Space Then Pattern Match makes Network Monitor wait until the buffer's filled to the point you chose; when it does, the trigger will fire when the specified pattern occurs in an incoming frame.

Once you've hit on the trigger condition that suits your needs, you can set a trigger action to be executed when the trigger is fired. Network Monitor can either do nothing (the default) or stop the capture. In either case, you can specify that an external program be run by checking the Execute checkbox and specifying the command line for the program in the Command Line field.

Starting, Pausing, and Stopping Capture

Once you've constructed a capture filter that will keep only the data that interests you, you're ready to capture data. Network Monitor provides a simple mechanism for logging network data: When you're ready to start, use the Capture | Start command (or the Start Capture toolbar button). If you're in normal capture mode, the statistics panes update in real-time to show you what's happening; if you're in dedicated mode, Network Monitor minimizes itself and displays a small dialog box with buttons for pausing or stopping the capture and a counter indicating the number of captured frames.

> **TIP:** If you try to start a capture before you've saved the current capture buffer, Network Monitor will ask you to confirm that you want to overwrite the original buffer's data if the Options | Prompt to Save Data option is enabled.

While you're capturing data, you can pause and restart the capture at any time with the Capture | Pause and Capture | Continue commands (or the Pause/Continue Capture toolbar button.) When in dedicated mode, use the buttons in the summary dialog box.

When you're ready to stop capturing data, you have two options. The Capture | Stop command will immediately stop the capture, while the Capture | Stop and View command will stop the capture and display the buffered data in a frame viewer window. Once capture has stopped, you can save captured data to a file with the File | Save As command or print it with the File | Print command.

Viewing and Analyzing Captured Data

Once you've stopped capturing data, you can move on to viewing and analyzing the packets that were captured by your filter. You can start viewing data in two ways: by selecting the Capture | Stop and View command when you stop capturing or the Capture | Display Captured Data command at any time after you've stopped the capture. In either case, Network Monitor will open a new summary window to show you what data was captured. The ordinary summary window is shown in Figure 18-3. The summary window shown in Figure 18-3 is titled Capture: 1 (Summary).

Network Monitor's user interface changes somewhat when you bring a summary window frontmost. The Capture menu changes its name to Display, and sprouts some additional options. An Edit menu appears; it can be used to copy data from the window and paste it into a text editor or other application..

Property and Protocol options are added to the Help menu (which protocols have help available depends on the network vendor; the standard Network Monitor installation only includes help for Microsoft's SMB protocol.)

The standard summary window will list a single entry for each captured frame. You can expand an entry to see more details of the frame by double-clicking an entry in the summary. The summary pane will shrink and two new panes will be added to the window, as shown in Figure 18-4. The middle pane is the Details pane, which shows you detailed data about the frame you selected; the bottom pane, the Hex pane, shows you the actual contents of the packets. Items in the Details pane may have subitems; you can collapse or expand these items by double-clicking them or single-clicking the plus or minus (shown as a plus in Figure 18-4) sign in the leftmost column.

> **TIP:** You can turn off the hex data or detail panes with the Window menu.

While you're looking at the frame summaries and details, you can move between frames with the Display menu's Next Frame, Previous Frame, and Goto Frame commands. Goto Frame requires you to pick a frame number, but the others go to the selected frame relative to the current frame. You can also use the Find Next Frame command to find frames that match your selection criteria; these criteria are identical to the ones you'll construct for display filters, so read the section on "Creating Display Filters" in this chapter for full details.

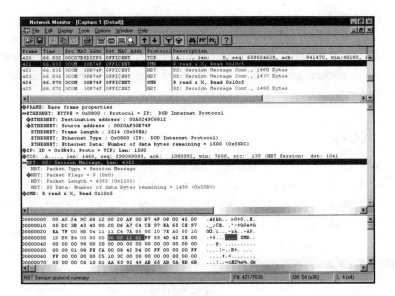

FIGURE 18-4

The Detail and Hex panes within the detail window (titled Network Monitor - [Capture:1 (Detail)]) show the exact contents of a specified frame.

The summary window display can be customized, too. Like the Session Stats and Station Stats panes of the capture window, you can adjust column widths and ordering by dragging the column rules or titles with the left mouse button. You can relabel the capture window, too. The default name for the summary window is the name of the capture buffer (the name you used to save the capture buffer or "Capture" if it hasn't been saved). You can relabel the capture window with the Window | Label command. Whatever label you type in will appear in the window's title bar when it's visible.

Network Monitor also lets you customize the font and color used to display the protocol information. Each protocol can have its own foreground and background colors, but the font you choose is used for all protocols. Use the Display | Font and Display | Colors commands to set these the way you like.

Designing Capture and Display Filters

There's an amazing amount of traffic passing over even small networks—browser broadcasts from newly-added shares, AppleTalk packets from the Macs down the hall, outgoing SMTP mail traffic, and the like. This means your Network Monitor capture session may end up deluging you with data. Network Monitor provides *capture filters* that you can use to selectively reject data that doesn't interest you. When you apply a capture filter, only data that matches the filter settings you provide is copied to the capture buffer. In addition, you can create *display filters* which further narrow the amount of data you see at one time. The difference between capture and display filters is that capture filters determine which network packets are captured (copied to the capture buffer) and display filters control which captured packets are displayed.

Capture Filters

The main control point for capture filtering is the Capture Filter dialog box, shown in Figure 18-5. The default filtering scheme, as shown in the dialog box, is to include any type of network packet sent between the Network Monitor's machine (which is named BUTLER in the example shown in Figure 18-5) and any other network address.

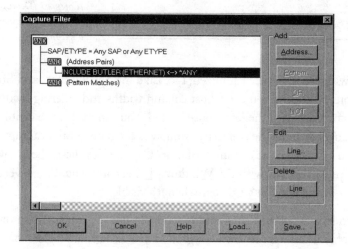

FIGURE 18-5

The Capture Filter dialog box lets you build complex filtering rules to discard uninteresting packets.

The button groups along the right edge of the Capture Filter dialog box let you add, edit, or delete filter criteria from the current tree. The buttons automatically enable or disable themselves depending on whether the selected item is changeable. You can edit criteria by using the Edit group's Line button or by double-clicking the item you want to edit; likewise, you can delete a filter item either with the Del key or the Delete group's Line button.

Filter criteria are organized in a tree structure. Each branch of the tree specifies a selection criteria; individual branches can use AND, OR, and NOT relationships to selectively add or remove matching packets from the capture set. The selection criteria become more specific as you move toward the bottom of the tree, since the topmost criteria are applied first.

TIP: You can reorder filter criteria or move them by dragging and dropping them with the left mouse button.

The default tree includes three fixed branches that are ANDed together; you can edit their criteria, but you can't remove them. The first branch of the tree specifies which Service Access Points (SAP) and Ethertypes (ETYPE) should be included in the filtering. The SAP and ETYPE identifiers mark particular protocols; for example, Xerox XNS packets will have an two-byte ETYPE value of 0x0600 or 0x0807. SAP filtering is the broadest filtering because you can choose to keep or drop whole protocols without regard to the addresses or contents of packets using that protocol. When you edit the SAP/ETYPE filter, you'll see the dialog box shown in Figure 18-6. This rather ornate dialog box lets you choose which SAPs and ETYPEs to include or exclude from your capture buffer. The sample in Figure 18-6 shows a filter that will trap traffic using any TCP or IP protocol while ignoring all others.

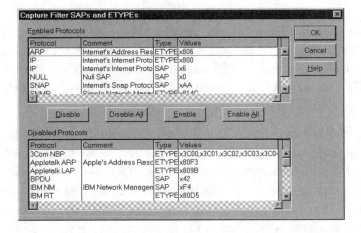

FIGURE 18-6

The Capture Filter SAP/ETYPE dialog box lets you select which SAPs and ETYPEs to use in your filter.

The next branch of the filter tree is the Address Pairs item, which you use to control which incoming and outgoing traffic is filtered. The NTS version of Network Monitor allows you to monitor only traffic sent from or received by your machine (including multicast and broadcast traffic), so the default address pair, which captures any traffic to or from your machine, is usually adequate. You can add other address pairs to this branch, or edit any existing pairs, using the Add group's Address button and the Edit group's Line button in the Capture Filter dialog box (refer to Figure 18-5). In either case, you'll see the Address Expression dialog box shown in Figure 18-7. The Include and Exclude radio buttons at the top of the dialog box let you select the direction in which this filter item works; the Station 1 and Station 2 groups let you set up expressions for traffic going in either or both directions—for example, you might want to see packets sent from one machine to another without wanting packets going the other way.

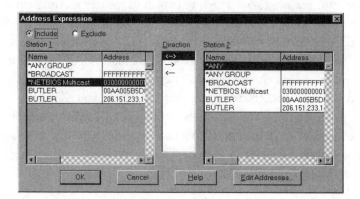

FIGURE 18-7

The Address Expression dialog box lets you construct an address pair to use in your filter.

The third default branch is the Pattern Match category. Any packets that match the SAP/ETYPE and address pair filters you provide must also match any pattern filters, or they'll be discarded. Unlike the SAP/ETYPE and address pair types, pattern matches can be joined with AND, OR, and NOT, so you can build a filter that requires multiple values within a packet to match your specifications.

The first step in building a pattern match item is to use the Add group's Pattern button in the Capture Filter dialog box (refer to Figure 18-5), which displays the Pattern Match dialog box pictured in Figure 18-8. Pattern matches are built up from two components: a data pattern to match, and an offset which tells Network Monitor where in the packet the pattern must occur. Specify the pattern you're looking for in the Pattern field, and use the Hex and ASCII radio buttons to indicate what format the pattern you provided is in. The Offset field tells Network Monitor where in the packet to start looking; its value is in hex and is modified by the two radio buttons below. If you select the From Start of Frame button, the offset starts at the first byte of the captured frame. When you select the From End of Topology Header button instead, the offset begins at the end of the physical topology section of the frame; this allows you to skip over the physical-layer data for a frame and base your filter on the network and protocol layer "payload" data within the frame.

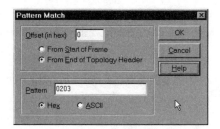

FIGURE 18-8

*Use the Pattern Match
dialog box to filter packets
based on their contents.*

You can add many pattern matches and specify their interrelationships with the Capture Filter dialog box's OR and NOT buttons. For example, you might match packets which contain a particular pattern at one offset and which do not have another pattern at a different offset. One example of how you could do this is shown in Figure 18-9.

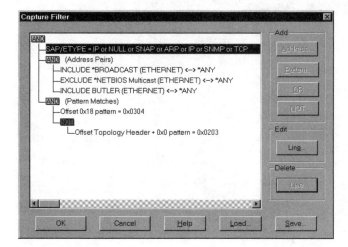

FIGURE 18-9

*Pattern match filters
can be conjoined with
AND, OR, and NOT
to allow arbitrarily
complex filtering.*

Since constructing filters can be a time-consuming and painstaking process, it's good that Network Monitor allows you to save and reload filter specifications with the Load and Save buttons of the Capture Filter dialog box. When you save a filter, you can specify a comment that describes exactly what the filter does. When you load filters, their comments are displayed as a memory aid.

Display Filters

The preceding section describes how to build a capture filter that restricts which network data is copied into the capture buffer. You can also define display filters that let you further restrict which data from the capture buffer is displayed in a summary window. The interface for building filters of either type is similar, so this section will only cover the features that are specific to building display filters.

The Display Filter dialog box is shown in Figure 18-10. It looks quite like the Capture Filter dialog box from Figure 18-5, but it adds some additional capabilities—in fact, it contains all the features of the SMS version's filter dialog boxes. The Add group is the same except for the presence of the Expression button. The Delete group includes buttons for deleting an entire branch of the tree, or the whole tree, with one click—which are not present in Capture Filter dialog box. The Edit group and the buttons along the bottom of the dialog box are the same as in the Capture Filter dialog box.

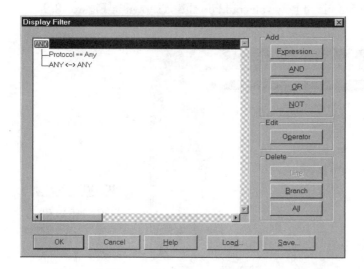

FIGURE 18-10

The Display Filter dialog box lets you build complex filters for controlling what Network Monitor displays.

The filter rules in the Display Filter dialog box are based on expressions that you can enter with the Add group's Expression button; you can edit existing expressions with the Edit group's Expression button. Both these buttons display the Expression dialog box. Network Monitor supports three kinds of expressions: address expressions, protocol expressions, and property expressions; the Expression dialog box has a tab for each expression type.

Address expressions are simply pairs of addresses, just like the Capture Filter dialog box uses. You can specify single address pairs or multi-/broadcast addresses. The Edit Addresses button opens the address database for you to browse and edit registered addresses. The Address tab of the Expressions dialog box is shown in Figure 18-11.

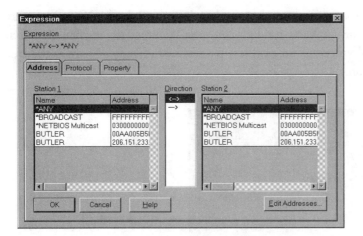

FIGURE 18-11

The Address tab of the Expressions dialog box lets you specify address pairs and types of interest.

Protocol expressions let you keep or discard packets based on the protocols they carry. When the Protocol tab (shown in Figure 18-12) is active, there are two protocol lists. Network Monitor will keep packets from those protocols listed in the E̲nabled Protocols list and filter out packets carrying protocols listed in the D̲isabled Protocols list. You can use the buttons between the two lists to enable or disable the protocols you want to include or exclude.

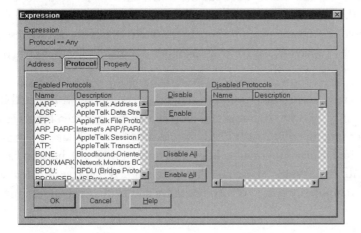

FIGURE 18-12

The Protocol tab of the Expressions dialog box lets you screen out packets based on the protocol used to encode them.

The Property tab is perhaps the most interesting, because it can create filter criteria based on the structures of many common network protocols. Using this tab, you can build expressions that look for packets that have specific values in protocol-specific fields.

Figure 18-13 shows a simple example; the filter shown will display IP packets whose destination address is the computer running Network Monitor. (Remember, the NTS version of Network Monitor will only capture packets sent directly to or from the Network Monitor workstation.)

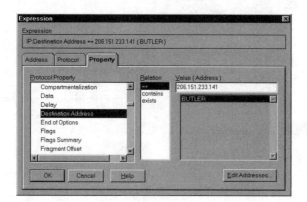

FIGURE 18-13

You can filter packets by content with the Property tab of the Expressions dialog box.

Property expressions can use the standard comparison operators—== (equal), <> (not equal), > (greater than), < (less than), >= (greater than or equal to), <= (less than or equal to)—as well as the "contains" and "exists" operators. "Contains" lets you search packets for a particular byte sequence, and "exists" flags packets which have the selected property at all, no matter what the property's value is. Network Monitor is smart about displaying operators; for example, it's meaningless to compare the ordering of network addresses with the >, <, >=, and <= operators, so Network Monitor doesn't display them when the property you've selected is an address.

Once you've constructed a display filter, you can conjoin its conditions with the AND, OR, and NOT operators, and you can drag and drop expressions between branches to get the precedence order set properly for your needs. The display filter will take effect as soon as you click OK in the Display Filter dialog box (refer to Figure 18-10), but you can turn filtering off again with the Display | Disable Filter command. When you disable the filter, it's not lost, just temporarily turned off. You can save and load display filters just like capture filters, too.

Using the Address Database

Network Monitor maintains a database of addresses that it finds; each entry in the database contains the address' name (which may be a NetBIOS name, domain name, or label), the physical address and its type, and a comment. Network Monitor includes some predefined entries for broadcast and monitoring packets, as well as entries for the computer running Network Monitor.

You can browse and edit the address database with the Capture | Addresses command. The Address Database dialog box is shown in Figure 18-14. The Add and Edit buttons display the same Address Information dialog box, in which you enter the address type (FDDI, Ethernet, IPX, and so on), the address, and a name and comment to be displayed in the database. You can change the address used with a name (as you might need to when replacing a failed network card in a computer) by editing the entry and changing its type without modifying the address. The Delete button removes the selected address from the database, and the Load and Save buttons allow you to save the database to disk and reload it at any time.

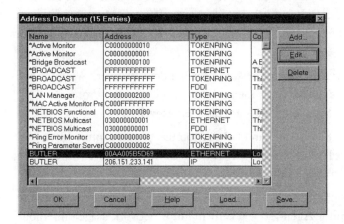

FIGURE 18-14

The Address Database dialog box shows which addresses Network Monitor has seen during its monitoring.

You can also scan the capture buffer for any network addresses that Network Monitor doesn't already have in its database. To start this scan, use the Capture | Find All Names command. Each unknown address will generate a name resolution query (the type of query depends on the protocol). Queries which succeed associate the network address with a human-readable name. Once the scan is finished, it displays a summary dialog box telling you how many names were found and how many of those found were added to the database.

> **TIP:** The Addresses and Find All Names commands are also available from the Display menu when you're looking at a capture summary window.

What's Missing from the NTS Network Monitor

If you've been reading this section while running Network Monitor, you've probably noticed that there are some commands not discussed. For some reason, Microsoft left a number of commands in the NTS version of Network Monitor that work only in the SMS version. Perhaps they wanted users to see clearly which features could only be used with the SMS version. Whatever the rationale, there are some commands that appear in the NTS version of Network Monitor's toolbars and menus that produce dialog boxes telling you they only work in the SMS version of Network Monitor. Here's a partial list:

- The Tools | Find Routers and Tools | Resolve Addresses From Name commands are disabled; if you choose them, Network Monitor will display a dialog box telling you that they only work in the SMS version of Network Monitor.

- When you're viewing a capture summary window, Network Monitor adds new commands to the Tools menu: Find Top Users and Protocol Distribution. These commands are disabled as well.

- The Capture | Filter command (which you use to edit capture filters) warns you that the NTS version can only capture traffic to and from the local s erver, not any traffic on the subnet.

- You cannot connect the NTS Network Monitor to a remote computer's Network Monitor Agent, so you can't monitor network usage on remote machines. If you install Network Monitor Agent on your server, however, SMS servers can monitor it.

Where to Go Next

This chapter discusses how to monitor your network's raw performance by using the Performance Monitor. In addition, it covers how to use the Network Monitor to do packet-level analysis of your network's traffic. The combination of these tools provides big-picture statistical data coupled with the ability to localize problems to an individual workstation, server, or router.

Other chapters are also relevant to these activities:

◆ Chapter 17, "Monitoring System Performance," discusses the details of using the Performance Monitor application.

◆ Chapter 19, "Performance Tuning and Optimization," covers adjustments to system configuration to improve overall and network performance.

◆ The section on "Controlling Network Browsing" in Chapter 15, "Planning and Using Domains and Workgroups," describes how to adjust the Browser service's behavior to reduce your network traffic.

Chapter | 19

Performance Tuning and Optimization

In This Chapter:

◆ System Performance Optimization

◆ Network Performance Optimization

How do I...

Chapter 17, "Monitoring System Performance" and Chapter 18, "Monitoring Network Performance" discuss how to use the Network Monitor and Performance Monitor tools to keep watch on your servers' network and system performance. However, no matter how vigilant you are, a time will probably come when you want to *improve* the machines' performance, not just watch it. This chapter shows how to build on your knowledge of NT's architecture and the specifics of your network and hardware to reduce performance bottlenecks and keep your network and its machines at maximum performance.

In general, you optimize performance in two steps. The first step is identifying system components that are bottlenecks; the second is minimizing the effect of the bottleneck or eliminating it. To identify bottlenecks, you use the Performance Monitor and Network Monitor, as discussed in Chapters 17 and 18. Once you've done so, you'll be ready to move on to the specific suggestions in this chapter.

System Performance Optimization

Unlike many other operating systems, Windows NT is specifically designed to need no adjustment. Most system components are designed to maximize performance for their most common tasks. Many subsystems whose performance affects the whole system, such as the virtual memory manager, are self-tuning and adjust their operation based on the system's capacity and loading.

Some components have configuration entries in the Registry that can be altered to affect their performance. Others provide a standard control panel or other easily accessible way for you to change their settings. There may be times when, despite the designers' good intentions, it's necessary for you to adjust "self-tuned" parameters to resolve a performance problem. It's important to realize that changing Registry parameters is a balance between optimization and risk. Every change can be be fatal to the system. Needless to say, if the system has crashed, performance is a moot issue.

Before we continue with optimizing tips, let us examine the way that Windows NT handles applications and threads.

Adjusting Task Scheduling and Priorities

When applications are written to take advantage of the Win32 specification, they adhere to an interesting model. The running instance of a program is defined as a process. This process is nothing more than an address and piece of memory space (4 gigabyte in size). This process has threads that actually do the work for the application.

The first thread created is termed the primary thread and it can in turn generate more threads. The operating system then assigns CPU time to each thread. Windows NT has the additional advantage of being able to use more than one CPU. In such cases, the operating system can assign a thread to a specific CPU. Because typically no more than one thread is running at any time, the access to the CPU is governed by priority; that is, each thread has a priority assigned to it. Altering this priority can change the amount of time the operating system allocates to an application.

When an application is written, priority classes are assigned to a process in the application by the programmers of the application. The following table defines these priorities and gives their relative value.

The thread scheduler simply assigns CPU time according to the process priority given a thread. In other words, a thread with a process priority of 13 can preempt a thread with a priority of 9. This scheduling of CPU time slices creates the preemptive multithreading design of Windows NT.

Table 19-1   **Priority classes govern how much CPU time is allocated to each thread.**

Priority Class	Relative Value (higher values get higher CPU priority)
Idle	4
Normal	7–9 (9 in foreground, 7 in background)
High	13
Realtime	24

Suppose you want to change the process priority in an application: Can it be done? In fact, you can, but you need to be aware of the consequences. First, running threads at realtime priority disrupts normal activity on the system. Mouse activity becomes slow and jerky and attempts to control cursor position are relatively futile. Second, and most important, the application can call threads at the internally-scheduled priorities. This implies that an application in realtime doesn't insure that all subsequent threads will run in realtime. In reality, there seldom is a reason to run applications in anything other than normal.

To run applications at thread priorities different from those assigned in the program, you must start applications from the command line. The full syntax of START at the command line is

```
START [title] [/Dpath] [/I] [/MIN] [/MAX] [/SEPARATE ¦ /SHARED]
►[/LOW ¦ /NORMAL ¦ /HIGH ¦ /REALTIME] [/WAIT] [/B] [command/program] [parameters]
```

Table 19-2 gives a detailed description of the individual items in the command line.

Table 19-2. The START command line options.

Option	Description
title	The title to display in the window title bar.
/Dpath	Starting directory.
/I	The new environment will be the original environment passed to cmd.exe and not the current environment.
/MIN	Start window minimized.
/MAX	Start window maximized.
/SEPARATE	Start 16-bit Windows program in separate memory space.
/SHARED	Start 16-bit Windows program in shared memory space.
/LOW	Start application in the IDLE priority class.

Option	Description
/NORMAL	Start application in the NORMAL priority class.
/HIGH	Start application in the HIGH priority class.
/REALTIME	Start application in the REALTIME priority class.
/WAIT	Start application and wait for it to terminate.
/B	Start application without creating a new window. The application has Ctrl+C handling ignored. Unless the application enables Ctrl+C processing, Ctrl+Break is the only way to interrupt the application *command/program*. If it's an internal cmd command or a batch file, the command processor is run with the /K switch to cmd.exe. This means that the window will remain after the command has been run. If it isn't an internal cmd command or batch file, it's a program, and will run as either a windowed application or a console application.
parameters	The parameters passed to *command/program*.

Notice the switches that control process priority; namely, /LOW; /NORMAL; /HIGH; and /REALTIME. A typical example of a START command that changes priority would be

```
start /high winword.exe
```

As a final note, you can adjust foreground/background values in the System Control Panel applet, on the Performance page. Recall that NORMAL has priorities assigned as 7 or 9. This applet enables you to adjust the given priority of the foreground. There are two common ways to adjust the priority. One is to allow all applications to have equal thread priorities. If you want to maximize multithreading, this is obviously the better choice. If you want to maintain a foreground focus with an application, set the foreground priority to maximum, as shown in Figure 19-1.

Tuning Virtual Memory

Virtual memory (VM) allows applications with large memory requirements to run on systems with relatively little physical RAM. The VM subsystem moves data from disk to RAM and back again so that each process has access to the data it needs at the current time; data for other processes, or data in the current process that's remained unused for a while, gets paged out to disk. VM is transparent to applications and system processes; the Windows NT executive handles the movement of data back and forth with no intervention from the process that owns the data.

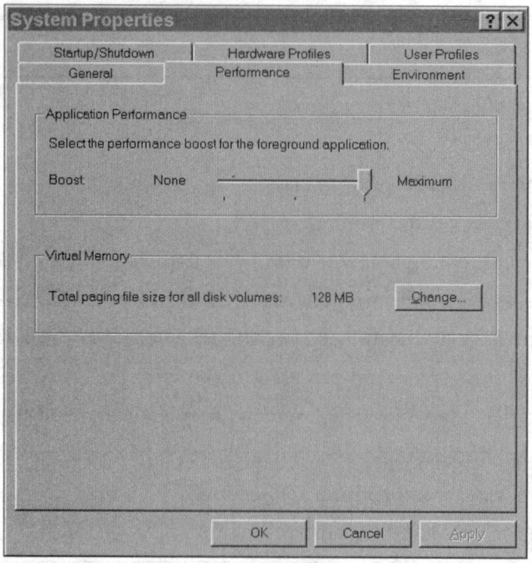

FIGURE 19-1

The System applet enables you to assign priorites to foreground/background applications by moving a single slider.

This behind-the-scenes swapping allows NTS to be run on a 16MB machine, although in reality the actual amount of virtual memory used while that server is running can be significantly greater. However, the benefits of VM come with a performance penalty. There's a small amount of overhead associated with deciding which chunks of data need to be sent to or read from the disk; more significant is the amount of time it actually takes to move data back and forth to the disk. Even the fastest hard disk is many times slower than RAM, so every page that must be moved incurs this penalty.

Unlike most UNIX variants, Windows NT's VM manager (VMM) is designed to be entirely self-tuning. The Windows NT VMM, which is described more fully in Chapter 2, "Understanding Windows NT Architecture," monitors the amount of physical and virtual RAM in use by each process in the system. It adjusts the amount of physical RAM available to a process dynamically depending on its priority and its allocation requests. The VMM is smart enough not to use VM for a process when there's enough physical RAM, so the first VM optimization you can make is to add more physical RAM to your servers. Because RAM prices fluctuate (as of this writing, 32MB of RAM costs about $350), this may not always be possible.

NOTE: The VMM is accessible via the Win32 programming interface, so programs can adjust their own VM use. This approach often helps performance significantly, since the application programmers know the application's memory use patterns and can tune its use of VM accordingly. If you're running custom in-house applications, consider asking the developers whether they've tuned VM usage for best performance.

Adjusting Paging File Behavior

Because the VMM is self-tuning, the only real adjustment you can make is to control where the system keeps data when it's swapped out to disk. These files, called *paging files*, are just big, contiguous files that contain data belonging to processes in memory. You can't modify them directly and you can't delete them while they're in use. If you boot into DOS or another OS and delete them, Windows NT re-creates them at the next boot.

You can control where the system puts its paging files and how much space it allocates to them with the Virtual Memory dialog box, shown in Figure 19-2. To open this dialog box, open the System Control Panel applet, choose the Performance tab, and click the change button in the Virtual Memory group.

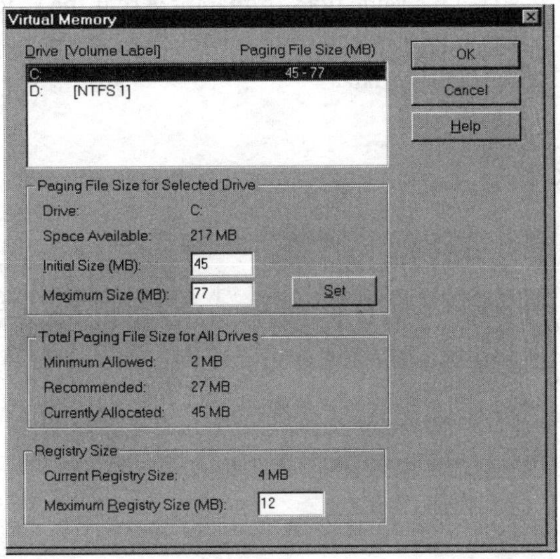

FIGURE 19-2

The Virtual Memory settings dialog box gives you control over where the system keeps its paging data.

These are the available options in the dialog box:

◆ The <u>D</u>rive list box shows each volume in the system; volumes that contain paging files show the paging file size range as well.

◆ The Paging File Size for Selected Drive group enables you to change the paging file settings for the drive selected in the Drive list. Once you enter the maximum and minimum sizes for the paging file, clicking the <u>S</u>et button triggers the change (you get an error if you assign a file that's too big to fit on the selected volume.) Entering a maximum size of 0 causes Windows NT to delete the paging file from that drive.

◆ The Total Paging File Size group shows how much paging file space is allocated on the disks on your system, along with the VMM's recommendation for how much space to allocate. Because the system creates paging files to match this recommendation, these figures agree unless you've reconfigured the paging files.

The default VMM suggestion for paging file size is the amount of physical RAM plus 0–12MB. You can make the files bigger, but the best balance between space usage and performace is to follow the VMM recommendation.

◆ The Registry Size group tells the system how much disk space you want to allocate to the system Registry. This value doesn't guarantee that the space will be available; it merely sets an upper limit for how much of the paging file space can be occupied by Registry data.

TIP: Because VM is disk-I/O bound, put paging files on the fastest disks and controllers on your server, not just on any random drive. If possible, keep a single paging file and put it on the fastest disk available.

You may wonder whether there is any performance advantage to placing a pagefile on each disk (assuming that the disks are serviced by separate controllers). Not really. Any time you split the file, you increase paging latency and overhead.

Improving Disk Performance

Disk drives and the related buses are clearly the worst bottlenecks on current high performance PCs. If you're running Pentium Pro machines, there is considerable idle time when the CPU is starved for data. In spite of rhetoric and marketing hype, the effective throughput on standard controllers and drives will never sustain any significant increase over 15MB/sec with current technology. Quite frankly, the bus and cable simply won't allow it. With the soon-to-be-released FC-AL drives and controllers, this might change but the entire bus needs to be redesigned.

Given the above, what options do you have to improve disk performance? Recall that Windows NT uses thread scheduling based upon priorities. Obviously, isolating the threads as much as possible can reduce their disruptive nature. The first step is to isolate slow and fast devices on a bus. Ideally, the controller with drives has only drives and similar speed ones at that. If you mix SCSI-II and wide SCSI devices on a controller, you won't take full advantage of the wide devices. The slower drives always degrade performance (obviously the degree of the disruption is related to the individual devices). Likewise, CD-ROMs, DAT drives, etc., need to be on a separate controller from the hard drives. For example, you can use a 3940w to handle your hard drives and a 3940u (both Adaptec controllers) to handle remaining devices. Because both of these controllers are bridged, you can use the PCI multiplexing and even place drives on separate buses on each controller. (The term *bridging* refers to a chipset that allows two controllers to be put together or *bridged*.) Place the wide boot drive on Bus A of the 3940w and the data drives on Bus B. Place the CD-ROMs on Bus A of the 3940u and the backup devices on Bus B. In such a scenario, you've maximized the capacity of the system to handle multitasking with the greatest assistance of the SCSI subsystem.

Suppose the speed obtained from conventional drives is simply not sufficient. Depending upon the depth of your wallet, this speed issue can be overcome. Set up multiple (at least three) RAID controllers (for example, Mylex PCI) and place the maximum amount of RAM on each controller (normally 64MB). Put four drives on each controller and make them RAID 0. Finally, connect the RAID 0 volumes with RAID 5. This gives you RAID 5+0, which provides you with redundancy and great speed. Systems using multimedia editing typically are set up in this fashion. The end result is complex, expensive, but very fast.

Upgrading Hardware

Disk subsystems are a good place to discuss hardware upgrades as a solution to performance problems. Disks and their controllers have steadily increased in speed over the last 15 years, and you can often upgrade to new, faster disks and controllers with little impact on the rest of the system. There are five relatively common types of hardware upgrades that you might consider when trying to solve a performance blockage:

♦ *System upgrades* are just what they sound like: wholesale replacement of one system with another, faster machine. This approach is easiest when you can add the new machine to the network, migrate files to it, and integrate it with the network before taking the old one offline.

♦ *Processor upgrades* have become increasingly common as manufacturers ship single-processor servers that can be upgraded to use multiple processors just by plugging them in. The impact of this upgrade is very low (provided you don't damage anything during the CPU insertion) and it can provide a significant boost for CPU-intensive applications.

♦ *Mass-storage upgrades* only help when the bottleneck is disk-related. Adding or replacing disks is relatively painless, but adding and configuring exotic controllers can be somewhat more difficult and expensive. See the earlier section "Improving Disk Performance" for more guidelines on when these upgrades are a good idea.

♦ At a minimum, *network upgrades* usually include replacing a network interface card with a more powerful model. Newer NICs have multiple buffers and onboard coprocessors that give them much better performance than older cards. You may also choose to upgrade your network itself, perhaps by moving from 10Base-T to 100Base-T or even ATM. Physical network upgrades usually require new NICs, too.

♦ *RAM upgrades* reduce the amount of virtual memory page swapping required by allowing more processes to execute from RAM. Adding RAM is reasonably easy and doesn't require any configuration changes; Windows NT recognizes the new memory automatically. (You may wonder whether there's a vanishing point for adding RAM. I have gone up to 512MB of RAM and the system gets better all the way. I've never seen "too much" RAM.)

When you upgrade hardware to improve performance, you need to be conscious of minimizing that hardware's impact on your system. For example, adding a faster network interface card to a server may cause the server's CPU to become a bottleneck—the old network card was keeping the CPU from being flooded, but the new card can deliver data faster than the CPU can handle it.

Network Performance Optimization

Besides optimizing the system's overall performance by adjusting system services and/or adding hardware, you can also optimize its use of the network. All network clients generate traffic, and this traffic is what makes the network useful—but you can reduce and reroute traffic to keep it from impairing your network's overall functionality.

Reducing Traffic

Sometimes the best way to increase your network's performance is to reduce the amount of traffic it carries. This is especially true when traffic has to cross low-speed network links, whether over a WAN (as between offices in different cities) or locally (as between a field site and the main office.)

Reducing Browse Traffic

Most browsing traffic is generated by users; however, a good bit of it is generated by system-level synchronization and communications that you can throttle back. Use the measures described in the section "Controlling Network Browsing" in Chapter 14, "Workgroups, Domains, and Browsing Explained." With these measures (including disabling the printer browser thread and changing the frequency of updates between domain browsers), you can balance browsing transmissions based on your network connections and update requirements.

You can even disable browsing altogether by keeping the Browser service from starting. Use the Services Control Panel applet to set the Browser service startup type to Disabled. Although this scheme prevents users from discovering resources by using the browser (meaning that they must know the exact path to all resources they want to use), at several large sites it has resulted in a 20 to 30 percent reduction in network traffic!

Reducing DHCP and WINS Requests

The DHCP and WINS protocols provide much-needed flexibility on networks. Chapter 24, "Interoperating with TCP/IP Clients," describes how DHCP dynamically assigns IP addresses and other network parameters to clients, while WINS ties NetBIOS names to TCP/IP addresses. Both of these protocols are highly dynamic: Clients request services at frequent intervals, and servers must communicate among themselves to keep synchronized. All of this communication can clog your network, but both protocols allow you to regulate the amount of traffic they generate.

For DHCP, the only changes you can make pertain to how long a client keeps its parameter lease before asking for a renewal. You can set the lease length for each scope in the DHCP Options dialog box; since DHCP databases aren't shared or replicated between machines, your control is somewhat limited. See Chapter 24 for more details.

WINS offers a greater range of possible adjustments (also described in Chapter 24):

- The renewal and verification intervals (which you set in the WINS Server Configuration dialog box) control how often clients and servers have to renew their use of particular names. Increasing these lessens the number of renewal broadcasts; setting them too high can cause the WINS server not to notice a name change or addition.

- The server replication interval (set in the WINS Preferences dialog box) controls how often each WINS server exchanges data with its replication partners. Increase this value to reduce the update frequency; set it too high, and changes take a long time to propagate between servers.

- The Replication Partners dialog box allows you to control how many database changes must occur before a replication is forced and how often a server should push data to its partners. Increasing these values reduces the number of WINS database replications; setting them too high can result in database staleness.

Subnetting Your Network

If a single network segment carries x amount of traffic, it seems reasonable that splitting the network into N pieces will reduce the load on each section to x divided by N. While this simple division is too simplistic for real networks, there's no denying that making subnets out of a single network can increase its capacity.

Consider the simple network shown in Figure 19-3. The four servers represent the four sample domains used in previous chapters. Each domain controller, and its associated clients, belongs to an independent department, but these departments all interchange data regularly. Although the network (the solid black line) is drawn as though the medium is a 10Base-2 network, it might just as easily be a 10Base-T connection instead. Any time two machines wish to communicate, their packets are intermixed with traffic from all other machines on the network—even if the two machines are in the same department! For example, packets going from HQ1 to the HEADQUARTERS PDC are using the same physical network as packets going between ENGR1 and ENGINEERING. This sharing greatly simplifies the network topology, but it results in congestion that affects every machine on the network.

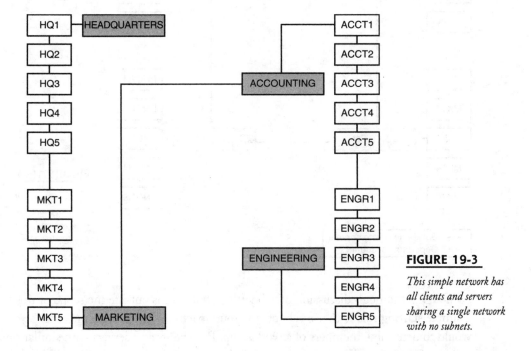

FIGURE 19-3

This simple network has all clients and servers sharing a single network with no subnets.

Figure 19-4 shows an alternative arrangement; in this figure, the same clients and servers shown in Figure 19-3 have been placed onto subnets, with one subnet for each department. The solid gray line between the servers represents a backbone network that links them; this backbone could be an ordinary 10BaseT line, Fast Ethernet, FDDI, or even a WAN connection. Each domain controller in this diagram is configured as a router with two network interface cards. One card connects the domain controller to the network segment that forwards traffic addressed to subnets controlled by other domain controllers. The second card connects to the subnet controlled by that domain controller. With this model, when two machines in the marketing department want to communicate, their packets don't appear on any of the other departments' subnets.

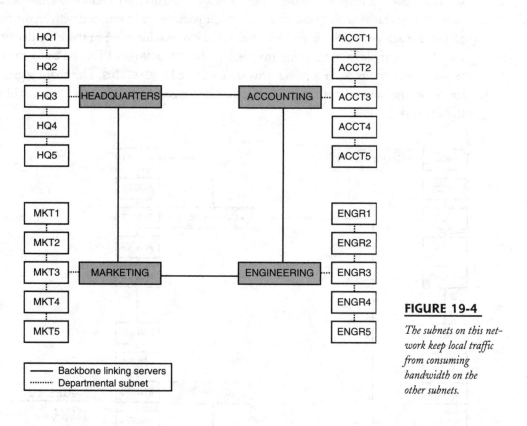

FIGURE 19-4

The subnets on this network keep local traffic from consuming bandwidth on the other subnets.

Although a thorough discussion of subnetting strategies is outside the scope of this book, a simple starting rule is to use subnets to group machines using the same criteria you would to determine members of a workgroup. Put clients and servers with similar organizational functions onto one subnet, then link the servers using a backbone. Taking this approach allows you to upgrade individual subnets gracefully when they need more bandwidth. In our example, if the engineering department needed to start using video conferencing on its subnet, you could upgrade only that subnet to 100Base-T without affecting any other departments. This upgrade wouldn't require any changes to the ENGINEERING PDC other than the addition of a faster network adapter—no configuration or protocol changes needed!

Configuring Network Adapters

Network adapters can be the bane of any installation. Some need software enabled in DOS, some use chipsets that don't reset properly, and some are quite frankly disasters in the making. For example, some early 3COM PCI cards would not function well with soft resets and the system would not boot into Windows NT. To circumvent this problem, you could disable the busmaster aspects of the card in the Registry. This is of course not what you wish to achieve. These problems can be bypassed.

The key to the establishment of a viable network is to determine a specific NIC (network interface card) and set of protocol stacks to enable. For most new systems, the cards chosen are PCI. Set up one system and see if there are any problems. Believe it or not, the installation process informs you of any problems. Specifically, if a card is detected that has no current NT 4.0 drivers, you receive a warning that the card might not function in NT 4.0. In fact, the warning is severe and absolves Microsoft from any blame. Take this warning very seriously. You may choose not to buy new NICs, but be aware of the consequences.

The steps involved in the installation of a network card are straightforward. Be certain that the card has NT 4.0 drivers and is on the current hardware compatibility list. If it isn't on the HCL, make certain that it does in fact work well in Windows NT 4.0. The installation steps are as follows:

1. Turn off the machine and insert the card, making sure that the card is seated properly.

2. If the card requires being software set, boot to a DOS floppy and run the setup tools (an example of such a card is the new Eagle NE2000). Be certain to pick IRQs and I/Os that don't overlap other cards. Generally, IRQ 10 and I/O 320 work fine. If the card is an ISA card, reserve the IRQ as ISA in the BIOS.

3. Boot into Windows NT and open the Network Control Panel applet. On the Adapter page, choose Add. A list of adapters is presented. Hopefully, your network card is on this list. Select the card in the list and set its parameters if appropriate.

4. When the NIC has been installed, the protocol stacks are bound to the NIC and you then have to reboot. If you're replacing a card, you can remove the old card prior to rebooting. If LMHOSTS is being used for TCP/IP name resolution, update the master lists.

5. Reboot into Windows NT.

Suppose the installation fails. How do you determine the cause of the failure? The following list shows the fundamentals of NIC installation troubleshooting:

♦ If the card isn't initialized properly, you receive an error message about a service not starting. Open Event Viewer and look for messages concerning the network card. If the NIC driver didn't start, you need to determine why.

♦ Always make certain that all cables are properly attached and configured. If you're using thinnet cable, check all terminators and "T"s and make certain that they're working properly. If you're on 10BaseT, check the hub and make sure that the physical connection is present.

♦ Open the Diagnostic tool in the Administrator folder to determine whether any overlap of IRQs or I/Os is occurring. Many times the Event Viewer tells you of an overlap and the Diagnostics tool gives you more information about the specific overlap or conflict.

♦ If the error you receive is an error 57, this means that the network isn't connected. This is clearly a fatal message for the network. Be certain to check the cables.

♦ As a final determination, boot to a DOS floppy and run the NIC diagnostic software. This software is typically a setup-and-diagnostic application that can test the card and connections.

♦ If you're running TCP/IP, attempt to ping the host to which you're connecting or ping the machine you're setting up (127.0.0.1 is the address reserved for pinging the local machine).

If after all these attempts the network still isn't working, you might have an incompatible or defective network card.

Clearly the troubleshooting of network and network card are very important on any network. Following a clear straightforward strategy helps considerably in this regard. Likewise, try to standardize on a specific NIC and set of stacks on the network. Such standardization helps a lot in setup of systems, including automated setups.

Setting the Optimal Binding Order

The installation process probably will install (or attempt to install) more than one stack— for example, IPX/SPX and NetBEUI. There's no reason to have more than one stack unless you need to connect to a different set of systems. For example, if you're connected to a Novell network, by all means load IPX/SPX, if you're not connected to Novell, don't load the stack. Likewise, if you go onto the Internet, you need to load TCP/IP. Choose the most appropriate protocol(s) for the network.

When a request for information goes from a client to a server, a complex chain of events occurs. On the client side, the application requests a file service on the server. This results in the formation of an I/O request packet, which is then passed to the file system driver or redirector. The redirector in turn passes the request to the network transport drivers. This is then passed to the actual hardware and travels to the server where the reverse occurs. The data-link headers are stripped off and then the network and transport headers are removed. The request goes to the server module or system. If all is appropriate, the command is sent to the local hard drive.

Notice that the requests go through the network transport drivers. If you've loaded more than one stack, this can result in poor or faulty communication unless the stacks are bound in the proper order. Always bind the master stack first and have all stacks in the same order on all machines in the network. If NetBEUI is your stack of choice, it should appear first in the bind list. If it doesn't appear first, highlight it on the bindings page in the network applet (show protocols in the lower window) and you can move it up or down.

Special Considerations

In attempts to increase throughput and performance, there's a delicate balance between improvement, cost, and RISK. Trying to maximize bus throughput is expensive. In the simple 2 controller suggestion above, the controller cost alone is 700-800 dollars. With the RAID 5+0 example, the cost is in the thousands and without the attached drives. Common sense must play a major role in the search for maximum speed. There's no magical formula or elixir. In all cases though, it's better to do all performance enhancing with hardware and not software solutions. Certain examples provide insight in specific hardware requirements.

Database Servers

Until recent years, database size wasn't huge—now we discuss gigabyte-sized databases. Two things seem to be the major requirements of servers that contain databases: the amount of memory and the number of CPUs present. Nearly all modern databases make good use of multiple processors. In fact, the truly large applications use massive parallel CPU arrays, which are still the hallmark of UNIX systems. A previous criticism of Windows NT was its inability to scale beyond four processors. In Version 4.0, this has been increased to eight processors but is markedly dependent on hardware configurations. In any event, make sure that you have an appropriate number of CPUs and memory. For the Microsoft SQL offerings, two CPUs and sufficient memory (try 128MB for a starting point) usually provide excellent server abilities.

Simply because NT can *use* 32 processors doesn't make it scalable for those processors. In fact, once you exceed four processors, the scalability (2 is twice as good as 1, for example) falls off dramatically. This problem is well recognized in the high-end database community. With Version 4.0, the developers indicate that the drop-off is now eight rather than four.

Web Servers

World Wide Web servers might seem to be network-bound, since they serve data to the network. For the most part, however, the amount of network traffic is reasonably low on the server end, and well within the capability of even a modest 75 MHz Pentium. The real potential bottleneck is actually the server's CPU: many servers run scripts or even small Java or JavaScript applets *every time* a client requests a page! Other servers fetch information from a database and dynamically build catalogs or other structures with it.

Although most WWW servers are multithreaded, a single CPU can be hard-pressed to keep pace with requests when each request requires the server to run an external application and return its output to the client. Adding a second CPU is an inexpensive way to boost WWW server performance (provided that your machine is upgradable to SMP!)

Remote-Access Servers

Remote access servers (RAS) are taxed heavily when multiple clients connect. The processing is obviously CPU and memory dependent. For each concurrent client, add a minimum of 2MB of RAM to the system. If there will be a reasonable number of con-current clients, use a dual CPU server. Try to keep the machine as RAS-ready as possible; in other words, don't also use it as a workstation. Of great importance is also the manner in which you add the modem banks.

Always use co-processed controllers such as Digiboard controllers or something similar. These cards can take a considerable load off the CPU and make the system run more efficiently. For large numbers of modems, use the PC-Card based modem banks such as the SCSI and IP based ones from Central Data and the IP based ones from Digiboard (LanaServer). Because of their small size, it's easy to set up the devices. Because both are based on PC-Card (PCMCIA) modems, it's also very easy to replace a failed modem.

Backup Servers

Backup servers have several limitations or bottlenecks. The first is CPU-related and the second is network-related. Interestingly, you won't see the CPU bottleneck on a server with only one backup device. On units running concurrent backups, the effects of the CPU speed and the amount of RAM are very real. In such situations, use multiple CPUs and a reasonable amount of RAM (32MB/processor as a minimum). Also of importance is placing the backup units on separate controllers or channels to maximize SCSI I/O.

A common problem for backup servers is inappropriate bandwidth and port handling. Most networks use passive hubs, which simply have all active ports contending for band-width. If you have 10 ports active on a 10BaseT hub, all ports are in contention for the same bandwidth. To get around this problem, use switches instead of hubs. A switch maximizes all active ports to the full bandwidth of the network (only stopped by error correction). This allows a far more efficient transport of files across the network.

Having all connections the same on the network isn't very efficient. The backbone (that is, the server-based cable) should be faster than the client-based ones. An optimal config-uration would have a 155-based ATM backbone with ATM 25 (large servers) and 10BaseT (workstations) clients. This optimizes the network throughput to the backup server. Conversely, you can use the other emerging technologies as backbone, or even use the newer, faster ATM protocols. In any event, plan the network to allow decent network performance. Backup is important, and it seems that there's never enough time to accom-plish it properly.

Video and Multimedia Servers

Delivering streamed or live video requires fast disks and controllers and adequate CPU power: in short, these servers exercise *all* their subsystems. For the most part, these machines tend to be purpose-built boxes from companies like Intergraph that include Ultra SCSI (SCSI-3), 100Base-T, and two or more Pentium Pro CPUs in the base models.

As with backup servers, servers that deliver video or multimedia content need as much bandwidth as they can possibly get. 100Base-T is practically the entry-level network for these systems; an increasing number of them are moving towards ATM because of its migration path up to 155Mbps.

Where to Go Next

Chapters 17 and 18 discuss how to use Windows NT tools to find performance problems; this chapter describes how to alleviate or completely fix them. The next chapter shows how to plan your network effectively to get the best utilization and capability for the least money.

At this point, you may find some of these chapters useful:

- ◆ Chapter 24, "Interoperating with TCP/IP Clients," discusses the details of the WINS and DHCP services, including how to change the configuration parameters discussed above.

- ◆ Chapter 14, "Workgroups, Domains, and Browsing Explained," discusses the changes you can make to affect the behavior of the browser service.

Chapter | 20

Estimating and
Planning Networks

In This Chapter:

 ♦ Planning Your LAN
 ♦ Planning for Remote Access

How do I...

At a very basic level, a network is nothing more that two or more computers linked together in some manner to share files and resources. In today's magic buzzwords, we hear internet, intranet, LANs (local area networks), MANs (Metropolitan Area Networks), WANs (Wide Area Networks) and GANs (Global Area Networks.) With imagination you can even think of other possibilities like RANs (Remote Area Networks) where all attachment to a server is remote. The amusing aspect of all these strange terms is that they rely on networking concepts that have been around for many years. A successful network is one that is thought out before and not a set of undesired hardware/software/cable malignancies. The first issue that seems critical is figuring out what factors are essential in the planning.

Planning Your LAN

Why do I want a network? This question reflects an interesting concept occurring today. Ten years ago, everyone was attached to a mainframe—probably via dumb terminal. As the personal computer (PC) evolved and the hard drive was invented, many people argued that local use was more important and efficient than working on a network. The resulting changes in computing habits were amazing. Users were working more and more on PCs, and it didn't take long for them to realize that the network had some very real advantages. Paramount of these advantages was the fact that files and printers could become a common resource. You had the power of the PC but the benefit of being able to share files and resources.

Now the view seems to be that the PC is dead and we need to go back to the big server/thin client ideas of the past. The mainframe is being replaced by the Internet and super servers. Our goal here is to discuss networks in the middle ground—that is, a combination of all possibilities.

Many factors go into the planning and setting up of networks. Some factors are obvious, some are not. The first important step is to determine the existing resources for the proposed network. Resources include:

- Determine the overall goal of the network and company. If the company is based on engineering, the network will have different components than one based on sales and support. Knowing this information also helps you predict the growth of the network.

- Human resources need to be evaluated in three basic categories: ability, quantity, and availability. If the network is very large, much of the network maintenance and support may be outsourced. In this case, much of the resource provided by Microsoft solution providers or similar networking specialists. This outside resource also needs to be evaluated and chosen carefully.

   In one case that I am aware of, a solution provider set up a regional restaurant chain and did such astute setups as ignore multiprocessor systems, caching high end SCSI controllers, and even set up switches as hubs. Although this might be an exception, it demonstrates the necessity of thoroughly evaluated both internal and external human resource.

- Be realistic about the scheduled network incorporation or upgrade. Don't try to use the 26-30 hours of the day to accomplish the upgrade. Most importantly, run small test environments to make certain that all hardware and design work as expected. No one can throw a network together overnight; in fact, you never want to throw a network together period.

- Plan systems according to task. Windows NT can function as a file server, a print server or an application server. The hardware demands are markedly different. Don't expect a Pentium 133 with 64MB of RAM to function well as a departmental SQL server. It simply won't happen. Yet this same system functions quite well as a RAS server for 12 or so modems and still has resources to spare. Don't allow the network to be put together in a haphazard manner.

- Inventory the existing hardware. In an NT environment, it's very easy to configure clients up as Windows 95, Windows for Workgroups or Windows NT Workstation. The inferred Microsoft choice has been Windows 95, but Workstation 4.0 is making the choice a bit more complex. In reality, the choice is relatively straightforward, if you have the resource to run NT 4.0 workstation and are more concerned with reliability than using legacy hardware, go with NT 4.0 Workstation. For systems with more modest resource and demands use Windows 95. Windows for Workgroups is the choice for older systems with minimal resource.

♦ If you decide to upgrade the hardware, be certain to deal with reputable vendors with known support records. In large networks, use manufacturers that produce well accepted systems and also ones that support Windows NT. This list includes Compaq, Hewlett Packard, IBM, and Digital Equipment. All these vendors have systems on the Hardware Compatibility List. Such systems are ideal because of the vendor support. If you decide to go with a custom builder, make certain that the vendor provides good support for Windows NT.

♦ It's difficult to give specific user load information with Windows NT. Different configurations have different requirements. We can, however, define certain types of systems. Assuming that you have segmented the network properly, server systems on the segment should be Pentium 133s (or higher) with 32-64M of RAM and reasonable hard drive systems; preferably wide SCSI. Workstations running NT can be more modest but 32M of RAM is a reasonable starting point. Servers and system on the backbone need to be very serious machines. For example, a backbone SQL server that will handle 2,000 users should use a quad Pentium 166 or higher with at least 2 gigabytes of RAM and a very fast disk subsystem, running RAID 50 and using the latest in disk controllers.

♦ Other factors that need to be considered are cost, training, and availability. All of these factors are crucial to the final decision process.

♦ Always follow a few simple rules:

   ♦ Generate hardware profiles that allow system flexibility and expandability. For example, specify two large SIMMs when ordering a machine rather than four small ones. This allows easy upgrades even if the system has only four SIMM slots.

- ◆ Purchase hardware that is scaleable; that is, the system can be easily upgraded if necessary.

- ◆ Eliminate components that are not on compatibility lists.

- ◆ Upgrade all software to known standard versions. Don't allow non-standard software versions on the network.

- ◆ Only accept known support teams. As stated earlier, don't take risks. They can be very expensive.

The most important initial question that you need to answer is what type of network do you want to set up. There are two basic types of network configurations: peer-to-peer and client/server. The setup and consequences of the two configurations are very different. Part of the decision is based on number of systems involved; part is based on the manner in which you want to deal with security and administration of the network. There are no magical formulas for determining the nature of the network. However, we have known for some time what works and what doesn't. A very crucial issue is the determination of user load.

User Loads

No absolute user load data is available for Windows NT—with several exceptions that we'll address shortly. The foremost issue is determining the basic type of network. In this case, the number of users (user load) dictates the type of network chosen.

For any LAN, the decision must be made as to the type of network desired. Of major importance in this decision is long-term planning. If the network never will grow beyond 10 computers, you can think one way, but if the network will soon encompass 4,000 computers, you need to think in a totally different manner.

Network Considerations: Peer-to-Peer

In general, networks composed of 10 or fewer systems can function very well on a peer-to-peer network. In this configuration, no serious hardware issues need to be solved. The demands are dictated exclusively by the task, and a dedicated server is unlikely to be found. Standard PCs based on a Pentium 100 and 16MB of RAM (32 gives far better performance) work fine.

If the system is much larger than 10 computers and users, peer-to-peer networking isn't the logical choice. First of all, as networks get larger, it's important to have individuals responsible for maintaining the network. Such an individual is part of the administration or information service core of a business. As the network gets larger, the administrator has more and more work to do and systems to control. Obviously, central administration is a very key component.

Network Considerations: Client/Server

In larger networks, centralization is key. Most likely there will be dedicated servers performing many tasks. Among these can be file and print servers, application servers, communication servers ranging from mail to fax—even remote access servers. It's obvious that this form of network requires system-wide policy to control the network effectively. In such a design, client/server is the network of choice. With this decision, however, comes inequality of hardware. Client machines are far less powerful than servers. Likewise, the positioning of those servers requires serious planning.

A *LAN plan* is simply an assessment of criteria to help you choose the appropriate network. Obviously, as stated earlier, if you have over 10 computers, peer-to-peer becomes very difficult to maintain and client/server is your best choice. There are other criteria that are as crucial as number of systems.

If you have any data or resources that need to be secure and carefully regulated, peer-to-peer won't work very well. If you only have six computers and everyone accesses a file server with specific and secure data, client/server is the only way to control such an environment.

Likewise, if you want to manage the network centrally, the only choice is client/server. In many companies, a central policy dictates type of software on systems, type of work done, and even mandatory desktops and applications. This system works only on a client/server network. In other words, criteria other than number of systems becomes relevant. As you can imagine, the larger the number, the greater management and control issues become. Central control is essential.

In truly large environments (the so-called *Enterprise environment*), additional concepts need planning. As the network becomes more and more segmented, you need more and more dedicated servers and even more sophisticated hardware. For example, if the network is contained in more than one building, having servers in all segments is probably easier than having clients cross segments to obtain data, or your servers can get more dedicated and specific and form global resources. In either case, you need to plan accordingly.

As networks get larger, the management of the network becomes more critical and needs more and more automation. With client/server designs, you can use an application like Systems Management Server (SMS) to deliver jobs across the network and to specified systems. On the one hand, this makes the network less flexible to the user (because of a strong central administration) but more secure. The following list shows the advantages of the client/server environment:

♦ Server-based resources are easy to control and to secure.

♦ All security can be maintained by one administrator.

♦ Backup and redundancy of data are far easier to maintain on dedicated servers than on random peers.

♦ A server-based environment can easily maintain thousands of users.

User Load and Hardware Requirements

The most obvious hardware requirement for Windows NT is related to the management of the SAM (Security Accounts Manager). The primary domain controller loads the SAM and it remains in RAM. Each user demands 1K of RAM. Microsoft recommends that a domain contain no more than 40,000 users. Assuming that bandwidth can handle such a number (very unlikely), this would mean that the SAM alone would be 40MB in size. Obviously, the PDC should be a dedicated server that isn't running any other applications. A Pentium 133/166 with 64MB of RAM should handle most network PDC requirements.

> **TIP:** Microsoft typically recommends a Pentium with 32MB as a starting point server. In fact, many networks are based on such systems. Given the fact that NT functions better and better as RAM increases, a increase to 64MB of RAM will show a sizable improvement in performance. It's well worth the money to increase the RAM to 64MB.

Unlike the PDC, a BDC (Backup Domain Controller) can serve other functions. Neither WINS nor DHCP use much resources. As such, these services can easily be placed on the BDC. Likewise, a BDC could function as a backup server because most backups occur when network use is at a minimum. If the system is simply functioning as a BDC with WINS/DHCP, our suggested Pentium 133/166 with 64MB of RAM will function very well. For small LANs, this system will function very well as a backup server. For large LANs, backup servers need to be dedicated systems with very serious hardware resources (refer to Chapter 19, "Performance Tuning and Optimization" for more details).

Specific database applications are very resource demanding. For example, The Microsoft SQL server should have a minimum of a Pentium 166 and 64MB of RAM. SQL will use as much memory as possible. The following Microsoft table demonstrates the relationship between system memory and SQL use:

Table 20-1. The relationship between the amount of total server memory and the amount claimed by SQL Server.

Machine memory (MB)	Approximate SQL Server memory allocation (MB)
16	4
24	8
32	16
48	28
64	40
128	100
256	216
512	464

This table clearly shows that SQL uses memory optimally. Of equal importance are the CPUs and disk I/O. As stated earlier, an optimized SQL server for a large number (several thousand) of users should have at least 2 gigabytes of RAM, 4 processors (either Pentiums or Pentium Pros of the Alpha equivalent) and a very fast Disk subsystem. As a general rule, with a moderate number of simultaneous users (40-50), it's worthwhile considering upgrading to a dual processor system with 256MB of RAM. In all cases, an SQL system should be a dedicated server.

If an SMS server is added to the domain, additional requirements must be met. SMS needs an SQL server, but the SMS and SQL servers should not be on the same system. SMS needs a minimum of 32MB of RAM. In fact, the minimum recommended is Pentium-based, 32MB RAM (dependent on function) and at least 1GB of disk space (depending on the number of clients and the number and size of packages). If you use SMS to distribute software packages, you need to allocate additional hardware space equivalent to the size of the packages.

The specific hardware requirements for Exchange server is dictated by the numbers of users and design of the Exchange system. Exchange requires a minimum of 32MB of RAM but also needs an optimized I/O system. If possible, install fast drives with caching controllers and striped drive arrays. The recommended file formats of the drives should be FAT for sequential reads and writes (message tracking logs, event logs) and NTFS for random reads and writes (public and private information stores). In general, use NTFS for both if security is an issue.

Microsoft Exchange needs a minimum of 32MB of RAM. However, the more memory you have in the computer, the less often the paging file is used. Accessing the paging files is several orders of magnitude slower than reading RAM; therefore, increasing the memory can improve performance. If your I/O system is fast and not a bottleneck, and you have enough memory to handle all the services of the server and additional services, then having a fast processor is going to improve performance. Microsoft Exchange processes are multithreaded and can make use of additional processors.

Exchange can be setup in two ways, distributed or centralized. Hardware that can be used with Microsoft Exchange ranges from single processor 486 computers with 32MB of RAM to the upper limits of Windows NT. It's possible, therefore, to set up a site of 50,000 users with all the Microsoft Exchange servers being small computers with 100 users each (the 486) or design the same site with powerful servers hosting 1,000 users each (quad processors with very fast disk subsystems and large amounts of RAM as dictated by the SQL example).

The choice of distributed versus centralized is difficult. In the distributed, disruption of Exchange is unlikely due to the number of servers. In the centralized, the main issue is cost and service. There are few vendors that can supply the needed hardware. If possible, use the centralized approach.

One final resource to consider is the Web server. Two items relative to the Web server should be looked at: basic hardware and connection bandwidth.

As far as basic hardware is concerned, our standard Pentium 133/166 with 64MB is an excellent starting point. If the system will be SQL based (not uncommon), then the size of the SQL system must also be adjusted accordingly.

With respect to bandwidth, if you assume a constant use by 45 or more users, then the adoption of a T1 line is clearly justified. If the number reaches 150 or more, the bandwidth should be the maximum that you can afford. You can use your ISP (Internet Service Provider) to assist you. Have the ISP notify you when the traffic reaches 60% of the available bandwidth. If this per cent is reached routinely, then you do need to increase the available bandwidth.

Physical Topography

The physical attributes of a network are referred to as the *network topology*. This topology includes computers, cables, and other components such as hubs, switches, and repeaters. Unfortunately, no single standard dictates the topology of a network. There are different types of cables, different types of network cards, different standards, and so on. The devices that you use to construct your network determine much of your network performance and maintenance.

Common Topologies

The simplest network is referred to as a *point-to-point* or *linear bus* topology. In this basic design, all computers are connected to a single bus (sometimes called a *backbone*). Information is sent on that bus across the backbone and is received by the appropriate computer. In this design, only one computer can send information at any one time.

When a signal travels on the backbone, it goes from one end to the other. This makes the linear bus design very fragile. First of all, the signal has to be absorbed (*terminated*) at each end so it doesn't simply bounce back and forth. Second, any break or discontinuity anywhere on the backbone will cause the entire network to fail. It therefore stands to reason that this simple bus design isn't efficient for a large network. In fact, it's sensible only on very small peer-to-peer LANs. To have a sizable LAN, you need to install repeaters (voltage boosting devices) on the linear bus to have any signal at all.

The term given to the types of cable used is *cable media*. The medium used in linear bus networks is standard coaxial cable. There are advantages to this medium:

♦ It's very resistant to electromagnetic interference (EMI). It's common to run cables over ceiling tile where it can touch or nearly touch other wiring. In such cases, interference between the cables can cause mutual disruption. Coaxial media reduces this risk.

◆ Although different standards have been used, the bulk of coaxial cable used is very thin—hence, the nickname *cheapnet*. The connectors used are the old BayoNet Connector or BNC such as you find on cable TV setups or VCRs.

The second most common type of network configuration is often called a *star topology*. In its simplest form, a star is nothing more than a number of computers connected to a centralized hub. In this design, all systems function by being attached to a port on that hub.

This type of network is very common on mainframes. It has the advantage of allowing one computer or link to fail without disrupting any other. On the other hand, wiring to a central hub can use lots of connecting cable and a loss of the hub disrupts the whole network.

The final type of common network is the *ring topology*. In this scheme, all systems are connected on a ring. At first glance, this topology is similar to that of the linear bus, but in reality most of the ring is accomplished in a hub or central node. In other words, a computer is attached to a hub and the internal wiring of the hub makes the ring. When a hub isn't fully populated, internal relays close that port.

Although presumably dying out, the ring environment is very efficient. The information travels around the ring in tokens. This is the IBM token ring environment. A token can travel around a 200-meter diameter ring 10,000 times a second.

Certain topologies have emerged as combination or so-called *mesh* topologies. These involve adding components to one aspect of a topology to expand it. For example, if you connect hubs via a single cable, you have a *star/bus* design. Each hub then becomes a segment of a larger network connected via a bus. All of these designs are being put forth to accommodate larger and larger networks. As you can see, the size and basic configuration is limited only by your imagination.

Cable Standards

It should be mentioned that cable standards have emerged. There are two major standards in existence: one defining Ethernet and one defining token ring. Each of these standards is discussed in the following sections.

Ethernet is the oldest LAN cabling still in use. It therefore stands to reason that more than one standard has arisen. The older standard is the 802.3 standard whereas most modern networks use the 802.2 (the IEEE standard).

Ethernet is the standard of the linear bus and most hubs. All devices share the same media and only one frame is allowed at any one time. The means of control of the media is called *CSMA/CD*, which stands for *Carrier Sense Multiple Access with Collision Detection*. The name describes exactly what occurs. Any device that wants to transmit data listens to see whether the bus is busy (carrier sense). Because all devices share the same media, any device can share the medium (*multiple access*). If two devices transmit at a time, the packets collide. The devices stop sending packets and actually issue a jamming signal. At this point in time, device access to the bus becomes random, but soon one sending device is capable of sending packets. Obviously, with low amounts of traffic, Ethernet is fine. As the LAN gets busier, packet collisions become a way of life; sooner or later, effective traffic on the LAN simply approaches a zero state. We'll discuss this issue momentarily.

There are two basic Ethernet standards. The *thin Ethernet* (coaxial cable) standard is the 10Base2 specification. This standard allows a network segment to be defined as a 10 Mbps bandwidth and a cable length of 185 meters. The maximum number of systems on this segment (the cable between two terminators) is 30, with an optimal spacing of one half-meter. Few systems are set up to these standards.

The cheapnet described earlier is rapidly being replaced by *twisted-pair cables*. This specification uses normal twisted-pair unshielded cable and RJ45 connectors. Needless to say, the type of network here is star-based. The primary advantage of the twisted-pair network is the ease of physical network management. For example, you don't have to shut down the network to add a device.

> **TIP:** Most of the new moderate speed network protocols (ATM 25 for example) will run over twisted pair cables. These cables should be the newer CAT5 cables rather than the older CAT3. When setting up a network, be sure to specify CAT5 cables.

Finally, Ethernet on most systems today consists of either IEEE 802.3 or Ethernet II. These frames are very similar, with only some minor tuning differences between them. If you're setting up an Ethernet environment, you need to know whether all frame types will be compatible.

Although token ring is a strong contender in the popular topology race, it's rapidly moving into obscurity. This is too bad because the basic network is better than Ethernet. The design of token ring is very elegant. A token travels around the ring. No device can place data onto the network until the token arrives and the device takes possession of the token. In theory, this should eliminate collision factors. In reality, however, tokens have been known to get lost. The standard for token ring is the 802.5 specification.

As you might suspect, much of the use of network standards is based on the physical design of the network. Neither standard Ethernet nor token ring will probably be sufficient in today's complex network. Much is an issue of pure bandwidth. At minimum, there needs to be a decent backbone (server cable/protocol onto the LAN). Many users are going to 100BaseT backbones but this will shortly also be too slow. The gigabyte Ethernet option stressed by some is a pure backbone solution. Far more realistic will be the emergence of ATM as a high end backbone as well as client.

Network Bandwidth Requirements

Bandwidth refers to the speed at which packets or tokens travel in a LAN environment. In many respects, it's similar to the width of highways. The greater the width of the road, the easier it is to sustain high speed in heavy traffic.

Certain factors need to be determined before you can ascertain whether standard Ethernet networks will suffice for you. It's generally thought that Ethernet works best if the maximum use of the bus is at 30 percent with burst rates no more than 60 percent. Obviously, really busy networks don't function well on Ethernet. So how can you use Ethernet in large environments? The solution is to subdivide the network into segments and combining the star-based segments with hub-to-hub bus connections. In other words, you maximize the local traffic by minimizing its amount. The only factor to consider is the type of connection between hubs (we'll get to that shortly). Ideally, each network segment has its own Windows NT server to minimize the need to cross segments.

It's reasonable to segment the network if there are more than 150 total systems. In doing so, the addition of a server to each segment is an excellent idea. Each segment should have a BDC which can also function as a DHCP server. In this way, everyone on the segment can log on even if the PDC is not functioning. A typical environment for a segmented network is shown in Figure 20-1. This is a simple model of such a network and doesn't include routers, servers, and other common devices. It does, however, depict a hub-to-hub connection.

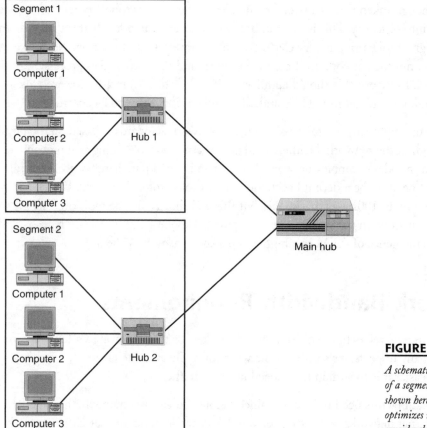

FIGURE 20-1

A schematic representation of a segmented network is shown here. This design optimizes network traffic considerably.

There's no doubt that the current major bottleneck on any system is bus I/O. Networks can afford to be slow because individual components are slow. With the beginning of FC-AL and fiber optic-based SCSI devices, the slowdown caused by the network will be far more apparent. Fortunately, network bandwidth hasn't remained static.

Hubs

The first change that's occurring is with the hubs themselves. In the standard hub, all ports are in contention for the same bandwidth. Manufacturers are aware of this limitation and have devised switching hubs, now formally called *switches*. In this design, the switches optimize every port to use maximum bandwidth with the limiting factor being error corrections. Switches are far superior to hubs in managing heavy network traffic.

Fast Ethernet Designs

Also becoming available over the past year has been the Fast Ethernet designs. These basically are targeted as using 100Base-T rather than 10Base-T. The underlying protocol is a fight right now between the IEEE-derived 802.3 specification and the 100VG-AnyLAN developed by Hewlett Packard.

100Base-T is reasonably well standardized. It's based on the same collision model as 10Base-T; namely, the CSMA/CD access. Switches are available that will accept both 10Base-T and 100Base-T connections. Likewise, there are Network Interface Cards (NIC) currently available that can function as either 10Base-T or 100Base-T. Consequently, segment traffic can easily be optimized. Fast systems can use 100 as standard while lower demand systems can function at 10.

The 100VG-AnyLAN approach advocated by HP is a better overall design than that of 100Base-T, but only Hewlett-Packard is currently supporting this specification (IEEE 802.12). The major advantage that 100VG-AnyLAN has is the elimination of collisions. This makes the design far more efficient and easier to enlarge. Likewise, the specification can handle both Ethernet and token ring connections, making it ideal for integrating different segments in legacy networks.

Fiber Dirstributed Data Interface (FDDI)

Shipping with NT 4.0 are drivers for *Fiber Distributed Data Interface* (FDDI) networks. The FDDE is basically a token-ring-like environment that can even function to redirect a broken link. Like token ring, FDDI is a better network topology than comparable Ethernet, but acceptance is very slow due to high cost.

Asynchronous Transfer Mode (ATM)

Also shipping with NT 4.0 are drivers for both Adaptec and Madge *Asynchronous Transfer Mode* (ATM) implementations. Unlike Ethernet's packets and ring topologies, ATM uses *cells*. These cells are very small (53 bytes) and are fully duplexed (they can send and receive at the same time). Cell collisions simply don't occur.

ATM is a connection-oriented technology. When one system calls another, a virtual circuit is made and all communication occurs over that circuit—*only* that circuit. Such an ATM circuit is called a *virtual circuit* (*VC*). Virtual circuits can be switched (*SVCs*) or permanent (*PVCs*). In the switched variety, once communication is finished the circuit is torn down. In contrast, some connections can be so critical that they're never torn down. These PVCs can be set up by the network administrator.

There are no ATM hubs. All ATM concentrators are switches and all seem to accept 10Base-T, ATM25, and ATM155 modules. Obviously, in such a configuration, you can use an ATM155 line as backbone, with ATM25 connections and 10Base-T to workstations. Such a design would clearly optimize throughput from backbone to server to workstation. Utilizing such connections, remote access can truly be optimized as well.

Planning for Remote Access

Sooner or later, you'll need to set up a *remote access server or RAS* (as opposed to *remote control*, which is a separate issue). Your salespeople are on the road; they need access to stored data, e-mail, and ordering systems. How do you accomplish this? Surprisingly, it's very easy to implement.

User Loads

RAS is very resource dependent. In general, users that log onto and use applications on the server, will soon bog down that server. For this type of RAS server, it's not unreasonable to add a second processor if there are more than 4 simultaneous users. In situations where the users are logging onto the RAS server but are using resources on other systems, then the server can be somewhat more modest. At a minimum, a Pentium 133 with 64MB of RAM using co-processed communications boards is an ideal starting point.

Likewise, systems using centralized modem banks are also convenient and easy to use. If the system access and use slows down excessively, add the additional CPU and RAM.

User Locations

Ideally, you want to use as many inexpensive components as possible. One such cost is long distance phone charges. In the best of all possible worlds, you'd dial into the Internet and connect to your home environment. Unfortunately, as this is being written, the use of the Internet in this regard is still somewhat premature (see the following sections). For many other reasons, including security, RAS servers are still probably the ideal way to go.

Access Methods

There are several basic methods for accessing a system remotely. In the first method, you set up a *Remote Access Server* (*RAS*) that has modems associated with it. A user simply calls a number and can log onto the network via that connection. In such a situation, access is the same as if logging on locally, but speed is far slower. If modems are an issue, you can use ISDN lines that connect to a PRI card in the server. When you dial in, you do so through ISDN PC Cards and can communicate ISDN to ISDN.

The best choices right now are dedicated servers with defined numbers of lines and modems. As stated earlier, a very convenient starting place is a Pentium 133 with 64MB of RAM and a bank of PC Card modems. Two superb examples of these banks are those from Digiboard and Central data. You call up the local phone company and obtain a *hunt group* of numbers (numbers that roll over to the next free number—your callers need to remember only one number). Of great importance is that the machine be reasonably-well dedicated. If not, performance will degrade very quickly. It's also important to have a high-speed NIC to connect the callers to the rest of the network. A card such as a 100Base-T would be even better and an ATM25 would be ideal.

When PPTP becomes a viable option, the optimal setup will be a system with a minimum of a dual B-Channel ISDN line with a permanent connection to the Internet. Individuals will dial into the Internet and gain access to the ISDN line, and the connection will be similar to a local LAN connection.

Security Requirements

Security requirements for any remote incoming connection are very serious. The optimal way to have security on the Remote Access Server is to use the call-back option. In this situation, the person is authenticated by RAS and then called back by the server. This allows the call to be inexpensive and provides a means of increasing the security of the remote connection. An example of such a connection permission is shown in Figure 20-2.

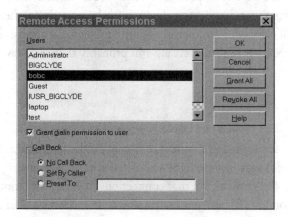

FIGURE 20-2

Using permissions in RAS server, you can set up dial–in permissions and call–back capabilities. This enables RAS to have excellent security.

Many will argue that Remote Access Servers are obsolete now that the Internet has gotten so popular. Such is not the case. RAS is far easier to set up and secure than the Internet currently is. Users can easily call in and gain access to all allowed resources. The major factor to consider is the serious nature of the hardware requirements of RAS.

Where to Go Next

Many of the issues covered in this chapter have also been mentioned or discussed throughout this book. Of particular note, look at the following chapters:

- Chapter 19, "Performance Tuning and Optimization," discusses in detail many of the issues involved in the performance tuning of Windows NT.

- Chapter 24, "Interoperating with TCP/IP Clients," discusses the details of the WINS and DHCP services and their significance.

PART VII

Integrating Windows NT with Your Network

Chapter | 21

Working with DOS
and Windows Clients

In This Chapter:

- ◆ Network Client Administrator
- ◆ Installing and Configuring Client 3.0 for MS-DOS
- ◆ Using Client 3.0 for MS-DOS and Windows
- ◆ Windows for Workgroups 3.11
- ◆ Windows 95
- ◆ Running Windows 95 from the Server
- ◆ Client Security
- ◆ Performance Issues

How do I...

Integrating the client into an NT Server based network can be a daunting task, especially when the client systems are a mixture of several different operating systems. One of the design goals of Windows NT networking was to make it as open and accessible as possible. Microsoft has done a very good job of reaching that goal, giving the network administrator several mechanisms to use when connecting clients to the network.

A client is defined as any computer that communicates with a server. As much as we may want to forget about them, there still is a need to make the NT server available to DOS and Windows 3.1 clients. The list of reasons one may include any or all of the following:

- ◆ Inability to upgrade clients due to hardware or financial constraints
- ◆ Specific applications that require the use of DOS or Windows 3.x
- ◆ The need to remote-boot a client workstation

This chapter details the use of the Network Client Administrator to install the included client software and the connection of existing client systems into your NT network. This chapter also covers all DOS and Windows-based clients and the individual configuration options for each. This chapter shows the use of the Windows 95 network setup tool, which allows you to install Windows 95 to the NT server and create a default setup installation script. (The Windows 95 network setup tool makes it very simple to deploy many Windows 95 workstations at once.) Finally this chapter discusses security and performance issues as they apply to each client.

Network Client Administrator

The Network Client Administrator is a versatile tool that is used to create a network installation boot disk and to create the floppy disks that can be used at the client to install the client software. The Network Client Administrator can also be used to install the client-based server administration tools and to view information related to using a remote-boot workstation. (These last two options are discussed in Chapter 10, "NT Server Management Tools.") As a network administrator, you may want to simplify the client installation process by using the network-based installation boot disk or you may simply want to create the disks that you need to install the DOS and Windows client.

When you start the Network Client Administrator you are given four options (see Figure 21-1). You can create a network installation startup disk, you can create an installation disk set, you can copy remote administration tools (discussed in Chapter 10) or you can view the help files regarding remote boot (which tell you to read the resource kit if you want to work with remote boot workstations).

FIGURE 21-1

The Network Client Administrator is used to install or update network clients.

Creating a Network Installation Disk

A network installation boot disk (described by NT Server as either a *network installation startup disk* or a *network startup disk*) is used to boot a client computer, attach the client to the network, and start an installation program for the client you have selected. This option is very useful when you have several client machines with identical network hardware and settings, as these settings are stored on the floppy disk. Because the client software is transferred to the client via the network, this installation method can only be used for clients that are already physically attached to the network.

When choosing to create a network startup disk, you are given four options: Use Existing Path, Share Files, Copy Files then Share, and Use Existing Share (see Figure 21-2). These options determine how your clients will access the installation files when booted from the floppy disk that's created here:

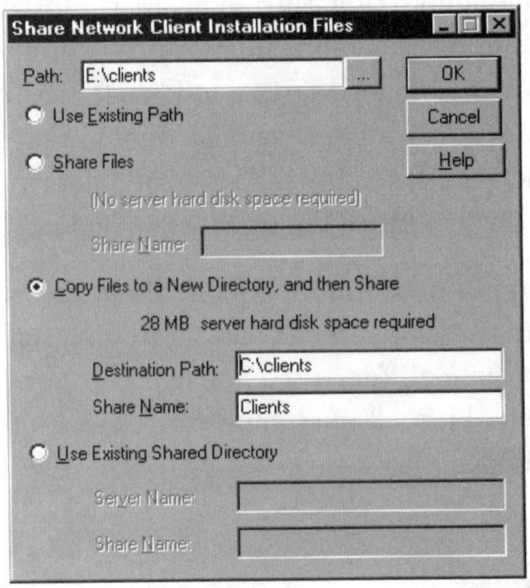

FIGURE 21-2

The Share Network Client Installation Files Window allows the Administrator to specify the location of the client source files.

◆ Use Existing Path—Choose this option when the Network Client Administrator has been used previously to copy the client files to the server's hard disk.

◆ Share Files—Choose this option when you don't wish to copy the client files to the server's hard disk. Remember, if you choose this option, you will have to make sure that the NT Server CD-ROM remains available on the server when you boot the client with the created network startup disk.

- ◆ Copy Files then Share—Choose this option when you wish to copy the client files from the CD-ROM to the server's hard disk. You want to examine the share permissions to make sure that the proper permissions have been granted. (There should be no reason for anyone to have any more than READ permissions to the share).

- ◆ Use Existing Share—Choose this option when the client files exist on another server and you want to point your client to that share.

> **CAUTION:** It's important to note that when you choose the Use Existing Share option, you don't specify the share using a Universal Naming Convention (UNC) name, instead you specify the name of the server in the first box and the name of the share in the second box, the client administrator automatically creates a UNC name (for example, \\Server\Share).

After selecting where to find the files to copy, you are brought to the workstation configuration screen, which allows you to specify the size of the floppy disk and the network interface card used at the client workstation. Once you select these options you are brought to the Network Startup Disk Configuration Window (see Figure 21-3). Here you select the various networking options for the client workstation:

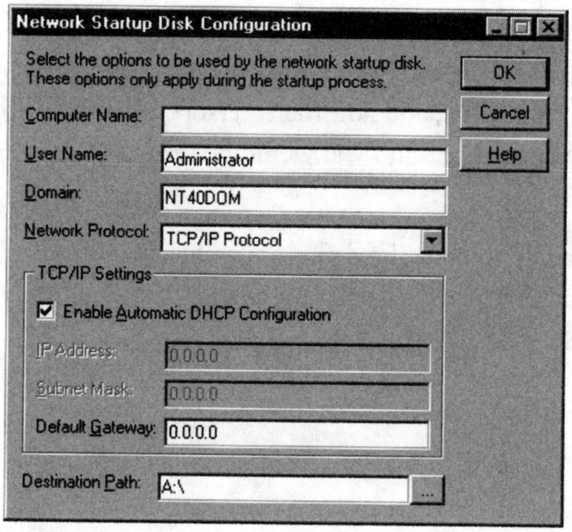

FIGURE 21-3

The Network Startup Disk Configuration Window allows you to select protocols and protocol options to install on the startup disk.

- Computer Name—The name of the client workstation when booted from the network startup disk. This name can be changed during the install, so it's a good idea to choose a generic name (such as install).

- User Name—The name you use to log onto the domain.

- Domain Name—The name of the domain you log onto.

- Network Protocol—The protocol used when communicating with the server. This selection is limited to the protocols installed on the server that's creating the network startup disk.

- Protocol Configuration—Various configuration options specific to the selected protocol. For example when configuring a disk to use the TCP/IP protocol, you must specify an IP address or to use DHCP to obtain one.

Once you select these options, you are asked to confirm your choices and place a floppy in the appropriate drive. After you comply, the network startup disk is then created.

You are never prompted to configure the settings for the network adapter. If you are using an adapter that isn't capable of "auto configuration" (for example, an NE2000 compatible adapter) then you need to edit the PROTOCOL.INI file manually. PROTOCOL.INI is created as part of the installation process and exists in the A:\NET directory.

When the installation process creates the PROTOCOL.INI file, it's configured for a "smart" card, which is capable of informing the system of its hardware configuration automatically. Accordingly, the hardware configuration options in the PROTOCOL.INI file, as installed, are commented out. You need to edit this file to include the proper hardware information, otherwise the disk won't work properly. Assuming you are using a Novell/Eagle NE2000 compatible adapter that's set to Port 340 and Interrupt 10, you would remove the semicolons (which are comment indicators) from both the IOBASE and INTERRUPT lines, add the port address to the IOBASE line, and add the Interrupt request (IRQ) to the INTERRUPT line (see Figure 21-4). Save the file and you would be ready to boot the disk at the client workstation.

Once the disk is created, you are ready to boot the disk from a client workstation. Remember that the disk will start the selected installation program automatically once booted, so be prepared to install the client software.

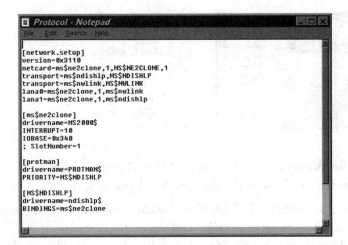

FIGURE 21-4

The PROTOCOL.INI *file after editing the hardware settings for a Novell/Eagle NE2000.*

Creating an Installation Disk Set

When selecting the installation disk set option, you are choosing to build the floppy disks needed to install the client. This option is useful when each client has different hardware settings, or if your clients aren't yet physically connected to the network (which means the client files can't be transferred over the network) and you wish to get them ready prior to connection.

When choosing to create an installation disk set, you are given four options: Use Existing Path, Share Files, Copy Files then Share, and Use Existing Share. These options allow the system administration to indicate where the source files are located.

After specifying where to find the files to copy, you are asked to indicate the Network Client or Service for which you want to create an installation disk set (see Figure 21-5). Your choices are as follows:

- ◆ Network Client 3.0 for DOS and Windows—This client software is used to connect either a DOS or a Windows 3.1 client to a Microsoft network. This software works especially well and has several installation options which will be discussed later in this chapter.

- ◆ Remote Access v1.1a for MS-DOS—This is a program that allows a DOS workstation to dial into an NT computer running the Remote Access Server.

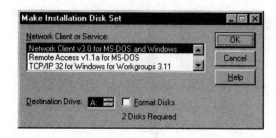

FIGURE 21-5

The Make Installation Disk Set dialog box enables the system administrator to select client software for the desired target client.

- TCP/IP 32 for Windows for Workgroups 3.11—This is the Microsoft TCP/IP suite that works with Windows for Workgroups 3.11.

- Lan Manager 2.2c client for MS-DOS—This client software is used mainly when you need either to set up a DOS workstation to communicate with both NT and NetWare or to provide access to remote-boot/diskless workstations. This software uses quite a bit of the workstation's memory and should only be used when absolutely essential.

- Lan Manager 2.2c Client for OS/2—This client software was designed to connect DOS and Windows workstations to Microsoft's LAN Manager product (An early precursor to Windows NT) and is the only Microsoft client software that will connect an OS/2 workstation to an NT domain.

Once you select the client software you wish to create, you are told how many floppy disks are required and prompted to insert the first one. As you comply, the client software is copied to the floppy disks.

Once the installation method is chosen and the disk set has been created, you can boot your client and run the installation program. (If you chose the network installation boot disk, the disk will automatically connect to the server and start the installation program).

If you want to connect a DOS or Windows 3.1 workstation to your Windows NT network, you need to install the Client 3.0 for MS-DOS. The following section is an overview of the process and will help you understand the steps involved installing this client.

Installing and Configuring Client 3.0 for MS-DOS

To install Network Client 3.0 you need to know the hardware configuration of the network adapter because the software has no mechanism to detect network cards or configuration.

Network Client 3.0 is installed either by running the installation program (called SETUP.EXE) that exists on the Installation Disk Set that you've created with Network Client Administrator or by booting the client with the Network Installation Startup disk.

Once the installation program starts, you are prompted to select the local directory where you wish to install the program. Next you are prompted to select the network adapter. Once the adapter is selected you are prompted to press Enter to optimize the network buffers. You are then prompted to enter a user name. This is the name that will be used by default at this workstation and should exist in the NT domain.

Next you will see the Command Prompt—Setup window (see Figure 21-6) in which you are presented with four options:

♦ Change Names—Configure your default user name, computer name, work-group name and domain name here. By default the installation program selects the user name as the computer name, WORKGROUP as the default workgroup name, and leaves the domain name blank. This is the only place during installation where you can modify these names.

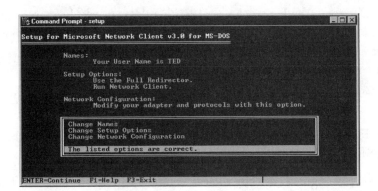

FIGURE 21-6

The Command Prompt—setup Window is used to set up the Network Client 3.0 program for the target client.

♦ Change Setup Options—After you choose Change Setup Options, the Command Prompt—setup Window will display the dialog shown in Figure 21-7. You can configure the operation of the client program from the dialog box.

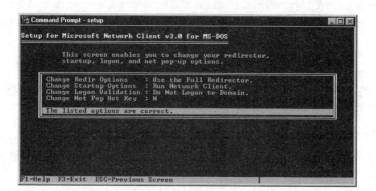

FIGURE 21-7

After choosing Change Setup Options, the Network options are displayed.

♦ Change Network Configuration—Here you can configure the network adapter's hardware settings, or add or remove protocols.

♦ Accept the listed options as correct.

These are the additional options:

♦ Redirector Options—You have a choice of using either the Full Redirector, which is capable of being validated by the Domain and is capable of using named pipes, or the Basic Redirector, which uses less memory but won't be validated by the domain or be able to use named pipes.

♦ Startup Options—You have a choice of starting the network client automatically or manually, and whether or not to load the NET TSR that gives hot-key access to the NET program (a DOS menu-based program that makes using the NET USE commands easier).

♦ Logon Validation—You have a choice of either logging on to a domain or not here.

♦ Change Hot Key—You can choose what key combination will activate the NET TSR.

Once the options are configured correctly you can continue with the installation. The program will prompt you to restart once it's done. By default, the installation program copies the Client 3.0 files to the C:\NET directory.

The installation program adds the line DEVICE=C:\NET\IFSHLP.SYS to the CONFIG.SYS file. This is the Installable File System driver that's required for Microsoft networking. If this file doesn't exist or if you inadvertently remove this line from CONFIG.SYS, you won't be able to start the Microsoft network client. The installation program also modifies AUTOEXEC.BAT by adding several lines that call programs related to the protocol you selected, and also includes the NET INITIALIZE command, which is the command that starts the Microsoft networking client.

Using Client 3.0 for MS-DOS and Windows

Once installed, Client 3.0 requires using the NET USE command, for example to connect drive G: to the DATA share on the NT server called NT1, use the command NET USE G: \\NT1\DATA. Or you can use the included NET TSR program to attach to network resources. These commands must be executed before Windows is started and are easiest when included in a logon script.

When installed with the Full Redirector option, Client 3.0 is capable of being validated by the domain controller, which makes it a full fledged member of the domain. The Full Redirector option also allows the client to use named pipes and Remote Procedure Calls (RPCs) to communicate with network resources (which is required when connecting to most application layer based resources such as SQL Server or Exchange Server). Full Redirector requires about 110K of system memory, but uses memory buffers for network communications, which makes this the fastest DOS client available.

When installed with the Basic Redirector option, Client 3.0 isn't capable of being validated by a domain controller, nor is it capable of using named pipes or RPCs to communicate with network resources. This means that the client won't be capable of using high-end e-mail packages such as Microsoft Exchange, nor will it be capable of operating as a client to SQL Server (or any similar product).

The Basic Redirector is capable of accessing domain resources, assuming your user id and password match an account in the domain database. Basic Redirector only uses about 10K of workstation memory, but doesn't buffer network communication, which makes using it slower than using the Full Redirector option.

There are no additional configuration options that need to be selected when using this client with Windows 3.x; however, there are some new features that are added to the Windows 3.x client, such as the ability to attach to shared directories through File Manager, and the ability to connect to shared printers via the Print Manager.

One thing to be careful of, if you connect to a shared directory or printer from a command shell within Windows, by default it is available only to that command shell and not the entire system.

Windows 3.x does not have any networking components built into the operating system. This requires the system administrator to install DOS-based networking if they wish to connect the desktop to a network. This creates a serious limitation in that adding additional DOS networking components consumes workstation resources such as memory. Microsoft recognized this program and developed Windows for Workgroups, which has the networking components built in, making life somewhat easier for the network administrator.

Windows for Workgroups 3.11

Prior to the release of Windows 95, Windows for Workgroups (WfW) was the operating system of choice for connecting 16 bit desktops to Windows NT. Windows for Workgroups 3.11 offers some 32 bit networking and 32 bit file access, which combine to improve performance considerably over Windows 3.1. WfW requires less system resources than Windows 95 or Windows NT Workstation and is capable of participating fully in the NT domain. This makes WfW an ideal client when you don't want the expense of upgrading your current hardware to run Windows 95 or Windows NT Workstation.

Configuring Windows for Workgroups 3.11

> **CAUTION:** The following section assumes that Windows for Workgroups has been installed previously with no network support. If it has been installed with network support, the steps will be slightly different.

It is a relatively simple task to configure Windows for Workgroups to operate with Microsoft networks and log onto a domain. Assuming that Windows for Workgroups has been previously installed without networking support, you start with the Network Setup program located in the Network group. The Network Setup dialog box (shown in Figure 21-8) provides you with the following options:

- ◆ Networks—Lets you select what type of network(s) to support (Microsoft and/or third-party networks such as Novell NetWare or Banyan Vines).

- ◆ Sharing—Allows you to select whether you want to make local files and printers available on the network.

- ◆ Drivers—Here you select the network hardware drivers, configuration, and protocols to support on the local machine.

FIGURE 21-8

The Network Setup dialog box in Windows for Workgroups allows you to configure network support.

Installing the Microsoft Windows Network

After selecting the Networks option, you are presented with a dialog box that allows you to specify the desired networks to support. The default here is No Windows support for networks, which means that Windows won't load any network drivers. Here you will need to select Install Microsoft Windows Network as shown in Figure 21-9. If you are selecting additional network support (such as Novell NetWare or Banyan Vines), you should install it now.

If you select the Sharing option (refer to Figure 21-8), you are presented with a dialog box that allows you to specify whether you want to make your local files and printers available on the network. This loads the server portion of Windows for Workgroups and does indeed allow you to share files and printers on the network, but remember that you can only protect these resources via share level security.

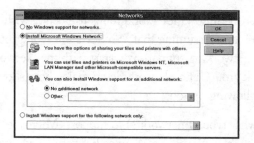

FIGURE 21-9

The Networks dialog box allows you to choose what network support is installed.

Configuring Network Drivers

When selecting the Drivers option (refer to Figure 21-8), you are presented with a dialog box (shown in Figure 21-10) that allows you to specify your network adapter drivers and what protocols are supported. If Windows for Workgroups didn't detect your network adapter automatically during the original installation, you will need to add it manually by selecting the Add Adapter button. You will then be presented with a list of available drivers, or you can select an NDIS driver from an OEM. Once you have installed the appropriate network driver, you may want to configure any OEM options by selecting the configure button.

FIGURE 21-10

The Network Driver dialog box allows you to select network drivers.

Configuring Network Names

Once the network adapter is installed and configured, select Close. The Network Names dialog box will appear (see Figure 21-11). Select your user name (the name as it exists in the NT domain), your workgroup name (you don't want your workgroup to have the same name as your domain), and your computer name (this name must be unique on the network).

FIGURE 21-11

The Microsoft Windows Network Name dialog box allow you to specify names to identify the client to others on the Network.

Once you have selected the appropriate names, select OK and the system will copy files, modify your startup files, and prompt you to restart the system. When the computer restarts you may notice some new programs being run automatically. Windows for Workgroups installs the IFSHLP.SYS file , which is the installable file system driver, into CONFIG.SYS, then loads real-mode networking support. Once the network drivers load properly the system will respond with The command completed successfully.

Logging on to the System

When Windows starts, you are first prompted to log on to the system (see Figure 21-12). This logon dialog box is for access to Windows, not your domain. The first time you log on to Windows you will be asked if you want to create a password file for the user logging on. Select YES to create the password list.

FIGURE 21-12

Logging on to the Microsoft Windows Network for the first time.

Once you have created your password list, open the Main group and start control panel, then select Network. The Microsoft Windows Network dialog box shown in Figure 21-13 appears. This is the main user configuration screen for Windows for Workgroups networking.

FIGURE 21-13

The Microsoft Windows Network applet.

Configuring Startup Options

Verify that the names of your default user and computer are correct, then select startup. The Startup Settings dialog box (shown in Figure 21-14) presents several options that affect the way your client will interact with the NT server:

- ♦ Log On at Startup—This option determines whether Windows for Workgroups prompts you to logon when you start Windows. If you turn this option off, you will need to log on to the system manually by selecting the Log On / Log Off icon in the network group. The default is to leave this option on.

- ♦ Ghosted Connections—This option defines whether Windows for Workgroups will actively connect all permanent network connections, or connect to them when they are accessed. The default is to connect to the resources when they are needed (Ghosted Connections).

- ♦ Enable Network DDE—This option enables the use of NetDDE from the client. NetDDE allows the client to use DDE connections over the network, such as Chat and the Clipbook. The default is to enable NetDDE.

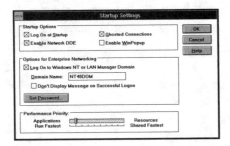

FIGURE 21-14

Select network startup options through the Startup Settings dialog box.

♦ Enable WinPOPUP—This option enables the client messaging system and allows Windows for Workgroups to receive administrative alerts from Windows NT and also receive various PopUp messages from other clients and servers. The default is to disable WinPOPUP. You want to enable WINPOPUP if you expect to receive any messages from the server or other users on the system.

♦ Log on to Windows NT or Lan Manager Domain—This option enables the domain validation of the client. If you want Windows for Workgroups to be validated by the NT domain controller this option must be checked and you must specify the name of the domain you want to log on to. The default is not to log on to any domain.

♦ Don't Display Message on Successful Logon—This options enables you to turn off the successful logon display, which notifies the user which domain controller validated them and what their priviledge level is in the domain. The default is to enable the display of the logon message, but you may find it annoying and your users most likely won't care what Domain controller validates them.

♦ Performance Priority—This option is presented in the form of a slider bar and affects the client only when it's also being used as a server. The left side of the scale sets aside less memory for network buffers and is for better local performance; the right side sets more memory aside for network buffers. You should only change this option when you want to use Windows for Workgroups as a server.

Once you have specified the appropriate options, exit Windows and restart. When Windows restarts you will be prompted again for your password, and assuming you chose to be validated by a domain, you will be prompted to enter your domain password. You will also be asked whether you want to cache that password on the local system. If you choose to cache your password on the local system, you will be logged onto the domain automatically when you provide the correct Windows password, even if it's different than your domain password. Once you enter the correct password, and assuming you chose to keep the successful logon message, the screen will display a message that tells you what domain controller validated you and what privilege you hold within the domain (see Figure 21-15).

FIGURE 21-15

Successful logon to the domain is announced by this dialog box.

You are now completely logged on to the domain and can access any resources that your user account is allowed. Your workstation is treated as a full-fledged member of the domain. One thing to remember is that user profiles aren't supported by Windows for Workgroups machines. The desktop in Windows for Workgroups and all user settings are saved on the local machine in the WIN.INI file; therefore, Windows for Workgroups is unable to implement NT profiles. You must also consider that Windows for Workgroups has no mechanism for user-level security.

If you need to support user profiles and user-level security, you will most likely want to consider using Windows 95 as your client. Windows 95 will support both Server based user profiles and user-level security.

Windows 95

Windows 95 is Microsoft's latest entry into the desktop operating system world. Windows 95 offers 32-bit file and network access, as well as a 32 bit kernel, which make it a very good choice for the desktop. Though it requires more resources than Windows for Workgroups, Windows 95 offers fast network communications and complete participation within the domain. Windows 95 offers the ability to participate in user-level security and is also capable of saving its profile information to a home directory on NT. All of these features work together to make Windows 95 the desktop of choice when you don't need the high-end features of Windows NT Workstation.

Configuring Windows 95

Configuring Windows 95 to participate in Windows NT domains is relatively simple. Assuming Windows 95 has been previously installed and your networking hardware has been correctly set up, you can start by right-clicking the Network Neighborhood icon and selecting Properties. This will display the Network Properties dialog box shown in

Figure 21-16. Here you will want to verify that your networking components have been installed.

Network Identification

Once you have verified that all networking components have been properly installed (refer to Figure 21-16), click the Identification tab (see Figure 21-17). Here you select your Computer Name, which must be unique on the network, and your Workgroup Name, which should not be the same name as your Domain. You are also able to type a comment to identify your computer during browsing.

Access Control

Once you have selected network names, click the Access Control tab (see Figure 21-18). You have a couple of options:

- Share Level Security—When sharing files and directories on the Windows 95 workstation, access to those resources are controlled by assigning two passwords to each share. The level of access that a user is granted depends on the password that they type.

- User Level Security—Access to local resources will be checked with a security provider (either a Windows NT machine or a Novell NetWare server) The level of access granted is based on the specific assignment on the local machine for that user.

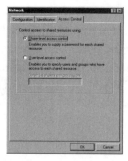

FIGURE 21-18

The Access Control Tab allows setting security.

Configuring Client for Microsoft Networks

Once you have selected the type of access control, you will want to go back to the configuration screen (click the Configuration tab and refer to Figure 21-16). You can continue the network configuration by selecting the Client for Microsoft Networks and choosing Properties. Doing so will display the Client for Microsoft Networks Properties dialog box. You then have the following options:

- Log on to Domain—Select the name of the Domain that you wish to validate you.

- Quick Logon—Selecting this option will reconnect any persistent network connections only when they are needed.

♦ Logon and Restore Connections—Selecting this option will reconnect any persistant network connections during logon so that they are available immediately when you attempt to access them.

Configuring the Primary Network Logon

Once you have selected the Domain options and choose OK, you are returned to the Configuration tab of the Network dialog box (refer to Figure 21-16). The next step is to specify the Primary Network Logon. The primary network logon determines what type prompt is displayed when first starting Windows 95 (such as a domain for Microsoft networks or a Server for NetWare networks). Selecting Client for Microsoft Networks as your primary network logon will ensure that you are validated by Windows NT and any logon scripts or profiles that are associated with the user will execute.

Configuring File and Print Sharing

Once you have selected the Primary Network Logon and clicked OK, you continue the configuration by selecting File and Print Sharing. The File and Print Sharing for Microsoft Networks Properties dialog box shown in Figure 21-19 is displayed. You have the following options:

♦ Browse Master—Selects whether the local workstation will become a master browser. Your choices are Automatic, which means that Windows 95 will automatically configure itself as browse master if needed, Disable, which means that Windows 95 won't become a browser, and Enable, which means that Windows 95 will become the master browser. The default setting for Browse Master is Automatic.

♦ LM Announce—If you are using any Lan Manager clients on your network, you will need to set this option to Yes so that Windows 95 will broadcast its information to the Lan Manager clients. The default for LM Announce is to NOT broadcast information to Lan Manager clients.

FIGURE 21-19

File and Print Sharing for Microsoft Networks.

Configuring the Network Adapter

Once you have selected the options for File and Print Sharing, you should verify the settings of your network adapter by selecting the adapter and clicking the Properties button (refer to Figure 21-16). Figure 21-20 shows the Adapter Properties dialog box for a PCI Ethernet adapter. You can specify options on the following tabs:

◆ Driver Type—Selects which network adapter that Windows 95 loads. Enhanced Mode NDIS driver is a 32 bit driver that fully supports Plug and Play. Real Mode NDIS driver is a 16 bit driver that doesn't support Plug and Play. Real Mode ODI driver is a 16 bit driver that supports the ODI specification. To participate in Windows NT domain authentication you should use the 32 bit driver. You will always want to use the 32 bit driver to utilize the networking functions of Windows 95 fully. Care must be taken when upgrading an existing system as Windows 95 will detect any 16 bit drivers currently in use and continue to use the 16 bit driver.

◆ Bindings—Select what protocols are associated with what adapters.

◆ Advanced—These are settings that are specific to the individual network adapter, such as the connection type (UTP or coax) or buffer size.

Once you have selected these options, click OK to save the configuration. You will be prompted to restart the computer. Once Windows 95 restarts, you will be prompted with the Domain Logon dialog box shown in Figure 21-21. After entering your password you are authenticated by the domain with whatever privileges that your NT user account possesses.

FIGURE 21-20

*Network Adapter
Properties for a PCI
Ethernet Adapter*

Once you have logged onto the domain, you can be sure that Windows 95 is configured to operate properly as a member of your domain.

There may come a time when you decide that working with each individual desktop is consuming too much of your time as an administrator. If this is the case, you may consider installing Windows 95 to run from the NT server. This will allow you to upgrade your machines and affect various changes to the desktop without actually visiting each one.

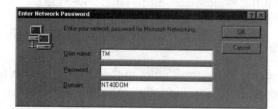

FIGURE 21-21

*Domain logon is provided
through the Enter Net-
work Password dialog box.*

Running Windows 95 from the Server

For administrators who are responsible for multiple workstations on their network, it makes sense to lighten their administrative load by placing as much information possible on a central file server, including running the operating system directly from the server. This can save the administrator hours of work when it comes to installing new software or upgrading the operating system itself. The downside to this is that it will definitely increase the amount of traffic on your network. (The exact amount of increased traffic is very hard to predict; it depends on several factors including the # of workstations running from the server and the amount of traffic generated by other applications on the network.)

If your network infrastructure can handle the increased traffic, you might consider installing Windows 95 on the NT Server, and install just the minimum files on the workstation to run Windows 95. This can be done with the Windows 95 NETSEUP program. The main reason to consider this is administrative ease: It's easier to control and administer every workstation when they are running from the same copy of Windows 95. The downside to this is that you will have slower clients as they will be pulling the files off the server for every operation. Your network traffic will definitely increase for the same reason. The actual amount of increased traffic depends upon your network infrastructure and how often these workstations are being used. Setting up Windows 95 to run from the server is done from an existing Windows 95 client.

Windows 95 Netsetup Program

Installing a shared copy of Windows 95 to the NT Server can be a time-consuming during initial setup, but it more than pays for itself in the long run when you consider the amount of time saved during application installs and upgrades. The program that performs the actual setup of the Windows 95 files on the server is NETSETUP.EXE. It's located in the \ADMIN\NETSETUP directory on the Windows 95 distribution CD-ROM.

Preparing to Run Netsetup

Prior to running Netsetup to install the Windows 95 files to the server, you must first configure the Windows NT server where you will install the Windows 95 files. You want to create a directory and assign the appropriate permissions. (Administrators should have full control and normal users should have read permission.) You should share the directory with a simple name, such as WIN95 or something similar.

Using Netsetup

The Windows 95 Netsetup program is on the Windows 95 CD-ROM in the ADMIN\NETTOOLS\NETSETUP directory. It must be executed from a Windows 95 workstation. Browse the CD and start NETSETUP.EXE. You will be asked to enter the path to install Windows 95 (shown in Figure 21-22). Once you enter this path Windows 95 will verify that the path is accessible.

FIGURE 21-22

*The Server Based
Netsetup program.*

Configuring the Client Installation Options

Once Windows 95 has verified that the path is accessible, you choose Install, which displays the Source Path dialog box shown in Figure 21-23.

> **TIP:** If your goal is to have a centralized location for Windows 95 source files, but not to run Windows 95 from the server, you want to select the "User's Choice" option, however to configure Windows 95 to run from the server.

You have the following options related to the location of the installed Windows 95 files at the client:

- ◆ Server—When clients attach to the server and run the setup program, Windows 95 setup will only allow them to use the shared copy of Windows 95. They won't be given the option to copy the files to their local hard disk. Select this option when you want your users to run Windows 95 only from the server.

- ◆ Local—When clients attach to the server and run the setup program, Windows 95 will only copy the files to their local hard drive. They won't be allowed to use the shared copy of Windows 95. Select this option when you want your users to run Windows 95 only from their own workstation.

- ◆ User's Choice—When clients attach to the server and run the setup program, Windows 95 will give them the option of either using the shared copy of Windows 95 or creating a local installation. Select this option when you wish to give your users a choice of where they want to run Windows 95.

FIGURE 21-23

Client installation options are shown in the Source Path dialog box.

Once you have selected the client install options, verify that the source path and destination path are correct, then click OK to continue. You will be asked if you wish to create an installation script manually or use the default installation script provided with Windows 95. If you choose Create Default, you will be brought to the setup editor program.

Creating a Default Installation Script

When installing Windows 95 onto the server, one of the things that the administrator can decide to do is create an installation script that makes the client installation easier for the person performing the installation. This script is created with the Setup Editor. These steps can be rather confusing are are presented here in overview format. For more information you may want to view the Windows 95 resource kit.

The Setup Editor is loosely based on the Windows 95 Policy Editor and is broken down into several sections. Each section corresponds to a major configuration item that's generally broken down into several subordinate options. You don't have to fill out any of the options here; however, the more completely you fill out the options, the less interaction is required from the user perfoming the installation. To select an option, click the option to activate it, then fill in the parameters in the second half of the screen.

For clarity, the Network Options are discussed in a separate section, "Network Options." The major configuration items within the Setup Editor are as follows:

- ◆ Setup Options—These are options that affect the setup of Windows 95:
    - ◆ Automated Installation—Selects whether the installation is automated or controlled by the user. If you select Automated, then you must select whether you will allow or not allow any input from the user during the installation process.

♦ Setup Mode—Selects what installation mode you will use for the client install. Your choices are Compact, which installs just the base operating system, Custom, which allows you to choose the options you want to install, Portable, which installs only the minimum files required to run Windows 95 on a portable computer, or Typical, which installs most options.

♦ Create Emergency Boot Disk—Specifies whether an emergency boot disk is created during the client installation. The emergency boot disk is used to recover from system failures.

♦ Install Verification—Specifies whether the setup program performs the installation or just verifies an installation.

♦ Enable Pen Windows Warning—Warns the user when setup is run about the effects of Pen Based Windows.

♦ Install Location—These are options related to the location of the Windows 95 files during instalation. When running Windows 95 from the server, you need a location to store the machine-specific operating system files. If you boot from the clients local hard drive this directory can be located on the client machines hard disk. If you boot from floppy or a remote boot server then the directory must exist on the server. The options are

♦ Install Directory—The name of the directory on the client where Windows 95 is stored.

♦ Server Based Setup—Specifies where the Windows files are stored (Either local to the workstation or the server) and what boot device is used. (Either a floppy, hard disk, or remote boot)

♦ Name and Organization—Choose whether the user will be allowed to type the user name and company or if setup fills in these options automatically

♦ Display Name and Organization Box—Allows the user to fill in the name and organization box during installation.

♦ Name—The name setup automatically fills in the Name box during installation.

- ◆ Organization—The name setup automatically fills in the Organization box during installation.
- ◆ Network Options—These are the options that are related to the network configuration of the client computer. The Network Options are discussed in detail in the section titled "Network Options."
- ◆ System Components—Determines which system components are installed on the client workstation.
  - ◆ Power Management—The power management model used by Windows 95.
  - ◆ Locale—The environment locale information.
  - ◆ Machine—Machine options.
  - ◆ Pen Windows—Pen Windows options.
  - ◆ Tablet—Input tablet options.
  - ◆ Keyboard—Type of keyboard support installed.
  - ◆ Monitor—The display type installed.
  - ◆ Display—The Video card configuration.
  - ◆ Mouse—The mouse type installed.
- ◆ Most Recently Used Paths (MRU)—This option will include up to 4 program names on the MRU list (Start | Run, pull-down box).

Once you have filled out the desired options, click OK. Windows 95 copies files to the directory you specified on the server. This process takes some time to complete. Once the files are copied to the NT server, you can attach a workstation to the server and run the setup program. Depending on the number of options that you filled in, Windows 95 will be installed with a minimum of user interaction.

Creating a Default Network Script: Network Options

The following are the options that are related to the network configuration of the client computer. These options are indeed the most complex of all, and for the most part your users will want to know nothing about their network setup, so be sure and fill out as much of this script as you can.

The major subheadings under the Network Options are as follows:

- Display network pages during custom setup—Determines whether the user will be prompted for network information or if setup will use the information provided in the following configuration options.

- Configuration—Various network configuration options are broken down separately in the following section.

- Identification—Determines how the client computer is identified on the network.

  - Computer Name—The NETBIOS name of the computer. If this option isn't blank, you will need to create a setup file for each computer that you install.

  - Workgroup—The name of the workgroup that the client will be a member of.

  - Description—The description of the client computer

- Access Control—Determines the type of access control on the client computer.

  - Security Type—Determines what type of sharing is installed on the client. Share level or User Level.

  - Pass Through Agent—If using user level security, where is the security controlled from. (Either a Windows NT Domain, Workstation, or NetWare server)

The above options relate to the configuration of the clients general networking environment, in the next section we deal with the client's hardware configuration and specific network client information.

Creating a Default Network Script: Network Configuration Options

- Clients—Information on the network client options.

  - Clients to Install—If you aren't using a Microsoft-supplied client, type the name of the client(s) here.

  - Client for Windows Networks—Configuration options related to the Windows Network client. The options are Validated Logon and

Logon Domain. Validated Logon determines whether or not Windows 95 will attempt to log on to a Windows NT Domain. Also determines if Windows is available for use if the user doesn't supply a valid username / password combination. Logon Domain determines what Domain Windows 95 will attempt to log on to.

- ◆ Client for NetWare Networks—Configuration options related to the NetWare client. The options are Preferred Server, which determines what NetWare server Windows 95 will attempt to log on to, and First Network Drive, which is the drive letter for the NetWare first drive (defaults to F:\).

- ◆ Protocols—Configuration options relative to the specific protocols installed during setup. The first level of Protocols is which Protocols to install.

  - ◆ IPX/SPX compatible protocol—Configuration options for the NWLINK protocol. The options are Frame Type and NetBios Support. Frame Type determines what frame type is configured on the client. The default here is Auto Detect, which does a good job of determining the IPX/SPX frame type. NetBIOS Support determines whether to enable NETBIOS on the IPX/SPX protocol. (Required unless you are also installing TCP/IP)

  - ◆ Microsoft TCP/IP—Configuration options related to the TCP/IP protocol. The option are whether the IP Address is automatically obtained from a DHCP Server or assigned manually. If you choose the manual option you will have to create a setup file for each workstation, as you can't have duplicate IP addresses on your network.

  - ◆ WINS configuration—Determines how WINS is used on the client workstation. You can Enable or Disable WINS, set address of the Primary and Secondary WINS Server (if you aren't using DHCP to set these addresses automatically), and set the NETBIOS scope ID (This parameter should be left blank. When this parameter isn't blank, the workstation can only communicate with other workstations and servers that have the same scope ID).

  - ◆ DNS configuration—Determines how DNS is used on the client workstation. You can Enable DNS, set the DNS host name, and set the workstation's Fully Qualified Domain Name (FQDN). In addition, you can specify the IP addresses of each of the DNS servers in the order that you want Windows 95 to search them and the order in which you want to search for host names (this option is generally left blank). Also, you can specify the path to the LMHOSTS file, which is used to resolve NETBIOS names to IP addresses when WINS is not used.

◆ Gateways—The gateways configured on the local workstation.

◆ Network Cards—Options related to the network interface cards installed in the system. You can specify the names of the network cards to install. This is used only when Windows 95 setup can't automatically detect the installed network adapter.

◆ Services—The services to install on the local workstation.

   ◆ Services to install—The names of any services that you want to install besides the File and Print sharing services.

   ◆ File and Print Sharing for NetWare Networks—Configuration options related to sharing resources to NetWare clients. Generally these won't be used in NT networks. They include SAP browsing, which turns SAP browsing on or off. SAP browsing induces quite a bit of traffic on the network and Browse Master, which determines whether the workstation is capable of being a browse master.

Client Security

One of the major concerns of any network manager should be security. Unfortunately each client operates differently in regards to Windows NT security. Determining the level of client security required will help to determine what client operating system you choose, and how you operate with that particular client.

DOS Clients and Security

The Client 3.0 for DOS and Windows supports logon validation when installed with the Full Redirector. This allows a network manager to configure a DOS client to force a user to enter a logon name and password. One problem that network managers face with DOS clients is that unfortunately there's no mechanism for preventing the use of the DOS workstation if the name and password are entered incorrectly. Another problem is that unless the Guest account in Windows NT has been disabled, the DOS workstation will be able to access domain resources, even when they haven't entered a valid user name and password combination.

This occurs due to the method that Microsoft networks attempt to utilize remote resources. Since the client wasn't validated by a domain controller it's considered to be part of a workgroup, which as discussed earlier is responsible for its own security. When the user at the DOS workstation attempts to access a resource on Windows NT, NT will check to see if that user exists in the domain database. If the user does indeed exist in the domain database, then NT checks the users password. If they don't match the NT will prompt the user for the correct password. If they do match then the access is granted to the resource (assuming the user has the appropriate rights to access the resource). If the users name doesn't exist in the domain database, then NT attempts to log on and access the resource as the Guest account. A good rule of thumb is to make sure that the guest account is always disabled, unless you have a specific requirement to support guest level access.

Windows Clients and Security

Since Windows 3.x clients are using the Client 3.0 for DOS, they have much the same issues related to security as the DOS clients do, however Windows for Workgroups introduces a new level of complexity into network security issues. One of the biggest complaints surrounding Windows for Workgroups as a network client is its perceived lack of any type of local access control. When Windows for Workgroups is first started, the system will prompt you for your user name and password. The user name isn't checked against any access control list, so any user can gain access to the desktop, whether they have a valid logon ID or not. This poses a problem when there are locally installed applications that need to be protected. (It also poses a problem when the Guest account hasn't been disabled in NT server, as resources available to Guest will be available to any user who makes up a name to type in the Windows for Workgroups login dialog box.)

For this reason, I recommend that any applications that need protection be installed on the server.

Windows 95 Clients and Security

Next to Windows NT Workstation, Windows 95 clients are probably the most secure. Through the use of Windows 95 system policies a user at a Windows 95 workstation can be forced to input a valid Windows NT user name and password before the desktop is available.

Performance Issues

There are several issues related to the performance of your client platform should be considered before calling your installation complete. For the vast majority of your users, the only interaction that they ever have with the network is from the client workstation. If the workstation isn't configured optimally, the perception of the users won't be completely favorable. A network manager should make every effort to ensure that the clients are configured properly. One of the major things to understand here is that when you are using an existing version of Windows for Workgroups (ie one that was not installed from the Windows NT server CD-ROM) you must upgrade it using the upgrade provided on the NT server CD-ROM.

Other things that must be considered by the administrator include:

♦ Network Protocols—Every effort should be taken to limit the number of protocols installed on the network. This will ensure that the traffic on the network is essential to communication and not just "chatter".

♦ Upgraded Components—In most cases, software manufactureres are constantly updating their products to fix minor problems and improve performance and useability. The administrator should make an effort to ensure that these upgrades are installed as necessary.

♦ Workstation Memory—When working with DOS and Windows clients, every effort should be taken to maximize the workstations memory efficiency. Programs such as the DOS MEMMAKER program, and Quarterdeck's QEMM should be used whenever possible to load as many of the network drivers as possible into upper DOS memory. This will make more memory available to applications, which tends to make those applications work faster and more efficiently.

Ensuring that the above guidelines are followed will help your network operate at peak efficiency.

The following section discusses an upgrade to the shipping version of Windows for Workgroups that should be applied when using these clients to communicate with Windows NT Server.

Upgrading Windows for Workgroups Clients

Since the release of Windows for Workgroups, there have been many improvements to the network redirector portion, which exists as the file VREDIR.386 and is located in \WINDOWS\SYSTEM. Among these improvements are the abilities to browse a wide area network and to direct-host with Windows NT. Earlier versions of Windows for Workgroups can't browse beyond the subnet that they are attached to. Installing the upgraded redirector allows Windows for Workgroups to browse for network resources that exist on the entire network and not just their subnet. Direct hosting bypasses the NETBIOS layer to improve speed when Windows for Workgroups initiates a conversation with Windows NT. Direct hosting can improve client speed by about 20 percent.

Included with the Windows NT Server 4.0 CD-ROM, in the CLIENTS\UPDATE.WFW directory are the files required to upgrade an existing Windows for Workgroups installation. The major files in this upgrade are

- ◆ NDIS.386—The new NDIS 3.1 driver for Windows for Workgroups.
- ◆ NET.EXE—The upgraded NET TSR program.
- ◆ NETAPI.DLL—The upgraded windows networking API.
- ◆ NWNBLINK.386—The upgraded NetBIOS over NWLINK driver. This is the file that allows for Direct Hosting over NWLINK.
- ◆ VNETSUP.386—The upgraded network support driver.
- ◆ VREDIR.386—The upgraded redirector. This file is the main file for the upgrade.
- ◆ VSERVER.386—The upgraded server service. This is the file that supports file and print sharing on the workstation.

Simply copy these files to the WINDOWS\SYSTEM directory on your Windows for Workgroups clients and restart. (With the exception of NET.*, which needs to be copied to the WINDOWS directory)

Windows 95 clients participate in wide area network browsing and direct hosting by default, so there is no need to worry about upgrading existing Windows 95 workstations.

Where to Go Next

This chapter discusses how to use the Network Client Administrator to create a boot disk or a client installation disk set. It shows how to configure the available clients for optimal network participation. The chapter also described how to install Windows 95 to run from the NT server and how to upgrade existing Windows for Workgroups clients to take advantage of some of the new browsing features and direct hosting.

For more information you might want to examine the Windows 95 Resource kit, which will give you detailed information on installing and configuring Windows 95 for use in the NT domain. It also presents a full discussion of Windows 95 system policies and the interaction with Windows NT domains.

Other chapters in this book which might be of interest are

- ◆ Chapter 1, "Introducing Windows NT" which has more information on the evolution of Windows clients.

- ◆ Chapter 10, "Network Management Tools" which has more information on managing NT servers.

Chapter | 22

Interoperability with Novell NetWare

In This Chapter:

♦ Coexisting with Novell NetWare

♦ Configuring NT Server/NetWare Communications with NWLINK

♦ Accessing NetWare Resources with GSNW

♦ Accessing NT Resources from NetWare Clients with FPNW

♦ Migrating from Novell NetWare to NT Server

How do I...

An important question that most network managers face today is whether a single network operating environment will solve all their business problems. In most corporate environments, the answer to that question may be a resounding "No." Though the goal of network operating system (NOS) vendors is to handle all of their customers' needs, network managers find pros and cons to each of the network operating systems that should be considered fully before deciding which one to use.

The goal toward which network managers should strive is interoperability between the network operating system. Interoperability allows a network manager to bring the best of all worlds to his or her users, accomplishing the overall business goals for which the network was designed.

One of the major strengths that Microsoft brings to the table with Windows NT is the capacity to interoperate with Novell NetWare on several levels. This chapter discusses the following related topics:

♦ Reasons for interoperating with Novell NetWare, covering both Novell Directory Services (NDS) and the Novell Bindery

♦ The capability of Windows NT to migrate users from Novell environments

- ◆ Configuring Windows NT in a NetWare environment
- ◆ Tools for working with Windows NT and NetWare

Coexisting with Novell NetWare

Though the Microsoft "marketing machine" would have you believe that Novell NetWare is a declining NOS, the fact is that Novell still has an extremely healthy market share. For that reason, there's still a fair amount of support for the NetWare environment, as well as a fair number of applications that run only on NetWare.

Using Windows NT as an Application Server

One of the most popular uses of Windows NT in a NetWare environment is as an application server. The use of the NWLINK protocol makes NT an ideal candidate for application services, as no additional network configuration is required of the client. The NWLINK protocol is 100 percent compatible with Novell's IPX/SPX protocol, making the addition of NT as an application server extremely easy. Integration of NetWare and NT application servers is discussed later in this chapter.

Using NetWare as a File and Print Server

Though Microsoft has made tremendous advances with NT's file and print services, it's still hard to beat NetWare in raw file and print speed. Because users generally rate the usefulness of the network by the amount of time needed to perform the basic tasks of retrieving and saving files, and by the time needed to start applications that are stored on the server, you might consider distributing file and print tasks onto NetWare servers. Of course, this strategy requires you as the network manager to have a plan to manage both environments. Microsoft has made available several tools to facilitate connecting to NetWare file and print services, but first you must understand how NetWare manages access to those resources.

NetWare Bindery

NetWare versions prior to NetWare 4.x use a server-based database called the *bindery*. The bindery stores all user account information as well as security information related to files and printers. This database pertains to only one server. Each NetWare server maintains its own database independent of the other servers, which can lead to problems when changes are made that must affect all servers. When using bindery-based NetWare resources, you must treat each server as a separate entity.

NetWare Directory Services (NDS)

NetWare Version 4.x uses a directory called NetWare Directory Services (NDS) that is loosely based on the X.500 standard. This directory can exist on all NetWare 4.x servers in the network, making it global in nature. If a resource exists in the database, any user who also exists in the database and has rights to a resource can access it. Because this database is global in nature, it can get very complicated to identify and access resources. If you're attempting to attach to NDS from a Windows NT client or server, you must first understand how those resources are identified.

NetWare Directory Services follows the X.500 naming convention, which divides objects into three categories: [ROOT], container, and leaf. These objects are organized in a hierarchical format called the *directory tree*.

The [ROOT] object is the top of the database and is used mainly as a placeholder. The only objects that can exist in [ROOT] are container objects. Each directory tree has only one [ROOT] object.

Container objects are broken down into the classifications Country, Organization, and Organizational Unit, each with its own set of unique attributes:

- The *Country* container can exist only in [ROOT] and is generally used to denote the country in which the subordinate objects reside. The Country container is optional, and is rarely used. The Country container is designated with the C attribute.
- The *Organization* container can exist in either the [ROOT] object or the Country container and is generally used to represent a company. The Organization

container is the first level of the directory tree that can contain leaf objects. Organization containers are designated with the O attribute.

♦ The *Organizational Unit* container can exist in Organization containers or other Organizational Unit containers and is generally used to represent either a business unit or a geographical location. Within a large NDS directory tree, the Organizational Unit container is the container type used most often. Organizational Unit containers are designated by the OU attribute.

Leaf objects represent network resources, such as users, file servers, hard disk volumes, printers, and so on. Leaf objects can exist in either Organization or Organizational Unit containers, and are designated with the CN (common name) attribute. The *full context name* of a leaf object is a combination of that object's common name and location in the directory tree. The full context name is sometimes referred to as the object's *address*. NDS uses a "bottom up" approach to identifying network resources. For example, to represent a user called User1, who is a member of the Administration team in Acme Corporation's Widgets division in North America, we might structure the tree like the tree shown in Figure 22-1. The resulting address of that user would be as follows:

```
CN=User1.OU=Administration.OU=WIDGETS.O=ACME.C=US
```

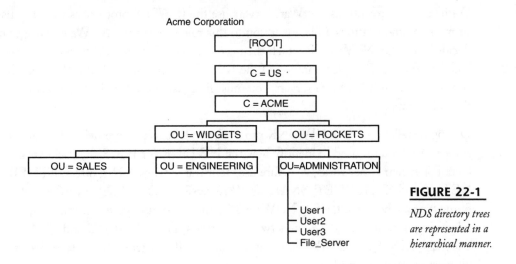

FIGURE 22-1

NDS directory trees are represented in a hierarchical manner.

To maintain backward compatibility with previous versions of NetWare, Version 4.x is capable of making resources that exist in the directory tree available to clients who can't communicate via directory services. This feature is known as *bindery emulation*. Bindery emulation is configured at the NetWare 4.x server console via a SET command, which points to the container (or containers) that you want to make available to bindery clients. In the example just cited, if you wanted to make all resources in the Administration container available to bindery clients, you would use this command at the NetWare console:

```
SET BINDERY CONTEXT=OU=ADMINISTRATION.OU=WIDGETS.O=ACME.C=US
```

> **CAUTION:** It's very important for the NT system administrator to understand the concept of bindery context, due to the fact that the Gateway Service for NetWare requires the use of bindery emulation on the NetWare server.

Configuring NT Server/NetWare Communications with NWLINK

With very few exceptions, NetWare servers use the IPX/SPX protocol as their mechanism of communications. (The exception to this rule is when the NetWare manager has decided to install NetWare IP, which then uses the TCP/IP protocol to communicate.) The Windows NT implementation of the IPX/SPX protocol is called *NWLINK.*. To communicate with NetWare servers, you must first install the NWLINK protocol on the NT server.

During installation of the NWLINK protocol, you'll be asked to provide the frame type. *Frame type* is a term used to identify how the NWLINK (or IPX/SPX) packet is assembled. For Ethernet networks, NetWare uses four frame types: 802.2, 802.3, ETHERNET_II, and ETHERNET_SNAP. NetWare version 3.11 and earlier used the 802.3 frame type as the default, while NetWare 3.12 and above use the 802.2 frame type. For token ring networks, NetWare uses two frame types, TOKEN_RING and TOKEN_RING_SNAP. It's important to note that the different frame types won't communicate with each another.

By default, Windows NT uses the Auto Detect frame type, where NT tries to determine what frame type is in use on the network by sending out a packet on each frame type, and setting the frame type to the first reply it receives. You must be very careful when using the Auto Detect frame type, especially if many different frame types are active on your network, because NT's Auto Detect algorithm does not sample the network and determine what the best frame type to use is, it simply sends out a packet on a given frame type and waits for an answer. The first answer it receives is the frame type that it choses. This can cause problems if you have some devices (such as HP Jet Direct print servers) that are configured to use multiple frame types, and your network servers use a specific frame type.

Installing NWLINK is a relatively simple procedure :

1. Open the Network dialog box (double-click the Network icon in Control Panel, or right-click the Network Neighborhood icon on the desktop and choose Properties from the pop-up menu). Figure 22-2 shows the Network dialog box. This figure displays a server with TCP/IP already installed.

2. On the Protocols tab, click Add to display the Select Network Protocol dialog box shown in Figure 22-3. Select the NWLINK IPX/SPX Compatible Transport and choose OK.

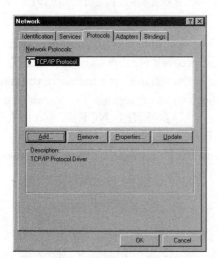

FIGURE 22-2

The Network dialog box enables you to install the NWLINK protocol.

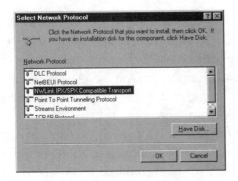

FIGURE 22-3

Selecting the NWLINK IPX/SPX Compatible Transport.

3. Verify the location of the Windows NT Server installation files; then choose Continue. The system copies the required files and then prompts you to restart the system.

> **CAUTION:** *Do not* restart the system—there are still some parameter settings that you need to verify.

4. The Network Settings dialog box reappears. Select the NWLINK protocol and click the Properties button to post a dialog box for configuring NWLINK (see Figure 22-4).

   This dialog box enables you to specify the advanced configuration options related to NWLINK, such as frame type and network number (see Figure 22-5). If you are going to specify the network number and frame type manually, you must ensure the number you specify is valid. You can determine the correct value to use by examining the NetWare server's AUTOEXEC.NCF file and look for a line containing the BIND command (for example, BIND IPX NE2000 NET=4E). The number following the NET= statement will be the network number that you should use.

> **NOTE:** Normally, you wouldn't need to change any of these options; however, you may want to specify the frame type and network numbers manually. Here's why.
>
> NetWare servers identify themselves by a combination of their internal IPX network number, the external network number, and the MAC address of the network adapter attached to that network. The external network number is defined by the network

manager and is common to all NetWare servers on that network segment. By default, Windows NT attempts to determine this number automatically by examining network traffic and extracting the network number from any received packets. This method works very well while there are NetWare clients and servers on a segment when the NT server is brought online.

However, when NT can't detect any packets on the network that contain network addresses (when the NetWare servers are offline), it chooses a random number for the external network number. This system works fine in a pristine NT environment, but when the NetWare servers come back online, they report a router configuration error because the external network number has been randomly assigned by NT and—unless you're extremely lucky—won't match the hard-coded network number in the NetWare servers configuration files. This problem can be solved by hard-coding the external network number for the NWLINK protocol.

5. After selecting the options you want, close the dialog boxes; then shut down and restart your system. Installation and configuration of NWLINK is complete.

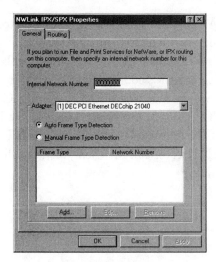

FIGURE 22-4

Here you can configure the various options related to the NWLINK protocol.

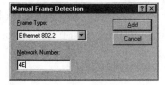

FIGURE 22-5

Configuring the frame type and network number manually.

Accessing NetWare Resources with GSNW

Once the NWLINK protocol has been installed successfully on the NT server, you need to determine how you want to access the resources that exist on the NetWare server. Microsoft-network-based clients use a protocol known as *Server Message Blocks* (*SMB*) to access resources, while NetWare-based clients use *NetWare Core Protocol* (*NCP*). Because most of the clients discussed in Chapter 21, "Working with Windows and DOS Clients," are capable of utilizing both SMB and NCP (the only client platform that isn't capable of using NCP is the Client 3.0 for DOS and Windows), you may consider installing redirectors for both operating systems at the client. Though this action seems to be an ideal solution, note that each redirector takes up client resources such as memory and processing power, and adds to network traffic.

One option that you have is to utilize the Gateway Service for NetWare to provide access to NCP resources from SMB clients. This will allow your NT clients to access NetWare resources without the overhead and traffic generated by an additional network redirector.

The Gateway Service for NetWare (GSNW) enables Windows NT managers to provide access to NetWare resources from clients that don't have any NetWare redirectors installed. GSNW allows network managers to minimize the number of protocols in use on the network by requiring only the NT server that is configured for GSNW to support NWLINK. The client computers that will be accessing resources through GSNW don't require NWLINK. (Unless NWLINK is the only protocol running on the NT server.) In other words, as long as the NWLINK protocol is installed on the NT server and a common protocol exists between the NT server and the client, then the client will be able to access NetWare resources via GSNW.

Installing GSNW

To install GSNW, follow these steps :

1. Open the Network dialog box (double-click the Network icon in Control Panel, or right-click the Network Neighborhood icon on the desktop and choose Properties from the pop-up menu). On the Services tab, choose <u>A</u>dd (see Figure 22-6).

2. Select Gateway (and Client) Services for NetWare, as shown in Figure 22-7. Then choose OK.

FIGURE 22-6

The Services dialog box allows you to add additional services, such as the Gateway Service for NetWare.

FIGURE 22-7

Selecting NetWare services.

3. Provide the location to the Windows NT Server installation files and choose Continue. The system copies the appropriate files and returns you to the Network dialog box. Choose Close, and then allow the system to restart.

4. After the system restarts and you enter your login information, you're prompted to select your default NetWare server via the Preferred Server dialog box shown in Figure 22-8. If a user on a NetWare server or within an NDS tree has the same name under which you've logged into NT, you can select the appropriate server or tree at this point; otherwise, select None. If the user trying to logon to NT does not have an account on the preferred NetWare server, the system

displays a dialog box that tells the user that he or she could not be authenticated to the server. The dialog box does not identify the server that the user can't be authenticated by, so the user can be quite confused by this dialog.

The Gateway Service for NetWare is now installed.

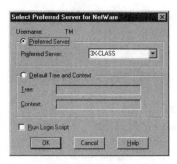

FIGURE 22-8

Configuring Windows NT Server to log into NetWare.

Configuring GSNW

Prior to configuring the GSNW service, you must first configure the NetWare server by creating a user account either on the server you want to access or in the bindery context of the NetWare 4.x server you want to access. This account must be a member of the NTGATEWAY group, which needs to be created in the same location as the user account.

Once GSNW is installed, it must be configured to allow access to NetWare resources. Follow these steps:

1. Open My Computer and select GSNW to open the Gateway Service for NetWare dialog box (see Figure 22-9).

2. Select the desired options. These options configure the client portion of the GSNW service, as well as the printing features. The following list describes the printing options:

   ◆ Add Form Feed—Select this box when you want to send a form feed at the completion of every print job. This feature allows the printer to eject partially completed pages from the printer.

   ◆ Notify When Printed—Select this box when you want to send a message to any user who prints a document on a NetWare printer connected via the Gateway Service.

- ◆ Print Banner—Select this option when you want to print a banner page before every print job. This isn't a very good option, though—the user who is listed on the banner page is the user who is configured to attach to the NetWare server and not the user who actually sent the print job.

FIGURE 22-9

The Gateway Service for NetWare configuration dialog allows you to specify various options related to the GSNW service.

3. Choose Gateway to post the Configure Gateway dialog box shown in Figure 22-10. In the Gateway Account text box, type the name of the user that you want to act as the gateway account. If you're accessing NetWare 3.x resources, provide the name of a user who exists on the server to which you're connecting. If you are accessing NetWare 4.x resources, provide the name of a user who exists in the bindery context of that server.

FIGURE 22-10

Configuring the account to be used to access NetWare resources.

4. Enter the password for this user in the Password field. (Note that this user *does not* need to have a valid account in Windows NT.)

5. Choose <u>A</u>dd to open the New Share dialog box shown in Figure 22-11.

FIGURE 22-11

Configuring Windows NT Server to access NetWare resources.

6. Provide a name for the shared resource. This name is the share that will be associated with the NT Server—but point to the path specified on the NetWare server. When entering the path to the share, you must use UNC names to reference the NetWare resources, for example to reference the APPS directory that exists on the SYS: volume of the NetWare server FS1, you would use \\FS1\SYS\APPS as the UNC reference. (Note that the : is dropped from the volume name).

7. (Optional) Supply a comment that will show up when clients attempt to browse the NT Server.

8. Select a drive letter to use and set the user limit if desired.

9. Choose OK to close the dialog box and return to the Configure Gateway dialog box. Then choose <u>P</u>ermissions to bring up the Access Through Share Permissions dialog box shown in Figure 22-12.

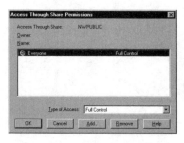

FIGURE 22-12

Securing access to NetWare resources via the Access through Share Permissions dialog box.

10. Choose the appropriate permissions.

11. Close the dialog boxes. The Gateway Service for NetWare is now configured and ready to use.

Understanding GSNW Resource Paths

NetWare bindery-based servers use a very interesting method of representing file system resources. Each volume is identified by a name, and the resource is located by specifying a combination of the volume name and its path on that volume. For example, PUBLIC is a directory that exists as a subdirectory of the SYS volume on all NetWare servers. If you want to provide access to this directory via the GSNW service, you enter *servername*\sys*public* as the path to the share.

NetWare servers utilizing Directory Services represent resources in a different manner. Each volume is identified by its object name within the database. The NetWare manager can use a "friendly name" to specify a volume's location. Assuming that the PUBLIC directory physically exists on the SYS volume on a NetWare 4.x server called NW1, the NetWare manager could create a *volume object* in the directory tree called NW1_SYS (any name could be used, but this format is the most common).

Assuming that the object exists in the Administration container of the ACME tree (using the earlier example from Figure 22-1), the UNC name for this object as specified by Windows NT would be as follows:

```
\\ACME\CN=NW1_SYS\OU=ADMINISTRATION\
➥ OU=WIDGETS\O=ACME\C=US\PUBLIC
```

Obviously, specifying the resource using the physical name would be easier: *nw1*\sys*public*. For this reason, GSNW always uses the physical path to the resource.

Accessing GSNW Resources

The beauty of using GSNW is that users never realize that the resources that they're accessing aren't located on Windows NT. When connecting to the gateway, they specify the server name of the GSNW server and the share name that you have specified. For example, your NT server is named NT1 and you have created a share called NWDATA via the GSNW service, your users would reference that directory by attaching to \\NT1\NWDATA, even though that directory actually exists on a NetWare server somewhere else. The same is true of printers, if you have a printer configured on your NT server that actually points to a NetWare print queue, your users need only know the name of your server and the printer's name in order to access it.

Accessing NT Resources from NetWare Clients with FPNW

Since it's probably true that most of the desktop clients in the corporate world today are NetWare-based, it would make sense to have a method of allowing those clients access to NT resources. Microsoft has introduced an add-on product for Windows NT called *File and Print Services for NetWare* (*FPNW*). This product retails for $99 and can be ordered directly from Microsoft.

When installed on an NT server, FPNW acts as an abstraction layer between the NCP client and the SMB server. FPNW receives the client's request via NCP, translates the request to SMB, sends it to the appropriate resource manager, translates the received reply to NCP, and returns it to the client. In essence, FPNW configures an NT server to "look and feel" exactly like a NetWare server. As a matter of fact, the client never realizes that the resource is located on anything other than a NetWare server.

FPNW is best suited for use when you plan to completely migrate your NetWare-based network to NT, but for any number of reasons want to keep the NetWare client platforms in place for a period of time. FPNW is also a good tool to use when your client workstations don't have the resources required to run a Microsoft-based networking client.

Installing FPNW

Installing FPNW is done via the Network Services tab within the Network dialog box. Follow these steps:

1. Open the Network dialog box by double-clicking the Network icon in Control Panel or by right-clicking the Network Neighborhood icon and choosing Properties from the pop-up menu.

2. Click the Services tab, the Add button, and then the Have Disk button.

3. Type the path to the installation point for FPNW and press Enter

   This brings you to the Select OEM Option dialog box (see Figure 22-13), which allows you to add components to Windows NT that are not part of the basic operating system.

FIGURE 22-13

The Select OEM Option dialog box enables you to add additional components to NT Server.

4. You are presented with 2 options here. Select File and Print Services for NetWare to install FPNW on this server, or choose File and Print Services for NetWare administrative tools only if you just want to install the tools to manage FPNW.; then choose OK. The files for the selected option will be copied to the appropriate directories, the Registry modified to include the FPNW options, and the management tools changed to include the FPNW extensions.

Once the system is finished copying files, the Install File and Print Services for NetWare dialog box appears, as shown in Figure 22-14. The options allow you to control the appearance of the FPNW server to NetWare clients, and what information will be available to those clients.

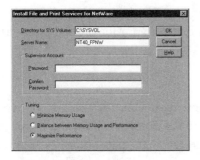

FIGURE 22-14

Use this dialog box to con-figure the various FPNW options related to the appearance of FPNW to NetWare clients.

5. Specify the appropriate directory on which to create the SYS volume. The SYS volume is where NetWare-specific information and tools will be stored. The default directory of C:\SYSVOL is okay, but you may want to make sure that this directory is stored on an NTFS partition. (If it isn't stored on NTFS, no permissions can be assigned, which allows all NetWare clients full access to the files contained there.)

6. Specify a name for the server. This name will be visible only to NetWare clients; it's the name they'll use to reference the server. You may want to use the name of an existing NetWare server from which you have migrated.

7. Assign a password to the Supervisor user. The Supervisor will have full rights to all files and directories under control of FPNW, so make sure that this password is secure.

8. If your FPNW server won't be used often, select the option <u>M</u>inimize Memory Usage; otherwise, select the default setting for memory. This option determines the percentage of RAM that will be set aside for file cache for the FPNW service.

9. After you're finished selecting options, close the dialog boxes.

   The system will review the bindings and then prompt you to restart the system. After the system has been restarted, you're ready to move on to configuring FPNW.

Configuring FPNW Services

You configure the FPNW service using the standard Windows NT administration tools. The following discussion details how prepare a Server to provide file and print services for NetWare Users..

Follow these steps:

1. To verify that FPNW was installed correctly, double-click the FPNW icon in Control Panel. This action brings you to the dialog box shown in Figure 22-15. (Notice the number of supported connections- it's quite a surprise to have a NetWare 3.x look-alike that supports more than 250 users.) Here you can configure several options:

   ◆ FPNW Server <u>N</u>ame—The name that NetWare clients use to reference the NT server running FPNW.

   ◆ <u>D</u>escription—A text description of the server that allows you to track it by listing a description in the browser that the clients will see when browsing the server.

FIGURE 22-15

Use this dialog box to confirm the installation of FPNW and to set various options related to the service.

- Ho**m**e Directory Root Path—When a user is created using the NetWare SYSCON utility, it uses this path as the base path for that directory.

- Default Queue—When a NetWare user issues the CAPTURE command without any options, this is the print queue to which he will attach.

- Allow New Users to Login—Enables or disables the ability of NetWare clients to attach to the NT server. This option doesn't affect existing users.

- Respond to Find_Nearest_Server Requests—Determines whether FPNW will advertise itself to clients looking for a NetWare server to attach to run the LOGIN command.

- Click the Users button to see a list of users who are currently logged on, as well as what they're accessing, as shown in Figure 22-16. Here you can disconnect a specific user, disconnect all users, or send a message to connected users, as shown in Figure 22-17.

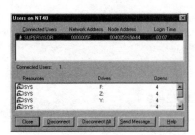

FIGURE 22-16

The Users dialog box enables you to view a list of connected users, disconnect them, and send messages to them.

◆ Use the <u>V</u>olumes button to see a list of available volumes and which users are accessing them, as shown in Figure 22-18.

FIGURE 22-17

Use the Send Message dialog box to send a message to a specific user or to all users.

FIGURE 22-18

Viewing currently-accessible volumes and which users are accessing them.

2. Change the settings as desired; then choose OK to close the dialog box.

3. Select the Network icon in Control Panel to open the Network dialog box.

4. Click the Services tab, select File and Print Services for NetWare, and click the <u>P</u>roperties button. This action displays the properties configuration for FPNW.

5. Click the Advanced button to open the Advanced Settings dialog box shown in Figure 22-19. Here you configure the frame type, network number, and adapters that use the FPNW service.

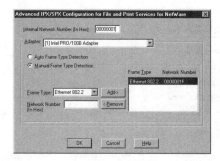

FIGURE 22-19

Here you can manually specify critical options, such as frame type and network numbers.

Configuring FPNW Users

When FPNW was installed, it modified the User Manager for Domains to take advantage of FPNW configuration items. A user who accesses resources as a NetWare client will need to have the right to log onto NT as a NetWare client. Set this up by accessing the user's properties and selecting the Maintain NetWare Compatible Login option in the User Properties dialog box.

You'll also notice a new button at the bottom of the dialog box: NW Compat (see Figure 22-20). Selecting this button brings you to the NetWare Compatible Properties dialog box shown in Figure 22-21.

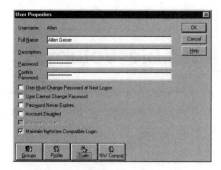

FIGURE 22-20

FPNW adds some extensions to the User Manager for Domains, including the NW Compat button.

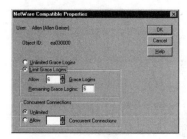

FIGURE 22-21

Configuring NetWare-compatible login parameters.

Here you can configure several NetWare-specific parameters for users:

  ◆ When a user's password expires, NetWare generally allows the user a certain number of logins in which to use the old password and not change it. This is called a *grace login*. If you want to allow grace logins for NetWare clients, specify the number of logins.

♦ NetWare enables you to configure the number of simultaneous logins that a user can use. Specify the desired number in the Concurrent Connections section of the dialog box.

Once you have set the appropriate NetWare restrictions, the user will be able to log into Windows NT just as if she were logging into NetWare.

> **NOTE:** All the options configured with User Manager for Domains can be accomplished through the NetWare SYSCON utility as well. This makes it easy for the NetWare administrator to modify accounts that "belong" to them, or allows a NetWare administrator to create an account on NT using tools that they are familiar with.

Configuring NetWare-Compatible Volumes

Before NetWare clients can access NT resources, you must configure NetWare-compatible volumes for them to access. You can use the Server Manager or File Manager to accomplish this task (see Figure 22-22).

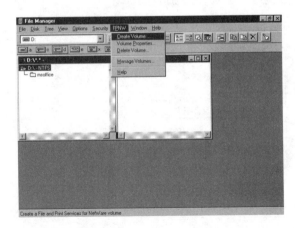

FIGURE 22-22

Using File Manager to manage FPNW file attributes.

> **TIP:** To access File Manager, choose Start | Run, type WinFile, and press Enter.

From File Manager's main screen, choose FPNW | Manage Volumes to display the Manage Volumes dialog box shown in Figure 22-23.

FIGURE 22-23

The Manage Volumes dialog box enables you to configure NetWare-accessible volumes and their properties.

You can choose from the following options:

- Create Volume—This option brings up another dialog box (see Figure 22-24). Here you can create a special share that relates to a NetWare-compatible volume and allows NetWare clients to access it as if it existed on a NetWare server. These are the available options in the Create Volume dialog box:

  - Volume Name—The name that NetWare clients will use to access this volume.

  - Path—The path on the NT server to which this volume points.

  - Permissions—The security assigned to the root of the volume.

  - User Limit—The number of concurrent users that can use this volume.

FIGURE 22-24

Creating a NetWare accessible volume.

- Properties—Choosing the Properties button in the Volumes dialog box displays yet another dialog box, which allows you to change the properties of existing NetWare-accessible volumes.

- Remove Volume—This button enables you to delete any NetWare-accessible volumes on the system.

The NetWare-accessible volume is nothing more than a shared directory that is advertised to NetWare clients. It should be treated just like any other shared directory on your system and rights should be assigned appropriately. To NT clients these directories are simply available directories; however, to NetWare clients, these are the ONLY directories made available.

Using Server Manager to Manage FPNW

Server Manager can be used to manage all aspects of NetWare file and print services on your NT machine. Server Manager is very convenient because it allows you to manage not only your local FPNW properties, but also the FPNW properties of any servers in your network that are running FPNW (see Figure 22-25).

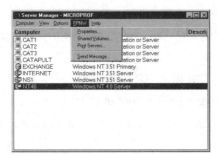

FIGURE 22-25

Server Manager allows you to manage FPNW servers throughout the enterprise.

The FPNW menu provides some useful options. The dialog box displayed when you choose the Properties option allows you to view the current configuration parameters of FPNW as well as change the name of the server (refer to Figure 22-15). Choosing Shared Volumes opens another familiar dialog box (refer to Figure 22-23). You can view the current status of the NetWare-compatible volumes, such as users attached and files opened. This dialog also enables you to create and remove NetWare volumes.

> **NOTE:** Even though you have created and configured NT printing, these printers are not available to NetWare clients until you have created a NetWare-compatible print server and a NetWare-compatible printer.

Choose the Print Servers option when you want to create NetWare-compatible print services. The system displays the Print Configuration dialog box shown in Figure 22-26.

FIGURE 22-26

Configuring NetWare-compatible print services.

This dialog box gives you a number of options. Use Add to create a new NetWare-compatible print server, which allows NetWare clients to print to NewWare-compatible printers (if they exist on the system). Remove allows you to remove any existing NetWare-compatible print servers.

If you want to protect your print server with a password, assign it with the Password button. (Remember that the print server logs on as a user, and be very careful. If the print server can't log on, the users can't print.)

Clicking the Printers button opens the Printers dialog box, where you can create NetWare-compatible printers, which are required for NetWare printing (see Figure 22-27).

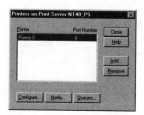

FIGURE 22-27

The Printers dialog box allows you to configure the options related to specific NetWare-compatible printers.

You can choose from a number of options when creating a printer:

◆ Add—Allows you to add a new printer via the Add Printer dialog box shown in Figure 22-28. Set the configuration options for this printer that are specific to NetWare. In the Printer text box, for example, specify the name of the printer as it will be used by NetWare users and the CAPTURE command. The queue service mode indicates how the print server handles incorrect form identifiers. The other options should be familiar.

♦ Remove—Allows you to delete an existing printer.

♦ Configure—Enables you to reconfigure an existing printer.

♦ Notify—Posts the Notify List shown in Figure 22-29, where you can specify whom to notify when a problem occurs.

♦ Queues—Specifies which NT printers are attached to the NetWare-compatible printers. (see Figure 22-30).

FIGURE 22-28

Adding a new printer to the NetWare-compatible printers list.

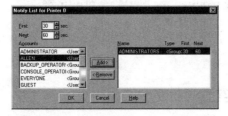

FIGURE 22-29

Use the Notify List to specify which users are notified when errors occur.

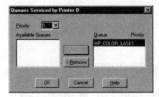

FIGURE 22-30

Indicating which NT printers are assigned to NetWare clients.

Once these options are configured, your NetWare clients will be able to access your NT resources as if they were NetWare resources. This makes for an easy migration path should you decide to move the NetWare servers to NT.

Migrating from Novell NetWare to NT Server

Though NetWare is a fast file and print server, you may find that the hassle of managing separate environments isn't worth the performance that you gain by staying with it. For this reason, Microsoft provides the NT manager with a very clear migration path from NetWare, and a tool called the *Migration Tool for NetWare* that facilitates this migration. The Migration Tool for NetWare allows an NT administrator to transfer user accounts and data from NetWare servers to a Windows NT server.

Philosophically speaking, you should think very hard before you decide to use a tool such as the Migration Tool for NetWare. Though this tool does indeed make the migration process go much more smoothly, consider the fact that moving from one network operating system to another might make for a good excuse to clean up some of the "fixes" that have inevitably found their way into your current operating environment. Using this migration tool will simply migrate those fixes over, leaving you with much the same problems in your new environment. It's generally a good idea to just start over and not consider migrating, unless of course you have a lot of data and users that need to be moved and very few changes that need to occur. In spite of these drawbacks, the migration tool is very handy when moving large groups of users or a large amount of data with minimal administrative overhead.

TIP: If you decide to keep your NetWare servers in place and distribute some of the file and print services to them, you'll need some method of managing both environments from a single location. Microsoft has taken this into consideration and created an add-on product called *Directory Service Manager for NetWare* (*DSMN*) which is available from Microsoft for $99.

DSMN allows NT administrators to copy account information from multiple NetWare servers to a single domain controller, and to control which accounts are propagated back to which NetWare servers. This feature lets you implement a single network login for all clients, which simplifies the lives of your users.

continues

Tip continued

Before installing and running DSMN, you should first follow some simple guidelines for account propagation:

♦ Make sure that the NetWare server's bindery is backed up properly. Good backups are always a rule when changing anything on your NOS.

♦ Determine which accounts will be propagated. You may not want all accounts to be propagated, as only users who have accounts on both NetWare and NT will benefit from DSMN.

♦ Resolve duplicate account names. You may want to run a trial migration from the server(s) that you want to manage via DSMN; this will help you to resolve duplicate names.

Once you have taken these items into consideration, you are ready to install and configure DSMN.

Using the Migration Tool for NetWare

Before starting the Migration Tool for NetWare, make sure that you are logged into NT as a user who has supervisory access to the NetWare server that you want to migrate, and that the Gateway Service for NetWare is installed and configured properly.

To access the Migration Tool for NetWare, choose Start | Programs | Administrative Tools. This action brings up the Migration configuration utility . The utility first asks you for the name of the NetWare server from which you want to migrate and then the name of the NT domain controller to which you're migrating (see Figure 22-31).

FIGURE 22-31

Selecting the NetWare server from which to migrate. You must be able to log into this server as a supervisor.

Configuring the Migration

Once you have specified the source and destination servers, the main Migration Tool for NetWare dialog box opens, as shown in Figure 22-32.

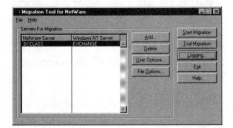

FIGURE 22-32

The Migration Tool for NetWare main configuration dialog enables you to specify all of the options related to migration.

The Add option in this dialog box adds servers to migrate from or to. Normally you will migrate one server at a time, but if you are a very brave soul you can migrate more than one server at a time. The Delete option obviously deletes servers from the migration list.

The User Options button brings up the User and Group Options dialog box (see Figure 22-33).

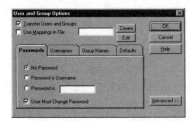

FIGURE 22-33

Controlling how users are migrated into NT.

This dialog box has its own set of options:

♦ Transfer Users and Groups—If you just want to migrate files and directories, deselect this option.

♦ Use Mappings in File—If you want to create a text file that maps specific users to specific groups and contains a specific password, select this option and click the Create box.

◆ Passwords—The options on this tab allow you to configure exactly how passwords are handled. Because NT can't read NetWare passwords, the password can't be migrated. The resulting Passwords dialog box has the following options:

   ◆ No Password—This option leaves the NT users' password blank.

   ◆ Password is Username—This option creates a password for the NT user that is identical to her username.

   ◆ Password is—This option allows you to specify the password of the NT user. Remember that this option is global for all users created during the migration.

   ◆ User must change password—This option forces the user to change his password the first time he logs onto NT.

◆ Usernames—The options on this tab allow you to configure exactly how user names are handled during the migration (see Figure 22-34):

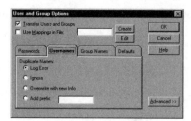

FIGURE 22-34

The Usernames tab allows you to take complete control over how users are migrated into the system.

   ◆ Log Error—This option causes an error to be written to the log file when a duplicate user account is encountered during the migration.

   ◆ Ignore—This option causes the migration tool to ignore any duplicate accounts and continue processing.

   ◆ Overwrite with New Info—This option causes the migration tool to overwrite any duplicate accounts with the new account. Any existing properties for that account will be lost.

   ◆ Add Prefix—Adds to any duplicate accounts a specific prefix that you select (for example: Jsmith, Jsmith1).

◆ Group Names—The options on this tab allow you to configure exactly how groups are handled during the migration (see Figure 22-35):

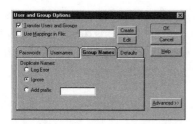

FIGURE 22-35

The Group Names tab allows you to configure exactly how groups are migrated into the system.

- ◆ Log Error—This option causes an error to be written to the log file when a duplicate group is encountered during the migration.

- ◆ Ignore—This option causes the migration tool to ignore any duplicate accounts and continue processing.

- ◆ Add Prefix—Adds a specified prefix to any duplicate groups.

◆ Defaults—The options on this tab allow you to specify exactly how the system handles NetWare-specific account information that isn't normally compatible with Windows NT (see Figure 22-36).

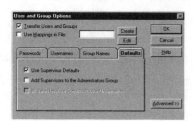

FIGURE 22-36

The Defaults options allow you to configure how NetWare-specific information is handled.

- ◆ Use Supervisor Defaults—This option allows you to specify whether to use the NetWare account restrictions or the Windows NT account restrictions. NetWare sets account restrictions (password expiration, and so on) on an account basis, whereas NT sets them globally. Selecting this option maintains the NetWare-specific account restrictions.

- ◆ Add Supervisors to Administrators Group—This option allows you to specify whether any user who has security equivalent to the Supervisor can be added to the Administrators group.

◆ Advanced—Selecting this button allows you to transfer the accounts to any trusted domains.

Once you have selected all desired user options, choose OK to return to the main migration options. Then choose File Options to open the File Options dialog box shown in Figure 22-37, which allows you to select which files and directories you want to migrate, and their destinations.

FIGURE 22-37

Here you can specify which files to migrate from the NetWare server.

These are the file options:

- ◆ Files—Allows you to specify the files before starting the migration.
- ◆ Add—Allows you to add new files to be migrated.
- ◆ Delete—Allows you to delete any files that were previously selected.
- ◆ Modify—Selecting this option brings up the Modify Destinations dialog box (see Figure 22-38), where you can select the destination options:
  - ◆ Share or New Share—These options allow you to modify the shared directory into which the files will be migrated, including creating a new directory and sharing it.
  - ◆ Subdirectory—Specifies how files will be copied into the share. You can copy just the directory or the entire tree.

FIGURE 22-38

The Modify Destination dialog box allows you to select the options pertaining to the shared directories on NT Server that will receive migrated files.

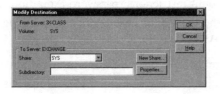

Running a Trial Migration

After selecting the files that you want to migrate (see Figure 22-39), click OK to return to the main migration options. At this point, you're ready to test your migration by running a trial migration. The trial migration allows you to correct any errors before running the migration.

FIGURE 22-39

The Files to Transfer dialog allows you to specify which files and directories are going to be copied.

Select the Trial Migration button to start the trial migration, as shown in Figure 22-40. The system simulates a migration by attaching to the NetWare server and activating the options that you have selected.

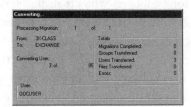

FIGURE 22-40

Running a trial migration.

Once the trial migration is completed, the Transfer Completed dialog box appears, as shown in Figure 22-41. This dialog box gives you a summary of the actions performed and allows you to view the migration log files, as shown in Figure 22-42.

FIGURE 22-41

The Transfer Completed dialog box gives a summary report on what happened during the trial migration.

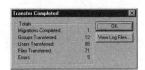

FIGURE 22-42

The log files allow you to view the details of the trial migration.

You may have to run several trial migrations to clean up errors and ensure that your real migration will run properly. Some of the more common errors that might occur are duplicate user accounts, or accounts that exist currently in both NT and NetWare. These errors can be minimized by ensuring that the user accounts are indeed unique between NT and NetWare prior to the migration.

Running a Live Migration

Once you have cleaned up the errors during the trial migration, you're ready to run a live migration. The first step here would be to force all users who are using NetWare to log out, type the NetWare console command **Disable Login** so that new users aren't allowed into the system, and ensure that no users are attempting to access the shared directory on NT into which you'll be migrating. Once you have accomplished these steps, you're ready to start. Make sure that you have selected the appropriate logging options (see Figure 22-43) so that any new errors that have popped up will be completely documented. After you've set the logging options, start the migration by selecting Start Migration.

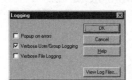

FIGURE 22-43

Use verbose logging during the migration to ensure that any new errors can be handled after the migration.

Once the migration is complete, you're ready to move forward in deciding how to handle existing NetWare clients. One method might be to leave the existing clients as they are, rename the FPNW server name to use the same name as the NetWare server, shut down the NetWare server, and make sure that the clients can still operate. This strategy gives you the ability to upgrade the clients to NT-based network at your leisure.

Where to Go Next

This chapter described how to co-exist with NetWare and migrate NetWare servers to NT (if the need arises) in a cost-effective manner. For additional information you might like to review:

◆ Chapter 2, "Understanding the NT Architecture," for more information on the NT architecture.

◆ Chapter 6, "Managing User and group Accounts," for more information on Managing Windows NT.

◆ Chapter 7, "Printer Management," for more information on managing printers.

Chapter | 23

Interoperating with Macintosh Clients

In This Chapter:

- ◆ Using the Services for Macintosh Package
- ◆ Installing Services for Macintosh
- ◆ Sharing Disks and Files with Macintosh Users
- ◆ Sharing Printers with Macintosh Users
- ◆ Sending Notifications to Macintosh Users
- ◆ Services for Macintosh Security Issues

How do I...

Despite continual press reports of its impending demise, Apple continues to produce Macintoshes and sell them to users all over the world. As of this writing, Apple just gave its 25 millionth Macintosh to an elementary school teacher. While the Mac isn't as common in the business world as Intel-based machines, it's still common to find islands of Macs on networks. These islands are typically made up of machines used for software development, graphic design, publishing, Internet content development, or other areas where the Mac's special talents make it valuable.

However, these islands often need to be integrated with the rest of their network neighbors. Although Macs can seamlessly read and write FAT floppies, networks are a much more efficient medium of exchange, especially because they also allow services like e-mail and video conferencing—hard to do those with floppies! This integration can proceed in two directions. First, you can install software on your Windows for Workgroups or Windows 95 clients to let them access files served from a Mac. There's relatively little software available to do this, however, and as of this writing none of it works on Windows NT anyway. The second, more popular, route is to use NT's Services for Macintosh package.

Services for Macintosh allows NTS machines to export NTFS volumes and printers so Macintosh users can use them without any changes on the Mac client side. This strategy is similar to the approach Microsoft has taken for its NetWare compatibility services; in most cases, it's much easier to configure a small number of servers than to install new software on every client on a network.

This chapter describes

+ How to install and use the Services for Macintosh software on your Windows NT Server computers

+ How to share files and printers between Windows and Mac clients

+ What security settings and precautions you should apply

Using the Services for Macintosh Package

Microsoft provides Macintosh compatibility in NTS via the Services for Macintosh package. This package actually contains several components that work together to make your NTS machines capable of communicating using the AppleTalk networking protocols. In addition, Services for Macintosh provides routing, file, and print services to AppleTalk clients by translating AppleTalk requests into the standard SMB protocol used by Windows Networking.

Mixing Macintosh and PC Network Clients

The Mac introduced the concept of inexpensive, easy-to-use peer networking. In 1984, you could network Macs and printers together with $15 cables and the operating system had file-access and sharing capabilities built in. However, both the Mac and PC networking worlds have changed significantly since then.

Most likely you won't have to make any changes to accommodate Mac clients on your network. Most Macs sold since 1994 have Ethernet on the motherboard. Those that don't can use an add-in NIC just like a PC. You can configure the Mac clients to use Ethernet as the medium for the AppleTalk protocol (this combination's called EtherTalk); when you do, Macs will be able to use TCP/IP and AppleTalk services on your network. If you're running a TokenRing network, you can run TokenTalk over it instead.

You may find that some of your Macs are using LocalTalk, Apple's original networking system. You can make them work on your network in several ways:

- Put a LocalTalk-capable NIC in your NTS machine and connect all the LocalTalk-only Macs to it;
- Add Ethernet capability to the Macs;
- Use a LocalTalk-to-Ethernet bridge (Shiva, Kinetics, and Apple all make them, as do several others)

In most cases, though, you don't have to do anything other than plug the Mac into your Ethernet network and start using it!

Understanding Services for Macintosh Components

The Services for Macintosh package extends NTS by adding a number of drivers to existing parts of the system. While you may choose to install the components individually, most networks require all of them for maximum interoperability.

AppleTalk Protocol Stack

The AppleTalk protocol stack, first introduced in 1984, is similar in many ways to other, more familiar, protocol families. It includes protocols for routing traffic, sharing printers and files over the network, and so on. The current revision includes enhancements for selective routing of broadcast or multicast traffic, which is quite useful on networks that carry audio or video conferences. The original AppleTalk protocols ran on a 230Kb/s network that was also called AppleTalk; that network is now called LocalTalk. EtherTalk and TokenTalk respectively describe the AppleTalk protocols running on Ethernet or Token Ring media.

The Microsoft AppleTalk implementation is an NDIS network driver that can coexist with other such drivers on a host machine. As with the NetWare IPX/SPX protocols and TCP/IP, the AppleTalk protocols can be bound simultaneously to one or more network adapters and can be used at the same time as any other bound protocols. The AppleTalk stack implements handlers for the Zone Information Protocol, the Datagram Delivery Protocol, the AppleTalk File Protocol, the AppleTalk Session Protocol, and a number of other, lesser-known but still necessary protocols.

There are two key AppleTalk concepts that you need to understand to get best use from Services for Macintosh. First is the idea of a network that is split up into *zones*. AppleTalk zones act like TCP/IP subnets and Windows NT workgroups. When Mac users browse the network for resources, they see resources in their local zone first. If they choose another zone, they see resources from the selected zone instead. Services for Macintosh can be told to offer its resources in any zone on the network, or in a new zone established as described below. Like TCP/IP subnets, traffic doesn't pass between zones on different subnets unless it is routed by a router or bridge on the network; however, a single physical network can still contain multiple logical zones—just like workgroups.

The second important AppleTalk concept is that of *seeding* a network. One device (either a computer or router) can seed other computers in a zone, in effect telling them what network addresses and settings to use. This process is very similar to the Dynamic Host Configuration Protocol (part of TCP/IP). The later section "Configuring the AppleTalk Protocol" provdes details on how to specify which zones you want to serve and/or seed from this NTS machine.

File Server for Macintosh

The File Server for Macintosh component (which you'll also see called *MacFile*) runs as an Windows NT service and provides a Windows NT file system driver that implements the Macintosh Hierarchical File System (HFS.) As described in Chapter 2, "Understanding Windows NT Architecture," Windows NT supports layering of drivers for precisely this reason. The MacFile driver is layered on top of the NTFS driver; it implements HFS-style volumes and folders by making appropriate calls to the NTFS driver and reformatting the data as necessary.

Because MacFile is layered on top of the NTFS driver, though, you can only share data on NTFS partitions. In addition, the NTFS and HFS security and naming schemes differ—HFS supports 31-character file names, and it supports fewer access controls than NTFS.

Print Server for Macintosh

The Print Server for Macintosh component, known as *MacPrint*, performs a similar service to MacFile. When MacPrint is running, Macintosh clients can print to printers shared by the NT server. As an added feature, MacPrint also allows Windows Net-working users to print to printers on the local AppleTalk network. This is a valuable feature because it enables you to spread the printing load on your network among more printers with virtually no extra effort. Even better, MacPrint can transparently translate PostScript output generated by Mac printer drivers into DIB files that can be printed to non-PostScript printers shared by the NTS machine.

Management Components

When you install Services for Macintosh, additional components are installed that change or extend the way existing Windows NT applications work. These extensions allow you to manage how your server makes resources available and gives you the same type of control over AppleTalk shares as you have with Windows Networking shares. These additional components include:

- ◆ The MacFile applet, which works like the Server applet and allows you to see lists of active users, disconnect users, list available volumes and open files, and send messages to Mac clients. MacFile can also accept command-line commands, so you can control Services for Macintosh operations from the command line or in scripts.

- ◆ The Server Manager gains a new MacFile menu with three commands for setting server properties, sending messages to users, and managing volumes shared by a server. You can use Server Manager to manage Services for Macintosh shares on remote servers, just as you can with Windows Networking shares.

- ◆ An extension DLL for the Windows File Manager; the DLL adds a MacFile menu to File Manager that you can use to quickly create and remove Mac volumes. Each Mac volume is an NTFS directory that appears on Mac desktops as a network disk.

Services for Macintosh Restrictions and Limitations

You should know about some restrictions and caveats before installing the Services for Macintosh package:

- The Mac services require a minimum of an additional 2Mb of RAM. Don't plan on running an NTS server with Services for Macintosh installed in 16Mb; although you can probably make it work, performance will suffer badly since 16Mb is the minimum usable RAM for NTS.

- Services for Macintosh can only share NTFS volumes, not FAT or other file system volumes.

- The share names you assign to Mac volumes are limited to 27 characters, and all the Mac-accessible share names served by one machine must fit into a single 4.5Kb AppleTalk buffer. With 20- to 30-character share names, that imposes a limit of around 150 Mac-compativle shares per server.

- Versions of the MacOS earlier than 7.5 won't support filesystems bigger than 2Gb; a bug in the MacOS Finder causes pre-7.5 Macs to crash when they see a Services for Macintosh volume bigger than 2Gb. Microsoft included a workaround in Windows NT 3.5 to prevent the problem, and in MacOS 7.5, Apple removed the 2Gb limit—but Microsoft didn't. If you set the value of HKEY_LOCAL_MACHINE\SYSTEM\CurrentControlSet\Services\ MacFile\Parameters\ServerOptions to be a REG_DWORD of value 0x13, this will allow NTS to report the correct size for volumes up to 4Gb. Above that size, volumes will work, but the Mac clients will only display the correct amount of free space on the disk when it falls below 4Gb. Be sure all Mac clients of your server are running MacOS 7.5 or later, or their machines may crash when mounting large volumes from your server.

- Services for Macintosh doesn't correctly enumerate any Macintosh path whose total length exceeds 260 characters. Because the limitation arises actually with a Win32 function used by Services for Macintosh, the File Manager, and other system components, you can't view the directory contents, set permissions, or do much of anything else with these directories. Microsoft's recommended workaround is to view the directory or set its permissions on a Macintosh client. In practice, this won't be a problem for most servers; however, if you use very long folder names on your server, you may run into this limitation.

◆ Macintosh security permissions are different from those for NT. For a complete discussion of the differences, see the later section "Services for Macintosh Security Issues."

Now that you understand how Services for Macintosh works, and what it can do for your network, it's time to install and configure the software itself.

Installing Services for Macintosh

Getting Services for Macintosh up and running is a three-step process. First, you have to install the Services for Macintosh package itself. Next, you have to configure the Apple-Talk Protocol (ATP) stack. Finally, you have to make your selected resources visible to Macintosh users on your network.

Installing the Services for Macintosh Components

Installing Services for Macintosh is identical to installing most other network software: open the Network Control Panel applet and select the Services tab. If you see Services for Macintosh listed, it's already installed; if not, click the Add button and select Services for Macintosh from the Select Network Service dialog box. When you click OK, Setup installs the Services for Macintosh package. After setup completes, you have an opportunity to configure the AppleTalk protocol before rebooting; see the later section "Configuring the AppleTalk Protocol" for more details on the configuration options.

Configuring Services for Macintosh

The Services for Macintosh package is well integrated with the Windows NT user interface. For the most part, you configure the network protocol and server components in the same way that you configure other native Windows NT components. Once you've installed Services for Macintosh, the first necessary task is configuring the

AppleTalk protocol device that allows the server to talk to Macintosh clients and other AppleTalk devices.

Configuring the AppleTalk Driver

In earlier versions of Windows NT, the AppleTalk stack was implemented as an ordinary network driver. With Windows NT 4.0, though, the stack is now a device driver that is managed through the Devices Control Panel applet. When you install Services for Macintosh, the AppleTalk Protocol service is set to start itself automatically at boot time; if you need to, you can start and stop it via the Devices Control Panel applet. There aren't any other configuration options for the AppleTalk driver itself.

Configuring the AppleTalk Protocol

Like most other Windows NT network protocols, you can configure protocol-specific options for the AppleTalk protocol by using the Protocols tab of the Network Control Panel applet. Select AppleTalk from the protocol list, then click Properties; you'll see the Microsoft AppleTalk Protocol Properties dialog box.

The General tab of this dialog box, pictured in Figure 23-1, lets you choose a default adapter for AppleTalk, EtherTalk, or TokenTalk operation; for example, if you know that you'll see AppleTalk traffic on one particular network adapter, you can tell the ATP stack to look there first. The Default Zone setting lets you control the zone in which the server advertises its resources; the Default Zone combo box will allow you to choose from a list of zones that the AppleTalk stack has noticed on the network, as well as any zones you manually add using the Routing tab (see Figure 23-2).

The Routing property page of the AppleTalk properties dialog box is shown in Figure 23-2. Since AppleTalk packets won't cross zones without routing, you'll probably want to use routing unless you have a very small number of Mac clients on your network. You can toggle routing with the Enable Routing check box. The Adapter combo box allows you to choose an adapter (if you have more than one) to bind to the AppleTalk stack; the settings for other fields will apply to the currently selected adapter.

The Use This Router to Seed The Network check box specifies whether this server should initialize the AppleTalk parameters on computers in the zone it's routing. When the seeding check box is on, the Windows NT server will seed network clients whose addresses fall in the range specified in the Network Range fields. The To and From fields can contain any valid AppleTalk address range (1 is the lowest address, and 65279 is the highest). Note that address ranges must not overlap; if you're seeding two zones, for example, they cannot both seed address 2112. The list at the bottom of the Routing property page shows the list of zones for this network adapter, as well as a *default zone*. Each AppleTalk device must belong to a zone, and the default zone is where devices with no specified home zone will appear. You can set a default zone, add or remove zones, or get a list of zones by querying the network using the buttons at the bottom of the property page.

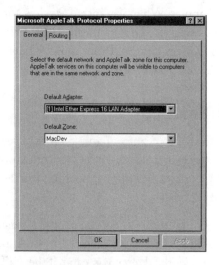

FIGURE 23-1

Configure the AppleTalk protocol with its Properties dialog box.

FIGURE 23-2

Control how your NTS machine routes AppleTalk traffic with the Routing property page.

Once you've set the AppleTalk protocol options to the desired values, you have to stop and restart the AppleTalk Protocol device driver manually by using the Devices Control Panel applet. One caveat: stopping the AppleTalk driver will also stop the MacPrint and MacFile services, which you must remember to restart after you restart the AppleTalk stack itself.

Setting Server Attributes

The final step in configuring your Services for Macintosh installation is to set server properties. These properties control how your server and its shares appear to AppleTalk clients. To do so, you use the MacFile Attributes dialog box, which you can open in two ways. From the MacFile applet, click the Attributes button; alternatively, you can open it from Server Manager by using the MacFile | Properties command, then clicking the Attributes button. The MacFile Attributes dialog box is shown in Figure 23-3; here's what its controls do:

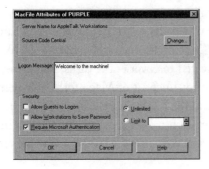

FIGURE 23-3

The MacFile Attributes dialog box lets you change the MacFile service's settings.

- ◆ The Server Name for AppleTalk Workstations group shows the current name that will appear in Macintosh users' network browsers. It can be the same as the machine's Windows Networking name, but it can also be any name up to 31 characters long. You can change the name with the Change button; the change won't take effect until you stop and restart the MacFile service.

- ◆ The Logon Message field lets you enter a message that Mac users will see after their logon has been authenticated.

♦ The Security group gives you control over whether guests (users who explicitly connect as the AppleTalk Guest account) can log on or not. You may also control whether or not users can choose to save their password on the client Mac and whether logon requests without Microsoft's User Authentication Module will be accepted. For more detail on these options, see the later section "Services for Macintosh Security Issues."

♦ The Sessions group, like its NetBEUI counterpart, gives you control over the number of concurrent connections you want your server to accept.

If you prefer the Windows NT command shell, you can also change the logon message, guest access, and concurrent session limit with the `macfile server` command's `/loginmessage`, `/guestsallowed`, and `/maxsessions` flags.

Sharing Disks and Files with Macintosh Users

Sharing files and data with Mac users is basically the same as sharing with other Windows clients, but there are some additional steps required. Before you can share any files on an NTFS partition, you must create a Macintosh-accessible volume (MAV) for each item you want to share. MAVs can be created to cover entire disks, folder trees, or individual folders. Each MAV can have its own distinct set of Macintosh-style permissions and access controls. Once you've created a MAV, Mac users can see it and use it as though it were a Mac volume—subject to access controls or security settings you impose. Let's start by examining the process by which you create new MAVs on your server.

> **NOTE:** If you prefer the command-line interface (or if you need to manipulate MAVs and Mac files in a script or batch file), you can use the `macfile` commands. Use the `macfile /?` command to get more detailed help on these commands; you can also use the online help provided in File Manager.

Creating and Removing Macintosh Volumes

When you create a MAV on your server, you're not actually creating a new volume; instead, you're creating an Windows NT object that the File Server for Macintosh software uses to map an NTFS directory or disk into a Macintosh volume. Although there are several ways to create Mac volumes (described in the next two sections), they all accomplish the same basic task. Once you've created the volume, you can still change its permissions and attributes at any time using the tools described in the following text.

> **CAUTION:** Microsoft warns that you shouldn't create Mac files on Services for Macintosh volumes that have the same names as Windows NT devices like NUL, LPT1, and so on. If you do, you may have trouble accessing files and directories on the NTS machine.

Creating Macintosh Volumes with File Manager

The old-style File Manager, which carries over from Windows NT 3.51 to 4.0, still offers the easiest interface for creating new MAVs.

The Windows NT Explorer doesn't include support for Services for Macintosh, but the File Manager adds a MacFile menu with several commands for managing MAVs. The MacFile | Create Volume command displays the Create Macintosh-Accessible Volume dialog box shown in Figure 23-4. Here's what each of the dialog box controls does:

- Use the Volume Name and Path fields to specify the name displayed to Mac clients and the path of the item you're creating a MAV for. The volume name displayed to Mac users can be up to 27 characters long and doesn't have to match the actual folder or disk name. If a disk or folder is selected when you choose the command, it will be used as the volume name and path.

- The two password fields let you specify a password that Mac clients must supply to mount the share. This serves in place of a Windows NT domain account, since Mac clients can't participate in domain security.

- The Volume Security group check boxes control access to the volume. The This Volume Is Read-Only box overrides whatever permissions you've set on the volume. When it's on, users will be able to mount the volume (subject to other permissions), but won't be able to make changes, no matter what other more permissive controls you've applied. The Guests Can Use the Volume check box allows you to allow or deny access from Macintosh clients when the user tries to log on using the AppleShare Guest account. Even when this option is set, Mac users can still log on by using the Windows NT Guest account if it's enabled.

♦ The User Limit group lets you limit the maximum number of concurrent users attached to this MAV.

♦ The Permissions button displays the clumsily-named Macintosh View of Directory Permissions dialog box, which is discussed in the later section "Setting Volume Permissions."

FIGURE 23-4

Use this dialog box to create new Macintosh-accessible volumes.

Clicking OK creates the MAV; you won't see any indication in the File Manager or Explorer that the object you just shared is now available to Macintosh clients.

Other Methods of Creating Macintosh Volumes

In addition to the File Manager, you can create volumes with other Windows NT system tools. From the Server Manager, use the MacFile | Volumes command, then click Create Volume in the resulting volume summary dialog. You can also create volumes with the macfile volume /add command.

Removing Macintosh Volumes

You can remove MAVs from the File Manager, Server Manager, or command line. In each case, you should remember that removing a MAV has no effect on the data itself—

it just makes that data inaccessible to Mac clients. Use the MacFile | Remove Volume command in File Manager or the Remove Volume button in the volume summary dialog box that appears when you use the Server Manager's MacFile | Volumes command. You'll be prompted to confirm your choice before it's actually deleted; if users are using the share, you'll have to disconnect them before you can remove the MAV.

> **CAUTION:** Make sure you don't remove a MAV until all clients have disconnected from it. Failure to do so can result in data loss on the clients *and* in files contained in the MAV.

Setting Volume Permissions and Attributes

Once you've created MAVs, Mac clients on your network can mount them as though they were AppleShare volumes. You may want to adjust the MAV's attributes or permissions once the MAV is created. As with the creation process itself, you can do so using File Manager, Server Manager, or the MacFile applet.

Setting Volume Permissions

The Macintosh file system supports access controls; unfortunately, they aren't exactly the same controls as the ones NTFS provides. You can set standard NTFS permissions and let Services for Macintosh translate them into their Mac equivalents. You can also set Mac permissions directly through an interface that resembles the standard AppleShare interface.

More important than the mechanics are the details of how the MacOS permissions correspond to their Windows NT counterparts. The MacOS supports three sets of permissions: one for the object's owner, one for a group, and one for everyone else. Each permission set contains three settings: See Files, See Folders, and Make Changes. These settings roughly correspond to the Windows NT read and change permissions, with a few small differences.

By default, the Windows NT account that owns the object being shared by the MAV will have full Mac permissions, as will users whose primary group is set to be the same as the group that owns the object. You can define which primary group the owner's account uses with the User Manager for Domains. Because the MacOS only supports one set of group permissions per object, Windows NT accounts that are in multiple groups must choose a primary group. The Everyone permissions will be set to allow read-only access, but not to allow changes.

You can modify the permissions by using the Permissions button in any of the property dialog boxes shown so far. When you use the one in the dialog box for a MAV, the dialog box in Figure 23-5 appears.

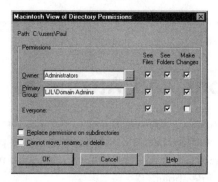

FIGURE 23-5

The Macintosh View of Directory Permissions dialog shows the mapping between MacOS and NTFS permissions.

The Owner and Primary Group fields, and their associated browse buttons, let you control the owner and group associated with the corresponding permission check boxes. In addition, the check boxes to the right of Everyone let you set permissions for any users other than the owner or members of the primary group. Of special note are the two check boxes below the Permissions group. When Replace Permissions on Subdirectories is checked, the permissions you set in this dialog box will be applied to all items contained in the MAV whose permissions you're setting. The Cannot Move, Rename, or Delete check box controls whether Mac clients can alter the MAV itself.

Setting Volume Attributes

You can reset the volume password, permissions, security settings, and connection limit in the Macintosh-Accessible Volume Properties dialog box; this dialog box is available by using the Properties button in the volume summary dialog boxes in Server Manager or File Manager. The fields of this dialog box work exactly like the fields described in the earlier section "Creating Macintosh Volumes with File Manager."

Controlling File Type Mappings and Forks

Macintosh files can contain data in two separate *forks*. You can think of each fork as an independent storage area, like an OLE structured storage container. The *data fork* contains a file's data (or PowerPC executable code for an application). Data forks are identical in concept and structure to ordinary binary files on Windows NT, Unix, NetWare, and so on. The *resource fork* is unique to Mac files. It contains resources that represent icons, window definitions, and the like.

Each file on a MacOS volume has a four-byte *type* code and a four-byte *creator* code. The type code indicates what kind of data is in the file and the creator code links a specific application to its file types. For example, an archive compressed with the Stuffit Deluxe application has a creator of SITD and a type of SIT!. The MacOS uses these codes to determine which icon to draw in the Mac Finder, as well as to let applications decide which types of data files they can open and use. Windows 95 and Windows NT 4.0 use a similar mechanism to map file extensions to data types via the File Types tab of the Explorer options dialog box.

Windows NT doesn't directly support either of these Mac-specific details. However, the NTFS designers gave NTFS the capability to store arbitrary attribute data as part of any file. The Services for Macintosh developers used this extension mechanism to attach two data blocks to every Macintosh file stored on an NTFS MAV: the first block contains the Finder information record (including the file's icon and its type and creator codes) and the second contains the contents of the resource fork. Services for Macintosh knows what to do with these extended attributes, but other applications—like Windows NT Backup, Explorer, and File Manager—see the files as ordinary NTFS files and treat them as such, carrying the extended attributes along with the files.

> **CAUTION:** FAT filesystems don't support these extended attributes, so if you copy a Mac file from an NTFS MAV to a FAT directory and back again—or onto a FAT floppy for use on a Mac—the resource fork, file type, and file creator data will be lost.

Associating Extensions with Mac File Types

Services for Macintosh includes a number of default file type associations for common files, including all of the Microsoft Office applications. You can change, remove, or add these mappings with the Associate dialog, shown in Figure 23-6. You can reach this dialog box with the File Manager's MacFile | Associate command.

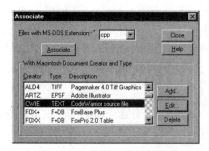

FIGURE 23-6

The Associate dialog box lets you bind file extensions to Mac type & creator codes.

You add new mappings in two steps. First, look in the With Macintosh Document Creator and Type list to see whether there's an entry for the Macintosh file type and creator you want to use. If not, use the Add button to create one. Once you have the right Mac type, select it in the list and type the file extension you want to map into the Files with MS-DOS Extension field, then click Associate to make the binding.

> **NOTE:** If you change or add an extension mapping, it won't apply to existing files. You have to use the `macfile forkize` command (described in the next section).

Combining Mac Forks

There may be times when you need to control manually what data appears in one or both forks of a Macintosh file. For example, you might want to create a new, Mac-compatible document by taking an existing PC document and copying its data to a Mac file with the correct type, creator, and fork layout. The MacFile service provides a command-line option to do just this: `macfile forkize`. The command gives you several options:

- ◆ `/resourcefork:file` tells MacFile to take resource fork data from the specified file. MacFile will blindly copy this data into the resource fork without any special processing.

- ◆ `/datafork:file` tells MacFile to copy data from the specified file into the Mac file's data fork.

- ◆ `/targetfile:file` specifies the target of the forkize operation.

◆ /type:*type-code* and /creator:*creator-code* let you force a particular type and creator on a file. You can use these to override associations made in the File Manager as described above.

◆ /server:*unc-name* lets you tell MacFile to change the file on a MAV on another server.

Because the command's syntax and capabilities are both a bit unusual, here are some examples that may help clear up what this command does:

```
macfile forkize /server:\\enigma /targetfile:"f:\mac\TestApp"
➥/resourcefork:"f:\debug\mac\TestApp 68K" /datafork:"
➥f:\debug\mac\TestApp PPC"
```

would combine the data from two separate files (TestApp 68K and TestApp PPC) into a third file (TestApp), as is commonly done when building a binary that can run on either PowerPC or 680x0 Macs, while

```
macfile forkize /type:"TEXT" /creator:"CWIE" /targetfile:"
➥f:\source\win32\login.cpp"
```

would reset the Mac type and creator of the specified file to make it visible to Metrowerks CodeWarrior, a development tool.

Viewing and Controlling MacFile Use

In addition to setting and changing attributes on volumes and files, Services for Macintosh provides a way for you to monitor who is using which MAVs and which files on each MAV are open. The MacFile applet displays a summary of MacFile usage as its main interface. The summary includes a count of the number of active AppleTalk connections, the number of open file forks, and the number of file locks. The dialog box also includes four buttons across the bottom. The Attributes button displays the MacFile Attributes dialog box (refer to Figure 23-3), while the Users, Volumes, and Files buttons each display independent dialog boxes.

The Server Manager's MacFile | Properties command displays the MacFile applet, so you can use Server Manager to manage the settings described below for the local server or any other machine where you have administrative privileges.

Viewing User Activity

The MacFile Users button displays the Macintosh Users dialog box shown in Figure 23-7. The Connected Users list at the top of the dialog box lists each connected user. Users who connect using the Guest button on the Mac client's Chooser will show up as Guest with an unknown computer name; registered users will appear with the name they used to log onto the server. When you select a user from this list, all volumes mounted by that user will be listed in the Volume list at the bottom of the dialog box.

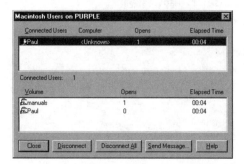

FIGURE 23-7

The Macintosh Users dialog box shows a summary of current user activity for shares on your server.

The Disconnect and Disconnect All buttons allow you to disconnect a single user or all users of the server forcibly. These buttons work like their Server Manager counterparts. You'll be asked to confirm the disconnection before it actually happens; the client will be forcibly disconnected, but can reconnect at any time. The Send Message button displays a dialog box with which you can send a text message to one or all users on the server.

Viewing Volume Usage

The MacFile Volumes button displays the MAV summary dialog box, shown in Figure 23-8, which shows the same basic information as the Users dialog box. Its organization focuses on the volumes shared by a server, not the users. In this dialog box, the list box at the top shows each MAV offered by the server and the user list at the bottom shows which users are connected to the selected volume. The Disconnect and Disconnect All buttons function identically to those in the Users dialog box.

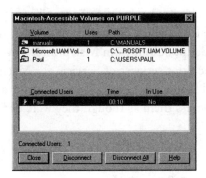

FIGURE 23-8

The Macintosh-Accessible Volumes dialog box shows a summary of volumes made available by your server.

Viewing File Usage

The MacFile applet's Files button allows you to see which files are open, who's using them, and what permissions are in effect. The Files Opened By Macintosh Users dialog box, shown in Figure 23-9, lists all the opened files (including the full path to the file on the server), who has them open, what permissions are in effect, and how many locks are active on the file. The Close Fork and Close All Forks buttons act like the Disconnect and Disconnect All buttons in the preceding dialog boxes—they allow you to summarily close a file while users have it open. Finally, you can refresh the list manually when needed with the Refresh button.

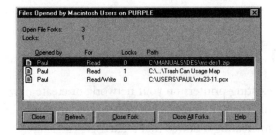

FIGURE 23-9

The Files Opened By Macintosh Users dialog box summarizes which files are in use.

Sharing Printers with Macintosh Users

As previously mentioned, Services for Macintosh gives Mac users on your network the ability to use printers shared by Windows Networking clients. Any printer that has a queue on your NTS machine can be made visible to AppleTalk clients. Clients that use this service reap the benefits of having the NTS machine act as a print spooler. In addition, the NTS machine will accept PostScript output from Mac printer drivers and render it on non-PostScript Printers. The print services of Services for Macintosh also offer the reverse capability: you can bind AppleTalk printers to your server and create queues to them so that PC users can access them as though they were ordinary shared printers.

Setting a User Account for MacPrint

The MacPrint service expects to be run under a user account, not as the default system account. Although theoretically you could use any account to do this, it's best to create an account just for the printer service. This avoids potential security hazards and allows you to maintain control over the printer service by controlling access to the account.

Use the User Manager to create a new account with whatever name you choose. Make sure to assign it a password. You can also assign logon time restrictions if you want to restrict access to shared Mac printers. Once the account is created, use the Services Control Panel applet to set the startup options for the Print Server for Macintosh service. Specifically, you must use the Log On As This Account button to specify the name of the account.

Sharing Printers with Mac Users

You can allow Mac users to access existing printers on your network, or create new ones, in much the same way that you would for Windows clients. There is a small number of differences; let's examine the steps to creating a device that Mac users can share.

> **NOTE:** For a detailed explanation of creating and removing printers, see Chapter 7, "Printer Management."

Sharing Existing Windows Printers

You can share an existing print device—whether it's driven over the network or is attached locally to the server—without doing anything extra. By default, Services for Macintosh will serve existing shared printers on your server to Mac clients. However, there are three things you need to know:

* Whatever restrictions you've applied to the account that MacPrint runs under will apply to printers. This lets you restrict access to printers for all Mac users by controlling the access settings for the MacPrint account.

* Network Macs can print to non-PostScript printers, but there's a catch: if the printer supports resolutions greater than 300 dpi, the Mac print jobs will still print at a maximum of 300 dpi. The standard Windows NT print drivers don't support 600 dpi printing from Services for Macintosh clients.

* For best-quality printing, the NTS print server must have a full set of TrueType fonts, available from Microsoft as the Win 3.1 TrueType Font Pack.

Capturing Existing AppleTalk Printers

By default, Mac clients will be able to see any AppleTalk printer (like an Apple LaserWriter) in any available zone on your network. Clients can normally access this printer by routing their print jobs directly to the printer. This saves you from needing to administer the printer and it keeps Windows users from printing to it as well. AppleTalk supports *capturing* a device so that only the captor can send jobs to it. The actual capture involves changing the device's address while simultaneously reassigning the original address to the captor. When clients send a print request to the printer, it goes to the captor, which can reroute it as needed. Services for Macintosh exploits this feature to solve both of these problems.

If you want only Mac users to have access to a printer, you must capture it but not share it. If you want Windows and Mac users to have access, you must capture it *and* share it. If you share it but don't capture it, Windows users will be able to use it, and Mac users will see the same printer listed twice in their browser—once with its AppleTalk name and once with the share name you supplied above.

To capture a printer, you have to create a Windows NT printer for it, just as though it were attached locally. Instead of specifying a standard port, though, you must add an

AppleTalk port to it. Once you locate the device on the network, you can capture or release it by using the ??? button in the Printer Properties dialog box.

Sending Notifications to Macintosh Users

You can send broadcast messages to Macintosh clients just as you can with Windows clients. Instead of using the Server Manager's Computer | Send Message command, you can use its MacFile | Send Message command or the Send Message button in the MacFile applet's Users dialog box. The Server Manager allows you to send messages only to all Mac clients currently using the server, while MacFile allows you to target individual users.

Services for Macintosh Security Issues

Because the security underpinnings of the MacOS and Windows NT are so different, there are some rough edges where the two intersect. None of them pose real security risks, but it's wise to be aware of them.

The Mac doesn't support user accounts, so access privileges fall into three groups: permissions for the owner of the shared item, permissions for the group that owns the item, and permissions for everyone else. MS automatically maps NTFS permissions into Mac-style permissions, but you can choose to see Mac-style permission information if you prefer. Mac users who have mounted the shared resource can also set permissions if they have adequate access rights.

Limiting Guest Access

There are two different types of guest access to Services for Macintosh volumes. The first, and most familiar, is via the Windows NT Guest account. Mac users can log onto the server with the Guest account if it's enabled. When they do, MacFile will correctly show that the Guest user is connected. The second type is actually a MacOS feature; instead of logging into a resource with a named account, the Mac Chooser provides a

Guest radio button—when selected, users access the resource as an AppleShare Guest, which is roughly similar to an anonymous FTP session.

If you use the MacFile Attributes dialog box to disable guest access, all you're really doing is keeping users from using the AppleShare Guest account to reach your server. If you leave the Windows NT Guest account active, users can log on with that account and still have guest access. In most cases, the Windows NT Guest account should already be disabled. It is wise to turn off AppleShare Guest access to Services for Macintosh volumes as well.

Automounting Volumes

The MacOS features *aliases*, which are small files that link to other files or network volumes—much like the Windows 95/Windows NT shortcuts, which are based on the alias concept. Users can create aliases that point to an Services for Macintosh volume. When they open the alias, the MacOS will remount the file server if it's not currently mounted. The pitfall here is that the alias mechanism always uses the default user authentication module (UAM), so if you've used the MacFile properties dialog box to require use of the Microsoft UAM alias users won't be able to log on cleanly. Make sure you warn your users about this.

Password Security

Unlike Windows NT passwords, Services for Macintosh volume passwords are case-insensitive. In addition, the MacOS has some features that complicate the use of passwords for resource accounts and shares.

Saving Passwords

When a user connects to an AppleShare or Services for Macintosh server as a registered user, they have the option of saving their password as part of the connection data. This allows fast remounting of shares and relieves the user from retyping their password; however, it also means that anyone who can gain access to the client Mac can remount the shares as well. The option called Allow Workstations to Save Password in the MacFile Properties dialog box lets you force users to type their passwords instead of keeping them on the server. If the box is checked, users won't be able to store their passwords on the client.

Using the Microsoft UAM

Unlike Windows NT, the MacOS sends username and password data in the clear when a user logs into a server. You can force the Mac clients to use the Windows NT password encryption scheme to authenticate themselves to the server by replacing the default AppleShare user authentication module (UAM) with the one Microsoft supplies. Copy the file `Microsoft UAM` from the server's `Microsoft UAM` volume into the `AppleShare` sub-folder of the `System Folder` on each Mac client. Once the UAM is installed on the client, lock it using the Macintosh Finder.

Putting the Microsoft UAM on the clients still allows clients that aren't using the UAM to connect. You can force all clients to use the Microsoft UAM by checking the Require Microsoft Authentication check box in the MacFile applet. If you do, Macs that don't have the UAM installed won't be able to log on as registered users (although they can still log on as guests if your server allows it.)

Where to Go Next

This chapter started with an overview of the components of the Services for Macintosh toolkit. From there, the text discussed how to use those tools to share disks and printers with Mac clients on your network. The next chapter completes the interoperability coverage by explaining how to integrate TCP/IP into a Windows NT network. At this point, though, you may find some of these chapters and resources useful:

- ◆ For more general information on managing shared printers, see Chapter 7, "Printer Management."
- ◆ Chapter 12, "Windows NT Security Fundamentals," covers the details of Windows NT and NTFS security.
- ◆ *Inside AppleTalk* (Gurshuran Sidhu; Addison-Wesley, 1990. ISBN 0201550210) is the definitive reference to the AppleTalk protocol stack from the team that designed it.

Chapter | 24

Interoperating with TCP/IP Clients

In This Chapter:

- ◆ Understanding NT's TCP/IP Services
- ◆ Using a Windows NT Server as a Router
- ◆ Using a Windows NT Server as a WINS Server
- ◆ Using a Windows NT Server as a DHCP Server
- ◆ Using a Windows NT Server as a DNS Server
- ◆ Troubleshooting TCP/IP Services

How do I...

TCP/IP is most familiar in its role as the common language of the Internet. It was originally developed as part of a Defense Department project to enable reliable transmission of data over and between networks; its use in the original Arpanet led to its role as the key to today's Internet. TCP/IP is actually two sets of protocols: the Transmission Control Protocol (TCP) and the Internet Protocol (IP). TCP contains protocols for transmitting and receiving information, and IP protocols route, translate, and monitor the information in transit.

TCP/IP is probably the closest thing to a universal network protocol there is; it runs on every class of machine from palmtops like Apple's Newton to giant IBM mainframes and Cray supercomputers. UNIX vendors have been supplying TCP/IP with their operating systems for years. The MacOS, Win95, OS/2, and WinNT all include full-featured TCP/IP implementations.

This chapter discusses the basics of some key TCP/IP services, then progresses on to how Windows NT implements them and, more importantly, how you can use them in your network. It closes by discussing some common TCP/IP problems—and their solutions.

Understanding NT's TCP/IP Services

Even though Windows defines its own set of network protocols, many Windows-only networks choose to use TCP/IP too. One reason is the NetBEUI-on-TCP/IP Transport (NBT) protocol, which uses TCP/IP to carry Windows networking data. Because NetBEUI packets aren't routable between subnets and TCP/IP packets are, many sites use NBT, which requires TCP/IP. A growing number of sites are also interested in TCP/IP so they can serve information over the Internet or an intranet with IIS or another Internet server suite. Because TCP/IP is so widely supported, it's also useful as a common protocol spoken by a wide range of systems.

Windows NT offers fairly complete support for the TCP and IP protocol suites. The TCP/IP protocol stack itself is provided as a network driver layer that runs as part of the executive; it is implemented as 32-bit code, runs on multiprocessor systems, and can cleanly coexist with other protocol stacks on one or more network cards.

In addition to the basic network protocols themselves, Windows NT includes support for several services of interest to network administrators, including the Dynamic Host Configuration Protocol (DHCP), the Windows Internet Name Service (WINS), and the Domain Name Service (DNS.) We'll cover each of these services in more detail.

Routing and How It Works

Routing is the process of determining where a packet of network data should go. Each router on a TCP/IP network maintains a table of its neighbors and their network addresses. By looking up the destination address of an incoming packet in that table, a routing device can determine which neighbor to send the packet to. You can think of IP routing as being like getting directions for a cross-country trip in the former Soviet Union. Because the government didn't allow civilians to possess maps, to get from Petropavlosk to Moscow you'd have to stop in each village you encounter and ask, "Which way to Moscow?" At each stop, you'd receive a new intermediate direction— "Go to Chelyabinsk; it's 200km west of here"—until you reached Moscow.

When one computer on a network wants to communicate with another, it creates one or more network packets, each containing the Media Access Control (MAC; also called the "hardware Ethernet" address) address of the destination computer. If the two machines are on the same physical network segment, nothing else is required; if not, the packet must be routed to reach its destination. Some protocols, like TCP/IP, are routable. Others, like NetBEUI, aren't.

Each routing device (whether it's a dedicated router or a Windows NT machine) maintains a table of routes. Each table entry maps a destination address to the address of a routing device; this mapping tells the router that a packet destined for an address should be redirected to the specified router instead. At each stop, the MAC address of the packet is changed so that the packet arrives at the next router. The final router replaces the destination MAC address and delivers the packet.

The route table can be built manually or automatically. There are a number of protocols that allow routers to exchange route data, just as drivers can swap the details about the fastest route between Atlanta and Indianapolis. However, Windows NT's routing service requires that you add routes to it manually. It can't share route data with other routers unless you install the Routing Information Protocol (RIP) service (see the later section "Enabling the RIP Protocol").

DHCP and How It Works

The Dynamic Host Configuration Protocol (DHCP) is a relatively new TCP/IP protocol, but an extremely useful one. DHCP provides a way for a server to configure the TCP/IP settings automatically for client workstations on the same network. This saves you from having to set IP addresses, gateways, and so forth manually on every client on your network. This is a *huge* time-saver for large networks.

> **NOTE:** Any NTS server can run the DHCP server service; however, if you move a DHCP server between network segments, you must reconfigure it. In addition, NT's DHCP server doesn't replicate its database between servers, so you must back-up each server independently.

DHCP servers must be configured with *scope* information before use; each scope is a range of IP addresses that the server has authority to dole out to clients. In addition to IP addresses, the server also supplies a set of additional parameters that you define. At a minimum, these parameters usually include the subnet mask, default gateway, and a list of DNS or WINS servers that each client should use. Once each DHCP server has been given a scope, it can begin assigning addresses to clients when they request it. In DHCP parlance, an address assignment to a particular client is called a *lease*; like any other kind of lease, DHCP leases are valid for a limited time. The Windows NT DHCP implementation defaults to a 3-day lease.

When a DHCP client is booted, it broadcasts a *discover* request on its subnet—in effect asking any listening DHCP server to respond. One or more servers may respond with *offer* packets. The offer is sent directly to the client's physical MAC address to avoid offering the same address to multiple clients. When the client accepts an offer, it sends a *request* back to all servers that sent offers. The request indicates which offer the client has accepted. Finally, the server whose offer was accepted sends an acknowledgment back to the client. The client then uses the data from the offer and acknowledgment packets to configure its TCP/IP stack. This back-and-forth negotiation is illustrated in Figure 24-1.

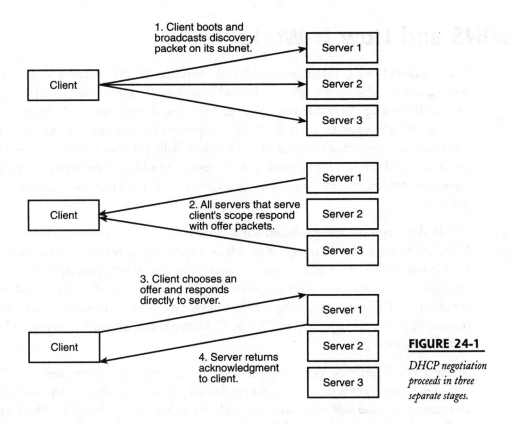

FIGURE 24-1

DHCP negotiation proceeds in three separate stages.

The DHCP client keeps its assigned data for the length of the lease. However, some time after the lease period is halfway over, the client will try to renew the lease. At this point (in Microsoft's DHCP implementation, it's after 7/8ths of the lease time has passed), the client will broadcast a lease request asking any server to give it a new lease. Just as with an office or apartment lease, it's best to try to renew it before it actually expires; this prevents the client from being unable to obtain a lease once its existing lease has expired. Any server whose scope includes the client can respond.

Leases may also be renegotiated due to changes in the network configuration. For example, moving a machine between subnets may result in a new DHCP lease assignment when that machine is first booted. You may also manually force a lease to expire by using the DHCP Manager (see the later section "The DHCP Server Manager").

WINS and How It Works

The Windows Internet Name Service (WINS) translates TCP/IP network addresses into human-readable names; however, instead of turning addresses into TCP/IP domain names, WINS maps NetBIOS computer names to their corresponding IP addresses. This functionality is required for using the NBT transport mentioned earlier. In addition, it can speed up services that run pure TCP/IP by eliminating the need for domain name lookups. WINS servers on a network provide on-request address translation, including support for tracking the dynamically-assigned addresses that DHCP-using clients will have.

WINS also supports name resolution across networks that contain routers. Without WINS, browsing a domain on the other side of a router will only work if there are NTW or Windows NT Server machines on *both* sides of the router; furthermore, those machines must have entries in their LMHOSTS files that point to the other domain's domain controllers. WINS removes this requirement and allows clients to browse across routers transparently by automatically providing an IP address corresponding to the required NetBIOS name.

In a non-WINS network, Windows Networking clients broadcast name queries to all machines on their network segment. As you'd expect, this broadcasting consumes a sizable amount of bandwidth— in some networks, WINS traffic can be up to 15% of all traffic. In addition, most routers don't forward the broadcast requests. By contrast, WINS network clients can directly query a WINS server to get the mapping between NetBIOS names and IP addresses. Only if the server query fails does the client send out name query broadcasts; if those broadcasts fail also, the local LMHOSTS file is used to resolve the name.

WINS works because NetBEUI clients dynamically register and unregister themselves with WINS servers. WINS clients send registration requests directly to the server by periodically announcing their names, in much the same manner as browsing. The server can accept the request if no one else has registered the same name or address; if the name or address is in use, the server challenges the registered holder of that name to see if it is still in use. If the name holder doesn't answer, or if it's not still using the name, the server accepts the request and stores it in the database.

Of course, there needs to be a way for the database to keep track of clients who aren't using their names. WINS implements this functionality in two ways: *name release* and *name renewal*. Name release is straightforward: when a WINS client shuts down, it sends a name release to the server that relinquishes its hold on that name–address mapping. If another client then requests that name, WINS will grant a registration to the new client. If the name stays released for a certain interval, it's marked as *extinct*, and requests for that name will be granted without challenge.

Name renewal works like leasing in DHCP. Each name grant from a WINS server includes a field that indicates how long it's valid; before that interval expires, the client must renew its registration. WINS treats that renewal request just like a new registration, and the renewal is subject to the same challenge process.

> **NOTE:** WINS and non-WINS machines can interoperate; instead of using a server, non-WINS machines are responsible for challenging other clients that attempt to use their names or addresses. In addition, you can make any NT machine a WINS proxy server; proxy servers can accept name requests from non-WINS clients, do a WINS lookup for the client, and return the data without requiring extensive broadcast queries. Finally, you can add static mappings to the WINS database as described in the later section "Static Mappings and the LMHOSTS File."

DNS and How It Works

By contrast to the Windows-specific WINS, the Domain Name Service (DNS) is a more-or-less universal address resolution service. DNS is a distributed protocol—on the Internet, a tree of DNS servers with a single root maps name *or* address queries into the corresponding name or address. Each top-level domain (.com, .edu, etc.) has a primary server, as does each second-level domain (like gatech.edu or netscape.com). Lower-level domains (say, paris.intergraph.com) may or may not have their own primary DNS servers. When a server gets a query that it can't answer, it can refer the query to another machine "above" it in the name server tree. Eventually, this buck-passing sends the query to a machine that can authoritatively answer the query and the result is returned to the original requester.

Each DNS server contains *resource records* (RRs); RRs provide the data that makes the DNS system work. *Statement of authority* (SOA) records indicate the domains for which a particular server has the authority to answer queries. *Name service* (NS) records indicate the name of the domain and its DNS servers. *Address* (A) records indicate the actual address for a host. These records can be cached by servers to reduce network overhead. Each record includes a *time-to-live* (TTL) field that acts like the freshness date on a milk carton.

When a client needs to turn a domain address (for example, enigma.ljl.com) into a TCP/IP address, the client first queries its local DNS server. The local server may have the answer in its cache; if so, it can return it quickly. If not, the local server will pass the query to one of the servers listed in its cache file. That server may return the requested address or an SOA record indicating what server has authority to answer the query. If an SOA record's returned, the local server will repeat the query to the authoritative server. Once an address is returned, the local server can cache it, as can the client. Address queries come in two forms: *forward* queries that request the address corresponding to a particular name and *reverse* queries that request the name corresponding to a TCP/IP address. Both types of queries are common.

DNS servers can act in two roles: *primary* and *secondary*. Primary servers keep the master copy of RRs for their domain, and they are the authoritative source of data for queries concerning that domain. Secondary servers keep read-only copies of the primary server's database. They can answer queries on behalf of the primary server, but their answers aren't considered authoritative. The process of copying data from the primary to the secondary server is called a *zone transfer*.

The Windows NT DNS server implementation looks and behaves very much like the UNIX equivalent, but with a GUI for controlling it. However, unlike UNIX servers, Windows NT Server 4.0 includes enhanced integration of WINS and DHCP with DNS. This allows the DNS server to answer queries by looking up data in the WINS database, and it allows users to connect to shares using UNC paths like `\\finance.abc-corp.com\budget`.

Any Windows NT Server can be a DNS server. In addition, your network may also include UNIX or other DNS servers that publish addresses to your Windows clients. The DNS server service can be turned on or off without affecting your Windows NT Server installation, but other network clients may rely on its availability.

Application Services

Besides the protocols already discussed, there are a number of vital application-level services that use TCP/IP as a transport mechanism. Whether you use these services on your network depends on the mix of clients you serve, what your network is for, and whether you can and do connect to the Internet.

FTP

The *File Transfer Protocol* defines a standard TCP/IP-based protocol for exchanging files between different machines. FTP transfers can move binary or ASCII files between two machines. Depending on the client that you use, you may be able to drag and drop files between your computer and the remote host. FTP is the most common method of exchanging files over the Internet, and it's a mainstay of networks that contain UNIX machines because there are good FTP clients for DOS, Win16, Win32, OS/2, and the Macintosh.

WWW

The World-Wide Web is one of the newest application services to appear atop TCP/IP. As a result of its rapid growth it now accounts for a large percentage of Internet traffic. By comparison with FTP, the *HyperText Transfer Protocol* (HTTP), on which the WWW is based, is simple: clients connect, make a single request, and get back the requested data—all over a single network connection.

NFS

Sun Microsystems invented the *Network File System* (NFS) to provide easy distributed file sharing for UNIX-only networks. Although NFS was originally available only for Sun workstations, then for other UNIX machines, its capability and good reliability have made it popular in mixed networks. For example, many design and engineering firms use NFS to share files between their UNIX and Windows NT CAD workstations using a Windows NT NFS package like Intergraph's DiskAccess.

ON THE

CD

> **NOTE:** The CD includes a 30-day trial version of DiskAccess. This version includes a completely new and very fast NFS redirector for improved performance.

Using a Windows NT Server as a Router

Windows NT Server 4.0 includes support for *multiprotocol routing*, or MPR. MPR allows a Windows NT server to route traffic between multiple network adapter cards in a single computer. The "multiprotocol" aspect is that a single computer running NTS can route NBT, TCP/IP, Novell IPX/SPX, and AppleTalk packets. This flexibility allows NTS machines to serve in place of dedicated routers (special-purpose boxes that do nothing but route network traffic) in some situations, and it provides the basis for the firewall features included as part of the Internet Information Server package.

You have to configure routing independently for each protocol you want routed. For example, you can choose to have a machine with three network interface cards route TCP/IP and AppleTalk, but not NetWare. Let's look at the TCP/IP routing features that Windows NT provides.

> **NOTE:** For more details on AppleTalk routing, see Chapter 23, "Interoperating with Macintosh Clients." For more details on IPX/SPX routing, see Chapter 22, "Interoperating with Novell NetWare."

TCP/IP Routing

TCP/IP networks are often made up of multiple subnets, and the distributed nature of the Internet means that a packet may traverse a dozen routers or more on the way to its final destination. Dedicated routers often handle routing tasks, but they're expensive. Because Windows NT supports routing, putting multiple network cards in a single computer can provide an effective substitute. Each card has its own TCP/IP address and can handle a separate network or subnet. The Windows NT TCP/IP stack handles routing packets that need to pass between subnets without sending the packets to another external router.

Routing data can come from two places: you or another router. Routes that you create in the routing table are called *static* routes, because they won't change without your intervention. *Dynamic* routes can change to reflect changes in network topology or the status of other routers, which may influence the path a packet takes. By default, Windows NT will expect you to provide static routes if you enable routing. You can get around this by installing an additional TCP/IP protocol.

Whether you choose static or dynamic route discovery, you control routing by using the Routing tab of the TCP/IP Properties dialog box. To reach this dialog box, open the Network Control Panel applet, click the Protocols tab, select TCP/IP from the list, and click Properties. When the TCP/IP Properties dialog box appears, click the Routing tab, then enable the Enable IP Forwarding check box (see Figure 24-2). When you change the routing setting, you'll have to reboot before it takes effect.

Enabling the RIP Protocol

The Routing Information Protocol (RIP) allows routing devices to advise each other of routes they discover. Although there are other more sophisticated routing advice protocols, RIP is popular because it's simple and fast. It works well with small- to medium-size networks. Because it's optional, if you want to use RIP you'll have to install it using the Add button of the Services tab in the Network Control Panel applet. Once you install RIP, you'll have to reboot before it becomes active.

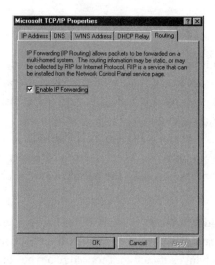

FIGURE 24-2

Enabling IP forwarding allows your NTS computer to act as a router.

NOTE: When you install RIP, you get two choices in the Select Network Service dialog box: RIP for Internet Protocol and RIP for NwLink. Make sure that you install RIP for Internet Protocol if you want to use TCP/IP routing.

Using the *LMHOSTS* File

NetBEUI packets can't be routed. This prevents NetBEUI users from browsing resources across routers, because the browser broadcasts don't pass over the routers. The NBT transport mechanism, which carries NetBEUI packets wrapped up in TCP/IP packets, provides a partial solution to this problem.

Windows NT also offers a low-tech but still workable routing system: the %SYSTEMROOT%\system32\drivers\etc\LMHOSTS file. This file acts like the /etc/hosts file in UNIX, but for Windows Networking clients. Each entry in the LMHOSTS file ties a TCP/IP address to a NetBIOS computer name. This mapping is used when broadcasts to the specified name have failed to elicit an answer. The NBT system maintains a cache of name-to-address mappings. This cache is filled with entries from successful WINS queries and entries from the LMHOSTS file.

The *LMHOSTS* File Format

The LMHOSTS file is a plain-text file with some simple formatting rules. Any line that begins with # is a comment and is ignored when the file is being read. The TCP/IP software reloads and reparses the entire file each time it's read, so comments slow performance.

Every line in the file provides one address-to-name mapping. At a minimum, an LMHOSTS entry looks like this:

```
128.158.222.45          freedom
```

The name and address can be separated by spaces or tabs.

Using the *#DOM* and *#PRE* Keywords

NBT keeps name mappings in a cache. As with other caching schemes, performance improves when you can preload the cache with entries you know will be requested. The #PRE keyword allows you to specify that an entry should be kept in the NBT cache; you append it to a name mapping like this:

```
206.151.233.126            armory #PRE
```

One of the primary uses of the LMHOSTS file is to allow you to make domain controllers on different subnets visible to all subnets by adding the #DOM keyword to entries into the LMHOSTS file. Without doing so, none of the special domain controller broadcasts (needed for login authentication, domain controller synchronization, and so on) will travel between subnets. To mark a machine as belonging to a domain, use the #DOM keyword with the domain name, like this:

```
206.151.233.180          purple #PRE #DOM:ENGINEERING
```

Note that #DOM requires the use of #PRE, or the entry won't stay in the cache and will thus be useless for resolving the PDC's address.

Including Other *LMHOSTS* Files

In a domain environment, it's very useful to be able to build a master LMHOSTS file that every machine can use to find all domain controllers. The trick is to build a file that contains entries for all of your PDCs and BDCs, as well as any other servers (like license or

RAS servers) that need to be visible throughout your network. Put this file in a share on a centrally located machine, then use the #INCLUDE directive to link its contents in to all the clients.

For example, if your master LMHOSTS file is kept at \\armory\config\hosts.1j1, here's what you'd put into each network client's LMHOSTS file:

```
206.151.233.126                 armory  #PRE
#include \\armory\config\hosts.1j1
```

The first line makes armory visible to the client. The second pulls in the include file itself. A variation on this scheme is to specify several include files. NBT will use the first one it can successfully load. You bracket these include statements with the #BEGIN_ALTERNATE and #END_ALTERNATE keywords, like this:

```
206.151.233.126     armory  #PRE
206.151.233.180     purple  #PRE
#BEGIN_ALTERNATE
#include \\armory\config\hosts.1j1
#include \\purple\config\armory.bak\hosts.1j1
#END_ALTERNATE
```

NBT will try each of the listed servers in order until it succeeds in including a file.

> **TIP:** When you modify an LMHOSTS file, you need to tell the NBT driver to flush its cache and reload it from the file you just changed. To do this, use the nbtstat -R command from an NT command shell. This forces NBT to purge and reload its name cache.

Using a Windows NT Server as a WINS Server

WINS serves as a bridge between the NetBEUI and TCP/IP worlds. NetBEUI names computers with names of up to 14 characters. These names must be unique, and there's no way to group them in a hierarchy. TCP/IP allows longer machine names and an arbitrary number of hierarchical groups. WINS allows you to combine the advantage of using

TCP/IP as a network transport protocol with the ability to let your users keep using the existing computer names they already know.

Because WINS is a Windows-only protocol, your network's WINS services will all come from Windows NT Server machines. The WINS server runs as an NT service, and you manage the database it keeps using the WINS Manager application, which is described in more detail in the later section "Using the WINS Manager." Before we discuss details of using WINS, let's examine some planning concerns.

Planning Your WINS Service

If you choose to use WINS on your network, it will be an important service, so some forethought before installation will help you get the best performance and reliability from your WINS servers. Microsoft claims that a pair of WINS servers (primary and backup) are required for every 10,000 computers on your network. However, as a practical matter you may want to use more servers for fewer computers. In particular, you should put a WINS server at any remote sites that are connected via WAN links to your main installation. This reduces overall network traffic by letting clients on a particular LAN get WINS requests answered by a nearby computer instead of one on the other side of your WAN connection.

The most common WINS failure is corruption of the WINS database. It's easy to recover (see the later section "Troubleshooting TCP/IP Services"), but recovery requires that you have a backup of the database. Make sure you include your WINS servers in your backup plan. WINS servers can also synchronize data with one another; each server can be in any number of *replication partnerships* with other servers. Servers in a partnership periodically communicate. Partnerships may be either one-way (server A sends updates to server B) or two-way (server A and B exchange updates.)

WINS servers are independent of Windows NT Server domains, so you don't necessarily need to have one WINS server per domain. In addition, the cross-router capabilities of WINS means that you don't have to put the server on any particular network segment. As an added bonus, the WINS Manager allows you to manage a remote server from another machine. This means that you can locate WINS servers physically wherever it's convenient (and secure!) without worrying about needing to put them on the same subnet as other equipment.

WINS servers are good candidates for inexpensive workstation-class machines, and you should consider using such machines as WINS servers instead of co-locating WINS on your other servers. (One exception: WINS and DHCP can easily share a machine.) Because WINS is designed to share the load by replicating its database, you can gain an overall performance increase by using multiple servers.

Installing the NT WINS Service

You must have Administrator privileges to install, start, or stop the WINS server service, and you must be a member of a WINS server's Administrators group to administer it with WINS Manager.

Installing the WINS service is straightforward. Because it's a network service, it's installed via the Network Control Panel applet. You can verify whether WINS is already installed by using the Services Control Panel applet; look for the Windows Internet Name Service entry.

If you need to install WINS, here's what to do: Open the Network Control Panel applet and click the Services tab, then click the Add button. The Select Network Service dialog box will appear. Select the Windows Internet Name Service entry, then click OK. Setup will prompt you for the location of the files it needs, then it will install the WINS service, the WINS Manager application, and some necessary DLLs and support files.

You can start or stop the WINS service using the Services Control Panel applet, the Server Manager, or the NT command line (`net start wins` and `net stop wins` are the commands to use).

Using the WINS Manager

In addition to the WINS service itself, installing WINS will add an icon for the WINS Manager application to the Administrative Tools group in the Programs section of the Start menu. Just as the User and Server Managers allow you to control user accounts and server behavior, the WINS Manager is the primary tool for monitoring and controlling the WINS servers in your network.

NOTE: Because WINS maps Windows names to TCP/IP addresses, the WINS Manager can use either NetBIOS names or IP addresses to refer to hosts on the network. Any time you specify a computer on the network, you can do so by using either the IP address or the NetBIOS name. If you specify an IP address, WINS Manager will connect via TCP/IP; if not, WINS Manager will use NetBEUI named pipes to connect. This feature is helpful in situations where you know only the IP address or only the NetBIOS name: either can get you connected.

When you start the WINS Manager, it will display its main window, shown in Figure 24-3. You can specify the initial server to use on the command line. For example, typing `start winsadmn \\semperfi` tells the server to establish its initial connection to the server running on the machine whose NetBIOS name is `semperfi`. If you don't specify an initial server, WINS Manager will connect to the WINS server on the local machine if there is one; if not, it will default to the first WINS server in the WINS Servers list.

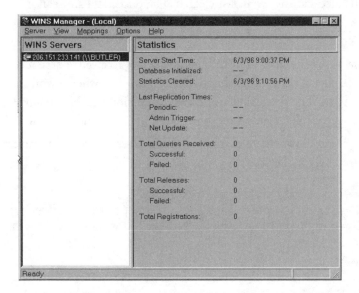

FIGURE 24-3

The WINS Manager's main window shows WINS statistics for the selected WINS server.

You can always add new WINS servers to the list of available servers by using the Server | Add WINS Server command. Just type the IP address or NetBIOS name of the server into the Add WINS Server dialog box and click Add; the server will be added to the main window's server list.

When you select a server in the WINS Servers list, the Statistics pane will display current WINS statistics for that server. Here's what each of the displayed statistics mean:

- *Database Initialized* shows the time when this WINS database was originally initialized.

- *Statistics Cleared* shows the time when statistics for this WINS server were last cleared. You can always clear the accumulated statistics by choosing View | Clear Statistics.

- *Last Replication Times.* Periodic indicates the last time the WINS database was replicated at the interval specified in the Preferences dialog box. Admin Trigger indicates the last time the WINS database was replicated due to use of the Replicate Now button in the Replication Partners dialog box. Finally, Net Update indicates the last time the WINS database was replicated due to receipt of a database push from a replication partner.

- *Total Queries Received* shows the total number of WINS requests this server has received since statistics were last cleared. The Successful and Failed counts show how many queries were successfully resolved and how many lookups failed.

- *Total Releases* shows number of WINS name releases received. These releases are sent when clients release their NetBIOS names—like when a workstation is shut down. The Successful and Failed counts indicate how many names were successfully released and how many attempted releases failed.

- *Total Registrations* shows the total number of messages received that indicate name registrations for clients.

> **TIP:** You can also see more detailed statistics for any particular server by selecting the server and choosing Server | Detailed Information.

Your primary control over the server's behavior is via the WINS Server Configuration dialog box (shown in Figure 24-4). You display this dialog box by selecting a server and choosing Server | Configuration. The dialog box's options fall into four main groups:

The WINS Server Configuration group allows you to control the four main intervals that govern the WINS server's actions. The renewal interval is how often every WINS client must reregister its name. The extinction interval is how much time will pass between when an entry is marked as released and it's marked as extinct. The extinction timeout sets the time between when an entry is marked as extinct and when it is deleted from the database. Finally, the verify interval sets the timer for when the WINS server must ask its partners to reconfirm name information for old names that they control.

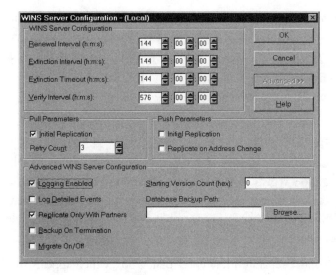

FIGURE 24-4

The WINS Server Configuration dialog box gives you control over the server's replication and timing behaviors.

The Pull Parameters group allows you to force your WINS server to pull database information from its replication partners at startup or when a replication parameter changes. To enable this automatic update, check the Initial Replication check box. The Retry Count field specifies how many times WINS should attempt the pull; this is necessary in case the pull partner is rebooting, offline, or otherwise unable to answer the initial pull request Each retry is initiated after the interval defined in the Preferences dialog box's Replication Interval field.

Similarly, you can control your WINS server's push actions with the Push Parameters group. If you check Initial Replication, your server will push an update to its partners when started or reinitialized. When Replicate on Address Change is checked, your server will push an update when address changes occur. (The number of changes required to trigger a push is adjustable from the Preferences dialog box.)

The final group, Advanced WINS Server Configuration, controls advanced options for the WINS server. The two logging options are self-explanatory—use them to control the

level of detail (none, some, or plenty) in the WINS log (The WINS log is in
`%SYSTEMROOT%\System32\WINS\JET.log`.) Here's what the other settings do:

♦ *Replicate Only With Partners* limits the server to exchanging data with replication partners that are defined in the server's replication partner list (discussed in the next section).

♦ *Backup On Termination* controls whether the WINS Manager will back up the WINS database when you quit the application or stop the WINS server.

♦ *Database Backup Path* controls where a backup database goes if Backup on Termination is enabled. If you don't change it, WINS Manager will use `%SYSTEMROOT%\SYSTEM32\WINS\BACKUP` as the backup path.

♦ *Migrate On/Off* controls how WINS treats static multihomed addresses. When it's on, new registration requests can overwrite static registrations.

♦ *Starting Version Count* is the next version count to use when storing WINS data. Each change to a registration gets a unique, and increasing, version number. When the database is replicated, the version number is replicated too. If your WINS database becomes corrupted, you'll need to set this field to a value higher than the version shown by any of its replication partners.

The WINS Manager also has a separate Preferences dialog box, which appears in Figure 24-5. Most of the options in this dialog box are self-explanatory. The exceptions are the Start Time, Replication Interval, and Update Count fields. Start Time controls when your server will first pull data from its replication partners. Replication Interval governs how often the servers will share their database changes. Update Count tells the server how many database changes (new registrations or changes to existing records) have to occur before the server pushes the changes to its partners.

Replicating WINS Data Between Servers

You may have multiple WINS servers on your network; using multiple servers distributes the load and can help minimize overall name service traffic. For example, if you place one WINS server on each network segment, client requests from that segment can be answered without routing to other segments. In order for multiple servers to stay synchronized, WINS servers must replicate their database information so that all servers have all name mappings for the entire network.

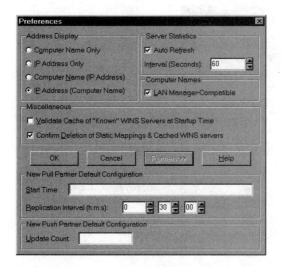

FIGURE 24-5

The WINS Manager's Preferences dialog box lets you set your preferences for the WINS server's settings.

NOTE: For more details on NT's directory replication capabilities, see the section "Controlling Directory Replication" in Chapter 9, "Managing NT Servers."

WINS servers that share data are called *replication partners,* and they come in two flavors: *pull partners* and *push partners.* A pulling replicator pulls database updates from its push partner by asking the partner to send its latest data. A push replicator, by contrast, will send an update notification to its pull partners when necessary; when the partner responds, the pusher will send its updates. These requests are called *replication triggers.* In either case, the WINS server uses the version number field for each database entry to decide whether to send replicas of that data to its partners.

TIP: Each WINS server can have multiple replication partners. To ensure that name queries can always be resolved, you should consider partnering each server with at least two others (if you have that many; Microsoft recommends at least one pair of servers for every 10,000 computers on your network.)

You can add, remove, and control a server's replication partners through the Replication Partners dialog box, available by choosing Server | Replication Partners. The Replication Partners dialog box is shown in Figure 24-6.

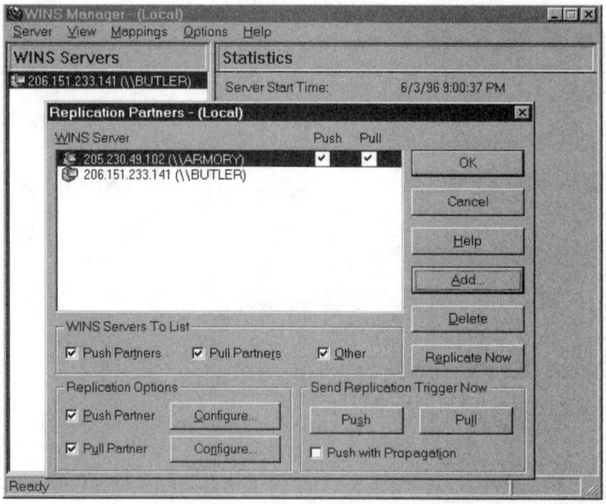

FIGURE 24-6

Add and remove replication partners for the WINS server with the Replication Partners dialog box.

To add replication partners, click Add to display the Add WINS Server dialog box, then specify the TCP/IP address or NetBIOS name of the server you're adding. WINS Manager will add the server to the list of replication partner servers, and then you can define its relationship with the server you're configuring.

To remove a replication partner, select it and click Delete or press Del. (You might or might not be asked to confirm the deletion, depending on how you set the appropriate preference in the Preferences dialog box.)

To control which servers are displayed in the list, use the three check boxes: Push Partners displays push partners of this server, Pull Partners displays pull partners of this server, and Other Servers shows other WINS servers that aren't partners.

Once you've added the servers you want to use as partners, you must set the replication parameters. Partnership is a two-way street: the way you configure a server will affect its partners, and the settings for push and pull partners are different. The Replication Partners dialog box takes that into account by offering separate configuration buttons for push and pull settings. To configure your server's interactions with its partners, choose either the push partner or pull partner Configure button.

For push partners, the only configuration you can do is to set the number of database changes required to trigger a push. (Remember, a push server sends a notification to its pull partners, which then pull the new data from the pusher.) This number includes additions and updates, but it doesn't include changes that the server received from its partners. Although the minimum number is 5, that's absurdly low, and a better value is around 10% of the number of clients on your network. You can always return to the value you specified in the Preferences dialog box by clicking the Set Default Values button.

For pull partners, you can specify two parameters: the start time when the server should first pull data from its push partners and the interval at which re-pulls should take place. The start time is just the time of day when the server will send its first pull trigger, and triggers will be re-sent at the specified interval. As with push partners, the Set Default Values button in the Preference dialog box will reset the pull partner configuration to match what you specified in the Preferences dialog box.

> **TIP:** If you checked the Initial Replication box in the server's configuration dialog box, the server will also pull data from its partners when the service starts. This ensures that the server keeps accurate data, because whenever it reboots it'll pull the latest updates.

Sometimes you'll want to force an immediate replication, like when you add a new WINS server to your network, or when you restore a corrupted database. The Replication Partners dialog box has three buttons to facilitate forced replication: Replicate Now and the Push and Pull buttons in the Send Replication Trigger Now group. As you'd expect, choosing the Replicate Now button forces an immediate replication for all partners of this server. The other buttons cause the server to send replication triggers to the appropriate partners, but replication may be delayed by the partners, because they may not immediately respond to the triggers. For example, if a partner is off the network, it won't respond, so you'll have to either retrigger the replication when the machine's available or let the WINS software retry afer the defined interval has passed.

Static Mappings and the LMHOSTS File

Ordinarily, the WINS server dynamically tracks name and address assignments. As described previously, the server can handle requests from WINS clients for other WINS clients, but what about machines that aren't WINS clients?

Static mappings provide the solution. These mappings stay in the WINS database and can't be challenged or unregistered. The only way to modify or remove a static mapping is for the administrator to do it through WINS Manager. You can only change mappings that are owned by the server you're administering.

You manage static mappings with the Static Mappings dialog box, shown in Figure 24-7. To bring up the dialog box, use the Mappings | Static Mappings command.

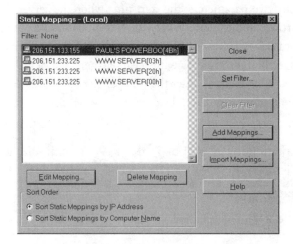

FIGURE 24-7

The Static Mappings dialog box is where you add, remove, and modify fixed WINS records.

CAUTION: When you add, change, or remove a mapping in the Static Mappings dialog box, the change takes place immediately, and there's no way to undo the change except by deleting and recreating the mapping. If you create mappings that mismatch names and addresses, or delete a needed mapping, WINS clients won't be able to find the resource they're looking for. Be careful!

First, let's talk about deleting static mappings. The process is very simple; just select the mappings you want to remove, then click Delete. The deletion is immediate, so be careful! Adding mappings is a bit more complex.

To add a static mapping, click the Add button. In the resulting Add Static Mappings dialog box, type the name and IP address of the computer, then set the type of WINS record you want to create:

- *Unique* is just an ordinary record. It maps a single IP address to a single name.

- *Group* records have names, but no assigned addresses. For example, a workgroup or domain is represented internally as a group—each workgroup or domain has a unique name, but no single resolvable address. Windows

Networking's browse services broadcast and listen to group addresses instead of individual computers.

♦ *Internet groups* extend group records to internetworks (not just the Internet!). WINS uses this record type to answer queries for domain controllers and Windows NT Server servers within domains. If you set the mapping record's type to internet group, additional controls are shown in the dialog box for adding up to 25 addresses to the specified name.

♦ *Multihomed* records associate a unique name with multiple network addresses. For example, it's common to see Windows NT Server servers with multiple Ethernet cards—each of which has a unique IP address, but all of which are in a single machine with a single NetBIOS name. If you set the record type to multihomed, additional controls are shown for adding up to 25 addresses to the specified name; however, the practical limit for the size of a multihomed record is the number of unique network addresses a single machine can contain.

You can also add groups of mappings by importing them from an LMHOSTS file (or any file using the LMHOSTS format.) Click the Import Mappings button, then select an appropriate file. WINS Manager will import the entries and add mappings. Existing mappings that use the same name or address will be overwritten. Entries for domain controllers (indicated with #DOM in the LMHOSTS file) will be added to an internet group. If no internet group exists, WINS Manager will create one.

Once you've added and imported your mappings, you might need to edit them. The only parameter you can edit is the IP address bound to a name. To change the name or record type of an entry, you have to delete it and re-add it.

> **NOTE:** Static mappings and DHCP don't mix well. Don't assign static mappings to DHCP clients; instead, tell the DHCP server to allocate the IP address in question statically, then assign the mapping through the WINS Manager

Administering the WINS Database

Over time, your WINS server's database will become clogged with obsolete data. Extinct registrations pile up and need to be removed. Due to occasional replication failures or other oddities, one server may still contain old data that no other server holds. The WINS server software provides for automatic or manual database cleanup. This process is called *scavenging*.

During a database scavenge, WINS will delete extinct names, mark unrenewed names as released, and mark old released names as extinct. WINS will periodically scavenge the database based on schedules it calculates from the renewal and extinction intervals you specify. Depending on how much your network changes over time, you may also need to cause a scavenge manually at any time with the Mappings | Initiate Scavenging command.

> **TIP:** Microsoft recommends that for best performance you periodically compact the WINS database; to do this, use the COMPACT.EXE tool provided in the %SYSTEMROOT%\System32 directory. Make sure to stop the WINS service (not just the WINS Manager) before compacting the database.

In addition to keeping the database cleaned and compacted, you should also make regular backups of it. The WINS database files themselves (wins.mdb, along with several temporary files) are kept in %SYSTEMROOT%\System32\WINS. Make sure you include them in your backup scripts. In addition, you can force WINS Manager to back up the database whenever you exit WINS Manager by enabling the Backup On Termination option in the Advanced WINS Server Configuration section of the server configuration dialog box. The Database Backup Path setting controls where your backup database is stored. Make sure it's local to the WINS server so that backups can succeed even if the network is down.

Configuring Windows NT WINS Clients

By default, Windows NT machines on your network won't have the address of a WINS server defined. You can tell the TCP/IP stack which WINS servers to use with the WINS Address property page of the TCP/IP Properties dialog. To reach this page, open the Network Control Panel applet, choose the Protocols tab, select TCP/IP from the list, and click Properties. When the TCP/IP Properties dialog box appears, click the WINS Address tab. The WINS Address page is shown in Figure 24-8.

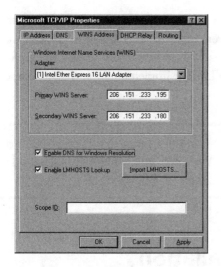

FIGURE 24-8

Use the WINS Address property page to specify a set of WINS servers to use for name queries.

The controls in the Windows Internet Name Services group let you specify which WINS servers to use for each network adapter in your computer. Each NIC can have its own independent settings. For maximum bandwidth savings, make sure that the WINS servers you specify are on the same subnet as the adapter card. If you only have a single WINS server, you can leave the Secondary WINS Server address field blank.

The two check boxes control where else TCP/IP will look for addresses. When Enable DNS for Windows Resolution is checked, the TCP/IP stack will forward unanswered WINS names to DNS. This is helpful when you have non-Windows computers that don't have static WINS mappings. Likewise, the Enable LMHOSTS Lookup option lets you look in the local LMHOSTS file to resolve queries for names WINS doesn't know.

Using a Windows NT Server as a DHCP Server

WINS is a useful protocol (especially in 100% Windows networks), but it doesn't provide a complete addressing solution. Although it can map NetBIOS names to network addresses, it doesn't provide a facility for assigning those addresses to clients. However, the TCP/IP protocol suite includes a protocol designed to do just that: the Dynamic Host Configuration Protocol, DHCP.

DHCP can be a real time-saver. Instead of configuring every workstation on your network manually, you can let the DHCP servers do it for you (though you'll still have to configure non-DHCP machines manually as well as the DHCP servers themselves.) However, there are some subtleties to NT's DHCP implementation that you should know.

> **CAUTION:** DHCP servers can't use DHCP themselves; they must instead use ordinary manual configuration. This is true even if you have routers or other dedicated DHCP-serving equipment on your network.

Planning Your DHCP Installation

The first step in planning your use of DHCP is to find out if your network routers can relay DHCP requests according to the Internet standard RFC 1524. Most routers can, but some can't. If your routers can forward requests, you can put DHCP servers anywhere on your network and client requests will reach them—any routers between the client and server will automatically send the request along. On the other hand, if your routers won't forward requests, you'll have to put a DHCP server on each network segment so that clients will "see" it. Even if your routers support RFC 1524, you should consider putting DHCP servers on your subnets to avoid broadcasting address queries across routers—especially if your internetwork spans WAN links.

Unlike WINS clients, DHCP clients won't be able to use their TCP/IP services if they can't contact a server at renewal time. This means that it's important to have multiple DHCP servers "visible" to every client on your network. Unfortunately, DHCP servers don't share database information like their WINS counterparts, so you must manually scope each DHCP server to make sure that no two servers are authorized to allocate the same address. For each scope, you should reserve part of the scope's address range (Microsoft recommends 30%, but you can probably get by with 20% if needed) to answer client requests from other subnets.

One nice feature of DHCP is that the servers and clients don't keep much information in their respective databases. This simplifies recovering from a server failure. Each server keeps a record of lease assignments, and each client keeps a record of its current configuration. Crash recovery is therefore simple: Make sure that the server has correct scope information, and then reboot all the clients. See the later section "Troubleshooting TCP/IP Services" for complete details.

Like WINS, DHCP will run happily on workstation-class machines. You can realize some cost savings by co-locating WINS and DHCP on a single machine—but make sure that the machine's backed up!

Installing the NT DHCP Service

You must have Administrator privileges to install, start, or stop the DHCP server service.

Like WINS, Microsoft's DHCP is implemented as an NT service that's installed through the Network Control Panel applet. If you need to install DHCP, follow the steps listed in the earlier section "Installing the NT WINS Service," but install the Microsoft DHCP Server package instead of (or in addition to) the WINS server.

Because DHCP runs as a service, you can start, pause, or stop it at any time using the Services Control Panel applet, the Server Manager, or the NT command line (`net start dhcpserver` and `net stop dhcpserver` are the commands to use.)

The DHCP Server Manager

Again like WINS, DHCP comes with a Manager of its own—the DHCP Manager, which shares the look and feel of its WINS cousin. Its icon is added to the Administrative Tools group in the Start menu's Programs group when you install the DHCP server. One important difference between the WINS and DHCP Managers is that the DHCP Manager only allows Internet-style domain names and IP addresses. Because DHCP is a non-Windows protocol the DHCP Manager won't accept Windows Networking names.

When you start the DHCP Manager, it will display its main window as shown in Figure 24-9. The first time you run it, there won't be any servers listed in the left-hand pane. You must add the servers you want by using the Server | Add command. You only need to specify the IP address *or* DNS name of the server in the dialog box. Whichever you specify, the server will be added to the DHCP Manager's known server list. (As with the other Manager applications, you can delete a server from the list by selecting it and pressing DEL or using the Server | Remove command.)

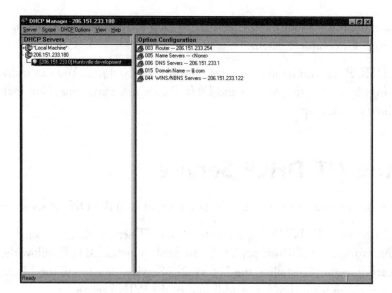

FIGURE 24-9

The DHCP Manager is the primary tool for configuring your network's DHCP servers.

Adding New Scopes

Your DHCP server won't do anything until you tell it to offer configuration data for a particular DHCP scope. The scope defines the range of addresses for which the server can assign configurations. It also defines the lease interval and lists any addresses within the scope's range that should be reserved. Adding scopes is a three-step process: you must add the scopes, configure the DHCP options for each scope, and activate the scopes. The server won't offer any data to clients in a scope until you activate the scope. Because DHCP doesn't replicate its databases, you may have many DHCP servers, each serving a different IP address range.

The first step in adding a new scope is to add it to the server. There are three key pieces of data for a scope: the range of IP addresses it has authority to assign, the subrange of addresses excluded from that range, and the lease duration for leases. For example, a scope might offer unlimited-duration leases for IP addresses between 129.135.253.1 and 129.135.253.255, except for 129.135.253.15 and the subrange between 129.135.253.128 and 129.135.253.192.

Use the DHCP Options | Scope command to bring up the DHCP Options: Scope dialog box as shown in Figure 24-10.

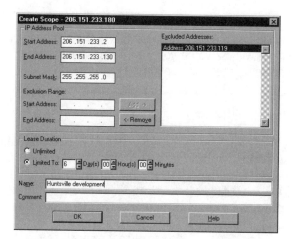

FIGURE 24-10

Use this dialog box to configure a new DHCP scope.

Once the DHCP Options: Scope dialog box is on the screen, enter the start and end of the scope's address pool in the appropriate fields. If you want to exclude a range of IP address from the lease pool, enter the range in the Exclusion Range fields. You can also enter individual addresses and add them. There are two classes of addresses you must remember to exclude from your DHCP scope:

♦ Addresses assigned to RAS clients: The RAS server will hand these out dynamically to callers, and the callers will configure themselves according to RAS.

♦ Addresses for which the DNS name must be resolvable: Because DNS records are static, if you let DHCP change the IP address of, say, your main web server, clients who depend on the DNS record for the server will find that the DNS record points to an out-of-date address that may be used by some other client.

You can set the length of the scope's leases using the Lease Options group. If you set the lease length to Unlimited, client leases will never expire. Because this will prevent the server from reassigning addresses that aren't being used, you should limit unlimited leases to clients whose address won't change often, if ever.

Finally, you can enter a name for the scope and a comment; these will be displayed next to the scope in the DHCP Manager's right-hand pane. When you're finished, click OK to add the new scope.

> **CAUTION:** Be sure not to activate a scope until you've set its options. When you add a new scope, DHCP Manager will ask you if you want to activate it; the correct answer is no—at least until you've set the scope options.

> **TIP:** Choose lease lengths based on how often your network changes. Leases that are too long can cause address shortages; leases that are too short cause unnecessary renewals. If you have many notebooks or other computers that migrate between subnets, a 7- or 14-day lease time is probably appropriate. On the other hand, if the only changes your network experiences is the occasional failure of a client machine or its network card (both of which will trigger DHCP renewals), a 30- or 45-day lease may make more sense.

Specifying DHCP Options

The DHCP specification details exactly what parameters a client can get from its DHCP server. As we've seen, the client needs at least an IP address, subnet mask, and gateway address to function, but the Internet RFC (RFC 1533) that defines the DHCP protocol also includes a large number of additional parameters. For example, DHCP can supply clients with the location of their WINS and DNS servers.

The NT DHCP server even specifies a way for you to add custom parameters that can be sent to the client (of course, this requires that the client understand them.) These parameters are mostly useful for sending application- or vendor-specific data to particular machines. The DHCP client on the receiving end must have a way to decode and use the parameter.

You can configure DHCP options for all scopes on a server, for a single scope, or for a single client. The order of precedence is global, then single, then client, so you can fine-tune individual clients by overriding the single-scope and global settings.

> **NOTE:** This section covers configuring a single scope; to configure all scopes on a server, use the DHCP Options | Global command instead of DHCP Options | Scope. To configure a client, see the later section "Configuring Individual Clients."

To set the DHCP options for a particular scope, choose the DHCP Options | Scope command to display the DHCP Options dialog box, shown in Figure 24-11. The dialog box contains two lists of options; the Active Options list contains all the parameters that DHCP will send to its clients, and the Unused Options list lists all the parameters that DHCP could be made to send to its clients. To move options back and forth between the two lists, use the Add and Remove buttons, located between the two lists.

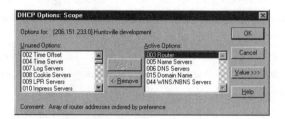

FIGURE 24-11

Tell DHCP which client parameters to set via the DHCP Options dialog box.

Table 24-1 lists the recommended parameters for DHCP's global and scope options. Choose the ones that are appropriate for your network. It's okay to use different settings for different scopes; some scopes may have multiple routers or DNS servers, or you may have one scope for machines outside your firewall and other scopes for those inside it.

Table 24-1   Recommended DHCP configuration options.

Option Name	Code	Purpose
Routers	003	Lists all routers on the client's subnet, in order of preference. Use this option to tell the client which routers to use.
DNS servers	006	Specifies IP addresses, in order of preference, for DNS servers that the client should use.
Host name	012	(Individual clients only) Specifies the TCP/IP hostname for an individual client. The name will be qualified with the DNS domain name if one exists.
Domain name	015	Specifies the DNS domain name the client should use for DNS host name resolution. By setting this option you can specify the fully-qualified domain name that clients within a scope should use.

continues

Table 24-1   Continued

Option Name	Code	Purpose
Static route	033	Specifies which static routes the client should preload in its routing cache. If you include more than one route to the same destination, clients will use them in the order you enter them. Each element in this option is a pair of IP addresses: the destination address and the router address. This option is particularly useful for channeling all Internet traffic to a proxy host or firewall machine.
WINS server	044	Specifies IP addresses, in order of preference, for WINS servers that the client should use. Use this option to tell clients within a scope to use the "nearest" WINS server to their subnet.
Renewal time	058	Specifies the interval (in seconds) from the time each client receives an address to when the client begins trying to renew its lease.

Some parameters (such as 012, the host name) may be appropriate only for individual clients, so remember the principle behind DHCP: It's better to configure your scope options once than it is to configure every individual client by hand. Setting individual client settings on the DHCP server offers you a way to centralize control and administration of those settings, meaning that you can change them on the server instead of wandering around reconfiguring each client.

Once you've set the global and scope options you want to use, you can proceed to the third step in setting up DHCP: activating the new scopes.

Activating and Deactivating Scopes

You must activate a new scope before clients can start to use it. If you don't, TCP/IP services won't work for DHCP clients that can't find anyone to give them a lease. To activate a scope, select it from the scope list and choose the Scope | Activate command. The DHCP service will activate the scope and immediately start issuing leases to clients who request them. To trigger these requests, reboot the clients or use the ipconfig /renew command.

You may occasionally need to deactivate a scope—perhaps because you're deleting it, or maybe because you need to give up a block of network addresses. In any case, deactivating a scope works just like activating one. DHCP Manager sets the menu command to Activate or Deactivate, depending on the state of the selected scope. Remember, you *must* deactivate a scope before you can delete it.

Configuring Individual Clients

There are three primary reasons why you might need to configure individual DHCP clients instead of doing everything at the global or scope level. The first is to reserve specific TCP/IP addresses for clients. Although doing this may seem odd, because DHCP is supposed to assign IP addresses automatically, there are actually reasons why you might need to do this. If your network has clients that can't use DHCP (for example, DOS or some types of UNIX clients), you need to reserve their IP addresses so DHCP won't assign them to one of its clients. The RAS service needs a pool of addresses to assign to its dial-in clients, and DHCP must be told not to assign those addresses either. Any machine that has to have a resolvable DNS record (like your main Internet server or your mail gateway machine) must have a static IP address, because DNS records are assigned statically and don't take advantage of DHCP.

The DHCP Manager allows you to make client address reservations through the Add Reserved Clients dialog box, which appears when you issue the Scope | Add Reservations command. The dialog box is shown in Figure 24-12. There are four fields: IP Address, Unique Identifier, Client Name, and Client Comment.

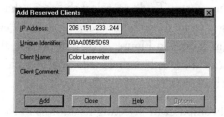

FIGURE 24-12

Add static address reservations using the Add Reserved Clients dialog box.

As you'd expect, the IP Address field should contain the IP address that you're reserving for this client. The Unique Identifier field should contain the "hardware Ethernet" or Media Access Control (MAC) address of the network adapter that owns the IP address you're reserving. The Client Name and Client Comment fields are for you to use to identify the client for your own reference. Neither DHCP nor WINS uses these settings. Once you've filled out the fields to your satisfaction, click Add to add the new reservation. To reserve more addresses, just repeat the procedure. When you're done, dismiss the Add Reserved Clients dialog box with Close.

> **NOTE:** The only way to change the address reserved for a client is to remove the existing reservation and add a new one.

> **CAUTION:** Be sure the client machine is finished with a reserved address before you delete the reservation. Release the address with the `ipconfig /release` command, then shut down the client before removing the reservation on the server.

The other time you might find it useful to configure options for an individual client is when you want to set specific options for reserved clients. For example, if your WWW server is outside the firewall you probably want it to use a different group of routers than other machines that are inside the firewall. To do this, we need to delve into how DHCP Manager lets us view and modify individual clients' data.

Viewing, Renewing, and Revoking Leases

The DHCP Manager offers a way for you to see what configuration and what lease expiration date apply to clients within a particular scope. To do so, select the scope that interests you from the left-hand DHCP Manager pane, then choose Scope | Active Leases. The Active Leases dialog box will appear (as it does in Figure 24-13), displaying all leases controlled by the scope you selected. (You can show only individually reserved addresses by checking the Show Reservations Only check box.)

You can view information for an individual computer by selecting its address in the Client list and clicking Properties. This will bring up the Client Properties dialog box. Note that the IP address is inactive, so you can't edit it—to change a reserved IP address, see the earlier section "Configuring Individual Clients." You *can*, however, change the DHCP options for a client, just as mentioned in the previous section. Select the client you want to affect and click the Options button (which will only be active for clients with reservations). This will display the DHCP Options dialog box (refer to Figure 24-11). The options you set in this version of the dialog box will apply only to the selected client.

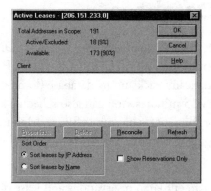

FIGURE 24-13

The Active Leases dialog box shows which leases a DHCP scope owns.

Finally, there's also a way you can force an individual lease to expire *right now*, whether the client's address is reserved or dynamically assigned. Select the client whose lease you want to revoke in the Client list of the Active Leases dialog box, then click the Delete button to remove the lease information. On individual NT clients, you can also force this expiration by using the `ipconfig /release` and `ipconfig /renew` commands. The first tells the client to relinquish its lease and the second tells the client to restart the DHCP negotiation process.

> **CAUTION:** Make sure that the client machine isn't using its address before you revoke its lease. Release the address by executing the `ipconfig /release` command only on the client, then shut down the client. Once that's done, then you can safely revoke the lease on the server.

Removing Scopes

Before you remove a scope, you must deactivate it *and leave it deactivated* until all clients' leases have expired and been denied renewal. You can ensure this by either booting the clients (thus forcing them to renegotiate their lease with another server) or waiting until all leases have expired. Once no clients are relying on the scope you want to remove, you can remove it by selecting it from the list and issuing the S*c*ope | *D*elete command.

Administering the DHCP Database

The DHCP service manages itself to a much greater extent than the WINS or DNS services. This in large measure is due to the small amount of data that the DHCP database contains. The DHCP service automatically backs up its database (located in %SYSTEMROOT%\System32\DHCP\DHCP.MDB) every 15 minutes. You can also schedule additional backups using the Replicator service or third-party backup software. Manual backups will work only if you do them after stopping the service, because otherwise the database files will be open while the backup is being done.

Over time, the DHCP database will accumulate outdated reservations and lease data. DHCP automatically scavenges its database to remove this obsolete data, and it will reload the backup database automatically if it detects that the working copy is corrupted when the DHCP service starts. However, there are some troubleshooting actions you can take; see the later section "Troubleshooting TCP/IP Services."

Registry-Only DHCP Settings

There are a number of DHCP settings that can only be changed in the Registry. These parameters all live in the following Registry key:

HKEY_LOCAL_MACHINE\SYSTEM\Current\CurrentControlSet\Services\DHCPServer\Parameters

> **CAUTION:** Be sure to stop the DHCP service before changing any of these values. Failure to do so can corrupt the DHCP database.

These are the most useful parameters:

♦ BackupDatabasePath and DatabasePath tell DHCP where to keep the database files. You can change them to any directory on the server, but don't set them to point to disks on other network machines.

- ◆ DebugFlag forces the server to log extra debugging information when it's set to 1. If you're having DHCP problems, you can toggle this setting, then examine the log files to look for problems.

- ◆ RestoreFlag can be used to force the server to restore its database from a backup, as described in the later section "Common Problems.".

- ◆ DatabaseCleanupInterval is the time interval, in minutes, that the DHCP server will wait between scavenge operations. The default is 24 hours (1440 minutes, or 05a0 hex). If your DHCP database changes frequently, lower the interval; if it changes infrequently, raise it.

Configuring Windows NT DHCP Clients

During installation, the Windows NT setup utility will ask whether your network has a DHCP server. If you say yes, and enter the address of a DHCP server, that server will be used to configure the TCP/IP stack. If you say no, you can always go back and re-enable DHCP later.

You can tell the TCP/IP stack that you want it to use DHCP-delivered configuration data with the IP Address property page of the TCP/IP Properties dialog box. To reach this page, open the Network Control Panel applet, choose the Protocols tab, select TCP/IP from the list, and click Properties. When the TCP/IP Properties dialog box appears, click the IP Address tab. The IP Address page is shown in Figure 24-14.

If you select the Specify an IP address button, you'll have to supply manually an IP address, subnet mask, and default gateway in the provided fields. However, if you instead select the Obtain an IP address from a DHCP server button, these parameters will be set from data sent by the DHCP server. In addition, if you've defined additional DHCP parameters (as described in the earlier section "Specifying DHCP Options"), these parameters will be set too.

Note that data you enter in the TCP/IP properties dialog will override any DHCP configuration data, so don't change settings in the properties dialog unless you want to overrule your DHCP server.

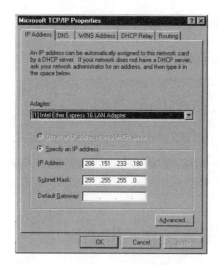

FIGURE 24-14

Turn on DHCP configuration in the IP Address page of the TCP/IP properties dialog.

Using the DHCP Relay Agent

Windows NT also includes a DHCP forwarder that can relay DHCP messages across an IP router. This is useful when you want a single DHCP server to answer queries from multiple subnets, even if the server isn't physically connected to all of them. To enable the relay agent, you have to take the following steps:

1. Install the relay agent: Open the Network Control Panel applet, click the Services tab, and use the Add button to install the DHCP Relay Service component.

2. Enable the relay agent: Open the TCP/IP Properties dialog, then click the DHCP Relay tab. The DHCP Relay property page is shown in Figure 24-15.

3. Specify a threshold (how long the broadcast should go unanswered before the relayer forwards it) and a maximum number of hops to allow the relayed packet to take.

4. Use the DHCP Servers group to specify which DHCP servers you want the relay agent to forward requests to. You can specify any number of servers.

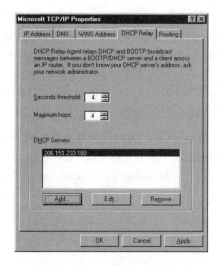

FIGURE 24-15

Enable the DHCP relay agent by specifying which servers it should relay broadcasts to.

Using a Windows NT Server as a DNS Server

TCP/IP addresses, consisting as they do of four numbers, aren't always easy to remember. The Domain Name Service (DNS) provides a robust, distributed mechanism for converting between IP addresses and human-readable names. Most DNS servers run on UNIX machines. Microsoft included a DNS server with the Windows NT 3.51 resource kit, and this same server has been revamped and made more stable for Windows NT 4.0. Although its user interface is good, configuring DNS is an error-prone and difficult task for the inexperienced. A good book like *DNS and BIND* (see "Where to Go Next" for a complete citation) is invaluable.

Planning Your DNS Installation

If you're running TCP/IP strictly on your internal network, you might be able to get by without using DNS. Instead, you can use WINS to serve queries for Windows clients and static host files for UNIX or other clients. However, it quickly becomes difficult to keep the hosts' files synchronized with network changes manually. It is easier to let a DNS server do the work for you. If you're using DHCP, you need to run DNS to map the automatically-assigned addresses to computer names effectively.

If you're connected to the Internet, DNS is a necessity. Not only do you need it so other net sites can find addresses for your resources, but you need a local server to answer requests from clients on your network. Your Internet service provider will probably give you the address of one of their DNS servers for your use; however, if you're connecting more than a few machines, you should probably establish your own local DNS servers to allow name resolution within your network.

Maintaining your own master server for your domain is worthwhile because it gives you control over host names and address-to-name mappings. It also keeps name queries from taking up bandwidth on your link to the Internet by handling local queries directly on your LAN.

Domains and Zones

Although the terms are often used interchangeably, domains and zones are actually two separate entities. A TCP/IP domain is a group of hosts that "belong" together; they don't have to have address ranges or anything else (save their domain name) in common. Even though the gatech.edu domain contains many different subnets and thousands of hosts, they all belong to the domain. A DNS zone is a group of machines whose addresses are served by a particular DNS server. For example, the cc.gatech.edu zone consists of all the machines whose name queries are answered by the College of Computing's DNS server.

Your network will consist of one or more TCP/IP domains. The general convention is to use one primary zone per network, with one secondary zone per domain and one DNS domain per TCP/IP domain. This approach keeps the primary and secondary servers separate for maximum redundancy, but still keeps a single authoritative source for the zone's address.

Within your primary zone, you may have as many DNS servers as you need. A good guideline is to put a DNS server anywhere you'd put a primary domain controller, especially at remote sites linked to your network via a WAN. Each TCP/IP domain on your network will need a corresponding DNS domain within your zone. For example, if your network has domains named atlanta.company.com, austin.company.com, and albuquerque.company.com, you should plan on having DNS domains with the same names somewhere within your group of DNS servers. By putting DNS servers in Albuquerque, Atlanta, and Austin, hosts in those respective cities can look up names without sending excess name queries over the WAN link.

Resource Records (RR)

Each zone will have SOA (Statement Of Authority) and NS (Name Server) records indicating what machines have information about the zone. Every DNS server will have an NS record (whether it's in a zone or a domain) that indicates the server's existence, and each host on your network that has a TCP/IP address should have a pair of resource records: an A record to map the hostname to an address, and a PTR record to map the address to a hostname. DNS Manager can automatically create PTR records when you add an A record, but you must first create a special domain to hold the PTR records as detailed in the later section "Enabling Reverse Lookups."

Installing the NT DNS Service

You must have Administrator privileges to install, start, or stop the DNS server service.

Like WINS and DHCP, Microsoft's DNS server is implemented as an NT service that's installed through the Network Control Panel applet. If you need to install DNS, follow the steps listed in the earlier section "Installing the NT WINS Service," but install the DNS server component, which is listed as the Microsoft DNS Server in the Network Control Panel applet.

You can start, pause, or stop the DNS service at any time using the Services Control Panel applet, the Server Manager, or the NT command line (net start dns and net stop dns are the commands to use.)

The DNS Server Manager

Microsoft's DNS implementation for Windows NT comes with a Manager of its own—the Domain Name Service Manager, which shares the look and feel of its WINS and DHCP relatives. When you start the DNS Manager, it will display its main window as shown in Figure 24-16. The left-hand pane shows a tree structure representing all the servers and zones known to this instance of DNS Manager. The contents of the right-hand pane vary, depending on what's selected on the left-hand side. In the figure, the right side shows a portion of the Internet domain served by a Microsoft DNS server.

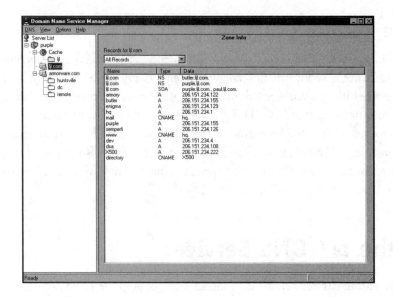

FIGURE 24-16

The Domain Name Service Manager is the primary tool for configuring your network's Windows NT DNS servers.

The first time you run DNS Manager, there won't be any servers listed in the left-hand pane. You must add the servers that interest you by using the <u>D</u>NS | <u>N</u>ew Server command. You'll be prompted to enter the TCP/IP address of another Microsoft DNS server; when you do, it will be added to the server list. As with the other Manager applications, you can delete a server, zone, or domain from the left-hand list by selecting it and pressing DEL or using the <u>D</u>NS | Delete command.)

TIP: Most of the DNS Manager's commands are also available by right-clicking the mouse over an object. The context menus contain whatever commands are appropriate to the selected object.

Creating and Deleting Zones

A DNS *zone* is a group of hosts or records. Zones can represent Internet domains, subnets, or groups of physical hosts. The most common use of zones is to group RRs for hosts within a domain so that a DNS server can offer information about the zone to requesting clients. Primary zones can answer queries with *authoritative* answers. These answers are guaranteed to be correct, and they indicate to the requestor that it doesn't need to query any other server to resolve the name. Secondary zones function like backup domain controllers and provide a redundant way to answer queries when the primary zone's server isn't available. To use DNS on your network, you'll need at least one primary zone, and for good measure you should have at least one secondary zone running on another server as well.

Figure 24-17 shows a subset of the domains owned by the Georgia Institute of Technology. All of the machines in the figure belong to the gatech.edu zone. The Colleges of Mathematics and Computing each maintain their own domains for their machines: math.gatech.edu and cc.gatech.edu are their names. The math domain is a secondary DNS zone that points back to the primary zone for the gatech.edu domain. By contrast, the College of Computing maintains its own primary DNS zone, which in turn has its own secondary zone. Each of the domains has many hosts in it, which are omitted for clarity.

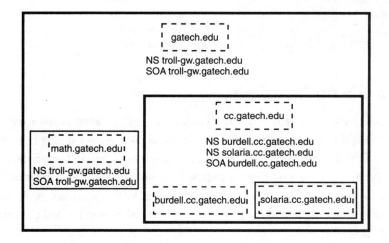

FIGURE 24-17

Domains, zones, and hosts fall into a hierarchy in the DNS.

Zones exist on servers, so you create new zones by selecting a server computer from the Server List pane and using the DNS | New Zone command. This command starts the zone creation wizard, which will interview you to get data it needs to set up the zone. The first dialog box asks whether you want to create a primary or secondary zone; the wizard's questions diverge at this point.

Creating a Primary Zone

The only step in creating a new primary zone is to name it, as shown in Figure 24-18. By convention, the zone name is the same as the Internet domain name. The default zone name for microsoft.com is microsoft.com. Once you specify a zone name, the wizard will suggest a zone file name. The zone file contains all the data about the zone. You can either use the suggested value or provide your own. The default name is the zone name you provide, plus an extension of .dns. Once you provide these two names, the new zone will be created and will appear in the Server List under the server you specified.

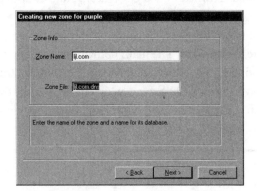

FIGURE 24-18

To create a new primary zone, start by providing a zone name and the file-name of the zone data file.

Creating a Secondary Zone

Creating a secondary zone is a little different, because a secondary zone is just a copy of a primary zone. When you select Secondary from the initial zone wizard dialog box, the Zone and Server fields become active, as shown in Figure 24-19. Fill in the primary zone and server for which you're creating this secondary. You can also grab the hand icon and drag it to a zone in the Server List to copy that zone's data. When you click Next, you'll be asked to specify a zone name and zone file name, just as when you created the primary zone.

The final step is to specify the IP Master for this zone. The IP Master is the IP address of the server from which the secondary zone server should get its updates. Because a domain's secondary zones must be on separate servers from the primary zone server to be useful, each secondary should point to the IP address of the primary server or servers for the zone.

FIGURE 24-19

To create a new secondary zone, start by specifying which primary zone this secondary is for.

Enabling Reverse Lookups

To answer reverse lookup queries (those where the caller has an IP address and wants the corresponding DNS name), you must create a special domain manually: the in-addr.arpa domain. This domain holds PTR records. Each PTR record corresponds to an A record somewhere in your network's zone. It's best to create this domain first. If it exists, DNS Manager will automatically populate it with PTR records when you add new A records for your hosts.

To create the domain, select the server you want to hold it and use the DNS | New Domain command, then specify in-addr.arpa as the name. DNS Manager will create it, as well as some automatic NS records that help speed reverse lookups. Once you've created it, you'll notice that DNS Manager automatically creates subdomains for each octet of your TCP/IP address—these subdomains contain the actual PTR records.

Populating a Primary Zone

When you create a new primary zone, DNS Manager automatically creates two RRs for the zone: an NS record, which tells the outside world which machine is the DNS server for the zone, and an SOA record, which tells the outside world which machine is the *authoritative* server for the zone. These will often point to the same machine. For large domains, they can point to different machines: the NS record points to the name server for the zone, while the SOA record points to the master server for the entire domain. For the zone to be useful, you must populate it with RRs representing the domains, hosts, and related data that you want your DNS server to return when queried.

Adding New Domains

A zone can be divided into multiple domains. This subdivision is common on large networks, where you might see separate domains for each regional office of a large company or for each school at a large college. For example, the gatech.edu zone contains many domains, including cc.gatech.edu for the College of Computing, alumni.gatech.edu for the alumni services office, and residence.gatech.edu for the dorm networks. In addition, it's common to see a single DNS server providing address service for a large number of domains. Internet service providers do this as a matter of course.

The DNS Manager supports an arbitrary number of domains in a single zone. You can create new domains with the DNS | New Domain command. The only data you must provide is the name of the new domain. Once you create the domain, it appears in the Server List beneath the zone that owns it.

Adding and Modifying Hosts

Domains can contain any number of host computers. The only limit is the number of available TCP/IP addresses within the domain. In the DNS, each host must have a unique TCP/IP address. This host-to-address mapping is represented by an A resource record. When you create a new host in the DNS Manager, you're actually adding a new A record to the zone or domain that contains the host.

When you select the DNS | New Host command, the New Host dialog box will appear, and you'll be prompted to enter the host name for the new host and its IP address. When you click the Add Host button, the new A record will appear in the zone view if you're looking at the zone that owns it. You can add several hosts one after another; click Done to close the New Host dialog box.

Once you've created a host, you may want to change its address. You can do so by selecting the host you want to change and using the DNS | Properties command to display the Host Properties dialog box. In this dialog box, you can change the TCP/IP address, but not any of the other fields.

Setting Domain and Zone Properties

Domains and zones have four sets of properties that you control with the Zone and Domain Properties dialog boxes (they're identical.) You reach this dialog box by selecting a zone or domain, then using the DNS | Properties command. The dialog box itself is shown in Figure 24-20.

FIGURE 24-20

Control the SOA, WINS, and notification settings for domains and zones with the Domain and Zone Properties dialog boxes.

Each of the four tabs lets you specify a group of parameters for the zone or domain:

◆ The General tab lets you change the name of the zone data file or switch the zone type between primary and secondary.

◆ The SOA Record tab (refer to Figure 24-20), gives you access to the SOA record for each domain or zone. With the SOA record, you can specify the primary DNS server for the domain/zone, the mail address of the domain/zone owner, (in user.domain instead of the more familiar user@domain format), and parameters controlling how often zone data is refreshed and replicated. See the later section "Controlling Database Updates" for more details.

- ◆ The Notify tab lets you tell a primary server which secondaries it should notify when changes to the DNS database occur. Normally, updates occur on a regular schedule. By adding secondaries to this list, you can force the primary to push updates out when changes occur.

- ◆ The WINS Lookup tab lets you take advantage of the tighter DNS-WINS integration in Windows NT 4.0. Its use is covered in the later section "Integrating WINS and DNS."

Adding and Modifying Resource Records (RR)

Resource records are what give the DNS its power. There are a number of RR types that can represent individual machines, zones, or domains. This section discusses four common types of RRs and the attributes you can set for each one.

You create most types of RRs in DNS Manager by selecting the host, domain, or zone you want the RR to apply to and choosing the DNS | New Record command. The New Resource Record dialog box, pictured in Figure 24-21, provides a common interface for creating any of the 18 RR types that DNS Manager supports. To create a new record, you must choose the RR type from the Record Type list. The fields in the Value group will change depending on what type you select.

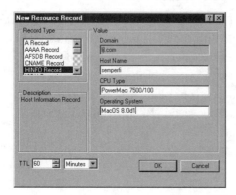

FIGURE 24-21

The New Resource Record dialog box lets you set the type and parameters of the RR you're creating.

Statement of Authority (SOA) Records

DNS Manager creates these records automatically when you create a new domain or zone. You can modify them only by using the Zone Properties dialog box. DNS Manager won't let you delete the SOA record for a zone or domain. When you delete the zone or domain itself, the SOA records are deleted too.

Nameserver (NS) Records

Each DNS server on a network must have an NS record. These records indicate to outside servers which machines within a domain are able to answer DNS queries. The SOA record states which nameserver in a domain or zone is authoritative, but other nameservers can still receive queries from hosts who don't need an authoritative answer. The only parameter you can specify when creating an NS record is the DNS name of the nameserver.

Canonical Name (CNAME) Records

Canonical name, or CNAME, records provide an alias linking a DNS name with an address *without* creating a new address record. For example, it's very common for companies to put a CNAME record in their DNS server to map www.company.com into another name. End users can use the canonical name without regard for the DNS name of the machine they wish to reach. CNAME RRs require two parameters: the alias name (say, www.microsoft.com) and the DNS name to which the alias points.

Mail Exchanger (MX) Records

A *mail exchanger* (MX) record tells outside systems where to route mail destined for a domain. A host with mail to deliver to a particular machine can query the DNS for an MX record to find out where to deliver the mail. Networks that map mail addresses from a single-level domain (like metrowerks.com) to an internal address (like austin.metrowerks.com) do so with MX records. Each MX record has a preference associated with it; most MX users have more than one record to keep mail moving in the event that one of the exchangers fails, and the preference serves as a weight to tell clients which exchanger to use first.

To create a new MX record, you must specify the host name of the domain or machine that is using the exchanger service (`metrowerks.com` in the preceding example), the DNS name of the mail exchanger itself (`austin.metrowerks.com`), and a preference.

Other RR Types

In addition to A, CNAME, MX, NS, and SOA records, the Windows NT DNS server supports several other, less often used, resource record types as shown in Table 24-2.

Table 24-2   Supported resource record types.

Resource	Type code	Purpose
IPv6 address	AAAA	Like an A record, but for Version 6 of the IP protocol. Not used much as of this writing.
AFS database	AFSDB	Points to the location of an Andrew File System (AFS) database. AFS is a distributed wide-area system for sharing disks on UNIX machines.
Host info	HINFO	Contains information (like CPU and OS types) for a network host.
ISDN number	ISDN	Contains the ISDN phone number used to establish an ISDN connection to the host.
Mailbox	MB	Points to an RFC822 e-mail address.
Mailbox info	MINFO	Points to RFC822 addresses used to contact the administrator of the host, plus an optional address used for reporting errors.
Responsible person	RP	Specifies the human being in charge of the host.
Route-through	RT	Specifies where to route traffic bound for this host.
Free-text	TXT	Contains arbitrary text associated with the host, as for a public cryptographic key.
Well-known	WKS	Lists the well-known Internet-standard services supported by this host.
X.25 address	X25	Like the ISDN record, specifies the X.25 address used to connect to this host.

Integrating WINS and DNS

WINS and DNS provide complementary services: WINS maps NetBIOS names to IP addresses and DNS maps IP address to domain names. Because the network clients keep the WINS database up to date automatically, integrating the WINS and DNS services—or at least letting them communicate—would allow machines running NBT to take advantage of the updated WINS database and ease the process of adding RR records manually. The Windows NT 4.0 DNS implementation does just that; it allows you to use WINS data to answer forward and reverse address queries. You configure WINS options with the WINS Lookup tab of the Zone Properties dialog box (refer to Figure 24-20).

Using WINS Lookups

To enable the use of WINS for forward lookups in a zone, open the Zone Properties dialog box by selecting the primary zone and using the DNS | Properties command. When the Zone Properties dialog box appears, click the WINS Lookup tab and turn on the Use WINS Resolution check box. Next, you must specify the TCP/IP addresses of at least one WINS server on your network. If you want data gathered from the WINS server to be transferred to secondary servers during a zone transfer, clear the Settings Only Affect Local Server check box. When it is on, WINS data won't be transferred during the zone transfer.

Using Reverse WINS Lookups

When you enable reverse WINS lookups, you're allowing queries to the in-addr.arpa subdomain for your domain to be answered with WINS database data. Enabling this option is simple: open the Zone Properties dialog box for the in-addr.arpa zone, then click the WINS Reverse Lookup tab. Check off the Use WINS Reverse Lookup check box. If you want data coming from the WINS database to be propagated during zone transfers, turn off the Settings only affect local server check box. The DNS Host Domain field lets you specify what domain name to add to the WINS name before it's returned. Because WINS names don't belong to any TCP/IP domain, you use this field to add on the proper DNS domain name.

Controlling the DNS Server

Now that you've created zones and domains for your network, and populated them with appropriate RRs representing the machines on your network, you need to be able to control how zone transfers and database updates take place, as well as how long your DNS data will be allowed to propagate before it's refreshed.

Controlling Database Updates

When you make changes in DNS Manager, these changes get propagated into the zone files on disk (hence to the outside world) in three ways: at predefined intervals, when you exit the DNS Manager, and when you stop the DNS server service. You can also force an update with the DNS | Update Server Data Files command, which updates the disk files to reflect any changes you've made to the zone.

However, just because you've updated the database on your server, it doesn't mean that those updates will automatically get out to other machines on the network. Three values specified in the zone's SOA record control this propagation. The *serial number* is incremented every time the primary zone database is modified. Secondary servers can compare the primary's serial number with their own to know whether the secondary database is out of date. The *refresh interval* defines how often secondary servers should ask the primary server for updates. The *time-to-live* (TTL) value controls how long data from the primary server can be cached by the server that receives it.

To force a zone transfer, you can modify the serial number field in the SOA Record tab of the Zone Properties database. When the next refresh interval is reached, the secondary zone servers will pull the database updates. You can also tell the DNS server service to notify secondaries when the primary database changes. To do this, open the Zone Properties dialog box of the primary zone, then use the Notify tab to add the IP address of each secondary server you want to be notified. When a change occurs, the primary will notify the listed secondaries, who will then start a zone transfer to get the changes.

> **TIP:** Zone transfers are logged on the primary and secondary servers' event logs. Look for events with a source of DNS.

Controlling DNS on Multiple Network Adapters

Some servers will have multiple network cards installed, each with its own TCP/IP address. Many networks use a Windows NT machine with two network adapters as a packet-filtering firewall. In a situation like this, you probably wouldn't want the "outside" network card to use the "inside" DNS server. The Interfaces tab of the Server Properties dialog box allows you to control which network adapters' IP addresses can respond to DNS queries. Figure 24-22 shows the Interfaces tab.

FIGURE 24-22

The Interfaces tab of the Server Properties dialog lets you block some IP addresses from responding to DNS queries.

Troubleshooting TCP/IP Services

Network addressing services can save you a great deal of work by quietly answering name and address queries with very little manual effort from you—however, if they stop working, users will quickly find out.

Because WINS, DNS, and DHCP all rely on a database of information, a good blanket remedy is to restore the database from a backup. DHCP and WINS can automatically do backups periodically. In addition, you should be doing regular backups of all your servers anyway.

> **TIP:** Configure the DHCP and WINS servers to keep their backups on a different disk than %SystemRoot%; this protects you in case of a disk failure. However, remember that neither DHCP nor WINS can store data on a network drive, so your backup disk must be physically mounted on the server.

Common Problems

There are a few problems so often reported with address services under NTS that I'm going to present them, along with solutions as follows:

Problem: I can't connect to my WINS server with WINS Manager. When I try, I get an RPC failure error message.

Solution: Make sure the client running WINS Manager has its WINS Client service running, and make sure the WINS server has the Windows Internet Name Service running. To verify that these services are up, check the appropriate line in the Control Panel's Services applet. (The same solution applies to DHCP and DNS servers that report this message, too.)

Problem: One of my WINS servers doesn't seem to be sharing data with any of its defined replication partners.

Solution: Replication, like marriage, is a two-way street. For A to push data to B, both A must be a push partner of B, and B must be a pull partner of A. If you only have a one-way relationship, the target server won't cooperate and no data will be exchanged.

Problem: One of my DHCP clients keeps changing its IP address almost at random.

Solution: If your client is part of more than one scope, every time it renegotiates its lease it may be getting a lease from a different server. Make sure the client is in only one scope.

Problem: I restarted my DHCP server because its database had been corrupted, but the original problem still occurs.

Solution: Force DHCP to restore its database from its backup copy by setting the DHCP service's `RestoreFlag` Registry key to 1. (Look in `HKEY_LOCAL_MACHINE\SYSTEM\current\currentcontrolset\services\DHCPServer\Parameters`). DHCP will reset this flag to 0 after it reloads the database.

Problem: One or more of my DHCP clients complain that they can't renew their leases, but for other clients lease renewals work fine.

Solution: The DHCP scope for the malfunctioning clients is probably on a server whose DHCP service has stopped. Check the Event Viewer log on the scope server, and make sure the server's DHCP service is running, then restart the client.

Problem: I get "duplicate name" errors for one or more WINS clients.

Solution: Static and dynamic mappings for the same name can't coexist in WINS. Check the database and remove any static mappings for the disputed name.

Restoring from a Database Backup

Your WINS, DNS, or DHCP database may become corrupted. Although this is never pleasant, and seldom predictable, recovery is usually fairly straightforward.

DHCP automatically restores its database from its backup at server startup if it detects that the database is corrupt. Alternatively, you can force it to reload from its local backup by setting RestoreFlag as mentioned in the preceding section.

WINS databases must be restored manually. You can restore from WINS' backup database by choosing Mappings | Restore Local Database from within WINS Manager and selecting the backup directory you specified in the WINS Preferences dialog box. Once you've done this, you can force all the server's replication partners to update themselves by sending replication triggers as described in the earlier section "Replicating WINS Data Between Servers."

Secondary DNS servers can restore themselves from the primary server; however, both primary and secondary servers keep their files in %SYSTEMROOT%\system32\DNS, so you should either replicate or back up these files at regular intervals. The DNS server service keeps a backup copy of the zone files in %SYSTEMROOT%\system32\DNS\backup as well.

There may be times when restoring from the local backup copy doesn't work. You can always recover (albeit the hard way), or you can move your database to a new machine (after installing the correct services, of course), by following these steps:

- ◆ On the server where the files will be restored, stop the NT service for the service you're restoring. Do this with the net stop command, the Services applet in Control Panel, or the Server Manager.

- ◆ Remove the database files in the database directory (%SystemRoot%\SYSTEM32*service*, where *service* is WINS, DNS, or DHCP.) The files to remove for WINS or DHCP are JET*.LOG, *service*.MDB, and any .TMP files. For DNS, remove all the files in the directory.

- For WINS and DHCP, if you're restoring the database to the exact path that it was in before, remove `SYSTEM.MDB` and restore it from a known-good backup. If you're putting the database in a different location from the original, don't remove `SYSTEM.MDB`from the new location.

- For WINS or DHCP, restore the `service.MDB` file from a known-good backup. For DNS, replace the files in the `%SYSTEMROOT%\system32\DNS` with copies from a backup or from the DNS backup directory.

- Restart the service of interest using the `net start` command or the Services applet in Control Panel.

Restoring After a Server Failure

Sometimes you'll need to restore address services because a server failed. If you have backup servers, you can just let them carry the load in the meantime, but when the failed machines are fixed you'll want to put them back online. The easiest way to do this is to log into the server with Administrator privileges and start the service manually, using either `net start` or the Services applet. To save yourself future trouble, you can use Services to make the service start automatically on boot.

Where to Go Next

This chapter explained how Windows NT implements TCP/IP, beginning with an overview of the key services that Windows NT provides and continuing into a detailed discussion of using the WINS, DHCP, and DNS services. In addition, we covered troubleshooting TCP/IP service problems.

The next chapter describes how to integrate Macintoshes into your Windows NT network. Later chapters will introduce the Dial-Up Networking subsystem and the Internet Information Server. For now, though, here are some other places you might find interesting:

- DNS configuration is a subtle art that can't be adequately covered here. All the ins and outs of the DNS system are explained in *DNS and BIND* (Paul Albitz & Cricket Liu; O'Reilly & Associates, 1992; ISBN 1-56592-010-4.)

♦ The DNS Resource Directory (http://www.dns.net/dnsrd) is an excellent source of DNS information. Of course, to access it you have to already have a working DNS server available, whether on your local network or via an Internet service provider.

♦ Douglas Comer's *Internetworking With TCP/IP* (Prentice-Hall, 1995; ISBN 0-132-16987-8) is probably the best single resource for understanding the technical details behind routing protocols and how they can impact your network planning.

♦ There are a number of useful, if slightly dated, white papers covering Windows NT's TCP/IP services on Microsoft's "Windows/Windows NT Server White Papers" page. Visit http://www.microsoft.com/ntserver/nts351/whtpap.htm for the full details.

PART VII

Extending Your Network

Chapter | 25

Providing Dial-Up
Access

In This Chapter:

- Understanding Dial-Up Networking
- Building a Dial-Up Networking Server

How do I...

Local area networks (LANs) exist to let people share information and resources on their computers. However, as the word *local* implies, these computers must be close to each other (for example, in the same office or building) to be part of the network. Employees increasingly want to be able to work away from their offices—working from their homes or while traveling. Sales personnel want to have access to corporate databases while on the road, network administrators want to be able to administer the corporate network remotely, and managers want to be able to do their jobs from wherever they may be.

As networks and information access become ever more important in today's online community, businesses must find a way to extend their networks across phone lines for these remote or mobile employees. Dial-up networking, in which a remote computer connects to a LAN using a modem and a phone line, can be a cost effective solution for connecting remote PCs to an existing LAN.

Understanding Dial-Up Networking

Most people understand a LAN as a series of cabling that connects a group of computers. The cabling connects each computer to the others by means of network adapters in those computers. Dial-up networking uses this same idea, except that it uses modems for the network adapters and the telephone system as the cabling. In broad terms, *dial-up networking* and *remote access* both refer to this type of networking. More specifically, the terms "client" and "server" are applied to this scenario, with "clients" *dialing out* to a remote network, and "servers" *accepting connections coming in* from the clients. In the Windows NT 3.51 environment, the term RAS Client was used to describe a workstation running the Remote Access Service client software to access a remote network, and the term RAS Server was used to describe a workstation or server running the Remote Access Service server software to accept connections from the RAS Clients.

However, with the release of Windows 95, Windows NT Workstation, and Windows NT Server version 4.0, Microsoft changed the name of the dial up client software that's bundled with those operating systems to *Dial-Up Networking*. Dial-Up Networking is the official name of the software that allows the workstation or server running it to dial and access a remote network. *Remote Access Service* is the official name of the software shipped with Windows NT Workstation and Server Version 4.0 that enables the workstation or server running it to accept incoming dial-up connection requests from clients, allowing remote workstations to access its network. As with Windows NT 3.51, Remote Access Service under Windows NT 4.0 Workstation is restricted to accept only one incoming dial-up connection, while RAS under Windows NT 4.0 Server can accept up to 256 incoming dial-up connection requests.

Some people who have used PCs/workstations with attached modems misunderstand dial-up networking because it sounds like other software they've used, such as:

◆ *Terminal software* creates a terminal session with the remote computer system, enabling the user to type commands or select options from a menu presented by the remote computer system. The remote computer system then executes those commands or menu options and sends the results back over the phone lines to the dialed-in computer. DataStorm's ProCOMM Plus and Windows NT's built-in HyperTerminal are examples of this type of software. Bulletin board systems (BBSs), mainframes, and Internet shell accounts are good examples of services that require this type of software.

◆ *Remote control software* enables a remote user to dial in and "take control" of the dialed-up computer system. In essence, this software displays to the dialed-in user the text and/or graphics displayed on the dialed-up computer system's screen. The dialed-in user then uses mouse and keyboard to work with the applications running on the dialed-up computer. Examples of this type of software are Symantec's Norton pcAnywhere/pcAnywhere32, InSync's CoSession Remote, Avalan Technology's Remotely Possible, and Microcom's Carbon Copy.

Dial-up networking isn't a terminal emulation program, and it doesn't "take control of" nor display applications running on a remote computer. Instead, dial-up networking is software that connects a remote workstation to an office server or network and makes that dialed-in workstation appear to that network as a directly-connected node. After connecting, the workstation's network services can be used just as if that workstation were connected to the LAN directly. Those network services include: File Manager, Explorer, and Network Neighborhood for file manipulation, the Printers folder for printer and print job management. Figure 25.1 shows an example of Dial-Up Networking and its components.

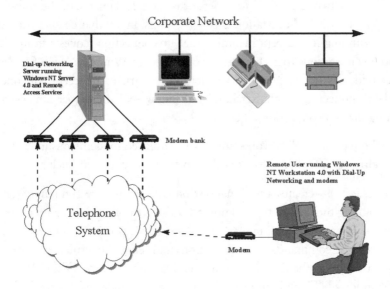

FIGURE 25.1

An example of dial-up networking.

Now that we know that Dial-Up Networking and Remote Access Service are truly ways of extending a network out over phone lines, you might ask what network protocols they support to do this. Both Dial-Up Networking and Remote Access Service support three major network protocols:

♦ *NetBEUI.* This is the standard protocol that is built-in to Microsoft Windows 3.1, Microsoft Windows for Workgroups 3.11, and Microsoft Windows 95. It is a non-routable protocol, which means that it can only be used to access network resources on the local area network. Any network resources beyond the local area network (for instance, file servers and print/plot servers on another LAN which is linked to the current LAN via a gateway or router) are not accessible with NetBEUI. In a LAN environment, NetBEUI relies upon the MAC (machine address code in ROM) of the installed network card in each system for addressing and communication. When a remote client (without an installed network card) dials-in over the phone lines to a Dial-Up Networking server, a MAC address is emulated on the client end.

♦ *IPX/SPX.* Internet Packet eXchange / Sequenced Packet eXchange is the standard protocol for Novell NetWare, and is in wide spread use. While IPX is not a routable protocol (as NetBEUI is not), SPX is, and can be used to access network resources on other networks. IPX/SPX, like NetBEUI, relies upon a MAC address for addressing and communication.

♦ *TCP/IP.* Transmission Control Protocol / Internet Protocol is the *lingua de fraca* of the Internet, and is the widest used protocol in the world. Unlike NetBEUI and IPX/SPX which use a hardware-assigned address (MAC), TCP/IP requires the use of *software-assigned* addresses. The advantage of this approach is that addresses can be assigned on the fly; either by selection from a static pool of addresses, or automatically via DHCP (Dynamic Host Configuration Protocol).

With Dial-Up Networking explained, we'll now move on to the individual components required to make Dial-Up Networking a reality.

Server Components

To extend a network onto the phone lines successfully, the remote users need a server on the network to dial into. Dial-up access can be provided for a LAN by one of the three major types of dial-up servers:

♦ A dedicated hardware device, such as a *communications server* (also known as a *terminal server*), with an attached bank of modems. This type of device is specialized hardware designed specifically for the job of accepting and authenticating incoming dial-up connection requests, and usually can't do anything else (in other words, you can't walk up to it, login, and use it like it was another workstation). Think of a communications server as a very special type of router.

♦ A workstation or server running Windows NT Server and Remote Access Service (RAS). This server would have installed in it a multiport serial adapter card. A bank of modems is then attached to that multiport serial adapter. Along with its role of acting as a dial-up server, this workstation or server can also serve multipurpose and also provide file or print sharing on the LAN, or even act as just another graphics workstation.

♦ A workstation or server running Windows NT Workstation and a single modem attached to one of the workstation's built-in serial ports. Windows NT Workstation's Remote Access Services allows one incoming dial-up connection, and for many small offices with only a few remote employees, this minimal setup proves sufficient.

Choosing which scheme to use as a dial-up server depends on cost, security considerations, whether spare equipment is already available to devote to this task, and so on. Communications servers tend to be proprietary, with setup and configuration varying wildly from vendor to vendor. Communications servers are purchased and used in instances where no spare PC or server equipment is available to fill the role of a dial-up server, and where there's a desire to have the users dialing in completely sealed-off from any well-known operating system when they initially connect. That is, communications servers run a special proprietary operating system (usually EPROM or floppy diskette based) that is closed and completely dedicated to the task of accepting and authenticating incoming dial-up connections—and nothing else. This closed operating system design is considered by many security experts to help further mitigate hacking/break-in attempts at the dial-up server.

With a machine running Windows NT Server and RAS, however, a business or corporation can provide a cost-effective dial-up server that's easy to install and maintain. This dial-up server can then also be used for other things (print server, plot spooler, file server, etc.). It's not a devoted piece of hardware like the communications server. RAS works with many network protocols and provides a network standards-based dial-up server (right out of the box) capable of client/server computing for remote users. Unlike the communications server, setting-up RAS is the same regardless of the hardware (such as Intel, MIPS, Alpha, PowerPC) on which Windows NT Server is running.

Security

Corporate and government organizations, deploying remote access solutions across the enterprise, require varying degrees of security, from virtual public access, to total discrete control. Microsoft's Windows NT, in combination with Remote Access Service, offers all of the tools necessary to implement whatever degree of security is desired.

Microsoft's RAS provides security at the operating system, file system, and network layers, as well as data encryption and event auditing. Some of the security features are inherited from the Windows NT operating system, while others are specific to RAS itself. Every stage of the process—such as user authentication, data transmission, resource access, logoff and auditing—can be secured.

Client Components

The components required for Dial-Up Networking are minimal, but they do include both hardware and software. For hardware, three items are required:

◆ *Modem.* Modem speed is usually the most important aspect of client hardware selection, although the computer can be the bottleneck instead of the modem if the CPU isn't fast enough, or if the computer doesn't have enough memory. Obviously, the computer requirements should meet or exceed the minimum hardware requirements of the operating system. Modem prices tend to be directly proportional to speed. The modem type should also directly correspond to the modem bank at the corporate site (in other words, only analog modems can be used to dial into an analog modem bank, and only ISDN Terminal Adapters can be used to dial into an ISDN Terminal Adapter bank).

NOTE: While some parts of the industry can be found using terminology like "ISDN Modems," it's important to realize that ISDN is purely digital, and doesn't require the modulation/demodulation that a standard modem provides. The device which connects to the ISDN service in place of a modem is actually called a Terminal Adapter.

♦ *Line service.* Naturally, to be able to use dial-up networking, a telephone circuit of some sort (analog, ISDN) must be available. Whether you choose analog or ISDN depends on your speed requirements and budgetary considerations.

♦ *Cabling.* This category includes all cabling required to interface the modem to the computer (in most cases, serial), and to interface the modem to the telephone circuit or ISDN Terminal Adapter to the ISDN line.

The client-side software component, Dial-Up Networking, is easy to install. Windows 95, Windows NT Workstation, and Windows NT Server even place a shortcut for the installation procedure right on the Start menu, under Programs | Accessories.

The following demonstrates an example installation of Dial-Up Networking under Windows NT Workstation 4.0 using an external U.S. Robotics 33.6Kbps Sportster on serial port COM1:

1. First, make sure that the settings for the serial port for your modem (or ISDN Terminal Adapter) are optimal. If you're using a 14.4Kbps or faster modem, it pays to turn on the serial port's 16550 UART. The serial port's UART, or *Universal Asynchronous Receiver Transmitter,* is a small buffer chip that temporarily stores data until the CPU gets around to receiving it (in the case of incoming data from the modem), or until the modem is ready to send it out (in the case of outgoing data). This buffer, called a "FIFO" under Windows NT, is turned on as shown in Figure 25.2. Notice also the speed of the port; this number is calculated by taking the carrier speed of the modem (for example, 28.8Kbps) and multiplying it by a theoretically perfect V.42bis compression ratio of 4.

2. To start the installation of Dial-Up Networking, click on the Start button, and navigate Programs | Accessories | Dial-Up Networking. You'll be prompted whether you want to continue the installation as shown in Figure 25.3. Click the Install button to continue.

3. Next, you'll be prompted for any RAS capable devices (modems, terminal adapters, etc.) you may have attached, as shown in Figure 25.4. Because the server-side Remote Access Service and the client-side Dial-Up Networking basically use the same type of communications hardware, the Dial-Up Networking installation procedure uses the terminology "RAS capable devices" to mean the same type of hardware that would be used for Remote Access Service.

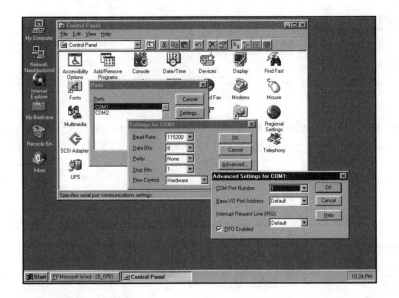

FIGURE 25.2

Recommended serial port settings for 28.8Kbps (and higher modems).

FIGURE 25.3

Installing Dial-Up Networking, as accessed via Start | Programs | Accessories | Dial-Up Networking.

FIGURE 25.4

Dial-Up Networking automatically prompts for the installation of RAS capable devices.

4. After the RAS capable devices are installed, click on the Configure button for each one to configure whether that device will be used for dial-out, receive only, or both. Figure 25.5 demonstrates this.

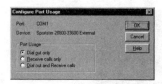

FIGURE 25.5

Configuring Port usage for the RAS device.

5. Next, we have to configure the network protocols that each RAS device will use, by clicking on the Network button as shown in Figure 25.6.

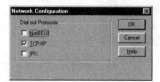

FIGURE 25.6

Configuring network protocols for the RAS device.

6. Finally, a reboot is required for the new software to take effect as shown in Figure 25.7.

FIGURE 25.7

Dial-Up Networking client software installation complete, ready to reboot for the new software to take effect.

Building a Dial-Up Networking Server

As we found out in "Understanding Dial-Up Networking," Microsoft changed the terminology they use to apply to dial-up networking such that "Remote Access Service" is no longer an umbrella term applied to both the client and the server as it was in Windows NT 3.51. A workstation or server running Windows NT 4.0 and Remote Access Services is now termed a *Dial-Up Networking Server*, a term used to describe the client-side software required to connect to it. The software which makes a Dial-Up Networking server is called Remote Access Service, and is bundled with both Windows NT Workstation and Windows NT Server (Windows NT Workstation's RAS accepts only one incoming connection, while Windows NT Server's RAS can accept up to 256 incoming connections). In the following section, we discuss what's required to build and implement a Dial-Up Networking server.

Server Requirements

To configure a dial-up server, the following components are needed:

- A workstation or server running Windows NT Server Version 4.0. This machine will act as the dial-up networking server.

- The installation media for Windows NT Server Version 4.0 (this requirement is so that you can load and configure the Remote Access Service on the workstation/server just mentioned).

- Telephone lines—these can be standard analog (voice) phone lines, or digital, as in the case of ISDN. Take a look at the number of remote/mobile employees needing simultaneous access, as well as the cost for each telephone line, to determine how many lines you need. These telephone lines can have a separate phone number, or you can arrange with your telephone company to group them with a common number that *automatically* "rolls through" each line until it finds one that's not busy. This plan is especially convenient for your remote users, as they won't have to dial multiple phone numbers on a trial-and-error basis, looking for one that's not busy.

- One modem for each phone line that you plan to service. Each modem should match the type of telephone circuit to which it connects (analog modem for standard analog phone line, ISDN terminal adapter for ISDN circuit, etc.). If you plan to service many phone lines, you might look into any of the various self-contained "integrated modem pools" offered by modem manufacturers. These systems essentially house 8 or 16 modems in a stackable (rack-mountable, in some cases) compact box.

♦ If you plan to connect more than four modems, you need a multiport serial adapter or cluster controller (see the following note) installed in this PC/server. These multiport serial adapters can come in different models that support 4, 8, 16, 32, and much higher numbers of serial ports. If you don't plan to connect more than four modems, you can use the PC/server's existing COM ports.

> **NOTE:** *Cluster controllers* are another option. A cluster controller is a special type of multiport serial adapter with a cable that leads into gangable concentrators (sometimes called *break-out boxes*). The concentrators have standard 9- or 15-pin serial ports, and are connected to the modems via standard serial cables. If more expansion is needed than is provided by a single concentrator, you can daisy-chain another concentrator from the first concentrator's expansion port. Depending on the product, cluster controllers with multiple ganged concentrators can sometimes support up to 1,024 simultaneously dialed-in users to a single PC/server!
>
> Because of the sheer large number of users a cluster controller can support, they are typically used in locations where large numbers of dial-up phone lines are concentrated. Internet Service Providers and large bulletin board systems are good examples of organizations which use cluster controllers in their dial-up modem banks to support large numbers of simultaneously dialed-in users.
>
> One company which manufactures cluster controllers listed as being supported on the Windows NT Hardware Compatibility List is Digi International; specifically their "C/X System" and "EPC/X System" cluster controllers.

♦ Cabling to connect the modems to the PC/server's COM ports or multiport serial adapter ports.

♦ Cabling to connect each modem to its phone line.

If you're planning to service no more than four phone lines with your dial-up server, you can forgo the multiport serial adapter or cluster controller, and use the PC/server's built-in COM ports instead. A workstation or PC typically comes with two physical serial ports, COM1 and COM2, and two logical (user-assignable) serial ports, COM3 and COM4. Most PC operating systems come preconfigured to recognize the four serial ports. This setup allows a maximum of four modems (thus four phone lines) to be connected to it: two external modems attached to the external COM1 and COM2 serial ports, and two internal modem cards configured for COM3 and COM4, respectively. (A variation on this idea is installing four internal modem cards configured for COM1 through COM4, leaving the external serial ports unused.) If your PC/server has a serial mouse (that is, it's not a PS/2-type mouse, but instead uses one of the external COM ports), a maximum of three phone lines can be served: one with an external modem, and the other two using internal modems.

> **TIP:** If you decide to go with using the PC/server's COM ports, be aware that COM ports *by default* share interrupts (IRQs). To be more specific, COM1 shares IRQ4 with COM3, and COM2 shares IRQ3 with COM4. If left configured that way, interrupt conflicts will occur between COM1 and COM3 (and likewise with COM2 and COM4)—with unpredictable results! Be sure to set the modem configured for COM3 to an alternate IRQ that isn't used by any other device (for example, IRQ5 or IRQ7, if they're currently unused), and do the same with the modem configured for COM4.

When choosing hardware for your Windows NT Server-based dial-up server, you should look at several issues for the most successful implementation:

♦ First is the PC/server hardware itself. Because the dial-up server is a gateway through which passes all data transferred between dial-up networking clients and the rest of the network, choosing its hardware is important for best performance.

♦ If you plan to support a large number of users (50 or more) dialing in, you'll want a fast Pentium or better CPU to keep up with the constant flow of interrupts (from the COM ports or multiport serial adapter) as users are tranferring data through the modems.

♦ Memory can also be an issue, with 32MB a recommended minimum for a light-duty (16 phone lines or less) dial-up server. If poor performance is experienced due to excessive paging or swapping, be prepared to add more physical memory to the system.

♦ The network adapter type and speed play a big role in the dial-up server's capacity to deliver data quickly to and from dialed-in clients. You should look at an EISA or preferably a PCI-based *bus mastering* network adapter, to avoid bottlenecks at the network card. In any network, the dialed-in users are going to access certain network resources (database servers, file servers, and so on) more than others. If you have a *multi-segmented* or subnetted network, try to locate the dial-up server either on or closest to the network segment having those network resources. This strategy gives the dial-up server the best access possible to those network resources, providing maximum performance for the dialed-in users. If an exceptionally large number of users (100 or more) are going to be dialing into that server simultaneously, locate the dial-up server on 100Megabit networking if and where available. A 100Megabit network (100BaseT, 100BaseVG, etc.) is a network which runs at 100 million bits per second, as opposed to the current standard 10Megabit network (10BaseT), which runs at 10 Million bits per second. The extra speed will prove valuable in keeping up with the increased demand from the dialed-in users for network resources.

♦ Finally, if the dial-up server *itself* is an information resource for the dialed-in users (for example, it serves dual-purpose as a database server, file server, etc.), a fast hard disk subsystem may be necessary to keep up with the constant demand for data.

Access Methods

Both Windows NT Workstation's Dial-Up Networking and Windows NT Server's Remote Access Service support several methods of dial-up access. This includes standard analog modems, ISDN terminal adapters, X.25, and Internet access (using Point-to-Point Tunneling Protocol). The following sections describe these methods.

Modem and ISDN Pools

Standard analog (voice) lines support a maximum transmission rate of 33.6Kbps, and ISDN lines can support up to 128Kbps. Remote Access Service can accommodate multiple modems ("modem pools") or ISDN Terminal Adapters. This type of RAS installation is one of the more common ones. Let's walk through a sample modem pool installation of RAS to see what information is required, and what options are available. In this sample installation, we'll install two U.S. Robotics 33.6Kbps Sportster modems to the serial ports (COM1 and COM2) of a server running Windows NT Server 4.0.

1. First, let's make sure the serial ports themselves are installed and setup properly. From the Start menu, navigate Settings | Control Panel | Ports. Since our example modems are U.S. Robotics 33,600bps Sportsters, we want to make sure that we set the highest possible speed on these ports (calculated as the carrier speed—33,600bps—multiplied by a "best case" 4x V.42bis compression ratio to equal over 115,200bps). It's also highly recommended to make sure that hardware handshaking and the 16550 UART circuit is enabled (refer to Figure 25.2).

2. Install Remote Access Service itself. From the Start menu, navigate Settings | Control Panel | Network. Pull the Services tab forward, and click the Add...button. Select Remote Access Service as shown in Figure 25.8, and click the OK button. Insert your Windows NT 4.0 installation media, and type the pathname to the installation files in the ensuing "Files Needed" dialog box.

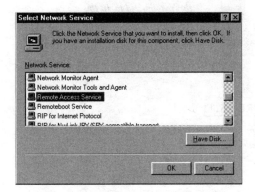

FIGURE 25.8

Installing Remote Access Service through the Control Panel.

3. If a modem has not been installed previously, a modem installer dialog box will appear as shown in Figure 25.9. Install the RAS capable devices by selecting the appropriate modem(s), and configure them for their respective serial ports. This is shown in Figure 25.10.

4. After each RAS capable device is installed, select each RAS capable device from the Remote Access Setup dialog box, and click on the Configure button to configure the port characteristics for each device. Decide whether the device will be used for dial-out only, receive calls only, or both dial-out and receive calls. Figure 25.11 illustrates that we're going to use our U.S. Robotics 33.6Kbps Sportster modems for receiving calls only (let's say the administrator for the server in our example has decided that it will act as a Dial-Up Networking Server only, and does not want her LAN users to use the server to dial-out).

FIGURE 25.9

If no modems were installed previously, Remote Access Service setup will prompt for them at install time.

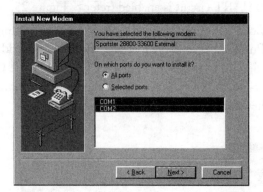

FIGURE 25.10

Configuring the modems for the serial ports that they're connected to. In this example, the U.S. Robotics Sportsters are connected to both COM1 and COM2.

FIGURE 25.11

Configuring the ports for each individual RAS device.

5. After the port characteristics for each RAS device have been configured, click on the Network button to configure the Network settings for each RAS device. The resulting dialog box allows you to configure Dial-Out Protocols, dial-in client protocols, and encryption settings. The "Server Settings" portion of this dialog is where the allowed protocol(s) are selected for the dial-up clients. Next to each protocol, a Configure button is available to configure that protocol. In our example, we've chosen to configure only TCP/IP for each RAS device as shown in

Figure 25.12. Also notice the RAS Server TCP/IP Configuration options in Figure 25.12; the RAS Server TCP/IP Configuration

allows setting:

◆ whether remote TCP/IP clients can access the entire network or just the RAS server itself only.

◆ how TCP/IP addresses are going to be assigned to the remote clients—either DHCP assigns an address dynamically, or selects an address from a static address pool.

◆ whether clients can request a predetermined IP address (this is useful in situations where network resources may only allow certain addresses have access to them).

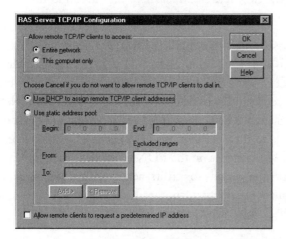

FIGURE 25.12

Configuring the network settings for each RAS device.

6. Click the OK button on each successive dialog box until you're back at the Network dialog box where you select the Services tab to load Remote Access Services. Click the OK button on this dialog box as well, and you should be prompted to restart the system for the new settings to take effect. Please do so.

X.25

Both Dial-Up Networking and Remote Access Service support X.25 networks. An X.25 network transfers data via packet switching, a method by which information is taken from many different users and combined into discrete data packets. These data packets are then forwarded to a kind of "network cloud" called the Packet Data Network (PDN). Each data packet is quickly routed through the PDN to its destination using self-contained routing information.

Using packet switching, an X.25 connection creates "virtual" circuits on the fly using standard analog phone lines. The data is characterized into packets which are switched in a logical fashion over a circuit shared by many different subscribers. Unlike the circuit switching that's used in a dedicated connection where the user actually has exclusive use of the circuit, a packet switched user has a "virtual" connection. The connection only appears to be dedicated. Instead of creating a permanent link between parties, the packet-switched circuit is set up on demand and lasts for the duration of that call only. A primary advantage of the X.25 network is that packet switching offers a significant cost savings compared to circuit switching. It is similar to a standard dial-up data modem connection but your business only pays for the time *used by actual traffic* on the connection, not the time the connection itself is open.

In an X.25 network, a Packet Assembler/Disassembler (PAD) is a device which assembles individual asynchronous transmissions from other nodes on the LAN into a single, synchronous X.25 packet. The PAD acts as a point-to-point 56Kbps multiplexer by buffering-up many X.25 packets, and sending this package out onto the Packet Data Network (the network cloud) to an X.25 switch. The X.25 switch then separates this package and routes the individual X.25 packets to their destination. Each packet then goes along its merry way though many other X.25 switches on the PDN to arrive at their destination. Each switch along the way checks the packets for errors, acknowledges receipt, and retransmits as necessary. Once at the destination, another X.25 PAD then disassembles each synchronous X.25 packet back into asynchronous LAN communications.

An X.25 network may be used in a variety of environments. For instance, X.25 is well suited in applications where:

- Line quality may not be good (X.25's error correction capabilities overcome poor line quality).
- Data volume is relatively small and "bursty."
- A company wants to use packet switching to decrease transmission expenses.

To set up Remote Access Service for X.25, you use the same technique as adding a modem, but instead of clicking on the Install Modem button on the Add RAS Device dialog box, you would click on the Install X.25 PAD button as shown in Figure 25.13. The type of X.25 PAD you select depends on your equipment and your service provider.

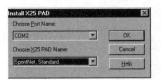

FIGURE 25.13

Installing an X.25 PAD as a RAS Device for use by a Dial-Up Networking server.

Next, select the X.25 PAD from the Remote Access Setup dialog, click on the Configure button, and select how that PAD is going to be used—whether it will be used for dial-out only, receive only, or both. This is shown in Figure 25.14.

FIGURE 25.14

Configuring the PAD for port usage.

Finally, we have to decide what networking protocols are going to be used for the X.25 PAD. On the Remote Access Setup dialog box, highlight the PAD, and click the Network button. Select the protocol(s) desired for the PAD, and click the Configure button next to each protocol to configure it, as the example in Figure 25.15 shows.

When finished, successively click the OK button all the way back to the Network Setup dialog, and reboot when prompted.

Configuring X.25 for client-side Dial-Up Networking is accomplished much the same way as creating a phonebook entry for a standard modem connection, except that you select an X.25 PAD instead of a modem.

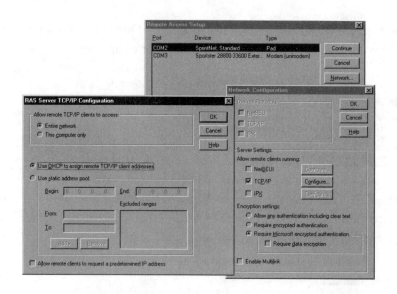

FIGURE 25.15

Configuring the network protocols for an X.25 PAD.

Internet

Dial-Up Networking and Remote Access Service can also be used as an "onramp" onto a network which is connected to the Internet. A common scenario is to configure a Windows NT Workstation or Server with the TCP/IP Protocol, Remote Access Service (with TCP/IP configured for the RAS devices), and the IP Forwarding checkbox enabled as shown in Figure 25.16

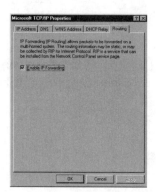

FIGURE 25.16

Enabling IP Forwarding in the TCP/IP Properties gives the Windows NT Workstation or Server the ability to act as a router.

When configured in this manner, users dialing into the Windows NT Workstation or Server can not only access the Dial-Up Networking server itself, but also the wide-area network it's connected to as well. Picture a remote user dialing into your network, and having at his/her disposal not only the resources on your network, but the Internet itself (if you've connected your network to the Internet) as well.

Where to Go Next

In this chapter, we discussed Dial-Up Networking and Remote Access Service, as well as how to size and configure a Dial-Up Networking Server. As with any new installation to, and modification of a network, prior planning is required to ensure the best possible results while minimizing unexpected "gotchas." Recommended reading for follow-up information is Chapter 24, for a discussion on Windows NT's implementation of the TCP/IP Protocol. The next chapter discusses connecting to the Internet, with some detailed discussion on how to approach some important decisions you'll have to make along the way.

Chapter | 26

Connecting to the Internet

In This Chapter:

♦ Planning for Your Internet Needs

♦ Securing Your Internet Connection

How do I...

With all the press the Internet is getting in today's online world, it's hard to turn on the TV, pick up a paper or magazine, and not see something related to the Internet. It can be in the form of an advertisement with an e-mail path or Web site address for the sponsoring company, or a story about something new happening or taking shape in the online world. Only a few years ago, it was unheard of to have Web site addresses or e-mail paths in TV advertisements. Today, not only are they commonplace, but more and more people and corporations are lured online; some to find out what this Internet thing is all about, some to take advantage of what may be a lucrative business opportunity. In a phone conversation only a few weeks ago, one of my remote family members said it best: "What're these 'http' things I keep seeing on commercials, and how do I use them?" For the home user, the Internet is a brand new world, full of adventure. For the corporation, Internet connectivity is (or can be, depending on how well it's used) a great business opportunity.

This chapter provides you, as a Windows NT system administrator, with the information and tools you need to make the leap to Internet connectivity. We discuss planning issues, identifying connectivity needs, choosing an Internet Service Provider (and the associated hardware), routing, and security.

That said, let's move to the first order of business: planning for your Internet needs.

Planning for Your Internet Needs

Internet connectivity is like electricity. You pay for it according to the amount you use, and you must be careful to choose the right kind of physical plant so that you have enough power. Internet connections are typically labelled—and priced—by the maximum peak bandwidth they support. For example, a T1 connection provides up to 1.544Mbps of bandwidth, even though your average usage might be less than that.

There are three necessary considerations to planning your Internet connection: what you use your connection for, where you get Internet service, and what kind of hardware you use. Let's look at each in detail.

Evaluating Your Internet Needs

Before you rush into planning, specifying, buying, and installing an Internet connection, stop and make sure you know why you're getting connected and what you're going to do with the connection once it's in place.

You may want an Internet connection to make it easier to communicate with suppliers and vendors, or you may want to set up a website of your products and services. As we saw in Chapter, planning for your likely eventual needs saves you money and time in the long run. Here are some questions you should ask during the planning process:

- Do you need a dedicated connection? If you're primarily going to be using the net for e-mail and letting your users access other servers' resources, an on-demand connection may suffice, and they are typically much less expensive than a dedicated connection.

- How much bandwidth to the Internet do you need? While most net surfers would reply, "As much as possible," you don't necessarily need a high-bandwidth connection for all uses. A 56Kbps line is probably the minimum acceptable speed for most corporate use and works well for e-mail exchange and some net access (of course, large numbers of users saturate this size link quickly.)

- If you plan to accept Network News Transport Protocol (NNTP) or Usenet traffic, or if your user base requires high-bandwidth access to net sites, you should consider stepping up to an ISDN or fractional T-1 line.

◆ How predictable are your bandwidth requirements? Some providers, like UUNet, allow you to buy bandwidth and pay extra if your peak usage exceeds what you've bought. Bandwidth demands for some applications, like e-mail exchange, are fairly constant, so reserving a certain bandwidth may be a less expensive option.

◆ Do you need to provide incoming access from the Internet? Just as with allowing RAS access, allowing the outside world to reach into your network is not something to undertake lightly; it requires careful security planning and load analysis before you start allowing outside access.

◆ Is your Internet connection a useful tool for employees or a critical part of your enterprise? Some enterprises depend absolutely on their Internet connection's uptime, while others can get by just fine during short outages. Decide which group you're in. If losing your connection means losing orders or not being able to communicate with important customers, you should find a provider who offers availability guarantees. Not all providers spend the extra money to install redundant hardware, backup power supplies, and the like. If you're planning on using redundant hardware to make sure your Internet server stays up, make sure your provider does the same.

◆ Have you allowed for the time required to administer and maintain the Internet connection? An Internet connection is not a one-time "do it and it's done" scenario. On the contrary, it requires sometimes many hours to administer and maintain. For example, there are ongoing maintenance requirements for access controls ("who can access my site from the outside", and "what Internet sites/services should I allow the people in my organization to use"), troubleshooting traffic bottlenecks, maintaining IP addresses and DNS lookup tables, implementation and maintenance of good virus protection, and upkeep of public FTP/WWW/GOPHER/NNTP servers.

◆ Can your current network configuration and topology be used as is, or do you need to reconfigure it to support the Internet connection? How about network traffic—will your current network configuration/topology support the additional traffic the Internet connection brings? An Internet connection almost always brings substantial additional traffic onto an existing network (end users using its services, outside Internet users visiting your FTP/WWW /GOPHER services, etc.). Your existing network might require redesign or tuning before the connection is established. Any discovered network problems need to be eliminated before the Internet connection is established.

- If you're planning a dedicated Internet connection and there's already a network in place, is that network running TCP/IP or not? TCP/IP is the de facto network protocol understood on the Internet. You won't find networks communicating over the Internet with IPX/SPX, AppleTalk, Banyan Vines, SNA, DLC, or any others—just TCP/IP. Some organizations claim to be communicating with one another over the Internet using one of the aforementioned non-standard protocols; however, what is happening in their case is that those network packets are being encapsulated inside of a TCP/IP packet before transmission onto the Internet. If your network isn't running TCP/IP, you must consider the costs of implementing at least one node (router, gateway, or firewall) that understands TCP/IP. This node in turn might be used as a gateway or protocol converter for the other nodes that don't have TCP/IP. Windows NT Server can be used as this node, or a dedicated multi-protocol router can be used.

One of the best things to do when trying to gauge the usefulness and cost analysis of an Internet connection is to consult with other organizations similar to yours that have already connected to the Internet. Ask them why they use the Internet, and what tangible or intangible benefits (as well as return on investment) they've gained from it. Ask them how often they use the Internet connection, what speed they're connected at, and how much a connection like their's costs.

When evaluating the cost of an Internet connection, you should consider both *hard* and *soft* cost items. Hard cost items are those for which an invoice or bill is created. Soft cost items are those items that are harder to quantify on paper, but are important nonetheless.

Hard costs include the cost of new phone lines or circuits, purchases of hardware (modems, terminal adapters, routers, and so on) , Internet Service Provider fees, and upgrades to existing hardware to make it *Internet ready*. Hard costs further break apart into two categories: fixed costs, which occur only once, and recurring costs, which accrue at regular intervals. Hardware purchases are fixed costs, while network access charges (usually paid both to the Internet service provider *and* whatever communications company provides the actual communications line) are recurring costs.

Soft costs include training and education of staff and end-users, deployment of new network-ready applications or network services such as FTP, GOPHER, WWW, and NNTP servers, centralized electronic mail services, or corporate-wide information systems. One way to look at soft costs is as people and organizational investments.

Identifying Your Connectivity Needs

There is a simple rule about Internet connectivity: the more you spend, the faster you can go and the more you can access. But when trying to identify your needs for an Internect connection, you should consider both speed and *why you want to use the Internet*. You should look at all the possible connection speeds and types that are available, not just the fastest, in light of your planned use of the Internet. This helps you arrive at a properly-sized Internet connection to get maximum return on investment. For example, to what Internet services do you need access, and which (if any) do you plan on providing for extenal customers? Here's a checklist of the most popular services:

- *Electronic mail.* This is the ability to exchange messages with other computer users over a network, such as the Internet. It's by far the most popular use of the Internet. These messages can be standard ASCII text, or have binary file attachments (such as word processing documents, spreadsheets, images or drawings, archived/compressed files, etc.). E-mail *by itself* presents a light load for an Internet connection because e-mail messages are usually very small. If that's the only Internet service your company will use, a dial-on-demand Internet solution probably would be sufficient. Individual e-mail messages can be sent immediately over an active dialed-up link to a local ISP access number or multiple messages can be spooled and sent or received in batches throughout the day to save on phone charges. However, if users are in the habit of attaching large files to Internet-bound e-mail messages, a larger pipe to the Internet might be needed, such as a dedicated connection.

- *File Transfer Protocol (FTP).* This is a protocol that allows a user on one networked computer to access, and transfer files to and from, another networked computer. *FTP* is also usually the *name* of the program the user invokes to access/transfer files using this protocol. Depending on the file sizes, the number of files transferred, and the number of simultaneous users using FTP, a dial-on-demand (for light usage) or dedicated connection (for heavy usage) might be needed.

- *Gopher.* This is a distributed information service that makes information available over the Internet using a hierarchical catalog. Gopher servers present simple menus of documents or directories they own; using a Gopher client, you select the item that interests you. Gopher is a fairly efficient protocol but has fallen into disuse since it's not as flexible as the protocol used to implement the World-Wide Web.

♦ *Internet news groups (USENET).* Commonly known as news groups, these are collections of message forums dedicated to individual topics of discussion. There are thousands of news groups on the Internet; choose any topic or subject, and there's probably a news group dedicated to it. You read news groups by *subscribing* to them; once subscribed, your news reader software will automatically check for new articles in that group the next time you start your news reader. USENET uses the Network News Transfer Protocol (NNTP).

Reading news requires the use of a news server that stores the articles as they arrive. This news server can be either be hosted by the Internet Service Provider or hosted on your site. One word of warning: hosting a news server is a big task, as it requires a fairly muscular server with lots of disk space and a robust dedicated Internet connection. If you consider that there are more than 16,000 news groups, with some individual news groups having 200 or more new articles a day, you can get a mental picture of the machine and Internet connection you would need.

Unless you're pondering your Internet connection for a large corporation, you should leave the news server hosting business to your Internet Service Provider and use what they provide. Otherwise, reading and posting news articles is just like e-mail; depending on how your news reader is set up (and how many news groups you're subscribed to), the impact on the Internet connection is minimal because the articles themselves are just plain ASCII text. A dial-up or dial-on-demand connection is usually fine to read news; however, if you have many users subscribed to many different news groups (especially very active news groups), you'll probably need a dedicated Internet connection.

♦ *The World Wide Web.* Ah yes, the ubiquitous WWW. One can't help but notice all the `http:` addresses in all the TV and media advertisements these days, nor help hearing an Internet discussion with the phrase *surfing the Web.* The World Wide Web is a collection of servers that make up hypertext-based distributed information system. You need a World Wide Web browser to view these servers' information services, but when viewed, the result is a very straightforward graphical or textual representation of the data.

Because the data is displayed as hypertext, navigation through the data is as easy as clicking or pressing Enter. Second only to e-mail in popularity,

Internet users have come to expect access to the World Wide Web; nontechnical Internet users in many cases (incorrectly) equate Internet access with WWW access. Web browsers can not only browse Web servers, but also FTP servers, Gopher servers, and several other types of servers as well. Web browsing can be done quite successfully with a dial-on-demand Internet connection; however, Web servers can and often do serve-up intense Web documents consisting of many large graphical images.

If there are many users in your institution who need access to Internet Web servers, you'll need a dedicated Internet connection. If you're planning on hosting a Web server to outside Internet users (possibly to advertise your group or institution's services), you have the choice of letting your Internet Service Provider host the Web documents to the Internet for you on their servers, or you can opt for an onsite Web server that you maintain. The former doesn't require you to maintain an active open connection to the Internet (because the Internet Service Provider always has an open pipe to the Internet 24 hours a day), so a dial-up or dial-on-demand Internet connection is fine. The latter instance of an onsite Web server requires a dedicated Internet connection, because you most likely want your Web server always available to outside Internet users (otherwise, in the case of a dial-up or dial-on-demand Internet connection, your Web server would only be available to outside users while the dial-up connection is actively established).

Often, usage versus price dictates a connection speed and type that is most appropriate for your requirements. The fastest dedicated connection might not offer the best return on investment (For an extreme example, having a 45 Mbps T3 connection to the Internet when it's only used for e-mail or other light load uses). So, when determining Internet connectivity needs, the following aspects should be considered:

♦ *Type of service.* Will your Internet usage dictate an always immediately-available, dedicated connection, or will a dial-on-demand connection suffice? A dial-on-demand connection is inexpensive and good for sporadic or light usage. Light usage might include Internet connection for a very small company or group that wants to send and receive e-mail and only occasionally browse Web pages and news groups or transfer files. A dedicated connection is much more expensive, but gives much faster access to Internet resources, can support more users, and allows outside Internet users better access to your company's resources.

♦ *Bandwidth.* How much traffic, both inbound (coming into your site) as well as outbound (going out from your site) do you expect? This depends strongly on what Internet services you plan to use (e-mail, transferring files, browsing the Web and/or news groups, etc.). Don't forget to consider the number of people in your organization, and how many of them require Internet services. (For more information on available bandwidths, see "Dedicated Connections" later in this chapter.)

♦ *Quality of service.* Will the Internet connection be a focal point of your institutions business/research, and/or do you foresee the Internet connection being used continuously? What impact would an interruption in the Internet connection have on your institution's workflow? Here it helps to select a reputable Internet Service Provider with a track record and comprehensive support infrastructure.

♦ *Growth considerations.* If your business or institution grows and creates a higher demand for Internet services, would the Internet connection allow for greater speed or bandwidth? Can it be easily upgraded with a minimum of hardware swap-outs or upgrades? As the Internet connection is more fully exploited, it helps to plan ahead and select a connection type that is easily upgraded. Once your connection is in place and users have climbed the learning curve, access becomes easier and uses that you never considered become practical.

Choosing a Connection Type

There are three basic types of connections that can be made to the Internet:

♦ Dial-up access to a connection service (shell account)

♦ Dial-up connection (dial-up analog SLIP/PPP, or ISDN)

♦ Dedicated connection (leased digital line)

Let's discuss each one.

Dial-Up Access to a Connection Service (Shell Account)

The first connection method is worth mentioning because it's so prevalent on Internet Service Provider's price sheets. It's the dial-up access to a connection service, as known as a shell account. It uses a workstation with modem attached and terminal emulation software (such as ProComm Plus or Windows NT 4.0's built-in HyperTerminal) to dial into a node that is connected to the Internet. The terminal emulation software sets up a terminal session with the Internet node to allow the user to use *that Internet node's services* to access Internet resources. This is called a shell account because the dialed-in user is using the Internet node's shell (or operating system) to gain access to Internet resources, and the Internet access is typically limited to just the dialed-in workstation (that is, it's usually not possible for other workstations on the LAN to access the Internet resources through the dialed-in workstation).

This type of connection usually requires some knowledge of the Internet node's core operating system (usually Unix), and sometimes entails using command-line based utilities in the terminal emulation window to access Internet resources. Typically, only character-based e-mail, remote login (rlogin or telnet), FTP, character-based Web browsing (e.g.: Lynx) or other limited functions are allowed using a shell account, although some allow the use of a command-line SLIP utility (on the Internet node) to switch from the shell to a full-featured SLIP connection on the fly. Shell accounts are typically the least expensive of the three access methods; however, with the graphical direction the World Wide Web is taking the Internet, and the fact that Internet access is limited to just the dialed-in workstation, the shell account's popularity is waning.

Dial-Up Connection

The second type of Internet connection, a dial-up connection, is one that uses a regular analog phone line (or digital in the special case of ISDN), and a workstation with appropriate networking software and a modem. When the connection to the Internet is needed, the workstation (and its accompanying network software) calls the Internet Service Provider over its modem and phone line and establishes a TCP/IP connection.. When the connection is no longer needed, the connection is dropped.

Establishing the connection can be done either manually or automatically as in *dial on demand*. Line speeds for this type of connection range from 9.6 Kbps to 128 Kbps, with speeds in the middle (14.4 Kbps, 28.8 Kbps, 33.6 Kbps) being the most common. This type of connection is the most popular. It can be used to connect a single workstation, or an entire local area network (LAN) if the workstation is configured for routing. Dial-up connections typically make use of SLIP (Serial Line Interface Protocol) or PPP (Point-to-Point Protocol), and can have either static or dynamic IP addressing. In static IP addressing the workstation has a fixed IP address assigned to it that is always used when dialing up the Internet Service Provider. In dynamic IP addressing, the ISP can assign that workstation an address automatically upon dial-up. The latter is by far the most common; static IP addresses are typically used only for remote networks within the same company (e.g.: remote offices, buildings or departments that do not share the same corporate backbone). These remote locations typically need access to company resources, but maybe for network configuration reasons need to stay within the company's fixed TCP/IP addressing scheme.

Dial-up connections are very popular with single individuals or small groups of individuals, and serve effectively for e-mail, reading USENET news, and light FTP, GOPHER, and WWW access. One thing to look out for in your area when evaluating a dial-up connection is the tariff structure of your phone company. Some phone companies charge on a per call basis, while others have a flat rate (with unlimited local calls). The former, depending on how far away the ISP is and how much the dial-up Internet connection is used, can run a phone bill that sometimes exceeds the cost of the dial-up connection itself. Check with your local phone company to find out what type calling plan you have.

A new and increasingly important high speed alternative to the standard analog dial-up connection is Integrated Services Digital Network (ISDN). It differs from the standard dial-up analog SLIP/PPP connection in that it's much faster (more than three times faster than a 33.6 Kbps connection), and it uses a digital phone line or a pair of digital lines. ISDN has the useful ability to double as a regular voice circuit, often simultaneously with an active data connection. ISDN service currently suffers from limited availability, but it has a very bright future. ISDN offers 64 or 128 Kbps capability (or 56/112 Kbps depending on the carrier), and is typically the next step up in price and performance. A dial-up digital service, ISDN was intended for short-lived sessions and thus normally costs the same as a normal analog telephone call. In certain areas, just like the dial-up analog SLIP/PPP connections described above, phone companies may impose an ISDN service tariff structure that might deter some companies from using it for full-time Internet access for fear of running up a big bill. In the areas where ISDN service has a flat charge, it is an attractive medium for accessing the Internet. Apart from any local phone company line charges, the ISP monthly charge for ISDN Internet service typically is between the price for a standard dial-up SLIP/PPP connection and a dedicated leased line. Be forewarned; because ISDN is comparatively new, the phone company (or ISP) may dictate the type and brand name of equipment you must purchase.

Dedicated Connection

A dedicated connection is a digital connection; it requires a point-to-point digital telecommunications link and an IP router to link the organization to the Internet. An IP router is a dedicated networking device that forwards traffic between IP networks. Line speeds for a dedicated connection range from 9.6 Kbps to 45 Mbps (because discussions of Internet or network communications always revolve around serial communications, the lowercase b means bits, not bytes). By far, the most common Internet connection speeds are 56/64 Kbps, Frame Relay (56 Kbps to T1 speeds), and T1 (1.54 Mbps). A dedicated connection is sometimes thought of as a *leased-line* connection, in that the telecommunications link to the Internet is always open and communicating. Dedicated connections require a permanently assigned IP address on the node that is used for the connection to the Internet.

There are six different types of dedicated Internet connections:

◆ *56/64 Kbps.* This is a common dedicated connection method, and it's good for smaller organizations. It requires a router, CSU/DSU, and digital phone circuit between you and your ISP (this phone circuit is used only by you— it's not shared with another Internet customer). The caveat to this dedicated connection type is that there's no growth potential without substantial hardware upgrade.

◆ *Frame Relay (56 Kbps—T1 speeds).* Frame Relay access is a popular means of Internet connectivity, and it's available in most major urban areas. Frame Relay allows an ISP to purchase a T1 line (1.544 Mbps) from the phone company and a router for connecting to the customer side. This router then connects dozens of 56 Kbps frame relay customers to the Internet. This translates into cost savings for the end user; frame relay is typically the lowest-cost leased digital circuit to the Internet. It allows you to get low-cost 56 Kbps access initially and to easily upgrade to T1 speeds in the future without a forklift upgrade of hardware or new leased-line installation charges. You simply tell your ISP you want to go faster (get out your checkbook) and tell the phone company to increase your line speed (and your monthly charge, of course). As of this writing, Frame Relay scalability up to T3 speeds (45 Mbps) is being formalized. The only caveat to Frame Relay (a minor one in most instances) is that you're sharing the ISP's T1 connection with other Frame Relay customers.

- *FT1 (also known as Fractional T1)*. This is a common dedicated Internet connection for mid-size organizations. It has good growth potential in that you pay for a T1 circuit on the local loop, but pay for fractional access to the Internet in 64 Kbps increments. The most common speeds for this type of service are 256, 512, 768, and 1024 Kbps.

- *T1 (1.544 Mbps)*. Common for large organizations, and for heavily accessed systems. Provides fast response to and from the Internet.

- *FT3 (also known as Fractional T3)*. This is for large organizations who foresee (or just plain need) scalability beyond T1's maximum speed. Fractional T3 is purchased in 1.544 Mbps increments, and approach a full T3's maximum speed of 45 Mbps. This type of Internet connection is common among Internet Service Providers themselves, so they can start up small, and work up to a full T3 as their customer base grows larger.

- *T3 (45 Mbps)*. As of this writing, the ultimate Internet connection. Very large companies, organizations, and large popular Internet Service Providers invest in this type of connection. Full T3 provides maximum bandwidth to and from the Internet. As can be expected, this is also the most expensive Internet connection, costing many thousands of dollars a month.

Choosing a Service Provider

One important and lasting decision to make when connecting to the Internet is the question of who will be your Internet Service Provider (ISP). There are many questions you should ask to evaluate and select the ISP that's right for you. We'll outline some of these questions to give you an idea of what to look for and what to watch out for. Probably the best tool you can have in your arsenal when shopping for an ISP is *experience*. If you haven't been exposed to the Internet before, now is the time. If you have a PC or Macintosh with a 14.4 or 28.8 Kbps modem, obtain a shell, SLIP, or PPP account with a local Internet Service Provider. If you're reading this book, you probably also receive some computer related periodicals. If so, many of these computer periodicals may have a floppy or two bundled with them advertising an ISP (The Pipeline and GNN come to mind). Many ISPs offer special deals where a certain number of startup hours are free. If you try a shell account, also try a SLIP/PPP account (or vice versa) to get an idea of the differences.

NOTE: Many *online services* (CompuServe, America Online, Prodigy, etc.) offer Internet connectivity as part of their bundles. Very often, a good number of their startup hours are free. However, their Internet services are often masked behind a proprietary graphical user interface (remember, they're targeting the general public). Keep in mind their presentation of the Internet to you is often not what you'll see from an Internet Service Provider (as opposed to an online service).

There are several thousand Internet service providers (ISPs) all across North America, ranging in size from the small (Airnet, which serves north Alabama and southern Tennessee) to the large (AT&T and MCI). Which type is right for you depends on how you answered the questions above, as well as your level of comfort with your ISP's local support personnel. Just as with most other types of service business, size can be an advantage or a disadvantage. Providers are like cars; they come in several different sizes, and which size is best for you depends on your individual needs.

The ISP market is very like a food chain. At the top of the food chain are the companies that operate the Internet's backbone, the main channel for traffic that needs to pass between large providers. The large providers come next. They sell bandwidth in large chunks to mid-size ISPs, who in turn sell it to small, local ISPs. There are exceptions; for example, some local providers buy their service directly from large companies like Sprint, without going through an intermediate provider.

In general, the large, national providers (including AT&T, MCI, UUNet, PSI, and Netcom) offer the widest range of services, from minimal installations (where the provider only supplies TCP/IP connectivity) to complete outsourcing arrangements (where the provider selects, installs, supports, and maintains all the Internet connectivity hardware and software.) Large providers typically also offer some type of service availability guarantee.

However, larger providers may not offer service in all areas, and they may not be able or willing to handle unusual configuration requests or requirements. Of course, many organizations prefer the comfort of dealing with a company like AT&T or MCI instead of a smaller, lesser-known entity.

Mid-size ISPs typically serve multi-state regions; examples include Mindspring (Alabama, Georgia, and parts of Tennessee) and iQuest (Indiana, Ohio, parts of

Kentucky and Michigan). These providers tend to be very flexible, and usually one or two mid-size providers provide the main regional access points to the Internet backbone. On the negative side, these ISPs frequently offer no availability guarantees, and they may not be able to supply integration or consulting services directly to you.

Small local ISPs, like interQuest (Huntsville, Alabama) and Rustnet (metro Detroit), are like local garages. There are good ones, with competent staff, fair policies, and good equipment—then there are some that aren't so good. Small ISPs are often the only option in small communities; even in larger areas, the hometown ISP often provides more individual and flexible support than larger, far-away competitors. Many companies prefer the idea of using a local vendor for Internet access.

Oddly, pricing is mostly independent of your provider's size. The increasing public awareness of the Internet has spurred a price war for personal Internet access, with rates in many areas hovering around $20/month for unlimited use. Price competition isn't as evident in the business connectivity market for the same reason it's not a factor for business airfares, but as the market consolidates you'll probably see prices drop somewhat.

No matter which category of ISPs seems best for you, here are some questions to ask your prospective ISP:

- ◆ Does the ISP have redundant hardware? What about backup power and redundant network links? If your enterprise depends on constant Internet access, don't pick a provider that can't guarantee their service.

- ◆ What sort of availability guarantee does the ISP offer, if any? Is there a dedicated network operations staff? How are support calls outside of normal business hours handled, if at all?

- ◆ What bandwidth connection does the ISP have? How many other customers will you be sharing it with? A T1 shared between many customers might become overloaded, and if you buy a full T1 to an ISP that only has a 512Kb link to the Internet you're wasting money.

- ◆ Where does the ISP get *its* connectivity from? Does it depend on a single provider? If so, damage to that provider can render redundant links useless. If the provider has a service guarantee, that's a good sign.

- ◆ What's the average response time to a network outage report? Does the ISP have agreements with its upstream providers to quickly investigate routing problems and outages?

♦ How much experience does the ISP have with clients like you? A small ISP whose business is 90% individual users may not have the expertise to provide a net connection for a 6000-user corporate campus, but a giant provider may not be the best choice for your small regional office.

♦ What does the type of service you need cost? What hardware, software, and support items are included in the cost? Things to consider: the circuit cost (installation and monthly charge), the router (cost of onsite router, cost of offsite router), hardware/software , membership fee.

♦ For dedicated connections, who fixes the equipment if it breaks? If they are responsible for these repairs,do they require 24 hour access to the physical location?

♦ Do they have an acceptable use policy?

♦ Are there limitations to connecting to other parts of the Internet (i.e., can you get everywhere you need to get)?

♦ To whom else do they provide service? Have them provide references.

TIP: Because Internet Service Providers usually only have experience with, or have a vested interest in, a certain brand of hardware or operating system, they might not be the best source for help with your particular integration plan. For example, some ISPs tell you that an Internet connection can still only be done using a machine running a flavor of Unix and that you must purchase such a machine! There are several hardware/operating system neutral companies that offer good consulting and integration services to help you make the right decisions when connecting to the Internet. These companies often have an extensive support infrastructure with specialists formally trained on a variety of hardware and operating systems. Intergraph (http://www.intergraph.com/network/; +1 800 345 4856) and UUnet (http://www.uu.net; +1 800 488 6383) are good starting points.

Where to Find ISPs for Your Area(s)

If you have a personal or single-user Internet connection (such as a shell account or a SLIP/PPP account), there are great resources on the World Wide Web to help you find an Internet Service Provider; just point your browser at the URLs indicated:

- CommerceNet's Internet Service Providers Directory: http://www.com-merce.net/jump/isp/index.html

- Network USA's ISP Catalog: http://www.netusa.net/ISP/

- Mecklermedia's *The List*: http://thelist.iworld.com/

Using these search databases, you can quickly locate an ISP that serves your area(s) and best suits your connectivity needs.

Choosing Hardware

We mentioned earlier that to communicate over the Internet and use its resources, you need to run the TCP/IP protocol on your network. Internet connectivity means TCP/IP connectivity, and the hardware you choose must support it.

For a shell account, all you need is a workstation with a good terminal program on it (ProComm Plus, or Windows NT's built-in HyperTerminal), a modem, and an analog (voice) phone line. The shell account is the only instance where TCP/IP isn't needed *on the local workstation*, because the node you're dialing into provides the TCP/IP services for you.

For a SLIP/PPP account, you need a workstation, a fast modem (14.4 Kbps or better), an analog phone line, and a dial-up TCP/IP suite. To browse the World Wide Web, you also need a Web browser, which often isn't included with the workstation's TCP/IP suite. Windows NT Workstation and Server both provide a dial-up TCP/IP suite as part of their Dial-Up Networking software. Microsoft's Internet Explorer Web browser is bundled in Version 4.0 of Windows NT Workstation and Server, so you have all the software tools you need for a successful SLIP/PPP Internet connection.

For a dedicated (digital) connection to the Internet, the following are to be considered *bare minimum*:

- *Channel Service Unit/Data Service Unit (CSU/DSU)*: This device connects to the digital phone line that the phone company provides. It performs many of the same functions that modems do, but it does not have to convert digital signals to/from analog (i.e.: modulate/demodulate like a standard modem does), because the end device and the underlying transmission facility are both digital. You can either purchase or lease a CSU/DSU.

- ◆ *Router*: a device that routes packets from the Internet to the local machines and from the local machines out onto the Internet. It does this through the use of internally stored routing tables that match each packet to its next target hop to find an optimal path. With today's concerns about security, this router should also include some kind of packet filtering capability (we discuss more about this capability in the section on security). One end of the router connects to the CSU/DSU, and the other connects to the local area network. You can purchase or lease a router, or you can use NT itself as a router.

- ◆ *A local area network (LAN)*: naturally, if you're connecting to the Internet with a dedicated link, you must have good reasons, and one of these reasons should be the fact that you have a LAN of workstations/servers that need Internet access. The router will directly connect to your LAN, and you'll have to treat it as a new node on your network.

Of course, this doesn't include the computers you use to offer services to Internet users (like your NT servers running IIS). It also doesn't include special-purpose hardware like firewalls or items needed for your Internet presence (gateways for routing e-mail between the Internet and your LAN mail system, IIS, or other net service software.)

Internet Traffic and Your Network

When you connect your network to the Internet, you have to ensure that traffic can flow between them as needed. There are two key requirements. First, your network must have legitimate network addresses. Second, you must have a way to route packets to their final destinations. Let's examine what changes your network may require to meet these requirements.

Routing Internet Traffic

Routing is the process by which TCP/IP packets get from their origin to their destination. The Internet Protocol—the "IP" in TCP/IP—is responsible for routing packets to their eventual destination. This section outlines how NTS routes TCP/IP packets, but the basic mechanism is the same for any TCP/IP router.

The IP layer gets packets from two sources: the network interface card passes incoming packets to IP for routing, and the higher-level TCP/IP protocols pass outgoing packets for distribution. Each packet contains the IP addresses of its origin and its destination.

The IP layer inspects the packet's destination address and compares it to a table of routing data that specifies where the packet should go next based on its destination. IP allows for three possibilities: the packet can be ignored and discarded, it can be forwarded to another intermediate address for further processing, or it can be passed up to a higher-level TCP/IP protocol.

If the packet is to be discarded, or passed to another TCP layer, no further routing is requierd. Routing *is* required for packets that are still in transit, and it's actually accomplished by modifying the packet's Media Access Control (MAC) address. Remember, the MAC address is the physical address of the device for which the packet is intended, not the IP address of the destination. When a packet sent from IP address 1.2.3.4 to IP address 5.6.7.8 is routed, the MAC address can change many times as individual routers along the path redirect the packet. The destination address, however, remains the same.

MAC addresses for the next hop come from the local routing table, which specifies where to send packets that match an address specified in each table entry. *Host routes* supply the destination MAC address for a host with a particular IP address. *Subnet* and *network* routes provide the MAC address of routers or gateways that provide routing for particular subnets or networks. The *default route* is where packets that don't match any table entry get sent; it usually points to the default gateway.

These routes are mostly automatically maintained. *The ICMP protocol* (another part of the TCP/IP suite) provides a way for routers, gateways, and computers to share routing information and negotiate data flow. *ICMP redirect* messages tell a router of a better route to reach a given MAC destination. NTS uses redirects to update its route table. *ICMP quench* messages are sent by a receiver to tell a sender to slow down, much like XON/XOFF on standard ASCII connections.

If you're considering a dial-up SLIP/PPP (or ISDN) connection to the Internet, have the dial-up workstation on a network, and want to use that workstation as a router for the other nodes on your network, you have to enable routing (shown as IP forwarding) for your TCP/IP Protocol configuration. This is done by bringing up the Windows NT Control Panel, double-clicking on Network, bringing the Protocols tab forward, double-clicking on TCP/IP Protocol, pulling the Routing tab forward, and placing a check mark in Enabling IP Forwarding as in Figure 26.1. Once this is done, your workstation acts as a router to the Internet while it is dialed-in with SLIP/PPP to your ISP. For more details on using NTS as a TCP/IP router, see the section titled, "Using a Windows NT Server as a Router" in Chapter 24.

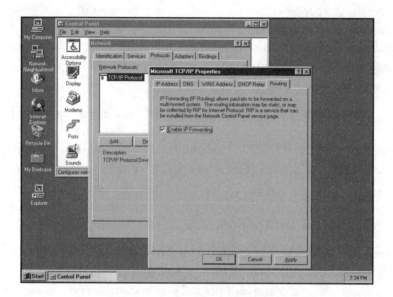

FIGURE 26-1

Windows NT allows you to configure a server as a router by enabling IP forwarding in your TCP/IP Protocol configuration.

NOTE: The description of routing above ignores many of the subtleties of the routing protocols and router behavior. For more details on the protocols that get packets from A to B, see Douglas Comer's book, listed in "Where To Go Next" at the end of this chapter.

Network Addressing and Your Network

As you contemplate connecting to the Internet, take note of the IP addresses (if you have one) that's in use in your organization. When making a dedicated digital connection to the Internet, you are required to have registered TCP/IP address(es) from the Network Information Center (you just can't pick TCP/IP addresses; they are assigned to you). If you already have registered addresses, then access to the Internet is basically seamless. If you have unregistered IP addresses in your organization or insufficient registered addresses to expand your network, you should draw up a plan of attack before the connection to the Internet is made. Your choices are limited when dealing with this problem: you can change all your addresses to registered ones, use a proxy server to isolate your network from the Internet, or use a network address translator (NAT) to represent your unregistered addresses to the Internet as registered addresses. Let's take a look at each option:

The first option—changing all your unregistered addresses to registered ones—presents a difficultproblem. First, medium to large organizations would have a problem acquiring sufficient addresses to meet their current and future needs. The NIC is *out* of class A addresses (there were 254 of those; 16 million hosts each), resists giving out class B addresses (64,000 total, having 64,000 hosts each), and will send you to your ISP for class C addresses (254 hosts each). Because of the inefficiencies of IP addressing, a class B network may only break out into enough addresses for 10,000 to 20,000 nodes. If you do acquire the address class of your choice, you must set about changing every computer and networking device's IP address in your organization. This is an incredible undertaking for large organizations.

The second choice is a proxy server (such as a machine running Microsoft's Catapult, http://www.microsoft.com./proxy/) and is the traditional means of dealing with this problem. A proxy server makes connections to the outside world on your behalf and uses a minimum number of addresses doing so. A proxy server gives the internal network a single point of contact for Internet access.

The proxy server usually listens on a specific TCP/IP port for connections from clients on the internal LAN. The client software sends a special message to the proxy server indicating where the client wants to connect (for example, most Web browsers are easily configured to use a proxy server, and once configured, it's seamless to the user—the Web browser takes care of sending this special message to the proxy server). The proxy server then makes the connection to the Internet destination on behalf of the inside client. For the rest of that client Internet session, the proxy server reads from one side and writing to the other.

Because the proxy server is a single point of contact for Internet resources, proxy servers also can provide access control down to the individual person level if the corporation needs it. This single point of Internet contact is also a caveat; because the proxy server is in the path of every single packet going to and from the Internet, performance can quickly become an issue for organizations with a hundred or more users. Another disadvantage to a proxy server is their configuration and maintenance; they have extensive setup and ongoing maintenance, which can carry a high cost.

The final choice is a fairly recent technology called network address translation (NAT). A NAT system placed at the boundary of your corporate IP network and the Internet allows you to represent your entire corporate IP network (which may consist of unregistered addresses) as a smaller set of *registered* addresses to the Internet. This allows you to build your internal IP network to meet your business requirements and have a small set of addresses for accessing the Internet. This has the useful side effect of hiding your internal IP addressing scheme from the outside world. A class C network (254 host addresses) in an NAT system can support a company with much more than 254 employees for connecting to the Internet.

Securing Your Internet Connection

Internet and *insecure* are two words that naturally seem to go well together. The original Internet protocols were developed in academia where the developers, for the most part, could trust each other. The TCP/IP protocol and many of the services that run on top of it, offer relatively weak security. To compound the problem, many of the protocol implementations suffer from vulnerabilities introduced by poor program design or sloppy coding (ask a Unix guru about sendmail bugs sometime for a practical example.)

There is some good news, though—NTS is not subject to all of the same security vulnerabilites as Unix servers, because it doesn't use the same code. For example, there's no standard NT equivalent of the Unix sendmail or telnetd processes, so attacks that exploit flaws in these programs won't work against NT hosts. Don't take this to mean that NT is secure; it just means that not as many security holes have been found in NTS yet.

You can implement Internet security at several levels. For best security, you should plan on implementing security measures on at least the packet and protocol levels.

Packet-Level Security

Packet-level security is where a *firewall* or router examines incoming and outgoing packets and rejects, logs, or ignores those that don't meet your security criteria. As the name implies, a firewall sits between the Internet and your internal LAN. The firewall's role is to block traffic that doesn't meet criteria you specify. A common example is a setting that allows SMTP connections on port 23 to pass through the firewall to LAN hosts, but rejects incoming connections on all other ports.

Dedicated firewalls typically include two network interfaces: one accepts packets from the Internet, and the other communicates only with the secure internal network. The firewall software decides which packets get copied from the open interface to the private one. Similar functionality is available in many off-the-shelf routers, brouters, and gateways.

You can implement an inexpensive firewall with an NTS machine, two network cards, and software from a number of third-party vendors. These firewalls use one NIC to connect to your LAN and one to connect to the Internet. The firewall software mediates the transfer of packets between the two.

At a minimum, you should include this level of security. Good packet-level security protects you against many kinds of attacks by screening out hostile traffic before it can reach into your network.

Protocol Security

Protocol security involves using features of the application protocol (like FTP or HTTP) to provide security. The best example of this today is Netscape's Secure Sockets Layer (SSL) protocol, which allows encryption and authentication of both ends of any TCP/IP stream. Protocol security can offer additional protection against spoofing attacks (when an attacker pretends to be a trusted host or user), which are more sophisticated than packet-based attacks but harder to track and prevent.

Windows NT Security Features

NTS itself offers several security features that can help reduce the risk of break-ins or damage from Internet intruders. At a minimum you should do the following:

♦ Turn off the default FTP service; it's insecure. If you want to serve files via FTP, use Microsoft's IIS instead, as described in Chapter 27, "Running Microsoft Internet Information Server."

♦ Disable the Guest account. Rename the Administrator account. Make sure that all user accounts have well-chosen passwords.

NOTE: The CD includes an evaluation version of the Kane Security Analyst from Intrusion Detection. KSA performs a rigorous check of your system's security and generates a fanatically detailed report of what it finds. Run it before you connect to the Internet—you might be surprised at what it finds.

♦ Carefully review the users and groups that have local accounts on machines visible to the Internet (for example, your WWW server). Double-check to be certain that none of the users on that machine have wide access throughout the domain to which the server belongs.

♦ Use NTFS. Set access controls on *all* files and directories on your server. Remove the default setting of allowing Everyone to have Full Control over shared files. Use the File Manager's Security menu to enable auditing of your NTFS partitions, then periodically review the audit logs.

♦ Subscribe to the advisory list put out by the Computer Emergency Response Team (CERT; their web site is at `http://www.cert.org`). CERT often offers the first early warning of newly discovered security flaws.

Where to Go Next

This chapter explained how to get your network connected to the worldwide Internet. Prior planning is strongly recommended, and you may find these references helpful as you plan and implement your connection:

♦ Chapter 24, "Interoperating with TCP/IP Clients" covers the Windows NT implementation of the Internet's TCP/IP protocol.

♦ Chapter 27, "Running Microsoft Internet Information Service" has more details on ensuring the security of your IIS server.

♦ The clearest and most concise guide to securing Internet hosts remains Bellovin and Cheswick's *Firewalls and Internet Security: Repelling the Wily Hacker* (Addison-Wesley, 1994; ISBN 0-201-63357-4).

♦ Likewise, the third edition of Douglas Comer's *Internetworking With TCP/IP* (Prentice-Hall, 1995; ISBN 0-132-16987-8) is probably the best single resource for understanding the technical details behind routing protocols and how they can impact your network planning.

Chapter | 27

Running Microsoft
Internet Information
Server

In This Chapter:

◆ Planning Your Internet Services

◆ Introducing Internet Information Server (IIS)

◆ Installing IIS

◆ Administering IIS

◆ IIS Security

How do I...

Bundled with Windows NT Server 4.0 is a powerful, flexible Internet server called Internet Information Server (IIS). This program offers secure FTP, Gopher, and World Wide Web (WWW) services. This chapter is about Microsoft's Internet Information Server, a component of Windows NT Server 4.0 that you can use for a presence on the Internet. Even if you're not connected to the Internet, you can still use IIS as a very robust solution for your company's *intranet*: think of it as your own local Internet.

ON THE

CD

> **NOTE:** The CD includes Process Software's Purveyor Web server. It's a competitor to IIS, but with some features (like search engine capability) that IIS lacks.

Planning Your Internet Services

Throughout this book, we've emphasized the benefits of good pre-installation planning. IIS is no different from any other NTS service; you'll get the most return from the least effort if you consider what you want to do before starting. (Throughout this section, we'll talk about Internet services, but this includes using IIS on your corporate network as well.) For complete details on connecting to the Internet, refer to Chapter 26, "Connecting to the Internet."

The most important decision you'll make is deciding what Internet services, if any, you provide to Internet or intranet users. Most organizations want to create an *Internet presence* after installing their Internet connection. That is, some kind of server that either advertises their organization or provides some kind of service back on the Internet to let outsiders know who they are.

Three main types of services are used to create an Internet presence:

- *FTP server*. As discussed in Chapter 26 FTP stands for *file transfer protocol*; it's the method by which files can be transferred back and forth between the FTP Server and the user. The program used to transfer files with the FTP protocol is also called *ftp*. It's usually a character-based (command-line) utility, although a World Wide Web browser can be used as a graphical way of browsing FTP servers. FTP servers can be configured to require username/password combinations for secure access. They can also accept guest users using a special username of anonymous, ftp, or guest, with their e-mail address as the password. FTP servers can log their sessions, which can include information such as the TCP/IP address of the connecting node, username entered, password entered, whether the connection was successful, and what documents/files were requested.

- *Gopher server*. A Gopher server is essentially a lookup-and-fetch service. It lists files, enabling the user to look for files or documents with relevant titles. These titles can include links to other Gopher servers—a primitive pre-WWW hyperlink. When the user selects an item, the Gopher client application then fetches the specified information for the user, using FTP. As with the FTP server, a Gopher server can be configured to log sessions, and includes the same type of audit information that the FTP server logs.

- *World Wide Web (WWW) server*. A server with a hypertext-based distributed information system. This server delivers documents formatted with the HyperText Markup Language (HTML), which are navigated and viewed on the client with a Web browser. HTML is a special language used to create "intuitive" documents; that is, documents including text and pictures that can be navigated by clicking or pressing Enter (for a character-based Web browser).

The current popularity of the Internet owes much to the success of the World

Wide Web, in that this method of propagating information doesn't alienate nontechnical users. You can't turn on the TV or pick up a periodical (newspaper, magazine, and so on) without noticing advertisements displaying a Web address. World Wide Web servers usually listen on TCP/IP port 80 (although exceptions to this rule are common), and communicate with clients—Web browsers—with Hypertext Transfer Protocol (HTTP). As with FTP and Gopher servers, sessions can be logged for later auditing purposes.

An organization desiring an Internet presence can deploy any or all of these services, on separate machines or integrated onto a single machine that offers all three services. When making the decision to have an Internet presence, consider what your organization does, what information about your organization would be useful to the Internet community, what services your organization offers that would be useful to Internetizens, and how you want to deliver the services.

Often, informational documents, software, image files, and other tangible files can be delivered with all three types of servers. To best serve the Internet community at large, you might set up all three services, as many people have preferences for how they want to retrieve information. Don't just set up a WWW server and neglect an FTP/Gopher server. Many long-time ("purist") Internet users don't like to use WWW servers simply because Web pages tend to be graphics-intensive and slow in comparison to FTP and Gopher servers—they want to retrieve what they're looking for (about you) *quickly* and with no fuss. In other words, don't limit yourself (or your organization's Internet presence) unnecessarily.

If you have databases (Microsoft Access, Microsoft or Sybase SQL Server, Oracle, Informix, and so on) that you want the Internet community to be able to query for "live" data, consider a Web server with special database connectors, that serves up HTML forms. These forms can be used by your Internet audience to query your database(s) and garner the information they need in the form of "dynamic" HTML documents; that is, HTML documents created on-the-fly that are essentially "wrappers" for the database data. This capability also works for accepting information from an Internet user (name, address, and so forth), and storing this information in a database for later use (for example, mailing list, shipping ordered products, and so on).

Once you've decided which services to offer, the next step is to install IIS from your distribution CD.

Introducing Internet Information Server (IIS)

Microsoft's IIS is a full-featured, extremely scalable, multi-threaded information server that provides FTP, Gopher, and World Wide Web services right out of the box—no additional software is needed.

IIS also has built into it a database connector called the *Internet Database Connector* (*IDC*). IDC is a fully ODBC-compliant database connector that enables you to create an information service with the ability to "snap in" to any ODBC-compliant database. You can then query the database, format the query results as a Web page on-the-fly (using an HTML template you create), and present the data to the user just as if it were a hard-coded, static HTML Web page. IDC also allows the database updates/modifications, giving you the opportunity to create an HTML form "front end" for your databases. This is useful for your data entry folks or database maintainers; using a standard Web browser on the HTML forms you create on the Web server, the data in the database can be kept up-to-date.

IIS is very secure; strict Windows NT C2-level security can be implemented on all three services, with full auditing and reporting. The IIS security goes one step further than the standard directory/file permissions of other Internet information services. When used with Microsoft's Internet Explorer Web browser, IISsupports a feature called *Windows NT Challenge/Response*, which allows the server to query the connecting workstation for the current user's SAM user information, and then use that information to allow or prevent access to all or certain portions of the information service. In addition (although it's not covered here), IIS supports Netscape's Secure Sockets Layer (SSL) protocol for encrypting and authenticating traffic with cryptography.

You can use any Web browser to view and check your installation of IIS. Windows NT 4.0 comes bundled with Version 2.0 of Microsoft's free browser, Internet Explorer. It's already installed and ready to use—it even has a shortcut on the desktop!

Installing IIS

Microsoft's Internet Information Server is easy to install. It's included on the Windows NT Server 4.0 installation CD. In fact, when you install Windows NT Server, the installer prompts you as to whether to install IIS. If you choose to install it, several very simple questions are presented about where to install it, what services to install, and what directories to use to create and install content.

The Installation Process

If you decide not to install IIS while installing Windows NT Server 4.0, it's very easy to install it at a later time. The Windows NT setup program will create a shortcut on your desktop named "Install Internet Information Server." If it's been deleted on your machine, you can use the Network control panel to install it.

Before you try to install IIS, check to see whether IIS is already installed. Open the Network control panel, click the Services tab, and look for the Microsoft Internet Information Server listing under Network Services (see Figure 27-1.) If IIS is already installed, you can pretty much forgo the rest of this installation procedure. If IIS isn't installed, you can install it via the control panel or the shortcut.

If you're using the shortcut, just open it by double-clicking it. If you'd rather use the control panel, make sure it's open and that the Services tab is active. Next, click the Add button, then select "Microsoft Internet Information Server 2.0" from the list in the Select Network Services dialog box . Click OK.

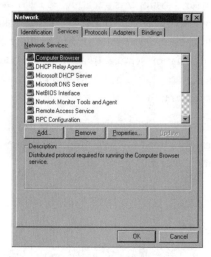

FIGURE 27-1

You can install IIS from the Services tab of the Network Control Panel applet.

Whichever route you choose to start the installation, the subsequent steps are the same. Here's what to do:

1. The first step is to enter the location of the NTS distribution files. When the Files Needed dialog box appears, type the full path to the Windows NT Server 4.0 installation files. If installing from CD-ROM, type the CD-ROM's drive letter followed by \i386 as in the following example, where the drive is d:

   ```
   d:\i386
   ```

   You can also use the Universal Naming Convention (UNC) pathname of a computer on the network, if you have the Windows NT Server 4.0 installation files on a network share. For example:

   ```
   \\filesrvr\delivery\ntsrvr40\i386
   ```

2. Choose OK or press Enter. The Microsoft Internet Information Server 2.0 Setup dialog box opens.

   This dialog box warns you that Setup can't install or update system files or shared components if they're in use by any other application. Check for open applications (word processing programs, office automation products or toolbars, graphics/image processing programs, etc.) and close them down before proceeding. Once all other applications are closed, click OK.

> **TIP:** A quick method to check for open applications is to press Shift + Ctrl + Esc on your keyboard, and click the Applications tab in the resulting window. No applications should be listed as running.

3. The IIS Setup window will appear, as shown in Figure 27-2. This window lets you control which components are installed and where they're installed. If you click an option in the Options list, the Description group on right-hand side of the window presents a short description of that option. These are the options you can install. They're all selected by default except for the HTML version of Internet Service Manager:

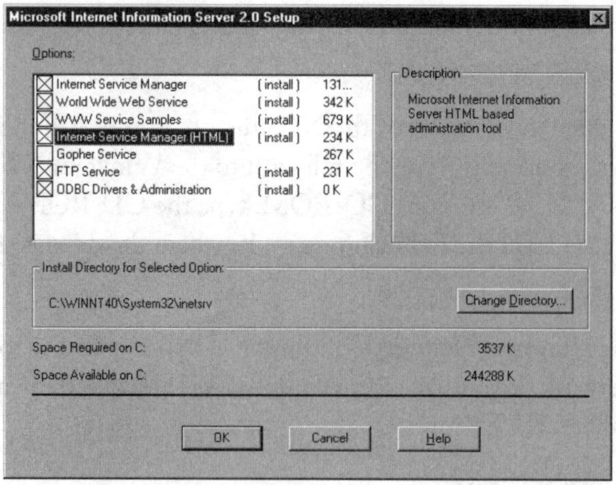

FIGURE 27-2

The IIS Setup window gives you control over what components of IIS are installed.

◆ *Internet Service Manager* is the Microsoft Internet Server Administrator tool. It's an intuitive and useful tool that you can use to stop, start, and configure the FTP, Gopher, and WWW Services. Because this feature requires only a trivial 423KB of disk space, be sure to leave it selected. Regardless of whether you install it, you can still start and stop the services using any of the methods described in Chapter 9, "Managing NT Servers."

◆ As the name implies, *World Wide Web Service* is the Microsoft World Wide Web Publishing Server, which enables you to serve Web documents in Web server style. If your Internet presence requirements dictate a Web server, leave this option selected.

◆ *Gopher Service* is the Microsoft Gopher Publishing Service. If you plan to offer a Gopher server, leave this option selected. However, Gopher service has been largely superseded by WWW, which uses a more efficient protocol. Unless you need Gopher, leave it off.

◆ *FTP Service* refers to the Microsoft FTP Publishing Service. To offer an FTP server, leave this option selected.

◆ The *Internet Service Manager (HTML)* option installs a set of Web pages and CGI scripts that allow you to manage an IIS server from any Web browser on the Internet. This can be a very valuable capability, especially for remote monitoring and administration.

- The *ODBC Drivers & Administration Tools* option installs the Microsoft ODBC (Open Database Connectivity) drivers and administration tools. They include various ODBC drivers to be used for session logging to databases, as well as the Internet Database Connector (IDC). As discussed earlier, IDC allows you to interface with databases via the WWW service, to create "dynamic" Web pages with data queried from the database, and so on. If you have no desire to interface with databases via the WWW service (or if you have chosen not to install the WWW service), you can deselect this option.

NOTE: Deselecting this option *disables* session logging to databases for audit trails on all services; you'll have to log to plain ASCII text files instead. If you have chosen to install the WWW service, and may need to interface with databases, leave this option checked.

- As their names imply, the *WWW Service Samples* are sample WWW and IDC files that you can use to help you get started. With this option, when IIS is done installing you'll have a fully-functional server that serves up helpful content right out of the box. Only if you're very low on disk space (or if you already know how to set up the FTP, Gopher, and WWW services) should you deselect this option.

A complete installation of IIS with all options selected requires about 3.8Mb of disk space; note that this doesn't include space for log files, databases, Web pages, or other files you want to serve.

4. Near the bottom of the dialog box is the default installation directory. This directory is where the IIS *software* (not your FTP/Gopher/WWW content) will go. By default, IIS will be installed in %SYSTEMROOT%\System32\inetsrv. If you need to change this directory, click the Change <u>D</u>irectory button, then navigate to the drive/directory where you want the IIS software to go. When the settings are correct, choose OK or press Enter. Click OK when you're happy with the installation directory.

5. Next, the program prompts for content locations (see Figure 27-3). The Publishing Directories dialog box allows you to specify where files published by the FTP, Gopher, and WWW services come from. If you elected to install the WWW sample files, these directories are where the samples will be copied, so

that you'll have a fully-functional server when you're done with the installation procedure.

If you want to change the default directories, type the new pathname for each of the three publishing directories (or use the Browse button to navigate to the new directories). When you're satisfied with the settings, choose OK. You'll be asked to confirm creation of any directories you specified if they don't already exist.

Various dialog boxes appear and disappear as files are copied from the Windows NT Server 4.0 installation media to your hard disk.

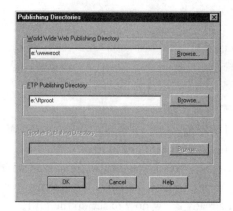

FIGURE 27-3

Selecting content directories.

6. When the IIS files have been copied and installed, the program presents the Install Drivers dialog box, in which you can select from a list of available ODBC drivers. Currently, the only ODBC driver bundled with IIS 2.0 is the SQL Server ODBC driver. If you are running (or plan to run) a SQL Server database, select the SQL Server driver and choose OK.

Another dialog box is displayed as the ODBC SQL Server driver is installed to your hard disk.

The next dialog box you see should congratulate you on your successful installation of Microsoft Internet Information Server 2.0.

TIP: The ODBC drivers for various databases are usually packaged with and delivered as part of the database installation media. If you don't have or can't find an ODBC driver for the database, you can contact Microsoft to obtain the ODBC Driver Pack 2.0 Fulfillment Kit, for a modest shipping fee. This kit contains a bundle of ODBC drivers for several popular databases. You can get more information about this kit (including a Q&A) at the following address:

```
http://www.microsoft.com./technet/technol/odbc/prodfact/odbcqa.htm
```

NOTE: If you get an error message about not being able to copy a file called `ODBCCP32.CPL`, leave the dialog box up and close Control Panel. IIS Setup can't install the ODBC Control panel applet when the Control Panel is open. Once it's closed, click the Retry button. The file should copy successfully.

Your First IIS Web Page

Start your Web browser. In its Address field, type the following URL and then press Enter:

```
http://localhost/
```

You should see a Web page displayed as in Figure 27-4, with some good information about IIS. This page includes an online tour of IIS, a sample site, programming examples for HTML and database connectivity, application ideas, and hot links to take you to pertinent information on Microsoft's WWW site on the Internet.

Naturally, you'll want to replace this default Web page with your own Web content, but take a minute or two to browse this information and familiarize yourself with it. It's full of good examples.

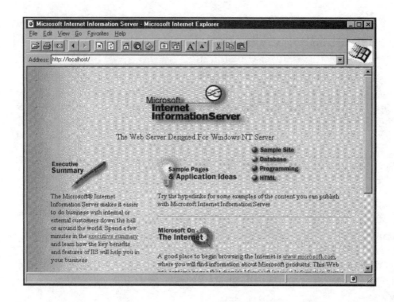

FIGURE 27-4

The default IIS page contains links to the sample pages.

NOTE: The database programming examples assume that you have SQL Server installed *with* the pubs sample database. If you don't have SQL Server installed (or have it installed without the pubs database), the programming examples won't work.

Administering IIS

Administering IIS is a simple matter with the Internet Service Manager. Internet Service Manager comes in two flavors: a standalone application, and a set of Web pages that provide the same functionality to any host on the network.

Internet Server Manager Basics

The stand-alone Internet Service Manager, whose main window is shown in Figure 27-5, is your primary interface to the IIS server components. To open the Internet Service Manager, choose Start | Programs | Microsoft Internet Server (Common) | Internet Service Manager.

FIGURE 27-5

Internet Service Manager is the control center for IIS.

When you first run Internet Service Manager, it displays a list of IIS services running on the local computer. The View menu lets you control which services are shown and how the display is sorted. You can also use the Servers View, Report View, and Services View commands to control whether servers are grouped by machine, by service type, or in the default report view.

In any of the views, you must select a service before you can do anything to it. Once you've done so, you can start, stop, or pause the service using either the commands in the Properties menu or the toolbar buttons. You can also set properties for the selected service as described below.

Not only can you manage the Internet services for the workstation/server on which the Internet Service Manager is currently running, but you can manage other Internet servers (other physical machines) on your network as well. The Properties | Find All Servers command (and its corresponding toolbar button) will search your network for other IIS servers and display them in the Internet Service Manager window. If you already know which machine you want to manage, you can use the Properties | Connect to Server command to manage its servers directly. Using these two buttons, you can connect to and manage additional Internet servers on the network from one central place.

Once you've selected the service you want to manage, you can use the Properties | Service Properties command to control its behavior.

Configuring the IIS Services

The WWW and FTP properties dialog boxes are very similar (except for the Messages tab of the FTP dialog, which is self-explanatory.) Figure 27-6 shows the Properties dialog box for the WWW service with some site-specific information being entered into the Comment field. This comment appears while browsing for Internet servers with Internet Service Manager.

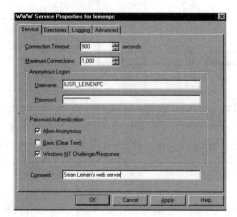

FIGURE 27-6

Managing the properties of the WWW Service.

Setting Service Properties

Along with the standard configuration values such as connection timeout and maximum number of connections, the Services tab in this dialog box lets you control the Windows NT username/password combination used when an anonymous (guest) user connects to the WWW Service. This is not a username or password that a Web browser must pass to the WWW service to get access to it, but rather the Windows NT username and password that the anonymous connection maps to. This mapping is used to set NT and NTFS permissions for anonymous accounts.

By default, Internet Information Server creates an account named IUSR_*computername* (if it doesn't exist) and uses it as the account which owns IIS. You can change the account that the IIS WWW Service uses by changing the settings in the Username and Password fields.

The Password Authentication group (only found in the WWW Properties dialog) controls what types of authentication IIS will accept. When A̲llow Anonymous is checked, users can connect without providing a username or password. When B̲asic (Clear Text) is on, clients using the standard WWW scheme of sending unencrypted user names and passwords will be allowed to connect. Finally, Windows N̲T Challenge/Response allows you to use SAM user data to authenticate clients who are running Internet Explorer 2.0 or later on NT machines.

Configuring Content Directory Settings

To configure the WWW (HTML) content directory for IIS, you use the options on the Directories tab, which is shown in Figure 27-7. The IIS default directories should be changed to the directories holding the custom content you want to serve to the Internet.

FIGURE 27-7

Managing the WWW content directories.

The list at the center of the property page shows which directories are currently able to serve documents. You can add or remove directories at any time. Each directory is independent of any others, and each can have its own set of permissions.

The WWW service page allows you to specify a default document name. This is the document that IIS serves if the Web client's browser doesn't ask for a specific HTML document by name. In this example, if the Web browser just connected with the path `http://leinenpc/`, the file `default.htm` would be served to the client browser.

Another very important option on this tab in the WWW dialog is Directory Browsing Allowed. When you enable this feature, if a Web client doesn't ask for a specific HTML document by name and IIS can't find a document with the name `default.htm`, IIS serves a directory listing that looks just like an FTP directory listing. This allows the client's Web browser to browse the directory structure of your Web server. In some cases, this might be desirable, but in most cases (especially Web servers presenting content to the Internet at large), this is highly undesirable. We recommend that you keep this option cleared.

For FTP servers, you can choose whether directory listings are formatted like MS-DOS or UNIX directory listings. Some FTP clients expect one format or the other.

You can also set properties for individual directories. Figure 27-8 illustrates the properties of a WWW service directory. In this case, the `Scripts` directory. We've chosen the `Scripts` directory to point out an important fact about IIS configuration. Directories containing server-side executable code—for example, CGI scripts, IDC files, or binary executables—must have their permissions set with Read off, and Execute on. Otherwise, IIS serves the CGI script, IDC file, or binary executable to the client browser *as is*, rather than executing it and serving its output to the Web client.

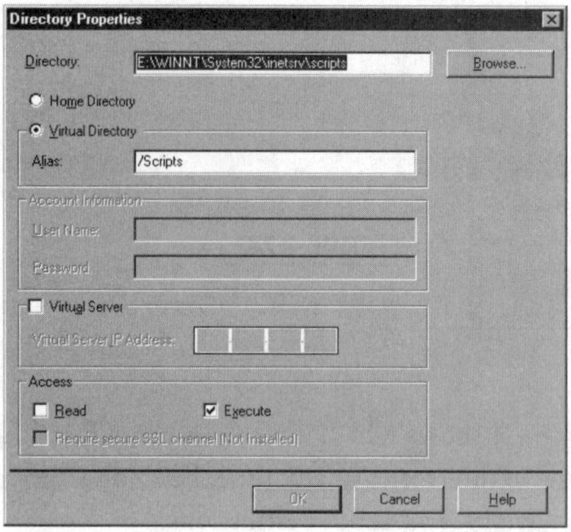

FIGURE 27-8

Setting the directory properties.

Controlling Logging

The Logging tab (shown in Figure 27-9) lets you specify how IIS should keep records of what data it's served. Once you enable logging with the Enable Logging checkbox, your next choice is between keeping data in plain text files or in an ODBC database.

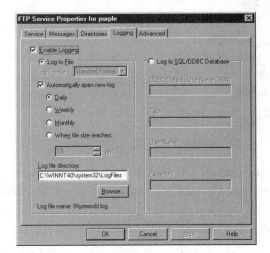

FIGURE 27-9

Control access logging with the Logging tab.

Plain-text log files can be recycled at periodic intervals. For example, the default setting of Daily creates a new log file every day, so that each day's accesses are in a separate file. You can roll logs over daily, weekly, monthly, or when the log reaches a certain size limit; you can also control where the log files are stored with the Log file directory field.

By comparison, when you keep log data in an ODBC database, you have to specify the user name and password required to connect to the database, the table name where you want the data stored, and the ODBC data source name. Logs aren't rolled over; you must use the database administration tools to clear out log data once you're done with it.

Configuring Access Control

The Advanced tab is somewhat of a misnomer, since it is really provides access controls for your IIS servers. It's shown in Figure 27-10. The most important controls are the pair of radio buttons at the top: Granted Access and Denied Access. Whatever setting you choose will apply to all incoming connection requests *except* those which match criteria in the list box.

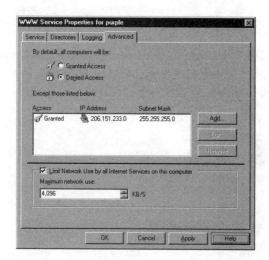

FIGURE 27-10

The Advanced tab lets you choose who can and cannot access your server.

For example, if you want to keep computers outside your domain from using your Web server, you could choose Denied Access and use the Add button to specify that hosts with addresses in your domain should be allowed access. Conversely, you can use Granted Access to let everyone in *except* machines you specifically ban in the exception list.

IIS also allows you to throttle the total amount of bandwidth it consumes. When Limit Network Use is turned on, IIS will honor the Maximum network use field so that the total traffic served by all IIS servers on the computer stays below that threshold. Note that this setting only applies to the computer it's set on, and not to other IIS machines in the domain.

Adding New Common Gateway Interface (CGI) Types

If you're already comfortable with HTML and CGI (Common Gateway Interface) programs, you'll be happy to know that Microsoft IIS is completely compatible with most CGI implementations, including the use of Perl (the *Practical Extraction and Report Language*) as CGI scripts. To get Perl to work with IIS, however, a value needs to be added to the Windows NT Registry, and the WWW Service subsequently stopped and restarted. Assuming that you already have Perl installed, just follow these steps to have IIS honor Perl scripts as valid CGI scripts:

1. Open the Registry Editor (regedit.exe).

2. Navigate to the following Registry key:

   HKEY_LOCAL_MACHINE\SYSTEM\CurrentControlSet\Services\W3SVC\Parameters\ScriptMap

3. Choose Edit | Add Value, then enter .pl in the Value Name field of the Add Value dialog. Click OK.

4. The String Editor dialog will appear. In the Value Data field, type the path to your Perl interpreter (the example assumes that the Perl software was installed in c:\perl5):

   c:\perl5\bin\perl.exe %s %s

   Figure 27-11 shows what the Registry Editor entry for this new key looks like.

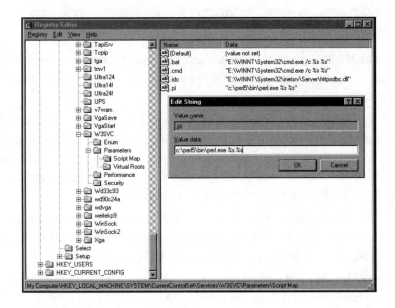

FIGURE 27-11

Installing the Registry value to support PERL scripts as CGI scripts under IIS.

5. Stop and restart the WWW service via the Internet Service Manager as described above.

Your Perl scripts should now work as valid CGI scripts under IIS, assuming that the directories in which they reside have Execute permission only (not Read permission) in the Internet Service Manager properties for the WWW Service.

This same procedure can also be modified for use with other types of CGI scripts you may have, based on the script's file extension and the program used to run it.

Once you have the servers configured the way you want them, it's time to examine how you can best secure your IIS resources to keep them safe from intrusion.

IIS Security

IIS uses a layered security policy. Each request it receives is checked to make sure the IP address, user, and permissions allow the client to get the requested data. If the server administrator has added rules which would cause these checks to fail, the client won't get the data. For these checks to be effective, though, you have to use them, and there are some other considerations you should be aware of too. Here are five basic steps you should take to secure your server:

1. Make sure the IUSR_*computername* account has appropriate permissions. Remove all rights from the account except for *Log on Locally* and *Access this computer from the network.*

2. If you want to allow anonymous access to several IIS servers within a domain, create a domain user account for anonymous access. Give it minimal rights, as with IUSR_*computername*, then instruct each computer running IIS to use that account instead of their own. Be certain that your new anonymous account isn't in any local or global groups where it doesn't belong.

3. Set NTFS permissions on your servers' files. Make sure any accounts which are used for anonymous access have appropriate rights (usually limited to Read, or Read + Execute for directories which contain CGI scripts.)

4. Use username/password and IP address access controls to keep unauthorized users and machines away from your data.

5. Use a security auditing tool, like the Kane Security Analyst (KSA—there's a demo on the included CD) to audit your server's security. Enable auditing on your IIS server and pay careful attention to the results.

Where to Go Next

This chapter explains how to plan, install, configure, and run Microsoft's Internet Information Server. With IIS, you can turn any NTS machine on your network into a full-featured net server for use on the Internet or your own corporate network. IIS relies on a number of other system components and protocols, so you may find these other chapters to be helpful:

◆ Chapter 24, "Interoperating with TCP/IP Clients" covers the intricacies of setting up Windows NT's TCP/IP protocol stack, which IIS requires.

◆ Chapter 26, "Connecting to the Internet" explains the rationale *and* details behind getting a part-time or dedicated Internet connection, including how to make your connection a secure one.

◆ Running a Web site with IIS can be a complex, wide-ranging endeavor, and we can't do it justice in the course of a single chapter. For a complete overview, see *Internet Information Server* (Allen Wyatt, Prima, ISBN 0-7615-0693-4).

Appendix

What's on the CD?

The CD that accompanies this book contains numerous tools and utilities to assist the NT network administrator in managing, securing, and monitoring the network. There are Internet servers, Windows NT tools and utilities, Internet tools, and more.

Running the CD

To make the CD more user-friendly and take up less of your disk space, no installation is required. This means that the only files transferred to your hard drive are the ones you choose to copy.

> **CAUTION:** Significant differences between the various Windows operating systems (Windows 3.1, Windows 95, and Windows NT) sometimes render files that work in one Windows environment inoperable in another. Prima has made every effort to insure that this problem is minimized. However, it is not possible to eliminate it entirely. Therefore you may find that some files or directories appear to be missing from the CD. Those files are, in reality, on the CD, but remain hidden from the operating system. To confirm this, view the CD using a different Windows operating system.
>
> **Note:** This problem most often occurs while viewing the CD in Windows 3.1.

Windows 3.1

To run the CD:

Insert the CD in the CD-ROM Drive.

1. From File Manager select File, Run to open the Run window.
2. In the Command Line text box type **D:\primacd.exe** (where D:\ is the CD-ROM drive).
3. Select OK.

Windows 95

Since there is no install routine, running the CD in Windows 95 is a breeze, especially if you have autorun enabled. Simply insert the CD in the CD-ROM Drive, close the tray, and wait for the CD to load.

If you have disabled autorun place the CD in the drive and follow these steps:

1. From the Start menu select Run.
2. Type **D:\primacd.exe** (where D:\ is the CD-ROM drive).
3. Select OK.

The Prima User Interface

Prima's user interface is designed to make viewing and using the CD contents quick and easy. It contains six category buttons, four options buttons, and a display window. Select a category button to show a list of available titles in the display window. Highlight a title in the window and choose an option button to perform the desired action.

Category Buttons

Sunbelt Tools—Sunbelt Software's entire Windows NT Web site, including all of their demo and evaluation software

NT Tools—A collection of essential NT tools and utilities

Internet—Web browsers, FTP clients, and other tools for getting the most from the Internet

Options Buttons

Install/Run—If the highlighted title contains an install routine, selecting this option begins the installation process. If the title has no install procedure, but contains an executable file the executable is run. If neither an install nor an executable file is present (as in the case of a graphics library), the folder containing the information is shown. In the event that an application contains an executable file that will not run from the CD the entire application is placed in a compressed ZIP file, which can be accessed by installing WinZip (included on the CD).

> **NOTE:** You can install some of the shareware programs that do not have installation routines by copying the program files from the CD to your hard drive and running the executable (.exe) file.

Information—Data about the selection is shown, if available. This information is usually in the form of a readme or help file.

Explore—This option allows you to view the folder containing the program files.

Exit—When you're finished and ready to move on, select exit.

The Software

This section gives you a brief description of some of the software you'll find on the CD. This is just a sampling. As you browse the CD, you will find much more.

DiskShare—A kernel-based network file system (NFS) server that enables UNIX and other NFS clients to mount file systems located on Microsoft's Windows NT Workstation and Windows NT Server-based systems.

DumpAcl—A Windows NT program that will dump the permissions and audit settings for the file system, registry, and printers in a concise, readable listbox format; so that "holes" in system security are readily apparent.

DumpEvt—A Windows NT program to dump the event log in a format suitable for importing into databases such as Access or SQL server.

DumpReg—A program for Microsoft Windows NT and Windows 95 that will dump registry values in an easy-to-use listbox.

RegEdit—A DLL that can be called from 32-bit Visual Basic programs. It allows a network administrator to write a short Visual Basic program to dump or modify the Windows NT user profiles for a large number of users or computers at once.

SnagIt—A Windows utility that provides users with an easy way to capture, print, or file Windows screen images. With SnagIt, you can capture an entire screen, a portion of the screen, or a specific window.

Sunbelt—Sunbelt Software's entire Windows NT Web site, including all of their demo and evaluation software.

INDEX

Notes

Notes

Notes

Notes

Notes

Notes

Notes

Notes

Notes

Notes

Notes

Notes

Notes

Notes

Essential Reporting for your Web Server

WebTrends analyzes the log files created by your World-Wide Web servers and automatically produces reports which include statistical information as well as colorful graphs that show user activity by market, interest level in specific pages or services, which products are most popular, whether a visitor has a local, national or international origin, and much more.

WebTrends reports are HTML files that can be viewed by any browser on your local system or remotely from anywhere on the Internet with any browser.

For more information check our website at www.WebTrends.com

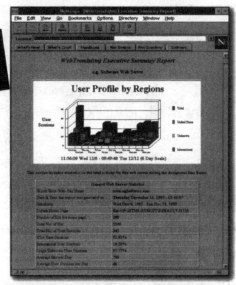

ORDER DIRECT SAVE 50%

MAIL OR FAX THIS COUPON TODAY AND ORDER WEBTRENDS FOR 1/2 OFF

NAME: _____

PHONE: _____ EXT: _____ FAX: _____

COMPANY: _____ TITLE: _____

ADDRESS: _____

CITY, STATE, ZIP: _____

METHOD OF PAYMENT: ☐ CHECK ☐ VISA ☐ MASTERCARD ☐ AMERICAN EXPRESS

CARD NUMBER: _____ EXP. DATE: _____

NAME ON CARD: _____

e.g. Software, Inc.
621 SW Morrison, Suite 1025
Portland, OR 97205 USA.
Phone: (503) 294-7025 • Fax: (503) 294-7130
www.WebTrends.com

Copyright 1995-96 e.g. Software, Inc. WebTrends is a trademark of e.g. Software, Inc.
Other trademarks are the properties of their respective owners.

WebTrends is compatible with NetScape, Microsoft, NCSA, WebSite, Quarterdeck, Purveyer, Apache, Cbuilder, Oracle, Emwac, and other Windows 3.x, NT, 95, Unix, and Macintosh Web servers.

System Requirements: Windows NT or Windows 95, 8MB of free memory, 10MB of free disk space

To Order Books

Please send me the following items:

Quantity	Title	Unit Price	Total
_____	_____	$ _____	$ _____
_____	_____	$ _____	$ _____
_____	_____	$ _____	$ _____
_____	_____	$ _____	$ _____
_____	_____	$ _____	$ _____

Subtotal $ _____

Deduct 10% when ordering 3-5 books $ _____

7.25% Sales Tax (CA only) $ _____

8.25% Sales Tax (TN only) $ _____

5.0% Sales Tax (MD and IN only) $ _____

Shipping and Handling* $ _____

Total Order $ _____

Shipping and Handling depend on Subtotal.

Subtotal	Shipping/Handling
$0.00–$14.99	$3.00
$15.00–$29.99	$4.00
$30.00–$49.99	$6.00
$50.00–$99.99	$10.00
$100.00–$199.99	$13.50
$200.00+	Call for Quote

Foreign and all Priority Request orders:
Call Order Entry department
for price quote at 916/632-4400

This chart represents the total retail price of books only
(before applicable discounts are taken).

By Telephone: With MC or Visa, call 800-632-8676, 916-632-4400. Mon-Fri, 8:30-4:30.
WWW {http://www.primapublishing.com}

Orders Placed Via Internet E-mail {sales@primapub.com}
By Mail: Just fill out the information below and send with your remittance to:

**Prima Publishing
P.O. Box 1260BK
Rocklin, CA 95677**

My name is _____

I live at _____

City_____ State_____ Zip _____

MC/Visa#_____ Exp._____

Check/Money Order enclosed for $ _____ Payable to Prima Publishing

Daytime Telephone _____

Signature _____

Other books from Prima Publishing, Computer Products Division

	Title	Price	Release Date
15-0801-5	ActiveX	$40.00	Available Now
15-0680-2	America Online Complete Handbook and Membership Kit	$24.99	Available Now
15-0915-1	Building Intranets with Internet Information Server and FrontPage	$45.00	Available Now
15-0417-6	CompuServe Complete Handbook and Membership Kit	$24.95	Available Now
15-0849-X	Corporate Intranet Development	$45.00	Fall '96
15-0692-6	Create Your First Web Page in a Weekend	$24.99	Fall '96
15-0503-2	Discover What's Online!	$24.95	Available Now
15-0693-4	Internet Information Server	$40.00	Available Now
15-0815-5	Introduction to ABAP/4 Programming for SAP	$45.00	Available Now
15-0678-0	Java Applet Powerpack	$30.00	Available Now
15-0685-3	JavaScript	$35.00	Available Now
15-0901-1	Leveraging Visual Basic with ActiveX Controls	$45.00	Available Now
15-0682-9	LiveWire Pro Master's Handbook	$45.00	Fall '96
15-0755-8	Moving Worlds	$35.00	Available Now
15-0690-X	Netscape Enterprise Server	$40.00	Available Now
15-0691-8	Netscape FastTrack Server	$40.00	Available Now
15-0852-X	Netscape Navigator 3 Complete Handbook	$24.99	Available Now
15-0751-5	Windows NT Server 4 Administrator's Guide	$50.00	Available Now
15-0759-0	Professional Web Design	$40.00	Available Now
15-0773-6	Programming Internet Controls	$45.00	Available Now
15-0780-9	Programming Web Server Applications	$40.00	Available Now
15-0063-4	Researching on the Internet	$29.95	Available Now
15-0686-1	Researching on the World Wide Web	$24.99	Available Now
15-0695-0	The Essential Photoshop Book	$35.00	Available Now
15-0752-3	The Essential Windows NT Book	$27.99	Available Now
15-0689-6	The Microsoft Exchange Productivity Guide	$24.99	Available Now
15-0769-8	VBScript Master's Handbook	$45.00	Available Now
15-0684-5	VBScript Web Page Interactivity	$40.00	Available Now
15-0903-8	Visual FoxPro 5 Enterprise Development	$45.00	Available Now
15-0814-7	Visual J++	$35.00	Available Now
15-0383-8	Web Advertising and Marketing	$34.95	Available Now
15-0726-4	Webmaster's Handbook	$40.00	Available Now

Margie @ clark.net